THE MARCH OF FOLLY

Barbara Tuchman (1912–1989) was awarded the Pulitzer Prize twice for her bestselling *August 1914* (1962) and for *Sand Against the Wind* (1971). Her other books published in Papermac are *A Distant Mirror, The Proud Tower, Bible and Sword, Practising History* and *August 1914*.

By the same author

Bible and Sword:
How the British Came to Palestine

Sand Against the Wind:
Stillwell and the American Experience in China 1911–1945

The Zimmerman Telegram:
How the USA Entered the Great War

The Proud Tower:
A Portrait of the World Before the War 1890–1914

A Distant Mirror:
The Calamitous Fourteenth Century

Practising History

August 1914

Barbara Tuchman

THE MARCH
OF FOLLY

From Troy to Vietnam

PAPERMAC

First published by 1984 Michael Joseph Ltd

First published in paperback in Abacus by Sphere Books Ltd, 1985

This edition published 1996 by Papermac
an imprint of Macmillan General Books
25 Eccleston Place, London SW1W 9NF
and Basingstoke

Associated companies throughout the world

ISBN 0 333 65686 5

Grateful acknowledgement is made to the
University of Chicago Press for permission to reprint an
excerpt from *The Iliad*, translated by Richard Lattimore.
Copyright 1951 by the University of Chicago.

1 3 5 7 9 8 6 4 2

A CIP catalogue record for this book is available
from the British Library.

Printed and bound in Great Britain by
Mackays of Chatham PLC, Chatham, Kent

'And I can see no reason why anyone should suppose that in the future the same motifs already heard will not be sounding still . . . put to use by reasonable men to reasonable ends, or by madmen to nonsense and disaster."

JOSEPH CAMPBELL

Foreword to *The Masks of God: Primitive Mythology*, 1969

Contents

Source references will be found in the notes
at the end of the book, located by page number
and an identifying phrase from the text.

Acknowledgments

I would like to express my thanks to those who have contributed in different ways to this book: to Professor William Wilcox, editor of the Benjamin Franklin Papers at Yale University, for a critical reading of Chapter IV; to Richard Dudman, former bureau chief of the *St. Louis Post-Dispatch* in Washington and author of *Forty Days with the Enemy* (a record of his captivity in Cambodia), for a reading of Chapter V; to Professor Nelson Minnich of the Catholic University of America for a reading of Chapter III. Reading does not imply agreement, particularly in the case of the last-named. I am solely responsible for all interpretations and opinions.

For consultation or help on various matters, I am grateful to Professor Bernard Bailyn of the History Department at Harvard University, to Dr. Peter Dunn for his researches on the return of the French troops to Vietnam in 1945, to Jeffrey Race for introducing me to the concept concealed under the jargon "Cognitive Dissonance," to Colonel Harry Summers of the Army War College, to Janis Kreslins of the library of the Council on Foreign Relations, and to all the persons listed under the references for Chapter V, who were kind enough to make themselves available for oral questioning.

The whole book owes a coherent existence to Mary McGuire of Alfred A. Knopf, who kept track of a stream of disconnected material and buttoned up loose ends. Extra thanks go to Robin Sommer for devoted and effective guardianship of accuracy in the proofs.

My further thanks go to my husband, Dr. Lester R. Tuchman, for suggesting Rehoboam and for discovering the references to ancient siege warfare and the illustration of an Assyrian siege engine; to my daughter and son-in-law, Lucy and David Eisenberg, and my daughter

Alma Tuchman for reading the manuscript as a whole, with helpful comments; to my agent, Timothy Seldes of Russell and Volkening, for availability and help whenever needed; and to my editor and publisher, Robert Gottlieb, for critical judgment and extended endurance of auctorial anxieties on the telephone.

THE MARCH OF FOLLY

Chapter One

PURSUIT OF POLICY CONTRARY TO SELF-INTEREST

A phenomenon noticeable throughout history regardless of place or period is the pursuit by governments of policies contrary to their own interests. Mankind, it seems, makes a poorer performance of government than of almost any other human activity. In this sphere, wisdom, which may be defined as the exercise of judgment acting on experience, common sense and available information, is less operative and more frustrated than it should be. Why do holders of high office so often act contrary to the way reason points and enlightened self-interest suggests? Why does intelligent mental process seem so often not to function?

Why, to begin at the beginning, did the Trojan rulers drag that suspicious-looking wooden horse inside their walls despite every reason to suspect a Greek trick? Why did successive ministries of George III insist on coercing rather than conciliating the American colonies though repeatedly advised by many counselors that the harm done must be greater than any possible gain? Why did Charles XII and Napoleon and successively Hitler invade Russia despite the disasters incurred by each predecessor? Why did Montezuma, master of fierce and eager armies and of a city of 300,000, succumb passively to a party of several hundred alien invaders even after they had shown themselves all too obviously human beings, not gods? Why did Chiang Kai-shek refuse to heed any voice of reform or alarm until he woke up to find his country had slid from under him? Why do the oil-importing nations engage in rivalry for the available supply when a firm united front vis-à-vis the exporters would gain them control of the situation? Why in recent times have British trade unions in a lunatic spectacle seemed periodically bent on dragging their country toward paralysis, apparently under the impression that they are separate from the whole? Why does American business insist on "growth" when it is demonstrably using up the three basics of life on our planet—land, water and unpolluted air? (While unions and business are not strictly government in the political sense, they represent governing situations.)

Elsewhere than in government man has accomplished marvels: invented the means in our lifetime to leave the earth and voyage to the moon; in the past, harnessed wind and electricity, raised earthbound stones into soaring cathedrals, woven silk brocades out of the spinnings of a worm, constructed the instruments of music, derived motor power from steam, controlled or eliminated diseases, pushed back the North Sea and created land in its place, classified the forms of nature, penetrated the mysteries of the cosmos. "While all other sciences have advanced," confessed our second President, John Adams, "government is at a stand; little better practiced now than three or four thousand years ago."

Misgovernment is of four kinds, often in combination. They are: 1) tyranny or oppression, of which history provides so many well-known examples that they do not need citing; 2) excessive ambition, such as Athens' attempted conquest of Sicily in the Peloponnesian War, Philip II's of England via the Armada, Germany's twice-attempted rule of Europe by a self-conceived master race, Japan's bid for an empire of Asia; 3) incompetence or decadence, as in the case of the late Roman empire, the last Romanovs and the last imperial dynasty of China; and finally 4) folly or perversity. This book is concerned with the last in a specific manifestation; that is, the pursuit of policy contrary to the self-interest of the constituency or state involved. Self-interest is whatever conduces to the welfare or advantage of the body being governed; folly is a policy that in these terms is counter-productive.

To qualify as folly for this inquiry, the policy adopted must meet three criteria: it must have been perceived as counter-productive in its own time, not merely by hindsight. This is important, because all policy is determined by the mores of its age. "Nothing is more unfair," as an English historian has well said, "than to judge men of the past by the ideas of the present. Whatever may be said of morality, political wisdom is certainly ambulatory." To avoid judging by present-day values, we must take the opinion of the time and investigate only those episodes whose injury to self-interest was recognized by contemporaries.

Secondly a feasible alternative course of action must have been available. To remove the problem from personality, a third criterion must be that the policy in question should be that of a group, not an individual ruler, and should persist beyond any one political lifetime. Misgovernment by a single sovereign or tyrant is too frequent and too individual to be worth a generalized inquiry. Collective government or a succession of rulers in the same office, as in the case of the Renaissance popes, raises a more significant problem. (The Trojan Horse, to be examined shortly, is an exception to the time requirement, and Rehoboam to the group requirement, but each is such a classic example and occurs so early in the known history of government as to illustrate how deeply the phenomenon of folly is ingrained.)

Folly's appearance is independent of era or locality; it is timeless and universal, although the habits and beliefs of a particular time and place determine the form it takes. It is unrelated to type of regime: monarchy, oligarchy and democracy produce it equally. Nor is it peculiar to nation or class. The working class as represented by Communist governments functions no more rationally or effectively in power than the middle class, as has been notably demonstrated in recent history. Mao Tse-tung may be admired for many things, but the Great Leap Forward, with a steel plant in every backyard, and the Cultural Revolution were exercises in unwisdom that greatly damaged China's progress and stability, not to mention the Chairman's reputation. The record of the Russian proletariat in power can hardly be called enlightened, although after sixty years of control it must be accorded a kind of brutal success. If the majority of Russians are materially better off than before, the cost in cruelty and tyranny has been no less and probably greater than under the czars.

The French Revolution, great prototype of populist government, reverted rapidly to crowned autocracy as soon as it acquired an able administrator. The revolutionary regimes of Jacobins and Directorate could muster the strength to exterminate internal foes and defeat foreign enemies, but they could not manage their own following sufficiently to maintain domestic order, install a competent administration or collect taxes. The new order was rescued only by Bonaparte's military campaigns, which brought the spoils of foreign wars to fill the treasury, and subsequently by his competence as an executive. He chose officials on the principle of "*la carrière ouverte aux talents*"—the desired talents being intelligence, energy, industry and obedience. That worked for a while until he too, the classic victim of hubris, destroyed himself through overextension.

It may be asked why, since folly or perversity is inherent in individuals, should we expect anything else of government? The reason for concern is that folly in government has more impact on more people than individual follies, and therefore governments have a greater duty to act according to reason. Just so, and since this has been known for a very long time, why has not our species taken precautions and erected safeguards against it? Some attempts have been made, beginning with Plato's proposal of selecting a class to be trained as professionals in government. According to his scheme, the ruling class in a just society should be men apprenticed to the art of ruling, drawn from the rational and wise. Since he recognized that in natural distribution these are few, he believed they would have to be eugenically bred and nurtured. Government, he said, was a special art in which competence, as in any other profession, could be acquired only by study of the discipline and could not be acquired otherwise. His solution, beautiful and unattainable, was philosopher-kings. "The philosophers must become kings in our cities or those who are now kings and potentates must learn to seek wisdom like true philosophers, and so political power and intellectual wisdom will be joined in one." Until that day, he acknowledged, "there can be no rest from the troubles for the cities, and I think for the whole human race." And so it has been.

Wooden-headedness, the source of self-deception, is a factor that plays a remarkably large role in government. It consists in assessing a situation in terms of preconceived fixed notions while ignoring or rejecting any contrary signs. It is acting according to wish while not allowing oneself to be deflected by the facts. It is epitomized in a historian's statement about Philip II of Spain, the surpassing wooden-head of all sovereigns: "No experience of the failure of his policy could shake his belief in its essential excellence."

A classic case in action was Plan 17, the French war plan of 1914, conceived in a mood of total dedication to the offensive. It concentrated everything on a French advance to the Rhine, allowing the French left to remain virtually unguarded, a strategy that could only be justified by the fixed belief that the Germans could not deploy enough manpower to extend their invasion around through western Belgium and the French coastal provinces. This assumption was based on the equally fixed belief that the Germans would never use reserves in the front line. Evidence to the contrary which began seeping through to the French General Staff in 1913 had to be, and was, resolutely ignored in order that no concern about a possible German invasion on the west should be allowed to divert strength from a direct French offensive eastward to the Rhine. When war came, the Germans could and did use reserves in the front line and did come the long way around on the west with results that determined a protracted war and its fearful consequences for our century.

Wooden-headedness is also the refusal to benefit from experience, a characteristic in which medieval rulers of the 14th century were supreme. No matter how often and obviously devaluation of the

currency disrupted the economy and angered the people, the Valois
monarchs of France resorted to it whenever they were desperate for
cash until they provoked insurrection by the bourgeoisie. In warfare,
the métier of the governing class, wooden-headedness was conspicuous.
No matter how often a campaign that depended on living off a hostile
country ran into want and even starvation, as in the English invasions
of France in the Hundred Years' War, campaigns for which this fate
was inevitable were regularly undertaken.

There was another King of Spain at the beginning of the 17th century, Philip III, who is said to have died of a fever he contracted from
sitting too long near a hot brazier, helplessly overheating himself because the functionary whose duty it was to remove the brazier, when
summoned, could not be found. In the late 20th century it begins to
appear as if mankind may be approaching a similar stage of suicidal
folly. Cases come so thick and fast that one can select only the overriding one: why do the superpowers not begin mutual divestment of
the means of human suicide? Why do we invest all our skills and resources in a contest for armed superiority which can never be attained
for long enough to make it worth having, rather than in an effort to
find a modus vivendi with our antagonist—that is to say, a way of
living, not dying?

For 2500 years, political philosophers from Plato and Aristotle
through Thomas Aquinas, Machiavelli, Hobbes, Locke, Rousseau,
Jefferson, Madison and Hamilton, Nietzsche and Marx, have devoted
their thinking to the major issues of ethics, sovereignty, the social contract, the rights of man, the corruption of power, the balance between
freedom and order. Few, except Machiavelli, who was concerned with
government as it is, not as it should be, bothered with mere folly, although folly has been a chronic and pervasive problem. Count Axel
Oxenstierna, Chancellor of Sweden during the turmoil of the Thirty
Years' War under the hyperactive Gustavus Adolphus, and actual
ruler of the country under his daughter, Christina, had ample experience on which to base his dying conclusion, "Know, my son, with how
little wisdom the world is governed."

Because individual sovereignty was government's normal form for
so long, it exhibits the human characteristics that have caused folly in
government as far back as we have records. Rehoboam, King of Israel,
son of King Solomon, succeeded his father at the age of 41 in approximately 930 B.C., about a century before Homer composed the
national epic of his people. Without loss of time, the new King com-

mitted the act of folly that was to divide his nation and lose forever its ten northern tribes, collectively called Israel. Among them were many who were disaffected by heavy taxation in the form of forced labor imposed under King Solomon, and had already in his reign made an effort to secede. They had gathered around one of Solomon's generals, Jeroboam, "a mighty man of valor," who undertook to lead them into revolt upon a prophecy that he would inherit rule of the ten tribes afterward. The Lord, speaking through the voice of a certain Ahijah the Shilonite, played a part in this affair, but his role then and later is obscure and seems to have been inserted by narrators who felt the Almighty's hand had to be present. When the revolt failed, Jeroboam fled to Egypt where Shishak, the King of that country, gave him shelter.

Acknowledged King without question by the two southern tribes of Judah and Benjamin, Rehoboam, clearly aware of unrest in Israel, traveled at once to Shechem, center of the north, to obtain the people's allegiance. He was met instead by a delegation of Israel's representatives who demanded that he lighten the heavy yoke of labor put upon them by his father and said that if he did so they would serve him as loyal subjects. Among the delegates was Jeroboam who had hurriedly been sent for from Egypt as soon as King Solomon died, and whose presence must certainly have warned Rehoboam that he faced a critical situation.

Temporizing, Rehoboam asked the delegation to depart and return after three days for his reply. Meanwhile he consulted with the old men of his father's council, who advised him to accede to the people's demand, and told him that if he would act graciously and "speak good words to them they will be thy servants forever." With the first sensation of sovereignty heating his blood, Rehoboam found this advice too tame and turned to the "young men that were grown up with him." They knew his disposition and, like counselors of any time who wish to consolidate their position in the "Oval Office," gave advice they knew would be palatable. He should make no concessions but tell the people outright that his rule would be not lighter but heavier than his father's. They composed for him the famous words that could be any despot's slogan: "And thus shalt thou say to them: 'Whereas my father laid upon you a heavy yoke, I will add to your yoke. Whereas my father chastised you with whips, I shall chastise you with scorpions.'" Delighted with this ferocious formula, Rehoboam faced the delegation when it returned on the third day and addressed them "roughly," word for word as the young men had suggested.

That his subjects might not be prepared to accept this reply meekly seems not to have occurred to Rehoboam beforehand. Not without reason he earned in Hebrew history the designation "ample in folly." Instantly—so instantly as to suggest that they had previously decided upon their course of action in case of a negative reply—the men of Israel announced their secession from the House of David with the battle cry "To thy tents, O Israel! See to thine own house, David!"

With as little wisdom as would have astonished even Count Oxenstierna, Rehoboam took the most provocative action possible in the circumstances. Calling upon the very man who represented the hated yoke, Adoram, the commander or overseer of the forced labor tribute, he ordered him, apparently without providing supporting forces, to establish his authority. The people stoned Adoram to death, upon which the rash and foolish King speedily summoned his chariot and fled to Jerusalem, where he summoned all the warriors of Judah and Benjamin for war to reunite the nation. At the same time, the people of Israel appointed Jeroboam their King. He reigned for twenty-two years and Rehoboam for seventeen, "and there was war between them all their days."

The protracted struggle weakened both states, encouraged the vassal lands conquered by David east of the Jordan—Moab, Edom, Ammon and others—to regain their independence and opened the way to invasion by Egypt. King Shishak "with a large army" captured fortified border posts and approached Jerusalem, which Rehoboam saved from conquest only by paying tribute to the enemy in the form of golden treasure from the Temple and royal palace. Shishak penetrated also into the territory of his former ally Jeroboam as far as Megiddo but, evidently lacking the resources necessary to establish control, faded back into Egypt.

The twelve tribes were never reunited. Torn by their conflict, the two states could not maintain the proud empire established by David and Solomon, which had extended from northern Syria to the borders of Egypt with dominion over the international caravan routes and access to foreign trade through the Red Sea. Reduced and divided, they were less able to withstand aggression by their neighbors. After two hundred years of separate existence, the ten tribes of Israel were conquered by the Assyrians in 722 B.C. and, in accordance with Assyrian policy toward conquered peoples, were driven from their land and forcibly dispersed, to vanish into one of the great unknowns and perennial speculations of history.

The kingdom of Judah, containing Jerusalem, lived on as the land of the Jewish people. Though regaining at different times much of the northern territory, it suffered conquest, too, and exile by the waters of Babylon, then revival, civil strife, foreign sovereignty, rebellion, another conquest, another farther exile and dispersion, oppression, ghetto and massacre—but not disappearance. The alternative course that Rehoboam might have taken, advised by the elders and so lightly rejected, exacted a long revenge that has left its mark for 2800 years.

Equal in ruin but opposite in cause was the folly that brought about the conquest of Mexico. While Rehoboam is not difficult to understand, the case of Montezuma serves to remind us that folly is not always explicable. The Aztec state of which he was Emperor from 1502 to 1520 was rich, sophisticated and predatory. Surrounded by mountains on a plateau in the interior (now the site of Mexico City), its capital was a city of 60,000 households built upon the piles, causeways and islets of a lake, with stucco houses, streets and temples, brilliant in pomp and ornament, strong in arms. With colonies extending east to the Gulf coast and west to the Pacific, the empire included an estimated five million people. The Aztec rulers were advanced in the arts and sciences and agriculture in contrast to their ferocious religion, whose rituals of human sacrifice were unsurpassed in blood and cruelty. Aztec armies conducted annual campaigns to capture slave labor and victims for sacrifice from neighboring tribes, and food supplies, of which they were always short, and to bring new areas into subjection or punish revolts. In the early years of his reign, Montezuma led such campaigns in person, greatly extending his boundaries.

Aztec culture was in thrall to the gods—to bird gods, serpent gods, jaguar gods, to the rain god Tlaloc and the sun god Tezcatlipoc, who was lord of the earth's surface, the "Tempter," who "whispered ideas of savagery into the human mind." The founding god of the state, Quetzalcoatl, had fallen from glory and departed into the eastern sea, whence his return to earth was expected, to be fore-shadowed by omens and apparitions and to portend the downfall of the empire.

In 1519 a party of Spanish conquistadors coming from Cuba under the command of Hernán Cortés landed on the Mexican Gulf coast at Vera Cruz. In the twenty-five years since Columbus had discovered the Caribbean islands, Spanish invaders had established a rule that rapidly devastated the native people. If their bodies could not survive Spanish labor, their souls, in Christian terms, were saved. In their mail and helmets, the Spaniards were not settlers with patience to clear forests and plant crops, but restless ruthless adventurers greedy for slaves and gold, and Cortés was their epitome. More or less at odds with the Governor of Cuba, he set forth on an expedition with 600 men, seventeen horses and ten artillery pieces, ostensibly for exploration and trade but more truly, as his conduct was to make plain, for glory and an independent domain under the Crown. His first act on landing was to burn his ships so that there could be no retreat.

Informed by the local inhabitants, who hated the Aztec overlords, of the riches and power of the capital, Cortés with the larger part of his force boldly set out to conquer the great city of the interior. Though reckless and daring, he was not foolhardy and made alliances along the way with tribes hostile to the Aztecs, especially with Tlaxcala, their chief rival. He sent word ahead representing himself as the ambassador of a foreign prince but made no effort to pose as a reincarnated Quetzalcoatl, which for the Spaniards would have been out of the question. They marched with their own priests in very visible presence carrying crucifixes and banners of the Virgin and with the proclaimed goal of winning souls for Christ.

On report of the advance, Montezuma summoned his council, some of whom strongly urged resisting the strangers by force or fraud, while others argued that if they were indeed ambassadors of a foreign prince, a friendly welcome would be advisable, and if they were supernatural beings, as their wondrous attributes suggested, resistance would be useless. Their "gray" faces, their "stone" garments, their arrival at the coast in waterborne houses with white wings, their magic fire that burst from tubes to kill at a distance, their strange beasts that carried the leaders on their backs, suggested the supernatural to a people for whom the gods were everywhere. The idea that their leader might be Quetzalcoatl seems, however, to have been Montezuma's own peculiar dread.

Uncertain and apprehensive, he did the worst thing he could have done in the circumstances: he sent splendid gifts that displayed his wealth, and letters urging the visitors to turn back that indicated his weakness. Borne by a hundred slaves, the gifts of jewels, textiles, gorgeous featherwork and two huge plates of gold and silver "as large as cart wheels" excited the Spaniards' greed, while the letters forbidding further approach to his capital and almost pleading with them to return to their homeland and couched in soft language designed to provoke neither gods nor ambassadors were not very formidable. The Spaniards marched on.

Montezuma made no move to stop them or bar their way when

they reached the city. Instead, they were greeted with ceremonial welcome and escorted to quarters in the palace and elsewhere. The Aztec army waiting in the hills for the signal to attack was never called, although it could have annihilated the invaders, cut off escape over the causeways or isolated and starved them into surrender. Just such plans had in fact been prepared, but were betrayed to Cortés by his interpreter. Alerted, he put Montezuma under house arrest in his own palace as a hostage against attack. The sovereign of a warlike people outnumbering their captors by a thousand to one, submitted. Through an excess of mysticism or superstition, he had apparently convinced himself that the Spaniards were indeed the party of Quetzalcoatl come to register the break-up of his empire and, believing himself doomed, made no effort to avert his fate.

Nevertheless it was plain enough from the visitors' ceaseless demands for gold and provisions that they were all too human, and from their constant rituals in worship of a naked man pinned to crossed sticks of wood and of a woman with a child, that they were not connected with Quetzalcoatl, to whose cult they showed themselves distinctly hostile. When, in a spasm of regret or at someone's persuasion, Montezuma ordered an ambush of the garrison that Cortés had left behind at Vera Cruz, his men killed two Spaniards and sent the head of one of them to the capital as evidence. Asking no parley or explanation, Cortés instantly put the Emperor in chains and forced him to yield the perpetrators whom he burned alive at the palace gates, not forgetting to exact an immense punitive tribute in gold and jewels. Any remaining illusion of a relationship to the gods vanished with the severed Spanish head.

Montezuma's nephew Cacama denounced Cortés as a murderer and thief and threatened to raise a revolt, but the Emperor remained silent and passive. So confident was Cortés that, on learning that a force from Cuba had arrived at the coast to apprehend him, he went back to deal with it, leaving a small occupying force which further angered the inhabitants by smashing altars and seizing food. The spirit of revolt rose. Having lost authority, Montezuma could neither take command nor suppress the people's anger. On Cortés' return, the Aztecs, under the Emperor's brother, rebelled. The Spaniards, who never had more than thirteen muskets among them, fought back with sword, pike and crossbow, and torches to set fire to houses. Hard pressed, though they had the advantage of steel, they brought out Montezuma to call for a halt in the fighting, but on his appearance his people stoned him as a coward and traitor. Carried back into the palace by the Spaniards, he died three days later and was refused funeral honors by his subjects. The Spaniards evacuated the city during the night with a loss of a third of their force and their loot.

Rallying his Mexican allies, Cortés defeated a superior Aztec army in battle outside the city. With the aid of the Tlaxcalans, he organized a siege, cut off the city's supply of fresh water and food and gradually penetrated it, shoveling the rubble of destroyed buildings into the lake as he advanced. On 13 August 1521, the remnant of the inhabitants, starving and leaderless, surrendered. The conquerors filled in the lake, built their own city on the debris and stamped their rule upon Mexico, Aztecs and allies alike, for the next three hundred years.

One cannot quarrel with religious beliefs, especially of a strange, remote, half-understood culture. But when the beliefs become a delusion maintained against natural evidence to the point of losing the independence of a people, they may fairly be called folly. The category is once again wooden-headedness, in the special variety of religious mania. It has never wrought a greater damage.

Follies need not have negative consequences for all parties concerned. The Reformation, brought on by the folly of the Renaissance Papacy, would not generally be declared a misfortune by Protestants. Americans on the whole would not consider their independence, provoked by the folly of the English, to be regrettable. Whether the Moorish conquest of Spain, which endured over the greater part of the country for three hundred years and over lesser parts for eight hundred, was positive or negative in its results may be arguable, depending on the position of the viewer, but that it was brought on by the folly of Spain's rulers at the time is clear.

These rulers were the Visigoths, who had invaded the Roman empire in the 4th century and by the end of the 5th century had established themselves in control of most of the Iberian peninsula over the numerically superior Hispano-Roman inhabitants. For two hundred years they remained at odds and often in armed contention with their subjects. Through the unrestrained self-interest normal for sovereigns of the time, they created only hostility and in the end became its victims. Hostility was sharpened by animosity in religion, the local inhabitants being Catholics of the Roman rite while the Visigoths belonged to the Arian sect. Further contention arose over the method of selecting the sovereign. The native nobility tried to maintain the customary elective principle, while the kings, afflicted by dynastic longings, were determined to make and keep the process hereditary. They used every means of exile or execution, confiscation of property, unequal taxation and unequal land distribution to eliminate rivals and weaken the local opposition. These procedures naturally caused the nobles to foment insurrection and hatreds to flourish.

Meanwhile, through the stronger organization and more active intolerance of the Roman Church and its bishops in Spain, Catholic influence was gaining, and in the late 6th century, it succeeded in converting two heirs to the throne. The first was put to death by his father, but the second, called Recared, reigned, at last a ruler conscious of the need for unity. He was the first of the Goths to recognize that for a ruler opposed by two inimical groups, it is folly to continue antagonizing both at once. Convinced that union could never be achieved under Arianism, Recared acted energetically against his former associates and proclaimed Catholicism the official religion. Several of his successors, too, made efforts to placate former adversaries, recalling the banished and restoring property, but divisions and cross-currents were too strong for them and they had lost influence to the Church, in which they had created their own Wooden Horse.

Confirmed in power, the Catholic episcopate lunged into secular government, proclaiming its laws, arrogating its powers, holding decisive Councils, legitimizing favored usurpers and fatefully promoting a relentless campaign of discrimination and punitive rules against anyone "not a Christian"—namely the Jews. Beneath the surface, Arian loyalties persisted; decadence and debauchery afflicted the court. Hastened by cabals and plots, usurpations, assassinations and uprisings, the turnover in kings during the 7th century was rapid, none holding the throne for more than ten years.

During this century, the Moslems, animated by a new religion, exploded in a wild career of conquest that extended from Persia to Egypt and, by the year 700, reached Morocco across the narrow straits from Spain. Their ships raided the Spanish coast and though beaten back, the new power on the opposite shore offered to every disaffected group under the Goths the ever-tempting prospect of foreign aid against the internal foe. No matter how often repeated in history, this ultimate resort ends in only one way, as the Byzantine emperors learned when they invited in the Turks against domestic enemies: the invited power stays and takes over control.

For Spain's Jews, the time had come. A once tolerated minority who had arrived with the Romans and prospered as merchants, they were now shunned, persecuted, subjected to forced conversion, deprived of rights, property, occupation, even of children forcibly taken from them and given to Christian slave owners. Threatened with extinction, they made contact with and provided intelligence to the Moors through their co-religionists in North Africa. For them anything would be better than Christian rule.

The precipitating act came, however, from the central flaw of disunity in the society. In 710, a conspiracy of nobles refused to acknowledge as King the son of the last sovereign, defeated and deposed him and elected to the throne one of their own number, Duke Rodrigo, throwing the country into dispute and confusion. The ousted King and his adherents crossed the straits and, on the theory that the Moors would obligingly regain their throne for them, invited their assistance.

The Moorish invasion of 711 smashed through a country at odds with itself. Rodrigo's army offered ineffective resistance and the Moors won control with a force of 12,000. Capturing city after city, they took the capital, established surrogates—in one case handing a city over to the Jews—and moved on. Within seven years their conquest of the peninsula was complete. The Gothic monarchy, having failed to develop a workable principle of government or to achieve fusion with its subjects, collapsed under assault because it had put down no roots.

In those dark ages between the fall of Rome and the medieval revival, government had no recognized theory or structure or instrumentality beyond arbitrary force. Since disorder is the least tolerable of social conditions, government began to take shape in the Middle Ages and afterward as a recognized function with recognized principles, methods, agencies, parliaments, bureaucracies. It acquired authority, mandates, improved means and capacity, but not a noticeable increase in wisdom or immunity from folly. This is not to say that crowned heads and ministries are incapable of governing wisely and well. Periodically the exception appears in strong and effective, occasionally even benign, rulership, even more occasionally wise. Like folly, these appearances exhibit no correlation with time and place. Solon of Athens, perhaps the wisest, was among the earliest. He is worth a glance.

Chosen archon, or chief magistrate, in the 6th century B.C., at a time of economic distress and social unrest, Solon was asked to save the state and compose its differences. Harsh debt laws permitting creditors to seize lands pledged as security, or even the debtor himself for slave labor, had impoverished and angered the plebeians and created a rising mood of insurrection. Having neither participated in the oppressions by the rich nor supported the cause of the poor, Solon enjoyed the unusual distinction of being acceptable to both; by the rich, according to Plutarch, because he was a man of wealth and substance, and by the poor because he was honest. In the body of laws he proclaimed, Solon's concern was not partisanship, but justice, fair dealing between strong and weak, and stable government. He abolished enslavement for debt, freed the enslaved, extended suffrage to the plebeians, re-formed the currency to encourage trade, regulated weights and measures, established legal codes governing inherited property, civil rights of citizens, penalties for crime and finally, taking no chances, exacted an oath from the Athenian Council to maintain his reforms for ten years.

Then he did an extraordinary thing, possibly unique among heads of state: purchasing a ship on the pretext of traveling to see the world, he sailed into voluntary exile for ten years. Fair and just as a states-man, Solon was no less wise as a man. He could have retained supreme control, enlarging his authority to that of tyrant, and was indeed reproached because he did not, but knowing that endless petitions and proposals to modify this or that law would only gain him ill-will if he did not comply, he determined to leave, in order to keep his laws intact because the Athenians could not repeal them without his sanc-tion. His decision suggests that an absence of overriding personal ambition together with shrewd common sense are among the essential components of wisdom. In the notes of his life, writing of himself in the third person, Solon put it differently: "Each day he grew older and learned something new."

Strong and effective rulers, if lacking the complete qualities of Solon, rise from time to time in heroic size above the rest, visible towers down the centuries. Pericles presided over Athens' greatest century with sound judgment, moderation and high renown. Rome had Julius Caesar, a man of remarkable governing talents, although a ruler who arouses opponents to assassination is probably not as wise as he might be. Later, under the four "good emperors" of the Antonine dynasty—Trajan and Hadrian, the organizers and builders; Antoninus Pius, the benevolent; Marcus Aurelius, the revered philosopher—Roman citizens enjoyed good government, prosperity and respect for about a century. In England, Alfred the Great repelled the invaders and fathered the unity of his countrymen. Charlemagne was able to impose order on a mass of contending elements. He fostered the arts of civilization no less than those of war and earned a prestige supreme in the Middle Ages, not equalled until four centuries later by Frederick II, called Stupor Mundi, or Wonder of the World. Frederick took a hand in everything: arts, sciences, laws, poetry, universities, crusades, parliaments, wars, politics and contention with the Papacy, which in the end, for all his remarkable talents, frustrated him. Lorenzo de' Medici, the Magnificent, promoted the glory of Florence but through his dynastic ambitions undermined the republic. Two queens, Elizabeth I of England and Maria Theresa of Austria, were both able and sagacious rulers who raised their countries to the highest estate.

The product of a new nation, George Washington, was a leader who shines among the best. While Jefferson was more learned, more cultivated, a more extraordinary mind, an unsurpassed intelligence, a truly universal man, Washington had a character of rock and a kind of nobility that exerted a natural dominion over others, together with the inner strength and perseverance that enabled him to prevail over a flood of obstacles. He made possible both the physical victory of American independence and the survival of the fractious and tottering young republic in its beginning years.

Around him in extraordinary fertility political talent bloomed as if touched by some tropical sun. For all their flaws and quarrels, the Founding Fathers have rightfully been called by Arthur M. Schlesinger, Sr., "the most remarkable generation of public men in the history of the United States or perhaps of any other nation." It is worth noting the qualities this historian ascribes to them: they were fearless, high-principled, deeply versed in ancient and modern political thought, astute and pragmatic, unafraid of experiment, and—this is significant—"convinced of man's power to improve his condition through the use of intelligence." That was the mark of the Age of Reason that formed them, and although the 18th century had a tendency to regard men as more rational than in fact they were, it evoked the best in government from these men.

It would be invaluable if we could know what produced this burst of talent from a base of only two and a half million inhabitants. Schlesinger suggests some contributing factors: wide diffusion of education, challenging economic opportunities, social mobility, training in self-government—all these encouraged citizens to cultivate their political aptitudes to the utmost. With the Church declining in prestige, and business, science and art not yet offering competing fields of endeavor, statecraft remained almost the only outlet for men of energy and purpose. Perhaps above all the need of the moment was what evoked the response, the opportunity to create a new political system. What could be more exciting, more likely to summon into action men of energy and purpose?

Not before or since has so much careful and reasonable thinking been invested in the formation of a governmental system. In the French, Russian and Chinese revolutions, too much class hatred and bloodshed were involved to allow for fair results or permanent constitutions. For two centuries, the American arrangement has always managed to right itself under pressure without discarding the system and trying another after every crisis, as have Italy and Germany, France and Spain. Under accelerating incompetence in America, this may change. Social systems can survive a good deal of folly when circumstances are historically favorable, or when bungling is cushioned by large resources or absorbed by sheer size as in the United States during its period of expansion. Today, when there are no more cushions, folly is less affordable. Yet the Founders remain a phenomenon to keep in mind to encourage our estimate of human possibilities, even if their example is too rare to be a basis of normal expectations.

In between flashes of good government, folly has its day. In the Bourbons of France, it burst into brilliant flower.

Louis XIV is usually considered a master monarch, largely because people tend to accept a successfully dramatized self-estimation. In reality he exhausted France's economic and human resources by his ceaseless wars and their cost in national debt, casualties, famine and disease, and he propelled France toward the collapse that could only result, as it did two reigns later, in the overturn of absolute monarchy, the Bourbon raison d'être. Seen in that light, Louis XIV is the prince of policy pursued contrary to ultimate self-interest. Not he, but the mistress of his successor, Mme de Pompadour, glimpsed the outcome: "After us the deluge."

By general agreement of historians, the most condemned act and worst error of Louis' career was his Revocation of the Edict of Nantes in 1685, cancelling his grandfather's decree of toleration and reopening persecution of the Huguenots. It lacks one qualification of complete folly in that, far from being reproved or admonished at the time, it was greeted with the greatest enthusiasm and still lauded thirty years later at the King's funeral as one of his most praiseworthy acts. This very fact, however, reinforces another criterion—that the policy must be the product of a group rather than of an individual. Recognition as folly was not long delayed. Within decades, Voltaire called it "one of the greatest calamities of France," with consequences "wholly contrary to the purpose in view."

Like all follies, it was conditioned by the attitudes and beliefs and politics of the time, and like some, if not all, it was unnecessary, an activist policy when doing nothing would have served as well. The force of the old religious schism and of Calvinist doctrinal ferocity was fading; the Huguenots, who numbered fewer than two million or about one-tenth of the population, were loyal hard-working citizens, too hard-working for Catholic comfort. That was the rub. Since Huguenots kept only the Sabbath as against more than a hundred saints' days and holy days kept by the Catholics, they were more productive and more successful in commerce. Their stores and workshops took away business, a consideration that operated behind the Catholic demand for their suppression. The demand was justified on the higher ground that religious dissidence was treason to the King and that abolition of freedom of conscience—"this deadly freedom"—would serve the nation as well as serve God.

The advice appealed to the King as he grew more autocratic after shedding the early tutelage of Cardinal Mazarin. The greater his autocracy, the more the existence of a dissident sect appeared to him an unacceptable rift in submission to the royal will. "One law, one King, one God" was his concept of the state, and after twenty-five years at its head, his political arteries had hardened and his capacity for tolerating differences atrophied. He had acquired the disease of divine mission so often disastrous to rulers, convincing himself that it was the Almighty's will "that I should be His instrument in bringing back to His ways all those who are subject to me." In addition, he had political motives. Given the Catholic leanings of James II in England, Louis believed that the balance of Europe was swinging back to Catholic supremacy and that he could assist it by a dramatic gesture against the Protestants. Further, because of quarrels with the Pope over other issues, he wished to show himself the champion of orthodoxy, reaffirming the ancient French title of "Most Christian King."

Persecution began in 1681 before the actual Revocation. Protestant services were banned, schools and churches closed, Catholic baptism enforced, children separated from their families at age seven to be brought up as Catholics, professions and occupations gradually restricted until prohibited, Huguenot officials ordered to resign, clerical conversion squads organized and monetary bounty offered to each convert. Decree followed decree separating and uprooting the Huguenots from their own community and from national life.

Persecution engenders its own brutality, and resort to violent measures was soon adopted, of which the most atrocious—and effective—were the *dragonnades*, or billeting of dragoons on Huguenot families with encouragement to behave as viciously as they wished. Notoriously rough and undisciplined, the enlisted troops of the dragoons spread carnage, beating and robbing the householders, raping the women, smashing and wrecking and leaving filth while the authorities offered exemption from the horror of billeting as inducement to convert. Mass conversions under these circumstances could hardly be regarded as genuine and caused resentment among Catholics because they involved the Church in perjury and sacrilege. Unwilling communicants were sometimes driven to Mass, among them resisters who spat and trampled on the Eucharist and were burned at the stake for profaning the sacrament.

Emigration of the Huguenots began in defiance of edicts forbidding them to leave under penalty, if caught, of sentence to the galleys. Their pastors on the other hand, if they refused to abjure, were forced into exile for fear they would preach in secret, encouraging converts to relapse. Obdurate pastors who continued to hold services were broken on the wheel, creating martyrs and stimulating the resistance of their following.

When mass conversions were reported to the King, as many as 60,000 in one region in three days, he took the decision to revoke the Edict of Nantes on the ground that it was no longer needed because there were no more Huguenots. Some doubts of the advisability of the policy by this time were rising. At a Council held on the eve of the Revocation, the Dauphin, probably expressing concerns privately conveyed to him, cautioned that revoking the Edict might cause revolts and mass emigration harmful to French commerce, but he seems to have raised the only contrary voice, doubtless because he was safe from reprisal. A week later, on 18 October 1685, Revocation was formally decreed and the act hailed as "the miracle of our times." "Never had there been such a triumph of joy," wrote the caustic Saint-Simon, who held his fire until after the King was dead, "never such a profusion of praise. . . . All the King heard was praise."

The ill effects were soon felt. Huguenot textile workers, paper makers and other artisans, whose techniques had been a monopoly of France, took their skills abroad to England and the German states; bankers and merchants took their capital; printers, bookmakers, shipbuilders, lawyers, doctors and many pastors escaped. Within four years, 8000–9000 men of the Navy, and 10,000–12,000 of the Army, plus 500–600 officers, made their way to the Netherlands to add their strength to the forces of Louis' enemy William III, soon a double enemy when he became King of England three years later in place of the ousted James II. The silk industry of Tours and Lyons is said to have been ruined and some important towns like Reims and Rouen to have lost half their workers.

Exaggeration, beginning with Saint-Simon's virulent censure claiming "depopulation" of the realm by as much as a quarter, was inevitable as it usually is when disadvantages are discovered after the event. The total number of émigrés is now estimated rather elastically at anywhere from 100,000 to 250,000. Whatever their number, their value to France's opponents was immediately recognized by Protestant states. Holland granted them rights of citizenship at once and exemption from taxes for three years. Frederick William, Elector of Brandenburg (the future Prussia), issued a decree within a week of the Revocation inviting the Huguenots into his territory where their industrial enterprise contributed greatly to the rise of Berlin.

Recent studies have concluded that the economic damage done to France by the Huguenot emigration has been overrated, it being only one element in the larger damage caused by the wars. Of the political damage, however, there is no question. The flood of anti-French pamphlets and satires issued by Huguenot printers and their friends in all the cities where they settled aroused antagonism to France to new heat. The Protestant coalition against France was strengthened when Brandenburg entered into alliance with Holland, and the smaller German principalities joined. In France itself the Protestant faith was reinvigorated by persecution and the feud with Catholics revived. A prolonged revolt of the Camisard Huguenots in the Cévennes, a mountainous region of the south, brought on a cruel war of repression, weakening the state. Here and among other Huguenot communities which remained in France, a receptive base was created for the Revolution to come.

More profound was the discredit left upon the concept of absolute monarchy. By the dissenters' rejection of the King's right to impose religious unity, the divine right of royal authority everywhere was laid open to question and stimulus given to the constitutional challenge that the next century held in store. When Louis XIV, outliving son and grandson, died in 1715 after a reign of 72 years, he bequeathed, not the national unity that had been his objective, but an enlivened and embittered dissent, not national aggrandizement in wealth and power, but a weakened, disordered and impoverished state. Never had so self-centered a ruler so effectively despoiled self-interest.

The feasible alternative would have been to leave the Huguenots alone or at most satisfy the cry against them by civil decrees rather than by force and atrocity. Although ministers, clergy and people thoroughly approved of the persecution, none of the reasons for it was exigent. The peculiarity of the whole affair was its needlessness, and this underlines two characteristics of folly: it often does not spring from a great design, and its consequences are frequently a surprise. The folly lies in persisting thereafter. With acute if unwitting significance, a French historian wrote of the Revocation that "Great designs are rare in politics; the King proceeded empirically and sometimes impulsively." His point is reinforced from an unexpected source in a perceptive comment by Ralph Waldo Emerson, who cautioned, "In analyzing history do not be too profound, for often the causes are quite superficial." This is a factor usually overlooked by political scientists who, in discussing the nature of power, always treat it, even when negatively, with immense respect. They fail to see it as sometimes a matter of ordinary men walking into water over their heads, acting unwisely or foolishly or perversely as people in ordinary circumstances frequently do. The trappings and impact of power deceive us, endowing the possessors with a quality larger than life. Shorn of his tremendous curled peruke, high heels and ermine, the Sun King was a man subject to misjudgment, error and impulse—like you and me.

The last French Bourbon to reign, Charles X, brother of the guillotined Louis XVI and of his brief successor, Louis XVIII, displayed a recurring type of folly best described as the Humpty-Dumpty type: that is to say, the effort to reinstate a fallen and shattered structure, turning back history. In the process, called reaction or counter-revolution, the reactionary right is bent on restoring the privileges and property of the old regime and somehow retrieving a strength it did not have before.

When Charles X at age 67 ascended the throne in 1824, France had passed through 35 years of the most radical changes in history up to that point, from complete revolution to Napoleonic empire to Waterloo and restoration of the Bourbons. Since it was then impossible to cancel all the rights and liberties and legal reforms incorporated in government since the Revolution, Louis XVIII accepted a constitution, though he could never accustom himself to the idea of a constitutional monarchy, and it was beyond the comprehension of his brother Charles. Having seen the process at work during exile in England, Charles said he would sooner earn his living as a woodcutter than be King of England. Not surprisingly, he was the hope of the émigrés who had returned with the Bourbons and who wanted the old regime put back together again, complete with rank, titles and especially their confiscated property.

In the National Assembly they were represented by the Ultras of the right, who, together with a splinter group of extreme Ultras, formed the strongest party. This had been accomplished by restricting the franchise to the wealthiest class by the interesting method of reducing the taxes of known opponents so they could not meet the tax qualification of 300 francs required for voters. Government office was similarly restricted. Ultras held all the ministerial posts, including a religious extremist as Minister of Justice whose political ideas, it was said, were formed by regular reading of the Apocalypse. His colleagues imposed strict laws of censorship and elastic laws of search and arrest and, as their primary achievement, created a fund to compensate approximately 70,000 émigrés or their heirs at an annual rate of 1377 francs. This was too little to satisfy them but enough to outrage the bourgeois whose taxes were paying for it.

The beneficiaries of the Revolution and of Napoleon's court were not prepared to make way for the émigrés and clergy of the old regime, and discontent was rising although still subdued. Surrounded by his Ultras, the King could probably have more or less comfortably completed his reign if he had not by aggravated unwisdom brought about its downfall. Charles was determined to rule and, while lightly endowed for the task intellectually, was rich in the Bourbon capacity to learn nothing and forget nothing. When opposition in the Assembly grew troublesome, he took the advice of his ministers to dissolve the session and, by bribes, threats and other pressures, to manipulate an acceptable election. Instead, the royalists lost by almost two to one. Refusing to acquiesce in the result like some helpless King of England, Charles decreed another dissolution and under a new and narrower franchise and sterner censorship, another election.

The opposition press called for resistance. While the King went hunting, not expecting overt conflict and having summoned no military support, the people of Paris, as so many times before and since, put up barricades and enthusiastically engaged in three days of street fighting known to the French as *les trois glorieuses*. Opposition deputies organized a provisional government. Charles abdicated and fled to the despised haven of limited monarchy across the Channel. No great tragedy, the episode was historically significant only in moving France a step forward from counter-revolution to the "bourgeois" monarchy of Louis-Philippe. More significant in the history of folly, it illustrates the futility of the recurrent attempt, not confined to Bourbons, to reconstruct a broken egg.

Throughout history cases of military folly have been innumerable, but they are outside the scope of this inquiry. Two of the most eventful, however, both involving war with the United States, represent policy decisions at the government level. They were the German decision to resume unrestricted submarine warfare in 1916 and the Japanese decision to attack Pearl Harbor in 1941. In both cases, contrary voices warned against the course taken, urgently and despairingly in Germany, discreetly but with profound doubt in Japan, unsuccessfully in both. The folly in both cases belongs to the category of self-imprisonment in the "we-have-no-alternative" argument and in the most frequent and fatal of self-delusions—underestimation of the opponent.

"Unrestricted" submarine warfare meant the sinking without warning of merchant ships found in a declared blockade zone, whether belligerent or neutral, armed or unarmed. Sternly protested by the United States on the dearly held principle of the neutral's right to freedom of the seas, the practice had been halted in 1915 after the frenzy over the *Lusitania*, less because of American outrage and threat to break relations, and the antagonizing of other neutrals, than because Germany did not have enough U-boats on hand to give assurance of decisive effect if she forced the issue.

By this time, indeed by the end of 1914 after the failure of the opening offensive to knock out either Russia or France, Germany's rulers recognized that they could not win the war against the three combined Allies if they held together, but rather, as the Chief of Staff told the Chancellor, that "It was more likely that we ourselves should become exhausted."

Political action to gain a separate peace with Russia was required, but this failed as did numerous other feelers and overtures made to or by Germany with regard to Belgium, France and even Britain during the next two years. All failed for the same reason—that Germany's terms in each case were punitive, as if by a victor, providing for the other party to leave the war while yielding annexations and indemnities. It was always the stick, never the carrot, and none of Germany's opponents was tempted to betray its allies on that basis.

By the end of 1916 both sides were approaching exhaustion in resources as well as military ideas, spending literally millions of lives at Verdun and the Somme for gains or losses measured in yards. Germany was living on a diet of potatoes and conscripting fifteen-year-olds for the Army. The Allies were holding on meagerly with no means of victory in sight unless the great fresh untapped strength of America were added to their side.

During these two years, while Kiel's shipyards were furiously turning out submarines toward a goal of 200, the Supreme High Command battled in high-level conferences over renewal of the torpedo campaign against the strongly negative advice of civilian ministers. To resume unrestricted sinkings, the civilians insisted, would, in the words of Chancellor Bethmann-Hollweg, "inevitably cause America to join our enemies." The High Command did not deny but discounted this possibility. Because it was plain that Germany could not win the war on land alone, their object had become to defeat Britain, already staggering under shortages, by cutting off her supplies by sea before the United States could mobilize, train and transport troops to Europe in any number sufficient to affect the outcome. They claimed this could be accomplished within three or four months. Admirals unrolled charts and graphs proving how many tons the U-boats could send to the bottom in a given time until they should have Britain "gasping in the reeds like a fish."

The contrary voices, beginning with the Chancellor's, countered that American belligerency would give the Allies enormous financial aid and a lift in morale encouraging them to hold out until aid in troops should arrive, besides giving them use of all the German tonnage interned in American ports and very likely bringing in other neutrals as well. Vice-Chancellor Karl Helfferich believed that releasing the U-boats would "lead to ruin." Foreign Office officials directly concerned with American affairs were equally opposed. Two leading bankers returned from a mission to the United States to warn against underestimating the potential energies of the American people, who, they said, if aroused and convinced of a good cause, could mobilize forces and resources on an unimagined scale.

Of all the dissuaders, the most urgent was the German Ambassador to Washington, Count von Bernstorff, whose non-Prussian birth and upbringing spared him many of the delusions of his peers. Well acquainted with America, Bernstorff repeatedly warned his government that American belligerency was certain to follow the U-boats and would lose Germany the war. As the military's insistence grew intense, he was straining in every message home to swerve his country from the course he believed would be fatal. He had become convinced that the only way to avert that outcome would be to stop the war itself through mediation for a compromise peace which President Wilson was preparing to offer. Bethmann too was anxious for it on the theory that if the Allies rejected such a peace, as expected, while Germany accepted, she could then be justified in resuming unrestricted submarine warfare *without* provoking American belligerency.

The war party clamoring for the U-boats included the Junkers and court circle, the expansionist war-aims associations, the right-wing parties and a majority of the public, which had been taught to pin its faith on the submarine as the means to break England's food blockade of Germany and vanquish the enemy. A few despised voices of Social Democrats in the Reichstag shouted, "The people don't want submarine warfare but *bread* and *peace!*" but little attention was paid to them because German citizens, no matter how hungry, remained obedient. Kaiser Wilhelm II, assailed by uncertainties but unwilling to appear any less bold than his commanders, added his voice to theirs.

Wilson's offer of December 1916 to bring together the belligerents for negotiation of a "peace without victory" was rejected by both sides. Neither was prepared to accept a settlement without some gain to justify its suffering and sacrifice in lives, and to pay for the war. Germany was not fighting for the status quo but for German hegemony of Europe and a greater empire overseas. She wanted not a mediated but a dictated peace and had no wish, as the Foreign Minister, Arthur Zimmermann, wrote to Bernstorff, "to risk being cheated of what we hope to gain from the war" by a neutral mediator. Any settlement requiring renunciations and indemnities by Germany—the only settlement the Allies would accept—would mean the end of the Hohenzollerns and the governing class. They also had to make someone pay for the war or go bankrupt. A peace without victory would not only terminate dreams of mastery but require enormous taxes to pay for years of fighting that had grown profitless. It would mean revolution. To the throne, the military caste, the landowners, industrialists and barons of business, only a war of gain offered any hope of their survival in power.

The decision was taken at a conference of the Kaiser and Chancellor and Supreme Command on 9 January 1917. Admiral von Holtzendorff, Naval Chief of Staff, presented a 200-page compilation of statistics on tonnage entering British ports, freight rates, cargo space, rationing systems, food prices, comparisons with last year's harvest and everything down to the calorie content of the British breakfast, and swore that his U-boats could sink 600,000 tons a month, forcing England to capitulate before the next harvest. He said this was Germany's last opportunity and he could see no other way to win the war "so as to guarantee our future as a world power."

Bethmann spoke for an hour in reply, marshaling all the arguments of the advisers who warned that American belligerency would mean Germany's defeat. Frowns and restless mutterings around the table confronted him. He knew that the Navy, deciding for itself, had already despatched the submarines. Slowly he knuckled under. True, the increased number of U-boats offered a better chance of success than before. Yes, the last harvest had been poor for the Allies. On the other hand, America . . . Field Marshal von Hindenburg inter- rupted to affirm that the Army could "take care of America," while von Holtzendorff offered his "guarantee" that "no American will set foot on the Continent!" The melancholy Chancellor gave way. "Of course," he said, "if success beckons, we must follow."

He did not resign. An official who found him later slumped in his chair, looking stricken, asked in alarm if there had been bad news from the front. "No," answered Bethmann, "but *finis Germaniae.*"

Nine months earlier, in a previous crisis over the U-boats, Kurt Riezler, Bethmann's assistant assigned to the General Staff, had reached a similar verdict when he wrote in his diary for 24 April 1916, "Ger- many is like a person staggering along an abyss, wishing for nothing more fervently than to throw himself into it."

So it proved. Although the sinkings took a terrible toll of Allied shipping before the convoy system took effect, the British, upheld by the American declaration of war, did not capitulate. Despite von Holtzendorff's guarantee, two million American troops eventually reached Europe and within eight months of the first major American offensive, the surrender that came was Germany's.

Was there an alternative? Given insistence on victory and refusal to admit reality, probably not. But a better outcome could have been won by accepting Wilson's proposal, knowing it would be a dead end, thus preventing or certainly postponing the addition of American strength to the enemy. Without America, the Allies could not have held out for victory, and as victory was probably beyond Germany's power too, both sides would have slogged to an exhausted but more or less equal peace. For the world the consequences of that unused alternative would have changed history; no victory, no reparations, no war guilt, no Hitler, possibly no Second World War.

Like many alternatives, however, it was psychologically impossible. Character is fate, as the Greeks believed. Germans were schooled in winning objectives by force, unschooled in adjustment. They could not bring themselves to forgo aggrandizement even at the risk of defeat. Riezler's abyss summoned them.

In 1941 Japan faced a similar decision. Her plan of empire, called the Greater East Asia Co-Prosperity Sphere, with the subjugation of China at its core, was a vision of Japanese rule stretching from Manchuria through the Philippines, Netherlands Indies, Malaya, Siam, Burma to (and sometimes including, depending on the discretion of the spokesman) Australia, New Zealand and India. Japan's appetite was in inverse proportion to her size, though not to her will. To move the forces necessary for this enterprise, access was essential to iron, oil, rubber, rice and other raw materials far beyond her own possession. The moment for accomplishment came when war broke out in Europe and the Western colonial powers, Japan's major opponents in the region, were fighting for survival or already helpless—France defeated, the Netherlands occupied though retaining a government in exile, Britain battered by the Luftwaffe and having little to spare for action on the other side of the world.

The obstacle in Japan's way was the United States, which persistently refused to recognize her progressive conquests in China and was increasingly disinclined to make available the materials to fuel further Japanese adventure. Atrocities in China, attack on the United States gunboat *Panay* and other provocations were factors in American opinion. In 1940 Japan concluded the Tripartite Treaty making herself a partner of the Axis powers and moved into French Indochina when France succumbed in Europe. The United States, in response, froze Japanese assets and embargoed the sale of scrap iron, oil and aviation gasoline. Prolonged diplomatic exchanges through 1940 and 1941 in the effort to reach a ground of agreement proved futile. Despite isolationist sentiment, America would not acquiesce in Japanese control of China while Japan would accept no limitations there or restraints on her freedom of movement elsewhere in Asia.

Responsible Japanese leaders, as distinct from the military extremists and political hotheads, did not want war with the United States. What they wanted was to keep America quiescent while they moved forward to gain the empire of Asia. They believed this could be managed by sheer insistence, augmented by bluster, fierce and pretentious demands, and intimidation implicit in partnership with the Axis. When these methods seemed only to stiffen American non-acquiescence, the Japanese became convinced, on too little examination, that if they moved to gain their first objective, the vital resources of the Netherlands Indies, the United States would go to war against them. How to achieve one without provoking the other was the problem that tortured them through 1940–41.

Strategy demanded that in order to seize the Indies and transport its raw materials to Japan, it was necessary to protect the Japanese flank from any threat of United States naval action in the Southwest Pacific. Admiral Yamamoto, Commander-in-Chief of the Japanese Navy and architect of the Pearl Harbor strike, knew that Japan had no hope of ultimate victory over the United States. As he told Premier Konoye, "I have utterly no confidence for the second or third year." Since he believed that operations against the Netherlands Indies "will lead to an early commencement of war with America," his plan was to force the issue and knock the United States out by a "fatal blow." Then, by conquering Southeast Asia, Japan could acquire the resources necessary for a protracted war to establish her hegemony over the Co-Prosperity Sphere. And so he proposed that Japan should "fiercely attack and destroy the United States main fleet at the outset of the war so that the morale of the United States Navy and her people [would] sink to an extent that it could not be recovered." This curious estimate came from a man who was not unacquainted with America, having attended Harvard and served as naval attaché in Washington.

Planning for the supremely audacious blow to smash the United States Pacific fleet at Pearl Harbor began in January 1941 while the ultimate decision continued to be the subject of intense maneuvering between the government and armed services throughout the year. Advocates of the preemptive strike promised, none too confidently, that it would remove the United States from all possibility of interference and, it was hoped, from further hostilities altogether. And if it did not, asked the doubtful, what then? They argued that Japan could not win a prolonged war against the United States, that the life of their nation was being staked on a gamble. At no time during the discussions were warning voices silent. The Prime Minister, Prince Konoye, resigned, commanders were at odds, advisers hesitant and reluctant, the Emperor glum. When he asked if the surprise attack would win as great a victory as the surprise attack on Port Arthur in the Russo-Japanese

War, Admiral Nagano, Chief of Naval General Staff, replied that it was doubtful that Japan would win at all. (It is possible that in speaking to the Emperor, this could have been a ritual bow of oriental self-disparagement, but at so serious a moment that would seem un-called for.)

In this atmosphere of doubt why was the extreme risk approved? Partly because exasperation at the failure of all her efforts at intimidation had led to an all-or-nothing state of mind and a helpless yielding like Bethmann's by the civilians to the military. Further, the grandiose mood of the fascist powers in which no conquest seemed impossible, must be taken into account. Japan had mobilized a military will of terrible force which was in fact to accomplish extraordinary triumphs, among them the capture of Singapore and the blow on Pearl Harbor itself, which brought the United States close to panic. Fundamentally the reason Japan took the risk was that she had either to go forward or content herself with the status quo, which no one was willing or could politically afford to suggest. Over a generation, pressure from the aggressive army in China and from its partisans at home had fused Japan to the goal of an impossible empire from which she could not now retreat. She had become a prisoner of her oversize ambitions.

An alternative strategy would have been to proceed against the Netherlands Indies while leaving the United States untouched. While this would have left an unknown quantity in Japan's rear, an unknown quantity would have been preferable to a certain enemy, especially one of potential vastly superior to her own.

Here was a strange miscalculation. At a time when at least half the United States was strongly isolationist, the Japanese did the one thing that could have united the American people and motivated the whole nation for war. So deep was the division in America in the months before Pearl Harbor that renewal of the one-year draft law was enacted in Congress by a majority of only one vote—a single vote. The fact is that Japan could have seized the Indies without any risk of American belligerency; no attack on Dutch, British or French colonial territory would have brought the United States into the war. Attack on American territory was just the thing—and the only thing—that could. Japan seems never to have considered that the effect of an attack on Pearl Harbor might be not to crush morale but to unite the nation for combat. This curious vacuum of understanding came from what might be called cultural ignorance, a frequent component of folly. (Although present on both sides, in Japan's case it was critical.) Judging America by themselves, the Japanese assumed that the American government could take the nation into war whenever it wished, as Japan would have done and indeed did. Whether from ignorance, miscalculation or pure recklessness, Japan gave her opponent the one blow necessary to bring her to purposeful and determined belligerency.

Although Japan was starting a war, not already deeply caught in one, her circumstances otherwise were strikingly similar to Germany's in 1916–17. Both sets of rulers staked the life of the nation and lives of the people on a gamble that, in the long run, as many of them were aware, was almost sure to be lost. The impulse came from the compelling lure of dominion, from pretensions of grandeur, from greed.

A principle that emerges in the cases so far mentioned is that folly is a child of power. We all know, from unending repetitions of Lord Acton's dictum, that power corrupts. We are less aware that it breeds folly; that the power to command frequently causes failure to think; that the responsibility of power often fades as its exercise augments. The overall responsibility of power is to govern as reasonably as possible in the interest of the state and its citizens. A duty in that process is to keep well-informed, to heed information, to keep mind and judgment open and to resist the insidious spell of wooden-headedness. If the mind is open enough to perceive that a given policy is harming rather than serving self-interest, and self-confident enough to acknowledge it, and wise enough to reverse it, that is a summit in the art of government.

The policy of the victors after World War II in contrast to the Treaty of Versailles and the reparations exacted after World War I is an actual case of learning from experience and putting what was learned into practice—an opportunity that does not often present itself. The occupation of Japan according to a post-surrender policy drafted in Washington, approved by the Allies and largely carried out by Americans, was a remarkable exercise in conqueror's restraint, political intelligence, reconstruction and creative change. Keeping the Emperor at the head of the Japanese state prevented political chaos and supplied a footing for obedience through him to the army of occupation and an acceptance that proved amazingly docile. Apart from disarmament, demilitarization and trials of war criminals to establish blame, the goal was democratization politically and economically through constitutional and representative government and through the breaking up of cartels and land reform. The power of the huge Japanese industrial enterprises proved in the end intransigent, but political democracy, which ordinarily should be impossible to achieve by fiat and only gained by inches through the slow struggle of centuries, was successfully transferred and on the whole adopted. The army of occupation ruled through offices of liaison with Japanese ministries rather than directly. The purge of former officials brought in juniors not perhaps essentially different from their predecessors but willing to accept change. Education and textbooks were revised and the status of the Emperor modified to that of symbol "deriving from the will of the people with whom resides sovereign power."

Mistakes were made, especially in military policy. The authoritarian nature of Japanese society seeped back. Yet the result on the whole was beneficial, rather than vindictive, and may be taken as an encouraging reminder that wisdom in government is still an arrow that remains, however rarely used, in the human quiver.

The rarest kind of reversal—that of a ruler recognizing that a policy was *not* serving self-interest and daring the dangers of reversing it by 180 degrees—occurred only yesterday, historically speaking. It was President Sadat's abandonment of a sterile enmity with Israel and his search, in defiance of outrage and threats by his neighbors, for a more useful relationship. Both in risk and potential gain, it was a major act, and in substituting common sense and courage for mindless continuance in negation, it ranks high and lonely in history, undiminished by the subsequent tragedy of assassination.

The pages that follow will tell a more familiar and—unhappily for mankind—a more persistent story. The ultimate outcome of a policy is not what determines its qualification as folly. All misgovernment is contrary to self-interest in the long run, but may actually strengthen a regime temporarily. It qualifies as folly when it is a perverse persistence in a policy demonstrably unworkable or counter-productive. It seems almost superfluous to say that the present study stems from the ubiquity of this problem in our time.

Chapter Two

PROTOTYPE:
THE TROJANS TAKE
THE WOODEN HORSE WITHIN
THEIR WALLS

The most famous story of the Western world, the prototype of all tales of human conflict, the epic that belongs to all people and all times since—and even before—literacy began, contains the legend, with or without some vestige of historical foundation, of the Wooden Horse.

The Trojan War has supplied themes to all subsequent literature and art from Euripides' heart-rending tragedy of *The Trojan Women* to Eugene O'Neill, Jean Giraudoux and the still enthralled writers of our time. Through Aeneas in Virgil's sequel, it provided the legendary founder and national epic of Rome. A favorite of medieval romancers, it supplied William Caxton with the subject of the first book printed in English, and Chaucer (and later Shakespeare) with the setting, if not the story, of Troilus and Cressida. Racine and Goethe tried to fathom the miserable sacrifice of Iphigenia. Wandering Ulysses inspired writers as far apart as Tennyson and James Joyce. Cassandra and avenging Electra have been made the protagonists of German drama and opera. Some thirty-five poets and scholars have offered English translations since George Chapman in Elizabethan times first opened the realms of gold. Countless painters have found the Judgment of Paris an irresistible scene, and as many poets fallen under the spell of the beauty of Helen.

All of human experience is in the tale of Troy, or Ilium, first put into epic form by Homer around 850–800 B.C.* Although the gods are its motivators, what it tells us about humanity is basic, even though—or perhaps because—the circumstances are ancient and primitive. It has endured deep in our minds and memories for twenty-eight centuries because it speaks to us of ourselves, not least when least rational. It mirrors, in the judgment of another storyteller, John Cowper Powys,

* Previously widely disputed, this is the span of time more or less agreed upon by scholars since the decipherment of Linear B in 1952.

"what happened, is happening and will happen to us all, from the very beginning until the end of human life upon this earth."

Troy falls at last after ten years of futile, indecisive, noble, mean, tricky, bitter, jealous and only occasionally heroic battle. As the culminating instrumentality for the fall, the story brings in the Wooden Horse. The episode of the Horse exemplifies policy pursued contrary to self-interest—in the face of urgent warning and a feasible alternative. Occurring in this earliest chronicle of Western man, it suggests that such pursuit is an old and inherent human habit. The story first appears, not in the *Iliad,* which ends before the climax of the war, but in the *Odyssey* through the mouth of the blind bard Demodocus, who, at Odysseus' bidding, recounts the exploit to the group gathered in the palace of Alcinous. Despite Odysseus' high praise of the bard's narrative talents, the story is told rather baldly, as if the main facts were already familiar. Minor details are added elsewhere in the poem by Odysseus himself and in what seems an impossible flight of fancy by two other participants, Helen and Menelaus.

Lifted by Homer out of dim mists and memories, the Wooden Horse instantly caught the imagination of his successors in the next two or three centuries and inspired them to elaborate on the episode, notably and importantly by the addition of Laocoon in one of the most striking incidents of the entire epic. He appears earliest in *The Sack of Ilium* by Arctinus of Miletus, composed probably a century or so after Homer. Personifying the Voice of Warning, Laocoon's dramatic role becomes central to the episode of the Horse in all versions thereafter.

The full story as we know it of the device that finally accomplished the fall of Troy took shape in Virgil's *Aeneid*, completed in 20 B.C. By that time the tale incorporated the accumulated versions of more than a thousand years. Arising from geographically separate districts of the Greek world, the various versions are full of discrepancies and inconsistencies. Greek legend is hopelessly contradictory. Incidents do not conform necessarily to narrative logic; motive and behavior are often irreconcilable. We must take the story of the Wooden Horse as it comes, as Aeneas told it to the enraptured Dido, and as it passed, with further revisions and embellishments by Latin successors, to the Middle Ages and from the medieval romancers to us.

It is the ninth year of inconclusive battle on the plains of Troy, where the Greeks are besieging the city of King Priam. The gods are intimately involved with the belligerents as a result of jealousies generated ten years earlier when Paris, Prince of Troy, offended Hera and Athena by giving the golden apple as the award of beauty to Aphrodite, goddess of love. Not playing fair (as the Olympians, molded by men, were not disposed to), she had promised him, if he gave her the prize, the most beautiful woman in the world as his bride. This led, as everyone knows, to Paris' abduction of Helen, wife of Menelaus, King of Sparta, and the forming of a federation under his brother, the Greek overlord Agamemnon, to enforce her return. War followed when Troy refused.

Taking sides and playing favorites, potent but fickle, conjuring deceptive images, altering the fortunes of battle to suit their desires, whispering, tricking, falsifying, even inducing the Greeks through deceit to continue when they are ready to give up and go home, the gods keep the combatants engaged while heroes die and homelands suffer. Poseidon, ruler of the sea, who, with Apollo, was said to have built Troy and its walls, has turned against the Trojans because their first king failed to pay him for his work and further because they have stoned to death a priest of his cult for failure to offer sacrifices necessary to arouse the waves against the Greek invasion. Apollo, on the other hand, still favors Troy as its traditional protector, the more so because Agamemnon has angered him by seizing the daughter of a priest of Apollo for his bed. Athena, busiest and most influential of all, is unforgivingly anti-Trojan and pro-Greek because of Paris' original offense. Zeus, ruler of Olympus, is not a strong partisan, and when appealed to by one or another of his extended family, is capable of exercising his influence on either side.

In rage and despair, Troy mourns the death of Hector, slain by Achilles, who brutally drags his corpse by the heels three times around the walls in the dust of his chariot wheels. The Greeks are no better off. The angry Achilles, their champion fighter, shot in his vulnerable heel by Paris with a poisoned arrow, dies. His armor, to be conferred on the most deserving of the Greeks, is awarded to Odysseus, the wisest, instead of to Ajax, the most valorous, whereupon Ajax, maddened by insulted pride, kills himself. His companions' spirits fail and many of the Greek host counsel departure, but Athena puts a stop to that. On her advice, Odysseus proposes a last effort to take Troy by a stratagem—the building of a wooden horse large enough to hold twenty or fifty (or in some versions, as many as three hundred) armed men concealed inside. His plan is for the rest of the army to pretend to sail for home while in fact hiding their ships offshore behind the island of Tenedos. The Wooden Horse will carry an inscription dedicating it to Athena as the Greeks' offering in the hope of her aid in ensuring their safe return home. The figure is intended to excite the veneration of the Trojans, to whom the horse is a sacred animal and who may well be moved to conduct it to their own temple of Athena within the city. If so, the sacred veil said to surround and protect the city will be torn apart, the concealed Greeks will emerge, open the gates to their fellows, summoned by signal, and seize their final opportunity.

In obedience to Athena, who appears to one Epeius in a dream with orders to build the Horse, the "thing of guile" is completed in three days, aided by the goddess' "divine art." Odysseus persuades the rather reluctant leaders and bravest soldiers to enter by rope ladder during the night and take their places "halfway between victory and death."

At dawn, Trojan scouts discover that the siege is lifted and the enemy gone, leaving only the strange and awesome figure at their gates. Priam and his council come out to examine it and fall into anxious and divided discussion. Taking the inscription at face value, Thymoetes, one of the elders, recommends bringing the Horse to Athena's temple in the citadel. "Knowing better," Capys, another of the elders, objects, saying Athena had for too long favored the Greeks, and Troy would be well advised either to burn the pretended offering at once or break it open with brazen axes to see what the belly contains. Here was the feasible alternative.

Hesitant, yet fearful of desecrating Athena's property, Priam decides in favor of bringing the Horse into the city, although the walls must be breached or, in another version, the lintel of the Scean Gate removed to allow it to enter. This is the first warning omen, for it has been prophesied that if ever the Scean lintel is taken down, Troy will fall.

Excited voices from the gathering crowd cry, "Burn it! Hurl it over the rocks into the sea! Cut it open!" Opponents shout as loudly in favor of preserving what they take to be a sacred image. Then occurs a dramatic intervention. Laocoon, a priest of Apollo's temple, comes rushing down from the citadel crying in alarm, "Are you mad, wretched people? Do you think the foe has gone? Do you think gifts of the Greeks lack treachery? What was Odysseus' reputation?

> *"Either the Greeks are hiding in this monster,*
> *Or it's some trick of war, a spy or engine,*
> *To come down on the city. Tricky business*
> *Is hiding in it. Do not trust it, Trojans;*
> *Do not believe this horse. Whatever it may be,*
> *I fear the Greeks, even when bringing gifts."*

With that warning that has echoed down the ages, he flings his spear with all his strength at the Horse, in whose flank it sticks quivering and setting off a moaning sound from the frightened souls within. The blow almost split the wood and let light into the interior, but fate or the gods blunted it; or else, as Aeneas says later, Troy would still be standing.

Just as Laocoon has convinced the majority, guards drag in Sinon, an ostensibly terrified Greek who pretends he has been left behind through the enmity of Odysseus, but who has actually been planted by Odysseus as part of his plan. Asked by Priam to tell the truth about the Wooden Horse, Sinon swears it is a genuine offering to Athena which the Greeks deliberately made huge so the Trojans would *not* take it into their city because that would signify an ultimate Trojan victory. If the Trojans destroy it they will doom themselves, but if they bring it inside they will ensure their city's safety.

Swung around by Sinon's story, the Trojans are wavering between the warning and the false persuasion when a fearful portent convinces them that Laocoon is wrong. Just as he cautions that Sinon's tale is another trick put into his mouth by Odysseus, two horrible serpents rise in gigantic black spirals out of the waves and advance across the sands,

> *Their burning eyes suffused with blood and fire,*
> *Their darting tongues licking their hissing mouths.*

As the crowd watches paralyzed in terror, they make straight for Laocoon and his two young sons, "fastening their fangs in those poor bodies," coiling around the father's waist and neck and arms and, as he utters strangled inhuman cries, crush him to death. The appalled watchers are now nearly all moved to believe that the ghastly event is Laocoon's punishment for sacrilege in striking what must indeed be a sacred offering.

Troublesome even to the ancient poets, the serpents have defied explanation; myth has its mysteries too, not always resolved. Some narrators say they were sent by Poseidon at Athena's request to prove that his animus against the Trojans was equal to hers. Others say they were sent by Apollo to warn the Trojans of approaching doom (although, since the effect worked the other way, this seems to have a built-in illogic). Virgil's explanation is that Athena herself was responsible in order to convince the Trojans of Sinon's story, thus sealing their doom, and in confirmation he has the serpents take refuge in her temple after the event. So difficult was the problem of the serpents that some collaborators of the time suggested that Laocoon's fate had nothing to do with the Wooden Horse, but was owed to the quite extraneous sin of profaning Apollo's temple by sleeping with his wife in front of the god's image.

The blind bard of the *Odyssey*, who knows nothing of Laocoon, simply states that the argument in favor of welcoming the Horse had to prevail because Troy was ordained to perish—or, as we might interpret it, that mankind in the form of Troy's citizens is addicted to pursuing policy contrary to self-interest.

The instrumentality of the serpents is not a fact of history to be explained, but a work of imagination, one of the most forceful ever described. It produced, in agonized and twisted marble, so vivid that the victims' cries seem almost to be heard, a major masterpiece of classical sculpture. Seeing it in the palace of the Emperor Titus in Rome, Pliny the Elder thought it a work to be preferred "above all that the arts of painting and sculpture have produced." Yet the statue is dumb as to cause and significance. Sophocles wrote a tragedy on the theme of Laocoon but the text disappeared and his thoughts are lost. The existence of the legend can tell us only one thing: that Laocoon was fatally punished for perceiving the truth and warning of it.

While on Priam's orders ropes and rollers are prepared to pull the Horse into the city, unnamed forces still try to warn Troy. Four times at the Gate's threshold, the Horse comes to a halt and four times from the interior the clang of arms sounds, yet though the halts are an omen, the Trojans press on, "heedless and blind with frenzy." They breach the walls and the Gate, unconcerned at thus tearing the sacred veil because they believe its protection is no longer needed. In post-*Aeneid* versions, other portents follow: smoke rises stained with blood, tears flow from the statues of the gods, towers groan as if in pain, mist covers the stars, wolves and jackals howl, laurel withers in the temple of Apollo, but the Trojans take no alarm. Fate drives fear from their minds "so that they might meet their doom and be destroyed."

That night they celebrate, feasting and drinking with carefree hearts. A last chance and a last warning are offered. Cassandra, Priam's daughter, possesses the gift of prophecy conferred on her by Apollo, who, on falling in love with her, gave it in exchange for her promise to lie with him. When Cassandra, dedicating herself to virginity, went back on her promise, the offended god added to his gift a curse providing that her prophecies would never be believed. Ten years before, when Paris first sailed for Sparta, Cassandra had indeed foretold that his voyage would bring doom upon his house, but Priam had paid no attention. "O miserable people," she now cries, "poor fools, you do not understand at all your evil fate." They are acting senselessly, she tells them, toward the very thing "that has your destruction within it." Laughing and drunken, the Trojans tell her she talks too much "windy nonsense." In the fury of the seer ignored, she seizes an axe and a burning brand and rushes at the Wooden Horse but is restrained before she can reach it.

Heavy with wine, the Trojans sleep. Sinon creeps from the hall and opens the trap door of the Horse to release Odysseus and his companions, some of whom, cooped up in the blackness, have been weeping under the tension and "trembling in their legs." They spread through the city to open the remaining gates while Sinon signals to the ships with a flaming torch. In ferocious triumph when the forces are joined, the Greeks fall upon the sleeping foe, slaughtering right and left, burning houses, looting treasure, raping the women. Greeks die too as the Trojans wield their swords, but the advantage has been gained by the invaders. Everywhere the dark blood flows, hacked corpses cover the ground, the crackle of flames rises over the shrieks and groans of the wounded and the wailing of women.

The tragedy is total; no heroics or pity mitigate the end. Achilles' son Pyrrhus (also called Neoptolemus), "mad with murder," pursues the wounded and fleeing Polites, Priam's youngest son, down a corridor of the palace and, "eager for the last thrust," hacks off his head in the sight of his father. When venerable Priam, slipping in his son's blood, flings a feeble spear, Pyrrhus kills him too. The wives and mothers of the defeated are dragged off in indignity to be allotted to the enemy chiefs along with other booty. Hecuba the Queen falls to Odysseus, Hector's wife, Andromache, to the murderer Pyrrhus. Cassandra, raped by another Ajax in the temple of Athena, is dragged out with hair flying and hands bound to be given to Agamemnon and ultimately to kill herself rather than serve his lust. Worse is the fate of Polyxena, another daughter of Priam once desired by Achilles and now demanded by his shade, who is sacrificed on his tomb by the victors. The crowning pity is reserved for the child Astyanax, son of Hector and Andromache, who on Odysseus' orders that no hero's son shall survive to seek vengeance, is hurled from the battlements to his death. Sacked and burned, Troy is left in ruins. Mount Ida groans; the river Xanthus weeps.

Singing of their victory that has ended the long war at last, the Greeks board their ships, offering prayers to Zeus for a safe return home. Few obtain it, but rather, through a balancing fate, suffer disaster parallel to that of their victims. Athena, enraged by the rapist's profanation of her temple, or because the Greeks, careless in victory, have failed to offer prayers to her, asks Zeus for the right to punish them and, given lightning and thunderbolts, raises the sea to a storm. Ships founder and sink or are smashed on the rocks, island shores are strewn with wrecks and the sea with floating corpses. The second Ajax is among those drowned; Odysseus, blown off course, is storm-tossed, shipwrecked and lost for twenty years; arriving home, Agamemnon is murdered by his faithless wife and her lover. The bloodthirsty Pyrrhus is killed by Orestes at Delphi. Curiously, Helen, the cause of it all, survives untouched in perfect beauty, to be forgiven by the bewitched Menelaus and to regain royal husband, home and prosperity. Aeneas too escapes. Because of his filial devotion in carrying his aged father on his back after the battle, he is allowed by Agamemnon to embark with his followers and follow the destiny that will lead him to Rome. With the circular justice that man likes to impose upon history, a survivor of Troy founds the city-state that will conquer Troy's conquerors.

How much fact lies behind the Trojan epic? Archeologists, as we know, have uncovered nine levels of an ancient settlement on the Asian shore of the Hellespont, or Dardanelles, opposite Gallipoli. Its site at the crossroads of Bronze Age trade routes would invite raids and sack and account for the evidence at different levels of frequent demolition and rebuilding. Level VIIA, containing fragments of gold and other artifacts of a royal city, and exhibiting signs of having been violently destroyed by human hands, has been identified as Priam's Troy and its fall dated near the end of the Bronze Age, around 1200 B.C. It is quite possible that Greek mercantile and maritime ambitions came into conflict with Troy and that the overlord of the several communities of the Greek peninsula could have gathered allies for a concerted attack on the city across the straits. The abduction of Helen, as Robert Graves suggests, might have been real in its retaliation for some prior Greek raid.

These were Mycenaean times in Greece, when Agamemnon, son of Atreus, was King at Mycenae in the citadel with the Lion Gate. Its dark remains still stand on a hill just south of Corinth where poppies spring so deeply red they seem forever stained by the blood of the Atridae. Some violent cause, in roughly the same age as the fall of Troy but probably over a more extended period, ended the primacy of Mycenae and of Knossus in Crete with which it was linked. Mycenaean culture was literate as we now know since the script called Linear B found in the ruins of Knossus has been identified as an early form of Greek.

The period following the Mycenaean collapse is a shadowy void of some two centuries called the Greek Dark Ages, whose only communication to us is through shards and artifacts. For some unexplained reason, written language seems to have vanished completely, although recitals of the exploits of ancestors of a past heroic age were clearly transmitted orally down the generations. Recovery, stimulated by the arrival of the Dorian people from the north, began around the 10th century B.C. and from that recovery burst the immortal celebrator whose epic fashioned from familiar tales and legends of his people started the stream of Western literature.

Homer is generally pictured as reciting his narrative poems to accompaniment on the lyre, but the 16,000 lines of the *Iliad* and 12,000 of the *Odyssey* were certainly also either written down by himself or dictated by him to a scribe. Texts were undoubtedly available to the several bards of the next two or three centuries who, in supplementary tales of Troy, introduced material from oral tradition to fill in the gaps left by Homer. The sacrifice of Iphigenia, Achilles' vulnerable heel, the appearance of Penthesilea, Queen of the Amazons, as an ally of Troy and many of the most memorable episodes belong to these poems of the post-Homeric cycle which have come down to us only through summaries made in the 2nd century A.D. of texts since lost. The *Cypria*, named for Cyprus, home of its supposed author, is the fullest and earliest of these, followed by, among others, *The Sack of Ilium* by Arctinus and the *Little Iliad* by a bard of Lesbos. After them, lyric poets and the three great tragic dramatists took up the Trojan themes, and Greek historians discussed the evidence. Latin authors elaborated further both before and especially after Virgil, adding jeweled eyes for the Wooden Horse and other glittering fables. Distinction between history and fable faded when the heroes of Troy and their adventures splendidly filled the tapestries and chronicles of the Middle Ages. Hector becomes one of the Nine Worthies on a par with Julius Caesar and Charlemagne.

The question of whether a historical underpinning existed for the Wooden Horse was raised by Pausanias, a Latin traveler and geographer with a true historian's curiosity, who wrote a *Description of Greece* in the 2nd century A.D. He decided the Horse must have represented some kind of "war machine" or siege engine because, he argues, to take the legend at face value would be to impute "utter folly" to the Trojans. The question still provokes speculation in the 20th century.

If the siege engine was a battering ram, why did not the Greeks use it as such? If it was the kind of housing that brought assaulters up to the walls, surely it would have been even greater folly for the Trojans to take it in without breaking it open first. One can be lured this way down endless paths of the hypothetical. The fact is that although early Assyrian monuments depict such a device, there is no evidence that any kind of siege engine was used in Greek warfare in Mycenaean or Homeric times. That anachronism would not have worried Pausanias, because it was normal in his, and indeed in much later, days to view the past dressed and equipped in the image of the present.

Ruse was indeed used in the siege of walled or fortified places in biblical lands in the warfare of the 2nd millenium B.C. (2000–1000), which covers the century generally given for the Trojan War. If unable to penetrate by force, the attacking army would attempt to enter by cunning, using some trick to gain the confidence of the defenders, and it has been said by a military historian that "the very existence of legends concerning the conquest of cities by stratagem testifies to a core of truth."

Although silent on the Wooden Horse, Herodotus in the 5th century B.C. wished to attribute more rational behavior to the Trojans than Homer allowed them. On the basis of what priests of Egypt told him in the course of his investigation, he states that Helen was never in Troy at all during the war, but remained in Egypt, where she had landed with Paris when their ship was blown off course following her abduction from Sparta. The local King, disgusted by Paris' ignoble seduction of a host's wife, ordered him to depart; only a phantom Helen came with him to Troy. Had she been real, Herodotus argues, surely Priam and Hector would have delivered her up to the Greeks rather than suffer so many deaths and calamities. They could not have been "so infatuated" as to sustain all that woe for her sake or for the sake of Paris, who was anything but admired by his family.

There speaks reason. As the Father of History, Herodotus might have known that in the lives of his subjects, common sense is rarely a determinant. He argues further that the Trojans assured the Greek envoys that Helen was not in Troy but were not believed because the gods wished for the war and the destruction of Troy to show that great wrongs bring great punishment. Probing for the meaning of the legend, here perhaps he comes closer to it.

In the search for meaning we must not forget that the gods (or God, for that matter) are a concept of the human mind; they are the creatures of man, not vice versa. They are needed and invented to give meaning and purpose to the puzzle that is life on earth, to explain strange and irregular phenomena of nature, haphazard events and, above all, irrational human conduct. They exist to bear the burden of all things that cannot be comprehended except by supernatural intervention or design.

This is especially true of the Greek pantheon, whose members are daily and intimately entangled with human beings and are susceptible to all the emotions of mortals if not to their limitations. What makes the gods so capricious and unprincipled is that in the Greek conception they are devoid of moral and ethical values—like a man lacking a shadow. Consequently, they have no compunction about maliciously deceiving mortals or causing them to violate oaths and commit other disloyal and disgraceful acts. Aphrodite's magic caused Helen to elope with Paris, Athena tricked Hector into fighting Achilles. What is shameful or foolish in mortals is attributed by them to the influence of the gods. "To the gods I owe this woeful war," laments Priam, forgetting that he could have removed the cause by sending Helen home at any time (presuming that she was there, as she very actively was in the Homeric cycle) or by yielding her when Menelaus and Odysseus came to demand her delivery.

The gods' interference does not acquit man of folly; rather, it is man's device for transferring the responsibility for folly. Homer understood this when he made Zeus complain in the opening section of the *Odyssey* how lamentable it was that men should blame the gods as the source of their troubles, "when it is through blindness of their own hearts" (or specifically their "greed and folly" in another translation) that sufferings "beyond that which is ordained" are brought upon them. This is a notable statement for, if the results are indeed worse than what fate had in store, it means that choice and free will were operating, not some implacable predestination. As an example, Zeus cites the case of Aegisthus, who stole Agamemnon's wife and murdered the King on his homecoming, "though he knew the ruin this would entail since we ourselves sent Hermes to warn him neither to kill the man nor to make love to his wife, for Orestes when he grew up was bound to avenge his father and desire his patrimony." In short, though Aegisthus well knew what evils would result from his conduct, he proceeded nevertheless, and paid the price.

"Infatuation," as Herodotus suggested, is what robs man of reason. The ancients knew it and the Greeks had a goddess for it. Named Atē, she was the daughter—and significantly in some genealogies, the eldest daughter—of Zeus. Her mother was Eris, or Discord, goddess of Strife (who in some versions is another identity of Atē). The daughter is the goddess, separately or together, of Infatuation, Mischief, Delusion and Blind Folly, rendering her victims "incapable of rational choice" and blind to distinctions of morality and expedience.

Given her combined heritage, Atē had potent capacity for harm and was in fact the original cause, prior to the Judgment of Paris, of the Trojan War, the prime struggle of the ancient world. Drawn from the earliest versions—the *Iliad*, the *Theogony* of Hesiod, roughly contemporary with Homer and the major authority on Olympian genealogy, and the *Cypria*—the tale of Atē ascribes her initial act to spite at not being invited by Zeus to the wedding of Peleus and the sea-nymph Thetis, future parents of Achilles. Entering the banquet hall unbidden, she maliciously rolls down the table the Golden Apple of Discord inscribed "For the Fairest," immediately setting off the rival claims of Hera, Athena and Aphrodite. As the husband of one and father of another of the quarreling ladies, Zeus, not wishing to invite trouble for himself by deciding the issue, sends the three disputants to Mount Ida, where a handsome young shepherd, reportedly adroit in matters of love, can make the difficult judgment. This, of course, is Paris, whose rustic phase is owed to circumstances that need not concern us here and from whose choice flows the conflict so much greater than perhaps even Atē intended.*

Undeterred from mischief, Atē on another occasion devised a complicated piece of trickery by which the birth of Zeus' son Heracles was delayed and an inferior child brought forth ahead of him, thus depriving Heracles of his birthright. Furious at the trick (which does indeed seem capricious even for an immortal), Zeus flung Atē out of Olympus, henceforward to live on earth among mankind. On her account the earth is called the Meadow of Atē—not the Meadow of Aphrodite, or the Garden of Demeter, or the Throne of Athena or

---

* In other versions, the origins of the war are associated with the Flood legend that circulated throughout Asia Minor, probably emanating from the region of the Euphrates, which frequently overflowed. Determined to eliminate the unsatisfactory human species, or alternatively, according to the *Cypria*, to "thin out" the population, which was over-burdening the all-nurturing earth, Zeus decided upon "the great struggle of the Ilian war, that its load of death might empty the world." He therefore contrived or took advantage of the goddesses' quarrel over the Apple to bring the war about. Euripides adopts this version when he makes Helen say in the play named for her that Zeus arranged the war that "he might lighten mother earth of her myriad hosts of men." Evidently, very early, there must have been a deep sense of human unworthiness to produce these legends.

some other more pleasing title, but, as the ancients already sadly knew it to be, the realm of folly.

Greek myths take care of every contingency. According to a legend told in the *Iliad*, Zeus, repenting of what he had done, created four daughters called *Litai*, or Prayers for Pardon, who offer mortals the means of escape from their folly, but only if they respond. "Lame, wrinkled things with eyes cast down," the Litai follow Atē, or passionate Folly (sometimes translated Ruin or Sin), as healers.

> *If a man*
> *Reveres the daughters of Zeus when they come near,*
> *He is rewarded and his prayers are heard;*
> *But if he spurns them and dismisses them*
> *They make their way back to Zeus again and ask*
> *That Folly dog that man till suffering*
> *Has taken arrogance out of him.*

Meanwhile, Atē came to live among men and lost no time in causing Achilles' famous quarrel with Agamemnon and his ensuing anger, which became the mainspring of the *Iliad* and has always seemed so disproportionate. When at last the feud which has so damaged the Greek cause and prolonged the war is reconciled, Agamemnon blames Atē, or Delusion, for his original infatuation for the girl he took from Achilles.

> *Delusion, the elder daughter of Zeus; the accursed*
> *Who deludes all and leads them astray. . . .*
> *. . . took my wife away from me.*
> *She has entangled others before me—*

and, we might add, many since, the Litai notwithstanding. She appears once again in Brutus' fearful vision when, gazing on the murdered corpse at his feet, he foresees how "Caesar's spirit, raging for revenge with Atē by his side, shall cry 'Havoc' and let slip the dogs of war."

Anthropologists have subjected myth to infinite classification and some wilder theorizing. As the product of the psyche, it is said to be the means of bringing hidden fears and wish fulfillments into the open or of reconciling us to the human condition or of revealing the contradictions and problems, social and personal, that people face in life. Myths are seen as "charters" or "rituals," or serving any number of other functions. All or some of this may or may not be valid; what we can be sure of is that myths are prototypes of human behavior and that one ritual they serve is that of the goat tied with a scarlet thread and sent off into the wilderness to carry away the mistakes and the sins of mankind.

Legend partakes of myth and of something else, a historical connection, however faint and far away and all but forgotten. The Wooden Horse is not myth in the sense of Cronus swallowing his children or Zeus transforming himself into a swan or a shower of gold for purposes of adultery. It is legend with no supernatural elements except for Athena's aid and the intrusion of the serpents, who were added, no doubt, to give the Trojans a reason for rejecting Laocoon's advice (and who are almost too compelling, for they seem to leave the Trojans with little option but to choose the course that contains their doom).

Yet the feasible alternative—that of destroying the Horse—is always open. Capys the Elder advised it before Laocoon's warning, and Cassandra afterward. Notwithstanding the frequent references in the epic to the fall of Troy being ordained, it was not fate but free choice that took the Horse within the walls. "Fate" as a character in legend represents the fulfillment of man's expectations of himself.

Chapter Three

THE RENAISSANCE POPES PROVOKE THE PROTESTANT SECESSION:

1470–1530

At about the time Columbus discovered America, the Renaissance—which is to say the period when the values of this world replaced those of the hereafter—was in full flower in Italy. Under its impulse the individual found in himself, rather than in God, the designer and captain of his fate. His needs, his ambitions and desires, his pleasures and possessions, his mind, his art, his power, his glory, were the house of life. His earthly passage was no longer, as in the medieval concept, a weary exile on the way to the spiritual destiny of his soul.

Over a period of sixty years, from roughly 1470 to 1530, the secular spirit of the age was exemplified in a succession of six popes—five Italians and a Spaniard*—who carried it to an excess of venality, amorality, avarice, and spectacularly calamitous power politics. Their governance dismayed the faithful, brought the Holy See into disrepute, left unanswered the cry for reform, ignored all protests, warnings and signs of rising revolt, and ended by breaking apart the unity of Christendom and losing half the papal constituency to the Protestant secession. Theirs was a folly of perversity, perhaps the most consequential in Western history, if measured by its result in centuries of ensuing hostility and fratricidal war.

The abuses of these six popes were not born full blown from the high Renaissance. Rather they were a crown of folly upon habits of papal government that had developed over the previous 150 years deriving from the exile of the Papacy in Avignon through most of the 14th century. The attempted return to Rome resulted in 1378 in a Schism, with one Pope in Rome and one in Avignon, and with the successors of each, for over half a century, claiming to be the true Pope. Thereafter each country's or kingdom's obedience to one claimant or the other was determined by political interests, thus thoroughly politicizing the Holy See. Dependence on lay rulers was

* Not counting one who reigned for 26 days and one foreigner for less than two years.

a fatal legacy of the Schism because rival popes found it necessary to make up for divided power by all kinds of bargains, concessions and alliances with kings and princes. Because income too was divided, the Schism commercialized as well as politicized the Papacy, making revenue its primary concern. From this time, the sale of everything spiritual or material in the grant of the Church, from absolution and salvation to episcopates and abbeys, swelled into a perpetual commerce, attractive for what it offered yet repellent for what it made of religion.

Under the heady humanism of the Renaissance, the popes, once the Holy See was definitively restored to Rome in the 1430s, adopted as their own the values and style of the piratical princes of the Italian city-states. Opulent, elegant, unprincipled and endlessly at odds with each other, the rulers of Italian life were, by reason of their disunity and limited territorial scope, no more than potentates of discord. In reproducing their avarice and luxury, the six popes did no better than their models and, because of their superior status, usually worse. Pursuing the spoils of office like hounds on a scent, each of the six, who included a Borgia and two Medicis, was obsessed by ambition to establish a family fortune that would outlive him. In this pursuit each in turn plunged into the temporal politics of the time, which meant into an incessantly shifting series of combinations, intrigues and maneuvers without permanent interest or guiding principle and regulated only by what appeared to be the balance of power at the moment. As the political balance was fragile and fluctuating, these arrangements were in a constant state of reversal and betrayal, allowing, indeed requiring, the exercise of deals, bribes and conspiracies as a substitute for thought or program.

The dominating political factor of the period was the repeated invasions of Italy, in league with one or another of the Italian states, by the three major powers—France, Spain and the Hapsburg Empire—competing for conquest of the peninsula or part of it. While the Papacy engaged to the hilt in this struggle, it lacked the military resources to make its role decisive. The more it took part in the temporal conflicts with consistently pernicious result, the more impotent among the monarchs it revealed itself, and in fact became. At the same time it shrank from the obvious task of religious reform because it feared loss of authority and of opportunity for private gain. As Italians, the Renaissance popes shared in the process that made their country the victim of war, foreign oppression and lost independence; as Vicars of Christ, they made their office a mockery and the cradle of Luther.

Was there a feasible alternative? The religious alternative in the form of response to the persistent cry for reform was difficult to achieve, owing to the vested interest of the entire hierarchy in corruption, but it was feasible. Warning voices were loud and constant and complaints of papal derelictions explicit. Inept and corrupt regimes like those of the terminal Romanovs or the Kuomintang cannot generally be reformed short of total upheaval or dissolution. In the case of the Renaissance Papacy, reform initiated at the top by a head of the Church with concern for his office, and pursued with vigor and tenacity by like-minded successors, could have cleansed the most detestable practices, answered the cry for worthiness in the Church and its priests and attempted to fill the need of spiritual reassurance, possibly averting the ultimate secession.

In the political sphere, the alternative would have been a consistent institutional policy consistently pursued. If the popes had directed their energies to that end instead of dissipating their efforts in the petty paths of private greed, they could have maneuvered the hostilities of the secular powers in the interests of the Papal States. It was not beyond them. Three of the six—Sixtus IV, Alexander VI and Julius II—were able and strong-willed men. Yet none, with the qualified exception of Julius, was to exercise a trace of statesmanship or be lifted by the prestige of Saint Peter's chair to an appropriate view of political responsibilities, much less spiritual mission.

The moral capacity and attitudes of the time might be said to have made the alternatives psychologically impossible. In that sense, *any* alternative not taken can be said to be beyond the grasp of the persons in question. That the Renaissance popes were shaped and directed by their society is undeniable, but the responsibility of power often requires resisting and redirecting a pervading condition. Instead, the popes succumbed, as we shall see, to the worst in society, and exhibited, in the face of mounting and visible social challenges, an unrelieved wooden-headedness.

Reform was the universal preoccupation of the age, expressed in literature, sermons, pamphlets, songs and political assemblies. The cry of those in every age alienated by the worldly footing of the Church and a yearning for a purer worship of God, it had become widespread and general since the 12th century. It was the cry Saint Francis had heard in a vision in the church of San Damiano, "My house is in ruins. Restore it!" It was dissatisfaction with materialism and unfit clergy, with pervasive corruption and money-grubbing at every level from the Papal Curia to the village parish—hence the cry for reform of "head and members." Dispensations were forged for sale, donations for crusade swallowed up by the Curia, indulgences peddled in common commerce so that the people, complained the Chancellor of Oxford in 1450, no longer cared what evils they did because they could buy remission of the penalty for sin for sixpence or win it "as a stake in a game of tennis."

Dissatisfaction was felt with absenteeism and plural holding of benefices, with the indifference of the hierarchy and its widening separation from the lower clergy, with the prelates' furred gowns and suites of retainers, with coarse and ignorant village priests, with clerical lives given to concubines and carousing, no different from the average man's. This was a source of deep resentment because in the common mind if not in doctrine priests were supposed to be holier as the appointed intermediaries between man and God. Where could man find forgiveness and salvation if these intermediaries failed in their office? People felt a sense of betrayal in the daily evidence of the gulf between what Christ's agents were supposed to be and what they had become. Basically, in the words of a sub-prior of Durham, people were "starved for the word of God," and could not obtain from unworthy ministers of God the "true faith and moral precepts in which the soul's salvation consists." Many priests "have never read the Old Testament, nor scarcely the Psalter-Book" and many came to the pulpit drunk. Rarely visiting their sees, prelates provided the minor clergy with no training or teaching or religious leadership so that they often did not know their own duties or how to conduct the rituals or give the sacraments. Although criticism of the clergy by lay preachers was forbidden, it was a subject that could be counted on to delight a congregation. "If the preacher just utters a word against priests or prelates, instantly the sleepers awake, the bored become cheerful . . . hunger and thirst are forgotten" and the most wicked see themselves as "righteous or holy compared to the clergy."

By the 14th century, protest had taken form and found a voice in the dissident movements of Lollards and Hussites, and in communal lay groups like the Brethren of the Common Life, where genuine piety found a warmer home outside the official Church. Here, many of the doctrinal dissents that were later to mark the Protestant revolt were already being expressed: denial of transubstantiation, rejection of confession, of the indulgence traffic, of pilgrimages and of the veneration of saints and relics. Separation from Rome was not unthinkable. In the 14th century, the famous doctor of theology William Ockham could envisage the Church without a pope and in 1453, a Roman, Stefano Porcaro, led a conspiracy aimed at total overthrow of the Papacy (although it seems to have been more political than religious in origin).

Printing and growing literacy nourished dissent especially through direct acquaintance with the Bible in the vernacular. Four hundred such editions appeared in the first sixty years of the printing press, and anyone who could read could find in the lore of the Gospels something missing from the hierarchy of his own day gowned in their purple and red.

The Church itself talked regularly of reform. At the Councils of Constance and Basle in the first half of the 15th century, renowned preachers harangued the delegates every Sunday on corrupt practices and loose morals, on simony in particular, on failure to generate the saving instrument of Christian revival, a crusade against the Turks, on all the sins that were causing the decay of Christian life. They called for action and positive measures. The Councils held endless discussions, debated countless proposals and issued a number of decrees dealing mainly with disputes between the hierarchy and Papacy over distribution of incomes and allocation of benefices. They did not reach down, however, to the places of basic need in such matters as bishops' visitation of their sees, education of the minor clergy, reorganization of the monastic orders.

The higher clergy were not solidly indifferent; among them were abbots, bishops, even certain cardinals who were earnest reformers. The popes too made intermittent gestures of response. Programs of reform were drawn up by order of both Nicholas V and Pius II in the 1440s and 1460s preceding the six of this study, in the latter case by a dedicated reformer and preacher, the German Cardinal and legate Nicholas of Cusa. On presenting his plan to Pius II, Nicholas said that the reforms were necessary "to transform all Christians beginning with the Pope into the likeness of Christ." His fellow reformer, Bishop Domenico de Domenichi, author of a *Tractatus* on reform for the same Pope, was equally unsparing. It was useless, he wrote, to uphold the sanctity of the Papacy to lawless princes because the evil lives of prelates and Curia caused laymen to call the Church "Babylon, the mother of all fornications and abominations of the earth!"

At the conclave to elect a successor to Pius II in 1464, Domenichi summarized the problem that should have earned the attention of Sixtus and his successors: "The dignity of the Church must be reasserted, her authority revived, morals reformed, the Curia regulated, the course of justice secured, the faith propagated," papal territory regained and, as he saw it, "the faithful armed for Holy War."

Little of this was to be accomplished by the six Renaissance popes. What frustrated reform was the absence of support, if not active dislike, for it by a hierarchy and Papacy whose personal fortunes were embedded in the existing system and who equated reform with Councils and the devolution of papal sovereignty. Throughout the century since the uprising of Hus, a religious revolution was in the making but the rulers of the Church failed to take notice. They regarded protest merely as dissent to be suppressed, not as a serious challenge to their validity.

Meanwhile a new faith, nationalism, and a new challenge in the rise of national churches were already undercutting Roman rule. Under the political pressure and deals made necessary by the Schism, the power of appointment, the essential source of papal power and revenue—which the Papacy had usurped from the local clergy, where it originally belonged—was gradually surrendered to the lay sovereigns or exercised at their dictation or in their interests. It had largely been lost already in France and England under forced arrangements with their rulers, and was to be further surrendered in this period to the Hapsburg Empire, Spain and other foreign potentates in the course of various political bargains.

To an unusual degree in the Renaissance good walked with evil in a wondrous development of the arts combined with political and moral degradation and vicious behavior. Discovery of classical antiquity with its focus on human capacity instead of on a ghostly Trinity was an exuberant experience that led to a passionate embrace of humanism, chiefly in Italy, where it was felt to be a return to ancient national glories. Its stress on earthly goods meant an abandonment of the Christian ideal of renunciation and its pride in the individual undermined submission to the word of God as conveyed by the Church. To the extent that they fell in love with pagan antiquity, Italians of the ruling class felt less reverence for Christianity, which, as Machiavelli wrote in *The Discourses*, makes the "supreme felicity to consist in humility, abnegation and contempt of things human," whereas pagan religion found the chief good in "grandeur of the soul, strength of body and all the qualities that make men redoubtable."

New economic enterprise, following the depression and miseries of the fading Middle Ages, accompanied humanism in the second half of the 15th century. Many explanations have been offered for this recovery: the invention of printing immensely extended the access to knowledge and ideas; advances in science enlarged understanding of the universe, and in applied science supplied new techniques; new methods of capitalist financing stimulated production; new techniques of navigation and shipbuilding enlarged trade and the geographical horizon; newly centralized power absorbed from the declining medieval communes was at the disposal of the monarchies and the growing nationalism of the past century gave it impetus; discovery of the New World and circumnavigation of the globe opened unlimited visions. Whether these were cause or coincidence or a turn of the tide in the mysterious ebb and flow of human affairs, they marked the beginnings of the period that historians call Early Modern.

Within these sixty years Copernicus worked out the true relationship of the earth to the sun, Portuguese vessels brought slaves, spices, gold dust and ivory from Africa, Cortés conquered Mexico, the Fuggers of Germany, investing profits from the wool trade in commerce, banking and real estate, created the wealthiest mercantile empire of Europe while the son of their founder, called Jacob the Rich, distilled the spirit of the time in his boast that he would continue to make money as long as there was breath in his body. His Italian counterpart, Agostino Chigi of Rome, employed 20,000 men in the branches of his business at Lyons, London, Antwerp and—undeterred from doing business with the infidel as long as it was lucrative—at Constantinople and Cairo. Having taken Constantinople in 1453 and advanced into the Balkans, the Turks were regarded much like the present Soviet Union as the overshadowing menace of Europe, but however fearful the alarms, the Christian nations were too immersed in conflict with one another to reunite in action against them.

In Spain, Ferdinand of Aragon and Isabella of Castile joined their kingdoms in marriage, reintroduced the Inquisition and expelled the Jews; Francis I of France met Henry VIII on the Field of the Cloth of Gold; Albrecht Dürer flourished in Germany, Hieronymus Bosch and Hans Memling in Flanders. Erasmus, welcomed in courts and capitals for his skeptical wit, was the Voltaire of his time. Sir Thomas More, toward the end of the sixty years, published *Utopia*, while Machiavelli, his opposite spirit in Italy, took a darker view of humanity in *The Prince*. Above all in Italy art and literature were honored as the supreme human achievement and, in being honored, produced an extraordinary fecundity of talent from Leonardo to Michelangelo to Titian and a host of others second only to the greatest. Literature was ornamented by Machiavelli's works, by Francesco Guicciardini's great *History of Italy*, by the comedies and satires of Pietro Aretino, by Ariosto's extravagantly admired epic poem *Orlando Furioso* on the struggle between Christians and Moslems, by Castiglione's *Book of the Courtier*.

Strangely, the efflorescence in culture reflected no comparable surge in human behavior but rather an astonishing debasement. Partly, this was owed to the absence in Italy of central authority in a monarch, which left the five major regions—Venice, Milan, Florence, Naples and the Papal States—plus the minor city-states like Mantua, Ferrara and the rest, in unrestrained and unending mutual conflict. Since the title to power of the ruling princes had originated in the degree of violence the founders had been ready to exercise, the measures they took to maintain or extend their sway were similarly uninhibited. Seizures, poison plots, treachery, murder and fratricide, imprisonment and torture were everyday methods employed without compunction.

To understand the popes we must look at the princes. When the subjects of Galeazzo Maria Sforza, ruler of Milan, murdered him in a church for his vices and oppressions, his brother, Ludovico il Moro, threw the heir, his nephew, into prison and seized the rule of Milan for himself. When the Pazzi family of Florence, antagonists of Lorenzo de' Medici the Magnificent, could endure the frustrations of their hatred no longer, they plotted to murder him and his handsome brother Giuliano during High Mass in the cathedral. The signal was to be the bell marking the elevation of the Host, and at this most solemn moment of the service, the swords of the attackers flashed. Giuliano was killed but Lorenzo alertly saved himself by his long sword and survived to direct a revenge of utter annihilation upon the Pazzi and their partisans. Assassinations were frequently planned to take place in churches, where the victim was less likely to be surrounded by an armed guard.

Most unpleasant of all were the kings of the Aragon house who ruled Naples. Ferrante (Ferdinand I), unscrupulous, ferocious, cynical and vindictive, concentrated all his efforts until his death in 1494 on the destruction of his opponents and in this process initiated more harm to Italy through internecine war than any other prince. His son and successor, Alfonso II, a brutal profligate, was described by the contemporary French historian Comines as "the cruelest, worst, most vicious and base man ever seen." Like others of his kind he openly avowed his contempt for religion. The condottieri on whom the princes' power rested shared the sentiment. As mercenaries, who fought for money, not loyalty, they were "full of contempt for all sacred things . . . caring nothing whether or not they died under the ban of the Church."

Rulers' habits could not fail of emulation by their subjects. The case of a physician and surgeon of the hospital of St. John Lateran, all the more grisly for being reported in the unemotional monotone of John Burchard, master of ceremonies of the papal court, whose daily record is the indispensable source, reveals Renaissance life in Rome. He "left the hospital every day early in the morning in a short tunic and with a cross bow and shot everyone who crossed his path and pocketed his money." He collaborated with the hospital's confessor, who named to him the patients who confessed to having money, whereat the physician gave these patients "an effective remedy" and divided the proceeds with his clerical informer. Burchard adds that the physician was subsequently hanged with seventeen other evil-doers.

Arbitrary power, with its inducements to self-indulgence and unrestraint and its chronic suspicions of rivals, tended to form erratic despots and to produce habits of senseless violence as often in the satellite rulers as in the great. Pandolfo Petrucci, tyrant of Siena in the 1490s, enjoyed a pastime of rolling down blocks of stone from a height regardless of whom they might hit. The Baglioni of Perugia and Malatesta of Rimini recorded sanguinary histories of feud and fratricidal crime. Others like the d'Este of Ferrara, the oldest princely family, and the Montefeltri of Urbino, whose court Castiglione celebrated in *The Courtier*, were honorable and well-conducted, even beloved. Duke Federigo of Urbino was said to be the only prince who moved about unarmed and unescorted or dared to walk in an open park. It is sadly typical that Urbino was to become the object of naked military aggression by one of the six popes, Leo X, who wished to acquire the duchy for his own nephew.

Alongside the rascals and the scandals, decency and piety existed as ever. No single characteristic ever overtakes an entire society. Many people of all classes in the Renaissance still worshipped God, trusted in the saints, wanted spiritual reassurance and led non-criminal lives. Indeed, it was *because* genuine religious and moral feeling was still present that dismay at the corruption of the clergy and especially of the Holy See was so acute and the yearning for reform so strong. If all Italians had lived by the amoral example of their leaders, the depravity of the popes would have been no cause for protest.

In the long struggle to end the chaos and dismay spread by the Schism and to restore the unity of the Church, laymen and churchmen resorted to the summoning of General Councils of the Church, supposed to have a supremacy over the Holy See, which that institution, whoever its occupant, violently resisted. Throughout the first half of the 15th century, the conciliar battle dominated Church affairs, and although Councils succeeded at last in establishing a single pontiff, they failed to bring any of the claimants to acknowledge conciliar supremacy. Successive popes gripped their prerogatives, dug in their heels and by virtue of divided opposition maintained their authority intact, though not unquestioned. Pius II, better known as the admired humanist and novelist Aeneas Sylvius Piccolomini, had been a Council advocate in his early career, but in 1460 he delivered as Pope the fearsome Bull *Exsecrabilis* threatening to excommunicate anyone who appealed from the Papacy to a General Council. His successors continued to regard Councils as hardly less dangerous than the Turk.

Reestablished in Rome, the popes became creatures of the Renaissance, outshining the princes in patronage of the arts, believing like them that the glories of painting and sculpture, music and letters, ornamented their courts and reflected their munificence. If Leonardo da Vinci adorned the court of Ludovico Sforza at Milan and the poet Torquato Tasso the court of the d'Este at Ferrara, other artists and writers flocked to Rome, where the popes were lavish in patronage. Whatever their failings in office, they bequeathed to the world immortal legacies in the works they commissioned: the Sistine ceiling by Michelangelo, the Vatican *stanze* by Raphael, the frescoes for the Cathedral Library in Siena by Pinturicchio, the Sistine wall frescoes by Botticelli, Ghirlandaio, Perugino, Signorelli. They repaired and beautified Rome, which, deserted during the Avignon exile, had dwindled to unkempt and underpopulated shabbiness. They uncovered its classical treasures, restored churches, paved the streets, assembled the incomparable Vatican Library and, as the crown of papal prestige—and, ironically, the trigger of the Protestant revolt—initiated the rebuilding of St. Peter's with Bramante and Michelangelo as architects.

Through visible beauties and grandeur, they believed, the Papacy would be dignified and the Church exert its hold upon the people. Nicholas V, who has been called the first Renaissance Pope, made the belief explicit on his deathbed in 1455. Urging the Cardinals to continue the renovation of Rome, he said, "To create solid and stable conviction there must be something that appeals to the eye. A faith sustained only by doctrine will never be anything but feeble and vacillating. . . . If the authority of the Holy See were visibly displayed in majestic buildings . . . all the world would accept and revere it. Noble edifices combining taste and beauty with imposing proportions would immensely exalt the chair of St. Peter." The Church had come a long way from Peter the fisherman.

1. Murder in a Cathedral:
Sixtus IV, 1471-84

Until the election in 1471 of Cardinal Francesco della Rovere, former General of the Franciscan Order, who took the name Sixtus IV, the popes of the early Renaissance, if without zeal for spiritual renewal, had maintained on the whole nominal respect for the dignity of their office. Sixtus introduced the period of unabashed, unconcealed, relentless pursuit of personal gain and power politics. He had attained prominence as a preacher and lecturer in theology at the universities of Bologna and Pavia, and as General of the Franciscans had acquired a reputation as an able and severe administrator. As a friar, he was supposedly chosen Pope in reaction to the worldliness of his predecessor, Paul II, a Venetian patrician and former merchant. In fact, he owed his election rather to the skillful maneuvering of the ambitious, unprincipled and very rich Cardinal Rodrigo Borgia, soon to acquire the papal tiara for himself. Borgia's support of Sixtus was in itself something of a character reference, and history has recognized the link by calling them, together with Innocent VIII, who came in between, the "three evil geniuses."

The Franciscan's gown concealed in Sixtus a hard, imperious, implacable character; a man of strong passions and a large, poor and exigent family. He proceeded to enrich its members and, using all the resources now at his command, to endow them with high office, papal territories and titled spouses. Upon taking office, he shocked public opinion by appointing as Cardinals two of his eleven nephews, Pietro and Girolamo Riario, both in their twenties, who rapidly became notorious for mad and spendthrift behavior. Before he had finished, Sixtus had conferred the red hat on three more nephews and a grandnephew, made another a Bishop, married four nephews and two nieces into the ruling families of Naples, Milan, Urbino, and to Orsinis and Farneses. Non-clerical relatives were placed in high positions of civil power as Prefect of Rome, Governor of Castel Sant' Angelo and to governorships of several of the Papal States with access to their revenues. He raised nepotism to a new level.

He packed the College of Cardinals with his personal appointees, creating no fewer than 34 in his thirteen-year papacy, although the College had been fixed at 24, and leaving at his death only five not beholden to him for their appointment. He made an established practice of political selection for the purpose of favoring this or that prince or sovereign, often choosing lords or barons or younger sons of great families without regard to merit or clerical qualification. He gave the archiepiscopal see of Lisbon to a child of eight and the see of Milan to a boy of eleven, both sons of princes. He so thoroughly secularized the College that his successors followed his example as if it were the rule. In the twenty years under Innocent VIII and Alexander VI, no fewer than fifty sees were given to youths under the canonical age for consecration.

Led by the wild behavior of Pietro Riario, the favorite nephew, whom the new fortunes of his family seem almost to have unbalanced, and augmented by the horde of newly rich della Roveres, the habit of unbridled extravagance became a fixed feature of the papal court. Cardinal Riario's excesses reached a peak in 1480 at a saturnalian banquet featuring a whole roasted bear holding a staff in its jaws, stags reconstructed in their skins, herons and peacocks in their feathers, and orgiastic behavior by the guests appropriate to the ancient Roman model. Reports of the affair were all the more shocking at a time of general dismay caused by the Turks having actually landed on the heel of Italy, where they seized Otranto, although they were not to hold it long. The advance of the Turks since the fall of Constantinople was generally considered to have been allowed by God in punishment for the sins of the Church.

Licentiousness in the hierarchy was promoted but not initiated by the della Roveres; it was already a problem in 1460 when Pius II, in a letter to Cardinal Borgia, reproved him for a party he had given in Siena where "none of the allurements of love was lacking," and "in order that lust be unrestrained," the husbands, fathers and brothers of the ladies present were not invited. Pius warned of the "disgrace" to the holy office. "This is the reason the princes and powers despise us and the laity mock us. . . . Contempt is the lot of Christ's Vicar because he seems to tolerate these actions." The situation under Sixtus was not new; the difference was that while Pius was concerned to arrest the deterioration, his successors neither tried nor cared.

Antagonism slowly gathered around Sixtus, especially in Germany, where anti-Romanism born of resentment of the clerical appetite for money was now aggravated by the financial exactions of the Papal Curia, the administrative arm of the Papacy. In 1479 the Assembly of Coblenz despatched to Rome a *gravamina*, or list of grievances. In

Bohemia, home of the Hussite dissent, a satiric manifesto appeared equating Sixtus with Satan priding himself on "total repudiation of the doctrine of Jesus." Accustomed to carping from one source or another for fifteen centuries, the Church had grown too thick a skin to bother about such straws blown in on the wind from the Empire.

To ensure efficient collection of revenues, Sixtus created an Apostolic Chamber of 100 lawyers to supervise the financial affairs of the Papal States and the law cases in which the Papacy had a financial interest. He devoted the income to multiplying the estates of his relatives and to embellishing the external glories of the Holy See. Posterity owes to him the restoration of the Vatican Library, whose holdings he increased threefold and to which he summoned scholars to register and catalogue them. He reopened the Academy of Rome, invited men of renown to its halls, encouraged dramatic performances, commissioned paintings. His name endures in the Sistine Chapel, built at his command for the renovation of old St. Peter's. Churches, hospitals, fallen bridges and muddy streets benefited from his repairs.

If admirable in his cultural concerns, he exhibited the worst qualities of the Renaissance prince in his feuds and machinations, conducting wars on Venice and Ferrara and an inveterate campaign to reduce the Colonna family, the dominant nobles of Rome. The most scandalous of his dealings was involvement in and possible instigation of the Pazzi plot to murder the Medici brothers. Allied to the Pazzi by complex family interests, he approved of or even shared in the conspiracy, or so it was widely charged and believed owing to the extremity of his reaction when the plot failed by half. In a rage at the violence of the Medicis' revenge upon the Pazzi, which had included the hanging of an Archbishop in violation of clerical immunity, he excommunicated Lorenzo de' Medici and all of Florence. This use of spiritual sanction for temporal motives, though certainly not new in Church practice, earned Sixtus wide discredit because of the harm done to the Florentines and their commerce and because of the suspicions it aroused of the Pope's personal involvement. Pious Louis XI, King of France, wrote worriedly, "Please God that Your Holiness is innocent of crimes so horrible!" The idea of the Holy Father plotting murder in a cathedral was not yet acceptable, though before long it would hardly seem abnormal.

The internal health of the Church did not interest Sixtus, and all calls for a Council, which were rising insistently, he roughly rejected on the precedent of *Exsecrabilis*. Denial did not end the demand. In 1481 the noise of reform sounded close at hand. Archbishop Zamometic, an envoy of the Emperor, arrived in Rome, where he voiced harsh criticisms of Sixtus and the Curia. Imprisoned by order of the Pope in Castel Sant' Angelo, he was released by a friendly cardinal and, though knowing the risk, relentlessly returned to his theme. He published a manifesto calling on Christian princes to summon a continuation of the Council of Basle in order to prevent the ruination of the Church by Pope Sixtus, whom he accused of heresy, simony, shameful vices, wasting Church patrimony, instigating the Pazzi conspiracy and entering into secret alliance with the Sultan. Sixtus retaliated by placing the city of Basle under anathema, effectively closing it off to outsiders, and by once more throwing the defiant Archbishop into prison, where, apparently severely treated, he died, an alleged suicide, two years later.

Prison does not silence ideas whose time has come, a fact that generally escapes despots, who by nature are rulers of little wisdom. In the last year of his life, Sixtus turned aside a reasonable program submitted to him by the Estates General of Tours in France. Agitated by the eloquence of a passionate reformer, Jean de Rély, the assembly proposed reform concerning fiscal abuse, plural benefices and the hated practice of *ad commendam*, by which temporary appointments, often of laymen, could be made "on recommendation" without the appointee's being required to fulfill their duties. One of those issues that arouse passion peculiar to their ages, *ad commendam* was a device that Sixtus could easily have prohibited, thereby earning himself immense credit with the reform movement. He was blind to the opportunity and ignored the program. A few months later he was dead. So rancorous had been his reign that Rome erupted in two weeks of riot and plunder led by soldiers of the Colonna faction he had attempted to smash. Unlamented, Sixtus IV had achieved nothing for the institution he had headed except discredit.

2. Host to the Infidel:
Innocent VIII, 1484–92

Amiable, indecisive, subject to stronger-minded associates, Sixtus' successor was a contrast to him in every way except in equally damaging the pontificate, in this case by omission and weakness of character. Originally named Giovanni Battista Cibo, the son of a well-to-do Genoese family, he was not at first designated for an ecclesiastical career, but entered it after a normally misspent youth during which he fathered and acknowledged an illegitimate son and daughter. No sudden conversion or dramatic circumstances propelled him into the Church, other than the accepted fact that to someone with the right connections the Church offered a substantial career. Cibo reached a bishopric at 37 and office in the Papal Curia under Sixtus, who, appreciating his malleable nature, made him one of his stable of Cardinals in 1473.

Elevation to the Papacy of this rather dim and mediocre person was the unplanned outcome, as often occurred when two fiercely ambitious candidates blocked each other's chances. The two, each of whom was subsequently to realize his ambition, were Cardinal Borgia, the future Alexander VI, and Cardinal Giuliano della Rovere, the most able of Sixtus' nephews, the future Julius II. As domineering and contentious as his uncle, but more effective, Giuliano, known as the Cardinal of St. Peter in Vincoli, could not as yet gather the votes of a majority of the College. Nor could Borgia, despite bribes of up to 25,000 ducats and promises of lucrative promotion spread among his colleagues. As the Florentine envoy reported home, Cardinal Borgia had a reputation for being "so false and proud that there is no danger of his being elected." In this impasse the rivals saw a danger of the election of Cardinal Marco Barbo of Venice, widely respected for his high character and strict principles, who would undoubtedly have limited the scope for a Borgia or a della Rovere and might even have contemplated reform. When Barbo came within five votes of election, Borgia and della Rovere joined forces behind the unassuming Cibo, indifferent to the affront to reformers of electing a pope with acknowledged children. Awarded their combined votes, their candidate was duly crowned as Innocent VIII.

As Pope, Innocent was distinguished chiefly by his extraordinary indulgence of his worthless son Franceschetto, the first time the son of a pope had been publicly recognized. In everything else he succumbed to the energy and will of Cardinal della Rovere. "Send a good letter to the Cardinal of St. Peter," wrote the envoy of Florence to Lorenzo de' Medici, "for he is Pope and more than Pope." Della Rovere moved into the Vatican and within two months raised his own brother Giovanni from Prefect of Rome to Captain-General of the Church. Innocent's other promoter, Cardinal Borgia, remained as Vice-Chancellor in control of the Curia.

Riches for Franceschetto, who was both greedy and dissolute, given to roaming the streets at night with bad companions for lewd purposes, absorbed Innocent's primary attention. In 1486, he succeeded in arranging his son's marriage to a daughter of Lorenzo de' Medici and celebrated it in the Vatican with a wedding party so elaborate that he was obliged, owing to chronic shortage of funds, to mortgage the papal tiara and treasures to pay for it. Two years later he staged an equal extravaganza, also in the Vatican, for the wedding of his granddaughter to a Genoese merchant.

While the Pope indulged himself, his more business-minded Vice-Chancellor created numerous new offices for apostolic officials for which the aspirants were required to pay—evidence that they looked forward to remunerative returns. Even the office of Vatican Librarian, hitherto reserved for merit, was put up for sale. A bureau was established for the sale of favors and pardons at inflated prices, of which 150 ducats of each transaction went to the Pope and what was left over to his son. When pardons instead of death penalties for manslaughter, murder and other major crimes were questioned, Cardinal Borgia defended the practice on the ground that "the Lord desireth not the death of a sinner but rather that he live and pay."

Under this regime and the influence of its predecessor, the moral standards of the Curia melted down like candle wax, reaching a stage of venality that could not be ignored. In 1488, halfway through Innocent's tenure, several high officials of the papal court were arrested, and two of them executed, for forging for sale fifty papal bulls of dispensation in two years. The extreme penalty, intended to display the moral indignation of the Pope, served to underline the conditions of his administration.

Swamped beneath the influx of Sixtus' cardinals, who included members of Italy's most powerful families, the Sacred College was a stage of pomp and pleasure. While a few of its members were worthy men sincere in their calling, the majority were worldly and covetous nobles, ostentatious in their splendor, players in the unending game of exerting influence in their own or their sovereigns' behalf. Among the relatives of princes were Cardinal Giovanni d'Aragona, son of the King of Naples, Cardinal Ascanio Sforza, brother of Ludovico, regent of Milan, Cardinals Battista Orsini and Giovanni di Colonna, members of the two rival and forever-feuding ruling families of Rome.

Cardinals at that time did not have to be priests—that is, qualified by ordination to administer the sacraments, and celebrate communion and the spiritual rites—though some of them might be. Those appointed from the episcopate, the highest level of the priesthood, continued to hold their sees, but the majority belonged to the officialdom of the Church without priestly function. Drawn from the upper ranks of the hierarchy, who were increasingly involved in administration, diplomacy and the financial business of the Church, they came from the Italian ruling families or, if foreigners, were usually more courtier than cleric. As secularization advanced, appointments went more frequently to laymen, sons and brothers of princes or designated agents of monarchs with no ecclesiastical careers behind them. One, Antoine Duprat, lay chancellor of Francis I, made a Cardinal by the last of the Renaissance six, Clement VII, entered his cathedral for the first time at his funeral.

As the popes of this period, using the red hat as political currency, enlarged the number of cardinals both to increase their own influence and to dilute that of the College, the cardinals collected plural offices— each involving another case of absenteeism—to augment their incomes, accumulating abbeys, bishoprics and other benefices, although by canon law only a cleric had the right to revenues and pensions derived from the goods of the Church. Canon law, however, was elastic like any other, and "by way of exception" allowed the Pope to grant benefices and pensions to laymen.

Regarding themselves as princes of the realm of the Church, the cardinals considered it their prerogative, not to mention their duty, to match in dignity and splendor the princes of the lay realm. Those who could afford to lived in palaces with several hundred servants, rode abroad in martial attire complete with sword, kept hounds and falcons for hunting, competed when they paraded through the streets in the number and magnificence of their mounted retainers, whose employment provided each prince of the Church with a faction among Rome's persistently riotous citizens. They sponsored masques and musicians and spectacular floats during Carnival; they gave banquets in the style of Pietro Riario's, including one by the opulent Cardinal Sforza which a chronicler said he could not venture to describe "lest he be mocked as a teller of fairy tales." They gambled at dice and cards—and cheated, according to a complaint by Franceschetto to his father after he had lost 14,000 ducats in one night to Cardinal Raffaele Riario. There may have been some substance to the charge, for on another night the same Riario, one of Sixtus' many nephews, won 8000 ducats gaming with a fellow Cardinal.

To arrest the thinning of their influence, the cardinals insisted as a condition of Innocent's election on a clause restoring their number to 24. As vacancies appeared, they refused consent to new appointments, limiting Innocent's scope for nepotism. The pressure of foreign monarchs for places, however, forced some openings, and among Innocent's first selections was his brother's natural son, Lorenzo Cibo. Illegitimacy was a canonical bar to ecclesiastical office which Sixtus had already overlooked on behalf of Cardinal Borgia's son Cesare, whom he started on the ecclesiastical ladder at age seven. Legitimizing a son or nephew became routine for the six Renaissance popes— yet another principle of the Church discarded.

Of the few he was allowed, Innocent's most notable appointment to the Sacred College was Franceschetto's new brother-in-law, Giovanni de' Medici, age fourteen, son of Lorenzo the Magnificent. In this case it was not Innocent's desire but the great Medici's pressure that made a Cardinal of the boy for whom his father had been procuring rich benefices since he was a child. Tonsured, that is, dedicated to the clerical life, at age seven, Giovanni had been made Abbot at eight with the nominal rule of an abbey conferred by the King of France, and at eleven, named *ad commendam* to the great Benedictine Abbey of Monte Cassino, since which time his father had pulled every wire at his command to secure a cardinalship as a step toward the Papacy itself. The young Medici was to fulfill his planned destiny as the fifth of the six popes of this story, Leo X.

After complying with Lorenzo's wish, Innocent, firm for once, insisted that the boy must wait three years before taking his place, devoting the time to the study of theology and canon law. The candidate was already more learned than most, Lorenzo having seen to a good education by distinguished tutors and scholars. When at last in 1492, Giovanni at sixteen took his place as Cardinal, his father wrote him a serious and significant letter. Warning of the evil influences of

Rome, "that sink of all iniquity," Lorenzo urged his son "to act so as to convince all who see you that the well-being and honor of the Church and the Holy See are more to you than anything else in the world." After this unique advice, Lorenzo does not neglect to point out that his son will have opportunities "to be of service to our city and our family," but he must beware the seductions to evil-doing of the College of Cardinals, which "is at this moment so poor in men of worth. . . . If the Cardinals were such as they ought to be, the whole world would be better for it, for they would always elect a good Pope and thus secure the peace of Christendom."

Here, expressed by the outstanding secular ruler of the Italian Renaissance, was the crux of the problem. If the cardinals had been worthy men they would have elected worthier popes, but both were parts of the same body. The popes *were* the cardinals in these sixty years, elected out of the Sacred College and in turn appointing cardinals of their own kind. Folly, in the form of absorption in shortsighted power struggles and perverse neglect of the Church's real needs, became endemic, passed on like a torch from each of the Renaissance six to the next.

If Innocent was ineffectual, it was partly owing to the perpetual discord of the Italian states and of the foreign powers as well. Naples, Florence and Milan were generally at war in one combination or another against each other or some smaller neighbor; Genoa "would not hesitate to set the world on fire," as the Pope, himself a Genoese, complained; the landward expansion of Venice was feared by all; Rome was a chronic battleground of the Orsini and Colonna; lesser states often erupted in the hereditary internal conflicts of their leading families. Though on taking office, Innocent earnestly wished to establish peace among the adversaries, he lacked the resolution to bring it about. Energy often failed him owing to recurrent illness.

The worst of his troubles was a campaign of brutal harassment periodically deepening into warfare by the unpleasant King of Naples, whose motive seems no more precise than simple malignity. He began with an insolent demand for certain territories, refused payment of Naples' customary tribute as a papal fief, conspired with the Orsini to foment trouble in Rome and threatened appeal to that awful weapon, a Council. When the barons of Naples rose in rebellion against his tyranny, the Pope took their side, upon which Ferrante's army marched on Rome and besieged it, while Innocent sought frantically for allies and armed forces. Venice held aloof but allowed the Pope to hire its mercenaries. Milan and Florence refused aid, and for convoluted reasons—perhaps a desire to see the Papal States weakened—opted for Naples. This was before Lorenzo de' Medici, the Florentine ruler, made family connections with Innocent, but these were not always decisive. In Italy, partners one day were antagonists the next.

The Pope's appeal for foreign aid against Ferrante aroused interest in France based on the worn-out Angevin claim to Naples, which, despite the disasters of previous pursuit, the French Crown could never bring itself to relinquish. The shadow of France frightened Ferrante, who suddenly, just when his siege of Rome had brought the city to desperation, agreed to a treaty of peace. His concessions to the Pope, which seemed amazing, were better understood when he later violated all of them, repudiated the treaty and returned to aggression.

He addressed the Pope with scorn and open insults while his agents stirred rebellion in the various Papal States. Endeavoring to cope with uprisings and conflicts in many places at once, Innocent vacillated and procrastinated. He drew up a Bull to excommunicate the King and Kingdom of Naples, but shrank from issuing it. The envoy of Ferrara reported comments in 1487 on "the pusillanimity, helplessness and incapacity of the Pope," which if not dispelled by some infusion of courage, he said, would have serious consequences. These were averted when Ferrante in another total about-face called off the war and offered an amicable settlement, which the Pope, despite all his humiliations, was only too glad to accept. To seal the brittle friendship, Ferrante's grandson was married to Innocent's niece.

Such were the combats of Italy, but though essentially frivolous and even meaningless, they were destructive, and the Papacy did not escape their consequences. The most serious was a lowering of status. Throughout the conflict with Naples the Papal States were treated like a poor relation and the Pope personally with diminished respect, reflecting Ferrante's insolence. Pamphlets distributed by the Orsini in Rome called for the Pope's overthrow, calling him a "Genoese sailor" who deserved to be thrown into the Tiber. Encroachments by the foreign powers on papal prerogatives increased, with the national churches filling benefices with their own appointees, withholding revenues, disputing obedience to papal decrees. Innocent was lax in resistance.

He built the famous villa and sculpture gallery on Vatican hill, named the Belvedere for its superb view over the Eternal City, and commissioned frescoes by Pinturicchio and Andrea Mantegna, which have since disappeared, as if to reflect their sponsor's place in history. Innocent lacked the time, funds and perhaps interest for much else in the patronage of arts, or for the pressing problem of reform. His concern in that sphere was concentrated on the least of its needs, crusade.

Public opinion, it is true, believed in crusade as the great restorative. Preachers to the Vatican who came by invitation about twice a month to address the court as Sacred Orators invariably included crusade in their exhortations. It was the Holy Father's duty and an essential part of his office, they reminded the incumbent, to bring peace among Christians; Pax-et-Concordia was the purpose of pontifical government. An end to strife among the Christian nations was the most frequent plea of the Orators, invariably coupled with a call to turn the arms of the Christian kings against the infidel. Only when dissuaded from their wars could the secular rulers unite against the common enemy, the Turk, the "beast of the Apocalypse," in Nicholas of Cusa's words, "the enemy of all nature and humanity." Offensive war against the Turks, it was argued, was the best defense of Italy. Constantinople and the Holy Places and other lost Christian territory could be regained. Religious unity of mankind under Christianity was the ultimate goal, and this too required the defeat of the Sultan. The whole enterprise would lift the Church from sin and initiate—or alternatively crown—reform.

Innocent made strenuous efforts to engage the powers in crusade, as had Pius II even more devotedly when the impact of the fall of Constantinople was still fresh. Yet the same deficiency which defeated Pius and others before him, disunity among the European powers equal to that among the princes of Italy, remained. "What mortal power," Pius had written, "could bring into harmony England and France, Genoese and Aragonese, Hungarians and Bohemians?" Neither Pope nor Emperor could any longer exert supremacy. Who then could persuade discordant and even hostile powers to join in a common venture? Without overall command and a single discipline, any army large enough to be effective would dissolve in its own chaos. Beyond these difficulties, a more fundamental impulse was missing: not defense but offense and an aggressive faith had inspired the first crusades. Since then, Holy War had lost credibility when trade with the infidel was profitable and Italian states negotiated regularly for the Sultan's aid against each other.

Nevertheless, Innocent, on the basis of what he took to be consent by the Emperor, announced crusade in a Bull of 1486, decreeing at the same time a tithe on all churches, benefices and ecclesiastical persons of all ranks, which may have been the real purpose. In the following year he succeeded in convening an international congress in Rome which went through the motions of planning objectives, discussing strategy, designating routes of march, commanders and size of national contingents. In the end, no forces ever assembled much less departed from the shores of Europe. The failure has been ascribed to the outbreak of civil conflict in Hungary and a renewal of dispute between France and the Empire, but these are pretexts for the absent impulse. No Holy War was to glorify Innocent's pontificate. Instead, by a reverse twist, the Papacy came to an unnatural accommodation with the enemy of Christianity in the remarkable case of Prince Djem.

A brother of the Sultan and a defeated but still dangerous contender for the Ottoman throne, Djem had escaped fraternal revenge and taken refuge across the gulf of creed with the Knights of St. John in Rhodes. Though originally founded for fighting the infidel, the Knights were sufficiently broadminded to recognize in Djem a valuable prize and to reach an agreement with the Sultan to keep him out of belligerent action in return for an annual subsidy of 45,000 ducats. The Grand Turk, as Djem became known, at once became a lever coveted by all. Venice and Hungary, France and Naples, and of course the Papacy vied for him. After a temporary sojourn in France, Djem was won by the Pope together with his subsidy at the price of two cardinalships, one for the Grand Master of Rhodes and one for a candidate of the French King.

Innocent's intention was to use Djem as a means of war on the Sultan, on a vague understanding that if assisted to his throne by the Christians, Djem would withdraw Turkish forces from Europe including Constantinople. Even if this had been believable, it is not clear how replacing one Moslem with another constituted Holy War.

The Grand Turk's arrival in Rome in 1489 was met with royal honors, sumptuous gifts, the Pope's white palfrey for his mount and escort by Franceschetto to the Vatican. An excited if puzzled populace packed the streets along his path, gazing in wonder in their belief that they were witnessing the fulfillment of a familiar prophecy that the Sultan would come to Rome to live with the Pope, heralding the descent of universal peace. Pope and cardinals received in audience the tall white-turbaned guest of gloomy countenance occasionally relieved by a savage glance from half-closed eyes. He was housed with his suite in the Vatican apartments reserved for royal guests and "provided with pastimes of all sorts such as hunting, music, banquets and other amusements." Thus the Grand Turk, brother of the "beast of the Apocalypse," took up his abode in the house of the Pope, the heart of Christendom.

Diplomatic maneuvers continued to swirl around him. The Sultan, fearing a Christian offensive with Djem as its spearhead, opened overtures to the Pope, sent envoys and the gift of a precious Christian relic, the Holy Spear, supposed to have pierced the side of Christ on the cross, which was received with immense ceremony in Rome. His brother's presence in papal custody at least served to restrain the Sultan, while Djem lived, from further attack on Christian territory. To that extent Innocent achieved something, but lost more. The general public was bewildered by the relationship, and papal status was compromised in the public mind by the strange comity extended to the Grand Turk.

Innocent's bouts of illness grew more frequent until the end was apparent in 1492. Summoning the cardinals to his deathbed, he asked forgiveness for his inadequacy and exhorted them to choose a better successor. His dying wish suffered the same futility as his life. The man the cardinals elected to Saint Peter's chair proved as close to the prince of darkness as human beings are likely to come.

3. Depravity:
Alexander VI, 1492-1503

When Rodrigo Borgia was 62, after 35 years as Cardinal and Vice-Chancellor, his character, habits, principles or lack of them, uses of power, methods of enrichment, mistresses and seven children were well enough known to his colleagues in the College and Curia to evoke from young Giovanni de' Medici at his first conclave the comment on Borgia's elevation to the Papacy, "Flee, we are in the hands of a wolf." To the wider circle of the princes of Italy and the rulers of Spain, Borgia's native land, and by repute abroad, the fact that, though cultivated and even charming, he was thoroughly cynical and utterly amoral was no secret and no surprise, although his reputation for depravity was not yet what it would become. His frame of mind was heartily temporal: to celebrate the final expulsion of the Moors from Spain, in 1492, the year of his election, he staged not a Te Deum of thanksgiving but a bullfight in the Piazza of St. Peter's with five bulls killed.

After serving under five popes and losing the last election, Borgia was not this time going to let the tiara pass from him. He simply bought the Papacy outright over his two chief rivals, Cardinals della Rovere and Ascanio Sforza. The latter, who preferred coin to promises, was brought round by four mule-loads of bullion that were despatched from Borgia's palace to Sforza's during the conclave, although it was supposedly to be held in camera. In later years, as the Pope's habits became more exposed, almost any tale of monstrosities could be told and believed about him, and the bullion train may be one of them. Yet it had an inherent credibility in that it would have taken a great deal to bring round so wealthy a rival as Ascanio Sforza, who in addition received the Vice-Chancellorship.

Borgia was himself the beneficiary of nepotism, having been made Cardinal at 26 by his aged uncle Pope Calixtus III, who had been elected at age 77 when signs of senility suggested the likelihood of another choice soon. Calixtus had had time enough, however, to reward his nephew with the Vice-Chancellorship for his success in recovering certain territories of the Papal States. From revenues of papal offices, of three bishoprics he held in Spain and of abbeys in Spain and Italy, from an annual stipend of 8000 ducats as Vice-Chancellor and 6000 as Cardinal and from private operations, Borgia amassed enough wealth to make him over the years the richest member of the Sacred College. In his early years as Cardinal he had already acquired enough to build himself a palace with three-storied loggias around a central courtyard where he lived amid sumptuous furniture upholstered in red satin and gold-embroidered velvets, harmonizing carpets, halls hung with Gobelin tapestries, gold plate, pearls and sacks of gold coin of which he reportedly boasted that he had enough to fill the Sistine Chapel. Pius II compared this residence to the Golden House of Nero, which had once stood not far away.

Borgia was said never to have missed a consistory, the business meeting of cardinals, in 35 years except when ill or away from Rome. There was nothing about the workings and opportunities of the papal bureaucracy that he did not grasp. Intelligent and energetic, he had fortified the approaches to Rome, and as legate of Sixtus had accomplished the complex task of persuading the nobles and hierarchy of Spain to support the marriage of Ferdinand and Isabella and the merger of their kingdoms. He was probably the ablest of the cardinals. Tall and large-framed, robust, urbane, he was dignified, even majestic in appearance, delighting in fine clothes of violet taffeta and crimson velvet and taking great care over the width of ermine stripes.

As described by contemporaries, he was usually smiling and good-tempered, even cheerful, and liked "to do unpleasant things in a pleasant way." An eloquent speaker and well-read, he was witty and "took pains to shine in conversation," was "brilliantly skilled in conducting affairs," combined zest with self-esteem and Spanish pride and had an amazing gift for exciting the affections of women, "who are attracted to him more powerfully than iron to a magnet," which suggests that he made his desire for them strongly felt. Another observer rather unnecessarily remarks that he "understood money matters thoroughly."

As a young Cardinal, he had fathered a son and two daughters of unrecorded mothers and subsequently, when in his forties, three more sons and a daughter, born to his acknowledged mistress, Vanozza de Cataneis, who reputedly succeeded her mother in that role. All were his acknowledged family. He was able to acquire for the eldest son, Pedro

Luis, the dukedom of Gandia in Spain and betrothal to a cousin of King Ferdinand. When Pedro died young, his title, lands and fiancée passed to his stepbrother Juan, his father's favorite, destined for a death of the kind that was to make the Borgia family a byword. Cesare and Lucrezia, the two famous Borgias who helped to make it so, were children of Vanozza, together with Juan and another brother, Jofré. The paternity of an eighth child named Giovanni, born during the Borgia Papacy, seems to have been uncertain even within the family. Two successive papal Bulls legitimized him first as the son of Cesare and then of the Pope himself, while public opinion considered him a bastard child of Lucrezia.

Whether for a veil of respectability or for the pleasure of cuckold-ing, Borgia liked his mistresses to have husbands, and arranged two successive marriages for Vanozza while she was his mistress and another for her successor, the beautiful Giulia Farnese. At nineteen, with golden hair reaching to her feet, Giulia was married to an Orsini in Borgia's palace and almost simultaneously became the Cardinal's mistress. While a licentious private life was no scandal in the high Renaissance, this liaison between an old man, as he was considered at 59, and a girl forty years younger was offensive to Italians, perhaps because they found it inartistic. Made the subject of lewd jokes, it helped to tarnish Borgia's reputation.

Upon Borgia's election as Pope, the disgraceful traffic that gained him the place soon became common knowledge through the fury of the disappointed della Rovere and his partisans. Borgia himself openly boasted of it. This was a mistake because simony was an official sin that was to give the new Pope's enemies a handle against him, which they very soon used. In the meantime, Alexander VI, as he now was, rode through Rome in a resplendent ceremony to take possession of the Lateran attended by thirteen squadrons of cavalry, 21 cardinals, each with a retinue of twelve, and ambassadors and noble dignitaries vying in the magnificence of their garments and equestrian draperies. Streets were decorated with garlands of flowers, triumphal arches, living statues formed by gilded naked youths and flags displaying the Borgia arms, a rather apt red bull rampant on a field of gold.

At this point, the shadow of France could be felt lengthening over Italy, preliminary to the era of foreign invasions that were to accelerate the decline of the Papacy and subject Italy to outside control. They were to ravage the peninsula for the next seventy years, wreck its prosperity, seize pieces of territory, diminish sovereignty and postpone the conditions for Italian unity by 400 years—all for no permanent gain to any of the parties involved. Fragmented by the incessant civil strife of its princes, Italy was an inviting and vulnerable target. It was envied too for its urban treasures, even if the region was not quite so tranquil, fertile, commercially prosperous and nobly adorned as in Guicciardini's famous description of his country on the eve of penetration. No economic need propelled the invasions, but war was still the assumed activity of the ruling class, indemnities and expected revenues from taxable conquered territories its source of profit, as well as the source of payment for the cost of the campaign itself. It may be, too, that just as the first medieval crusades were a vent for baronial aggression, the campaigns in Italy represented simply a mood for nationalist expansion. France had recovered from the Hundred Years' War, Spain had finally expelled the Moors, both acquiring national cohesion in the process. Italy, under its warm sun, divided against itself, was an attractive place to exert aggression.

In Italy, the scandal of Alexander's election might have suggested to him that it would be useful to give some time and thought to religious governance. Instead, he immediately set about attending to his political fences. He married his daughter Lucrezia to a Sforza and his son Jofré to a granddaughter of the troublesome King of Naples, and in his first year as Pope, enlarged the Sacred College, to the rage and resentment of the opposition cardinals, who, as known partisans of della Rovere at the conclave, had not shared in the golden shower. Prevailing over their bitter resistance, Alexander named eleven new cardinals including Alessandro Farnese, brother of his mistress; a scion of the d'Estes, age fifteen, and his own son Cesare, whose unsuitability to an ecclesiastical career was so patent that he soon resigned it for the more congenial occupations of war, murder and associated skills. The other appointees were judiciously selected to please all the powers, one each for the Empire, France, England, Spain, Hungary, Venice, Milan and Rome, among them several men of piety and learning. The influx consolidated Alexander's control of the College and caused della Rovere, when he learned of the appointments, to utter "a loud exclamation" and fall ill from outrage. Alexander was eventually to appoint a total of 43 cardinals, including seventeen Spaniards and five members of his own family, with the exact sum that each paid for his hat being meticulously recorded by Burchard in his diary.

The Papacy's detachment from religion over the preceding fifty years, its sinking reputation and aversion to reform, gave the French plans for invasion an added impulse. In the general weakening of papal authority and revenues caused by the suction of the national churches over the past century, the French Church had won considerable autonomy. At the same time, it was troubled by ecclesiastical corruption in its own realm. Preachers castigated the decline in flaming sermons, serious critics discussed it, synods were held to draw up measures of reform—all without much practical effect. In these years, wrote a Frenchman, reform was the most frequent topic of conversation. In 1493, when the campaign to make good the French royal claim to Naples was under discussion, Charles VIII summoned a commission at Tours to prepare a program which would validate his march through Italy as a crusade for reform, with the understood if not explicit intention of calling a Council to depose Alexander VI on grounds of simony. This was not a spontaneous idea of the King's. A poor ungainly creature of the decrepit Valois line, with his head full of dreams of chivalric glory and crusade against the Turks, he had added religious reform to his concerns under the fierce persuasions of Cardinal della Rovere, who, in his ungovernable hatred of Alexander, had come to France for the express purpose of destroying him. A Pope "so full of vices, so abominable in the eyes of the world" must be removed, he insisted to the King, in order that a new Pope might be elected.

Just such action, initiated by the Cardinals and resting on the support of France, had caused the Schism of recent memory, and nothing in Christian history had done the Church such irretrievable harm. That della Rovere and his party could even contemplate a repetition, no matter what argument Alexander's crimes provided, was irresponsibility hardly explicable except by virtue of the folly that infected each of the Renaissance rulers of the Church.

Alexander had good reason to fear della Rovere's influence on the King of France, especially if he were to direct the befuddled royal mind toward a reformation of the Church. According to Guicciardini, no admirer of the popes, reform was to Alexander a thought "terrible beyond anything else." Considering that as time went on, Alexander poisoned, imprisoned or otherwise immobilized inconvenient opponents, including cardinals, it is a wonder that he did not lock up della Rovere, but his enemy and successor was already too outstanding, and besides, he was careful to stay outside Rome and take up his residence in a fortress.

Reports coming out of France set the Italian states into a frantic commotion of combining and recombining in preparation to resist the foreigner—or, if necessary, join him. The great question for the papal and secular rulers was whether larger advantage could be gained by siding with Naples or with France. Ferrante of Naples, whose kingdom was the French objective, engaged in a blizzard of deals and counter-deals with the Pope and princes, but, as a life-long conspirator, he could not wean himself from secretly arranging to undercut his own alliances. He died of his efforts within a year, succeeded by his son Alfonso. Mutual mistrust governed his neighbors while they gave themselves over (as George Meredith wrote in a very different context) to "drifting into vanities, congregating in absurdities, planning short-sightedly, plotting dementedly."

The move by Milan that precipitated the French invasion qualified in all these respects. It began with a complaint to Ferrante by his granddaughter Isabella, daughter of Alfonso and wife of the rightful heir to Milan, Gian Galeazzo Sforza, that she and her husband were deprived of their rightful place and made subordinate in everything to the regent, Ludovico il Moro, and his wife, the capable Beatrice d'Este. Ferrante responded with such furious menaces as to convince Ludovico that his regency, which he had no intention of resigning, would be safer if Ferrante and his house were deposed. Ludovico allied himself with the disaffected barons of Naples who shared this aim, and, to make sure of the outcome, he invited Charles VIII to enter Italy and establish his claim to the Neapolitan throne. This was taking a serious risk, because the French monarchy through the Orléans line had a stronger claim to Milan than to Naples, but Ludovico, an adventurer at heart, felt confident he could contain that threat. That was an error as events proved.

Out of such motives and calculations, Italy was opened to invasion, although at the last moment it almost failed to take place. Charles' advisers, doubtful of the enterprise, caused the King so much worry by stressing the difficulties that lay ahead and the untrustworthiness of Ludovico and Italians in general that he halted his army when it was already on the march. The timely appearance of della Rovere, fervent in exhortation, rekindled his enthusiasm. In September 1494, a French army of 60,000 crossed the Alps carrying with them, in Guicciardini's words, for once not exaggerated, "the seeds of innumerable calamities."

At the outset, after swinging this way and that in something of a panic, Alexander joined a league of defense with Florence and Naples, which came apart as soon as made. Florence defected owing to a crisis of nerves on the part of Piero de' Medici, eldest son of Lorenzo the Magnificent, who had died two years earlier. Suddenly faint-hearted in the face of the enemy, Piero secretly arranged terms for opening his city to the French. From this triumph in Florence, Charles' army moved on unresisted to Rome, where the Pope, after desperate twists to avoid receiving him, succumbed to superior might. The invaders' armed parade on entering Rome took six hours to pass, in a train of cavalry and foot, archers and crossbowmen, Swiss mercenaries with halberds and lances, mailed knights, royal bodyguard carrying iron maces on their shoulders, all followed by the fearful rumble of 36 wheeled cannon drawn over the cobblestones. The city quaked under the huge influx. "Requisitions are fearful," reported the envoy of Mantua, "murders innumerable, one hears nothing but moaning and weeping. In all the memory of man the Church has never been in such evil plight."

Negotiations between the conquerors and the Papacy were pressed hard. Though forced to abandon Naples and hand over Prince Djem (who shortly died in French custody), Alexander held firm against two demands: he refused to deliver Castel Sant' Angelo into French hands, or formally to invest Charles with the crown of Naples. Beleaguered as Alexander was, this took strength of mind, even if he had to give the French the right of passage to Naples through papal territory. The one subject that was not at issue during all the sessions was reform. Despite constant prodding by Cardinal della Rovere and his party, the frayed, fumbling French King was no man to shoulder a Council, sponsor reform or depose a Pope. That cup passed from Alexander; he was left in place. The French moved out and on to Naples without meeting combat; the only violence was their own sack and brutality in places seized along the way. King Alfonso avoided the crisis by abdicating and entering a monastery; his son Ferrante II threw away his sword and fled.

The reality of French presence in southern Italy galvanized at last a union of resistance, initiated by Spain. Determined not to allow French control of Naples, which Spain wanted for herself, King Ferdinand induced the Emperor Maximilian, who already feared French expansion, to join him, offering as inducement his daughter Joanna in a marriage of fateful consequence to Maximilian's son Philip. With Spain and the Empire as allies, the Papacy and Milan could now safely turn against France. When even Venice joined, a combination called the League of Venice, later called the Holy League, came into being in 1495, causing the French, who had made themselves hated in Naples, to fear being cut off in the Italian boot. They marched for home and, after fighting at Fornovo in Lombardy on their way out, the only battle of the campaign, a scrambled combat without decisive effect, made their way back to France. Alfonso and his son promptly reappeared to resume the rule of Naples.

Although no one, least of all France, emerged with profit from this momentous if senseless adventure, the powers, undeterred by empty result, returned again and again to the same arena to compete over Italy's body. From this time on, wars, leagues, battles, tangled diplomacy, fluid and shifting alignments succeeded one another until they were to culminate in ferocious climax—the Sack of Rome in 1527 by Spanish and Imperial troops. Every twist and maneuver of the Italian wars of these 33 years has been devotedly followed and exhaustively recorded in the history books far beyond the general interest they can sustain today. The significance of the particulars in history's permanent annals is virtually nil except as a study in the human capacity for conflict. There were certain historic consequences, some important, some minor but memorable: the Florentines, outraged by Piero's surrender, rose against him, threw out the Medici and declared a republic; the Spanish-Hapsburg marriage produced in the future Emperor Charles V the controlling factor of the next century; Ludovico il Moro, the hotspur of Milan, paid for his folly in a French prison, where he died; at Pavia in the most famous battle of the wars, a King of France, Francis I, was captured and grasped immortality in the quotation books with "All is lost save honor."

Otherwise, the Italian wars are significant for their effect in further politicizing and debasing the Papacy. Taking the same part as any secular state, treating and dealing, raising armies and fighting, it became entirely absorbed in the things that are Caesar's, with the result that it was perceived as no better than secular—a factor that was to make possible the Sack of Rome. In proportion to their absorption in the realm of Caesar, the popes had less time or concern for the things of God. Continually engaged in the quid pro quos of one alliance or another, they neglected more than ever the internal problems of the Church and the religious community and hardly noticed the signs of coming crisis in their own sphere.

In Florence, beginning in 1490, the frenzied preaching of a Dominican friar, Girolamo Savonarola, prior of San Marco, was a voice of religious distress which Alexander managed to ignore for seven years while it took control of an entire city and aroused echoes throughout Italy. Savonarola was not so much a forerunner of Luther as the type of zealot and scourge of sin that can arise in any disturbed time and sway mobs by his fanaticism. He represented his own time in that his impulse came from revulsion at the low estate and corruption of the Church and in his espousal of reform as necessary to reopen the way to Heaven through a purified clergy. His prophecy that reform would be followed by a period of happiness and well-being for all Christendom exerted a strong appeal. Preaching neither doctrinal reform nor separation from Rome, he poured wrath upon the sins of the people and clergy, whose source he traced to the wickedness of popes and hierarchy. His scoldings and apocalyptic prophesies, according to Pico della Mirandola, "caused such terror, alarm, sobbing and tears that everybody went about the city bewildered, more dead than alive." His prophecy that Lorenzo the Magnificent and Innocent VIII would both die in 1492, which they shortly did, endowed him with awesome power. He inspired bonfires into which crowds with sobs and hysteria threw their luxuries and valuables, their paintings, fine garments and jewelry. He roused bands of children to scour the city for "vanities" to be burned. He called upon his followers to reform their own lives, to renounce profane festivals and games, usury and vendettas, and to restore religious observance.

It was when he castigated the Church that Savonarola's outrage rang fiercest. "Popes and prelates speak against pride and ambition and they are plunged in it up to their ears. They preach chastity and keep mistresses. . . . They think only of the world and worldly things; they care nothing for souls." They have made the Church "a house of ill-fame . . . a prostitute who sits upon the throne of Solomon and signals to the passers-by. Whoever can pay enters and does what he wishes, but he who wishes for good is thrown out. Thus, O prostituted Church, you have unveiled your abuse before the eyes of the entire world and your poisoned breath rises to the heavens."

That there was some truth in this verbiage did not excite Rome, long accustomed to censorious zealots. Savonarola became politically dangerous, however, when he hailed Charles VIII as the instrument of reform sent by the Lord, "as I have long predicted," to cure the ills of Italy and reform the Church. Championship of the French was his fatal move, for it made him a threat to the new rulers of Florence and brought him unpleasantly to the notice of the Pope. The former demanded his suppression, but Alexander, anxious to avoid a popular outcry, took action only when Savonarola's denunciations of himself and the hierarchy became too pointed to ignore, most especially when Savonarola called for a Council to remove the Pope on grounds of simony.

At first, Alexander attempted to silence Savonarola quietly by simply forbidding him to preach, but prophets filled with the voice of

God are not easily silenced. Savonarola defied the order on the ground that Alexander, by his crimes, had lost his authority as Holy Father and "is no longer a Christian. He is an infidel, a heretic and as such has ceased to be Pope." Alexander's answer was excommunication, which Savonarola promptly defied by giving communion and celebrating Mass. Alexander then ordered the Florentine authorities to silence the preacher themselves under pain of excommunicating the whole city. Public sentiment had by now turned against Savonarola owing to a test by fire into which he was drawn by his enemies and could not sustain. Imprisoned by the authorities of Florence and tortured to extract a confession of fraud, tortured again by papal examiners for a confession of heresy, he was turned back for execution by the civil arm. To the howls and hisses of the mob, he was hanged and burned in 1498. The thunder was silenced but the hostility to the hierarchy it had voiced remained.

Itinerant preachers, hermits and friars took up the theme. Some fanatic, some mad, all had disgust with the Church in common and responded to a widespread public sentiment. Anyone who assumed a mission to preach reform could be sure of an audience. They were not a new phenomenon. As a form of entertainment for the common people, one of the few they had, lay preachers and preaching friars had long wandered from town to town attracting huge multitudes who listened patiently for hours at a time to lengthy sermons held in the public squares because the churches could not hold the throngs. In 1448 as many as 15,000 were reported to have come to hear a famous Franciscan, Roberto da Lecce, preach for four hours in Perugia. Lashing the evils of the time, exhorting the people to lead better lives and abandon sin, the preachers were important for the popular response they evoked. Their sermons usually ended with mass "conversions" and gifts of gratitude to the speaker. A favorite prophecy as the century turned was of an "angelic Pope" who would initiate reform, to be followed, as Savonarola had promised, by a better world. A group of some twenty working-class disciples in Florence elected their own "pope," who told the followers that until reform was accomplished, it was useless to go to confession because there were no priests worthy of the name. His words spread as token of some great approaching change.

Borgia family affairs had now succeeded in scandalizing an age inured to most excesses. Conceiving that marriage ties to the royal family of Naples would be in his interest, Alexander annulled the marriage of his daughter Lucrezia to Giovanni Sforza in order to marry her to Alfonso, the Neapolitan heir. The outraged husband, fiercely denying the charge of non-consummation, resisted the divorce loudly and publicly, but under heavy political and financial pressures engineered by the Pope was forced to give way, and even to return his wife's dowry. Amid revelry in the Vatican, Lucrezia was married to a handsome new husband, whom according to all accounts she genuinely loved, but the insult to the Sforzas and offense to the marriage sacrament increased Alexander's disrepute. Giovanni Sforza added to it with the charge that Alexander had been activated by incestuous desire for his own daughter. Though hard to sustain in view of her rapid remarriage, the tale aided the accretion of ever more lurid slanders that clustered around Alexander and gathered credibility from the vices of his son Cesare.

In the year of Lucrezia's remarriage, the Pope's eldest surviving son, Juan, Duke of Gandia, was found floating one morning in the Tiber, his corpse pierced by nine stab wounds. Although he had numerous enemies, owing to the large slices of papal property bestowed upon him by his father, no assassin was identified. The longer the mystery and whispers lasted, the more suspicion came to rest on Cesare based on a supposed desire to supplant his brother in the paternal largesse or, alternatively, as the outcome of an incestuous triangle with brother and sister. In the bubbling stew of Rome's rumors, no depravity appeared beyond the scope of the Borgias (although historians have since absolved Cesare of the murder of his brother).

Stunned with grief at—or perhaps frightened by—the death of his son, Alexander was afflicted with remorse and a sudden rare introspection. "The most grievous danger for any Pope," he told a consistory of cardinals, "lies in the fact that encompassed as he is by flatterers, he never hears the truth about his own person and ends by not wishing to hear it." It was an unheard message to every autocrat in history. In his moral crisis the Pope further announced that the blow he had suffered was God's judgment upon him for his sins and that he was resolved to amend his life and reform the Church. "We will begin the reform with ourselves and so proceed through all levels of the Church till the whole work is accomplished." He at once appointed a commission of several of the most respected cardinals to draw up a program, but, except for a provision to reduce plural benefices, it hardly went to the heart of the matter. Beginning with the cardinals, it required reduction of incomes, which had evidently climbed, to 6000 ducats each; reduction of households to no more than eighty (of whom at least twelve should be in holy orders) and of mounted escorts to thirty; greater restraint at table with only one boiled and one roast meat per meal and with entertainment by musicians and actors to be replaced by reading of Holy Scriptures. Cardinals were no longer to take part in tournaments or carnivals or attend secular theatricals or employ miscellaneous "youⁿhs" as body servants. A provision that all concubines were to be dismissed within ten days of publication of the Bull embodying the reforms may have modified the Holy Father's interest in the program. A further provision calling for a Council to enact the reforms was enough to bring him back to normal. The proposed Bull, *In apostolicae sedis specula*, was never issued and the subject of reform was dropped.

In 1499, the French under a new King, Louis XII, returned, now claiming through the Orléans line the succession to Milan. Another churchman, the Archbishop of Rouen, as the King's chief adviser, was the mover behind this effort. He was himself moved by ambition to be Pope and believed he could make a great thrust in the papal stakes through French control of Milan. Alexander's role in the new invasion, doubtless affected by his experience in the last, was entirely cynical. Louis had applied for an annulment of his marriage to his sad, crippled wife, Jeanne, sister of Charles VIII, in order to marry the much coveted Anne of Brittany, widow of Charles VIII, for the sake of finally attaching her duchy to the French Crown.

Although Louis' plea for annulment was furiously condemned by Oliver Maillard, the late King's Franciscan confessor, and resented by the French people, who warmly sympathized with the discarded Queen, Alexander was indifferent to public opinion. He saw a means toward gold for his coffers and advancement for Cesare, who, having renounced his ecclesiastical career, had ambitions to marry the daughter of Alfonso of Naples, a ward and resident of the French court. Cesare's unprecedented resignation of the red hat, antagonizing many of the cardinals, evoked from a Venetian diarist of events a sigh that summarized the Renaissance Papacy. "Thus now in God's Church *tutto va al contrario*" (everything is upside-down). In return for 30,000 ducats and support for Cesare's project, the Pope granted Louis' annulment plus a dispensation to marry Anne of Brittany and threw in a red hat for the Archbishop of Rouen, who became Cardinal d'Amboise.

In this second scandalous annulment and its consequences, folly was compounded. In ducal splendor, Cesare bearing the dispensation journeyed to France, where he discussed with the King the projected campaign for Milan on the basis of papal support. Alexander's partnership with France, arranged for the sake of his maligned son, whom he now described as more dear to him than anything else on earth, angered a field of opponents—the Sforzas, the Colonnas, the rulers of Naples and, of course, Spain. Acting for Spain, Portuguese envoys visited the Pope to reprimand him for his nepotism, simony and French policy, which they said endangered the peace of Italy and indeed of all Christendom. They, too, raised the threat of a Council unless he changed course. He did not. Sterner Spanish envoys followed on the same mission, ostensibly for the welfare of the Church although their motive—to frustrate France—was as political as Alexander's. Conferences were heated; reform by Council was again used as a threat. A wrathful envoy told Alexander to his face that his election was invalid, his title as Pope void. In return, Alexander threatened to have him thrown into the Tiber, and scolded the Spanish King and Queen in insulting terms for their interference.

When Cesare's marriage fell through, owing to the princess' stubborn aversion to her suitor, the French alliance threatened to crumble, leaving Alexander deserted. He felt so endangered that he held audiences accompanied by an armed guard. Rumors circulated in Rome of withdrawal of obedience by the powers and a possible schism. The French King, however, arranged another marriage for Cesare with the sister of the King of Navarre, rejoicing Alexander, who in return endorsed Louis' claim to Milan and joined France in a league with Venice, always ready to oppose Milan. The French army crossed the Alps once more, reinforced by Swiss mercenaries. When Milan fell to this assault, Alexander expressed delight regardless of the odium this aroused throughout Europe. In the midst of war and turmoil, pilgrims arriving in Rome for the Jubilee Year of 1500 found no security, but instead public disorder, robberies, muggings and murders.

Cesare was now embarked on a full military career to regain control of those regions of the Papal States which had strayed too far into autonomy. That his objective was a temporal domain, even a kingdom for himself in central Italy, was the belief of some contemporaries. The cost of his campaigns drained huge sums from the papal revenues, amounting in one period of two months to 132,000 ducats, about half the Papacy's normal income, and in another period of eight months to 182,000 ducats. In Rome he was overlord, callous in tyranny, an able administrator served by spies and informers, strong in the martial arts, capable of beheading a bull at one blow. He too loved art, patronized poets and painters, yet did not hesitate to cut off the tongue and hand of a man reported to have repeated a joke about him. A Venetian supposed to have circulated a slanderous pamphlet about the Pope and his son was murdered and thrown into the Tiber. "Every night," reported the helpless Venetian Ambassador, "four or five murdered men are discovered, bishops, prelates and others, so that all Rome trembles for fear of being murdered by the Duke." Sinister and vindictive, the Duke disposed of opponents by the most direct means, sowing dragon's teeth in their place. Whether for self-protection or to hide the blotches that disfigured his face, he never left his residence without wearing a mask.

In 1501 Lucrezia's second husband, Alfonso, was attacked by five assailants but escaped although severely wounded. While devotedly nursed by Lucrezia, he was convinced that Cesare was the perpetrator and would try to finish the deed by poison. In this fear Alfonso rejected all physicians and was nevertheless recovering when he saw from a window his hated brother-in-law walking below in the garden. Seizing a bow and arrow, he shot at Cesare and fatally missed. Within minutes he was hacked to death by the Duke's bodyguard. Alexander, perhaps by now himself intimidated by the tiger he had reared, did nothing.

For his son-in-law the Pope suffered no further spasms of morality. Rather, judging from Burchard's diary, the last inhibitions, if any, dropped away. Two months after Alfonso's death, the Pope presided over a banquet given by Cesare in the Vatican, famous in the annals of pornography as the Ballet of the Chestnuts. Soberly recorded by Burchard, fifty courtesans danced after dinner with the guests, "at first clothed, then naked." Chestnuts were then scattered among candelabra placed on the floor, "which the courtesans, crawling on hands and knees among the candelabra, picked up, while the Pope, Cesare and his sister Lucrezia looked on." Coupling of guests and courtesans followed, with prizes in the form of fine silken tunics and cloaks offered "for those who could perform the act most often with the courtesans." A month later Burchard records a scene in which mares and stallions were driven into a courtyard of the Vatican and equine coupling encouraged while from a balcony the Pope and Lucrezia "watched with loud laughter and much pleasure." Later they watched again while Cesare shot down a mass of unarmed criminals driven like the horses into the same courtyard.

The Pope's expenses emptied the treasury. On the last day of 1501, Lucrezia, robed in gold brocade and crimson velvet trimmed with ermine and draped in pearls, was married off for the third time to the heir of the d'Estes of Ferrara in a ceremony of magnificent pomp followed by a week of joyous and gorgeous festivities, feasts, theatricals, races and bullfights to celebrate the Borgia tie to the most distinguished family of Italy. Alexander himself counted out 100,000 ducats of gold to the bridegroom's brothers for Lucrezia's dowry. To finance such extravagance as well as Cesare's continuing campaigns, the Pope, between March and May 1503, created eighty new offices in the Curia to be sold for 780 ducats each, and appointed nine new cardinals at one blow, five of them Spaniards, realizing from their payments for the red hat a total of 120,000 to 130,000 ducats. In the same period, great wealth was seized on the death of the rich Venetian Cardinal, Giovanni Michele, who expired after two days of violent intestinal illness, generally believed to have been poisoned for his money by Cesare.

This was the last year of Alexander's life. Hostilities surrounded him. The Orsini with many partisans were fighting an extended war against Cesare. Spanish forces had landed in the south and were fighting the French for control of Naples, which they were shortly to win, establishing Spanish control of the kingdom for the next three and a half centuries. Serious churchmen concerned for the faith were raising more insistently the issue of a Council—a treatise by Cardinal Sangiorgio, one of Alexander's own appointees, stated that continued papal refusal to call one harmed the Church and scandalized all Christian people, and if all remedies failed, the cardinals themselves had a duty to convene a Council.

In August 1503 at the age of 73, Alexander VI died, not of poison, as was of course the immediate supposition, but probably of susceptibility at his age to Rome's summer fevers. Public emotion, released as if at the death of a monster, exploded in ghastly tales of a black and swollen corpse with tongue protruding from a foaming mouth, so horrible that no one would touch it, leaving it to be dragged to the grave by a rope fastened around the feet. The late Pontiff was said to have gained the tiara by a pact with the Devil at the price of his soul. Scandal sheets, to which Romans were much given, appeared every day hung around the neck of *Pasquino*, an ancient statue dug up in 1501 which served the Romans as a display center for anonymous satire.

Cesare, for all his military might, proved unable to sustain himself without the support of Rome, where an old enemy had succeeded a fond father. The dragon's teeth now rose around him. He surrendered at Naples under a Spanish promise of safe conduct, promptly violated by his captors, who took him to prison in Spain. Escaping after two years, he made his way to Navarre and was killed there in a local battle within a year.

So many had been Alexander's offenses that his contemporaries' judgments tend to be extreme, but Burchard, his Master of Ceremonies, was neither antagonist nor apologist. The impression from his toneless diary of Alexander's Papacy is of continuous violence, murders in churches, bodies in the Tiber, fighting of factions, burnings and lootings, arrests, tortures and executions, combined with scandal, frivolities and continuous ceremony—reception of ambassadors, princes and sovereigns, obsessive attention to garments and jewels, protocol of processions, entertainments and horse races with cardinals winning prizes—with a running record throughout of the costs and finances of the whole.

Certain revisionists have taken a fancy to the Borgia Pope and worked hard to rehabilitate him by intricate arguments that dispose of the charges against him as either exaggeration or forgeries or gossip or unexplained malice until all are made to vanish in a cloud of invention. The revision fails to account for one thing: the hatred, disgust and fear that Alexander had engendered by the time he died.

In the history books the pontificate is treated in terms of political wars and maneuvers. Religion, except for an occasional reference to Alexander's observance of Lenten fasts or his concern to maintain the purity of Catholic doctrine by censorship of books, is barely mentioned. The last word may belong to Egidio of Viterbo, General of the Augustinians and a major figure in the reform movement. Rome under Pope Alexander VI, he said in a sermon, knows "No law, no divinity; Gold, force and Venus rule."

4. The Warrior:
Julius II, 1503-13

The papal crown having eluded him twice, Cardinal della Rovere now missed it a third time. His strongest opponent, and an arrogant contender, was the French Cardinal d'Amboise. Cesare Borgia too, controlling a solid group of eleven Spanish cardinals, was a third force grimly bent on the election of a Spaniard who would be his ally. Armed forces of France, Spain, of the Borgia, the Orsini and various Italian factions exerted pressure for their several interests by an intimidating presence. Under the circumstances, the Cardinals retreated for their conclave within the fortress walls of Castel Sant' Angelo, and only when they had hired mercenary troops for protection, removed to the Vatican.

Might-have-beens haunted the election. Once more an accidental pope emerged when the leading candidates cancelled each other out. The Spanish votes were nullified by tumultuous mobs, shouting hate for the Borgias, which made election of another Spaniard impossible. D'Amboise was cut out by the dire warnings of della Rovere that his election would result in the Papacy being removed to France. The Italian cardinals, although holding an overwhelming majority of the College, were divided in support of several candidates. Della Rovere received a majority of the votes, but two short of the necessary two-thirds. Finding himself blocked, he threw his support to the pious and worthy Cardinal of Siena, Francesco Piccolomini, whose age and ill health indicated a short tenure. In the deadlock Piccolomini was elected, taking the name Pius III in honor of his uncle, the former Aeneas Sylvius Piccolomini, who had been Pius II.

The new Pope's first public announcement was that reform, beginning at the top with the papal court, would be his earliest care. A cultivated and learned man like his uncle, though of more studious and secluded temperament, Piccolomini had been a Cardinal for over forty years. Active in the service of Pius II, but out of place in the worldliness of Rome since that time, he had stayed away in Siena through the last pontificates. Though hardly known, he had a reputation for kindness and charity instantly seized upon by the public craving for a "good" Pope who would be the opposite of Alexander VI. The announcement of his election excited tumults of popular rejoicing. Reformist prelates were happy that the government of the Church was at last entrusted to a pontiff who was "the storehouse of all virtues and the abode of the Holy Spirit of God." All are filled, wrote the Bishop of Arezzo, "with the highest hopes for reform of the Church and the return of peace." The new Pope's religious and virtuous life promised "a new era in the history of the Church."

The new era was not to be. At 64, Pius III was old for his time and debilitated by gout. Under the burden of audiences, consistories and the long ceremonials of consecration and coronation, he weakened daily and died after holding office for 26 days.

The fervor and hope that had welcomed Pius III was a measure of the craving for a change, and warning enough that a Papacy concentrating on temporal aims was not serving the underlying interest of the Church. If this was recognized by perhaps a third of the Sacred College, they were chaff in the wind of a single fierce ambition. In the new election, Giuliano della Rovere, using "immoderate and unbounded promises," and bribery where necessary, and to the general astonishment sweeping all factions and erstwhile opponents into his camp, secured the papal tiara at last. He was chosen in a conclave of less than 24 hours, the shortest ever recorded. A monumental ego expressed itself in the change of his given name by only a syllable to the papal name of Giulio, or Julius, II.

Julius is ranked among the great popes because of his temporal accomplishments, not least his fertile partnership with Michelangelo—for art, next to war, is the great immortalizer of reputations. He was, however, as oblivious as his three predecessors to the extent of disaffection in the constituency he governed. His two consuming passions, motivated by neither personal greed nor nepotism, were restoration of the political and territorial integrity of the Papal States and embellishment of his See and memorialization of himself through the triumphs of art. He achieved important results in both these endeavors, which, being visible, have received ample notice as the visibles of history usually do, while the significant aspect of his reign, its failure of concern for the religious crisis, has been overlooked as the invisibles of history usually are. The goals of his policy were entirely temporal. For all his dynamic force, he missed his opportunity, as Guicciardini wrote, "to promote the salvation of souls for which he was Christ's Vicar on earth."

Impetuous, hot-tempered, self-willed, reckless and difficult to manage, Julius was an activist, too impatient to consult, hardly able to listen to advice. In body and soul, reported the Venetian Ambassador, he "had the nature of a giant. Anything that he had been thinking overnight has to be carried out immediately next morning and he insists on doing everything himself." Faced by resistance or contrary views, "he looks grim and breaks off the conversation or interrupts the speaker with a little bell kept on the table next to him." He, too, suffered from gout, as well as kidney trouble and other ills, but no infirmities of body restrained his spirit. His tight mouth, high color, dark "terrible" eyes, marked an implacable temperament unprepared to give way to any obstacles. *Terribilità*, or awesomeness, was the word Italians used of him.

Having broken the power of Cesare Borgia, he moved on to neutralize the feuding baronial factions of Rome by judicious marriages of della Rovere relatives to Orsinis and Colonnas. He reorganized and stiffened the papal administration, improved order in the city by stern measures against bandits and the paid assassins and duelists who had flourished under Alexander. He hired the Swiss Guard as the Vatican's protectors and conducted tours of inspection through the papal territories.

His program to consolidate papal rule began with a campaign against Venice to regain the cities of the Romagna, which Venice had seized from the Holy See, and in this venture he brought France to his aid in alliance with Louis XII. Negotiations streamed from him in local and multi-national diplomacy: to neutralize Florence, to engage the Emperor, to activate allies, to dislocate opponents. In their common if conflicting greeds, all participants in the Italian wars had designs on the expanded possessions of Venice, and in 1508 the parties coalesced in a liquid coalition called the League of Cambrai. The wars of the League of Cambrai over the next five years exhibit all the logical consistency of opera librettos. They were largely directed against Venice until the parties shifted around against France. The Papacy, the Empire, Spain and a major contingent of Swiss mercenaries took part in one permutation of alliance after another. By masterful manipulation of finances, politics and arms, aided by excommunication when the conflict grew rough, the Pope succeeded ultimately in regaining from Venice the estates of the patrimony it had absorbed.

In the meantime against all cautionary advice, Julius' pugnacity extended to the recovery of Bologna and Perugia, the two most important cities of the papal domain, whose despots, besides oppressing their subjects, virtually ignored the authority of Rome. Announcing his intention of taking personal command, and overriding the shocked objections of many of the cardinals, the Pope stunned Europe by riding forth at the head of his army on its march northward in 1506.

Years of belligerence, conquests, losses and violent disputes engaged him. When in the normal course of Italian politics Ferrara, a papal fief, changed sides, Julius in his rage at the rebellion and the dilatory progress of his punitive forces, again took physical command at the front. In helmet and mail, the white-bearded Pope, lately risen from an illness so near death that arrangements for a conclave had been made, conducted a snow-bound siege through the rigors of a severe winter. Making his quarters in a peasant's hut, he was continually on horseback, directing deployment and batteries, riding among the troops, scolding or encouraging and personally leading them through a breach in the fortress. "It was certainly a sight very uncommon to behold the High Priest, the Vicar of Christ on earth . . . employed in person in managing a war excited by himself among Christians . . . and retaining nothing of the Pontiff but the name and the robes."

Guicciardini's judgments are weighted by his scorn for all the popes of this period, but to many others besides himself the spectacle of the Holy Father as warrior and instigator of wars was dismaying. Good Christians were scandalized.

Julius was carried forward in this enterprise by fury against the French, who through a long series of disputes had now become his enemies and with whom Ferrara had joined. The aggressive Cardinal d'Amboise, as determined to be Pope as Julius before him, had persuaded Louis XII to demand three French cardinalships as the price of his aid. Against his will, Julius had complied for the sake of French support, but relations with his old rival were embittered and new disputes arose. The Pope's relations with the League, it was said, depended on whether his hatred of d'Amboise proved greater than his enmity for Venice. When Julius supported Genoa in its effort to overthrow French control, Louis XII, needled by d'Amboise, made enlarged claims of Gallican rights in appointment of benefices. As the area of conflict spread, Julius realized that the Papal States would never be firmly established while the French exercised power in Italy. Having once been the "fatal instrument" of their invasion, he now bent every effort upon their expulsion. His reversal of policy, requiring a whole new set of alliances and arrangements, awed his compatriots and even his enemy. Louis XII, reported Machiavelli, then Florentine envoy in France, "is determined to vindicate his honor even if he loses everything he possesses in Italy." Vacillating between moral and military procedure, the King threatened at times "to hang a Council around [the Pope's] neck" and at other times, with d'Amboise pressing at his elbow, "to lead an army to Rome and himself depose the Pope." A vision of not merely succeeding but replacing the Pope lured Cardinal d'Amboise. He too had become infected by the virus of folly—or ambition, its large component.

In July 1510 Julius ruptured relations with Louis, closing the Vatican door to the French Ambassador. "The French in Rome," gleefully reported the envoy of Venice, "stole about looking like corpses." Julius, on the contrary, was invigorated by visions of himself winning glory as the liberator of Italy. Thereafter *Fuori i barbari!* (Out with the barbarians!) was his battle cry.

Bold in his new cause, he executed a complete about-face to join with Venice against France. Joined also by Spain, ever eager to drive the French out of Italy, the new combination, designated the Holy League, was given a fighting edge by the addition of the Swiss. Recruited by Julius on terms of a five-year annual subsidy, their commander was the martial Bishop of Sion, Matthäus Schinner. A kindred spirit to the Pope, Schinner hated his overbearing neighbors, the French, even more than Julius hated them and was dedicated in his heart, soul and talents to their defeat. Gaunt, long-nosed, limitless in energy, he was an intrepid soldier and spell-binding orator, whose eloquence before battle moved his troops "as the wind moves the waves." Schinner's tongue, complained the next King of France, Francis I, gave the French more trouble than the formidable Swiss pikes. Julius made him a Cardinal on his entering the Holy League. In later days in battle against Francis I, Schinner rode to war wearing his cardinal's red hat and robes after announcing to his troops that he wished to bathe in French blood.

The addition of another martial cleric, Archbishop Bainbridge of York, whom Julius made a Cardinal at the same time he elevated Schinner, deepened the impression of a Papacy addicted to the sword. "What have the helmet and mitre in common?" asked Erasmus, clearly referring to Julius although prudently waiting until after his death to do so. "What association is there between the cross and the sword, between the Holy Book and the shield? How do you dare, Bishop who holds the place of the Apostle, school your people in war?" If Erasmus, always so adept at ambiguity, could say as much, many others were made yet more uncomfortable. Satiric verses referring to the armored heir of Saint Peter appeared in Rome and caricatures and burlesques in France, instigated by the King, who used Julius' warrior image for propaganda against him. He was said to "pose as a warrior but only looks like a monk dancing in spurs." Serious churchmen and cardinals were antagonized and begged him not to lead armies in person. But all arguments about exciting the world's disapproval or supplying added reason to those agitating for his removal were in vain.

Julius pursued his aims with an absolute disregard of obstacles that helped to make him irresistible, but his pursuit disregarded the primary purpose of the Church. Folly, in one of its aspects, is the obstinate attachment to a disserviceable goal. Giovanni Acciaiuoli, Florentine Ambassador in Rome at this time, sensed that affairs were out of control. Schooled in the Florentine theory of political science based on rational calculations, the Ambassador found in the wild swings of Julius' policy and in his often demonic behavior disturbing evidence that events were proceeding "outside of all reason."

As a builder and sponsor of the arts the Pope was as passionate and arbitrary as in his policies. He aroused many against him by deciding to demolish the old basilica of St. Peter's for replacement by a grander edifice suitable to a greater Holy See and a Rome that he would make the world's capital. More than that, it was to house his own tomb, to be built in his lifetime from a design by Michelangelo which surpassed, in Vasari's words, "for beauty and magnificence, abundance of ornament and richness of statuary, every ancient and imperial mausoleum." Thirty-six feet high, adorned by forty larger-than-life statues, surmounted by two angels supporting the sarcophagus, it was expected by the artist to be his masterpiece and by the client his apotheosis. According to Vasari, the design for the tomb preceded the design of the new church and so excited the Pope that he conceived the plan of a new St. Peter's as suitable housing for it. If the motive of his Papacy, as his admirers claim, was the greater glory of the Church, he identified it with the greater glory of the Supreme Pontiff, himself.

His decision was widely deplored, not because men did not want a handsome new church, said a critic, "but because they grieved that the old one should be pulled down, revered as it was by the whole world, ennobled by the sepulchres of so many saints and illustrious for so many things that had been done in it."

Ignoring disapproval as always, Julius plunged ahead, commissioning the architectural design by Bramante and pressing the work so

vehemently that 2500 laborers were employed at one time in de-
molishing the old basilica. Under the pressure of his impatience, the
accumulated contents of centuries—tombs, paintings, mosaics, statues
—were discarded without inventory and lost beyond recall, earning
Bramante the title *il ruinante*. If Julius shared in the title, he cared not
at all. In 1506 he climbed down a ladder to the bottom of a steep shaft
constructed for a pier of the new building, there to lay the foundation
stone for the "world's cathedral," which was inscribed of course with
his name. The cost of construction far exceeded papal revenues and
had to be met by a device of fateful consequence, the public sale of
indulgences. Extended to Germany in the next pontificate, it completed the disillusion of one angry cleric, precipitating the most
divisive document in Church history.

In Michelangelo the Pope had recognized an incomparable artist
from the time of his first sculpture in Rome, the *Pietà*, a requiem in
marble which no one from that day to this can view without emotion.
Finished in 1499 on commission from a French cardinal who wished
to present a great work to St. Peter's on his departure from Rome, it
made Michelangelo famous at 24 and was followed within five years
by his overpowering *David* for the cathedral of his native Florence.
Clearly the supreme Pope had to be glorified by the supreme artist,
but the temperaments of the two *terribili* clashed. After Michelangelo
had spent eight months cutting and transporting the finest marble
from Carrara for the tomb, Julius suddenly abandoned the project,
refused to pay or speak with the artist, who returned to Florence in a
rage, swearing never to work for the Pope again. What had taken
place inside the dark truculence of the della Roveran mind no one
can say, and his arrogance would not permit him to offer any explanation to Michelangelo.

When Bologna was conquered, however, the triumph had to have
a monument by no other hand. After repeated and stubborn refusals
and through the persistent efforts of intermediaries, Michelangelo was
eventually won back and consented to model a huge statue of Julius
three times life size as ordered by Julius himself. When it was viewed
by the subject while still in clay, Michelangelo asked whether he should
place a book in the left hand. "Put a sword there," answered the
warrior Pope, "I know nothing of letters." Cast in bronze, the colossal
figure was toppled and melted down when the city changed hands
during the wars, and made into a cannon derisively named *La Giulia*
by papal enemies.

In the Renaissance spirit, Julius' Papacy, carrying on the work of
his uncle Sixtus IV, poured energies and funds into the renovation of

the city. Everywhere laborers were building. Cardinals created palaces, enlarged and restored churches. New and rebuilt churches—Santa Maria del Popolo and Santa Maria della Pace—arose. Bramante built the sculpture garden of the Belvedere and the loggias connecting it to the Vatican. Major painters, sculptors, carvers and goldsmiths were called on for ornamentation. Raphael exalted the Church in frescoes for the papal apartments, newly occupied by Julius because he refused to inhabit the same suite as his late enemy Alexander. Michelangelo, dragooned against his will by the importunate Pope, painted the Sistine ceiling and, caught by his own art, worked alone on a scaffold for four years, allowing no one but the Pope to inspect his progress. Climbing a ladder to the platform, the aging Pope would criticize and quarrel with the painter, and lived just long enough to see the unveiling, when "the whole world came running" to gaze and acknowledge the marvel of a new masterpiece.

Art and war absorbed papal interest and resources to the neglect of internal reform. While the exterior bloomed, the interior decayed. A strange reminder of ancient folly appeared at this time: the classic marble *Laocoon* was rediscovered, as if to warn the Church—as its prototype had once warned Troy. It was dug up by a householder named Felice de Fredi when clearing his vineyard of ancient walls in the vicinity of the former Baths of Titus, built over the ruins of Nero's Golden House. Although the find was broken into four large and three smaller pieces, every Roman knew a classical statue when he saw one. Word was immediately sent to the Pope's architect, Giuliano de Sangallo, who set out at once on horseback with his son riding behind him and accompanied by Michelangelo, who happened to be visiting his house at the moment. Taking one look at the half-buried pieces as he dismounted, Sangallo cried, "It is the *Laocoon* that Pliny describes!" The observers watched in anxiety and excitement as the earth was carefully scraped away and then reported to the Pope, who bought the statue at once for 4140 ducats.

The ancient earth-stained *Laocoon* was welcomed like royalty. Transported to the Vatican amid cheering crowds and over roads strewn with flowers, it was reassembled and placed in the Belvedere sculpture garden along with the *Apollo Belvedere*, "the two first statues of the world." Such was the éclat that de Fredi and his son were rewarded with an annual pension for life of 600 ducats (derived from tolls of the city gates), and the finder's role was recorded by him on his tombstone.

From the antique marvel sprang new concepts of art. Its tortured motion profoundly influenced Michelangelo. Leading sculptors came to examine it; goldsmiths made copies; a poetic Cardinal wrote an ode to it (". . . from the heart of mighty ruins, lo!/Time once more has brought Laocoon home. . . ."); Francis I tried to claim it as a prize of victory from the next Pope; in the 18th century it became the centerpiece of studies by Winckelmann, Lessing and Goethe; Napoleon seized it in transitory triumph for the Louvre, whence, on his downfall, it was returned to Rome. The *Laocoon* was art, style, virtue, struggle, antiquity, philosophy, but as a voice of warning against self-destruction it was not heard.

Julius was no Alexander, but his autocracy and bellicosity had aroused almost as much antagonism. Dissident cardinals were already moving into the camp of Louis XII, who was determined to oust Julius before Julius drove him from Italy. The ouster had become an accepted objective, as if the awful example of the last century's Schism had never happened. Secularization had worked too well; the aura of the Pope had shriveled until he was, in political if not in popular eyes, no different from prince or sovereign, and subject to handling on those terms. In 1511, Louis XII in association with the German Emperor and nine dissident cardinals (three of whom later denied their consent) summoned a General Council. Prelates, orders, universities, secular rulers and the Pope himself were called upon to attend in person or through delegations for the stated purpose of "Reform of the Church in Head and Members." This was everywhere understood as a euphemism for war on Julius.

He was now in the same position as he had once tried to place Alexander, with French troops advancing and a Council looming. Deposition and Schism were openly discussed. The French-sponsored Council, with the schismatic cardinals taking the position that Julius had failed to carry out his original promise to hold a Council, convened at Pisa. French troops re-entered the Romagna; Bologna fell once more to the enemy. Rome trembled and felt the approach of doom. Worn out by his exertions at the front, tired and ill at 68, his territory and authority both under attack, Julius, as a last resort, took the one measure he and his predecessors had so long resisted: he convoked a General Council under his own authority to meet in Rome. This was the origin, in desperation rather than in conviction, of the only major effort in religious affairs by the Holy See during this period. Though carefully circumscribed, it became a forum for, if not a solution of, the issues.

The Fifth Lateran Council, as it was named, convened at St. John

Lateran, the first-ranking church of Rome, in May 1512. In the history of the Church the hour was late, and there were many who recognized it as such, with an urgency close to despair. Three months earlier, the Dean of St. Paul's in London, John Colet, scholar and theologian, preaching to a convention of clergy on the need for reform, had cried, "never did the state of the Church more need your endeavors!" In all the rushing after revenues, he said, in "the breathless race from benefice to benefice," in covetousness and corruption, the dignity of priests was dishonored, the laity scandalized, the face of the Church marred, her influence destroyed, worse than by the invasion of heresies because when worldliness absorbs the clergy, "the root of all spiritual life is extinguished." This was indeed the problem.

A savage defeat in the Romagna, just before the convening of Lateran V, reinforced the sense of crisis. On Easter Sunday, the Swiss having not yet taken the field, the French, with the help of 5000 German mercenaries, overpowered the papal and Spanish armies in a sanguinary and terrible triumph at Ravenna. It was an ill omen. In a treatise addressed to the Pope on the eve of the Council, a Bolognese jurist warned, "Unless we take thought and reform, a just God himself will take terrible vengeance, and that before long!"

Egidio of Viterbo, General of the Augustinians, who gave the opening oration at the Lateran Council in the presence of the Pope, was another who saw Divine Providence in the defeat at Ravenna and did not hesitate to use it in words of unmistakable challenge to the old man glowering from the throne. The defeat showed, said Egidio, the vanity of relying on worldly weapons and it summoned the Church to resume her true weapons, "piety, religion, probity and prayer," the armor of faith and the sword of light. In her present condition the Church had been lying on the ground "like the dead leaves of a tree in winter. . . . When has there been among the people a greater neglect and greater contempt for the sacred, for the sacraments and for the holy commandments? When has our religion and faith been more open to the derision even of the lowest classes? When, O Sorrow, has there been a more disastrous split in the Church? When has war been more dangerous, the enemy more powerful, armies more cruel? . . . Do you see the slaughter? Do you see the destruction, and the battlefield buried under piles of the slain? Do you see that in this year the earth has drunk more blood than water, more gore than rain? Do you see that as much Christian strength lies in the grave as would be enough to wage war against the enemies of the faith . . . ?"—that is to say, against Mohammed, "the public enemy of Christ."

Egidio moved on to hail the Council as the long-awaited harbinger of reform. As a reformer of long standing and author of a history of the Papacy composed for the express purpose of reminding the popes of their duty in that regard, he was a churchman of great distinction, and interested enough in clerical appearances to preserve his ascetic pallor, so it was said, by inhaling the smoke of wet straw. He was later made Cardinal by Leo X. Listening to the Lateran voices at a distance of 470 years, it is hard to tell whether his words were the practiced eloquence of a renowned preacher delivering the keynote address, or an impassioned and genuine cry for a change of course before it was too late.

For all its solemnity and ceremonial and five years' labors and many sincere and earnest speakers, the Fifth Lateran was to achieve neither peace nor reform. Continuing into the next Papacy, it acknowledged the multitude of abuses and provided for their correction in a Bull of 1514. This covered as usual the "nefarious pest" of simony, the holding of multiple benefices, the appointment of incompetent or unsuitable abbots, bishops and vicars, neglect of the divine office, the unchaste lives of clerics and even the practice of *ad commendam*, which was henceforth to be granted only in exceptional circumstances. Cardinals as a special class were ordered to abstain from pomp and luxury, from serving as partisan advocates of princes, from enriching their relatives from the revenues of the Church, from plural benefices and absenteeism. They were enjoined to adopt sober living, perform divine office, visit their titular church and town at least once a year and donate to it the maintenance of at least one priest, provide suitable clerics for the offices in their charge and obey further rules for the proper ordering of their households. It is a picture of what was wrong at every level.

Subsequent decrees, more concerned with silencing criticism than with reform, indicated that the scolding of preachers had begun to hurt. Henceforth preachers were forbidden to prophesy or predict the coming of Anti-Christ or the end of the world. They were to keep to the Gospels and abstain from scandalous denunciation of the faults of bishops and other prelates and the wrongdoing of their superiors, and refrain from mentioning names. Censorship of printed books was another measure intended to stop attacks on clerics holding offices of "dignity and trust."

Few if any of the Council's decrees ever left paper. A serious effort to put them into practice might have made an impression, but none was made. Considering that Leo X, the then presiding Pope, was engaged in all the practices that the rules forbade, the will was missing. Change of course must come either from will at the top or from irresistible external pressure. The first was not present in the Renaissance Papacy; the second was approaching.

In the battle of Ravenna the vital French commander Gaston de Foix had been killed and his forces, losing impetus, had failed to exploit their victory. D'Amboise had died, Louis was hesitant, support for the Council of Pisa, condemned as schismatic and null and void by the Pope, was leaking away. When 20,000 Swiss reached Italy the tide turned. Beaten at the battle of Novara outside Milan and compelled by the Swiss to yield the duchy, expelled by Genoa, forced backward to the base of the Alps, the French "vanished like mist before the sun"—for the time being. Ravenna and Bologna returned in allegiance to the Pope; all of the Romagna was reabsorbed into the Papal States; the Council of Pisa picked up its skirts and fled over the Alps to Lyons, where it soon faded and fell apart. Because of the underlying fear of another schism and the superior status and dignity of the Lateran, it had never had a firm foundation.

The indomitable old Pope had accomplished his aims. Rome exploded in celebration of the flight of the French; fireworks blazed, cannon boomed in salute from Castel Sant' Angelo, crowds screaming "Giulio! Giulio!" hailed him as the liberator of Italy and the Holy See. A thanksgiving procession was staged in his honor in which he was represented in the guise of a secular emperor holding a scepter and globe as emblems of sovereignty, and escorted by figures representing Scipio, conqueror of Carthage, and Camillus, who saved Rome from the Gauls.

Politics still ruled. The Holy League was crippled when Venice turned around to ally herself with France against her old rival Genoa. The Pope in his last year pursued complex connections with the Emperor and the King of England, and it was not long after his death before the French returned and the wars began again. Nevertheless, Julius had succeeded in halting the dismemberment of papal territory and consolidating the temporal structure of the Papal States, and for this he has received high marks in history. In reference books he can be found designated as "true founder of the Papal State," and even "Saviour of the Church." That the cost had been to bathe his country in blood and violence and that all the temporal gains could not prevent the authority of the Church from cracking at the core within ten years are not reckoned in these estimates.

When Julius died in 1513, he was honored and mourned by many because he was thought to have freed them from the detested invader. Shortly after his death Erasmus offered the contrary view in a satiric dialogue called *Julius Exclusus*, which, though published anonymously, has been generally attributed to him by the knowledgeable. Identifying himself at the gates of Heaven to Saint Peter, Julius says, ". . . I have done more for the Church and Christ than any pope before me. . . . I annexed Bologna to the Holy See, I beat the Venetians. I jockeyed the duke of Ferrara. I defeated a schismatical Council by a sham Council of my own. I drove the French out of Italy, and I would have driven out the Spaniards too, if the Fates had not brought me here. I have set all the princes of Europe by the ears. I have torn up treaties, kept great armies in the field, I have covered Rome with palaces. . . . And I have done it all myself, too. I owe nothing to my birth for I don't know who my father was; nothing to learning for I have none; nothing to youth for I was old when I began; nothing to popularity for I was hated all round. . . . This is the modest truth and my friends at Rome call me more god than man."

Defenders of Julius II credit him with following a conscious policy based on the conviction that "virtue without power," as a speaker had said at the Council of Basle half a century earlier, "will only be mocked, and that the Roman Pope without the patrimony of the Church would be a mere slave of Kings and princes," that, in short, in order to exercise its authority, the Papacy had first to achieve temporal solidity before undertaking reform. It is the persuasive argument of *realpolitik*, which, as history has often demonstrated, has a corollary: that the process of gaining power employs means that degrade or brutalize the seeker, who wakes to find that power has been possessed at the price of virtue—or moral purpose—lost.

5. The Protestant Break: Leo X, 1513-21

"God has given us the Papacy—let us enjoy it," wrote the former Cardinal Giovanni de' Medici, now Pope Leo X, to his brother Giuliano. There is some question whether the remark is authentic but none that it is perfectly characteristic. Leo's principle was to enjoy life. If Julius was a warrior, the new Pope was a hedonist, the only similarity between them being that their primary interests were equally secular. All the care of Lorenzo the Magnificent for the education and advancement of the cleverest of his sons had produced a cultivated bon vivant devoted to fostering art and culture and the gratification of his tastes, with as little concern for cost as if the source of funds were some self-filling magic cornucopia. One of the great spenders of his time, undoubtedly the most profligate who ever sat on the papal throne, Leo was much admired for his largesse by his Renaissance constituents, who dubbed his reign the Golden Age. It was golden for the coins that rained into their pockets from commissions, continuous festivities and entertainment, the rebuilding of St. Peter's and city improvement. Since the money to pay for these came from no magic source but from ever-more extortionate and unscrupulous levies by papal agents, the effect, added to other embittering discontents, was to bring Leo's reign to culmination as the last of united Christianity under the Roman See.

The luster of a Medici on the papal throne bringing with him the glow of money, power and patronage of the great Florentine house, augured, as it seemed, a happy pontificate, promising peace and benevolence in contrast to the blood and rigors of Julius. Consciously planned to reinforce that impression, Leo's procession to the Lateran following his coronation was the supreme Renaissance festival. It represented what the Holy See signified to the occupant of its last undivided hour—a pedestal for the display of the world's beauties and delights, and a triumph of splendor in honor of a Medici Pope.

A thousand artists decorated the route with arches, altars, statuary, wreaths of flowers and replicas of the Medici "pawnshop balls" sprouting wine. Every group in the procession—prelates, lay nobles, ambassadors, cardinals and retinues, foreign dignitaries—was richly and resplendently costumed as never before, the clerical as magnificent as the lay. A brilliant symphony of banners displaying ecclesiastical and princely heraldry waved over them. In red silk and ermine, two by two, 112 equerries escorted the sweating but happy Leo on his white horse. His mitres and tiaras and orbs required four bearers to carry them in full view. Cavalry and foot soldiers enlarged the parade. Medici munificence was exhibited by papal chamberlains throwing gold coins among the spectators. A banquet at the Lateran and a return procession illuminated by torchlight and fireworks terminated the occasion. The celebration cost 100,000 ducats, one-seventh of the reserve Julius had left in the treasury.

From then on extravagance only increased. The Pope's plans for St. Peter's, exuberantly designed by Raphael as successor to Bramante, were estimated to cost over a million ducats. For the celebration of a French royal marriage arranged for his brother Giuliano, the Pope spent 150,000 ducats, fifty percent more than the papal household's annual expenses and three times what these had been under Julius. Tapestries of gold and silk for the upper halls of the Vatican, woven to order in Brussels from cartoons by Raphael, cost half as much as his brother's wedding. To keep up with his expenditures, his chancery created over 2000 saleable offices during his Papacy, including an order of 400 papal Knights of St. Peter, who paid 1000 ducats each for the title and privileges plus an annual interest of ten percent on the purchase price. The total realized from all the offices sold has been estimated at 3 million ducats, six times the Papacy's annual revenue—and still proved insufficient.

To glorify his family and native city by a monument in recognition of himself and the "divine craftsman" who was his fellow Florentine, Leo initiated what was to be an unsurpassed work of art of his time, Michelangelo's Medici Chapel in the Church of San Lorenzo, where three generations of Medici were already buried. Having heard that the most beautiful marble was to be had from the Pietrasanta range 120 miles away in Tuscany, which Michelangelo said would be too costly to bring out, Leo would consent to nothing less. He had a road built through untrodden country for the marble alone and succeeded in bringing out enough for five incomparable columns. At this stage, he ran out of funds, besides finding Michelangelo "impossible to deal with." He preferred the genial courtliness of Raphael and the easy beauties of his art. Work on the Chapel stopped, to be resumed and completed in the Papacy of Leo's cousin Giulio, the future Clement VII.

For the University of Rome, Leo recruited more than a hundred scholars and professors for courses in law, letters, philosophy, medicine, astrology, botany, Greek and Hebrew, but owing to corrupt appointments and dwindling funds, the program, like many of his projects, faded rapidly from brilliant beginnings. An avid collector of books and manuscripts, whose contents he would often quote from memory, he founded a press for the printing of Greek classics to indulge his enthusiasm. He dispensed privileges and purses like confetti, showered endless favors on Raphael, employed brigades of assistant artists to execute his designs for ornaments, scenes and figures, decorative floors and carved embellishments for the Papal Palace. He would have made Raphael a Cardinal if the artist had not forestalled him by dying at 37, allegedly of amorous excess, before he could wear the red robes.

Conspicuous and useless expenditure by potentates for the sake of effect was a habitual gesture of the age. At a never-forgotten banquet given by the plutocrat Agostino Chigi, the gold dishes, after serving tongues of parrots and fish brought from Byzantium, were thrown out the window into the Tiber—a little short of the ultimate gesture, in that a net was laid below the surface for retrieval. In Florence, money was perfumed. The apogee of display was the Field of the Cloth of Gold prepared for the meeting of Francis I and Henry VIII in 1520. It left France with a deficit of four million livres, which took nearly a decade to liquidate. As a Medici born to conspicuous expenditure, Leo, had he been a layman, could not have been faulted for reflecting his times, even to the point of neurotic excess. But it was pure folly not to perceive any contradiction of his role in a display of ultra materialism, or ever seriously to consider that because of his position as head of the Church the effect on the public mind might be negative. Easygoing, indolent, intelligent, seemingly sociable and friendly, Leo was careless in office but conscientious in religious ritual, keeping fasts and celebrating Mass daily, and on one occasion, on report of a Turkish victory, walking barefoot through the city at the head of a procession bearing relics to pray for deliverance from the peril of Islam. Danger reminded him of God. Otherwise, the atmosphere of his court was relaxed. Cardinals and members of the Curia who made up the audience for the Sacred Orators chatted during the sermons, which in Leo's time were reduced to half an hour and then to fifteen minutes.

The Pope enjoyed contests of impromptu versifying, gambling at cards, prolonged banquets with music and especially every form of theatricals. He loved laughter and amusement, wrote a contemporary biographer, Paolo Giovio, "either from a natural liking for this kind of pastime or because he believed that by avoiding vexation and care, he might thereby lengthen his days." His health was a major concern because, although only 37 when elected, he suffered from an unpleasant anal ulcer which gave him great trouble in processions, although it aided his election because he allowed his doctors to spread word that he would not live long—always a persuasive factor to fellow cardinals. Physically he hardly resembled the Renaissance ideal of noble manhood that Michelangelo embodied in the figure of his brother for the Medici Chapel, even though that too bore small resemblance to the original. ("A thousand years from now," said the artist, "who will care whether these were the real features?") Leo was short, fat and flabby, with a head too heavy and legs too puny for his body. Soft white hands were his pride; he took great care of them and adorned them with sparkling rings.

He loved hunting accompanied by retinues of a hundred or more, hawking at Viterbo, stag-hunting at Corneto, fishing in the Lake of Bolsena. In winter, the Papal Court enjoyed musical programs, poetry readings, ballets and plays, including the risqué comedies of Ariosto, Machiavelli, and *La Calandria* by Leo's former tutor, Bernardo da Bibbiena, who accompanied the Pope to Rome and was made a Cardinal. When Giuliano de' Medici came to Rome with his wife, Cardinal Bibbiena wrote to him, "God be praised, for here we lack nothing but a court with ladies." A clever, cultivated Tuscan and skilled diplomatist of great wit, high spirits and earthy tastes, Bibbiena was the Pope's close companion and adviser.

Leo's taste for the classical and the theatrical filled Rome with endless spectacles in a strange mixture of paganism and Christianity: pageants of ancient mythology, carnival masquerades, dramas of Roman history, spectacles of the Passion played in the Colosseum, classical orations and splendid Church feasts. None was more memorable than the famous procession of the white elephant bearing gifts to the Pope from the King of Portugal to celebrate a victory over the Moors. The elephant, led by a Moor with another riding on his neck, carried under a jeweled howdah a chest decorated with silver towers and battlements and containing rich vestments, gold chalices and books in fine bindings for Leo's delight. At the bridge of Sant' Angelo, the elephant, on command, bowed three times to the Pope and sprinkled the assembled spectators with water to their screams of glee.

On occasion, paganism invaded the Vatican. In the course of one of the Sacred Orations, the speaker invoked the "immortals" of the Greek pantheon, causing both laughter and some anger in the audience, but the Pope listened complacently and tolerated the blunder "in keeping with his nature." He liked the sermons to be above all learned, reflecting classical style and content.

In political affairs Leo's lax attitude accomplished no triumphs and undid some of Julius'. His principle was to avoid trouble as far as he could and accept the inevitable when he had to. His method followed Medici statecraft, which allowed, not to say prescribed, arrangements with both sides. "Having made a treaty with one party," Leo used to say, "there is no reason why one should not treat with the other." While acknowledging French claim to Milan, he secretly dealt with Venice to defeat the French re-occupation. When allied to Spain, he likewise colluded with Venice to drive the Spaniards out of Italy. Dissimulation became his habit, more pronounced the deeper his Papacy advanced into trouble. Evasive and smiling, he eluded inquiries and never explained what his policy was, if indeed he had one.

In 1515 the French returned under Francis I at the head of an imposing army with 3000 noble cavalry, skilled artillery and infantry of German mercenaries to launch themselves upon the reconquest of Milan. After judicious consideration, the Pope joined the none too energetic members of the Holy League in resistance, relying on the Swiss for combative force. Unhappily, at the hard-fought battle of Marignano outside Milan, the French were victorious. Though the combat was touch-and-go for two days, papal forces camped at Piacenza less than fifty miles away took no part.

Once more in control of the great northern duchy, the French sealed it by a treaty of "eternal peace" with the Swiss. They were now in too strong a position for the Pope to contend with them, so he reasonably changed sides and, meeting with Francis at Bologna, reached an accommodation which was largely a cession. He yielded Parma and Piacenza, long contested by Milan and the Papacy, and settled the old struggle over Gallican rights concerning Church appointments and revenues. One provision, designed to improve the quality of appointees, required bishops to be over the age of 27 and trained in theology or law, but these qualifications could conveniently be suspended if the nominees were blood relatives of the King or noblemen. Undertaken in such a spirit, these reforms, like those of the Lateran Council, accomplished small improvement.

On the whole, the Concordat of Bologna, even though the French Church found some of its provisions objectionable, marked a further surrender by the Papacy of ecclesiastical power, just as the French reconquest of Milan marked the final crippling, for this period, of Italian independence. Though obvious to bitter critics like Machiavelli and Guicciardini, that result, if he noticed it, did not greatly trouble Leo. *Fuori i barbari!* was not his battle cry. He preferred harmony. Never able to refuse, he promised at Francis' request to give him the *Laocoon*, planning to palm off a copy, which he subsequently ordered from the sculptor Baccio Bandinelli (and which is now in the Uffizi). He obtained a French princess for his brother and another for his nephew Lorenzo, and remained happy enough with the French until power shifted with the accession of Charles V as Emperor in 1519, uniting the Spanish and Hapsburg thrones. Finding it expedient to change sides again, Leo allied himself with the new Emperor. The wars continued, largely as conflicts of the great powers fighting out their rivalry on Italy's soil while the Italian states in their inveterate separation shuffled futilely among them.

The peculiar family passion of the popes which seemed to make family fortunes more important to them than the Holy See was fully shared by Leo, to his undoing. Having no children of his own, he focused his efforts on his closest relatives, beginning with his first cousin Giulio de' Medici, bastard son of the Giuliano killed in the cathedral by the Pazzi. Leo disposed of the birth barrier by an affidavit stating that Giulio's parents had been legally if secretly married, and, thus legitimized, Giulio became a Cardinal and his cousin's chief minister, eventually to occupy his seat as Clement VII. Altogether Leo distributed among his family five cardinalships, to two first cousins and three nephews, each a son of one of his three sisters. This was merely routine. The trouble came when, on the death of his brother, Leo determined to make their common nephew Lorenzo, son of their deceased elder brother Piero, the carrier of Medici fortunes. To obtain the duchy of Urbino for Lorenzo became Leo's obsession.

Seizing the domain by force of arms from the existing Duke, whom he excommunicated, the Pope endowed the title and territory upon Lorenzo, requiring the College of Cardinals to confirm the deed. The incumbent Duke, a della Rovere nephew of Julius' who shared his late uncle's vigor, fought back. When his envoy came to Rome, bearing the Duke's challenge to Lorenzo, he was seized despite a safe-conduct and tortured for information. To prosecute his war on Urbino, the Pope imposed taxes throughout the Papal States on the ground that the Duke was a rebel. This shameless campaign turned opinion against him, but, like Julius or any other autocrat, Leo ignored the effect of his actions on the public. With relentlessness he showed in little else, he pursued the war for two years. At the end of that time, Lorenzo and his French wife were both dead, leaving only an infant daughter whose unexpected destiny as Catherine de' Medici was to marry the son of Francis I and to become Queen—and ruler—of France. This whirl of fortune's wheel, however, came too late for Leo; nor did it prevent the decline of the Medici. Into the empty war on Urbino Leo had poured a total of 800,000 ducats, a plunge into indebtedness that meant the financial wreck of the Papacy. It led the wrecker not to retrenchment, but, through more tortuous devices, to the greatest scandal of the age.

The Petrucci conspiracy was an obscure and vicious affair that has baffled everyone from that day to this. Leo professed to discover through betrayal by a servant a conspiracy of several cardinals to assassinate him. Led by the young Cardinal Alfonso Petrucci of Siena, who nursed a personal grievance, the plot depended on poison to be injected by a suborned doctor in the course of lancing a boil on the Pope's buttock. Arrests were made, informers tortured, suspect cardinals grilled. Lured to Rome on a safe-conduct, Petrucci and others of the accused were imprisoned, the violation being condoned by Leo on the ground that no poisoner could be considered a safe risk. Hearings produced awful revelations; confessions were induced; whispered reports of the proceedings bewildered and terrified Rome. Forced to plead guilty, Cardinal Petrucci was executed by strangling with an appropriate red silk noose at the hand of a Moor because protocol did not permit a Christian to put to death a Prince of the Church. Faced with this example, the other accused cardinals accepted pardons at a cost of enormous fines, up to 150,000 ducats from the richest, Cardinal Raffaele Riario, yet another of the *nipoti* of Sixtus IV, in this case a great-nephew.

So farfetched was the plot that the inference could not be avoided that the Pope, perhaps seizing upon some informer's tattle, had promoted the whole affair for the sake of the fines. Recent investigations in Vatican archives suggest that the plot may in fact have been real, but what counts is the impression made at the time. Coming on top of public indignation at Leo's war on Urbino, the Petrucci conspiracy further discredited the Papacy, besides alarming and antagonizing the cardinals. Whether to nullify their hostility or to fend off bankruptcy, or both, Leo in an act of astonishing boldness created 31 new cardinals in a single day, collecting from the recruits over 300,000 ducats. The wholesale creation is said to have been conceived by Cardinal Giulio de' Medici as a paving stone on his own path to the Papacy. Demoralization by now was such that no movement of rebellion in the College followed.

The amiable Leo, foundering in his own transactions, turned less amiable, or perhaps had never been so benign as popularly supposed. The Petrucci affair was not the only unpleasantness. To incorporate Perugia into the Papal States, its dynastic ruler, Gianpaolo Baglioni, had to be eliminated. A "monster of iniquity," Baglioni deserved no mercy, but the Pope once again resorted to treachery. He invited Baglioni to Rome on a safe-conduct, seized and imprisoned him on arrival and after the usual torture had him beheaded.

Why anyone trusted the safe-conducts of the time is the least of the questions. The greater question is what kind of apostleship of Christianity did the Supreme Pontiff and his four predecessors see themselves as filling? Elevated to the chair of Saint Peter, Holy Fathers to the faithful, they had a duty to their constituency to which they seem rarely to have given a thought. What of the believers who looked up to them, who wished to revere holiness and trust in the Pope as supreme priest? A sense of "the perpetual majesty of the pontificate," in Guicciardini's phrase, seems to have meant only its tangible attributes to these popes. They made no pretense of holiness or any gestures of religious vocation, while those in their charge had never clamored for it more loudly.

Unconcerned, Leo ignored the indignation his methods caused and made no attempt to curtail his extravagance. He never tried economizing; nor did he reduce his household or gave up gambling. In 1519 in the midst of bankruptcy he staged a bullfight—Alexander's legacy to the Holy See—on Carnival Sunday with resplendent costumes donated to all the toreadors and their attendants by a Pope already irredeemably in debt.

The year of the Petrucci scandal was 1517, a year destined to turn over a page in history. Since the beginning of the century, dissatisfaction with the Church had grown and widened, expressing itself clerically in synods and sermons, popularly in tracts and satires, letters, poems, songs and the apocalyptic prophecies of preachers. To everyone but the government of the Church, it was plain that an outbreak of dissent was approaching. In 1513, an Italian preaching friar felt it close at hand, predicting the downfall of Rome and of all priests and friars in a holocaust that would leave no unworthy clergy alive and no Mass said for three years. The respectable middle class was made indignant by the reckless extravagance and debts of the Papacy, and every class and group in every nation resented the insatiable papal taxation.

Sermons at the reopening of the Lateran Council under Leo made the discontent explicit. The warning of Giovanni Cortese, legal adviser to the Curia, who had advised Leo on his election that the task of reform was dangerously overdue, was repeated. Many years later, Cortese as a Cardinal was to prepare the agenda for the Council of Trent, which tried to repair the damage. In a notable address at the closing of the Lateran in March 1517, Gianfrancesco Pico della Mirandola, ruler of a small duchy and nephew of a more famous uncle, concluded a summary of all the needed reforms with a succinct statement of the choice between the secular and religious: "If we are to win back the enemy and the apostate to our faith, it is more important to restore fallen morality to its ancient rule of virtue than that we should sweep with our fleet the Euxine Sea." If its proper task were neglected, the speaker finished, heavy would be the judgment that would fall upon the Church. Representing the devout Christian layman, Pico's speech indicated the spread of discontent.

Alienated by the worldly values of the Papacy, humanists and intellectuals turned back, as did Jacques Lefèvre of France, to the Scriptures to find the meaning of their faith, or like Erasmus to satire, which, while it may have been motivated by genuine religious distress, helped to lower respect for the Church. "As to these Supreme Pontiffs who take the place of Christ," he wrote in the *Colloquies*, "were wisdom to descend upon them, how it would inconvenience them! . . . It would lose them all that wealth and honor, all those possessions, triumphal progresses, offices, dispensations, tributes and indulgences. . . ." It would require prayers, vigils, studies, sermons "and a thousand troublesome tasks of that sort." Copyists, notaries, advocates, secretaries, muleteers, grooms, bankers, pimps—"I was about to add something more tender, though rougher, I am afraid, on the ears"—would be out of work.

The popes' wars also earned Erasmus' scorn, directed as they were against so-called enemies of the Church. "As if the Church had any enemies more pestilential than impious pontiffs who by their silence allow Christ to be forgotten, enchain Him by mercenary rules . . . and crucify Him afresh by their scandalous life!" In a private letter he put the matter briefly. "The monarchy of the Pope at Rome, as it is now, is a pestilence to Christendom."

Writing in the same years, 1510–20, Machiavelli found proof of decadence in the fact "that the nearer people are to the Church of Rome, which is the head of our religion, the less religious are they." Whoever examined the gap between the principles upon which the Christian religion was founded and their present application by the Church "will judge that her ruin and chastisement are near at hand." Machiavelli's anger was at the harm done to Italy. "The evil example of the court of Rome has destroyed all piety and religion in Italy," resulting in "infinite mischief and disorders" which "keep our country divided." This is "the cause of our ruin." Whenever fearing loss of temporal power, the Church, never strong enough to be supreme, calls in some foreign aid, and "this barbarous domination stinks in the nostrils of everyone."

The indictment was summarized in one sentence by Guicciardini: "Reverence for the Papacy has been utterly lost in the hearts of men."

The abuse that precipitated the ultimate break was the commercialization of indulgences, and the place where the break came, as everyone knows, was at Wittenberg in northeastern Germany. Anti-Roman sentiment was strongest, and protest most vocal, in the German principalities owing to the absence of a national centralized power able to resist papal taxation as in France. Also, Rome's exactions were heavier because of ancient connections with the Empire and the great estates held there by the Church. Besides feeling themselves directly robbed by papal agents, the populace felt their faith insulted by the ring of coin in everything to do with the Church, by the wickedness of Rome and its popes and their refusal to reform. A revolt against the Holy See could be expected, warned Girolamo Alessandro, Papal Nuncio to the Empire and a future Bishop and Cardinal. Thousands in Germany, he wrote to the Pope in 1516, were only waiting for the moment to speak their minds openly. Immersed in money and marble monuments, Leo was not listening. Within a year, the awaited moment came through the instrumentality of his agent for the sale of papal indulgences in Germany, Johann Tetzel.

Indulgences were not new, nor were they invented by Leo. Originally granted as a release from all or part of the good works required of a sinner to satisfy a penance imposed by his priest, indulgence gradually came to be considered a release from the guilt of the sin itself. This was a usage severely condemned by purists and protesters. More objectionable was the commercial sale of a spiritual grace. The grace once granted in return for pious donations for church repairs, hospitals, ransom of captives of the Turks and other good works had grown into a vast traffic of which a half or third of the receipts customarily went to Rome and the rest to the local domain, with various percentages to the agents and pardoners who held the concessions. The Church had become a machine for making money, declared John Colet in 1513, with the fee considered as the effective factor rather than repentance and good works. Employing charlatans, misleading the credulous, this traffic became one of the persistent evils of organized religion.

When pardoners allowed the belief—though never explicitly stated by the popes—that indulgences could take care of future sins not yet committed, the Church had reached the point of virtually encouraging sin, as its critics did not fail to point out. To enlarge the market, Sixtus IV ruled in 1476 that indulgences applied to souls in Purgatory, causing the common people to believe that they must pay for the relief of departed relatives. The more prayers and masses and indulgences bought for the deceased, the shorter their terms in Purgatory, and since this arrangement favored the rich, it was naturally resented by the poor and made them readier when the moment came to reject all official sacraments.

Julius had already issued a distribution of indulgences to help pay for the new St. Peter's. Leo in his first year of office authorized another issue for the same purpose and again in 1515 for special sale in Germany, to offset the costs of his war on Urbino. Offering "complete absolution and remission of all sins," this one was to be sold over an unusual eight-year term. The financial arrangements, of Byzantine complexity, were designed to enable a young noble, Albrecht of Brandenburg, brother of the Elector of Brandenburg, to pay for three benefices to which the Pope had appointed him. At age 24 he had received the archbishoprics of Mainz and Magdeburg and the bishopric of Halberstadt for a total price variously stated to be 24,000 or 30,000 ducats. Representing simony, plural benefices and an unqualified nominee, this transaction was arranged while the Lateran Council was engaged in outlawing the same practices. Unable to raise the money, Albrecht had borrowed from the Fuggers, whom he was now to reimburse through the proceeds from the indulgences.

Tetzel, a Dominican monk, was a promoter who might have made Barnum blush. Upon arrival in a town, he would be greeted by a pre-arranged procession of clergy and commoners coming out to meet him with flags and lighted candles while church bells rang joyful tunes. Traveling with a brass-bound chest and a bag of printed receipts, and preceded by an assistant friar bearing the Bull of Indulgence on a velvet cushion, he would set up shop in the nave of the principal church in front of a huge cross raised for the occasion and draped with the papal banner. At his side an agent of the Fuggers kept careful count of the money that purchasers dropped into a bowl placed on top of the chest, as each received a printed indulgence from the bag.

"I have here," Tetzel would call out, "the passports . . . to lead the human soul to the celestial joys of Paradise." For a mortal sin, seven years of penance were due. "Who then would hesitate for a quarter-florin to secure one of these letters of remission?" Warming up, he would say that if a Christian had slept with his mother and put money in the Pope's bowl, "the Holy Father had the power in Heaven and earth to forgive the sin, and if he forgave it, God must do so also." In behalf of the deceased, he said that "as soon as the coin rang in the bowl, the soul for whom it was paid would fly out of Purgatory straight to Heaven."

The ring of these coins was the summons to Luther. Tetzel's crass equation of the mercenary and the spiritual was the ultimate expression of the message emanating from the Papacy over the past fifty years. It was not the cause but the signal for the Protestant secession, whose doctrinal, personal, political, religious and economic causes were old and various and long-developing.

In response to Tetzel's campaign, Luther in 1517 nailed his 95 theses on the church door at Wittenberg, assailing the abuse of indulgence as sacrilegious, although without yet suggesting a break with Rome. In the same year the Fifth Lateran held its final session—the last chance for reform. Luther's challenge provoked a counter-attack by Tetzel affirming the efficacy of indulgences followed by a reply by Luther in a vernacular tract, *Indulgence and Grace*. His fellow Augustinians took up the debate, opponents entered the dispute and within two months a German Archbishop in Rome called for heresy proceedings. Summoned to Rome in 1518, Luther petitioned for hearings in his native land, to which the Papal Legate in Germany and the lay authorities agreed in order not to exacerbate feelings during the imminent meeting of the German Diet which was supposed to vote taxes. The death of the Emperor Maximilian shortly afterward, requiring election of a successor by the Diet, was a further reason to avoid trouble.

Enclosed, like his predecessors, in the Italian drama, the Pope was unaware of the issues and incapable of understanding the protest that had been developing for the century and a half since Wycliffe had repudiated priesthood as necessary to salvation, as well as the sacraments and the Papacy itself. Leo hardly noticed the fracas in Germany except as a heresy to be suppressed like any other. His response was a Bull in November 1518 providing excommunication for all who failed to preach and believe that the Pope has the right to grant indulgences. It proved as effective as Canute's admonition to the waves. Leo, however, was soon to be more distressed by the shock of Raphael's death than by the challenge of Luther.

Once the protest became overt, revolt against Rome followed in a rush. When the Diet of Augsburg in 1518 was asked to vote a special tax for crusade against the Turks, it replied that the real enemy of Christendom was "the hell-hound in Rome." At his hearings in Leipzig in 1519, Luther now repudiated the authority of both the Papacy and a General Council, and subsequently published in 1520 his definitive statement of the Protestant position, *To the Christian Nobility of the German Nation*. Claiming that baptism consecrated every man a priest with direct access to salvation, it denounced popes and hierarchy for all their sins and unrighteousness and called for national churches independent of Rome. Taken up by other Church rebels and reformers, his doctrine swept in a torrent of illustrated sheets and pamphlets and tracts to eager readers in towns and cities from Bremen to Nuremberg. In the Swiss city of Zurich, a fellow protester, Ulrich Zwingli, already preaching the same theses as Luther, extended the protest which was soon to fall into doctrinal disputes that were to fragment the movement forever after.

Informed by papal envoys of the spreading dissent, the Papacy saw itself dealing with "a wild boar which has invaded the Lord's vineyard," so described in a new Bull, *Exsurge Domine*, in 1520. Upon examination, the Bull condemned 41 of Luther's theses as heretical or dangerous and ordered him to recant. When he refused, he was excommunicated and his punishment as a declared heretic was asked from the civil arm. The new Emperor, Charles V, young but sage and not anxious to draw popular anger upon himself, handed the hot coal to the Diet at Worms, where Luther in 1521 again refused to recant. As a devout Catholic, Charles V was forced to denounce him, perhaps less from orthodoxy than in return for a political pact with the Pope to join in ejecting the French from Milan. The Edict of Worms obediently put Luther and his followers under the ban of the Empire, promptly rendered null by his friends, who removed him to safety.

The Imperial forces triumphed over the French at Milan in 1521, enabling their papal allies to regain the northern jewels of the patrimony, Parma and Piacenza. Characteristically celebrating the victory by one of his favorite all-night banquets in December, Leo caught a chill, developed a fever and died. In seven years he had spent, as estimated by his financial controller, Cardinal Armellini, five million ducats, and left debts of more than 800,000. Between his death and burial, the customary plunder on the death of a pontiff was so thorough that the only candles that could be found to light his coffin were half-used ones from the recent funeral of a Cardinal. His hectic extravagance, lacking even Julius' justification of political purpose, was the compulsive spending of a spoiled son of wealth and the acquisitiveness of a collector and connoisseur. Unlike Chigi's gold plate, it had no waiting net in the river. It nourished immortal works of art, but however much these have graced the world, the proper business of the Church was something else.

Leo left the Papacy and the Church in the "lowest possible repute," wrote the contemporary historian Francesco Vettori, "because of the continued advance of the Lutheran sect." A lampoon suggested that if the Pope had lived longer, he would have sold Rome too, and then Christ, and then himself. People in the street hissed the cardinals going to the conclave to choose his successor.

6. The Sack of Rome: Clement VII, 1523-34

At this belated moment, as if fate were taunting the Church, a reformer was elected Pope, not through conscious intent but by a fluke during a deadlock of leading contenders. When neither Cardinal Alessandro Farnese nor Giulio de' Medici could gain a majority and the bellicose Cardinal Schinner missed election by two votes, the nomination of someone not present was proposed, "just to waste the morning," as Guicciardini says. The name of the Dutch-born Cardinal Adrian of Utrecht, former Chancellor of the University of Louvain, former tutor of Charles V and presently his Vicroy in Spain, was put forward. As the virtues of this reform-minded, austere but otherwise unfamiliar person were extolled, the Cardinals began to follow each other in voting for him until suddenly they found they had elected him—a virtual unknown, and what was worse, a foreigner! When this remarkable result could not be explained rationally, it was attributed to the intervention of the Holy Ghost.

Curia, cardinals, citizens and all expectant beneficiaries of papal patronage were appalled, Romans outraged at the advent of a non-Italian, ergo a "barbarian," and the Pope-Elect himself anything but eager. Reformers, however, encouraged by Adrian's reputation, were hopeful at last. They drew up programs for a Reform Council and lists of enforcements of long-disregarded Church rules needed to cleanse the clergy of corruption. Their case was summarized in the stern reminder of one adviser: "Under pain of eternal damnation, the Pope is bound to appoint shepherds, not wolves."

Adrian did not appear in Rome until late in August 1521, almost eight months after his election, owing in part to an outbreak of plague. He made his intent clear at once. Addressing the College of Cardinals at his first consistory, he said that evils in the clergy and Papacy had reached such a pitch that, in the words of Saint Bernard, "those steeped in sin could no longer perceive the stench of their own iniquities." The ill repute of Rome, he said, was the talk of the whole world, and he implored the Cardinals to banish corruption and luxury from their lives and, as their sacred duty, to set a good example to the world by joining him in the cause of reform. His audience was deaf to the plea. No one was prepared to separate personal fortune from ecclesiastical office, or do without the annuities and revenues of plural benefices. When the Pope announced austerity measures for all, he met only sullen resistance.

Adrian persisted. Curia officials, former favorites, even Cardinals were summoned for rebuke or for trials and penalties. "Everyone trembles," reported the Venetian Ambassador, "owing to the things done by the Pope in the space of eight days."

He issued rules to prohibit simony, reduce expenses, curb the sale of dispensations and indulgences, appoint only qualified clerics to benefices and limit each to one, on the innovative theory that benefices should be supplied with priests, not priests with benefices. At each effort, he was told that he would bankrupt or weaken the Church. Served only by two personal attendants, isolated by language, despised for his lack of interest in arts and antiquities, in every way the contrary of an Italian, he could do nothing acceptable. His letter to the German Diet demanding the suppression of Luther as decreed by the Diet of Worms was ignored, while his admission that in the Roman Church "sacred things have been misused, the commandments have been transgressed and in everything there has been a turn for the worse" alienated the papal court. Against popular protests and demonstrations, satiric *pasquinate*, insults scribbled on walls and the non-cooperation of officials, Adrian found the system too entrenched for him to dislodge. "How much," he sorrowfully acknowledged, "does a man's efforts depend on the age in which his work is cast!" Utterly frustrated, the outsider died unmourned in September 1523, after a year and two weeks in active office.

Rome went back to normal. The conclave, taking no chances, elected another Medici, Cardinal Giulio, who perversely chose the name of the murderous, if able, first Anti-Pope of the Schism, Clement VII. The new Clement's reign proved to be a pyramid of catastrophes. Protestantism continued its advance. The German states—Hesse, Brunswick, Saxony, Brandenburg—one by one signed the Lutheran confession, breaking with Rome and defying the Emperor. Economic gain from disendowing Church properties and eliminating papal taxes interested them as much as doctrine, while doctrinal feuds, reflecting the quarrel of Zwingli and Luther, riddled the movement from the moment it was born. Meanwhile the Danish Church virtually seceded and the Reformed Doctrine steadily advanced in Sweden. In 1527 Henry VIII, in the act of so much consequence, asked the Pope to annul his marriage to Catherine of Aragon, who inconveniently for Clement was the aunt of Charles V. Otherwise the Pope might usefully have decided, like his predecessors, that in such cases expedience was the better part of principle. But Charles V, double monarch of the Empire and Spain, loomed larger than Henry VIII, causing the Pope consistently to refuse the divorce on grounds, as he claimed, of his respect for canonical law. He made the wrong choice, and lost England.

Supreme office, like sudden disaster, often reveals the man, and revealed Clement as less adequate than expected. Knowledgeable and effective as a subordinate, Guicciardini writes, he fell victim when in charge to timidity, perplexity and habitual irresolution. He lacked popular support because, disappointing expectations of a Medici, he "gives away nothing and does not bestow the property of others, therefore the people of Rome grumble." Responsibility made him "morose and disagreeable," which was not surprising as in his conduct of policy every choice proved unwise and the outcome of every venture worse than the last. "From a great and renowned Cardinal," wrote Vettori, he was transformed "into a little and despised Pope."

The rivalry of France and the Hapsburg-Spanish combination was now working itself out in Italy. Trying to play off one against the other after the Italian habit, Clement managed only to gain the mistrust of both and lose a dependable alliance with either. When Francis renewed the war for Milan in 1524, his initial success decided Clement, in spite of the Papacy's recent pact with the Empire, to enter into a secret treaty with Francis in return for his promise to respect the Papal States and Medici rule of Florence, Clement's primary interest. On discovering the Pope's double dealing, Charles swore to go to Italy in person to "revenge myself on those who have injured me, particularly that fool of a Pope." In the following year at the decisive and climactic battle of Pavia, the Spanish-Imperialists defeated and took prisoner the King of France. Upon this disaster for his ally, Clement reached a new agreement with the Emperor while retaining the secret hope that it would not be long before France would re-establish the balance of power, allowing him to regain his power of maneuver between the two. He seems to have seen no advantage in constancy, no disadvantage in infidelity, but only the momentary dictates of unstable fortune.

A year later, Charles released Francis from prison on condition of his pledge, incorporated in a treaty, to renounce French claim to Milan,

Genoa, Naples and everything else in Italy, besides ceding Burgundy. It was not a pledge the proud King of France, once back on his own ground, was likely to obey, nor did he. On regaining his throne, he opened overtures to Clement, who saw his awaited opportunity to liberate the Papacy from the heavy Spanish hand, even though past experience of inviting France into Italy had a bitter history. He nevertheless took Francis as a partner in a Holy League with Venice and Florence on condition that he would take up arms against the Emperor while the Pope would absolve him from breaking his word to his erstwhile captor. Needless to say, the Italian states were engaged in all these arrangements and when it came to hostilities were trampled and battered.

By 1527, hardly a part of Italy had escaped violence to life and land, plunder, destruction, misery and famines. Regions that were spared profited from the distress of others. Two English envoys traveling through Lombardy reported that "the most goodly countree for corne and vynes that may be seen is so desolate that in all that ways we sawe [not] oon man or woman in the fylde, nor yet creatour stirring, but in great villaiges five or six myserable persons," and in Pavia children crying in the streets and dying of hunger.

Clement's misjudgments having prepared the way, Rome itself was now to be engulfed by war. Imperial forces made up of German *Landsknechte* and Spanish companies, with a French renegade, the Constable de Bourbon, in command, crossed the Alps to combat the Holy League and take control of Rome and the Papacy, forestalling any similar intent by the French. As it turned out, French promises having outrun depleted capacity, no French army was to enter Italy that year to support the Pope. At the same time, and probably with a helpful hint from Charles V, an uprising by the pro-Imperial Colonna party erupted in Rome, led by Cardinal Pompeo Colonna, whose fury of ambition and hatred of the Medici fired him with a scheme to bring about Clement's death and impose his own election upon a conclave by force of arms. His raiders raised havoc, bloodied and killed fellow-citizens, looted the Vatican but missed the Pope, who escaped through a private passageway—built for such emergencies by Alexander VI—to refuge in Castel Sant' Angelo. Decked in the papal robes, some of Colonna's men strutted in mockery in the piazza of St. Peter's. Terms were agreed upon and the raiders withdrawn, following which the Pope, doubtless absolving himself, violated the agreements and assembled sufficient forces to lay waste Colonna properties.

The Colonna raid suggested to Clement no necessity to organize defense. He clung to negotiations. His maneuvers and treaties over the next months with the Spanish Ambassador acting for Charles V and with this state and that are too twisted to follow and were, in any event, fruitless. Concerted policy and determined action could have disabled the invaders in Lombardy, whose mixed forces were mutually hostile, unpaid, undisciplined, hungry and mutinous. All that held them was their commanders' promise of loot and rich ransoms in Rome and Florence. The difficulty was that the Holy League's available forces were in no better condition, and unity and leadership as always conspicuously absent. Charles V, bred in Spanish orthodoxy and reluctant to attack the Holy See, agreed to an eight-month armistice in return for payment of 60,000 ducats to his troops. Enraged by this postponement of plunder, the troops mutinied and marched for Rome. Their way south was actively aided by food and free passage provided by the dukes of Ferrara and Urbino in revenge for wrongs each had suffered at the hands of Medici popes.

Commanders of the Imperial force, fearful of the savagery they felt preparing to break loose on the Eternal City, were amazed to meet no signs of defense, receive no overtures for parley, no reply to their ultimatum. Rome was demoralized; among its several thousands of armed men, not 500 could be rallied into bands to defend or even to blow up the bridges. Clement seems to have counted on Rome's sacred status as its shield of defense, or else was paralyzed by irresolution. "We are on the brink of ruin," wrote a papal secretary of state to the Papal Nuncio in England. "Fate has let loose upon us every kind of evil so that it is impossible to add to our misery. It seems to me that the sentence of death has been passed on us and that we are only awaiting its execution which cannot be long delayed."

On 6 May 1527, the Spanish-German invaders breached the walls and poured into the city. The orgy of human barbarity that followed in the See of St. Peter's, the capital of Christendom for 1200 years, was a measure of how far the image of Rome had been demeaned by its rulers. Massacre, plunder, fire and rape raged out of control; commanders were helpless and their chief, the Constable de Bourbon, was dead, having been killed the first day by a shot from the Roman walls.

The ferocity and bloodthirstiness of the attackers "would have moved a stone to compassion," according to a report in the Mantua archives, "written in a trembling hand." The soldiers looted house by house, killing anyone who offered resistance. Women were violated regardless of age. Screams and groans filled every quarter; the Tiber floated with dead bodies. Pope, cardinals, Curia and lay officials piled into Sant' Angelo in such haste and crush that one cardinal was drawn up in a basket after the portcullis was dropped. Ransoms were fixed on the wealthy and atrocious tortures devised to make them pay; if they could not, they were killed. Priests, monks and other clergy were victimized with extra brutality; nuns dragged to brothels or sold to soldiers in the streets. Palaces were plundered and left in flames; churches and monasteries sacked for their treasures, relics trampled after being stripped of jeweled covers, tombs broken open in the search for more treasure, the Vatican used as a stable. Archives and libraries were burned, their contents scattered or used as bedding for horses. Surveying the scene, even a Colonna wept. "Hell has nothing to compare with the present state of Rome," a Venetian reported.

Lutherans of the feared *Landsknechte* delighted in the scene, parodied the papal rites, paraded through the streets in the rich vestments of prelates and the red robes and hats of cardinals, with a leader playing the part of Pope riding on an ass. The first wave of carnage lasted eight days. For weeks Rome smoked and stank of unburied corpses gnawed by dogs. The occupation lasted nine months, inflicting irreparable damage. Two thousand bodies were estimated to have been thrown into the Tiber, 9800 buried, loot and ransoms estimated at between three and four million ducats. Only when plague appeared and food vanished, leaving famine, did the drunken satiated hordes recede from the "stinking slaughterhouse" they had made of Rome.

It was a sack, too, of spiritual authority. The Vandals who perpetrated the sack of A.D. 455 were aliens and so-called barbarians, but these were fellow-Christians, propelled, so it seemed, by an extra lust in defiling the tarnished lords of the Church. Troy too had once believed in a sacred veil of protection; when the moment came, Rome counted on its sacred status but it was found to have vanished.

No one could doubt that the Sack was divine punishment for the worldly sins of popes and hierarchy, and few questioned the belief that the fault came from within. The aggressors agreed. Appalled by the event and fearing the Emperor's displeasure at "these outrages on the Catholic religion and the Apostolic See," the Commissary of the Imperial Army wrote to Charles V, "In truth everyone is convinced that all this has happened as a judgment of God on the great tyranny and disorders of the Papal court." A sadder insight was articulated by Cardinal Cajetan, General of the Dominicans, reform spokesman at the Lateran, Papal Legate in Germany in the dealings with Luther: "For we who should have been the salt of the earth have decayed until we are good for nothing beyond outward ceremonials."

Clement's humiliation was twofold. He had to accept terms imposed by the victors and remain their prisoner in Sant' Angelo until he found funds for his ransom, while at news of his helplessness, Florence promptly expelled the agents of Medici rule and re-established a republic. Elsewhere a shift of opinion against the scandal of an imprisoned Pope caused the Emperor to open the doors of Sant' Angelo, whence, disguised as a merchant, Clement was escorted to a shabby refuge in Orvieto, where he remained, still hoping that France would come to redress the balance. In the following year, Francis came indeed, launching an army against Naples. When he was defeated once again and again required to renounce all claims in Italy, the Pope was forced to come to terms with Charles V, now the undisputed master of Italy. In cold and penury, sleeping on straw, he journeyed to Bologna to reach the best agreement he could, with little room now for maneuver. He was obliged to invest Charles, as King of Spain, with the Kingdom of Naples and crown him as Emperor. Charles in return was to provide the military aid to restore the Medici to Florence. In one thing the Pope had his way: as Pope he still retained authority to refuse the General Council for reform that Charles wanted. His underlying objection was personal: a fear that his illegitimate birth, rather casually overcome by Leo, might be invoked to invalidate his title.

Clement's major activity thereafter was a war to restore his family's rule of Florence. Under Imperial command, the dregs of the troops that had sacked Rome were among those used to besiege his native city, which, after holding out for ten months, was forced to yield. He spent on this enterprise as much as Leo on Urbino and for similar purposes of family power. The problems of Medici succession, now resting on two dubious Medici bastards, one a mulatto, distracted him from the problem of the Protestant advance or any serious consideration of how the Church should meet it. In his last years the German states reached a formal divorce from the Papacy and formed the Protestant League.

Clement died despised by the Curia (according to Guicciardini), distrusted by monarchs, detested by Florentines, who celebrated his death with bonfires, and by Romans, who held him responsible for the Sack. They dragged his corpse from its grave and left it hacked and mutilated, with a sword thrust through the heart.

Terrible in its physical impact, the Sack had seemed unmistakable as a punishment. The significance of the Protestant secession took longer to register on the Church. Time and perspective are needed before people can see where they have been. Recognition by the Papacy of its misgovernment developed slowly. Midway in the pontificate of Clement's successor, Paul III (the former Cardinal Alessandro Farnese), not quite thirty years after Luther's overt break, with the summoning of the Council of Trent in 1544, the long laborious recovery "of what had been lost" began.

What principles of folly emerge from the record of the Renaissance six? First, it must be recognized that their attitudes to power and their resultant behavior were shaped to an unusual degree by the mores and conditions of their time and surroundings. This is of course true of every person in every time, but more so in this case because the mores and conditions of the Italian governing class of this period were in fact so exotic. The local determinants of papal conduct—in foreign relations, political struggles, beliefs, manners and human relationships—must be sifted out in the hope that abiding principles may appear.

The folly of the popes was not pursuit of counter-productive policy so much as rejection of any steady or coherent policy either political or religious that would have improved their situation or arrested the rising discontent. Disregard of the movements and sentiments developing around them was a primary folly. They were deaf to disaffection, blind to the alternative ideas it gave rise to, blandly impervious to challenge, unconcerned by the dismay at their misconduct and the rising wrath at their misgovernment, fixed in refusal to change, almost stupidly stubborn in maintaining a corrupt existing system. They could not change it because they were part of it, grew out of it, depended on it.

Their grotesque extravagance and fixation on personal gain was a second and equal governing factor. Once, when reproved for putting the temporal power of the Papacy before "the welfare of the True Church which consists of the peace of Christendom," Clement VII had replied that if he had so acted he would have been plundered to his last farthing, "unable to recover anything of my own." This may stand as the excuse of all six. None had the wit to see that the head of the Church had a greater task than the pursuit of his "own." When private interest is placed before public interests, and private ambition, greed and the bewitchment of exercising power determine policy, the public interest necessarily loses, never more conspicuously than under the continuing madness from Sixtus to Clement. The succession from Pope to Pope multiplied the harm. Each of the six handed on his conception of the Papacy unchanged. To each—with some larger view in the case of Julius—the vehicle of Church government, Saint Peter's See, was the supreme pork barrel. Through sixty years this conception suffered no penetration by doubt, no enlightenment. The values of the time brought it to extremes, but personal self-interest belongs to every time and becomes folly when it dominates government.

Illusion of permanence, of the inviolability of their power and status, was a third folly. The incumbents assumed that the Papacy was forever; that challenges could always be suppressed as they had been for centuries by Inquisition, excommunication and the stake; that the only real danger was the threat of superior authority in the form of a Council, which needed only to be fended off or controlled to leave them secure. No understanding of the protest, no recognition of their own unpopularity or vulnerability, disturbed the six minds. Their view of the interests of the institution they were appointed to govern was so short-sighted as to amount almost to perversity. They possessed no sense of spiritual mission, provided no meaningful religious guidance, performed no moral service for the Christian world.

Their three outstanding attitudes—obliviousness to the growing disaffection of constituents, primacy of self-aggrandizement, illusion of invulnerable status—are persistent aspects of folly. While in the case of the Renaissance popes, these were bred in and exaggerated by the surrounding culture, all are independent of time and recurrent in governorship.

Chapter Four

THE BRITISH LOSE
AMERICA

1. Who's In, Who's Out: 1763-65

Britain's self-interest as regards her empire on the American continent in the 18th century was clearly to maintain her sovereignty, and for every reason of trade, peace and profit to maintain it with the goodwill and by the voluntary desire of the colonies. Yet, through the fifteen years of deteriorating relations that led up to the shot heard round the world, successive British ministries, in the face of constant warnings by men and events, repeatedly took measures that injured the relationship. However justifiable in principle, these measures, insofar as they progressively destroyed goodwill and the voluntary connection, were demonstrably unwise in practice, besides being impossible to implement except by force. Since force could only mean enmity, the cost of the effort, even if successful, was clearly greater than the possible gain. In the end Britain made rebels where there had been none.

The major issue, as we all know, was the right of Parliament as the supreme legislative body of the state—but not of the empire, according to the colonists—to tax the colonies. The mother country claimed the right and the colonists denied it. Whether this "right" did or did not constitutionally exist defies, even now, a definitive answer, and for purposes of this inquiry is essentially irrelevant. What was at stake was a vast territorial empire planted by a vigorous productive people of British blood. As a contemporary Laocoon, the unavoidable Edmund Burke, perceived and said, "The retention of America was worth far more to the mother country economically, politically and even morally than any sum which might be raised by taxation, or even than any principle so-called of the Constitution." In short, although possession was of greater value than principle, nevertheless the greater was thrown away for the less, the unworkable pursued at the sacrifice of the possible. This phenomenon is one of the commonest of governmental follies.

Trouble arose out of the British triumph in 1763 over the French and Indians in the Seven Years' War. With the cession by France of Canada and its hinterlands, Britain became possessed of the great trans-Allegheny plains in the valleys of the Ohio and Mississippi populated by unruly Indian tribes and some 8000 or 9000 French-Canadian Catholics. Not entirely expelled from the continent, the French still held Louisiana and the mouth of the Mississippi, from where it was possible they might stage a comeback. Administration and defense of the new area would mean increased expense for the British over and above interest payments on the national debt, which the costs of the war had almost doubled from £72 to £130 million. At the same time, supply bills (the budget) had risen tenfold from £14.5 to £145 million.

The immediate necessity of victory was to establish an armed force, projected at 10,000 men, in North America for defense against Indian troubles and French resurgence and, at the same time, to raise revenue from the colonies to pay for it—for their own defense, as the British saw it. The mere whisper of a standing army, which carried in the 18th-century mind the worst connotations of tyranny, aroused the politically sensitive among the colonials to instant antagonized alert. They suspected the British of suspecting them, now that they were freed of threat from the French, of harboring intent to throw off the British yoke, and they thus believed the mother country was planning "to fix upon us a large number of Troops under pretense of our Defence but rather designed as a rod and check over us"; to keep them, as another colonial wrote, "in proper subjection." While this thought was certainly not absent from some British minds, it does not seem to have been as primary or determining as the jumpy Americans believed. The attitude of the home government was not so much fear of colonial rebellion as a sense that colonial fractiousness and failure to give adequate support to defense must not be allowed to continue and that measures were needed to require the colonies to assume their share of the burden.

The prospect of taxation excited in the colonies even more pugnacity than the prospect of a standing army. Until now funds for local government in the several colonies had been voted and appropriated by their own assemblies. Except in the form of customs duties, which regulated trade for the benefit of Britain, America had not been subject to metropolitan taxation, and the fact that this had not been exercised gradually created the assumption that the "right" was lacking. Since they were not represented in Parliament, the colonials grounded their resistance on the principle of an Englishman's right not to be taxed except by his own representatives, but the underpinning was the universal reaction to any new tax: we won't pay. While acknowledging allegiance to the Crown, the colonies considered themselves independent of Parliament and their assemblies coequal with it. Rights and obligations of the relationship, however, were unformulated, and by dint of avoiding definition, the parties on either side of the ocean had managed to rumble along, though not always smoothly, without anyone being sure of the rules, but as soon as it was suggested, prospective taxation, like the standing army, was denounced in the colonies as a breach of their liberties, a creeping encroachment of tyranny. The ground for conflict was laid.

At this point, some notice of the limits, scope and hazards of this essay is required. What follows is not intended as yet another properly balanced account of developments precipitating the American Revolution, of which a superfluity already exists. My theme is narrower: a depiction of folly on the British side because it was on that side that policy contrary to self-interest was pursued. The Americans overreacted, blundered, quarreled, but were acting, if not always admirably, in their own interest and did not lose sight of it. If the folly we are concerned with is the contradiction of self-interest, we must in this case follow the British.

The first thing to be said about the British relation to America was that while the colonies were considered of vital importance to the prosperity and world status of Britain, very little thought or attention was paid to them. The American problem, even while it grew progressively more acute, was never, except during a brief turmoil over repeal of the Stamp Act, a primary concern of British politics until the actual outbreak of hostilities. The all-pervading, all-important problem that absorbed major attention was the game of faction, the obtaining of office, the manipulating of connections, the making and breaking of political alliances—in sum, the business, more urgent, more vital, more passionate than any other, of who's in, who's out. In the absence of fixed political parties, the forming of a government was more subject to personal maneuvering than at any time since. "The parliamentary cabals" which harassed the first twelve years of George III, wrote Lord Holland, nephew of Charles James Fox, "being mere struggles for favor and power, created more real blood and personal rancour between individuals than the great questions of policy and principle which arose on the American and French wars."

The second interest was trade. Trade was felt to be the bloodstream of British prosperity. To an island nation it represented the wealth of the world, the factor that made the difference between rich and poor nations. The economic philosophy of the time (later to be termed mercantilism) held that the colonial role in trade was to serve as the source of raw materials and the market for British manufacture, and never never to usurp the manufacturing function. This symbiosis was regarded as unalterable. Transportation both ways in British bottoms and re-export of colonial produce by way of Britain to foreign markets were aspects of the system, which was regulated by some thirty Navigation Acts and by the Board of Trade, the most organized and professional arm of the British government. Enjoined under the Navigation Acts from exporting so much as a horseshoe nail as a manufacture and from trading with the enemy during Britain's unending wars in the first half of the century, colonial merchants and ship captains resorted routinely to smuggling and privateering. Customs duties were evaded or ignored, producing barely £1800 a year for the British Treasury. A remedy for this situation offered hope of revenue to the depleted Treasury after the Peace of 1763.

Even before the end of the Seven Years' War, an effort to augment revenue from the colonies evoked a cry of outrage that supplied the slogan of future resistance. To enforce the collection of customs duties, Britain issued Writs of Assistance, or search warrants, permitting customs officers to enter homes, shops and warehouses to search for smuggled goods. The merchants of Boston, who, like all of the eastern seaboard, lived by trade that evaded customs, challenged the Writs in court with James Otis as their advocate. His plea in a "torrent of impetuous eloquence" enunciated the basic colonial principle that "taxation without representation is tyranny." The signal of trouble in America was plain from then on—to anyone who listened.

Otis did not invent it. Colonial governors—if not their principals at home, who did not suppose that provincials had or should have political opinions—knew well enough the strength of the American aversion to any taxes not imposed by themselves, and reported as far back as 1732 that "Parliament would find it no easy matter to put such an Act in Execution." The indications were clear enough to Sir Robert Walpole, the presiding statesman of that time, who, when taxing America was suggested to him, replied, "No! it is too hazardous a measure for me; I shall leave it to my successors." Proposed taxes grew more frequent during the Seven Years' War in reaction to the stinginess of the colonies in providing men and funds to support the war, but none was adopted because the home government at that time could not risk alienating the testy provincials.

Six months after Otis' plea, England took the first in what was to be her long train of counter-productive measures when the Attorney General in London ruled that the Writs of Assistance were legal to enforce the Navigation Acts. The resulting cost in alienation far outweighed the revenue collected from the ensuing duties and fines.

In the meantime the Peace Treaty of 1763 was divisive and fiercely opposed as too yielding by William Pitt, architect and national hero of Britain's victories in the war. Under the celebrated thunders of his scorn, the House of Commons shook and ministers blanched, but nevertheless voted for the Peace Treaty by a majority of five to one, chiefly out of desire to return to peacetime expenditures and a reduced land tax. That proved illusory. Instead, Lord Bute, George III's choice to replace Pitt, who had haughtily removed himself when overruled on the war issue, levied an excise tax in Britain on cider with calamitous effect. Like the Writs in America, the act empowered inspectors to visit premises, even live with owners of cider mills to keep count of the number of gallons produced. So loud was the English cry of tyranny at this invasion and so violent the protest that troops had to be called out in apple country, while at Westminster Pitt was inspired to his immortal statement of principle: "The poorest man in his cottage may bid defiance to all the force of the Crown. It may be frail; its roof may shake; the wind may blow through it; the storms may enter; the rain may enter—but the King of England cannot enter; all his forces dare not cross the threshold of the ruined tenement!" This was the voice that but for tragic flaws in the man might have prevented all the wrong turnings.

No one having calculated the expected return from the cider tax, it was not clear how much of the deficit it could make up before resentment would bring down the Government. The Chancellor of the Exchequer was a prominent rake, Sir Francis Dashwood, shortly to succeed as 15th Baron Le Despencer. A founder of the notorious Hellfire Club, which was given to exercises of debauchery in a reconstructed monastery, he was not a competent financier: his knowledge of accounts, said a contemporary, "was confined to the reckoning of tavern bills," and a sum of five figures was to him "an impenetrable secret." He seems to have discerned that the cider tax would not bring him glory. "People will point at me," he said, "and cry, 'There goes the worst Chancellor of the Exchequer that ever appeared!'"

Consciousness of their inadequacy for the work of government commonly afflicted the noble lords who filled the offices, not least when rank was their only qualification. The extra importance of high rank was accepted by all classes in the 18th-century world from yeoman to

King; the enlightenment of the age did not extend to egalitarianism. George III made it quite clear: "Lord North cannot seriously think that a private gentleman like Mr. Penton is to stand in the way of the eldest son of an Earl, undoubtedly if that idea holds good it is diametrically opposed to what I have known all my life."

As a qualification for office, however, rank did not necessarily confer self-confidence. Regard for rank and riches propelled the Marquess of Rockingham and the Duke of Grafton to the premiership and the Duke of Richmond to office as Secretary of State in the 1760s. Rockingham, even when First Minister (the title Premier, though describing the office in fact, was not used), had the greatest difficulty in speaking on his feet, and Grafton complained regularly of feeling unequal to his task. The Duke of Newcastle, who inherited estates in twelve counties and an income of £40,000 a year, who served several times as First Minister and controlled political patronage for forty years, was timorous, anxious, jealous and probably the only Duke on record who went about always expecting to be snubbed. Lord North, who headed the government throughout the crucial decade of the 1770s protesting most of the way, and George III himself bemoaned their responsibilities as being beyond their capacities.

The cider tax provided the final tumult in unseating the hated Earl of Bute, who was suspected of subverting the King by Tory advocacy of the royal "prerogative." He resigned in 1763, to be succeeded by Pitt's brother-in-law, George Grenville. Although the cider tax had clearly failed and was repealed within two years, the Government in its search for revenue was to attempt the same method of taxation in America.

George Grenville, when he assumed the first office at 51, was a serious man, industrious among dilettantes, inflexibly honest among the venal, narrow-minded, self-righteous and pedantic. An economist by temperament, he made it a rule to live on his income and save his salary. Though ambitious, he lacked the graces that oil the way for ambition. Horace Walpole, the ultimate insider, considered him the "ablest man of business in the House of Commons." Though not a peer or heir to a peerage, Grenville, through his background and family, was connected with the Whig ruling families who monopolized government office. His mother was a Temple, through whom his elder brother Richard inherited a title as Lord Temple; his maternal uncle Viscount Cobham was proprietor of Stowe, one of the most superb estates of the era. George followed the classic path through Eton and Christ Church, Oxford, studied law at the Inner Temple and was admitted to the Bar at 23, entered Parliament at 29 in 1741 for a family borough, which he represented until his death, pursued ministerial rank with the unusual intention of earning it by mastery of the business, served in most of the important offices under the aegis of Pitt, who had married his sister, while he himself had not neglected to marry a sister of the Earl of Egremont, a principal Secretary of State.

This was the pattern of the British minister. They came from some 200 families inclusive of 174 peerages in 1760, knew each other from school and university, were related through chains of cousins, in-laws, stepparents and siblings of second and third marriages, married each other's sisters, daughters and widows and consistently exchanged mistresses (a Mrs. Armstead served in that role to Lord George Germain, to his nephew the Duke of Dorset, to Lord Derby, to the Prince of Wales and to Charles James Fox, whom she eventually married), appointed each other to office and secured for each other places and pensions. Of some 27 persons who filled high office in the period 1760–80, twenty had attended either Eton or Westminster, went on either to Christ Church or Trinity College at Oxford or to Trinity or Kings at Cambridge, followed in most cases by the Grand Tour in Europe. Two of the 27 were dukes, two marquises, ten earls, one a Scottish and one an Irish peer; six were younger sons of peers and only five were commoners, among them Pitt, the outstanding statesman of the time, and three who through the avenue of the law became Lords Chancellor. As the only professional education open to peers' younger sons and gentlemen-commoners (the army and clergy could be entered without training) law was the path for the ambitious.

Peers and other landowners of comfortable estate enjoyed annual incomes of £15,000 or more from the rent-rolls, mines and resources of their properties. They managed great households, farms, stables, kennels, parks and gardens, entertained endless guests, employed armies of servants, grooms, gamekeepers, gardeners, field laborers, artisans. The Marquess of Rockingham, the wealthiest to hold high office in this period except for the dukes, received an income of about £20,000 a year from properties in Yorkshire, Northamptonshire and Ireland, lived in one of the largest homes of England, married an heiress, disposed of three parliamentary boroughs, 23 clerical livings and five chaplaincies, served locally as Lord-Lieutenant of the West Riding of Yorkshire and of the city of York.

Why did possessors of wealth, privilege and great estate enter government? Partly because they felt government was their province and responsibility. Noblesse oblige had roots in the feudal obligation that originally obliged nobles to serve in the King's council, and they had long governed as landlords and Justices of the Peace in their home counties. Governing went with territorial title; it was the employment of gentlemen, the duty of landed nobility. In the election of 1761, 23 eldest sons of peers entered the House of Commons at their first opportunity after reaching 21, all but two of them under the age of 26.

For another thing, high office offered the means of support for dependent relatives. Because estates were entailed by primogeniture on the eldest son, private wealth was rarely enough to support younger sons, nephews, poor cousins and deserving retainers. "Place" was necessary because these dependents had no other means of support. Except for law, there were no professions for which the gentry were trained. Through patronage and connections at court, a minister could take care of his own. Salaried sinecures of rather misty duties were limitlessly available. Sir Robert Walpole, dominant minister of the previous reign, distributed among his three sons, including Horace, the post of Auditor of the Exchange, Usher of the Exchange, and Clerk of the Pells, while two of the sons shared a Collectorship of Customs. George Selwyn, a fashionable libertine and connoisseur of public hangings, was appointed and served as Registrar to the Court of Chancery in Barbados without his ever gracing the island by his presence. One reason for the meager returns from American customs was that appointees to the Collectorships often remained comfortably at home in England, leaving their duties to poorly paid and easily bribed substitutes.

More than patronage, the lure of power and status has bewitched men of all times and conditions, in comfortable circumstances no less than in needy. The Earl of Shelburne, one of the more intelligent ministers of the time, stated it plainly: "The only pleasure I propose by employment is not the profit, but to act a part suitable to my rank and capacity, such as it is." The aristocracy of 18th-century England succumbed to the lure like other men; even the Duke of Newcastle's fear of office was surmounted, says Horace Walpole, by "his passion for the front rank of power." They entered young, were rarely prepared or trained for the tasks, could become restless or bored under difficulties and usually retreated for half the year to the charms of their country homes, their racing stables, hunting fields and adventures in landscaping. Individual temperaments and capabilities differed as much as in any group: some were conscientious, some casual about their duties, some liberal in thought, some reactionary, some spoiled by gambling and drink, some more thoughtful, able, better educated than others, but on the whole, their attitude toward government was less than professional.

Indeed the profession of government did not exist; the idea would have shocked those who practiced it. Social pleasures tended to come first; office was attended to in the time remaining. Cabinet meetings, unscheduled and haphazard affairs, were generally held at dinner in the First Minister's London residence. Sense of commitment was not always strong. Lord Shelburne, in whom it was strong, once commiserated with a colleague on how provoking it was to have Lord Camden and the Duke of Grafton "come down [to London] with their lounging opinions to outvote you in the Cabinet."

When gambling was the craze of the fashionable world, when ladies filled their homes with card parties which they advertised in the papers and men sat up until dawn at Brooks' betting huge sums on the turn of a card or in meaningless wagers about tomorrow's rain or next week's opera singer, when fortunes were easily lost and debt was a normal condition, how did such men, as ministers, adapt themselves to the unforgiving figures of supply bills and tax rates and national debt?

Noble circumstances did not nurture realism in government. At home, a word or a nod to servitors accomplished any desired end. At the fiat of Capability Brown or another landscape designer, rolling contours were fashioned from level land; lakes, vistas, groves of trees created; sweeps of curving lawn laid from lake to house. When the village of Stowe interfered with the designer's planned view, all the inhabitants were moved to new houses two miles away and the old village razed, plowed over and planted with trees. Lord George Germain, the minister responsible for conducting the military operations of the American Revolution, was born a Sackville and brought up at Knole, a family domain so extensive, with its seven courtyards and multiple roofs of different heights, that it looked from a distance like a town. In his boyhood his father planted in one grand sweep the seedlings of 200 pear trees, 300 crabapple, 200 cherry, 500 holly, 700 hazel, another 1000 holly to screen the kitchen garden and 2000 beeches for the park.

Tastes were not in all cases confined to the outdoors and the clubs. Education at school and university was supposed to have provided a respectable acquaintance with the Latin classics and some Greek, and the continental Grand Tour some acquaintance with the arts, embellished by the purchase of paintings and casts of classical sculpture to bring home. The Tour usually included Rome, which seems not to have greatly changed since the times of the Renaissance popes. Its government was "the worst possible," wrote an English visitor. "Of the population a quarter are priests, a quarter are statues, a quarter are people who do nothing."

Counsel from outside their narrow class was available to British rulers, if they wished, through the employment of outstanding intellectuals in advisory capacities. Rockingham, when thrust into the chief office following Grenville, and perhaps conscious of his shortcomings, had the wit to select the brilliant young Irish lawyer Edmund Burke as his private secretary. Lord Shelburne employed the scientist Joseph Priestley as his librarian and literary companion with a house for himself and an annuity for life. General Henry Seymour Conway, Secretary of State and a future Commander-in-Chief, appointed the political philosopher David Hume as his departmental under-secretary and, on Hume's plea, secured a pension of £100 a year for Jean Jacques Rousseau, then in England. Conway himself, as an occasional author, wrote a comedy adapted from the French and produced at Drury Lane. The Earl of Dartmouth, Secretary of State in the ministry of his stepbrother Lord North, was principal benefactor of Eleazar Wheelock's school for Indians, which became Dartmouth College. He sat for eighteen portraits, including one by Romney, and was a devoted patron of the poet William Cowper, whom he provided with a sinecure and a quiet home to shelter him in his bouts of insanity.

For all their cultivated tastes, the upper crust of the governing class produced during this period few of outstanding mind. Dr. Johnson declared he knew "but two men who had risen considerably above the common standard": William Pitt and Edmund Burke, neither wholly of the upper crust. Pitt suggested a factor, doubtless subjective, in his remark that he hardly knew a boy "who was not cowed for life at Eton." He kept his own children at home to be educated privately. The general state of mind was better understood by William Murray, the Scottish lawyer and, as Earl of Mansfield, future Chief Justice and Lord Chancellor. He had tried without much success to direct a course of study in history, oratory and the classics for his nephew, the future Marquis of Rockingham, and wrote to him when he turned 21, "You could not entertain me with a more uncommon sight than a man of your age, surrounded by all the baits and instruments of folly, daring to be wise; in a season of dissatisfaction, daring to think." That was the condition of the period 1760–80; daring to be wise, daring to think was not its forte. But then, how often has it ever been of any period?

The young monarch presiding over this establishment was not widely admired in these years. On George III's accession to the throne in 1760 at the age of 21, Horace Walpole found him tall, florid, dignified and "amiable," but the amiability was painfully assumed. Fatherless since the age of twelve, George had been brought up in an atmosphere of the harshest rancor between his grandfather George II and his father, Frederick, Prince of Wales. While common among royalty, the paternal-filial hatred in this case was extreme, leaving young George inimical to all who had served his grandfather and persuaded that the world whose rule he inherited was deeply wicked and its moral improvement his duty. In the narrow family circle at Leicester House, he was poorly educated with no contacts with the outside world and grew up obstinate, limited, troubled and unsure of himself. He liked to retire to his study, reported his tutor, Lord Waldegrave, "to indulge the melancholy enjoyment of his own ill humor." He would seldom do wrong, "except when he mistakes wrong for right" and, when this happens, "it will be difficult to undeceive him because he is uncommonly indolent and has strong prejudices."

Strong prejudices in an ill-formed mind are hazardous to government, and when combined with a position of power even more so. In a boyhood essay on King Alfred, George wrote that when Alfred came to the throne, "there was scarce a man in office that was not totally unfit for it and generally extremely corrupt in the execution of it." Removing the incorrigibles, "reclaiming" the others, Alfred had "raised the glory and happiness of his country" with the help of the Almighty Power that "wrecks the cunning of proud, ambitious and deceitful men." Such was George's view of his ministers and such his own program. He must clean out the system, restore righteous rule—his own— and carry out his mother's injunction, "George, be a *King*." His efforts from the first day of his reign to unseat the Whig grandees who complacently ruled through a pervasive distribution of patronage, by acquiring control of the patronage in his own hands, not unnaturally convinced many of his intention to restore the royal absolutism defeated at such cost in the previous century.

In need of a father substitute, George had fixed on the Earl of Bute with a neurotic adoration that was bound to—and did—end in disillusion. Thereafter, until he found the comfortable Lord North, he either disliked or despised every First Minister, or swung over into dependence, and since he had power to appoint and dismiss within certain limits, his swings kept government unstable. Because Pitt had left the Prince of Wales' circle to serve under George II, George called him "the blackest of hearts" and a "true snake in the grass," and vowed to make other ministers "smart for their ingratitude." Often confessing to Bute the torture of his self-distrust and irresolution, he was convinced at the same time of his own righteousness, which had as its basic assumption that because he wished nothing but good, everyone who did not agree with him was a scoundrel. This was not a sovereign likely to understand or try to understand insubordinate colonials.

A weakness of England's government was lack of cohesion or of a concept of collective responsibility. Ministers were appointed by the Crown as individuals and pursued their own ideas of policy often without consulting their colleagues. Because government derived from the Crown, aspirants to office had to find favor and work in partnership with the King, which proved a more ticklish job under George III than it had been under the thick-witted, foreign-born first Hanoverians. The sovereign was, within limits, chief of the executive with the right to choose his own ministers although not on the basis of royal favor alone. The First Minister and his associates had to have the support of the electorate in the sense that, even without a political party, they had to muster a majority of Parliament and rely on it to enact and approve their policies. Even when this was achieved, George III's erratic and emotional exercise of his right of choice made for extreme uncertainty of governments in his first decade, the brewing years of the American conflict, besides fostering personal rancor in the struggle of factions for favor and power.

The Cabinet was a fluid body constantly being reshuffled and not charged with a specific policy. Its chief was called simply First Minister; resistance to the title of Premier, which Grenville called "odious," was a legacy from the twenty-year tenure of Sir Robert Walpole and the fear of renewed aggregation of power in one man. The function, insofar as it had to be exercised, inhered in the First Lord of the Treasury. The working Cabinet numbered five or six including, besides the First Lord, two Secretaries of State, for home and foreign affairs—oddly designated the Northern and Southern departments—the Lord Chancellor for law and the Lord President of the Council, meaning the Privy Council, a large floating group of ministers, former ministers and important officials of the realm. The First Lord of the Admiralty, representing the major service, was sometimes though not always a member of the inner Cabinet. The Army had a Secretary at War without a seat in the Cabinet and a Paymaster-General, who, through control of pay and supplies, held the most lucrative post in the government, but it had no representative in policy councils. Until 1768, no department was specifically charged with administration of the colonies or execution of measures pertaining to them. Pragmatically, colonial affairs became the business of the Board of Trade and Plantations; equally pragmatically, the Navy, which maintained contact across the ocean, served as policy's instrument.

Junior Lords, Under-Secretaries, Commissioners of boards and customs, performed the daily business of government, suggested and drafted the bills for Parliament. These members of the civil service, as far down as clerks, were appointed through patronage and "connexions," as were the colonial governors and their staffs and the Admiralty officials in the colonies. "Connexion" was the cement of the governing class and the operative word of the time, often to the detriment of the function. This did not go unrecognized. Asked by the Duke of Newcastle to appoint to his staff an unqualified M.P. for the sake of assuring his vote, Admiral George Anson, who became First Lord after his celebrated voyage around the world, bluntly stated the disservice to the Navy: "I must now beg your Grace will seriously consider what must be the condition of your Fleet if these burrough recommendations which must be frequent are to be complied with"; the custom "has done more mischief to the publick than the loss of a vote in the House of Commons."

Beyond ministers, beyond the Crown, Parliament held supremacy, bitterly won in the last century at the cost of revolution, civil war, regicide, restoration and a second royal ouster. In the calm that at last settled under the rule of the imported Hanoverians, the House of Commons was no longer the fiery tribunal of a great constitutional struggle. It had settled into a more or less satisfied, more or less static body of members who owed their seats to "connexions" and family-controlled "rotten" boroughs and bought elections, and gave their votes in return for government patronage in the form of positions, favors and direct money payments. In 1770, it has been calculated, 190 members of the House of Commons held remunerative positions in the gift of the Government. Though regularly denounced as corruption, the system was so ubiquitous and routine that it carried no aura of disgrace.

Members were associated in no organized political parties, and they were attached to no identifiable political principles. Their identity came from social or economic or even geographical groups: the country gentlemen, the business and mercantile classes of the cities, the 45 members from Scotland, a parcel of West Indian planters who lived on their island revenues in English homes—a total of 558 in the Commons. In theory, members were of two kinds: knights of the shire or county, of whom two were elected at large for each county, and burgesses representing the boroughs, that is, any town empowered by its charter to be represented in Parliament. Since the knights of the shire were qualified by holding land worth £600 a year, they belonged to the substantial gentry or were sons of peers. Combining with them in interest were the members from the smaller boroughs, who had so few voters that they could be bought or were so tiny that the local landlord held them in his pocket. They generally chose members belonging to the gentry who could further their interests at Westminster. Hence the landed gentry or country party were by far the largest group in the House of Commons and claimed to represent popular opinion, although in fact they were elected by only some 160,000 voters.

The larger urban boroughs had virtually democratic suffrage and held contested, often rowdy, elections. Their members were lawyers, merchants, contractors, shipowners, Army and Navy officers, government officials and nabobs of the India trade. Though influential in themselves, they represented an even smaller electorate, hardly more than 85,000, because the country party managed to keep the urban population largely disenfranchised.

About half the seats, it was estimated, could be bought and sold through patronage vividly portrayed in Lord North's instructions to the Treasury Secretary at the time of the general election of 1774. He was to inform Lord Falmouth, who controlled six seats in Cornwall, that North agreed to terms of £2500 for each of three seats to fill by his own nomination; further that "Mr. Legge can only afford £400. If he comes in for Lostwithiel he will cost the public some 2000 guineas. Gascoign should have the refusal of Tregony if he will pay £1000"; further, "Let Cooper know whether you promised £2500 or £3000 for each of Lord Edgcumbe's [five] seats. I was going to pay him £12,500 but he demanded £15,000."

Political patrons controlled sometimes as many as seven or eight seats, often in family groups depending from a peer in the Lords, whose members acted together under direction from the patron, although when an issue took fire, dividing opinion, individuals sometimes voted their own convictions. The knights of the counties whose electorates were too large to be dominated by any patron, and thirty or forty independent boroughs not controlled by estates, considered themselves the country party. Here the Tory idea still existed, a residue of the Crown party of the 17th century, exiled from the central government, grown crusty. Long accustomed to local government, the counties resented interference from London and despised court and capital on principle, although this was not incompatible with supporting Whig ministries. Attached to no faction, following no leaders, soliciting no titles or "place," serving their constituency, the county members voted according to that interest and their own beliefs. A Yorkshire M.P. wrote in a letter that he had "sat twelve hours in the House of Commons without moving, with which I was well satisfied, as it gave me some power, from the various arguments on both sides, of determining clearly by my vote my opinion." Men thinking for themselves will defeat the slush funds—if there are enough of them.

George Grenville's primary concern when he took office was Britain's financial solvency. With the Peace of Paris in hand, he was able to reduce the Army from 120,000 to 30,000 men; his economies at the expense of the Navy, involving a drastic cutting back of dockyard facilities and maintenance, was to have crippling consequences when the test of action came. At the same time, he prepared legislation for taxing American trade, in no ignorance of the sentiments likely to be aroused. Agents or lobbyists retained by the colonies to represent their interests in London, given their lack of representation in Parliament, were often M.P.s themselves or other persons with access to government. Richard Jackson, a prominent M.P., merchant and barrister, and agent at different times of Connecticut and Pennsylvania, Massachusetts and New York, was Grenville's private secretary. "I have access to almost every place any friends of the Colonys wd wish to have access to," he wrote to Franklin, "but I am not sensible of my making any impression proportional to my Endeavors." He and his colleagues did what they could, against a cloud of indifference, to make colonial opinion known in the capital.

In addition to Jackson as a channel, Grenville was in correspondence with the colonial governors and the Surveyor General of Customs in the northern colonies, whose advice he asked before drafting a bill for enforcement of the customs. It was no secret that Americans would regard enforced collection, so long allowed to lapse, as a form of taxation they were prepared to resist. Grenville's preliminary order of November 1763 instructing customs officers to collect existing duties to the full was reported by Governor Francis Bernard of Massachusetts to have caused "greater alarm" in America than had the French capture of Fort William Henry six years earlier. For the record, the Board of Trade was asked to advise by what method "least Burthensome and most Palatable to the Colonies" they would contribute to the costs of "Civil and Military Establishments." Since there was no way that burden could be made palatable, and Grenville had already made up his mind, a reply was perhaps not seriously expected.

If prospects of trouble did not greatly disturb the ministry, it was because, as Grenville said reasonably enough, "All men wish not to be taxed," and because he was determined in any event that America could and should contribute to the costs of its own government and defense. His two Secretaries of State, the Earl of Halifax and the Earl of Egremont, were not men to dissuade him. Lord Halifax had inherited his peerage at 23 and enriched it by the acquisition of a wife who brought him, from a father in textiles, a huge fortune of £110,000. With these qualifications, he served as Groom of the Bedchamber and Master of Buckhounds and in other ornamental court posts until the political roundabout dropped him in the Presidency of the Board of Trade, where his tenure at the time of the founding of Nova Scotia caused its capital to be named for him. Considered weak but amiable, he was a hard drinker and a victim of early senility, of which he was to die at 55 while serving in the first Cabinet of his nephew Lord North.

The heavy drinking of the age was often a diminisher of life, or ability. Even the universally admired Marquess of Granby, Commander-in-Chief of armed forces in England in 1766–70, a noble soldier of noble character, did not escape: according to Horace Walpole, "his constant excesses in wine hurried him out of the world at 49." In the general election of 1774, Charles James Fox, no mean consumer himself, complained of the entertaining he had to do while canvassing. Eight guests came on one afternoon, stayed from three to ten, and drank "ten bottles of wine and sixteen bowls of punch, each of which would hold four bottles"—the equivalent of nine bottles per man.

Grenville's other Secretary of State, the Earl of Egremont, his brother-in-law, was incompetent and arrogant in equal parts, taking after a ducal grandfather known as "the proud Duke of Somerset." He was a composite, reports the always uncharitable Horace, "of pride, ill-nature and strict good breeding . . . [with] neither the knowledge of business nor the smallest share of parliamentary abilities," and reputedly untrustworthy besides. He looked down on Americans but disappeared from their affairs when a stroke of apoplexy brought on by overeating (according to Walpole) carried him off while the Revenue Bill was still being drafted.

His successor, the Earl of Sandwich, a former and later First Lord of the Admiralty, was a change only in temperament. Hearty, good-humored and corrupt, he used his control of appointments and provisions for the Navy for private profit. Although not a dilettante but a hard-working enthusiast of the fleet, his inveterate jobbery left dockyards a scandal, provisioners defrauded and ships unseaworthy. The condition of the Navy, when revealed by the war with America, was to earn him a vote of censure by both Houses. Socially he was a crony of Dashwood's Hellfire circle and so addicted to gambling that, sparing no time for meals, he would slap a slice of meat between two slices of bread to eat while gaming, thus bequeathing his name to the indispensable edible artifact of the Western world.

While under the aegis of these ministers the Revenue Bill was being prepared, a measure fertile in discord was taken without act of Parliament. The Boundaries Proclamation of 1763 prohibited white settlement west of the Alleghenies, reserving these lands to the Indians. Prompted by the ferocious Indian uprising called Pontiac's Rebellion, which swept up the tribes from the Great Lakes to Pennsylvania and threatened at one stage to drive the British from the area, the Proclamation was intended to appease the Indians by keeping the colonists from invading their hunting grounds and provoking them to renewed war. Another Indian rising could be a stalking horse for the French besides requiring new expenditure to combat it that Britain could ill afford. Behind the stated motive was a desire to restrict the colonists to the Atlantic seaboard, where they would continue to import British goods, and to prevent debtors and adventurers from crossing the mountains and planting a settlement free of British sovereignty in the heart of America. Here, out of contact with the seaports, they would manufacture their own necessities, in the dire prediction of the Board of Trade, "to the infinite prejudice of Britain."

The Proclamation was hardly welcome to colonists who were already forming stock companies to promote migration for profit or, like George Washington and Benjamin Franklin, obtaining grants of land across the mountains for speculation. To the restless homesteader it was infuriating interference. A century and a half of winning the wilderness had not made Americans amenable to the idea that a faraway government of lords in silk knee-breeches had the right to prevent their taking possession of land they could conquer with axe and rifle. They saw in the Proclamation not protection of the Indians—whom their own volunteer forces had done more than the redcoats to combat in Pontiac's Rebellion—but corrupt plans of Whitehall to grant great tracts of Crown lands to court favorites.

Getting acquainted is supposed to generate mutual understanding, and joining in the same fight to weld fellow-feeling, yet the reverse was the effect of contact between regulars and provincial forces in the Seven Years' War. At the end of operations they liked, respected and understood each other less than before. Colonials naturally resented the British Army's snobbery, the officers who disdained to accord equal rank to colonial officers, the rituals of spit and polish (British troops used 6500 tons of flour a year for whitening wigs and breeches), the extension of supreme command over provincial forces and superior airs in general. That could be expected.

On the other hand, British contempt for the colonial soldier, who was eventually (with French help) to take the British sword in surrender, was the oddest, deepest, most disserviceable misjudgment of the years leading to the conflict. How could General Wolfe, the hero who at 32 captured Quebec and died on the battlefield, call the rangers who fought with him "the worst soldiers in the universe"? He added in another letter, "The Americans are in general the dirtiest most contemptible cowardly dogs you can conceive . . . rather an encumbrance than any real strength to an army." Dirty the woodsmen-rangers certainly were in comparison with the white-wigged redcoats. Brilliant exterior had become so much the criterion of a European army that it determined judgment. Sir Jeffery Amherst had a "very poor opinion" of the rangers and Wolfe's successor, General James Murray, declared the Americans "very unfit for and very impatient of war." Others who saw service in the woods and camps of America alongside the rangers called them rabble, unsoldierly, cowardly. Such judgments swelled at home into fatuous boasts like that of General Thomas Clarke, aide-de-camp to the King, who said in the presence of Benjamin Franklin that "with a thousand Grenadiers he would undertake to go from one end of America to the other and geld all the males partly by force and partly by a little coaxing."

A possible cause for the fatal misjudgment has been found in the different nature of military service experienced on the one hand by British professionals and on the other by provincials, who were recruited by their local assemblies under contract for a specific mission, a limited time and prescribed conditions of pay and supply. When these failed, as in all wars they must, colonial troops balked, refused duty, and if the grievances were not met, simply marched off for home, not in solitary hidden desertions but openly in a body as a natural response to breach of contract. This was behavior quite incomprehensible to Hussars, Light Dragoons and Grenadier Guards steeped in regimental pride and tradition. British commanders tried to apply the Rules and Articles of War; the colonials, doggedly civilian soldiers and determined that nothing should transform them into regulars, stubbornly rejected them, to the point of group desertion if necessary. Hence their reputation as rabble.

Ill feeling found another source in the effort of the Anglican Church to establish an episcopate in New England. With religion's peculiar capacity to stimulate enmity, the episcopal prospect aroused the fiercest suspicions in Americans. A bishop to them was a bridgehead of tyranny, an instrument for suppressing freedom of conscience (which no one practiced less than New Englanders), a hidden door to popery and a sure source of new taxes to support the hierarchy. In fact the British government, as distinct from the Church, had no intention whatever of sponsoring a separate American episcopate. Nevertheless, "No bishop!" continued to be a cry as potent as "No tax!" or later, "No tea!" Even masts for the British Navy were a source of friction through the White Pine Acts, which prohibited the felling of tall trees to preserve them for masting.

It is possible these multifarious quarrels might have been composed if an American Department to give steady attention and coherent management to the colonies had been created at the close of the Seven Years' War when the need for a uniform reorganized administration was recognized. The moment was exigent; a large new territory had to be incorporated; the diverse charters of the colonies had already proved troublesome. But the need was not met. Lord Bute's iniquities and the maneuvering of colleagues and rivals in his wake absorbed political activity. The fractious affairs of empire were left to the Board of Trade, which had three successive presidents in the year 1763 alone.

The Revenue Bill presented to Parliament in February 1764 contained provisions bound for trouble. It reduced the long-ignored duty on molasses, the fulcrum of New England commerce, but required that collection of a new duty of 3d. a gallon be enforced; it removed trials of suspected violators from common-law courts, with juries of fellow-citizens not inclined to convict, to a special non-jury Admiralty Court in Halifax, with judges not readily bribed by colonial merchants and where the accused would have to travel to defend his case. The Bill did not disguise but proclaimed that its purpose was "to raise a revenue in America for defraying the expenses of defending, protecting and securing the same." This was its red flag. Yet it was plain that while the Crown's right to regulate trade was more or less fitfully acknowledged by the Americans, they were bent on denying the right of taxation for revenue except by themselves. More compelling was their fear of a ruined trade, profitable while customs duties had long been hardly more than a fiction, but with no margin of profit left under an enforced duty of 3d. a gallon.

The colonies' agents in England had already made the point that a dwindling trade would be of no benefit to Britain and insisted that molasses could not tolerate a duty of more than a penny a gallon although merchants might "silently acquiesce" to 2d.* Locally, the assemblies of Massachusetts and New York were already growling about violation of their "natural rights" in the principle of taxation and urging Connecticut and Rhode Island to join in protesting a "Mortal Wound to the Peace of these Colonies." They resisted the principle as strongly as the actual threat to the pocket because they believed that acceptance of a precedent in parliamentary taxation would open the way to future taxes and other impositions. Colonial opinion, however, was at this stage meagerly reported, or regarded, in London.

The Board of Trade fixed the duty at 3d. and the Revenue Bill (generally known afterward as the Sugar Act) was enacted by Parliament in April 1764 with only one negative vote, by a member named John Huske, who had been born in Boston.

The Act carried a sting in its tail—as yet only in embryo—in the announcement of a projected Stamp Tax to follow. This was no horrendous device to torture Americans but one of numerous ad hoc levies used in England, in this case, a tax on letters, wills, contracts, bills of sale and other mailed or legal documents. Grenville inserted the advance notice because he was indeed aware of a lurking question about Parliament's right to tax unrepresented subjects, which he himself considered beyond question, and he hoped "in God's name" that it would not be made an issue in Parliament. A premise of England's government in an age tired of struggle was to maintain a wide base of acceptable policy that would awake no sleeping dogs, the eternal wish for "consensus." Grenville was less concerned about colonial reaction than about disturbance of a nicely reliable Parliament. He embodied notice of the Stamp Tax in the Revenue Bill, perhaps hoping that enactment would establish without fuss the principle of Parliament's right to impose a revenue tax, or he may have intended a hint to the colonies to tax themselves, though his subsequent actions do not bear this out. A more Machiavellian motive has been advanced in the suggestion that he knew the notice would incite such bellows of colonial protest as would unite Parliament in angry assertion of its sovereignty.

The cry was indeed loud and unrestrained, but by the time it was

---

* It has been suggested that the merchants' objections were muted because at that stage the leading colonial agent, Benjamin Franklin of Pennsylvania, kept in mind that his position as Deputy Postmaster General in America and his son's as Governor of New Jersey were held at the pleasure of the Crown.

heard, England's attention was absorbed in an issue that awoke every sleeping dog in the country—the Wilkes case. Not that John Wilkes diverted attention from America, because there was little as yet to divert. The measures of 1763–64 were not unreasonable, nor were they folly per se, except in failing to take into account the quality, the temperament and the vital local concerns of the people to whom they applied. But heeding local concerns is not in the nature of an imperial government. The colonists were not a primitive "fluttered folk and wild" but offspring of exceptionally strong-minded and enterprising dissidents of the British breed. Essentially, the problem was attitude. The British behaved—and what is more, thought—in imperial terms as governors to the governed. The colonials considered themselves equals, resented interference and sniffed tyranny in every breeze coming over the Atlantic.

Liberty was the most intense political sentiment of the time. Government was disliked; although the streets of London were beset by assault and robbery, resistance to a police force was strong, and when Lord Shelburne was to suggest, after the days of violence, flames and deaths during the Gordon riots of 1780, that the time had come for an organized police, he was regarded as advocating a thing only suitable to French absolutism. The idea of a census was considered an intolerable intrusion. Providing information to "place-men and tax-masters," it was denounced by a Member of Parliament in 1753 as "totally subversive of the last remains of English liberty." If any officer should demand information about his household and family he would refuse it and if the officer persisted he would have him thrown into the horsepond. It was sentiments such as these that animated the fervor with regard to taxation and Wilkes.

The Wilkes case, which blew up into a constitutional issue of alarming virulence, was important for America because it was to create allies in the cause of "liberty." Because parliamentary rights, represented by Wilkes, and American rights were both seen as issues of liberty, those who became opponents of the government in the Wilkes affair became ipso facto friends of the American cause. John Wilkes himself was an M.P. and a coarse but witty man-about-town of the type that gains notoriety by being abusive. In 1763 in his journal, *The North Briton,* he published a ferocious attack on the terms of the settlement with France of the Seven Years' War laced with insults to the King. He was arrested under a general warrant on a charge of seditious libel and imprisoned in the Tower. Chief Justice Pratt (the future Lord Camden) ordered his release on grounds of his parliamentary privilege. Expelled from the House of Commons by the government majority he fled to France, while in England he was tried in absentia for libel of the King and, irrelevantly, for obscenity for privately publishing a pornographic *Essay on Women,* which his erstwhile friend Lord Sandwich insisted on reading aloud word for word in the House of Lords.

These attentions secured Wilkes' conviction and sentence of outlawry and succeeded in raising a crisis when parliamentary opposition, now free of defending the man, rallied around a resolution declaring his arrest by general warrant illegal. When it was barely defeated by a government majority that sank to fourteen, the vote revealed the weakness of patronage when the House scented abuse of its rights. The King angrily ordered Grenville to dismiss all the renegade voters who held positions in the royal household or in the ministry, thus creating a nucleus of opposition that was to grow. George III was not the most astute politician.

2. "Asserting a Right You Know You Cannot Exert": 1765

The Stamp Tax, introduced by Grenville in 1765, will be remembered "as long as the globe lasts." So proclaimed Macaulay in one of his bugle calls to historical grandeur. It was the act, he wrote, destined to "produce a great revolution, the effects of which will long be felt by the whole human race," and he blamed Grenville for not foreseeing the consequences. That is hindsight; even the colonies' agents did not foresee them. But enough information was available to the English to forecast determined resistance by the Americans and prospects of serious trouble.

Reports were now being received and published in the *London Chronicle* and other journals of colonial resentment of the Sugar Act and indignation at the proposed Stamp Tax. Emphatic protests were delivered by Massachusetts, Rhode Island, New York, Connecticut, Pennsylvania, Virginia and South Carolina, each affirming the "right" to tax itself and denying Parliament's right. The fallacy inherent in the British Government's position was laid bare by the ill-fated Thomas Hutchinson, Lieutenant-Governor of Massachusetts, who was to suffer so much worse from his colony than he deserved. He pointed out in a treatise, of which he sent copies to the government in London, that revenue was a fallacious goal because England's natural profit from colonial trade, which would be endangered by ill-will, was greater than any prospective yield from the tax. A tragic figure, vilified by one side and ignored by the other, Hutchinson thus early identified England's folly. It was evident also to others. Benjamin Franklin noted in a memorandum to himself that while Americans at present loved British modes, customs and manufactures, "A disgust of these will ensue. Trade will suffer more than the tax profits." He added a thought that should have been a creed for the British government: "Everything one has a right to do is not best to be done." This in essence was to be the Burke thesis: that principle does not have to be demonstrated when the demonstration is inexpedient.

By the time the protests and petitions were received in London—the eastbound crossing took anywhere from four to six weeks, and it took longer the other way—Grenville was preparing the Stamp Act. Anxious to prevent it, four of the agents, Benjamin Franklin, Richard Jackson, Charles Garth, an M.P. agent for Maryland and South Carolina, and Jared Ingersoll, newly arrived from Connecticut, waited on him in a body. Discussion focused on the alternative of the colonies taxing themselves. Asked by Grenville if they could state how much each was prepared to raise, the agents, uninstructed on that point, could give no answer, and Grenville did not really want one. What he wanted was to establish Parliament's right to tax for now and thereafter. He avoided pressing the question and remained deliberately vague in responding to the agents' queries about the amounts needed.

Here at the very start was the feasible alternative. If revenue from the colonies to pay the cost of their defense was what Britain wanted—which was reasonable enough—she could and should have put it to the colonies to raise it themselves. They were prepared to respond. The Massachusetts Assembly petitioned Governor Francis Bernard in 1764 for a special session to enable the colony to tax itself rather than be taxed by Parliament, but the Governor, though he favored that procedure, refused because he thought it would be useless without specific requisitions from Grenville. Pennsylvania instructed its agent in London to signify its willingness to raise revenue if requested in a regular manner for a specific sum. "Most of the colonies," according to the agent Charles Garth, "had signified their inclinations to assist their Mother Country upon proper requisitions from hence."

The firmness of colonial objection was made equally explicit. When Thomas Whately, the Treasury Secretary and M.P. responsible for drafting the Stamp bill, asked the agents for likely American reactions, they told him the tax was neither "expedient" nor "prudent." Ingersoll of Connecticut said the New England colonies were "filled with the most dreadful apprehensions of such a step's taking place," and if it did, many gentlemen of property had said they would "remove themselves with their families and fortunes into some foreign Kingdom." Whately was unimpressed because, as he said indisputably, "some taxes are absolutely necessary." He was to hear more. Britain's own representative, the Royal Governor of Rhode Island, Stephen Hopkins, stated in a published pamphlet, *The Rights of the Colonies Examined*, the fixed opposition of His Majesty's American subjects to taxation except "by their own representatives as Your Majesty's other free subjects are." The Rhode Island Assembly sent his pamphlet to their agent in London along with a petition to the King confirming its sentiments. The New York Assembly likewise, in petitions to the King and to both Houses of Parliament, expressed its "most earnest Supplication" that apart from necessary regulation of trade, Parliament should "leave it to the legislative power of the Colony to impose all other Burthens upon its own people which the publick Exigencies require."

The evidence was ample that taxation by Parliament would meet adamant resistance in the colonies. It was ignored because the policymakers regarded Britain as sovereign and the colonials as subjects, because Americans were not taken too seriously, and because Grenville and his associates, having some doubts themselves as to the rights in the case, wanted to obtain the revenue in a way that would establish Parliament's eminent domain. It was a classic and ultimately self-defeating case of proceeding against all negative indications. Grenville made no formal "requisitions from hence" upon the colonies to tax themselves and by rejecting this alternative opened the path to the Revolution.

In Parliament, the colonial petitions were rejected unheard on the ground that they concerned a money bill for which petitions were disallowed. Jackson and Garth spoke in the House denying Parliament's right to tax "until or unless the Americans are allowed to send Members to Parliament." Rising to answer, the President of the Board of Trade, Charles Townshend, soon to be a critical figure in the conflict, provoked the first moment of excitement in the American drama. Shall the Americans, he asked, "children planted by our Arms, shall they grudge to contribute their mite to relieve us from the heavy weight of that burden we lie under?"

Unable to contain himself, Colonel Isaac Barré, a fierce one-eyed former soldier who had fought with Wolfe and Amherst in America, sprang to his feet. "They planted by your Care? No! Your Oppressions planted 'em in America. . . . They nourished up by *your* Indulgence? They grew up by your neglect of 'em. . . . They protected by *your* arms? They have nobly taken up arms in your defence. . . . And believe me, and remember that I this day told you so, that same spirit of freedom which actuated that people at first, will accompany them still. . . . They are a people jealous of their liberties and who will vindicate them if ever they should be violated—but the Subject is too delicate and I will say no more." These sentiments, recorded Ingersoll, were thrown out so spontaneously, "so forcibly and firmly, and the breaking off so beautifully abrupt, that the whole House sat awile as Amazed, intently looking and without answering a Word." It may have been the first moment when perhaps a few realized what loomed ahead.

Barré, who looked on the world with a "savage glare" from a face scarred by the bullet that took out his eye at Quebec, was to become one of the leading defenders of America and orators of the Opposition. Of Huguenot ancestry, born in Dublin and educated at Dublin's Trinity College (described by the father of Thomas Sheridan as "half bear garden and half brothel"), he had left the Army when his promotion was blocked by the King and was elected to Parliament through the influence of Lord Shelburne, Irish-born like himself. His staunch support of America, joined with that of another champion, of a sort, is commemorated in the town of Wilkes-Barre, Pennsylvania.

A more explicit warning was heard at the second reading, when General Conway warmly protested the exclusion of the colonial petitions and moved that they be heard. "From whom unless from themselves are we to learn the circumstances of the colonies," he asked, "and the fatal consequences that may attend the imposing of this tax?" His motion was of course rejected by the well-schooled majority. A professional soldier, he seems to have been the first to glimpse a possibility of "fatal consequences." He was a cousin and close friend of Horace Walpole, a handsome, likable, honorable man, who, having voted against the government in the Wilkes case, was one of those deprived by royal vindictiveness of a court post and also of command of his regiment, on which he depended for income. Nevertheless, he refused financial assistance from friends and joined with Barré, Richard Jackson and Lord Shelburne in the nucleus of those who were beginning to oppose the Government's American policy and who met in association under Shelburne's roof.

The Earl of Shelburne, 32 at this time, was the most able of Pitt's disciples and after him the most independent-minded among the ministers, perhaps because he escaped schooling at Westminster or Eton, although his early education in Ireland, he said, was "neglected to the greatest degree." Considered too clever and known as "the Jesuit," he was disliked and mistrusted by colleagues. Needed for his talent, he was never to be long out of office and, despite mistrust, was to reach the premiership in 1782 in time to negotiate the treaty confirming American independence. The dislike he inspired may have sprung from fear of his ideas, which tended to be cynical about men and progressive in policy. He voted against the expulsion of Wilkes, favored Catholic emancipation, free trade and even, in contrast to Burke, the French Revolution when it came.

While owner of enormous rent-rolls in Ireland and England, and one of the richest absentee proprietors of Irish land, he was the only minister, according to Jeremy Bentham, who did not fear the people, and the first, according to Disraeli, to comprehend the rising importance of the middle class. He conformed to noble style in having his country estate landscaped by Capability Brown, his town house designed by Robert Adam and his portrait painted by Joshua Reynolds, several times. He went beyond it in amassing a vast library of books, maps and manuscripts, whose sale at auction after his death lasted 31 days, and a collection of historical documents bought for the nation by a special grant of Parliament. Like Pitt and Burke, he had no trouble discerning the inexpediency of coercing America, and no hesitation in warning against it.

At its third reading, the Stamp Tax, the first direct tax ever levied on America, was enacted by 249 to 49, the usual five-to-one majority, by whom, says Horace Walpole, it was "little understood . . . and less attended to." The professionals understood it well enough. It was the "great measure" of the session, said Whately, because it established "the Right of Parliament to lay an internal tax upon the Colonies." A colleague, Edward Sedgewick, Under-Secretary of State, acknowledged that it had been done deliberately, in the face of strong resolutions by the American assemblies, "because it was thought to establish the Right by a new execution of it."

Americans reacted widely and strenuously. Because the Act not only required a stamp on all printed matter and legal and business documents, but extended to such things as ships' papers, tavern licenses and even dice and playing cards, it touched every activity in every class in every colony, not only New England, and coming on top of the Sugar Act confirmed the suspicion of a deliberate plan by the British first to undermine the economy and then to enslave the colonies. The Virginia House of Burgesses, meeting to denounce the Act, heard Patrick Henry skirt treason in the famous words reminding George III of the fate of Caesar and Charles I. When Boston learned of the Virginia resolves, "the universal voice of all the people," wrote Hutchinson, supported them in the conviction that "if the Stamp Act must take place, we are all slaves." Sons of Liberty were organized in the towns to foment resistance. In response to a general movement to force stamp agents to resign, mobs rampaged and pillaged and wrecked their homes and paraded with the agents' figures hanged in effigy. Heeding the warning, the agents in Boston and Newport resigned in August, and by November, when the Act took effect, not an agent remained in office to execute it.

Agitators and pamphleteers kept passions excited. Hardly a family from Canada to Florida had not heard of the Act though many had little idea what it threatened. A country gentleman whose servant was afraid to go out to the barn on a dark night asked him, "Afraid of what?" "Of the Stamp Act," the servant replied. In Connecticut, three out of four were ready to take up the sword, as reported by Ezra Stiles, preacher and future President of Yale. More astonishing and, to any Englishmen who took notice, ominous was the agreement of nine colonies at a Stamp Act Congress in October in New York. After a mere two and a half weeks of bickering, they united on a petition for repeal, and agreed also to abandon the troublesome distinction that figured so largely in the whole American dispute between acceptable "external" taxation in the form of duties on trade and unacceptable "internal" taxation on domestic processes.

Beyond all words and petitions, the effective protest was boycott, known as Non-Importation. Already set in motion in response to the Sugar Act, a program to cut off imports of English goods was now formally adopted by groups of merchants in Boston, New York and Philadelphia. The call swept through the colonies on winds of enthusiasm. Women brought their spinning wheels to the minister's parlor or to the courthouse to compete in the number of skeins they could turn out for homespun to replace English cloth. Flax was spun for shirts "fine enough for the best gentlemen in America." By the end of the year, imports were £305,000 less than the year before out of a total of some £2 million.

What of the alternative available to the British? It was, as many thought, to give the Americans the representation in Parliament they claimed and let taxation follow. At one stroke, this would have invalidated American resistance. While other dynamics of conflict were present, nothing raises tempers like money, and taxation was the Americans' most vibrant issue. They were ready enough to claim representation as a right but the fact was that they did not really want it in the flesh. The Stamp Act Congress agreed to declare it "impractical."

In all discussions of representation, much was made of the 3000-mile distance, where "seas roll and months pass" between order and execution. Yet distance did not prevent Americans from ordering English furnishings, clothes and books, adopting English fashions, sending children to English schools, corresponding steadily with colleagues in Europe, sending botanical specimens, absorbing ideas and generally maintaining a close cultural relationship. It was not so much the "vast and hazardous ocean" that was the deterrent as a growing realization in the colonies that what they really wanted was less interference and greater home rule. Although separation, much less independence, was not contemplated, many did not want a closer connection for they shuddered at the corruption of English society. John Adams believed that England had reached the same stage as the Roman Republic, "a venal city, ripe for destruction." Visiting Americans were shocked at the corrupt politics, the vice, the gap between the "Wealth, Magnificence and splendour" of the rich and the "extreme Misery and distresses of the Poor . . . amazing on the one hand and disgusting on the other."

They viewed the patronage system as hostile and dangerous to liberty, for when government rested on purchased support, true political liberty was a dead letter. Englishmen were the only people to have gained that liberty; pervading American polemic in these years was a sense of America's mission, as inheritor, to foster and preserve it for mankind. Colonial members in Parliament were believed likely to be corrupted by English decadence and in practice would be a helpless minority always outvoted. It was also clear that if the colonies gained representation, they would no longer have grounds for resisting Parliament's right to tax. Americans recognized this ahead of the English, who, indeed, never seriously considered the advantage to themselves of admitting American representation.

Attitude was again the obstacle; the English could not visualize Americans in terms of equality. Should uncouth provincials, the "spawn of our [prisoners'] transports," rabble-rousers "with manners no better than Mohawks," be invited, asked the *Gentleman's Magazine*, to occupy the "highest seats of our commonwealth?" To the *Morning Post*, Americans were "a mongrel breed of Irish, Scotch and Germans leavened with convicts and outcasts." Deeper than social disdain was fear of the colonials as "levellers" of class, whose representation in Parliament would encourage unrepresented English towns and districts to demand seats, destroying property rights in the boroughs and overturning the system.

The English had contrived a convenient theory of "virtual representation" to cover the masses who lacked votes or members to represent them. Every member of the House, it was maintained, represented the whole body politic, not a particular constituency, and if Manchester, Sheffield and Birmingham had no seats and London had only six while Devon and Cornwall had seventy, the former could take comfort in being "virtually represented" by the bluff gentlemen from the country. These gentlemen on the whole, bearing the main weight of the land tax, heartily favored taxing the colonies for their share of the burden and firmly believed in the assertion of parliamentary sovereignty.

An alternative to conflict that serious men gave thought to, and proposed, was colonial union followed by some form of federation with Britain, and with colonial representation in an imperial parliament. In 1754, a Plan of Union to meet the French and Indian threat had been proposed by Benjamin Franklin, with advice from Thomas Hutchinson, at the Albany Congress and found no takers. During the Stamp Act crisis the idea was revived by persons who held governing responsibility in the colonies and were worried by the growing alienation from the mother country. Franklin himself, Thomas Pownall, a former Governor of Massachusetts, now an M.P., Thomas Crowley, a Quaker merchant familiar with America, and Francis Bernard, the current Governor of Massachusetts, all proposed various plans for rationalization of the colonial government and definitive settlement through debate of reciprocal rights and obligations leading to federation. Pownall complained at a later crisis in 1775 that as no one in government paid any attention to his views, he would offer them no more. Francis Bernard, who formulated a detailed plan of 97 propositions which he sent to Lord Halifax and others, was told by Halifax that the plan was "the best thing of the kind by much that he had ever read," and that was the last he heard.

Benjamin Franklin urged his British correspondents to recognize the inevitability of American growth and development and to make no laws intended to cramp its trade and manufacture, for natural expansion would sweep them aside, but rather to work toward an Atlantic world peopled by Americans and English possessing equal rights in which the colonists would enrich the mother country and extend its "empire round the whole globe and awe the world!" It was a splendid vision which had enthralled him since the Albany Plan of Union. "I am still of the opinion," he wrote years later in his autobiography, "that the Plan of Union would have been happy for both Sides of the Water if it had been adopted. The Colonies so united would have been sufficiently strong to have defended themselves; there would have been no need of Troops from England; of course the subsequent Pretence for Taxing America, and the bloody Contest it occasioned would have been avoided." Franklin ends with a sigh: "But such Mistakes are not new; History is full of the Errors of States and Princes."

Repeal became an issue in England almost as soon as the Stamp Act became law. As Non-Importation emptied the ports, and shippers and handlers and factory workers lost employment and merchants lost money, Britain awoke to American sentiment. For the next six months the Stamp Act was a leading topic in the press. With the 18th century's passion for political principle, all the issues—the rights of Parliament, the iniquity of taxation without representation, "virual representation," external versus internal taxation—were debated in comments, columns and angry letters.

Great impact was made by a pamphlet published by Soame Jenyns, a Commissioner of the Board of Trade, who insisted that both the right to tax and the expediency of exerting it were "propositions so indisputably clear" that they needed no defense, were it not for arguments challenging them "with insolence equal to their absurdity." The phrase "liberty of an Englishman," snorted Mr. Jenyns, had lately been used "as a synonymous term for blasphemy, bawdry, treason, libels, strong beer and cyder," and the American argument that people cannot be taxed without their consent was "the reverse of truth, for no man I know is taxed by his own consent."

Lord Chesterfield, observing affairs, like Horace Walpole, from the sidelines, had a way of picking out the essence in contrast to the stilted etiquette he preached to his nephew. The "absurdity" of the Stamp Act, he wrote to Newcastle, equaled "the mischief of it by asserting a right you know you cannot exert." Even if effective, he wrote, the tax should bring in no more than £80,000 a year (the government calculated on no more than £60,000), which could not compensate for the loss to Britain in trade worth at least a million a year (it was worth two million). A harder truth came from General Thomas Gage, commander of British forces in the colonies, who reported in November that resistance was widespread throughout the colonies, and that "Unless the Act from its own nature enforces itself, nothing but a very considerable military force can do it." The gentlemen of England could not envisage this necessity vis-à-vis rabble.

By the time the crisis that Grenville's Stamp Act had engendered was at hand, he had lost office. The King, long irritated and bored by Grenville's habit of lecturing him on economic policy, became enraged when his mother's name was eliminated by Grenville's faction for devious political reasons from a Regency Bill drawn up in consequence of the King's illness early in 1765.* George dismissed him, unfortunately before locating someone sufficiently master of the conflicts stirred up by the Regency Bill to form a ministry in his place. At a loss, George turned to his uncle, the Duke of Cumberland, a person of un-

---

* Much has been written on whether this was or was not an early manifestation of the King's later insanity. Since no other attack occurred until the definite onset of his mental illness in 1788, more than twenty years later, the King may be taken as sane throughout the period of the American conflict.

Hanoverian ability and considerable prestige. The Duke offered the premiership to Pitt, who obstinately refused for reasons not easily discerned in this complex and opaque character. He may have been already determined on repeal and not sure whether he could command it and too stiff-necked to compromise or, given that he had been absent from affairs for the past year, the physical and sometimes mental disturbances that afflicted him from time to time may have been active.

Historians have suggested that, had Pitt taken office in 1765, the course of the next decade might have been different, but that is a supposition dependent on his continuing to function, which, as events soon proved, he could not. Pitt's intransigence and exaggerated demands for an autonomous hand unquestionably weakened the government during the conflict with America. With his immense popularity, reputation and influence, and his incomparable sway over the House of Commons, he was an epic figure who had won, and could not save, an empire.

Pitt owed his rise as a younger son of what Lord Chesterfield called "a very new family" to force of character and his own abilities. His grandfather, called "Diamond" Pitt, was a nabob of the East India Company, of brutal temperament and wild and tyrannical habits, who had made the family fortune in the Indian trade and held a share of command for a while as Governor of Madras. The diamond for which he was known was bought by the French Crown for more than two million livres. In England the family acquired the rotten borough of Old Sarum in Wiltshire, whose seat Pitt held from 1735. He took it over at 27 from his elder brother, who, having dissipated his fortune and alienated all friends in the process, retired abroad "in very bad circumstances" and intermittently mad, "though not confined but obliged to lead a very retired life." The streak of madness in the blood, whether or not stemming from the grandfather, appeared also in Pitt's sisters, one of whom was confined and two others more or less so.

Throughout his life Pitt suffered from incapacitating gout, which had afflicted him since schooldays at Eton. Rare in youth, gout at that age was evidence of a severe form. Its recurring pain caused the irritability common to gout-sufferers and required a gout-stool and huge boot to be built into the front of Pitt's carriage and sedan chair.

His political career gained notoriety by a much publicized refusal as Paymaster of the Forces to take commissions or hold back for personal investment the sums assigned for pay, both customary perquisites of office. As Secretary of State during the Seven Years' War, he was able to abide shared command with the Duke of Newcastle as premier because Newcastle stayed within his specialty, the handling of patronage, and left policy to Pitt.

Pitt was driven by conviction that England's destiny was maritime supremacy and that her resources could prevail in the rivalry with France by destruction of French trade and trading bases. With passionate application of funds and forces to this object, and infusion of his own assurance, which once expressed itself in the statement "I know I can save this country and that I alone can," he reconditioned and manned the fleet, recruited fellow-countrymen to replace foreign mercenaries, and turned feckless campaigning into a national war and tide of victory. Louisburg, on Cape Breton, Guadeloupe, Ticonderoga, Quebec, Minden in Europe, naval triumph in the Bay of Biscay—such a series of successes, wrote Horace Walpole, that "we are forced to ask every morning what victory there has been for fear of missing one." Captured French flags were hung from St. Paul's amid roars of the multitude. Supplies were voted without discussion. Pitt dominated his colleagues and, as the Great Commoner, was the idol of the public, who admired his absence of title and felt that in him they had a representative. This feeling carried as far as New England, where, according to Ezra Stiles, he was "idolized." Fort Duquesne, captured from the French in 1758, was renamed Fort Pitt and its wooden village Pittsburgh.

Only when he wanted to carry the war to Spain, the other maritime rival, his dominance failed against the resistance to increased taxes and against the new King's determination to turn out the Newcastle Whigs and take patronage into his own hands. When Pitt resigned in 1761, cheers followed his coach from the palace, ladies waved their handkerchiefs from windows, the populace "clung to the wheels, shook hands with the footmen and even kissed the horses."

Thereafter Pitt was too unbending, too arrogant, too vain to enter into bargaining for place. He did not fit into the system, having no interest in groups and cabals. His interest was in policy commanded by himself. On leaving office in 1761 he told the House that he would not govern when his advice was not taken. "Being responsible, I *will* direct and will be responsible for nothing I do not direct." A member thought this was "the most insolent declaration ever made by a Minister," but it was Pitt to the core. He was of the rare type incapable of acting in association with others. "Unattached to any party, I am and wish to be entirely single," he said, and more starkly on another occasion, "I cannot bear the least touch of command." Perhaps what spoke here was a touch of megalomania. Pitt may have suffered from what in our time would be called delusions of grandeur and manic depression, but these had no names in his time and were not recognized as mental illness.

Tall, pale, thin-faced, with a hawk nose and piercing eye, ankles swollen with the gout that caused him to hobble, he was grand, proud, imposing, appearing always in full dress and full peruke, in manner "sage and awful as a Cato." He was always acting, always enveloping himself in artificiality, perhaps to conceal the volcano within. His glance of scorn or indignation could wither an opponent, his invective and sarcasm were "terrible"; he had the same quality of *terribilità* as Julius II. His gift for oratory at a time when political success resided in it was literally spellbinding though few could explain why. His eloquence, vehement, fiery, original, bold, could win the support of the independents in Parliament. Theatrical, even bombastic in language, spoken with an actor's gestures and plays of tone, employing "very brilliant and striking phrases," his most successful speeches were composed on his feet, although of a particularly striking phrase he told Shelburne that he had "tried it on paper three times" before deciding to use it. At a whisper his voice could be heard to the remotest benches, and when swelling like a great organ to its fullest register, the volume filled the House and could be heard in the lobbies and down the stairs. All fell silent to listen when Pitt stood up to speak.

Failing Pitt, the Duke of Cumberland put together a mixed ministry whose three principal offices were filled by personal acquaintances from the turf and the Army, none of whom had held ministerial office before. The chief was the young grandee, the Marquess of Rockingham, one of the wealthiest nobles of England, with baronies in three counties, wide estates in Ireland and Yorkshire, the lord-lieutenancy of his home county, an Irish peerage and suitable titles as Knight of the Garter and Lord of the Bedchamber to add to his status. At 35, he was a "new Whig" of the younger generation, untried and uncertain how to proceed. The Secretaries of State were General Conway, who had been the Duke's aide-de-camp, and Augustus Henry Fitzroy, 3rd Duke of Grafton, a fellow-patron of the turf like Rockingham, known to Cumberland from the Jockey Club. A rather lax young man of thirty, Grafton had no great ambition to make a name in history and was more interested in racing than government, but he was ready from a sense of noblesse oblige to serve his country as well as he could. When rank won him unanimous election as Chancellor of Cambridge University in 1768, the poet Thomas Gray, author of "Elegy in a Country Churchyard," for whom Grafton had secured appointment as Regius Professor of History, wrote an ode that was set to music for the Duke's installation. In government Grafton was less happy, uneasy in his duties and given to frequent proposals to resign.

Leading the King's friends in the Cabinet as Lord Chancellor was the gouty, profane, boisterous Lord Northington, who though frequently the worse for drink had held all the various law posts over the last nine years and was willing to concede the effects of too much port, saying, "If I had known that these legs were one day to carry a Lord Chancellor, I would have taken more care of them when I was a lad." The Secretary at War, who accepted his post at the King's express wish, was Viscount Barrington, an amiable man with one brother an Admiral and another a Bishop. He made it a principle, he said, to refuse no office on the theory that "some fortune may at last make me pope." He remained at the War Office, still waiting, for the next thirteen years, one of the longest tenures of the period. The disunion permissible within a Cabinet is illustrated by his making it a condition of his accepting the post that he be permitted to vote against the ministry both on the Stamp Act and on General Warrants.

Divided and weak, the new ministry headed into the Stamp Act crisis, losing Cumberland by death after only four months, which left Rockingham unsheltered and without guidance. He tried to recruit Pitt without success and when he repeatedly asked what he should do about repeal, Pitt refused to communicate. Suffering from some debility, he was out of affairs throughout 1765.

Non-Importation was cutting into the economy, distressing merchants and labor. Alarming articles appeared in the press, inspired in many cases by an organized merchants' campaign for repeal, reporting factory closings and an army of unemployed preparing to march on London to obtain repeal by threat of violence to the House of Commons. London's merchants formed a committee to write to their fellows in thirty manufacturing and port towns urging them to petition Parliament for repeal. The Government was torn between "Stamp Men" and "No Stamp Men," with Rockingham, Grafton and Conway and the old Duke of Newcastle in favor of repeal, against the Stamp Men, who wanted a demonstration of sovereignty and argued that repeal would destroy Britain's authority and give the colonies impetus toward outright independence. Openly at odds with the Rockingham faction, Lord Northington announced he would attend no more Cabinet meetings, but rather than resigning, he remained to work through intrigue to bring the government down.

While not himself the possessor of forceful opinions, Rockingham acquired a policy by transfusion from his secretary, Edmund Burke.

He became persuaded that the violent American reaction indicated that an attempt to enforce the Act would be inexpedient, that England would be poorly advised to lose her colonial trade through ill-will, and that if harmony could be restored by repeal, so much the better. Through conciliation, Burke explained, the two Whig principles of liberty of the subject and sovereignty of Parliament could be reconciled.

With a majority determined to teach the colonies a lesson in sovereignty and eager for a reduction in their own land tax in consequence of revenue from America, the hope of moving Parliament to vote for repeal was slight. Grenville fulminated about the "outrageous Tumults and Insurrections" in North America, and Lord Northington declared that to "give up the law" by repeal would mean for Britain to "be conquered in America and become a Province to her own Colonies." Efforts to elicit an opinion from Pitt during the Christmas recess were unavailing and when Parliament reconvened on 14 January 1766, Rockingham, trying to maintain a government weakened by dissension, was uncertain what to do.

Pitt appeared. The benches hushed. He said to them that the subject before them was "of greater importance than ever engaged the attention of this House" since their own liberties were at stake in the revolution of the last century and that "the outcome will decide the judgment of posterity on the glory of this kingdom and the wisdom of government during the present reign." Taxation was "no part of the governing or legislative power"; it was a "voluntary gift" of representative assemblies. The idea of "virtual representation of America in this House is the most contemptible idea that ever entered into the head of man and it does not deserve a serious refutation." Referring to remarks by Grenville denouncing those in England who encouraged colonial resistance, he retorted, "I rejoice that America has resisted. Three millions of people so dead to all feelings of liberty as voluntarily to submit to be slaves would have been fit instruments to make slaves of the rest." A member cried out that the speaker should be sent to the Tower, evoking, according to a witness, "such shouts of applause as I never heard." Shaken but not diverted, Pitt went on to announce that the Stamp Act must be repealed "absolutely, totally, immediately" and at the same time accompanied by a statement of "sovereign authority over the colonies . . . in as strong terms as can be devised and be made to extend to every point of legislation whatsoever—that we may bind their trade, confine their manufactures, and exercise every power whatsoever except that of taking their money out of their pockets without their consent."

Here was a fine obfuscation. Was not binding their trade by customs duties another way of taking money out of their pockets without their consent? If Parliament had supreme legislative power, how could taxation not be "part of that sovereign power"? Grenville, in making these points, refused to accept the distinction between external and internal taxation. Pitt was a firm mercantilist and his reply was unequivocal: "Let it be forever ascertained; taxation is theirs, commercial regulation is ours." His distinction left others unconvinced. "If you understand the difference," wrote Lord George Germain to a friend, "it is more than I do, but I assure you it was very fine when I heard it."

It was enough for Rockingham; he had his signal. A declaration of parliamentary sovereignty, which it was hoped would satisfy the demand for assertiveness, was immediately drafted and introduced along with the bill for repeal. The King's sullen consent was secured by informing him that the choice was either repeal or armed enforcement requiring additional military forces for which it would be hard to find funds. The House resumed debate. In the Lords the Duke of Bedford, leader of the Grenville faction, insisted that the Stamp Act "if suffered to be removed puts a final period to the British Empire in America." Rockingham, however, had found allies. He encouraged the merchants' campaign in order to shift emphasis from controversial "rights" to economic consequences. Provincial mayors and leading citizens from 35 cities arrived each day to present petitions from their cities for repeal. Letters from American traders to English shippers canceling orders were presented. More than a hundred merchants gathered in London to exert by their presence in the Visitors Gallery a silent pressure. Twenty riders were kept waiting to gallop with news of the vote.

Forty witnesses, including colonial agents, merchants and visiting Americans were called to testify on Non-Importation. Among them, Benjamin Franklin at his famous examination in February 1766 firmly told the House that Americans would never pay the Stamp duties "unless compelled by force of arms," and armed forces would be useless because "they cannot compel a man to take stamps who chuses to do without them. They will not find a rebellion; they may indeed make one." That could stand as Britain's epitaph for the decade, for at the time Franklin spoke, "an overwhelming majority" of his countrymen, as an English historian has stated, "had never contemplated the idea of severing the connection with the mother country."

The dilemma was real. To leave the Act in place would be to assure, as the witnesses testified, lasting disaffection, even "total alienation" in the colonies, while to concede repeal would be to acknowledge loss of authority in America. Horace Walpole, in his memoirs written two years later, added another disturbing factor: enforcement which could "risk lighting up a rebellion" might be a cause of the colonies' "flinging themselves into the arms of France and Spain." On the other hand, repeal of a revenue bill was "setting a precedent of the most fatal complexion."

The Declaratory Act, stating that "The Parliament of Great Britain had, hath, and by right ought to have full power and authority to make laws and statutes of sufficient force and validity to bind the Colonies and people of America in all cases whatsoever," won unanimous approval in the Commons and the votes in the Lords of all but five, who included, interestingly enough, Lord Cornwallis. Another was Lord Camden, formerly Chief Justice Pratt, the only minister to speak against the Declaratory Act, who insisted that the very ground of the objection was that taxation without representation was illegal and that "there are some things you cannot do." The fact that the Act did not mention taxation, the whole point of the dispute, was questioned by the Attorney-General, Charles Yorke, who moved to insert "in cases of taxation" but was overruled by the assurance that "in all cases whatsoever" covered the necessity. That satisfied enough members to win a majority for repeal. But though convenient the Declaratory Act was rash because it locked Parliament into a statutory position that foreclosed compromise. It returned to haunt many who had voted for it when in the next decade the Rockingham party was trying to avert war. For the moment it accomplished its purpose. Repeal was enacted over 167 hold-outs. The Lords still resisted and gave their assent only when the King was induced to let it be known that he favored repeal.

The thing was done. General Conway's face shone, reported Burke, "as it were the face of an angel." The messengers galloped away with the glad news, bells rang in Bristol, ship captains raised their flags and fired salutes, huzzahs resounded in the seaports, and when the news reached America, rejoicing was double. John Hancock, a merchant-shipper himself, gave a great party with Madeira and fireworks, militias paraded with drum and fife, taverns burst with celebrators, gala balls were held, loyal thanks offered to King and Parliament and 500 sermons of thanksgiving preached throughout New England. Orders for English merchandise were renewed and itchy homespun garments given to the poor. Eight months later, John Adams wrote that the people were now "as quiet and submissive to Government as any people under the sun"; repeal had "composed every wave of popular disorder." The Declaratory Act made no impression for the very reason that it contained no reference to taxation. The Americans may also have assumed that it was a gesture of hurt pride which would not be implemented.

How shall we assess the Stamp Act and its repeal? Although framed in the face of information assuring trouble, the policy behind the Act was not yet classic folly in the sense of mindless persistence in conduct clearly counter-productive. It was natural to want revenue from the colonies and natural to try to obtain it. Repeal likewise fell short of folly because it lacked a clearly available alternative. Enforcement was impossible; repeal unavoidable. It was inauspicious because Americans, no matter how joyful, could hardly escape the conclusion that parliamentary supremacy was vulnerable to riot, agitation and boycott. Yet the great majority at this time, apart from the few activists, had never contemplated rebellion or separation, and if no further British provocation had followed, combat might never have come to Lexington Common.

3. Folly Under Full Sail:
1766-72

After a mistake so absolute as to require repeal, British policy-makers might well have stopped to reconsider the relationship with the colonies, and ask themselves what course they might follow to induce a beneficial allegiance on the one hand and ensure a secure sovereignty on the other. Many Englishmen outside government did consider this problem, and Pitt and Shelburne, who were shortly to come to power, entered office intending to calm the suspicions and restore the equanimity of the colonies. Fate, as we shall see, interfered.

Policy was not reconsidered because the governing group had no habit of purposeful consultation, had the King over their heads and were at odds with one another. It did not occur to them that it might be wise to avoid provocative measures for long enough to reassure the colonies of Britain's respect for their rights while leaving their agitators no excuse. The riotous reaction to the Stamp Act only confirmed the British in their belief that the colonies, led by "wicked and designing men" (as stated in a House of Lords resolution), were bent on rebellion. Confronted by menace, or what is perceived as menace, governments will usually attempt to smash it, rarely to examine it, understand it, define it.

A new provocation emerged in the annual Quartering Act of 1766 for the billeting, provisioning and discipline of British forces. It carried a clause requiring colonial assemblies to provide barracks and supplies such as candles, fuel, vinegar, beer and salt for the regulars. Little thought would have been needed for Parliament to recognize that this would be resented as another form of internal taxation, as it immediately was in New York, where the troops were mainly stationed. Colonists saw themselves soon being required to pay all the costs of the Army in America at the "dictate" of Parliament. The New York Assembly refused to appropriate the required funds, causing wrath in Britain at such new evidence of disobedience and ingratitude. "If we once lose the superintendency of the colonys, this nation is undone," declared Charles Townshend to thunderous applause in the House. Parliament responded with the New York Suspending Act rendering acts of the Assembly null and void until it voted the funds. Mother country and colonies were off again in quarrel.

A political upheaval took place at this time when the King, having found cause to quarrel with Rockingham, obeyed the injunctions of Providence "to dismiss my ministry." Immensely complicated negotiations brought in Pitt at the head of an ill-assorted ministry while the Rockinghams, insulted, moved into opposition. The new government contained more discordant opinions and characters than usual because Pitt, in a position to bargain hard for his terms and determined to command unfettered, deliberately put together a mixed group that he could dominate unbeholden to any "connexion." The financial cost was high because holdovers had to be given handsome pensions to persuade them to make way for successors.

On the one hand, Shelburne was brought in as Secretary of State with responsibility for the colonies, Grafton and Conway were retained and Lord Camden, another of the Pitt circle, was named Lord Chancellor. On the other hand, the King's agent, Lord Northington, was named Lord President of the Council, a place was found for Lord Bute's brother, the unpredictable Charles Townshend became Chancellor of the Exchequer and the Earl of Hillsborough, as unfriendly to the colonies as Shelburne was the opposite, was added as President of the Board of Trade. Hillsborough was a compound of "conceit, wrongheadedness, obstinacy and passion," according to Benjamin Franklin, whom he had treated rudely. The private disconnections of these people, more apparent then than now, inspired Burke's elaborate sarcasm about "a piece of diversified mosaic; a tesselated pavement . . . here a piece of black stone, there a piece of white. . . ." Burke was, of course, a disgruntled Rockingham follower.

What opened the way to folly was not the mosaic but Pitt's collapse. With catastrophic effect on his popular standing, he accepted a peerage and left the House of Commons to enter the House of Lords as Earl of Chatham. His decision was owed in part to a desire to avoid, because of his inferior health, the First Minister's extra task of leadership of the House of Commons. The public reacted as if Jesus Christ had joined the money-changers in the temple. Celebrations of the hero's return to office were canceled, bunting taken down from the Guildhall and pamphlets and lampoons gave themselves up to abuse. The Great Commoner was seen as having abandoned the people, who felt him to be their representative; as having sold himself to the court for a coronet.

In the Lords, with a smaller, less responsive audience, the new Earl had diminished effect as a speaker and lost his customary base in the larger house. His gout attacked in force; he grew peevish and sullen; his treatment of colleagues became rude and tyrannical. "Such language as Lord Chatham's," said General Conway, "had never been heard west of Constantinople." In chronic pain, hurt by public condemnation and a sense of lost greatness, frustrated by the negative turn of events in America, he sank into depression, attended no Cabinet meetings, remained inaccessible, though not beyond communicating in an unbridled letter his wrath at "the spirit of infatuation that has taken possession of New York. . . . Their spirit of disobedience will justly create a great ferment here. . . . The late Stamp Act has frightened those irritable and umbrageous people quite out of their senses."

Without its master, the tesselated Government fell into disorder. "Continuous cabals, factions and intrigues among the ins and outs," reported Benjamin Franklin, "keep everything in confusion." The Duke of Grafton, who had unhappily accepted the Treasury, for which he knew himself unfit, in order to leave Pitt free of administrative office, now at age 32 had to take over as acting chief. Feeling more than ever at a loss in that role, he would come to London "but once a week or once a fortnight to sign papers at the Treasury, and as seldom to see the King." He postponed a Cabinet Council to attend the races at Newmarket and a second time because of entertaining a large house party at his estate. The vessel of government was left virtually unsteered. Lord Shelburne, who had begun to work through the colonial agents to restore colonial goodwill, fell out with his colleagues. Lord Camden, who apart from the law was something of a dilettante in politics, failed to speak out. There was no one able to restrain the most brilliant, most irresponsible member of the Cabinet, Charles Townshend.

"The delight and ornament of the Commons and the charm of every private society," according to Burke, Townshend could make a stunning speech even when inebriated and had the intelligence and capacity that might have made him, according to Horace Walpole, "the greatest man of this age," if his faults had only been moderate. But they were not. He was arrogant, flippant, unscrupulous and unreliable, given to reversing himself by 180 degrees if expedience beckoned. "Will Charles Townshend do less harm in the War Office or in the Treasury?" the Duke of Newcastle once asked when considering him for office.

Wanted for his abilities, he had filled various offices at the Board of Trade, the Admiralty and the War Office, interspersed with resignations and refusals to serve. "He studied nothing with accuracy or with attention," wrote Walpole, "had parts that embraced all knowledge with such quickness that he seemed to create knowledge instead of searching for it" and with such abundant wit "that in him it seemed loss of time to think." The dazzle of these talents concealed a meagerness of substance, as David Hume, for one, suggested in the phrase "He passes for the cleverest fellow in England."

The spoiling fault was Townshend's "immoderate passion for fame," which may have had something to do with being a younger son and possibly with having notoriously scandalous parents who lived apart. The dissolute and eccentric father, 3rd Viscount Townshend, was in Walpole's words to a friend, "not the least mad of your countrymen." A further disability of the son was his being subject to falling fits, now thought to have been epilepsy, though described by Walpole rather casually: "he drops down in a fit, has a resurrection, thunders in the Capitol. . . ." Emulating Pitt without Pitt's sense of direction, Townshend was determined "to have *no* party, to follow *no* leader, to be governed absolutely by my own judgment." Judgment was unfortunately his weakest faculty.

While at the Board of Trade, where his several terms of service caused him to be regarded as the most knowledgeable on American affairs, he had been the first in 1763 to propose raising revenue from the colonies to pay for their defense and also to pay fixed salaries to colonial officials and judges, rendering them "no longer dependent upon the pleasure of any Assembly." This was the bugbear of the colonies, seen as an unmistakable step toward suppression of their rights.

Townshend now revived both ideas, carelessly, almost without planning. When he introduced his budget in January 1767 calling for a continuance of the land tax at 4s., it raised great rumbles of discontent among the country members. Ever eager to be popular, he said the tax could go back to 3s. if the Government did not have to spend over £400,000 on the administration of the colonies. At this, Grenville, unmoved by the fate of his Stamp Tax, promptly suggested that the budget could be cut if the colonies were assessed the greater part of the cost of their defense and administration. As if to say "No problem," Townshend, to the astonishment of his ministerial colleagues, jauntily "pledged himself to find a revenue in America sufficient for the purposes that were required." He assured the House he could do it "without offense" to the Americans, meaning by external taxes, while at the same time saying that the distinction between external and internal was "ridiculous in everybody's opinion except the Americans'." By this time the Americans themselves had rejected the distinction at the Stamp Act Congress and in public discourse, but American opinion was not a factor on which Townshend bothered to inform himself.

Given the prospect of lightening their own taxes, the House blithely accepted Townshend's assurance, the more willingly because they had been impressed by Benjamin Franklin's curiously complacent testimony during the Stamp Act hearings that the colonies would not object to external taxes even for revenue. Prodded by the discarded Rockinghams and the Bedfords on the right,* who wished to embarrass the Government, the country members carried a motion to reduce the land tax from 4s. to 3s. in the pound, thus depriving the Government of about £500,000 a year and facing the Chancellor of the Exchequer with the necessity of making good on his pledge.

Without consulting his Cabinet colleagues or giving them any notice of his intention, Townshend proposed a series of customs duties on imports into America of glass, paint, lead, paper and all grades of tea for the stated purpose not of controlling trade but of raising revenue. The expected return according to his own calculations was £20,000 from the tea duty and a little less than £20,000 from the rest, altogether £40,000, amounting to a tenth of the total cost of governing the colonies and less than a tenth of the loss from the reduced land tax. For this pittance, which would barely reduce and would very likely add to the national deficit by costing more to collect than it would bring in, Townshend was ready to wreck what repeal of the Stamp Act had been intended to gain. As with most follies, personal self-interest paralyzed concern for the greater interest of the state. In Chatham's absence, Townshend saw a way open to make himself First Minister and, toward that end, a way to enhance his stature in the House of Commons, fame's "chosen temple," as Burke called it.

His proposal seems to have dumbfounded his colleagues in the literal sense of striking them dumb. Although raising revenues from the colonies, Grafton admitted, was "contrary to the known decision of every member of the Cabinet," and the Chancellor's unilateral action "was such as no Cabinet will, I am confident, ever submit to," the

---

* This is an unhistorical term not then in use, but because it carries an exact connotation to the modern reader that no other word equals, I have decided with an uneasy conscience to use it.

Cabinet in fact submitted. When Townshend threatened to resign unless allowed to carry out his pledge, the Cabinet, in the belief that his departure would bring down the Government, meekly acquiesced. As it has ever been, staying in office was the primary thought.

Parliament in its prevailing frame of mind was happy to teach the Americans another lesson, no matter that the last one had boomeranged. In May 1767 the Revenue Act embodying the Townshend Duties passed both Houses easily without a division, that is, without need to count votes. As if deliberately trying to be provocative, Townshend wakened America's phobia in the preamble to the Act, which announced that the proceeds were to be used for raising revenue to help meet the cost of the colonies' defense and "for defraying the cost of the administration of justice and support of the civil list." Without this statement, his duties might well have raised no storm. Folly had now set sail.

How could it have happened? Townshend himself was a reckless self-aggrandizer; the real responsibility lay with Government and Parliament. The Duke of Grafton's excuse in his memoirs that only Chatham had the authority to dismiss Townshend and that "nothing less could have stopped the measure" is frail. A united Cabinet with any sense of the responsibility of government could simply have accepted the threatened resignation and taken its chances of survival. The Parliament of England, Europe's oldest representative assembly in national experience, could have given thought to possible consequences before rushing into enactment. Even the Rockinghams raised no voice to halt the measure. "The friends of America are too few," wrote Charles Garth, agent for South Carolina, "to have any share in a struggle with the Chancellor of the Exchequer." Irate articles in the press and indignant pamphlets were demanding that the ingrate colonies be made to recognize British sovereignty. Rather than conciliate the Americans, Government and Parliament were in a mood for a rap on the knuckles. The Townshend Duties fitted right in.

Their author did not live to witness the fate of his measure. He contracted what was called a "fever" that summer and after several false recoveries, the inconstant career of such short but momentous import for America ended in death in September 1767 at the age of 42. "Poor Charles Townshend is fixed at last," commented a fellow-member.

Through these events the great Chatham was beyond reach. The distracted Duke of Grafton kept entreating to see him, to consult him just for half an hour, for ten minutes, and the King added his pleas in letter after letter, even proposing to visit the sick man himself. Replies came from Lady Chatham, the ailing man's beloved wife and blessing of his tortured existence, who refused for him because of his "utter disability . . . increase of illness . . . unspeakable affliction." Colleagues thought he might be malingering but when Grafton at last, after repeated pressure, was admitted for a few moments' visit, he found a shattered man, "nerves and spirits affected to a dreadful degree . . . the great mind bowed down and thus weakened by disorder."

Isolated at Pynsent, Chatham in a manic upswing ordered the gardener to have the bare hill that bounded the view covered by a planting of evergreens. Told that "all the nurseries in this county would not furnish a hundredth part" of what would be needed, he nonetheless ordered the man to obtain the trees from London, from where they were brought down by wagon. Pynsent was an estate willed to Pitt by its irascible owner, a kinsman of Lord North, who had been so enraged by North's vote for the cider tax that he had him burnt in effigy and changed his will, leaving his estate to the national hero. To occupy it, Pitt had sold his own estate of Hayes, where he had spent great sums buying up nearby houses to "free himself from the neighborhood." Now he was seized by an insistent desire to recover Hayes and could not rest until his wife, forced to beg the influence of her brothers, with whom Chatham had quarreled, was able to persuade the new owner to sell it back.

No happier at Hayes, in the grip of gout and despair, Chatham could bear no contact. He refused to see or communicate with anyone, could not suffer his own children in the house, would not speak to servants, sometimes not even to his wife. Meals had to be kept hot at all times to be wheeled in at irregular hours when he sounded his bell. His temper erupted at the slightest defect. For days at a time he sat staring vacantly out the window. No visitor was admitted, but Lord Camden, told of the condition, said, "Then he is mad." Others called it "gout in the head."

Gout in the days of heavy diet and heavy drinking of fortified wines played a role in the fate of nations. It was a cause of the abdication of Charles V, Emperor in the time of the Renaissance Popes. A leading physician of Chatham's time, Dr. William Cadogan, maintained that the disease had three causes, "Indolence, Intemperance and Vexation" (in modern times ascertained to be an overproduction of uric acid in the blood, which, when not absorbed, causes the inflammation and pain), and that an active and frugal life was the best preventive and possible cure. That physical exercise and a vegetarian diet were remedial was known, but the theory of opposites, one of the least helpful precepts of 18th-century medicine, was preferred by Chatham's physician, a Dr. Addington. A specialist in lunacy, or "mad-doctor," he hoped to induce a violent fit of gout on the theory that this would drive out the mental disorder. He therefore prescribed two glasses of white wine and two of port every day, double his patient's usual intake, over and above Madeira and port at other intervals. The patient was also to continue eating meat and avoid exercise in the open air, with the natural result that the affliction grew worse. Chatham took no part in government through 1767 and 1768. That he survived at all under Dr. Addington's regimen and was, indeed, to recover his sanity represents one of man's occasional triumphs over medicine.

While sometimes linked to gout, probably through pain, madness appeared not infrequently in the 18th-century governing class. Two central figures in the American crisis, Chatham during and George III afterward, showed symptoms of it, and in America, James Otis, who had been acting wildly for some time, went definitely insane in 1768. Walpole's nephew, the Earl of Orford, from whom he was to inherit the title, was intermittently insane, as were Lord George Germain's two brothers, one of whom, heir to the Sackville earldom, cut down all the trees at Knole and was declared mentally incompetent by his family and eventually died "in a fit." The other, Lord John Sackville, a victim of melancholia, spent a wandering life in Europe in secluded poverty "fighting off madness." The Duchess of Queensberry was "very clever, very whimsical and just not mad." The poet William Cowper, as already noticed, was mad and so too was the minor poet Christopher Smart, whom Dr. Johnson visited in Bedlam. Lord George Gordon, who led the Gordon riots in 1780, was generally considered crazed. While occasional such cases mentioned in the memoirs may not represent a high incidence, they suggest the likelihood of others that are not mentioned. On the basis of such evidence one cannot say anything significant about madness in the governing class, but only that if Chatham had been healthy the history of America would have been different.

The Townshend Duties met a delayed reaction in America. Many citizens and future loyalists, disturbed by the mob action against lives and property during the Stamp Act crisis, had begun to fear the "patriotic" movement as the vanguard of class "levelling." They were not anxious to provoke a break with Britain. The New York Assembly, rather than accept suspension, had soberly complied with the Quartering Act. Friction, however, developed soon through harassment by agents of the new American Customs Board, created along with the Townshend Act to administer the new duties. At the same time, Writs of Assistance to allow search of premises had been legalized. Eager to make their fortunes from the penalties they could impose, the Customs agents, with infuriating zeal, halted and inspected everything that floated, boarding ships in every port and on every waterway down to the farmer ferrying chickens across a river in his riverboat.

While tempers rose, America's cause suddenly found a voice that made everybody listen. It was heard in the *Farmer's Letters*, which began appearing in the Pennsylvania *Chronicle* in December 1767, written by John Dickinson, a Philadelphia lawyer of a prosperous farming family and a future delegate to the Continental Congress. The letters laid out the colonies' case so cogently and convincingly that they joined the historic company of writings that persuade and move people to action. Newspapers throughout the colonies reprinted them and Governor Bernard of Massachusetts sent a complete set to the agent Richard Jackson in London, warning that unless refuted they could become "a Bill of Rights in the opinion of the Americans."

Dickinson's theme was the necessity for unity among the colonies to protest against the New York Suspending Act, which he called a "dreadful stroke," and the Revenue Act. He asserted that any tax raised for revenue was unconstitutional and that therefore there was no difference between the Townshend Duties and the Stamp Tax. The colonies owed no contribution to governing costs since Britain already reaped profit from control of their trade. To apply the duties toward the civil list and judges' salaries was the "worst stroke," absolutely destructive of local control, potentially reducing the colonies to the status of poor Ireland. Dickinson's most telling point was his suggestion that the reason the duties were so petty was that the British hoped to have them pass virtually unnoticed, thereby establishing a precedent for future taxation. Therefore they must be challenged at once.

Readers sprang to action even if Dickinson's argument supplied Townshend with a more rational motive for his policy than he in fact had. Americans tended to see a conscious plan to enslave them in every British measure. They assumed the British were more rational, just as the British government assumed they were more rebellious, than was true in either case.

The effect of the *Farmer's Letters* was to fire up resistance to the Revenue Act, set Sam Adams on the stump with his calls to the mob and elicit from the Massachusetts Assembly a circular letter summoning the other colonies to resist any tax revenue. Britain's response came from a figure of new consequence, Lord Hillsborough, whom fate seems to have selected to ensure that Townshend's death would not empty the cornucopia of mischief. Hillsborough had moved into control of American affairs in place of Lord Shelburne, whom the Duke of Grafton, under pressure from the King and from the Bedfords, whose alliance Grafton needed, had been forced to remove. Not a man for the axe, Grafton split Shelburne's office to create a new office of Secretary for the Colonies, to which Hillsborough was named. Because he held an Irish peerage with large estate, Hillsborough opposed any softening toward the colonies in fear, shared by other Irish landowners, of his tenants' migrating to America and emptying his rent-rolls. Though he had held many offices, he was not known for tact or reason; even George III, who shared the same deficiency, said he did not know "a man of less judgment than Lord Hillsborough." This shortcoming promptly made itself felt.

In a peremptory letter, the new Secretary ordered the Massachusetts Assembly to rescind its circular letter under pain of dissolution if it refused and informed other governors that any other assembly that followed Massachusetts' seditious example was likewise to be dissolved. The punitive tone of his letter and its implication that Americans were to be compelled to accept taxation or have their representative assemblies closed down ignited outrage where there had been little before. When Massachusetts refused loudly and passionately to rescind, Pennsylvania and other colonies that had refused her first call now adopted resolutions on the Massachusetts model in defiance of Hillsborough. Self-interest in preserving the empire was not doing well in his hands.

At the same time the Customs Board, growing nervous, appealed in February 1768 for a warship and troops for protection. The arrival of H.M.S. *Romney* in Boston harbor from Halifax emboldened the Customs Board to seize John Hancock's ship *Liberty*, setting off such a riot that the Customs Commissioners fled aboard the *Romney* in fear for their lives. Fearful of the mounting disorder, General Gage ordered two regiments down from Halifax; two more arrived from the mother country in November. "To have a standing army! Good God!" wrote a Bostonian, after watching the redcoats parade through the city. "What can be worse to a people who have tasted the sweets of liberty!" It would "hasten that independency which at present the warmest among us deprecate."

Without any plan or decision, the use of armed force for coercion had entered the conflict. The unwisdom of this procedure disturbed many Englishmen including the Duke of Newcastle, now 75, who had administered the colonies as Secretary of State for a quarter century in his early days and believed that "Measures of Power and Force" should be avoided in dealing with them. "The measure of conquering the colonies and obliging them to submit is now becoming more popular," he wrote to Rockingham. "I must in conscience protest against it and I hope our friends will well consider before they give in to so destructive a measure."

The weight of the Cabinet, gradually infused by Bedfords and the King's friends, was tipping the other way. Conway, who alone had tried to check Townshend and curtail the New York Suspending Act, resigned as Secretary of State, though retaining a minor post. His place was filled by a port-loving lord of small account except as a Bedford "connexion," Viscount Weymouth, whose specialty was gambling all night and losing so consistently that his house was filled with bailiffs. As Secretary of State, he continued in his habits, going to bed at 6:00 a.m. and rising after noon "to the total neglect of the affairs of his office, the business of which was managed as much as it could be by Mr. Wood, his under-secretary." Townshend's empty place as Chancellor of the Exchequer was taken over by Lord North, an equable, comfortable person with a good deal of common sense and few strong opinions, though belonging to the no-compromise side. Two other places were filled by peers of the Bedford faction: Earl Gower when Lord Northington died, and the Earl of Rochford, recently Ambassador to Spain, where in order to leave Madrid he had to pawn his silver plate and jewels for £6000 to pay his debts. He was now named Secretary of State when Shelburne, the only Cabinet member to oppose Hillsborough's coercive measures, finally resigned —or was pushed—after holding on to the rump of his office for eight months. Informed of his departure, Chatham, on the way to recovery, sent in the Privy Seal, officially resigning his office.

What had once been Chatham's government now belonged to the Bloomsbury Gang, so called from the Duke of Bedford's residence in Bloomsbury Square. The Duke himself, aside from great wealth and the many offices he had held in the previous reign and aside from his powers, positions and titles in Bedfordshire, owed his influence to a supremely developed sense of status and self-assurance. He was said to be the only man who could speak openly against Pitt in his great days. He had served as Lord President of the Council and real head of the Grenville government, generally spoken of as the Bedford ministry, but now, afflicted by gout, he exerted his influence through his followers while spending most of his time at Woburn Abbey, his country home. Together with his brother-in-law Earl Gower and his son-in-law the 4th Duke of Marlborough, he controlled thirteen seats in the House of Commons. Though intelligent and warm-hearted, Bedford was hot-tempered, wrong-headed and obstinate. His entourage included masters of jobbing and electioneering and the strongest advocates of coercing the colonies. Six frigates and a brigade, they kept telling the King, would be enough to suppress American insolence.

King George had only one idea of policy with regard to the colonies: that "it was the indispensable duty of his subjects in America to obey the Acts of the Legislature of Great Britain," and that the King "expects and requires a cheerful obedience to the same." In the conduct of government, his influence was more pernicious because he was convinced of his royal duty to purify it after the model of his schoolboy idol, Alfred the Great. Through the Bedfords, he now interfered more than ever, appointing and dismissing ministers at will, controlling patronage, accepting no collective policy from the Cabinet but dealing with individual ministers in reference only to their own departments, even suggesting who was to speak in debates in the House of Commons. His choices for office tended to be courtiers of rank who had made themselves agreeable to him but whose talent or training for government was not likely to be greater than his own.

American eruptions at every tax and every measure proved to the Bedfords that the colonists were bent on breaking the mercantilist system and obtaining free trade and would raise the cry of "Tyranny!" at every act of Parliament. If given in to, their protest would soon leave not a shred of sovereignty remaining.

As regards trade, these apprehensions were not misplaced. Breaking the mercantilist yoke while developing home industries was indeed an idea that had taken hold of the Americans, prompted by the success of Non-Importation. By provoking the colonists' turn to homemade cloth and other goods, Britain had brought upon herself the very impulse toward commercial independence she was most determined to prevent. Even to Pitt, mercantilist regulation had always been the essence of colonial policy. "Not a hobnail or a horseshoe," he once declared, should the colonies be allowed to manufacture. Now the impulse was reinvigorated. In August and September 1768, the merchants of Boston and New York agreed to cease importing from Britain until the Townshend Duties were repealed. Philadelphia's merchants joined the agreement a few months later, followed by most of the other colonies through the course of 1769. Home weaving by organized groups of "Daughters of Liberty" had in fact continued since the Stamp Act. The graduating class of Harvard College in 1768 and the first graduating class and President of Rhode Island College (now Brown) in 1769 all appeared in clothes of American homespun.

At home the return of Wilkes reawakened a furor of resentment against the Government when he was re-elected to Parliament from Middlesex, London's county, and re-expelled by the government majority in the House. At once his cause rallied all opponents of the royal prerogative and invigorated the Radicals' movement for parliamentary reform to replace the patronage system by genuine elections. All the causes of "Liberty," including the friends of America opposed to coercion, coalesced, lending one another strength.

The cry "Wilkes and Liberty!" resounded as the protagonist stood again for Middlesex, was defiantly returned by its voters, again expelled, again elected and expelled a third time. He became both a constitutional symbol and a popular hero, focus of the commoners' discontents. When the Government put up its own candidate for Middlesex and declared him elected by ruling out the votes for Wilkes, tumult and agitation convulsed London. The city "is a daily scene of lawless riots and confusion," wrote Benjamin Franklin. "Mobs patrol the streets at noonday, some knocking down all that will not roar for Wilkes and liberty." Coalers, sailors, watermen and all sorts of rioters overturned carriages, looted shops, broke into noble residences, while the ministry was "divided in their counsels" and apprehensive of what might come.

By its fatuous suppression of the Middlesex vote, the Government aroused the ever-ready cry of alarm about English liberties. The connection with American liberties, constantly propounded among the Wilkesites by the more active American agents, was confirmed. "The persons who wish to enslave America, would, if it lay in their power, enslave us," said a linen draper and elector of London during the canvass for votes in 1768. The 236 elected councilmen and 26 aldermen, mainly shopkeepers and self-employed artisans, who made up the London Court of Common Council, condemned virtually every measure for coercion of the colonies.

At the head of the advocates was the Lord Mayor himself, the spirited merchant William Beckford, who, like most partisans of America, reached that position through his advocacy of Wilkes; to oppose the Government on one was to oppose it on both. As the scion of a wealthy Jamaica family of sugar planters and the island's largest

landowner, Beckford enlarged his fortune in English commerce, rose
from alderman to sheriff to Lord Mayor and addressed to the King the
protest of the city of London against the doctoring of the Middlesex
election. Though snobbishly said by Walpole to act from "a confused
heap of knowledge . . . so uncorrected by judgment that his absurdities
were made but more conspicuous by his vanity," he made a bold voice
among the critics of American policy. English Radicals reflected the
colonists' view of a ministerial conspiracy to suppress their liberties.
Josiah Wedgwood, a leading Radical, believed the Townshend Act
was a deliberate effort toward that end, although he thought it would
be counter-productive in that it would accelerate American independence by a century.

The *London Magazine* in August 1768 compared the authors and
abettors of "the present impolitick measures against America" to the
Crown and its "wretched ministers" of the 17th century. "From our
own observations we will venture to say that nine persons in ten, even
in this country, are friends to the Americans" and believe they "have
right on their side." Nine out of ten was certainly exaggerated; some
journals estimated the proportions just in reverse. Ralph Izard, an
American resident in London, judged that four out of five Britons were
opposed to America and that Parliament's support of the Government
correctly reflected public opinion. When the opposition regularly
produced no more than eighty votes, "you may depend on it, the
measure is not thought a bad one, for corruption does not reach that
deep." Public opinion is hard to judge from the contemporary press
because many of the pro-American articles were contributed anonymously or under pseudonyms by Americans in London. Nevertheless,
English printers would not have given the fair amount of space they
did to paragraphs and letters favorable to the colonies if an important
section of public opinion had not opposed the Government's policies.

It should be added that the political concerns of public opinion are
often overestimated by posterity. The real interest in 1768 among the
governing class was not the Americans or even Wilkes but the scandal
caused by the Duke of Grafton in "defying all decency" by escorting
his mistress, Nancy Parsons, to the opera in the presence of his divorced
Duchess and the Queen. Grafton was at least divorced, which most
men who kept mistresses were not, but this did not reduce the scandal.
Daughter of a Bond Street tailor and former mistress of a West Indies
merchant, Nancy was also known as Mrs. Hoghton, having acquired
marital status along her way, but that too failed to palliate society's
scorn. The fact that Grafton "paraded" her in public and sat her at

the head of his table excited a peculiar indignation. It was the sensation
of the season. Nancy quite blanketed out the obstreperous colonists.

Indignant protests in Parliament from Virginia, Pennsylvania and
other colonies showed that resistance to the Revenue Act was spreading
and cold figures confirmed the fact. From 1768 to 1769, English exports to America dropped by a third, from £2,400,000 to £1,600,000.
New York cut its imports to one-seventh of what they had been in
1764, from £482,000 in that year to £74,000 in 1769. Boston's imports were cut in half, those of other colonies, where compliance with
Non-Importation was uneven, by less. Receipts from the Townshend
Duties in their first year amounted to £16,000, compared to military
expenditures for America of £170,000. Even Hillsborough, as Secretary for the Colonies, had to admit that the Townshend Act was "so
anti-commercial that he wished it had never existed," while the new
Chancellor of the Exchequer, Lord North, said the duties were "so
preposterous that he was amazed that they had ever been passed by
the British Parliament." Both gentlemen had voted for the Act they
now deplored.

Rather than conciliate for the sake of quickly terminating Non-
Importation, the Government's instinct was punitive. Having maneuvered itself into a situation of challenge from its subjects, it felt
obliged to make a demonstration of authority, the more so as it was
feared that American protest, if it succeeded, would inspire the spirit
of emulation in English and Irish mobs. Hillsborough, like Rehoboam,
believed effective demonstration lay in being as rough as possible. He
resurrected from the autocratic era of Henry VIII an ancient statute
providing for trial in England of persons accused of treason outside
the kingdom and this was moved by the Duke of Bedford as a parliamentary resolution with reference to the offenses of Massachusetts.
The Commons concurred, the Chathamites of Grafton's group in the
Government seem to have raised no objection and the order was duly
transmitted to Governor Bernard in Boston. Reaction was naturally
violent. Citizens to be snatched from home and delivered to trial in
hostile surroundings 3000 miles from friends and defenders! Here was
tyranny unconcealed!

At the same time in England the basic fear of the encouragement
being given to American industry by the Non-Importation movement
was taking effect. Having recklessly provoked the boycott, Government and Parliament now began to consider how to undo the damage
by repeal. The Stamp Act experience was re-enacted as if the governing establishment of Britain were under a gambler's compulsion

to keep placing its chips on the same squares where they had lost before. The process of repealing the Townshend Act took more than a year, from March 1769 to May 1770, during which other measures taken to discipline the colonies were as counter-productive as the one undergoing cancellation.

By now accumulated folly was fully perceived and explicitly and derisively denounced in the year's debates. Opposition speakers roused to outrage against the Government over the non-seating of Wilkes, which was considered a "violation of the sacred right of election" and an "overturn of the whole constitution," felt free to castigate the Government equally severely on America. Burke launched his sarcasm, Colonel Barré his scorn; Lord Mayor Beckford observed "that it was a strange piece of policy to expend £500,000 a year to assist the Customs-House officers in collecting £295, which was the whole net produce of the taxes there." The hero of the debates was none of these but former Governor Thomas Pownall speaking from seven years' experience in America in the administration of four different colonies. In long, cogent, irrefutable argument and evidence, he was perhaps the only one to speak from genuine disinterest and genuine concern to restore good relations with America. Other critics, with scoffing invective and exaggerated sympathy for the oppressed colonists—whom Barré described as the "honest, faithful, loyal, and till that moment, as subjects, irreproachable people of Massachusetts"—were more concerned to bring down the Government than to reconcile it with America. The Government complacently ignored the criticism, secure in its large majority.

Pownall laid bare the follies. Instead of ordering the billeting and supply of troops by the Quartering Act, which instantly aroused colonial protest, the process should be left "to the people themselves to do it in their own way, and by their own modes of doing business" as they had done during the Seven Years' War. The commanding officer of any body of soldiers should be empowered to treat with local magistrates to quarter the troops by mutual agreement. In moving repeal of the Townshend Act, he showed how the preamble in announcing the purpose to be revenue for civil government was a "total change" of the system by which the colonies had always controlled public servants by their own legislatures having the grant and disposal of funds for government. In changing that system, the Act was not only unnecessary, since the Declaratory Act already established Parliament's sovereignty, but "unjust and a grievance in every degree."

As regards trade, he showed how the Act was "directly contrary to all the principles of commerce respecting your own interests": it served as a bounty to American manufactures, encouraged contraband and recourse to foreign markets, rendered the colonies "every day less beneficial and advantageous to us and will in the end break off their dependence on us." If this occasion for rectifying the error were lost, "it is lost forever. If this session elapses with Parliament's doing nothing, American affairs will perhaps be impracticable forever after. You may exert power over, but you can never govern an unwilling people." Almost unintentionally, Pownall had formulated a principle worth the attention of all who rule at any time—that government must conduct itself with regard to the feelings of the governed, and ignores them at its peril.

Despite the fact that Pownall's motion won general agreement (or perhaps because of it), the ministry complained that it was too late in the session to debate a matter of so much consequence for which they were not prepared, and carried a motion to put it off to the next session. This was a fumble because their own desire was to end Non-Importation as quickly as possible. The Cabinet took up the problem during the recess. Grafton and his group, who voted for total repeal, were outvoted by Hillsborough, North and the three Bedford ministers, who insisted on retaining the duty on tea in order to retain the preamble as token of the right to tax for revenue. A resolution of painful straddling was adopted: that no measure would be taken "to derogate in any way from the legislative authority of Great Britain over the colonies"; at the same time it was not the intention to lay "any further taxes" upon America for revenue, and it was the intention at the next session of Parliament "to take off the duties upon paper, glass and colours." When Hillsborough informed the colonial governors of the intended repeal, he managed to vitiate its effect by omitting "the soothing and conciliatory expressions" which the Grafton group had won consent to introduce. Since the omission of tea indicated that the Act as a whole was not to be repealed, the colonies were not persuaded to call off Non-Importation.

"If you would be but steady in any scheme," despairingly wrote Thomas Hutchinson to Richard Jackson, "we should come to some sort of settlement in the colonies. . . . Let me beseech you, repeal as many of the laws now in force as you please," but implement those that remain effectively. "The longer you delay the more difficult it will be." He was close to the evidence in Boston, where the press reported that 300 "mistresses of families," aware that the consumption of tea supported the Customs Commissioners "and other tools of power," agreed to abstain from tea "until those creatures, together with the Boston Standing Army, are removed and the Revenue Acts repealed."

Hardly was Parliament reconvened and the debate on America renewed when a crisis emptied the ministry of Grafton, its nominal chief, and his associates. Chatham, returned from the shadows, had risen to express alarm over the Americans' success in supplying themselves with their own manufactures, and to say, in echo of Pownall's principle, that "the discontent of two millions* of people deserved consideration and the foundation of it ought to be removed." That was the only way to stop the "combinations and manufactures" in America. Chatham's major eloquence, however, was spent on the non-seating of Wilkes, and when he proposed a motion condemning it, Lord Chancellor Camden, with independent courage, voted for the motion, against the Government of which he was a member, and was accordingly dismissed from office. Perhaps he welcomed the result for he confessed in Parliament that often in the Cabinet he merely hung his head in silence to register disapproval of measures which he knew overt opposition could not prevent.

A tragedy was the result. When Charles Yorke, former Attorney-General and son of a former Lord Chancellor, was offered the post that was his life's ambition in a government that he and his family and friends opposed, and was strongly pressed by the King with promise of a peerage, he accepted against his conscience. That evening, reproached by associates and tortured by ambivalence, he committed suicide. As the man who had offered Yorke the post, Grafton, shaken by the death and dispirited by inability to control policy, resigned, followed by the two generals, Conway and Granby.

The new First Minister, forever to be associated with the American Revolution, was the amiable Lord North, who during his years of increasingly distracted office was to gain a clear idea of what a chief minister's qualifications should be—and was sure he did not have them. In one of his periodic letters to the King begging to be allowed to resign, he wrote that the office should be held by "a man of great abilities, and who is confident of his abilities, who can choose decisively,

---

* The discrepancy between this figure and the three million of Chatham's speech of January 1766 may reflect inexact knowledge of the facts or inexact parliamentary reporting, both of which were features of the time. The actual population is estimated to have been approximately 2.5 million.

and carry his determination authoritatively into execution . . . and be capable of forming wise plans and of combining and connecting the whole force and operations of government." It was an excellent prescription and it concluded, "I am certainly not such a man."

Nevertheless, as the King's personal choice, North was to last, however unwillingly, for twelve critical years in the office that had had five occupants in the last decade. Fat-cheeked and corpulent, with bulging eyes, he bore a startling resemblance to George III, which was often made the subject of ribald suggestion, referring to the close connection of North's parents with the household of Frederick, Prince of Wales, father of George III. At the time of North's birth his father, the Earl of Guilford, served the Prince as Lord of the Bedchamber. North was christened Frederick for the Prince, who was his godfather, if nothing closer. In addition to physical resemblance, both North and George III suffered blindness in their last years.

In temperament, Lord North happily escaped resemblance to the King, being known, in Gibbon's words, for "the felicity of his incomparable temper." It was said that only one man, a drunken stupid groom, had ever been known to make him angry; unimproved and always forgiven, the man died still in North's service. Elected from the family-controlled pocket borough of Banbury with thirteen voters, North entered the House of Commons at 22 and represented the same borough for the rest of his life. When appointed chief minister, he was 38, awkward in movement with weak eyesight and a tongue too large for his mouth "which rendered his articulation somewhat thick though not at all indistinct." One who profited from education at Eton, at Oxford and on a three-year Grand Tour, he was proficient in Greek and Latin, spoke French, German and Italian, and when wide enough awake, sprinkled his speeches with classical allusions, foreign phrases and flashes of wit and genial humor.

If he could not hide from the harassments of office, he took refuge from them by sleeping on the front bench during debates. Asking to be wakened when Grenville in the course of a ponderous and long-winded discourse should reach modern times, and nudged when the speaker was citing a precedent of 1688, he opened an eye, muttered "a hundred years too soon" and relapsed into somnolence. He carried the habit to Cabinet meetings, where, according to Charles James Fox, who later served with him, "he was so far from leading the opinions of other ministers that he seldom gave his own and generally slept the greater part of the time he was with them." This did not conduce to firm collective policy.

If seldom voiced, North's opinions were firmly on the Right. He voted for the cider tax, for the expulsion of Wilkes, for the Stamp Act and against its repeal. Although against compromise with America, he was in practice ready to proceed by conciliation toward a possible middle ground, and "heartily wished to repeal the whole of the [Townshend] law" if he could have done it without giving up "that just right which I shall ever wish the mother country to possess, the right of taxing the Americans." Though not a member of the Bedford clique, he was acceptable to them or he could not have been named First Minister. His chief disability lay in the extended and tight-fisted life of his father, who lived to be 86, depriving his son of the inheritance of a considerable fortune until he was old and blind and within two years of his own death. The result was that with a large family to support and an important position to keep up, North was in financial straits throughout his political life, dependant on office and obligated to the King, who, however kindly and tactfully, gave his First Minister £20,000 to pay his debts. Under such circumstances, independence of mind or action was less than likely.

When debate was renewed from March to May 1770, opposition speakers unsparingly depicted the Government's record in America since the Townshend Act as a series of infirm policies, contradictory measures, irresolute and in some cases unconstitutional action and judgments contrary to Britain's interest—in short, as folly. The terrible Colonel Barré excoriated the Cabinet for taking it upon itself to inform the Americans of its intention to repeal the duties before Parliament had acted, thus inspiring them "with a most contemptible idea of the measures of Parliament and the imbecility of those by whom lawful government is administered." He scolded them further for reviving the statute from "the tyrannical reign of Henry VIII" and yet, "with weakness no less conspicuous than their wickedness . . . they had not the resolution to execute it."

Pownall explained that it was the preamble to the Act "which gives the offence and raises the alarm in America"; in order to remove it, the whole Townshend Act must be repealed and exclude tea, and he so moved. Grenville, acknowledging himself the originator of the controversy with America, offered the unhelpful opinion that partial repeal would not satisfy the colonies while total repeal would not "sufficiently provide for the dignity of the nation," and therefore he would abstain from voting. An independent member, Sir William Meredith, found the Government "so perversely, so inflexibly persisting in error on every occasion" as to cause surprise, in Dryden's phrase, "that 'they never deviate into sense' nor stumble upon propriety by downright accident." Since the tea duty, he added, would never pay for the cost of collecting it and the deficiency would have to be made up from the "coffers of this kingdom," the result would merely be "to plunder ourselves." Although Government majority prevailed over common sense, defeating Pownall's motion by 204 to 142, common sense made an impression, for the yeas were almost twice the regular number of pro-American votes.

Again Pownall returned to the offensive when the debate turned to American policy as a whole. He showed that the real apprehension of the colonies, apart from taxation, was of a British "design to alter their civil constitution." They found it confirmed in Hillsborough's order dissolving their assemblies and in the Townshend Act preamble, which they feared would "render all their assemblies useless." By this time news had reached England of the so-called Boston Massacre, which had raised local emotions to such a pitch that to prevent further incident, the redcoats who had been sent to cow Boston had to be removed, with less than glory to British arms, to the safety of Castle William in Boston Harbor. The withdrawal gave opportunity for the "infinite wit and raillery" of Mr. Edmund Burke, who of all the speakers of his time is the best known to posterity.

Burke's ideas had the great advantage of being housed in mastery and felicity of language. Had his ideas been fuzzy, verbal beauties would not have helped, but his political thinking was acute and incisive. Though often prolix and overstated, his remarks became epigrams because they were so well phrased. He had a way of "winding into his subject like a serpent," said Oliver Goldsmith, who thought him in conversation the equal of Dr. Johnson. Dr. Johnson agreed. "Burke talks because his mind is full. . . . No man of sense could meet Mr. Burke by accident under a gateway to avoid a shower without being convinced that he was the first man in England." He often talked at such length as to empty the House and so vehemently that his friends had to hold him down by the skirts of his coat to restrain his passion, but his wit and intelligence prevailed. The bite of his speeches on America, wrote Horace Walpole, excited "continual bursts of laughter even from Lord North and the Ministers themselves." His pathos "drew iron tears from Barré's cheek"; his scorn would have excited strangers, if they had not been excluded from a certain debate, "to tear ministers to pieces as they went out of the House."

Burke had no difficulty in making the Government look foolish with his list of its infirm chastisements of the colonies: how the Massachusetts Assembly, after being ordered to rescind its seditious resolution or suffer dissolution, was permitted to sit again without rescinding; how the other assemblies under the same threat defied the penalty and "treated the Secretary of State's letter with contempt"; how the pains of the Henry VIII statute "never were, as it was known they never would be, carried into execution"; how a fleet and army sent to Boston to control the situation "are now withdrawn out of the town"; how in sum "the malignity of your will is abhorred and the debility of your power is condemned," which has ever been the case of "government without wisdom."

The majority, of course, defeated Burke's eight resolutions of censure, and the same fate met a similar censure moved in the House of Lords by the young Duke of Richmond, a new and important, if rather too independent, recruit to the American cause who was to become an eminent opponent of Government policy.

Richmond was a glittering personage who personified in many ways the unreality of 18th-century English government. He was so heavily weighted with fortune's goods that they hampered his thorough performance of any one task. A great-grandson of Charles II by his mistress Louise de Kéroualle, Duchess of Portsmouth, a brother of the lovely Lady Sarah Lennox, whom George III wanted to marry, he was dignified, courteous, strikingly handsome and together with his wife, also of a ducal family, made "the prettiest couple in England." Duke at fifteen, colonel of his regiment at 23, Ambassador to France and briefly Secretary of State under Rockingham at 31, he had youth, beauty, great riches, highest rank, military valor, intelligence and capacity for hard work, a network of political connections and "all the blood of kings from Bruce to Charles II." Not surprisingly, with these attributes, he was tactless, hot-tempered, unable to bend to other men or to political necessities, intolerant of inadequacies in others and given to quarreling with family, friends, subordinates and with the King in the first year of his reign so that he resigned from a post in the royal household and was pursued by royal animosity thereafter.

Intent on exposing abuses, Richmond harassed Army, Admiralty and Treasury with his searching questions, which did not make him popular. He could arrive in town on the morning of a debate, master the issues in a quick study and speak on them effectively the same afternoon. Defeat of his aims and purposes, however, turned him quickly sour, causing repeated threats to retire from politics altogether. He suffered periods of depression, one in 1769 of which he wrote to

Rockingham, "I must for some time at least indulge myself in my present disposition which I will give no name to." At home in Sussex he spent vast sums on new wings to Goodwood House, on dog kennels and race track, yacht, hunting and the local militia and, after inheriting a great estate worth £68,000 with an additional annual income of £20,000 from coal duties, found himself £95,000 in debt forty years later. His interest in government, like that of others of his kind, often slipped below other matters. It was unreasonable of Burke, Richmond once wrote to him, to want him to come down to London before Parliament convened. His opinion carried "little weight," therefore for him to confer with political associates had no purpose. "No, let me enjoy myself here till the meeting, and then at your desire I will go to town and look about me for a few days."

Unrestrained in the 1770 debate, he described ministerial conduct in America as that of either "artful knave or incorrigible fool" and either way, "the ministers are a disgrace to the very name of government." He proposed eighteen resolutions of censure covering all acts and measures since 1768 and concluding that "these many and ill-judged proceedings have been a principal cause of the aforesaid disorders." Goaded to reply, Hillsborough made the usual defense of the need to establish authority, and added a charge that "our patriots" of the opposition were stimulating colonial protest and "continually throwing obstacles in the way of reconciliation" out of "the patriotic wish of getting into place. . . . In fact, my lords, their whole patriotism is a despicable avarice of employment . . . so they can succeed to office."

While obviously underrating the colonies' native resistance, Hillsborough had a point about the motives of the opposition. Their "avarice" for office, however, was not as strong as their inertia of political organization. They were ineffectual because, owing to feuds and differences, they could not find common ground to form a solid front. "Dowdeswell [former Chancellor of the Exchequer under Rockingham] was devilish sulky at Lord Chatham," wrote Richmond to Rockingham at this time, "and Burke is all combustible." Burke could not take Chatham's arrogance and Chatham could not endure a strong-minded intellectual equal as an ally. Although Rockingham tried to bring Chatham into a team that would work together under his captaincy, Chatham would accept only on conditions establishing his own dominion. Shelburne, disgusted with the helplessness of being in a perpetual minority, went abroad with Barré in 1771. Richmond and Rockingham were lured by their country acres and, as a contemporary satire put it,

With hound and horn her truant schoolboys roam
And for a fox-hunt quit St. Stephen's dome.*

In America, no heightened protest followed Parliament's maintenance of the Townshend preamble and tea duty. As often happens, the
logical course of events suffered quirks and diversions. Among the
colonial propertied class, fear of mobs and social upheaval had begun
to erode their support of the "patriotic" movement. Its impetus
dwindled. Wearying of Non-Importation, New York proposed a conference of the northern seaports to decide on a common policy. Merchants of Boston and Philadelphia, also eager to resume trade, were
prevented by the agitators. When the proposed conference fell
through, New York, rather than be cheated while "starving on the
slender Meals of patriotism," abandoned Non-Importation and opened
its port in 1772. Separately, at different times, the other colonies followed, agitation subsided and the absence of unity confirmed Britain
in the assumption that the colonies would never join in a common front
and that loyalist sentiment and economic self-interest would prevail
over seditious impulse.

With feelings intense in Parliament over the Wilkes issue, Lord
North's policy was to keep American affairs out of the House of
Commons, and for two years, owing to the lull in the colonies, he
succeeded. This could have been a period of compromise and possible
reunion if a positive effort had been made. The colonies were bent on
redress of grievances and autonomy in their own affairs, not on
independence. On the contrary, the Stamp Act Congress had asserted
that they "most ardently" desired "perpetual continuance" of the
ancient tie with Britain. Even the Massachusetts Assembly, the most
aggressive in sentiment, had disavowed in 1768 "the most distant
thought of independence," claiming that the colonies "would refuse
it if offered to them and would deem it the greatest misfortune to be
obliged to accept it." George III, Lord North, Hillsborough and the
Bedfords, however, were not equipped for positive effort or creative
government. In the lull, the sails of folly were furled for the moment—
until the affair of the *Gaspée* in 1772.

---

* St. Stephen's represents the Houses of Parliament.

4. *"Remember Rehoboam!"*:
1772-75

The *Gaspée* was a British customs schooner under a bellicose commander, Lieutenant Dudington, who pursued his task as if he carried a personal warrant from the King to stamp out smuggling in the thousand isles and inlets of Narragansett Bay. Boarding and examining every ship he met, threatening to blow recalcitrant skippers out of the water, he aroused a lust for revenge in the Rhode Islanders that found its moment when his schooner ran aground below Providence. Within hours local seafarers organized eight boatloads of men who attacked the ship, wounded Lieutenant Dudington, put him and his crew ashore and burned the *Gaspée*.

As so often, Britain's response started out sternly and ended feebly. The Attorney-General and Solicitor-General decided that the attack on the *Gaspée* was an act of war on the King and as such was treasonable, requiring the culprits to be sent to England for trial. First they had to be discovered. A Royal Proclamation offered a £500 reward and the King's pardon to informants, and an imposing Commission of Inquiry consisting of the Governor of Rhode Island and the chief justices of New York, New Jersey and Massachusetts and of the Vice-Admiralty Court of Boston was appointed to indict the suspects. This announcement revived every slumbering suspicion of a conspiracy against liberty. Rhode Island, together with Massachusetts the most intractable of the colonies, shook with cries of "Tyranny!" and "Slavery!" "Ten thousand deaths by the *haltar* and the *ax*," proclaimed the *Newport Mercury* in outraged italics, were preferable "to a miserable life of slavery in chains under a pack of worse than Egyptian tyrants." No informants came forward; no suspects could be found although every neighbor knew who they were. After several hollow sessions in Newport, the Court of Inquiry in all their wigs and scarlet sheepishly adjourned, never to reconvene. One more chastisement went unexecuted, confirming the perception of Britain as both despotic in intent and ineffectual in execution.

The consequence was important because Rhode Island's roars of protest caused a decisive step toward unity. Following a model created among the towns of Massachusetts, Virginia's House of Burgesses invited the colonies to form Committees of Correspondence to consult on joint acts and methods of resistance. Thomas Jefferson and Patrick Henry served on Virginia's Committee. This was the beginning of the development toward intercolonial union, which Britain remained confident could never occur and on whose non-occurrence her confidence rested. The Committees excited little attention—except in moments of confrontation, American affairs on the whole did not. The letters of Mrs. Delany, a well-connected lady and wife of an Anglican dean who corresponded actively throughout this period with friends and relatives in social and literary circles, do not notice America at all.

The two legal officers of the home government who were immediately responsible for the *Gaspée* order, Edward Thurlow, the Attorney-General, and Alexander Wedderburn, the Solicitor-General, were an unpleasant pair. Unmanageable as a schoolboy, expelled from Cambridge University for insolence and misconduct, surly and assertive in the law, Thurlow had a savage temper and reputedly the foulest mouth in London. He was nevertheless an impressive figure, although according to Charles James Fox his deep voice and solemn aspect proved him dishonest "since no man could be as wise as he looked." His treatment of defendants in court was often offensive. In policy he was inflexible on the demonstration of British sovereignty over America and, although Lord North was known to hate him, the King eventually rewarded his firm support with appointment as Lord Chancellor and a barony to go with it. Equally coercive as regards America, Wedderburn was a Scot of voracious ambition who would use any means, suck up to or betray any associate, to gain advancement. "There was something about him," said an acquaintance, "that even treachery could not trust." Although despised by the King, he too eventually became Lord Chancellor.

Yet it was the Cabinet, in which Thurlow and Wedderburn had no place, that ordered the Court of Inquiry and the summons for trial in England, and it was "the good Lord Dartmouth," as Hillsborough's successor, who signed the order. In response to an attack on the state, they acted with every conviction of righteousness, and if it was the proper response from the ruler's point of view, it was utter folly as practical politics. Given the known outrage at the idea of transporting Americans to trial in England, and the obvious unreality of expecting Rhode Islanders to mark their fellows for that fate, the mischief once more lay "in asserting a right you know you cannot exert." This became very openly apparent at Newport, the hub of coastal communication, from where the impression of the mother country as ineffectual quickly spread.

Lord Dartmouth, although a stepbrother of Lord North, with whom he had grown up and shared the Grand Tour, was an earnest friend of America, possibly as a result of his having joined the Methodists, whose missions and preaching in America were a major activity. Amiable and pious and said to be the model of the virtuous Sir Charles Grandison in Samuel Richardson's novel of that name, Dartmouth was nicknamed the "psalm-singer." He had served as President of the Board of Trade in the Rockingham ministry, though credited with very little administrative capacity. Lord North brought him in as Secretary of State for the Colonies when Hillsborough, as a result of an intrigue against him by the Bedfords for reasons of place, not policy, was forced to resign. Alone in the Cabinet as pro-American, Dartmouth "wishes sincerely a good understanding with the colonies," wrote Benjamin Franklin, "but does not have strength equal to his wishes" and while wishing "for the best measure is easily prevailed with to join in the worst." Gradually, as American intransigence defeated his well-meant paternalism, he was to turn against conciliation in favor of repression.

At this point tea becomes the catalyst. The financial troubles and notorious abuses of the East India Company and its complex financial connections with the Crown had for years been a problem almost as intractable as Wilkes and are relevant here only because they precipitated the period of no return in the British-American quarrel. To evade the tea duty, Americans had been smuggling Dutch tea, reducing the sale of the Company's tea by almost two-thirds. To rescue the Company, whose solvency was essential to London for an amount of £400,000 a year, Lord North devised a scheme by which the surplus tea piling up in Company warehouses could be sold directly to America, skipping England and the English customs duty. If the duty in America was reduced to 3d. a pound, the tea could be sold at 10s. instead of 20s. a pound. Considering the Americans' known extraordinary fondness for tea, the lowered price was expected to overcome their patriotic resistance to paying duty. A million Americans reportedly drank tea twice a day, and according to one report from Philadelphia "the women are such slaves to it that they would rather go without their dinner than without a dish of tea." Since the collapse of Non-Importation, restored trade, apart from tea, had mollified both sides and many people thought past troubles were now a bygone issue.

The Tea Act of May 1773 accordingly passed by Parliament with no expectation of another American outburst.

That the British were invincibly uninformed—and stayed uninformed—about the people they insisted on ruling was a major problem of the imperial-colonial relationship. Only some fifteen years had elapsed, Colonel Barré told Josiah Quincy, agent of Massachusetts, since two-thirds of the people of Great Britain were of the opinion that Americans were Negroes. Americans in London like Arthur Lee of Virginia, who had been partly educated in England and lived there for ten years prior to hostilities, and Henry Laurens, a wealthy merchant-planter of Charleston and future President of the Continental Congress, and such other South Carolina planters as Ralph Izard and Charles Pinckney associated mostly with merchants and men of the City. Although friendly with Burke, Shelburne and other partisans, they had no entrée into aristocratic society, which in turn knew nothing of them.

Pamphlets and petitions, Dickinson's *Letters*, Jefferson's *Summary View of the Rights of British America* and many other polemics on issues and sentiments of the colonies were published in London, but the peers and country squires hardly read them. Special agents like Josiah Quincy were more often than not refused hearings in the Commons on one technical ground or another. "In *all* companies I have endeavored to give a true state of the affairs of the Continent and of the genuine sentiments of its inhabitants," Quincy wrote home, but he added no assurance of a successful effort. Fixed in the preconception of "our inherent pre-eminence," in Hillsborough's phrase, Englishmen held to the view of Americans as uncouth obstreperous trouble-makers, regardless of the example in their midst, among others, of Benjamin Franklin, as variously talented and politically sophisticated as anyone in Europe, and thoroughly dedicated to the goal of reconciliation.

The attitude of America's friends was also wide of the mark. Rockingham thought of Britain as the parent and the colonies as "the children [who] ought to be dutiful." Chatham shared this view, although if either had visited America, attended the colonial assemblies, experienced the mood of the people, he might have come away with some remedial knowledge. It is an astonishing fact that, apart from Army and Navy officers, no minister of a British government from 1763 to 1775, much less before or after, ever visited the trans-Atlantic provinces upon which they felt the empire depended.

They were more determined to maintain a firm hold because they believed that the Americans were bent on rebellion and their independence would mean England's ruin. Chatham's insistence on conciliation was based on his fear that if America were driven to resistance by force and the empire were lost, France or Spain would acquire it and "if this happens, England is no more." Losing that tremendous stake, she would be cut off from development as a world power. Murkily, the King had something of this in mind when he wrote, "We must get the Colonies in order before we engage our neighbors."

In another sense, too, Chatham felt, as many did, that England's fate was tied to the colonies, "for if liberty be not countenanced in America, it will sicken, fade and die in this country." That was the argument of liberty. The argument of power held that if untaxed, the colonies would attract many English skilled workmen and manufacturers to settle there, would prosper and eventually dominate, leaving old England "A poor deserted deplorable Kingdom." Letters to the press worried this theme, some predicting that America would soon surpass in population the mother country "and then how are we to rule them?" or even become the seat of empire after two centuries. If Americans outnumbered Englishmen, stated the *St. James Chronicle* on Christmas Eve 1772, then only natural interest and friendship in some form of commonwealth could keep America attached to Britain, so that united they might "defy the world in arms."

The Tea Act proved a startling disappointment. Instead of happily acquiescing in cheap tea, Americans exploded in wrath not so much from popular feeling as from agitation inspired by the merchants, who saw themselves eliminated as wholesalers and their trade ruined through underselling by the East India Company. Ship owners and builders, captains and crews, whose livelihood was in smuggling, also felt threatened. Political agitators, delighted to have a cause again, accommodated them. They raised the horrid cry of "Monopoly" about to grip America by a company notorious for its "black, sordid and Cruel Avarice." If established in tea, it would soon extend to spices, silks, chinaware and other commodities. Once India tea was accepted in America, the 3 d. duty would "enter the bulwark of our sacred liberties" and would accomplish Parliament's purpose of taxation for revenue; nor would its authors desist "till they have made a conquest of the whole."

Peace-makers in the colonies hoped to arrange return of the tea ships before any cargo was unloaded and duty paid. This was accomplished in ports other than Boston by raising the threat of mobs and frightening the Company's consignees into resigning as purveyors to the retail grocers. In Boston, two of the consignees were sons of Governor Hutchinson, who had come to believe in a firm stand against the agitators. They stood ready to take delivery. The first tea ship docked at a Boston wharf on 1 December 1773, followed by two more. Because unloaded cargoes after a stated period were liable to seizure by customs commissioners for nonpayment of duty, the patriots suspected the commissioners would sell the confiscated cargo under the counter for revenue. To forestall them and perhaps also to intimidate any hopeful purchasers, they boarded the ships during the night of 16 December and in the enterprise to be known forever after as the Boston Tea Party, slashed open the tea chests and dumped the contents into the water.

News of this criminal attack on property, which reached London as early as 20 January, exasperated the British. It wrecked the plan for quiet establishment of a revenue tax, jeopardized the finances of the East India Company and proved the people of Massachusetts to be incorrigible insurrectionists. Britain's interest might have suggested at this point a review of the series of increasingly negative results in the colonies with the aim of re-directing the by now alarming course of events. That would have required thought instead of mere reaction, and pause for serious thought is not a habit of governments. The ministers of George III were no exception.

They launched themselves instead upon that series of measures generally called the Coercive or Punitive Acts, and in America the Intolerable Acts, which served to advance antagonism in the direction it was already pointing and to pass the fork in the road at which another path might have led to another outcome.

As an act of war upon Crown property, the Tea Party was adjudged another case of treason. Judiciously deciding to avoid the embarrassment of the *Gaspée* procedure, the Cabinet chose instead to punish Boston as a whole by act of Parliament. Accordingly, a bill was presented to close the port of Boston to all commerce until indemnity had been paid to the East India Company and reparations to the customs commissioners for damages suffered, and until "peace and obedience to the Laws" was assured sufficiently that trade might be safely carried on and customs duly collected.

While preparing the bill, the Cabinet, having learned nothing from the ten years of angry protests since Grenville's first tax, expected, as always, no trouble. Ministers believed the other colonies would condemn the Bostonians' destruction of property, would not intervene on their behalf and might indeed be happy to absorb the tea diverted to their ports by the closing of Boston. Wooden-headedness enjoyed no finer hour. To respond angrily and positively to the grand larceny on the wharves was natural and lawful, but to suppose that the Boston Port Bill would contribute to control of the situation or to the stability of empire or be regarded with equanimity by Massachusetts' neighbors was to let emotional reaction prevail over every indication of recent evidence.

Emotionalism is always a contributory source of folly. It showed itself at this time in the savage glee of which Benjamin Franklin was made a target at the hearings in the affair of the Hutchinson letters. These letters to Thomas Whately, the Treasury Secretary, advising more emphatic measures to suppress the rebelliousness of Massachusetts had been acquired by Franklin sub rosa and when published caused Massachusetts, in a fury against Hutchinson, to petition Parliament for his dismissal as Governor. Wedderburn conducted the examination of Franklin in hearings on the petition in a chamber aptly called the Cock-pit before 35 members of the Privy Council, the largest number ever to attend such a hearing, and an eager audience of peers, M.P.s and other guests. They responded with snickering delight and open laughter as Wedderburn rose through sneers and jibes to heights of brilliant and malevolent invective depicting the most influential American in London as a thief and a traitor. Lord North was reported to be the only listener who did not laugh. Franklin was dismissed next day by the Crown from his post as Deputy Postmaster of the colonies, which did nothing to encourage the man who was the strongest advocate of accommodation, and Franklin did not forget. Four years later, when signing the Treaty of Alliance with France that confirmed the birth of his nation, he dressed himself in the same suit of Manchester velvet he had worn under Wedderburn's torment.

Sentiment against Boston was so strongly with the Government that the Port Bill excited no disapproval at its first two readings; even Barré and Henry Conway spoke in favor of firm action. At the third reading, opposition speakers found their voice, pointing out that other ports had sent the tea back to England and urging that Boston be given a chance to pay the indemnity before her commerce was cut off. The most important statement was made by a person with experience on the spot, former Governor George Johnstone of West Florida, who warned "that the effect of the present Bill must be productive of a General Confederation, to resist the power of this country." Few listened to his prophecy. Opposition speakers, admitted Burke, who was one of them, "made so little impression" that the House did not need to divide for the vote. In the Lords, Shelburne, Camden and the Duke of Richmond deplored the bill with no greater effect. The Boston Port Bill passed through Parliament like melted butter.

Three more Coercive Acts followed in rapid succession. First was the Massachusetts Regulatory Act, virtually annulling the charter of the Bay colony. Rights of election and appointment of officials, representatives, judges and juries and the basic right to summon town meetings, all that had been at "the sole disposal of her own internal government," in Burke's phrase, were taken over by the Crown acting through the Governor. Not unnaturally, this suggested to other colonies that what was done to Massachusetts could be done to them. The Administration of Justice Act followed, which allowed Crown officials accused of crime in Massachusetts who claimed they could not be assured a fair trial to be tried in England or in another colony. This was an insult considering that Boston had leaned over backward to give Captain Preston, commanding officer in the "Massacre," a fair trial with defense by John Adams and had acquitted him. Next, the annual Quartering Act added a new provision authorizing, in case of any refusal to furnish barracks, the billeting of troops in citizens' homes, taverns and other buildings. At the same time, General Gage was ordered to Boston to take over from Hutchinson as Governor.

The most furiously resented of the measures, though it was not one of the Coercive Acts, was the simultaneous Quebec Act extending Canada's boundaries to the Ohio River, where Virginia and other colonies had territorial claims. The Act also formulated terms of civil government in Canada providing for the right of taxation by Parliament, for trial without jury according to the French manner and for toleration of the Catholic religion. Since 95 percent of Canadians were Catholic, this was a surprisingly sensible measure of toleration, but it gave the colonists and their friends in England a fiery issue. Roars of "Popery" thundered. The Inquisition was forecast for Pennsylvania, the "carnage of a St. Batholomew's Day" foreseen in Philadelphia, the whore of Babylon invoked, a "Popish army" and "Popish hordes" pictured by Lord Camden as ready to subvert the liberties of the Protestant colonies. As for the elimination of trial by jury, it was declared by the *St. James Chronicle* "too scandalous a clause to have been framed by any Englishman." A motive for this strangely ill-timed act granting favors to the Canadians may have been the hope of winning their loyalty in order that they might help to check any American outbreak. Yet if any intention remained of calming and eventually reconciling the colonies, passage of the Quebec Act on top of the Coercive Acts was a perfect model of how not to proceed.

How much of the Government's ineptitude was ignorance and how much deliberate provocation, as the opposition firmly believed, is impossible to say. Governor Johnstone once remarked rather helplessly in the Commons that he noticed "a great disposition in this House to proceed in this business without knowing anything of the constitution of America." Ignorance was certainly a factor.

The measures of March–June 1774 roused the opposition to real apprehension and to explicit warnings of dire consequences. Coming use of force could be sensed and the prospect of its use against people of English blood and tradition appalled many. John Dunning, a liberal-minded lawyer who had served as Solicitor-General in Grafton's ministry and who would later summarize matters toward the end of the war in the memorable Dunning's Resolution, saw in the Coercive Acts a trend toward "war, severe revenge and hatred against our own subjects." It was the lack of chance of success that disturbed others. Major General William Howe, who had scaled the Heights of Abraham with Wolfe at Quebec, told his constituents while canvassing for the election of 1774 that the whole British Army together would not be enough to conquer America. General John Burgoyne, who also held a seat in Parliament, said he would like "to see America convinced by persuasion rather than the sword."

Ministers too were warned. Henry Laurens, when consulted by Dartmouth as to the probable effect of the Coercive Acts, prophesied, as had Governor Johnstone in Parliament, that the people "from Georgia to New Hampshire would be animated to form such an Union and phalanx of resistance" as had hitherto been thought only a miracle could accomplish. But the fate of warnings in political affairs is to be futile when the recipient wishes to believe otherwise. In formulating Cassandra's curse—that she would tell the truth and not be believed—the ancient Greeks showed their remarkable early insight into the human psyche.

In the debate of 19 April 1774, on a motion by the opposition for repeal of the tea duty, Burke delivered the foundation speech of his views on the American question. It was an immense peroration on the successive acts and repeals, the vacillations and equivocations, the empty menaces, false assumptions and history of colonial policy all the way back to the Navigation Acts and forward to "the distempered vigor and insane alacrity with which you are rushing to your ruin." Never, he said, "have the servants of the state looked at the whole of your complicated interests in one connected view. . . . They never had any system of right or wrong but only invented occasionally some miserable tale for the day in order meanly to sneak out of difficulties into which they had proudly strutted. . . . By such management, by the irresistible operation of feeble councils . . . they have shaken the pillars

of a commercial empire that circled the globe." Striking at the token
assertion of authority—what today would be called credibility—he
said, in words with a long echo, "They tell you that your dignity is tied
to it. . . . This dignity is a terrible encumbrance to you for it has of late
been ever at war with your interest, your equity and every idea of your
policy."

That "terrible encumbrance" has pursued policy-makers in every
century. Benjamin Franklin, a wise man and one of the few who derived
principles from political experience and were able to state them, wrote
during the Stamp Act crisis that it should not be supposed that honor
and dignity are better served "by persisting in a wrong measure once
entered into than by rectifying an error as soon as it is discovered."

In America, the Boston Port Bill ignited solidarity. In May, Rhode
Island issued the first call for an intercolonial congress, while Connecticut towns held indignation meetings and took vows to rush aid in
money and provisions to Boston and "to sprinkle American altars with
our hearts' blood" if occasion arose. The old Indian fighter and ranger
of the Seven Years' War, Colonel Israel Putnam, chairman of the
Connecticut Committee of Correspondence, personally drove 130
sheep 100 miles from his home in Pomfret to Boston. Baltimore sent
1000 bushels of corn and ultimately gifts were received from all thirteen colonies. Patriot leaders demanded a complete denial of tea
throughout the colonies, smuggling was stopped, the "hurtful trash"
was burned on village greens and unappetizing herb potions called
Liberty Tea substituted.

The summons to a congress was quickly supported by New York
and Philadelphia and brought acceptances from twelve colonies during
the summer. Many Americans had become convinced that, as Jefferson
wrote in a draft of instructions to the Virginia delegates to the congress,
Britain's series of oppressions "pursued unalterably through every
change of ministers, too plainly prove a deliberate and systematical plan
of reducing us to slavery."

This became an article of faith in America. George Washington
endorsed it, speaking of "a regular systematic plan [to] fix the shackles
of slavery upon us." Tom Paine maintained "it was the fixed determination of the British Cabinet to quarrel with America at all events" in
order to suppress her charters and control her progress in population
and property. The accusation was convenient because it justified the
ultimate rebellion, and indeed if Britain had really been pursuing a plan
to goad the colonies to insurrection in order to subjugate them, then her
conduct of policy becomes rational. Unhappily for reason, that version

cannot be reconciled to the repeals, the backings and fillings, the hap-hazard or individual decisions. Rather than "deliberate and systemati-cal," English policy, its critics complained, was exactly the opposite. "What enforcing and what repealing," cried Burke; "what bullying and what submitting; what doing and undoing; what straining and what relaxing. . . . Let us embrace some sort of system before we end this session. . . . Let us hold some sort of consistent conduct."

Believing, on the contrary, that England's policy *was* consistent, Americans moved toward the overt break. By uniting the colonies into a whole, the Coercive Acts accomplished the same cohesion in the adversary as the Japanese attack on Pearl Harbor accomplished two centuries later—and with ultimately the same result. The first Con-tinental Congress of 56 members representing all colonies except Georgia convened at Philadelphia in September 1774. They declared all acts of Parliament respecting the colonies since 1763 to have violated American rights and pledged themselves to renew Non-Importation until all were repealed. If there were no redress of grievances within a year, they would move to Non-Intercourse, that is, cessation of exports as well as imports. They adopted ten resolutions on the rights of self-government, including self-taxation by their own legislatures, and under pressure by the radicals, endorsed the Resolves taken by Suffolk County in Massachusetts, which declared the Coercive Acts to be unconstitu-tional and invalid, authorized no obedience until they were repealed and advised citizens to arm and form militia for defense if attacked. While acknowledging allegiance to the Crown, they considered themselves a "dominion" not subject to Parliament. In order not to alienate the con-servatives among them, they issued no call for independence, "a Hob-goblin of so frightful mien," declared John Adams, "that it would throw a delicate Person into Fits to look it in the face."

Some were ready, however, for the alternative, as Jefferson phrased it in his instructions to the delegates of Virginia, of "union on a generous plan." His conditions were that there must be no limitation of the col-onies' external trade and no taxation or regulation of their properties "by any power on earth except our own." Joseph Galloway of Penn-sylvania, leader of the conservatives at the Congress, officially presented a similar plan of "Proposed Union between Great Britain and her Colonies" but it found few delegates to support it. They were men who had no wish to combine with a Britain they thought of as corrupt, decadent and hostile to liberty. "When I consider," wrote Franklin to Galloway, "the extreme corruption prevalent among all orders of men in this old rotten state" with its "numberless and needless places, enormous salaries, pensions, perquisites, bribes, groundless quarrels, foolish expeditions, false accounts or no accounts, contracts and jobs [that] devour all revenue . . ." he would fear more mischief than benefit from closer union.

As the crisis in relations worsened, the idea of union found advocates among progressive thinkers in England. In 1776, Adam Smith was to propose it in *The Wealth of Nations* as the means "to the prosperity, to the splendour, and to the duration of the empire." In the same year, Dr. Richard Price, intellectual leader of the Non-conformists, proposed Anglo-American union on a basis of equality in his *Observations on the Nature of Civil Liberty and War with America*. Wrapped in Enlightenment, he based his case on the civil liberties that "reason and equity and the rights of humanity give."

Here was the alternative to force on the one hand and rebellion on the other, although to say it was feasible at that time would be an overstatement. Majority opinion in Britain did not for a moment tolerate the idea of equality with the Americans, and federation could not have been reached in any case, for no one in power in England would have yielded the right to regulate trade. These were not, however, everyone's conditions, and had there been desire and will on both sides to achieve it, some form of federation might have been slowly worked out. At that time it was too soon. Fixed ideas and biases were against it and the technology of overseas communication was a hundred years away.

England saw treason in the unpleasing unity of the Continental Congress. By now, resort to force had become an accepted idea. Increasingly alarming letters had been coming from General Gage, who reported that "the Flame of Sedition" was spreading rapidly, that it was not confined to a "faction" of agitators but shared by the generality of freeholders and farmers in Massachusetts and its neighbors, that they were assembling arms and ammunition and even artillery, and finally that all New England must be considered in open rebellion. In November the King acknowledged that "blows must decide" whether the colonies were to be subject or independent, and that he was "not sorry that the line of conduct seems now chalked out."

The Cabinet reached a decision to send three warships with reinforcements, but with everyone busy canvassing for the election of that fall, action was postponed until the new Parliament should convene. Meanwhile within the Ministry, if not in the inner Cabinet, Viscount Barrington, the long-serving Secretary at War, entered a dissent. Although formerly in favor of a hard line toward America, he was one of the few in any group who allowed facts and developments to penetrate and influence their thinking. By 1774 he had come to believe that to coerce the colonies to the point of armed resistance would be disastrous. He had not turned pro-American or changed his political loyalties in any way; he had simply come to the professional conclusion, as he explained to Dartmouth in two letters of November and December 1774, that a land war in America would be useless, costly and impossible to win. Useless because it was plain that Britain could never successfully impose internal taxation; costly and impossible to win because conquered areas must be held by large armies and fortresses, "the expense of which would be ruinous and endless," besides producing "the horrors and bloodshed of civil war." Britain's only war aim was proving supremacy without being able to use it; "I repeat, our contest is merely a point of honor" and "will cost us more than we can ever gain by success."

Barrington proposed that rather than reinforcing the Army in Massachusetts, the troops should be withdrawn from Boston, leaving that city in its present "distracted state" until it should be better disposed to cooperate. Without small successes and the "violence of persecution" to animate the colonies, their rebelliousness would fade and they would eventually be ready to treat.

The earmark of so many follies—disproportion between effort and possible gain—and the "terrible encumbrance" of honor were here clearly expressed by Barrington, but since his office was not policy-making, merely administrative, his views had no effect. Required to implement a policy he did not believe in, he asked to resign, but the King and North held on to him, not wishing to reveal the doubters in their ranks.

In the City, popular opinion was strongly with the colonies to the extent that the freemen of London chose two Americans, Stephen Sayre of Long Island and William Lee of Virginia, as sheriffs. Candidates for the London seats were required to sign a pledge to support a bill giving America the right to elect its own Parliament and tax itself. With equal if opposite conviction a more notable Londoner, Dr. Samuel Johnson, expressed his view that the Americans were "a race of convicts and ought to be grateful for anything we allow them short of hanging." His thumping pamphlet *Taxation No Tyranny* delighted the country squires, the universities, the Anglican clergy and all the firmly anti-American community. Privately, however, he acknowledged to Boswell that "administration is feeble and timid" and, as the year went on, that "the character of our own government at present is imbecility."

The last chance for Britain to guard her own interest, to grasp an alternative that was feasible, was offered when Parliament convened in January 1775 by the outstanding statesman of his time, Lord Chatham, now ill and failing. On 20 January he moved for the immediate withdrawal of British forces from Boston as evidence that England could afford to "make the first advances for concord." He said the troops were provocative without being effective. They might march from town to town enforcing a temporary submission, "but how shall you be able to secure the obedience of the country you leave behind you . . . ?" Resistance to "your arbitrary system of taxation might have been foreseen." What forces now would be required to put it down? "What, my Lords, a few regiments in America and 17,000 or 18,000 men at home! The idea is ridiculous." To subdue a region extending over 1800 miles, populous in numbers, valorous and infused with the spirit of liberty would be impossible. To "establish despotism over such a mighty nation must be vain, must be fatal. We shall be forced ultimately to retreat: let us retreat when we can, not when we must."

It was the masterful eloquence of the old Pitt, but arrogant in his mastery, he had ignored political necessities, failed to assemble supporters to vote for his motion, failed even to tell anyone except Shelburne that he was going to speak or make a motion. All he told Shelburne was that he was going to knock on the door of "this sleeping and confounded ministry." His realism was hard, his foresight precisely on target, but the House did not want realities; it wanted to whip the Americans. Presented with Chatham's unexpected motion, "the opposition stared and shrugged; the courtiers stared and laughed," wrote Walpole, and the motion won only 18 votes against 68 nays.

Although his magic dominance was gone, Chatham had not lost the sense that "I know I can save this country and that I alone can." After privately consulting with Benjamin Franklin and other Americans, he introduced on 1 February a bill for settlement of the American crisis which provided for repeal of the Coercive Acts, freedom from taxation for revenue without consent, recognition of the Continental Congress, which would then be responsible for assessing the colonies for self-taxation to raise revenue for the Crown in return for its expenses, and an independent judiciary with juries and no removal of accused for trial in England. The regulation of external trade and the right to deploy an army when necessary were to be retained by the Crown. Lord Gower, leader of the Bedfords since the Duke's death, "rose in great heat" to condemn the bill as a betrayal of the rights of Parliament. "Every tie of interest, every motive of dignity, and every principle of good government," he said, required the assertion of "legislative supremacy entire and undiminished."

Thirty-two peers voted in favor of Chatham's plan of settlement, although it was of course rejected by the majority. He could not save an empire for the unwilling. Embittered by sneers in the debate, he vented his frustration in a summary indictment as savage and unsparing as any government is ever likely to hear: "The whole of your political conduct has been one continued series of weakness, temerity, despotism, ignorance, futility, negligence, and notorious servility, incapacity and corruption."

The next day the Government presented a bill declaring New England to be in rebellion and asking for augmented forces to reduce it to obedience. The nays in the Commons rose to 106, although the bill was quickly passed, together with a Restraining Act to bring economic pressure by excluding the New England colonies from the Newfoundland fisheries and prohibiting them from trade with any but British ports. The Cabinet nominated three general officers to serve in America: Major Generals William Howe, John Burgoyne, and Henry Clinton. That their future held recall and a surrender was then unimaginable.

At the same time, three regiments were sent to reinforce General Gage, and the King asked Sir Jeffery Amherst, former Commander-in-Chief during the Seven Years' War, to take command again of the forces in America on the ambivalent theory that as someone known and trusted in the colonies he might bring the "deluded people to due obedience without putting a dagger to their throats." Whether from doubts of the outcome or distaste of the policy, Amherst, though offered a peerage, declined to serve against the Americans, "to whom he had been so much obliged." He was not the last to make that refusal.

Suddenly North too seemed to vacillate. Pushed by Dartmouth, who was still trying for a peaceful settlement, he presented his own Conciliatory Proposition, which offered to exempt from taxation any individual colony that raised its own revenue for administration and defense in amounts that the King and Parliament approved. "Uncertainty, surprise, and distraction were seated on every countenance" until it became apparent that the plan was designed to divide the colonies against each other and that, since it offered no repeal of the Coercive Acts, it would not be accepted anyway.

Burke prolonged the last chance in a major effort and another enormous outpouring—for he never spoke in less than a torrent. His main point was "the absolute necessity of keeping up a concord of this empire by a unity of spirit." This could only be managed, he said, by possessing the sovereignty but not exercising it. Whether they liked it or not, the American spirit of liberty existed; their forebears emigrated because of it, and it remained stronger in the English colonists than probably in any other people on earth. "It cannot be removed, it cannot be suppressed, therefore the only way that remains is to comply with it, or if you please, to submit to it as a necessary evil." Here he reached the great prescription: "Magnanimity in politics is not seldom the truest wisdom; and a great empire and little minds go ill together." Let the Coercive Acts be repealed, let the Americans tax themselves "by grant and not by imposition." Allow them freedom and opportunity to grow rich and they will supply all the more resources against France and Spain.

Large minds are needed for magnanimity. George III and his ministers and their majority in Parliament, heedless of reason and their ultimate interest, proceeded on their course toward suppression. It was plain that even if they should win, which experienced soldiers like Amherst and Howe thought doubtful, they would lose through the enmity created. This was not a hidden perception. "It is that kind of war in which even victory will ruin us," wrote Walpole at this hour to his friend Horace Mann. Why were King and Cabinet blind to that outcome? Because they could think no further ahead than affirming supremacy and assumed without thinking about it that military victory over the "rabble" was a matter of course. They never doubted that Americans must succumb to British arms. This was the governing factor. A Colonel Grant, who said he had served in America and knew the Americans well, assured the House of Commons that "they would not fight. They would never dare to face an English army and did not possess any of the qualifications necessary to make a good soldier." The House of Lords heard the same kind of thing. Lord Sandwich, replying to an opposition member who warned that the colonies would draw on unlimited numbers, said fatuously, "What does that signify? They are raw undisciplined cowardly men," and the more the better because "if they did not run away, they would starve themselves into compliance with our measures." He and his colleagues were glad to have the interminable quarrel with the colonies finally settled by force, which to those who feel themselves stronger always seems the easiest solution.

Further, they continued to believe, as Lord Gower put it, that the rebellious language of the Americans "was the language of the rabble and a few factional leaders," and that the delegates to the Continental Congress, "far from expressing the true sense of the respectable part of their constituents," had been chosen "by a kind of force in which people of consequence were afraid to interpose." While there may have been a certain validity to his idea about the people of consequence, it was not as determining or as general as he supposed.

Lazy preparation was a product of these assumptions. Although the coming of hostilities was a predictable consequence of the Coercive Acts of the year before, no measures for military readiness had been undertaken in the interim. The swaggering Sandwich, long an advocate of forceful action, had done nothing as First Lord of the Admiralty to prepare the Navy, essential for transportation and blockade; in fact, he had reduced its strength by 4000 men, or a fifth of the total, as late as December 1774. "We took a step as decisive as the passage of the Rubicon," General Burgoyne was to say some months later, "and now find ourselves plunged at once in a most serious war without a single requisition, gunpowder excepted, for carrying it on."

In April 1775, General Gage, upon learning of a large quantity of rebel arms stored at Concord, twenty miles away, took the obvious decision to despatch a force to destroy the stores. Despite his attempted secrecy of movement, the warning signal lights flashed, the messengers rode, the Minute Men gathered at Lexington, exchanged fire and were scattered. While the redcoats marched on to Concord, the alerted countryside rose, men with their muskets poured in from every village and farm, and engaged the returning British troops in relentless pursuit with deadly accuracy of fire until the redcoats themselves had to be rescued by two regiments sent out from Boston. "The horrid Tragedy is commenced," sadly acknowledged Stephen Sayre when news of the event reached London.

That actual war had commenced beyond retrieval seemed still uncertain in England, and the event inspired a last impassioned appeal to common sense from John Wesley, the Methodist leader. In a letter to Lord Dartmouth on 14 June, he wrote, "Waiving all considerations of right and wrong, I ask is it common sense to use force toward the Americans? Not 20,000 troops, not treble that number, fighting 3,000 miles away from home and supplies could hope to conquer a nation fighting for liberty." From the reports of his preachers in America he knew that the colonists were not peasants ready to run at the sight of a redcoat or the sound of a musket, but hardy frontiersmen fit for war. They would not be easily defeated. "No, my Lord, they are terribly united. . . . For God's sake," Wesley concluded, "Remember Rehoboam! Remember Philip the Second! Remember King Charles the First!"

5. "... A Disease, a Delirium":
1775-83

Crisis does not necessarily purge a system of folly; old habits and attitudes die hard. Conduct of the war by the Government was to be marked by sluggishness, negligence, divided counsel and fatal misjudgments of the opponent. Lax management at home translated into lax generalship in the field. Generals Howe and Burgoyne had been disbelievers to start with; when Howe was in command his indolence became a byword. Other military men doubted the use of land forces to conquer America. The Adjutant-General, General Edward Harvey, had judged the whole project to be "as wild an idea as ever controverted common sense."

Ministers underestimated the task and the needs. Materials and men were inadequate, ships unseaworthy, too few and short of able seamen; problems of transport and communication were unappreciated in London, where direction of the war was retained at a distance that required of two to three months for letter and reply. Overall, performance was affected by the unpopularity of a war against fellow-subjects. "The ardor of the nation in this cause," acknowledged Lord North after Lexington and Bunker Hill, "has not arisen to the pitch one could wish." Meager results in recruiting, with fewer than 200 enlistments in three months, led to the mercenary employment of Hessians from Germany (amounting ultimately to one-third of all British forces in America). While employment of mercenaries was customary in England's wars at a time when military service was very low in the esteem of the common man, the use of the Hessians did more than anything else to antagonize the colonists, convince them of British tyranny and stiffen their resolve. The American Revolution, given its own errors and failures, cabals and disgruntlements, succeeded by virtue of British mishandling.

It was not until four months after Lexington and Concord, and a month after news of the battle of Bunker Hill, that America was declared in "open and avowed rebellion," the interim being consumed by ambivalent policies, quarrels over office and customary absences for the grouse and salmon season. The King, during this time, had been pressing for a declaration of rebellion and of determination to prosecute "with vigor every measure that may tend to force those deluded people into submission." Lord Dartmouth as Secretary for the Colonies was still seeking any opening for a non-violent settlement; moderates outside the Cabinet and the experienced under-secretaries hoped to avert a break; the Bedfords were hot for action; Lord Barrington was insisting that the colonies could be subdued by naval action alone through blockade and interruption of trade; the brothers Howe—General Sir William and Admiral Lord Richard—named Commanders-in-Chief respectively of the land and sea forces in America, believed a negotiated settlement preferable to a fight and were seeking joint appointment as peace commissioners to accomplish this purpose; Lord North, averse to the definitive, was trying to delay anything irreversible.

Against the pressure of the Bedford Cabinet and the King, he had to give way. His Majesty's Proclamation for Suppressing Rebellion and Sedition was issued on 23 August. In announcing the Americans' "traitorous" levying of war upon the Crown, it clung to the view that the uprising was the work of a conspiracy of "dangerous and ill-designing men," in spite of the stream of reports from General Gage and governors on the spot that it was inclusive of all kinds and classes. Insistence on a rooted notion regardless of contrary evidence is the source of the self-deception that characterizes folly. By hiding the reality, it underestimates the needed degree of effort.

Meanwhile, in Philadelphia moderates of the Continental Congress succeeded in obtaining the Olive Branch Petition, which professed loyalty and allegiance to the Crown, appealed to the King to halt hostilities and repeal the oppressive measures enacted since 1763, and expressed the hope that a reconciliation might be worked out. George III's refusal to receive the petition when it reached London in August and his Proclamation for Suppressing Rebellion, which followed within a few days, effectively terminated the American overture, for what it was worth. In Parliament, a motion by the opposition to consider the Olive Branch a basis for negotiation met with the usual rejection by the majority.

Following the Proclamation, the definitive act was the removal of Dartmouth to the office of Lord Privy Seal and his replacement as Secretary for the Colonies by a vigorous advocate of "bringing the rebels to their knees" by armed force, Lord George Germain. A Sack-ville of Knole by birth* and younger son of the 7th Earl and 1st Duke of Dorset, he had overcome a strange history of court-martial and ostracism to maneuver himself into favor with the King and, by plying him with the advice he wanted to hear, to gain the critical American post in the Cabinet.

As a Lieutenant-General and commander of the British cavalry at the battle of Minden in 1759, Lord George had inexplicably refused to obey the order of his superior, Prince Ferdinand of Brunswick, to lead a cavalry charge to finish off a victory over the French. Dismissed from the service, called a coward by society, tried for disobedience to orders, he was declared by verdict of the court-martial "unfit to serve His Majesty in any military capacity whatever," the sentence being re-corded in the order book of every British regiment. "I always told you," wrote his poor half-mad brother Lord John, "that my brother George was no better than myself."

Although the tag of cowardice fitted queerly with a strenuous mili-tary career of more than twenty years, Lord George never explained his conduct at Minden. Hard and arrogant, he stemmed from one ances-tor who "lived in the greatest splendour of any nobleman in England," from a grandfather who avoided a charge of murder only by the friendly intercession of Charles II, from a father created a Duke when George was four years old, whose house was so crowded with suitors and visitors on a Sunday as to give it the appearance of a royal levee. Not a likable man, Lord George had already made enemies by his criticisms of fellow-officers, yet he was able after some years, with Sack-ville support and an aggressive will, to rise above disgrace and retrieve the status owed to his rank and family. Made harder if not wiser by his experience, he was now to become the minister in active charge of the war.

Opposed like the rest of the Cabinet and the King's friends to any effort at conciliation, Lord George resisted rigorously the plan of a peace commission to treat with the colonies. When Lord North carried this point, to which he was previously committed, Germain insisted on drafting the instructions. His terms required the colonies to ac-knowledge, prior to a parley, the "supreme authority of the legislature to make laws binding on the Colonies in all cases whatsoever." Since their consistent rejection of this principle for ten years was what had

---

* The surname Germain was adopted in 1770 upon an inheritance from a family friend by that name.

led them to rebellion, it was fairly obvious, as Lord North pointed out, that this formula would condemn the peace commission to failure. Dartmouth said flatly he would resign as Privy Seal if the instructions stood; North hinted that he would go if his stepbrother did.

Interminable discussions of the terms followed: whether the phrase "in all cases whatsoever" should be in or out; whether colonial acceptance of the supremacy principle must precede or be part of negotiations; whether the commissioners should have discretionary powers; whether Admiral Howe should hold both the naval command and membership on the peace commission. Mingled with these disputes were intrigues about who should fill several court and sub-Cabinet posts from which opponents of the war had resigned, while Parliament, upon reconvening in January 1776, spent its time arguing over contested elections and the high prices charged by German princes for the hire of their troops. The peace proposals as finally settled went no further than North's conciliation plan of the year before, already spurned by the Continental Congress. Neither King nor Cabinet had any thought of considering American terms for a form of autonomy under the Crown; the peace commission was intended mainly for public effect and the still persisting illusion of dividing the colonies. Under Germain's domineering direction, wrote Franklin's friend the scientist Dr. Joseph Priestley, "anything like reason and moderation" could not be expected. "Everything breathes rancor and desperation."

By the time terms and appointments were settled in May 1776, events had made them obsolete. Thomas Paine's pamphlet *Common Sense*, calling boldly for independence, had electrified the colonists, convinced thousands of the necessity of rebellion and brought them with their muskets to the recruiting centers. George Washington had been named Commander-in-Chief; Fort Ticonderoga had yielded to Ethan Allen's company of 83 men; General William Howe, prompted by the Americans' remarkable hauling of cannon from Ticonderoga to Dorchester Heights, had been forced to evacuate Boston; British forces in full combat were gaining in the south and in Canada. In June the Continental Congress heard a resolution offered by Richard Henry Lee of Virginia that the United Colonies "are, and of right ought to be, free and independent States." On 2 July the formal Declaration of Independence was voted without dissent, with revisions added in a second vote on 4 July.

In September, after Howe's victory in the battle of Long Island, his brother the Admiral arranged in his alternate capacity as peace commissioner a conference with Franklin and John Adams representing the

Continental Congress, but as he had no authority to negotiate unless the colonies resumed allegiance and revoked the Declaration of Independence, the meeting was fruitless. So passed on both sides the attempt to forestall and then reverse the rupture.

Opponents of the war were vocal from the beginning although outnumbered by the war's supporters. Following Amherst's example, others in the Army and Navy refused to serve against the Americans. Admiral Augustus Keppel, who had fought throughout the Seven Years' War, declared himself out of this one. The Earl of Effingham resigned his Army commission, unwilling to bear arms in what "is not so clear a cause." Chatham's oldest son, John, serving with a regiment in Canada, resigned and came home, while another officer who remained with the Army in America expressed the opinion that because "This is an unpopular war, men of ability do not choose to risk their reputations by taking an active part in it." This freedom of action found its justifier in General Conway, who declared in Parliament that although a soldier owed unquestioning obedience in foreign war, in case of domestic conflict he must satisfy himself that the cause is just, and he personally "could never draw his sword" in the present conflict.

Animating these sentiments was the belief that the Americans were fighting for the liberties of England. Interdependent, both would either be "buried in one grave," said the opposition speaker, Lord John Cavendish, or endure forever. London's four members in Parliament and all its sheriffs and aldermen remained steadfast partisans of the colonies. Motions were made in both the Commons and the Lords opposing the hiring of foreign mercenaries without prior approval by Parliament. The Duke of Richmond moved in December 1776 for a settlement based on concessions to America, whose resistance he termed "perfectly justifiable in every political and moral sense." A public subscription was raised for the widows and orphans and parents of Americans "inhumanly murdered by the King's troops at or near Lexington and Concord."

Recognizing the contradiction of self-interest in the American war, a political cartoon of 1776 pictured the British lion asleep while ministers were busily engaged in slaughtering the goose that lays the golden egg. Observers like Walpole saw the contradiction too. Whether America was conquered or lost, Britain could expect "no good issue," for if governed by an army, the country, instead of inviting settlers and trade, "will be deserted and a burden to us as Peru or Mexico with all their mines have been to Spain. . . . Oh the folly, the madness, the guilt of having plunged us into this abyss!" Even Boswell in private thought the measures of the Government were "ill-digested and violent" and the ministry "mad in undertaking this desperate war."

Governing opinion in support of the war was no less forward and more general. Not all would have joined in Dr. Johnson's intemperate outburst, "I am willing to love all mankind *except an American*," or gone to the extreme of absurdity of the Marquess of Carmarthen, one of the King's friends, who demanded in a debate, "For what purpose were [the colonists] suffered to go to that country, unless the profit of their labor should return to their masters here?" But gradations of such sentiments were widely shared. (A notable factor in the British attitude was a bland ignorance of how and why the colonies had been settled.)

Business sentiment was expressed by Bristol, Burke's constituency, which he addressed in his *Letter to the Sheriffs of Bristol* with implacable logic and small effect, for the merchants, tradesmen and clergy of the busy port sent a loyal address to the King urging firm coercion. Landed gentry and fashionable society agreed. All motions of the opposition were routinely defeated in Parliament, where the majority sustained the Government faithfully, not merely from purchased loyalty but from the gruff conviction of the country party that supremacy must be made good and the colonies brought to submit.

The impotence of the opposition, which numbered about a hundred, was owed not only to the power of the incumbents but to their own lack of cohesion. Chatham, sunk in another period of debility, was out of combat from the spring of 1775 to the spring of 1777 but, like Hamlet, not so mad that when the wind was in the right quarter, he failed to know a hawk from a handsaw. After the American Declaration of Independence, he predicted to his physician, Dr. Addington, that unless England changed her policy, France would espouse the cause of the Americans. She was only waiting until England was more deeply engaged in this "ruinous war against herself" before taking an overt part.

Yet when active, Chatham always played his own hand, scorning association. His arrogance and his refusal to act as a functioning leader left the opposition subject to separation and to the vagaries of its chief figures. Richmond, who had emerged as the most aggressive and outspoken voice in the Lords, hated Chatham and was not temperamentally either a leader or a follower. Charles James Fox, rising young star of the opposition, glittered in the Commons with wit and invective, as Townshend once had, but he too played a solo role. Others were ambivalent. Though believing in the justice of the American cause, they could not help fearing that a victory for American democracy represented a threat to parliamentary supremacy and a dangerous stimulus to the Reform movement.

To feel dismayed by their own government and always to be out-voted were dispiriting. Richmond confessed it in replying to Rocking-ham, who was trying to maintain the opposition front and had sum-moned him to come to vote on a bill prohibiting trade with the thirteen colonies during the rebellion. "I confess I feel very languid about this American business," he wrote. There was no use going on opposing this bill and that; "the whole system must be opposed." He did not come down to London and later took himself off to France to deal with legalities regarding a French peerage he possessed. It might be "a happy thing to have," he wrote to Burke, for the day might not be distant "when England will be reduced to a state of slavery," and if he were "among the proscribed . . . and America not be open to us, France is some retreat, and a peerage here is something." With the French Revolution coming in the next decade, probably no historical prophecy has ever been so upside down. "About English politics," Richmond concluded, "I must freely confess to you that I am quite sick and wore out with the too melancholy state of them."

Rockingham, as leader, grew so frustrated that in 1776 he proposed a "secession" by opponents of the war, that is, a deliberate absenting of themselves from Parliament as their most visible protest against minis-terial policy. Solidarity on this issue too was unobtainable; only his own followers agreed. Dignified and stately, the Rockingham Whigs retired to their estates, but after a year of ineffectiveness drifted back. They were "amiable people," wrote Charles Fox to Burke, but "unfit to storm a citadel." Burke, making an essential point about these men as minis-ters, replied that their virtues were the result of "plentiful fortunes, assured rank and quiet homes."

Submission of the rebels was no nearer. For all their disadvantage in shortage of arms and supplies and of trained and disciplined troops and in the short-term enlistments that were their most disabling factor, they had a cause to fight for, a commander of heroic stature and unflinching will and occasional stunning limited victories as at Trenton and Prince-ton to reinvigorate morale. Britain's enemies abroad were supplying arms and British resort to deliberate wrecking and pillage of property and to recruitment of Indians for terrorist tactics stimulated American fighting spirit when it faded under hardship. British overestimation of the internal support to be expected from Loyalists and the failure—which owed something still to scorn of colonials even on their own side —to mobilize and organize a Loyalist fighting force left them depen-

dent on the long trans-Atlantic haul of Europeans. Fear that France and
Spain would take advantage of their trouble by a naval offensive or even
invasion required maintenance of troops for home defense and hard-to-
spare ships in home waters. The drain of the whole enterprise alarmed
many. "The *thinking* friends of the Government are by no means san-
guine," wrote Edward Gibbon, who had been elected to Parliament in
1774 as a supporter of North.

In February 1777, General Burgoyne came home to plan with
Germain a knockout campaign that by effecting a juncture on the Hudson of British forces coming down from Canada and others coming up
from New York would cut off New England from the rest of the colonies and end the war before the next Christmas. Burgoyne returned
to lead the northern force in a march pointed at Albany, but the pincer
movement suffered from a fatal deficiency in having only one arm. The
bulk of the southern arm under the Commander-in-Chief, Sir William
Howe, who had designed his own campaign without reference to his
colleague, was moving in the other direction, against Philadelphia. Sir
Henry Clinton, in command of the remaining forces in New York,
could not move up the Hudson without the main Army. Burgoyne had
started in June. As the summer progressed, reports were disquieting:
Burgoyne's supplies were dwindling dangerously; a foray to capture
stores at Bennington was sharply defeated; an American Army was
gathering in strength. Howe was still occupying himself in Pennsylvania; Clinton, though given to fits of paralysis of will, made a last-
minute move northward in desperation; no juncture had yet been made.
Washington, engaged against Howe outside Philadelphia and discovering from his movements that there was no danger of Howe's turning
north, wrote to General Putnam on learning of the victory at Bennington that he hoped now "the whole force of New England will turn out
and . . . intirely crush General Burgoyne."

Less concerned with these events than with the threat of France,
Lord Chatham rose to his feet on 20 November 1777 to demand an
"immediate cessation of hostilities." Speaking before news was known
of the event that was to mark the watershed of the war and justify his
argument, he said, "I know that the conquest of English America is an
impossibility. You cannot, I venture to say it, you CANNOT conquer
America. . . ." Defense of unalienable rights was not rebellion. The
war was "unjust in its principles, impracticable in its means, and ruinous
in its consequences." The employment of "mercenary sons of rapine
and plunder" had aroused incurable resentment. "If I were an American
as I am an Englishman, while a foreign troop was landed in my country,

I would never lay down my arms, never—never—never!" By insisting on submission, Britain would lose all benefit from the colonies through their trade and their support against the French and gain for herself only renewed war against France and Spain. The only remedy was to terminate hostilities and negotiate a treaty of settlement. Chatham did not call for recognition of American independence as a condition of settlement, for he believed to his dying day in the unalterable relationship of colony and Crown, and, in paraphrase of a successor, would have gladly declared that he had not served as First Minister to acquiesce in the liquidation of the British empire. His proposal of an end to hostilities made no appeal to the Lords, who rejected his motion by four to one.

In the Commons, Charles Fox pursued the same vein in a military analysis that was to be uncannily verified. Conquest of America, he said, was "in the nature of things absolutely impossible" because there was "a fundamental error in the proceedings which would forever prevent our generals from acting with success"—that they were placed too far apart to aid each other. Twelve days later a courier arrived with the awful report that General Burgoyne with all that was left of his battered, starving and outnumbered force had surrendered to the Continental Army at Saratoga near Albany on 17 October. General Clinton, who had advanced no farther than Kingston, fifty miles below Albany, had on the previous day turned back to New York for reinforcements.

The result of Saratoga was a matchless encouragement to American morale that warmed the thin blood of survival through the snows and miseries of that winter at Valley Forge. Saratoga lost the British, through casualties and the terms of surrender, which required Burgoyne's men to lay down their arms and be shipped back to Britain under pledge not to serve again in the war against America, an entire army of almost 8000. Above all, it realized Britain's greatest dread, the entry of the French into the war in alliance with America. Within two weeks of the news of the surrender, the French, in fear that the British might now offer acceptable peace terms to their former colonies, hastened to inform the American envoys of their decision to recognize the newborn United States, and three weeks later of their readiness to enter into alliance. The treaty, which for its share in bringing into existence a new nation was one of the most momentous in history, was negotiated in less than a month. Besides recognizing American independence and including the usual articles of amity and commerce, it provided that in the event of war between Britain and France, neither of the treaty partners would make a separate peace.

Chatham's prediction of French entry was now confirmed, but even before this was known he rose in the House of Lords on 11 December 1777 to declare again his view that England had engaged herself in a "ruinous" war. The nation had been betrayed into it, he said in a devastating summary that could apply to wars and follies of many ages before and since, "by the arts of imposition, by its own credulity, through the means of false hope, false pride and promised advantages of the most romantic and improbable nature."

In England, the incredible fact of a British Army surrendering to colonials stunned government and public and awoke many who had hardly concerned themselves about the war until then. "You have no idea what effect this news has had on the minds of people in town," wrote a friend to George Selwyn. "Those who never felt before, feel now. Those who were almost indifferent to American affairs are now awakened out of their lethargy and see to what a dreadful situation we are reduced." Stocks fell, "universal dejection" ruled the City, people murmured of a "disgraced nation" and talked of a change of government. Gibbon wrote that although the majority held in Parliament, "if it had not been for shame there were not 20 men in the House but were ready to vote for peace," even "on the humblest conditions."

The opposition bounded into virulent attack, castigating every minister individually and the Government collectively for mismanagement of the war and the measures that had led to it. Burke accused Germain of having lost America through "wilful blindness"; Fox called for Germain's dismissal; Wedderburn, who came to Germain's defense, challenged Burke to a duel; Barré said the plan of campaign was "unworthy of a British minister and rather too absurd for an Indian chief." Even Germain himself was flustered but survived the onslaught with the King's and North's support. They could see that if they let responsibility be brought home to Germain, it would be carried next to his superiors—themselves.

The Government too survived on its carefully carpentered structure of votes. Although uneasy about the war, the country party were uneasier about change, and though burdened with a war that was costing them money instead of bringing in revenue, they sat tight. Only the King, encased in his armor of righteousness, was impervious to the general anxiety. "I know that I am doing my duty and therefore can never wish to retreat," he had told North at the beginning of the war, and that was all he needed to know. No actualities could dent the armor. The King was convinced of the rectitude and therefore the necessary triumph of his actions. Later, as fortunes faded, he believed that a victory for American independence would mean the dissolution of the empire under his sovereignty and he prayed Heaven "to guide me so to act that posterity may not lay the downfall of this once respectable empire at my door." The prospect of defeat under "my" command pleases no ruler, and rather than face it, George tried obstinately to prolong the war long after it held any hope of success.

Howe's resignation, Burgoyne's return, Clinton's mistrust and disillusion, recriminations and official inquiries followed in the wake of Saratoga. The generals, who blamed their failures on the ineptitude of the ministry, were treated with forbearance not only because of the general feeling that the fault indeed lay with Germain, but also because they held seats in Parliament and the Government had no wish to drive them into opposition. Germain's failure to coordinate Howe's campaign at Philadelphia with Burgoyne's on the Hudson was clearly the hinge of the disaster and like his strange conduct at Minden seemed to have no explanation—other than a languid attitude.

Afterward, to feed the general dislike of Germain, a story was advanced that during the initial planning, Germain on his way to his country estate had stopped at his office to sign despatches. His Under-Secretary, William Knox, had pointed out to him that no letter had been written to Howe acquainting him with the plan and what was expected of him in consequence. "His Lordship started, and D'Oyley [a second secretary] stared," and then hurriedly offered to write the despatch for his lordship's signature. Having "a particular aversion to being put out of his way on any occasion," Lord George brusquely refused because it would mean that "my poor horses must stand in the street all the time and I shan't be to my time anywhere." He instructed D'Oyley to write the letter to Howe enclosing Burgoyne's instructions, "which would tell him all that he would want to know." Expected to go by the same ship as the despatches, the letter missed it and did not reach Howe until much later.

It would be tempting to claim that the comfort of carriage horses lost America, but distance, time, uncertain planning and incoherent generalship were the greater faults. Lord George's nonchalant way with despatches was only a symptom of a larger carelessness. It would be tempting, too, to say that this carelessness might be traced to the overprivileged lives of Georgian ministers, but then, what of another famous failure of communications: when American commanders were not warned of probable attack on Pearl Harbor? Failure of communications appears to be endemic to the human condition.

. . .

The immediate necessity was to relieve Britain of a profitless war in order that she might be free to meet the French challenge, and the only way was settlement with the colonies. With rumors buzzing of a coming Franco-American treaty, North, who had lost hope of victory after Saratoga, was trying to put together another peace commission against the resistance of Germain, Sandwich, Thurlow and other diehards whose minds were set against any parley with the rebels. While North agonized over what terms could be offered—not so mortifying as to be rejected by Parliament yet sufficiently attractive to be accepted by the Americans—word was received through secret intelligence that the alliance of France and America had been signed.

Ten days later North presented to Parliament a set of proposals for the peace commission so extensive in concessions that had they been ceded before the war they could well have averted it altogether. They were virtually the same as Chatham's bill of settlement that Parliament had rejected the year before. They renounced the right to tax for revenue, agreed to treat with Congress as a constitutional body, to suspend the Coercive Acts, the Tea Act, and other objectionable measures passed since 1763, to discuss seating American representatives in the House of Commons and to appoint peace commissioners with full powers "to act, discuss and conclude upon every point whatever." They did not yield, as Chatham had not yielded, independence or control of trade; the intention was to reattach the colonies, not to give them up.

A "full melancholy silence" fell upon the House as it heard North's long explanation, which lasted two hours. He seemed to have abandoned the principles the Government had been maintaining for the past ten years. "Such a bundle of imbecility never disgraced a nation," commented Dr. Johnson acidly. Friends were confounded, opponents staggered, and Walpole, the Greek chorus, sobered. He called it an "ignominious" day for government and an admission "that the Opposition had been right from beginning to end." He thought the concessions were such as the Americans could accept, "and yet, my friend," he wrote to Mann, "such accommodating facility had one defect—it came too late." The French treaty had already been signed; instead of peace there would be greater war. The House was ready to approve the plan "with a rapidity that will do everything but overtake time past." He was right; historical mistakes are often irretrievable.

To abandon a policy that is turning sour is more laudable than ignominious, if the change is genuine and carried out purposefully. The peace commission was something less. North, ever amiable but uncertain, was anything but firm. Under the turmoil of debate and the wrath of the diehards in his Cabinet, he wavered, modified terms, withdrew the discretionary powers of the commissioners and promised there would be no discussion of independence; the Americans would have to treat "as subjects or not at all." He set twelve months from June (it was then March) as the time limit for the mission, which suggested no great anxiety to succeed. Indeed, the fortunes of war were sufficiently changeable and the American situation sufficiently uncertain as to allow the King and the diehards to persuade themselves they might still prevail.

Many suspected, as was said by John Wilkes (seated in Parliament at last), that the peace commission was only meant "to keep the minds of the people quiet here . . . not to regain the colonies." A show was needed to keep the Government's supporters from fading away. Fall of the Bedfords seemed possible and might have been forced if the opposition's political action had been as vigorous as their words. In debate they were magnificent, in effect, weak because incurably divided over the issue of independence. Chatham, followed by Shelburne and others, remained utterly and unalterably opposed to dismembering the empire he had brought to triumph in the Seven Years' War. Rockingham and Richmond had come to believe that the colonies were lost forever and that the only course was to acknowledge their independence "instantly and publicly" in order to win them away from France and concentrate all forces against the major opponent.

On 7 April 1778, Richmond moved in a speech of passion and urgency to request the King to dismiss the incumbent ministry, withdraw the troops from the colonies, recognize their independence and negotiate to "recover their friendship at heart if not their allegiance."

Chatham should have concurred because concentration against France was always his object and because it was obvious that the colonies' Declaration of Independence and the Articles of Confederation that had followed could not be annulled except by a military defeat, which Chatham himself had declared to be impossible. Yet personal outrage extinguished logic; the break-up of empire was to him intolerable. Informed by Richmond that he was going to move the recognition of independence, Chatham summoned all his flickering strength, invested all the remnants of his once great authority in a sad offensive against his own side and against history.

Supported by his nineteen-year-old son, soon to make the name of William Pitt again the awe of Europe, and by a son-in-law, he limped to his seat, as always in full dress, with his legs wrapped in flannel. Beneath a huge peruke, the piercing glance still gleamed from eyes sunk in an emaciated face. When the Duke of Richmond closed, Chatham rose, but his voice was at first inaudible and when the words became distinct, they were confused. He spoke of "ignominious surrender" of the nation's "rights and fairest possessions" and of falling "prostrate before the House of Bourbon." Then he lost track, repeated phrases, mumbled, while around him the embarrassed peers, whether in pity or respect, sat in silence so profound it seemed tangible. Richmond replied courteously. Unyielding, Chatham rose again, opened his mouth soundlessly, flung a hand to his chest, collapsed and fell to the floor. Carried to a nearby residence, he recovered enough to be taken to his country home at Hayes, where in the next three weeks he sank slowly toward death. At the end, he asked his son to read to him from the *Iliad* about the death of Hector.

Forgetting the great statesman's decline and failings, the country felt a sense of ominous loss. Parliament voted unanimously for a state funeral and burial in Westminster Abbey. "He is dead," wrote the unknown author of the *Letters of Junius*, for once forgoing his usual venom, "and the sense and honor and character and understanding of the nation are dead with him." Dr. Addington thought his death was the mercy of Providence, "that he might not be a spectator of the total ruin of a country which he was not permitted to save."

It is striking how often the prospect of losing America inspired predictions of ruin, and how mistaken they were, for Britain was to survive the loss well enough and go on to world domination and the apogee of imperial power in the next century. "We shall no longer be a powerful or respectable people," declared Shelburne, if American independence were recognized. On that day, "the sun of Great Britain is set." Richmond foresaw the Franco-American alliance as "a Measure which must be our ruin." Walpole scattered his letters with gloomy prognoses, predicting, "whatever way this war ends it will be fatal for this country," or just before the end, foreseeing dire consequences of defeat: "We shall be reduced to a miserable little island, and from a mighty empire sink into as insignificant a country as Denmark or Sardinia!" With her trade and marine gone, Britain would lose the East Indies next, and "then France will dictate to us more imperiously than ever we did to Ireland."

These dark expectations derived from two assumptions of the age: that the trade with colonies was essential to the prosperity of Britain, and that the Bourbon monarchies of France and Spain were a dangerous threat. Though only eleven years ahead, the French Revolution was as yet unimaginable; rather, Englishmen felt themselves to be in a

stage of decline. Complaining of public apathy in a letter to Rockingham, Burke wrote that without a great change in national character
and leadership, the nation could slide down "from the highest point
of grandeur and prosperity to the lowest state of imbecility and mean-
ness. . . . I am certain that if great and immediate pains are not taken
to prevent it, such must be the fate of this country." Since no conscious
effort can arrest a national slide if it is indeed taking place, Burke in this
instance was talking nonsense as, given his enormous outpouring of
words, he frequently did.

Chatham's death in May opened an opportunity for Rockingham
to assert leadership, unite factions, win over adherents of the Government who were growing doubtful of the war and its expenses. The
King had been advised that some changes were necessary, and this was
Rockingham's chance to press for office on a policy of ending hostilities and recognizing the inevitable independence of the colonies. Fox
tried to persuade the hesitant Marquess of this course, suggesting that
he propose a partial replacement of ministers to the King so as not to
upset him and to retain his support. To refuse office if offered "in a
manner consistent with his private honor," Fox said, "was irreconcilable
with the duty of a public man." Burke too tried to argue the theme of
consistent responsibility, but in both Rockingham and Richmond, although they saw the issues clearly and perceived the remedies, the
sense of public duty tended to fade when the outlook was depressing
or the political necessities distasteful. Rockingham's followers were
unready, and his own principles and conditions for accepting office
precluded his obtaining it. The opposition "have been too inert," wrote
Walpole. The opportunity passed and the King's ministers, "though
despised everywhere and by everybody," according to Fox, "will still
continue ministers."

A peace commission was duly appointed headed by Frederick
Howard, 5th Earl of Carlisle, a young man of wealth and fashion, owner
of the splendid Castle Howard and otherwise qualified only as the son-
in-law of Lord Gower. He was to be assisted by two more experienced and hardheaded men: former Governor Johnstone, who sided
with the opposition, and William Eden, an accomplished politician
and under-secretary, manager of secret intelligence in the war, former
secretary of the Board of Trade, an old school companion of Carlisle
and a friend of Wedderburn, Germain and North. The combined
procedures of this group and of the Government that sent them
confirm the impression that a pervasive and peculiar folly was controlling events.

When, on reaching Philadelphia, the Commissioners requested a conference with representatives of the Continental Congress, they were told that the only terms to be discussed were withdrawal of British forces and recognition of American independence. Governor Johnstone thereafter attempted to bribe two leading figures of the Congress, Joseph Reed and Robert Morris, to persuade Congress to accept British conditions of negotiation. This insult, on being exposed, deepened American distaste for the British Government and created a scandal that caused Johnstone to resign from the Commission. In the meantime, without informing the Commissioners, Germain had issued secret orders to Sir Henry Clinton, Howe's successor, to send 8000 troops to strengthen the West Indies against France, thereby reducing his forces in Philadelphia from 14,000 to 6000, rendering the city no longer defensible, and requiring him in consequence to evacuate it.

Forced to move to New York, Carlisle was infuriated by the embarrassment and at not having been informed of Germain's intention in advance. The only instrument that could make the Americans come to a settlement was the prospect of forceful military action if they refused, and this sanction being now withdrawn, he was a toothless tiger. His little daughter Caroline, he wrote privately, could have told the Government that under such conditions the Peace Commission was a farce. "Our offers of peace," he wrote later, "were too much the appearance of supplications for mercy from a vanquished and exhausted state." It was not the last case of the peculiar foolishness of withdrawing forces while trying to make an enemy come to terms. In one of history's malicious ironies, the United States that was born of this folly repeated it against an enemy two hundred years later with the same result.

Carlisle and his colleagues put as good a face on their mission as possible, pointing out that the causes of the war were now canceled— the tea duty and other punitive acts repealed, "exemption from any tax by the Parliament of Great Britain" declared, representation in Parliament open for discussion and Congress itself recognized as a legitimate body. Short of recognition of independence, however, the Congress maintained its refusal to treat or even confer. In last resort, the Commissioners appealed to the colonies over the head of Congress to deal separately, in the belief that most Americans really wanted to return to their former allegiance. They issued a public proclamation on 3 October 1778, which, after reiterating the removal of the original grievances and promising pardon for all treasons committed before that date, tried to revive the threat of punitive action: for, when a country "mortgages herself and her resources to our enemies . . . Britain may by every means in her power destroy or render useless a connexion contrived for her ruin."

The real intention behind this threat was expressed in Carlisle's first draft of the proclamation, proposing that as a result of America's "malice and perfidy" in contracting with France and obstinacy in persevering in rebellion, Britain had no choice but to employ the "extremity of distress . . . by a scheme of universal devastation" and to apply "this dreadful system" to the greatest extent to which her armies and fleet could carry it. This argument, he believed, "will have *effect*," but he was evidently advised to moderate the language. So that the proclamation should be widely known, copies were sent to all members of the Continental Congress, to George Washington and all generals, to all provincial governors and assemblies, to ministers of the gospel and to commanders of the British forces and prison camps.

Since every colony had already suffered the deliberate pillage and destruction of homes and properties by British and Hessians, the burning of villages and the laying waste of farms, fields and timberlands, the threat from a weakened force carried no great terror. Rather, Congress recommended to state authorities that the British text should be published in local gazettes "more fully to convince the good people of these states of the insidious designs of the Commissioners." Having reached fiasco in six months, whether by design or blunder, the Peace Commission returned home in November.

Possibly the mission really was intended to fail. Yet Eden wrote to his brother that if "my wishes and cares" could accomplish it, "this noble country . . . would soon belong once more to Great Britain." He regretted "most heartily that our Rulers instead of making the Tour of Europe did not finish their education round the Coast and Rivers of the Western Side of the Atlantic." Privately he wrote to Wedderburn the astonishing confession that "It is impossible to see what I can see of this Magnificent Country and not go nearly mad at the long Train of Misconducts and Mistakes by which we have lost it."

It is a significant letter. Here is a member of inner government circles not only recognizing that the colonies were already lost, but that his government's mistakes had lost them. Eden's admission reveals the tragic side of folly: that its perpetrators sometimes realize that they are engaged in it and cannot break the pattern. The unavailing war was to continue at a cost of more lives, devastation and deepening hatred for four more years. During these years, George III simply could not conceive that he might preside over defeat. While Parliament and public grew increasingly sour on the war, the King persisted in its continuance partly because he believed the loss of empire would bring shame and ruin, and more because he could not live with the thought that it would be *his* reign that would forever bear the stigma of the loss.

In persisting, he could take heart from the fact that the Americans were often beset by trouble. Without central funds, Congress could not keep the armies in pay or supplies, which meant deserting soldiers and another winter of deprivation worse than Valley Forge, with rations at one-eighth normal and mutinies on more than one occasion. Washington was harassed by political cabals, betrayed by Benedict Arnold, disobeyed by General Charles Lee, subjected to scattered but savage warfare by Loyalist and Indian groups, disappointed by the failure of the attempt in combination with the French fleet to regain Newport and by British success in the Carolinas including the capture of Charleston. On the other hand, he had the immense accretion of French naval and land forces, which altered the balance of the war, and he had been joined by Baron von Steuben and other European professionals who drilled the ragged Americans into disciplined formations. In 1779 Congress appointed John Adams to negotiate peace on a basis of independence and total British withdrawal, but to the King and the hard-line ministers this was still unthinkable.

The English, under a First Minister who hated his position and longed only to be released and have nothing more to do with the war, and with a War Minister, Germain, whom he disliked and distrusted and who was still under a cloud of investigation, were not well equipped to win. They were incapable of forming an overall strategy for the war and could think only in terms of saving some colonies for the Crown, perhaps in the south, and of continuing a war of harassment and disruption of trade until the colonists were made to yield. Commanders and ministers alike, everyone but the King, knew this was illusion; that to subdue the country was beyond their power. Meanwhile, the French had appeared in the Channel. Though Lord Sandwich had boasted that he had 35 ships ready and manned and fit for war, Admiral Keppel was to find no more than six "fit to meet a seaman's eye" and dockyards empty of stores when the French entered the war. The battle off Ushant in June 1778 ended in a draw although the British took some encouragement in claiming it as a victory.

Worse than the war were political developments in England. Fueled by the American revolt, the movement for political reform spread through the country with demands for annual Parliaments, manhood suffrage, elimination of rotten boroughs, abolition of sinecures and contracts awarded to members of Parliament. The election of 1779 created bitter feeling between parties. Government majorities shrank. Protest reached a climax in the Yorkshire Petition of February 1780, which demanded a halt in appropriations and pensions until reforms were enacted. Petitions like Yorkshire's flooded Westminster from 28 other counties and many cities. Permanent reform associations were formed. The King was seen, as he had been since the days of Bute, as the promoter of absolutism. Dunning's bold resolution on the power of the Crown, that it "has increased, is increasing and ought to be diminished," was actually carried by a narrow majority with many country members among the ayes. In June, in response to the repeal of certain penal laws against the Catholics and the mad agitation of Lord George Gordon, the mobs gathered and burst in frightening riot. To cries of "No Popery!" and demands for repeal of the Quebec Act, they attacked ministers, tore their wigs, raided and robbed their houses, burned Catholic chapels, rushed the Bank of England and for three days held the city in terror until the troops gained control.

The unpopularity of the Government and the war grew with these events while other troubles mounted. Spain declared war on Britain, Holland was helping the rebels, Russia was disputing the British blockade of the colonies and the war in America itself was dragging along vainly.

In May 1781, Lord Cornwallis, commander in the south, set out to consolidate his front by abandoning South Carolina for Virginia, where he established a base at Yorktown on the coast at the mouth of Chesapeake Bay. From here he could maintain contact by sea with Clinton's forces in New York. Reinforced by other British troops in the area, his strength was 7500. Washington, stationed on the Hudson at this time, was joined by the Comte de Rochambeau with French troops from Rhode Island for a planned attack on New York. At this moment a communication from Admiral de Grasse in the West Indies informed them that he was sailing with 3000 French troops for Chesapeake Bay and could reach there by the end of August. Washington and Rochambeau turned and marched for Virginia, which they reached early in September, hemming in Cornwallis by land.

In the meantime, a British fleet met de Grasse in action off Chesapeake Bay and after some mutual damage returned to New York for repairs, leaving the French in command of the waters off Yorktown. Cornwallis was now blocked by land and sea. A desperate effort to break out in rowboats across the York River was frustrated by a storm. His only hope was return of the British fleet with help from

New York. The fleet did not come. The allied army of some 9000 Americans and nearly 8000 French moved forward against the Yorktown redcoats. Waiting for rescue, Cornwallis progressively drew in his lines while the besiegers advanced theirs. After three weeks the British situation was hopeless. On 17 October 1781, four years to the day after Saratoga, Cornwallis opened parley for surrender and two days later, in a historic ceremony, his army laid down its arms while the band played, as everybody knows, a tune called "The World Turned Upside Down." The fleet bringing Clinton's forces from New York arrived five days later, when it was too late.

"Oh God, it is all over!" cried Lord North when the news was brought to him on 25 November. Doubtless it was a cry of relief. That it was all over was not realized everywhere at once, but weariness of a losing struggle and the demand to make an end of it began to lap at the King. A barrage of motions by the opposition to terminate hostilities slowly gained votes as the country gentlemen, fearing more and more taxes, deserted the Government. In December a motion against the war gained 178 votes. In February 1782 the issue was brought to finality by the independent-minded General Conway. As he had been the first at the time of the Stamp Act to foresee "fatal consequences" lying in wait for the Government along the path it was taking, so he was now to sound their knell. He moved "That the war on the continent of North America might no longer be pursued for the impracticable purpose of reducing the inhabitants of that country to obedience." In a supporting speech as eloquent and effective as any heard in the House within living memory, he roused members to a fervor that swept them to within one vote of the majority: the tally was 194 to 193. The opposition, uniting at last behind the powerful scent of office, threw itself against the Government's fingerhold. Votes of censure followed one upon another, but after the peak reached by Conway's motion, the Government recovered just enough to hold on.

When Lord North, still held in office by the King, asked Parliament for a further large war loan, the House finally balked, the Government's majority broke and the King in his misery drafted, though he did not deliver, a message of abdication. In it he said that the change in sentiment in the Commons incapacitated him from conducting the war effectively and from making a peace that was not destructive "to the commerce as well as the essential rights of the British nation." At the same time he expressed his fidelity to the constitution, overlooking the fact that unless he abdicated, the constitution required him to obey the opinion of Parliament.

In March, the Government's fingerhold was pried loose. A bill authorizing the Crown to make peace passed on 4 March without a division. On 8 March the Government survived a vote of censure by only ten votes. On 15 March, on a motion expressing no confidence in ministers who had spent £100,000,000 to lose thirteen colonies, the margin was reduced to nine. Notice was given of two more motions of no confidence to follow. Earlier, Lord North had at last informed the King resolutely and definitively that he must go, and on 20 March, forestalling another test of confidence, his resignation and that of his Cabinet took effect. On 27 March a new government, headed by Rockingham, took office, with Shelburne and Fox as Secretaries of State, Camden, Richmond, Grafton, Dunning and Admiral Keppel in other posts, General Conway as Commander-in-Chief, and Burke and Barré as Paymasters of the Army and Navy, respectively.

Even with such partisans of America—as they had been when in opposition—now in office, Britain's acknowledgment of the nationhood of her former colonies was ungracious in the extreme. No minister, peer or even M.P. or Under-Secretary was named to conduct the peace negotiations. The single envoy sent to open preliminary talks with Franklin in Paris was a successful merchant and contractor for the British Army named Richard Oswald. A friend of Adam Smith, who had recommended him to Shelburne, he was to remain, unsupported by any formal delegation, the lone negotiator throughout.

Rockingham died suddenly in July 1782, to be succeeded as First Minister by Shelburne, who shrank from irrevocably and explicitly recognizing independence. He thought now of federation, but it was too late for statesmanship that Britain might earlier have used. The Americans insisted that their independent status was the sine qua non to be recognized in the preamble, and so it had to be. With some stalling, formal negotiations with Franklin, Adams, Laurens and John Jay began in September and the Treaty of Paris was concluded in November, to take effect in January 1783. The King's final comment gained nothing in graciousness. He felt less unhappy, he wrote to Lord Shelburne, about the "dismemberment of America from this Empire," in the knowledge "that knavery seems to be so much the striking feature of its inhabitants that it may not be in the end an evil that they become aliens to this Kingdom."

In summary, Britain's follies were not so perverse as the Popes'. Ministers were not deaf to rising discontent, because they had no chance to be; expressed by their equals, it rang in their ears in every debate and rudely impinged on them in the action of riots and mobs. They remained unresponsive by virtue of their majority in Parliament, but they worried about losing it, worked hard and spent heavily to hold it and could not enjoy the popes' illusion of invulnerability. Nor was private avarice their besetting sin although they were as subject as most men to the stings of ambition. Being accustomed to wealth, property and privilege and most of them born to it, they were not so driven by desire for gain as to make it a primary obsession.

Given the intention to retain sovereignty, insistence on the right to tax was justifiable per se; but it was insistence on a right "you know you cannot exert," and in the face of evidence that the attempt would be fatal to the voluntary allegiance of the colonies, that was folly. Furthermore, method rather than motivation was at fault. Implementation of policy grew progressively more inept, ineffective and profoundly provocative. Finally, it came down to attitude.

The attitude was a sense of superiority so dense as to be impenetrable. A feeling of this kind leads to ignorance of the world and of others because it suppresses curiosity. The Grenville, Rockingham, Chatham-Grafton and North ministries went through a full decade of mounting conflict with the colonies without any of them sending a representative, much less a minister, across the Atlantic to make acquaintance, to discuss, to find out what was spoiling, even endangering, the relationship and how it might be better managed. They were not interested in the Americans because they considered them rabble or at best children whom it was inconceivable to treat—or even fight— as equals. In all their communications, the British could not bring themselves to refer to the opposite Commander-in-Chief as General Washington but only as Mister. In his wistful regret that "our rulers" had not toured America instead of Europe to finish their education, William Eden was supposing that a view of the magnificence of the country would have made them more anxious to retain it, but nothing suggests that it would have improved their dealings with the people.

Americans were the settlers and colonizers of a territory deemed so essential that its loss would spell ruin, but the British wall of superiority precluded knowledge and promoted fatal underestimation. Meeting it during the peace negotiations, John Adams wrote, "The pride and vanity of that nation is a disease; it is a delirium; it has been flattered and inflamed so long by themselves and others that it perverts everything."

Unsuitability for government, while an unwilled folly, was a folly of the system, which was peculiarly vulnerable to the lack of an effective head. At his dynamic best, Pitt had engineered England's triumph in the Seven Years' War, and his son was to hold the controls effectively against Napoleon. In between, a hapless government shuffled and blundered. Dukes and noble lords in the reign of George III did not take well to official responsibility. Grafton, in his reluctance and sense of unfitness and once-a-week attendance, Townshend in his recklessness, Hillsborough in his arrogant obtuseness, Sandwich, Northington, Weymouth and others in their gambling and drinking, Germain in his haughty incapacity, Richmond and Rockingham in their moods of aloofness and devotion to their country pursuits, poor Lord North in his intense dislike of his job, made a mess of a situation that would have been difficult even for the wisest. One cannot escape the impression that the level of British intelligence and competence in both civil and military positions in the period 1763–83 was, on the whole, though not in every case, low. Whether that was bad luck or was owing to the almost exclusive hold of the ultraprivileged on decision-making positions is not clear beyond question. The underprivileged and the middle class often do no better. What is clear is that when incapacity is joined by complacency, the result is the worst possible combination.

Finally there is the "terrible encumbrance" of dignity and honor; of putting false value on these and mistaking them for self-interest; of sacrificing the possible to principle, when the principle represents "a right you know you cannot exert." If Lord Chesterfield could remark this in 1765 and Burke and others repeatedly plead for expediency rather than token display of authority, the government's refusal to see it for themselves must be designated folly. They persisted in first pursuing, then fighting for an aim whose result would be harmful whether they won or lost. Self-interest lay in retaining the colonies in goodwill, and if this was considered the hinge of British prosperity and yet incompatible with legislative supremacy, then supremacy should have remained, as so many advised, unexercised. Conciliation, Rockingham once said, could be brought about by "tacit compact" and much remaining "unascertained."

Although the war and the humiliation poisoned Anglo-American relations for a long time, Britain learned from the experience. Fifty years later, after a period of troubled relations with Canada, Commonwealth status began to emerge from the Durham Report, which resulted from England's recognition that any other course would lead to a repetition of the American rebellion. The haunting question that remains is whether, if the ministers of George III had been other than they were, some such status or form of union between Britain and

America might have been attainable and in that case might have created a preponderance of trans-Atlantic power that would have deterred challengers and perhaps spared the world the Great War of 1914–18 and its unending sequels.

It has been said that if the protagonists of *Hamlet* and *Othello* were reversed, there would have been no tragedy: Hamlet would have seen through Iago in no time and Othello would not have hesitated to kill King Claudius. If the British actors before and after 1775 had been other than they were, there might have been statesmanship instead of folly, with a train of altered consequences reaching to the present. The hypothetical has charm, but the actuality of government makes history.

Chapter Five

AMERICA BETRAYS HERSELF
IN VIETNAM

1. In Embryo:
1945-46

Ignorance was not a factor in the American endeavor in Vietnam pursued through five successive presidencies, although it was to become an excuse. Ignorance of country and culture there may have been, but not ignorance of the contra-indications, even the barriers, to achieving the objectives of American policy. All the conditions and reasons precluding a successful outcome were recognized or foreseen at one time or another during the thirty years of our involvement. American intervention was not a progress sucked step by step into an unsuspected quagmire. At no time were policy-makers unaware of the hazards, obstacles and negative developments. American intelligence was adequate, informed observation flowed steadily from the field to the capital, special investigative missions were repeatedly sent out, independent reportage to balance professional optimism—when that prevailed—was never lacking. The folly consisted not in pursuit of a goal in ignorance of the obstacles but in persistence in the pursuit despite accumulating evidence that the goal was unattainable, and the effect disproportionate to the American interest and eventually damaging to American society, reputation and disposable power in the world.

The question raised is why did the policy-makers close their minds to the evidence and its implications? This is the classic symptom of folly: refusal to draw conclusions from the evidence, addiction to the counter-productive. The "why" of this refusal and this addiction may disclose itself in the course of retracing the tale of American policy-making in Vietnam.

The beginning lay in the reversal during the last months of World War II of President Roosevelt's previous determination not to allow, and certainly not to assist, the restoration of French colonial rule in Indochina. The engine of reversal was the belief, in response to strident French demand and damaged French pride resulting from the German occupation, that it was essential to strengthen France as the linchpin in Western Europe against Soviet expansion, which, as victory approached, had become the dominant concern in Washington. Until this time Roosevelt's disgust with colonialism and his intention to see it eliminated in Asia had been firm (and a cause of basic dispute with Britain). He believed French misrule of Indochina represented colonialism in its worst form. Indochina "should not go back to France," he told Secretary of State Cordell Hull in January 1943; "the case is perfectly clear. France has had the country—thirty million inhabitants —for nearly a hundred years and the people are worse off than they were at the beginning. [They] are entitled to something better than that."

The President "has been more outspoken to me on that subject," Churchill informed Anthony Eden, "than on any other colonial matter, and I imagine that it is one of his principal war aims to liberate Indochina from France." Indeed it was. At the Cairo Conference in 1943, the President's plans for Indochina made emphatic capital letters in General Stilwell's diary: "NOT TO GO BACK TO FRANCE!" Roosevelt proposed trusteeship "for 25 years or so till we put them on their feet, just like the Philippines." The idea thoroughly alarmed the British and evoked no interest from a former ruler of Vietnam, China. "I asked Chiang Kai-shek if he wanted Indochina," Roosevelt told General Stilwell, "and he said point blank 'Under no circumstances!' Just like that—'Under no circumstances!' "

The possibility of self-rule seems not to have occurred to Roosevelt, although Vietnam—the nation uniting Cochin China, Annam and Tonkin—had before the advent of the French been an independent kingdom with a long devotion to self-government in its many struggles against Chinese rule. This deficiency in Roosevelt's view of the problem was typical of the prevailing attitude toward subject peoples at the time. Regardless of their history, they were not considered "ready" for self-rule until prepared for it under Western tutelage.

The British were adamantly opposed to trusteeship as a "bad precedent" for their own return to India, Burma and Malaya, and Roosevelt did not insist. He was not eager to add another controversy to the problem of India, which made Churchill rave every time the President raised it. Thereafter, with liberated France emerging in 1944 under an implacable Charles de Gaulle and insisting on her "right" of return, and with China as a trustee ruled out by her own now too obvious frailties, the President did not know what to do.

International trusteeship slowly collapsed from unpopularity. Roosevelt's military advisers disliked it because they felt it might jeopardize United States freedom of control over former Japanese islands as naval bases. Europeanists of the State Department, always pro-French, thoroughly adopted the premise of French Foreign Minister Georges Bidault that unless there was "whole-hearted cooperation with France," a Soviet-dominated Europe would threaten "Western civilization." Cooperation, as viewed by the Europeanists, meant meeting French demands. On the other hand, their colleagues of the Far East (later the Southeast Asia) desk were urging that the goal of American policy should be eventual independence after some form of interim government which could "teach" the Vietnamese "to resume the responsibilities of self-government."

In the struggle of policies, the future of Asians could not weigh against the Soviet shadow looming over Europe. In August 1944, at the Dumbarton Oaks Conference on post-war organization, the United States proposal for the colonies made no mention of future independence and offered only a weak-kneed trusteeship to be arranged with the "voluntary" consent of the former colonial power.

Already Indochina was beginning to present the recalcitrance to solution that would only deepen over the next thirty years. During the war, by arrangement with the Japanese conquerors of Indochina and the Vichy government, the French Colonial administration with its armed forces and civilian colonists had remained in the country as surrogate rulers. When, at the eleventh hour, in March 1945, the Japanese ousted them from control, some French groups joined the native resistance under the Viet-Minh, a coalition of nationalist groups including Communists which had been agitating for independence since 1939 and conducting resistance against the Japanese. SEAC (Southeast Asia Command), controlled by the British, made contact with them and invited collaboration. Because any aid to resistance groups would now unavoidably help the French return, Roosevelt shied away from the issue; he did not want to get "mixed up" in liberating Indochina from the Japanese, he irritably told Hull in January 1945. He refused a French request for American ships to transport French troops to Indochina and disallowed aid to the resistance, then reversed himself, insisting that any aid must be limited to action against the Japanese and not construed in the French interest.

Yet who was to take over when the war against Japan was won? Experience with China in the past year had been disillusioning, while the French voice was growing shrill and more imperative. Caught between the pressure of his Allies and his own deep-seated feeling that France should not "go back," Roosevelt, worn out and near his end, tried to avoid the explicit and postpone decisions.

At Yalta in February 1945, when every other Allied problem was developing strain with the approach of victory, the conference skirted the subject, leaving it to the forthcoming organizing conference of the UN at San Francisco. Still worrying the problem, Roosevelt discussed it with a State Department adviser in preparation for the San Francisco meeting. He now retreated to the suggestion that France herself might be the trustee "with the proviso that independence was the ultimate goal." Asked if he would settle for dominion status, he said no, "it must be independence . . . and you can quote me in the State Department." A month later, on 15 April 1945, he died.

With the way now clear, Secretary of State Stettinius told the French at San Francisco ten days after Roosevelt's death that the United States did not question French sovereignty over Indochina. He was responding to a tantrum staged by de Gaulle for the benefit of the American Ambassador in Paris in which the General had said that he had an expeditionary force ready to go to Indochina whose departure was prevented by the American refusal of transport, and that "if you are against us in Indochina" this would cause "terrific disappointment" in France, which could drive her into the Soviet orbit. "We do not want to become Communist . . . but I hope you do not push us into it." The blackmail was primitive but tailored to suit what the Europeanists of American diplomacy wished to report. In May at San Francisco, Acting Secretary of State Joseph Grew, the dynamic former Ambassador to Japan and polished veteran of the Foreign Service, assured Bidault with remarkable aplomb that "the record is entirely innocent of any official statement of this government questioning, even by implication, French sovereignty over that area." Recognition is a rather different thing from absence of questioning. In the hands of an expert, that is how policy is made.

Roosevelt had been right about the French record in Indochina; it was the most exploitative in Asia. The French administration concentrated on promoting the production of those goods—rice, coal, rubber, silk and certain spices and minerals—most profitable to export while manipulating the native economy as a market for French products. It provided an easy and comfortable living for some 45,000 French bureaucrats, usually those of mediocre talent, among whom a French survey in 1910 discovered three who could speak a reasonably fluent Vietnamese. It recruited as interpreters and middlemen an assistant bureaucracy of "dependable" Vietnamese from the native upper class, awarding jobs as well as land grants and scholarships for higher education mainly to converts to Catholicism. It eliminated traditional village schools in favor of a French-style education which, for lack of qualified teachers, reached barely a fifth of the school-age population and, according to a French writer, left the Vietnamese "more illiterate than their fathers had been before the French occupation." Its public health and medical services hardly functioned, with one doctor to every 38,000 inhabitants, compared with one for every 3000 in the American-governed Philippines. It substituted an alien French legal code for the traditional judicial system and created a Colonial Council in Cochin China whose minority of Vietnamese members were referred to as "representatives of the conquered race." Above all, through the development of large company-owned plantations and the opportunities for corruption open to the collaborating class, it transformed a land-owning peasantry into landless sharecroppers who numbered over 50 percent of the population on the eve of World War II.

The French called their colonial system *la mission civilisatrice*, which satisfied self-image if not reality. It did not lack outspoken opponents on the left in France or well-intentioned governors and civil servants in the colony who made efforts toward reform from time to time which the vested interests of empire frustrated.

Protests and risings against French rule began with its inception. A people proud of their ancient overthrow of a thousand years of Chinese rule and of later more short-lived Chinese conquests, who had frequently rebelled against and deposed oppressive native dynasties, and who still celebrated the revolutionary heroes and guerrilla tactics of those feats, did not acquiesce passively in a foreign rule far more alien than the Chinese. Twice, in the 1880s and in 1916, Vietnamese emperors themselves had sponsored revolts that failed. While the collaborating class enriched itself from the French table, other men throbbed with the rising blood of the nationalistic impulse in the 20th century. Sects, parties, secret societies—nationalist, constitutionalist, quasi-religious—were formed, agitated, demonstrated and led strikes that ended in French prisons, deportations and firing squads. In 1919, at the Versailles Peace Conference, Ho Chi Minh tried to present an appeal for Vietnamese independence but was turned away without being heard. He subsequently joined the Indochinese Communist Party, organized from Moscow in the 1920s like the Chinese, which gradually took over leadership of the independence movement and raised peasant insurrections in the early 1930s. Thousands were arrested and imprisoned, many executed and some 500 sentenced for life.

Amnestied when the Popular Front government came to power in France, the survivors slowly reconstructed the movement and formed the coalition of the Viet-Minh in 1939. When France capitulated to the Nazis in 1940, the moment seemed at hand for renewed revolt. This too was ferociously suppressed, but the spirit and the aim revived in subsequent resistance to the Japanese, in which the Communists, led by Ho Chi Minh, took the most active part. As in China, the Japanese invasion endowed them with a nationalist cause and when the colonial French let the Japanese enter without a fight, the resistance groups learned contempt and found renewed opportunity.

During the war clandestine American OSS groups operated in Indochina, joining or aiding the resistance. Through airdrops they supplied weapons and on one occasion quinine and sulfa drugs that saved Ho Chi Minh's life from an attack of malaria and dysentery. In talks with OSS officers, Ho said he knew the history of America's own struggle for independence from colonial rule and he was sure "the United States would help in throwing out the French and in establishing an independent country." Impressed by the American pledge to the Philippines, he said he believed that "America was for free popular governments all over the world and that it opposed colonialism in all its forms." This of course was not disinterested conversation. He wanted his message to go further; he wanted arms and aid for a government that he said was "organized and ready to go." The OSS officers were sympathetic but their district chief in China insisted on a policy of "giving no help to individuals such as Ho who were known Communists and therefore sources of trouble."

At Potsdam in July 1945, just before the Japanese defeat, the question of who would take control of Indochina and accept the Japanese surrender was resolved by a secret decision of the Allies that the country below the 16th parallel would be placed under British command and that north of the 16th under Chinese. Since the British were obviously dedicated to colonial restoration, this decision ensured a French return. The United States acquiesced because Roosevelt was dead, because American sentiment is always more concerned with bringing the boys home than with caretaking after a war and because, given Europe's weakened condition, America was reluctant to enter into a quarrel with her Allies. Pressed by the French offer of an army corps of 62,000 for the Pacific front, to be commanded by a hero of the liberation, General Jacques Leclerc, the Combined Chiefs at Potsdam accepted in principle on the understanding that the force would come under American or British command in an area to be determined later, and that transport would not be available until the spring of 1946. It was hardly a secret that the area would be Indochina and the mission its reconquest.

French restoration thus slid into American policy. Although President Truman meant to carry out Roosevelt's intentions, he felt no sense of personal crusade against colonialism and found no written directives left by his predecessor. He was moreover surrounded by military chiefs who, according to Admiral Ernest J. King, the Naval Chief of Staff, "are by no means in favor of keeping the French out of Indochina." Rather, they thought in terms of Western military power replacing the Japanese.

American acceptance was confirmed in August when General de Gaulle descended upon Washington and was told by President Truman, now thoroughly indoctrinated in the threat of Soviet expansion, "My government offers no opposition to the return of the French army and authority in Indochina." De Gaulle promptly announced this statement to a press conference next day, adding that "of course [France] also intends to introduce a new regime" of political reform, "but for us sovereignty is a major question."

He was nothing if not explicit. He had told the Free French at their conference at Brazzaville in January 1944 that they must recognize that political evolution of the colonies had been hastened by the war and that France would meet it "nobly, liberally" but with no intention of yielding sovereignty. The Brazzaville Declaration on colonial policy stated that "the aims of the *mission civilisatrice* . . . exclude any idea of autonomy and any possibility of development outside the French empire bloc. The attainment of 'self-government' in the colonies, even in the distant future, must be excluded."

A week after the Japanese surrender in August 1945, a Viet-Minh congress in Hanoi proclaimed the Democratic Republic of Vietnam and after taking control in Saigon declared its independence, quoting the opening phrases of the American Declaration of Independence of 1776. In a message to the UN transmitted by the OSS, Ho Chi Minh warned that if the UN failed to fulfill the promise of its charter and failed to grant independence to Indochina, "we will keep on fighting until we get it."

A moving message to de Gaulle composed in the name of the last Emperor, the flexible Bao Dai, who had first served the French, then the Japanese, and had now amiably abdicated in favor of the Democratic Republic, was no less prophetic. "You would understand better if you could see what is happening here, if you could feel this desire for independence which is in everyone's heart and which no human force can any longer restrain. Even if you come to re-establish a French administration here, it will no longer be obeyed: each village will be a nest of resistance, each former collaborator an enemy, and your officials and colonists will themselves ask to leave this atmosphere which they will be unable to breathe."

It was one more prophecy to fall on deaf ears. De Gaulle, who received the message while he was in Washington, doubtless did not transmit it to his American hosts, but nothing suggests that it would have had any effect if he had. A few weeks later, Washington informed American agents in Hanoi that steps were being taken to "facilitate the recovery of power by the French."

Self-declared independence lasted less than a month. Ferried from Ceylon by American C-47s, a British general and British troops with a scattering of French units entered Saigon on 12 September, supplemented by 1500 French troops who arrived on French warships two days later. Meanwhile, the bulk of two French divisions had sailed from Marseilles and Madagascar on board two American troopships in the first significant act of American aid. Since the shipping pool was controlled by the Combined Chiefs and the policy decision had already been taken at Potsdam, SEAC could request and be allocated the transports from those available in the pool. Afterward, the State Department, closing the stable door, advised the War Department that it was contrary to United States policy "to employ American flag vessels or aircraft to transport troops of any nationality to or from the Netherlands East Indies or French Indochina, or to permit the use of such craft to carry arms, ammunition or military equipment to those areas."

Until the French arrived, the British command in Saigon used Japanese units, whose disarming was postponed, against the rebel regime.* When a delegation of the Viet-Minh waited on General Douglas Gracey, the British commander, with proposals for maintaining order, "They said, 'welcome' and all that sort of thing," he recalled. "It was an unpleasant situation and I promptly kicked them out." Though characteristically British, the remark was indicative of an attitude that was to infiltrate and deeply affect the future American endeavor as it developed in Vietnam. Finding expression in the terms "slopeys" and "gooks," it reflected not only the view of Asians as inferior to whites but of the people of Indochina, and therefore their pretensions to

---

* Lord Louis Mountbatten, the Theater Commander, reported on 2 October 1945 to the Combined Chiefs of Staff that the only way he could avoid involving British/Indian forces was "to continue using the Japanese for maintaining law and order and this means I can*not* begin to disarm them for another three months."

independence, as of lesser account than, say, the Japanese or Chinese. The Japanese, notwithstanding their unspeakable atrocities, had guns and battleships and modern industry; the Chinese were both admired through the influence of the missionaries and feared as the Yellow Peril and had to be appreciated for sheer land mass and numbers. Without such endowments, the Indochinese commanded less respect. Foreshadowed in General Gracey's words, the result was to be a fatal underestimation of the opponent.

The French divisions from Europe arrived in October and November, some of them wearing uniforms of American issue and carrying American equipment. They plunged into the old business of armed suppression during the first fierce days of arrests and massacre. While they regained control of Saigon, the Viet-Minh faded into the countryside, but this time colonial restoration was incomplete. In the northern zone assigned to the Chinese, the Vietnamese, armed with weapons from the Japanese surrender which the Chinese sold them, retained control under Ho's Provisional Government in Hanoi. The Chinese did not interfere and, loaded with booty from their occupation, eventually withdrew over the border.

In the confusion of peoples and parties, OSS units suffered from a "lack of directives" from Washington which reflected the confusion of policy at home. Traditional anti-colonialism had left a reservoir of ambivalence, but the governing assumption that a "stable, strong and friendly" France was essential to fill the vacuum in Europe tipped the balance of policy. Late in 1945, $160 million of equipment was sold to the French for use in Indochina and remaining OSS units were instructed to serve as "observers to punitive missions against the rebellious Annamites." Eight separate appeals addressed by Ho Chi Minh to President Truman and the Secretary of State over a period of five months asking for support and economic aid went unanswered on the ground that his government was not recognized by the United States.

The snub was not given in ignorance of conditions in Vietnam. A report in October by Arthur Hale, of the United States Information Service in Hanoi, made it apparent that French promises of reform and some vague shape of autonomy, which American policy counted on, were not going to satisfy. The people wanted the French out. Posters crying "Independence or Death!" in all towns and villages of the north "scream at the passerby from every wall and window." Communist influence was not concealed; the flag of the Provisional Government resembled the Soviet flag, Marxist pamphlets lay on official desks, but the same might be said for American influence. The promise to the Philippines was a constant theme, and a vigorous enthusiasm was felt for American prowess in the war and for American productive capacity and technical and social progress. Given, however, the lack of any American response to the Viet-Minh and such incidents "as the recent shipment of French troops to Saigon in American vessels," the goodwill had faded. Hale's report too was prophetic: if the French overcome the Provisional Government, "it can be assumed as a certainty that the movement for independence will not die." The certainty was there at the start.

Other observers concurred. The French might take the cities in the north, wrote a correspondent of the *Christian Science Monitor*, "but it is extremely doubtful if they will ever be able to put down the independence movement as a whole. They have not enough troops to root out every guerrilla band in the north and they have shown little capacity to cope with guerrilla fighting."

Asked by the State Department for an evaluation of American prestige in Asia, which it suspected was "seriously deteriorating," Charles Yost, political officer in Bangkok and a future Ambassador to the UN, confirmed the Department's impression, and he too cited the use of American vessels to transport French troops and "the use of American equipment by these troops." Goodwill toward America as the champion of subject peoples had been very great after the war, but American failure to support the nationalist movement "does not seem likely to contribute to long-term stability in Southeast Asia." The restoration of colonial regimes, Yost warned, was unsuited to existing conditions "and cannot for that reason long be maintained except by force."

That American policy nevertheless supported the French effort was a choice of the more compelling necessity over what seemed a lesser one. George Marshall as Secretary of State acknowledged the existence of "dangerously outmoded colonial outlook and methods in the area," but "on the other hand . . . we are not interested in seeing colonial empire administrations supplanted by philosophy and political organizations emanating from and controlled by Kremlin." This was the crux. The French peppered Washington with "proof" of Ho Chi Minh's contacts with Moscow, and Dean Acheson, Under-Secretary of State, was in no doubt. "Keep in mind," he cabled Abbot Low Moffat, chief for Southeast Asia affairs, who went to Hanoi in December 1946, "Ho's clear record as agent international communism, absence evidence recantation."

Moffat, a warm partisan of the Asian cause, reported that in conversation Ho had disclaimed Communism as his aim, saying that if he could secure independence, that was enough for his lifetime. "Perhaps," he had added wryly, "fifty years from now the United States will be Communist and then Vietnam can be also." Moffat concluded that the group in charge of Vietnam "are at this stage nationalist first" and an effective nationalist state must precede a Communist state, which as an objective "must for the time being be secondary." Whether he was deluded history cannot answer, for who can be certain that, at the time Ho was seeking American support, the development of the Democratic Republic of Vietnam (DRV) was as irrevocably Communist as the course of events was to make it?

The compulsion of the French to regain their empire derived, after the humiliation of World War II, from a sense that their future as a great power was at stake, but they realized the necessity of some adjustment, at least pro forma. During temporary truces with the Viet-Minh in 1946 they tried to negotiate a basis of agreement with promises of some unspecified form of self-government at some unspecified date, so worded as never to ruffle the edges of sovereignty. These were "paper concessions," according to the State Department's Far East desk. When they failed, hostilities resumed and by the end of 1946 the first, or French, Indochina war was fully under way. There was no illusion. If the French resumed the repressive measures and policy of force of the past, reported the American Consul in Saigon, "no settlement of situation can be expected foreseeable future and period guerrilla warfare will follow." The French commander assigned to carry out the reconquest himself saw, or felt, the truth. After his first survey of the situation, General Leclerc said to his political adviser, "It would take 500,000 men to do it and even then it could not be done." In one sentence he laid out the future, and his estimate would still be valid when 500,000 American soldiers were actually in the field two decades later.

Was American policy already folly in 1945–46? Even judged in terms of the thinking of the time, the answer must be affirmative, for most Americans concerned with foreign policy understood that the colonial era had come to an end and that its revival was an exercise in putting Humpty-Dumpty back on the wall. No matter how strong the arguments for bolstering France, folly lay in attaching policy to a cause that prevailing information indicated was hopeless. Policy-makers assured themselves they were not attaching the United States to that cause. They took comfort in French pledges of future autonomy or else in the belief that France lacked the power to regain her empire and would have to come to terms with the Vietnamese eventually. Both Truman and Acheson assured the American public that the U.S. position was "predicated on the assumption that the French claim to have the support of the population of Indochina is borne out by future events." To assist her now for the sake of a strong presence in Europe was therefore no crime—though it was a losing proposition.

The alternative was present and available: to gain for America an enviable primacy among Western nations and confirm the foundation of goodwill in Asia by aligning ourselves with, even supporting, the independence movements. If this seemed indicated to some, particularly at the Far East desk, it was less persuasive to others for whom self-government by Asians was not something to base a policy on and insignificant in comparison to the security of Europe. In Indochina choice of the alternative would have required imagination, which is never a long suit with governments, and willingness to take the risk of supporting a Communist when Communism was still seen as a solid bloc. Tito was then its only splinter, and the possibility of another deviation was not envisaged. Moreover, it would be divisive of the Allies. Support of Humpty-Dumpty was chosen instead, and once a policy has been adopted and implemented, all subsequent activity becomes an effort to justify it.

An uneasy suspicion that we were pursuing folly was to haunt the American engagement in Vietnam from beginning to end, revealing itself in sometimes contorted policy directives. In a summary of the American position for diplomats in Paris, Saigon and Hanoi, the French desk in 1947 drafted for Secretary George Marshall a directive of wishful thinking combined with uncertainty. It saw the independence movements of the new nations of Southeast Asia, representing, so it said, a quarter of the world's inhabitants, as a "momentous factor in world stability"; it believed the best safeguard against this struggle's succumbing to anti-Western tendencies and Communist influence was continued association with former colonial powers; it acknowledged on the one hand that the association "must be voluntary" and on the other hand that the war in Indochina could only destroy voluntary cooperation, and "irrevocably alienate Vietnamese"; it said that the United States wanted to be helpful without wishing to intervene or offer any solution of its own, yet was "inescapably concerned" with the developments in Indochina. Whether foreign service officers were enlightened by this document is questionable.

2. Self-Hypnosis:
1946-54

Inchoate cold war entered maturity with Churchill's "iron curtain" speech at Fulton, Missouri, in March 1946, in which he stated that no one knew "the limits, if any, to [the] expansive and proselytising tendencies" of the Soviet Union and its Communist International.

The situation was in fact alarming. Roosevelt's vision of a postwar partnership of wartime allies to maintain international order had vanished, as he knew before he died, when on his last day in Washington he acknowledged that Stalin "has broken every one of the promises he made at Yalta." By 1946, Soviet control had been extended over Poland, East Germany, Rumania, Hungary, Bulgaria, Albania and more or less over Yugoslavia. Domestic Communist parties in France and Italy appeared as further threats. From the Embassy in Moscow George Kennan formulated "a long-term patient but firm and vigilant containment of Russian expansionist tendencies." In 1947, Secretary Marshall summoned America to develop "a sense of responsibility for world order and security" and a recognition of the "overwhelming importance" of United States acts and failures to act in this regard. Moscow answered by a declaration that all Communist parties in the world were united in common resistance to American imperialism. The Truman Doctrine was announced, committing America to support of free peoples resisting subjugation by "armed minorities" or by external pressure, and the Marshall Plan adopted for economic aid to revive the weakened countries of Europe. A major effort was launched and succeeded in obstructing a Communist takeover in Greece and Turkey.

In February 1948, Soviet Russia absorbed Czechoslovakia. The United States re-enacted the draft for military service. In April of that year Russia imposed the Berlin blockade. America responded with the bold airlift and kept it flying for a year until the blockade was withdrawn. In 1949, NATO (North Atlantic Treaty Organization) was formed for a common defense against attack on any one of its member countries.

The event that shook the balance of forces was the Communist victory in China in October 1949, a shock as stunning as Pearl Harbor. Hysteria over the "loss" of China took hold of America and rabid spokesmen of the China Lobby in Congress and the business world became the loudest voices in political life. The shock was the more dismaying because only a few weeks earlier, in September, Russia had successfully exploded an atomic bomb. As 1950 opened, Senator Joseph McCarthy announced that he had a list of 205 "card-carrying" Communists in the employ of the State Department, and for the next four years Americans joined in more than they opposed his vilification of fellow citizens as Communist infiltrators of American society. In June 1950, North Korea, a Soviet client, invaded South Korea, an American client, and President Truman ordered American military response under United Nations authority. During these abject years the Rosenbergs were tried for treason, convicted in 1951, and when President Eisenhower refused to commute a death sentence that would make orphans of two children, were subsequently executed.

These were the components of the cold war that shaped the course of events in Indochina. Its central belief was that every movement bearing the label Communist represented a single conspiracy for world conquest under the Soviet aegis. The effect of Mao's victory in China seemed a terrible affirmation and when followed by the attack on South Korea induced a panic period in American policy regarding Asia. It was now "clear" to the National Security Council "that Southeast Asia is the target for a coordinated offensive directed by the Kremlin." Indochina was viewed as the focus, partly because a war was already in progress there with European troops pitted against an indigenous force under Communist leadership. It was declared to be the "key area," which, if allowed to fall to the Communists, would drag Burma and Thailand in its wake. At first, the Communist offensive was seen as generated by Soviet Russia. After Chinese troops entered the Korean combat, China was seen as the main mover, with Vietnam as its next target. Ho and the Viet-Minh took on a more sinister aspect as agents of the international Communist conspiracy and ipso facto hostile to the United States. When Chinese Communist amphibious forces seized the island of Hainan in the Gulf of Tonkin, held until then by Chiang Kai-shek, the level of alarm rose. In response, on 8 May 1950, President Truman announced the first direct grant of military aid to France and the Associated States of Indochina in the amount of $10 million.

The Associated States, comprising Laos, Cambodia and Vietnam, were a creation of France in the previous year under the Elysée Agreement, which had recognized the "independence" of Vietnam and resurrected Bao Dai as its chief of state. Thereupon, the Soviet Union and China, in February 1950, promptly recognized the Democratic Republic in Hanoi as the legitimate government, followed in the same month by the United States' recognition of Bao Dai. No actual transfer of administrative powers or authority into Vietnamese hands resulted from the Elysée Agreement, and the French retained control of the Vietnamese army as before. The Bao Dai regime, with officials more efficient in graft than in government, was inept and corrupt. Yet Americans tried to persuade themselves that Bao Dai was a valid nationalist alternative to Ho Chi Minh and that they could thus support France, his sponsor, without incurring the stigma of colonialism. As the hoped-for alternative, however, the Bao Dai solution proved empty, as even its titular figure acknowledged. "Present political conditions," he said to an adviser, Dr. Phan Quang Dan, "make it impossible to convince the people and troops that they have something worthwhile fighting for." If he expanded his army, as the Americans were urging, it could be dangerous because they might defect en masse to the Viet-Minh. Dr. Dan, a sincere nationalist, was more emphatic. The Vietnamese army, he said, officered by the French and with virtually no leaders of its own, was "without ideology, without objective, without enthusiasm, without fighting spirit and without popular backing."

American government was in no ignorance of this state of affairs. Robert Blum, of the American Technical and Economic Mission accredited to Vietnam, reported that Bao Dai's government "gives little promise of developing competence or winning the loyalty of the population," that the situation "shows no substantial prospect of improving," that in the circumstances no decisive military victory was likely to be achieved by the French, leading to the gloomy conclusion that "the attainment of American objectives is remote." After eighteen months of frustration, Blum returned home in 1952.

While Washington departments continually assured each other that the "development of genuine nationalism" in Indochina was essential to its defense, and repeatedly tried to push France and the passive Bao Dai himself to perform more actively in that direction, they continued to ignore the implications of their own knowledge. Regardless of the absence of popular backing for the Bao Dai regime, the specter of advancing Communism demanded aid to France against the Viet-Minh. Immediately following the invasion of Korea, Truman announced the first despatch to Indochina of American personnel. Called the Military Assistance Advisory Group (MAAG), starting with 35 men at the opening of the Korean war and increasing to about 200, it was supposed to introduce American know-how—which the French did not want and persistently resented—and supervise the use of American equipment, the first consignment of which was airlifted to Saigon in July. At French insistence, the matériel was delivered directly to the French themselves, not to the Associated States, demonstrating all too patently the fiction of independence.

With this step onto the ground of the struggle, American policy-makers felt impelled to assert the American interests that justified it. Policy statements about the vital importance of Southeast Asia began to pour from the government. It was presented as an area "vital to the future of the free world," whose strategic position and rich natural resources must be held available to the free nations and denied to international Communism. Communist rulers of the Kremlin, President Truman told the American people in a radio address, were engaged in a "monstrous conspiracy to stamp out freedom all over the world." If they succeeded the United States would be among "their principal victims." He called the situation a "clear and present danger" and raised the Munich argument that was to become a staple: if the free nations had then acted together and in time to crush the aggression of the dictators, World War II might have been averted.

The lesson may have been true, but it was misapplied. The aggression of the 1930s in Manchuria, North China, Ethiopia, the Rhineland, Spain and the Sudetenland was overt, with armed invasions, planes and bombs, and occupying forces; the envisaged aggression against Indochina of 1950 was a self-induced state of mind in the observers. In a revealing appraisal, the National Security Council (NSC) in February 1950 called the threat to Indochina only one phase of "anticipated" Communist plans to "seize all of Southeast Asia." Yet a State Department team investigating Communist infiltration of Southeast Asia in 1948 had found no traces of the Kremlin in Indochina. "If there is a Moscow-directed conspiracy in Southeast Asia," it reported, "Indochina is an anomaly so far."

That the Russian danger in the world was nevertheless real, that the Communist system was hostile to American democracy and American interests, that Soviet Communism was expansionist and directed toward the absorption of neighboring and other vulnerable states, was undeniable. That it was joined in aggressive partnership with Communist China was a natural conclusion, but exaggerated and soon to prove mistaken. That it was right and proper in the national interest for American policy-makers to try to contain this inimical system and to thwart it where possible goes without question. That the Communist system threatened American security through Indochina, however, was an extrapolation leading to folly.

American security entered the equation when China entered the Korean war, a development that President Truman said put the United States in "grave danger" from "Communist aggression." Doubtless General MacArthur's crossing of the 38th parallel into Communist-held territory—the action which provoked the Chinese entry—put China's security in grave danger from the Chinese point of view, but the opponent's point of view is rarely considered in the paranoia of war. From the moment the Chinese were engaged in actual combat against Americans, Washington was gripped by the assumption from then on that Chinese Communism was on the march and would next appear over China's southern border in Indochina.

Battered and abused by charges of having "lost" China and having invited the attack on Korea by Acheson's "perimeter" speech—leaving Korea outside the perimeter—the Truman administration was determined to show itself combatively confronting the Communist conspiracy. The menace to all Southeast Asia became doctrine. Soviet rulers, Truman told Congress in a special message announcing a program of $930 million in military and economic aid for Southeast Asia, had already reduced China to a satellite, were preparing the same fate for Korea, Indochina, Burma and the Philippines and thus threatened "to absorb the manpower and vital resources of the East into the Soviet design of world conquest." This would "deprive the free nations of some of their most vitally needed raw materials" and transform the peaceful millions of the East into "pawns of the Kremlin." The otherwise suave Acheson echoed the rhetoric on repeated occasions. He found proof of the Communist conspiracy in Russia's and China's recognition of Ho Chi Minh, which should "remove any illusions" as to Ho's nationalism and reveal him "in his true colors as the mortal enemy of native independence in Indochina."

A new voice, that of Dean Rusk, Assistant Secretary of State for Far Eastern Affairs, who was to prove the most unwavering, the most convinced, the most sincere, the most rigid and the longest-lasting of all the policy-makers on Vietnam, found a way to put Vietnam's struggle for independence, the source of so much American ambivalence, in a new light. The issue, he told the Senate Foreign Relations Committee, was not French colonialism but whether the people of

Vietnam were to be "absorbed by force into a new colonialism of a Soviet Communist empire." The Viet-Minh were a "tool of the Politburo" and therefore "part of an international war."

By these arguments the American government convinced itself that it was a vital American interest to keep Indochina out of the Communist orbit and that therefore French victory in Indochina, whether colonial or not, was "essential to the security of the free world." (The question of what France was fighting for if Vietnam was indeed to be "independent" was not discussed.) The word passed to the public in a *New York Times* editorial that proclaimed, "It should now be clear to all Americans that France is holding a front-line section of great importance to the whole free world." While there was no impulse to send American troops, the United States was determined to "save for the West the Indochinese rice bowl, the strategic position, the prestige that could be shaken throughout Southeast Asia and all the way to Tunisia and Morocco." The NSC at this time drew a prospect of even Japan succumbing if it were cut off from the rubber and tin and oil of Malaya and Indonesia and its rice imports from Burma and Thailand.

The process of self-hypnosis came to its logical conclusion: if the preservation of Indochina from Communist control was indeed so vital to American interest, should we not be actively engaged in its defense? Armed intervention, given the fear that it might precipitate a Chinese military response as it had in Korea, aroused no eagerness in the American military establishment. "No land war in Asia" was an old and trusted dogma in the Army. Cautionary voices were not lacking. Back in 1950, at the time of China's intervention in Korea, a State Department memorandum by John Ohly, Deputy Director in the Office of Mutual Defense Assistance, had suggested the advisability of taking a second look at where we were going in Indochina. Not only might we fail, wasting resources in the process, but we were moving toward a point when our responsibilities would "tend to supplant rather than complement the French," and we would become a scapegoat for the French and be sucked into direct intervention. "These situations have a way of snowballing," Ohly concluded. As is the fate of so many prescient memoranda, his counsel made no impact on, if it ever reached, the upper echelon but lay silently in the files while history validated its every word.

Before it went out of office, the Truman Administration adopted a policy paper by NSC which recommended, in the event of overt Chinese intervention in Indochina, naval and air action by the United

States in support of the French and against targets on the Chinese mainland but made no mention of land forces.

The advent of the Republicans under General Eisenhower in the election of 1952 brought in an Administration pushed from the right by extremists of anti-Communism and the China Lobby. Opinions of the Lobby were epitomized in a remark of the new Assistant Secretary of State, Walter Robertson, a fervent partisan of Chiang Kai-shek, who, when given a CIA estimate of Red China's steel production, replied indignantly that the figures must be wrong because "No regime as malevolent as the Chinese Communists could ever produce five million tons of steel." The extremists were led by Senator William Knowland of California, Majority Leader of the Senate, who accused the Democrats of "placing Asia in danger of Soviet conquest," fulminated regularly against Red China and swore to hold the Administration accountable if Mao's People's Republic were admitted to the UN. The pressure of the far right on the Administration was a constant factor. This was "the Great Beast to be feared," as Lyndon Johnson, though under far less pressure, was to testify to its power nearly fifteen years later.

The Republicans also brought to office a domineering policy-maker in foreign affairs, John Foster Dulles, a man devoted to the offensive by training and temperament. If Truman and Acheson adopted cold war rhetoric even to excess, it was at least partly in reaction to being accused of belonging to the "party of treason," as McCarthy called the Democrats, and to the peculiar national frenzy over the "loss" of China. Dulles, the new Secretary of State, was a cold war extremist naturally, a drum-beater with the instincts of a bully, deliberately combative because that was the way he believed foreign relations should be conducted. Brinksmanship was his contribution, counteroffensive rather than containment was his policy, "a passion to control events" was his motor.

When a Senator in 1949, following the fall of Nationalist China, he stated that "our Pacific front" was now "wide open to encirclement from the East. . . . Today the situation is critical." His concept of encirclement was a Chinese Communist advance to Formosa and from there to the Philippines, and a capacity, if once allowed to push beyond the Chinese mainland, "to move and keep on moving." When MacArthur's forces in Korea were thrown back by the Chinese, Dulles' estimate of the enemy grew more bloodcurdling. Huk banditry in the Philippines, Ho Chi Minh's war in Indochina, a Communist rising in Malaya, Communist revolution in China and the attack on Korea were "all part of a single pattern of violence planned and plotted for 35 years and finally brought to a consummation of fighting and disorder" across the length of Asia.

This melding of the several countries of East Asia as if they had no individuality, no history, no differences or circumstances of their own was the thinking, either uninformed and shallow or knowingly false, that created the domino theory and allowed it to become dogma. Because Orientals on the whole looked alike to Western eyes, they were expected to act alike and perform with the uniformity of dominoes.

As the son of a Presbyterian minister, a relative of missionaries and himself a devoted churchman, Dulles possessed the zeal and self-righteousness that such connections endow, not precluding the behavior, in some of his official dealings, of a scoundrel. His perception of Chiang Kai-shek and Syngman Rhee was that "these two gentlemen are modern-day equivalents of the founders of the Church. They are Christian gentlemen who have suffered for their faith." Far from a source of suffering, their adopted faith had in fact been a source of power for both.

Under the title "A Policy of Boldness," Dulles published in *Life* magazine in 1952 his belief that with regard to Communist-dominated countries, America must demonstrate that "it wants and expects liberation to occur"—"liberation" meaning of course overthrow of Communist regimes. As author of the foreign-policy section of the Republican platform in that year, he rejected containment as "negative, futile and immoral," and spoke in a muffled jargon of encouraging "liberating influences . . . in the captive world," which would cause such stresses as would make "the rulers impotent to continue their monstrous ways and mark the beginning of the end." If the rhetoric was more than the usual bluster even for an election year platform, it characterized the man who was to be a policy-making, not merely an office-holding, Secretary of State throughout the next seven years. During his tenure Dulles became the supreme public relations officer of American intervention in Vietnam.

Stalin's death in March 1953 was the event that opened a path to the Geneva Conference of 1954 and an international settlement of the war in Indochina. Taut confrontation in Europe loosened when the new Russian premier, Georgi Malenkov, used the funeral oration to speak of the need for "peaceful coexistence." Foreign Minister Molotov followed with overtures toward a conference of the powers. President Eisenhower responded, much to Dulles' distaste, with a speech welcoming signs of détente and expressing Americans' desire, once an "honorable armistice" was concluded in Korea, for "a peace that is true and total" throughout Asia and the world. *Pravda* and *Izvestia* paid him the compliment of printing the speech verbatim. Dulles had attempted to write into it a condition linking American agreement to a Korean armistice dependent on the Kremlin's explicit promise to end the Viet-Minh's rebellion against the French; he was making his usual assumption that Moscow pulled the operative strings in Hanoi. In this case his suggestion did not prevail, but his premise of the Soviet Union as an omnipotent master criminal of world conspiracy never wavered.

Conclusion of the Korean armistice in July 1953 had raised a new alarm that China might transfer its forces to aid a Communist victory in Vietnam. The Viet-Minh had succeeded in opening supply lines to China and they were receiving fuel and ammunition that had risen from a trickle of ten tons a month to more than 500 tons a month. The option of American military intervention was now intensively debated in the government. As the arm that would bear the burden of land war, and sullen from the experience of limited war in Korea, the Army did not want to fight under such restrictions again. The Plans Division of the General Staff struck the central issue when it asked for a "re-evaluation of the importance of Indochina and Southeast Asia in relation to the possible cost of saving it." The same concern had once worried Lord Barrington when he argued that if Britain made war on its colonies, "the contest will cost us more than we can ever gain by success." This crucial question of relative value was never answered for Vietnam, as it never had been in the case of the colonies.

While several naval and air commanders in the discussions urged a decision in favor of combat, Vice-Admiral A. C. Davis, the adviser on foreign military affairs to the Secretary of Defense, counseled that involvement in the Indochina war "should be avoided at all practical costs," but if national policy determined no other alternative, "the United States should not be self-duped into believing in the possibility of partial involvement such as 'Naval and Air units only.'" Air strength, to be worth anything, he reminded the group, would require land bases and bases would require ground force personnel and these would require ground combat units for protection. "It must be understood that there is no cheap way to fight a war, once committed."

"Partial involvement" was—not without reason—the key objection. Pentagon chiefs in advice to the Executive deplored a "static" defense of Indochina and stated their belief that war should be carried to the aggressor, "in this instance Communist China." That was the enemy in Asia; the Vietnamese, in the Pentagon's view, were only pawns. The chiefs added a warning that would echo through the years to come: "Once United States forces and prestige have been committed, disengagement will not be possible short of victory."

The factors that could make any victory elusive were known to Washington—known, that is, if we assume that department heads and presidents avail themselves of the information they have sent government agents to obtain. A CIA report, speaking of the "xenophobia" of the indigenous population, stated that "Even if the United States defeated the Viet-Minh field forces, guerrilla action could be continued indefinitely," precluding non-Communist control of the region. In such circumstances, the United States "might have to maintain a military commitment in Indochina for years to come."

The debate of the departments—State, Defense, NSC and the intelligence agencies—continued without a solution, knotted as it was in a tangle of what-ifs: what if the Chinese entered; what if the French asked for active United States participation, or, alternatively, pulled out, as a strong current of French opinion was demanding, abandoning Indochina to Communism. Every contingency was examined; an interagency Working Group delivered exhaustive reports of its studies. Again there were few illusions. It was recognized that the French could win only if they gained the genuine political and military partnership of the Vietnamese people; that this was not developing and would not, given French reluctance to transfer real authority; that no valid native non-Communist leadership had emerged; that the French effort was deteriorating and that United States naval and air action alone could not turn the tide in France's favor. The conclusion reached by President Eisenhower was that armed American intervention must be conditional on three requirements: joint action with allies, Congressional approval and French "acceleration" of the independence of the Associated States.

In the meantime, in proportion as a French slide appeared imminent, American aid increased. Bombers, cargo planes, naval craft, tanks, trucks, automatic weapons, small arms and ammunition, artillery shells, radios, hospital and engineering equipment plus financial support flowed heavily in 1953. Over the previous three years, 350 ships (or more than two every week) had been delivering war matériel to the French. Yet in June 1953 a National Intelligence estimate judged that the French effort "will probably deteriorate" during the following twelve months and if current trends continued could subsequently "deteriorate very rapidly"; that "popular apathy" would continue and the Viet-Minh "will retain the military initiative." Whether taken as a prescription to withdraw from an inherently flawed cause or to bolster it by increased aid, the Intelligence estimate should at least have resulted in sober second thought. That it did not was due to fear that a cut-off of aid would mean losing French cooperation in Europe.

"The French blackmailed us," as Acheson put it; aid in Indochina was France's price for joining the European Defense Community (EDC). American policy in Europe was tied to this scheme for an integrated coalition of the major nations, which France feared and resisted because it included her late conqueror, Germany. If the United States wanted France's membership and her twelve divisions for NATO, it must in turn pay for her holding back Communism—and incidentally holding on to her empire—in Asia. EDC would become operative only if France joined. The United States was committed to it, and paid.

The reason why the French with superior manpower and American resources were doing so poorly was not beyond all conjecture. The people of Indochina, of whom more than 200,000 were in the colonial army together with some 80,000 French, 48,000 North Africans and 20,000 Foreign Legionnaires, simply had no reason to fight for France. Americans were always talking about freedom from Communism, whereas the freedom that the mass of Vietnamese wanted was freedom from their exploiters, both French and indigenous. The assumption that humanity at large shared the democratic Western idea of freedom was an American delusion. "The freedom we cherish and defend in Europe," stated President Eisenhower on taking office, "is no different than the freedom that is imperiled in Asia." He was mistaken. Humanity may have common ground, but needs and aspirations vary according to circumstances.

There was no delusion or ignorance about the absence of will to fight in the Associated States. A high-ranking officer, Major General Thomas Trapnell, returning from service with MAAG in 1954, reported a war of paradoxes, in which "there is no popular will to win on the part of the Vietnamese" and in which "the leader of the Rebels is more popular than the Vietnamese Chief of State." His recognition of absent will, however, did not preclude this officer from recommending more vigorous prosecution of the war. Eisenhower, too, had to admit at a press conference to "a lack of enthusiasm which we would like to have there." In his memoirs, published in 1963 (well before his successors took America into the war), he acknowledged that "the mass of the population supported the enemy," making it impossible for the French to rely on their Vietnamese troops. American aid "could not cure the defect."

By 1953 French domestic opinion had grown weary and disgusted with an endless war for a cause unacceptable to many French citizens. The conviction was growing that France could not at the same time maintain guns in Indochina and guns for the defense of Europe while providing the butter of domestic needs. Although the United States was paying most of the bill, the French people, assisted by Communist propaganda, were raising increasing clamor against the war and mounting heavy political pressure for a negotiated settlement.

Dulles' desperate effort was now exerted to keep the French fighting lest the awful prospect of losing Indochina to the Communists become a reality. Early in 1954 forty B-26 bombers with 200 United States Air Force technicians in civilian clothes were despatched to Indochina, and Congress appropriated $400 million plus another $385 million to finance the offensive planned by General Henri Navarre, in a last fevered burst of French military effort. By the time of the terminal catastrophe at Dien Bien Phu a few months later, American investment in Indochina since 1946 had reached $2 billion and the United States was paying 80 percent of the French expenditure for the war, not counting aid to the Associated States intended to stabilize their governments and strengthen their resistance to the Viet-Minh. Like most such aid, the bulk of it trickled away into the pockets of profiteering officials. As the Ohly memorandum had predicted, the United States was ineluctably approaching the point of supplanting rather than supplementing the French in what remained, whether we liked it or not, a colonial war.

Knowing what was wrong, American officials kept insisting in endless policy papers addressed to one another and in hortatory advice to the French that independence must be "accelerated" and genuine. Here was folly shining bright. How could the French be persuaded to fight more energetically to hold Vietnam and simultaneously be brought to pledge eventual true independence? Why should they invest a greater effort to retain a colonial possession if they were not going to retain it?

The contradiction was clear enough to the French, who, whether they were for or against the war, wanted some form of limited sovereignty that would keep Indochina within the French Union, a postwar euphemism for empire. French pride, French glory, French sacrifice, not to mention French commerce, demanded it, the more so as France feared the example for Algeria if Indochina succeeded in breaking loose. In American policy the underlying absurdity of expecting both battle and renunciation from the French was possible because Americans thought of the war only in terms of fighting Communism, which could include independence, and closed their eyes to its aspect as the dying grip of colonialism, which obviously could not.

Mesmerized by a vision of Chinese intervention, Dulles and Admiral Arthur Radford, Chairman of the Joint Chiefs of Staff, and others believed that as long as the Chinese were discouraged from entering by subtle warnings of "massive"—meaning nuclear—retaliation or other American action against the mainland, the balance in Indochina would eventually swing toward the French. Characteristically this ignored the Viet-Minh and a hundred years of Vietnamese nationalism, a miscalculation that would dog the United States to the end.

At the same time, policy-makers understood, as their anxious memoranda show, that the United States was becoming tainted in Asian eyes as the partner in a white man's war; that French success via the Navarre Plan was illusory; that, in spite of the optimism expressed by General "Iron Mike" O'Daniel, chief of MAAG, increased American supply could not assure General Navarre's victory. American aid remained somehow ineffectual. They knew that unless the Chinese supplies, which had now reached 1500 tons a month, could be cut off, Hanoi would not give up; they were painfully conscious of the growing disaffection of the French public and the French National Assembly and the possibility that the war might be terminated by political crisis, leaving the United States with a wasted effort or the alternative of taking on the ill-omened cause for itself. They knew that without American support, the Associated States could not sustain themselves. In this knowledge and this awareness, what was the rationale of continued American investment in a non-viable client on the other side of the world?

Having invented Indochina as the main target of a coordinated Communist aggression, and having in every policy advice and public pronouncement repeated the operating assumption that its preservation from Communism was vital to American security, the United States was lodged in the trap of its own propaganda. The exaggerated rhetoric of the cold war had bewitched its formulators. The administration believed, or had convinced itself under Dulles' guidance, that to stop the advance of the Communist octopus into Southeast Asia was imperative. Morever, to "lose" Indochina after the "loss" of China would have invited political catastrophe. Liberals, too, joined the consensus. Justice William O. Douglas, after visiting five regions of Southeast Asia in 1953, pronounced his judgment that "each front is indeed an overt act of a Communist conspiracy to expand the Russian empire. . . . The fall of Vietnam today would imperil all of Southeast Asia." Senator Mike Mansfield, normally a steadying influence in foreign policy and an influential member of the Foreign Relations Committee with a special interest in Asia dating from his years as a professor of Far Eastern history, returned in 1953 from a survey of the situation on the spot. He reported to the Senate that "World peace hangs in the balance" along the avenues of Communist expansion in the Far East; "Hence the security of the United States is no less involved in Indochina than in Korea." Our aid in the conflict was being given in recognition of Indochina's "great importance to the non-Communist world and to our own national security."

The matrix of this exaggeration was the state of the union under the paws of the Great Beast. The witch-hunts of McCarthyism, of the House Un-American Activities Committee, the informers, the blacklists and the fire-eaters of the Republican right and the China Lobby, the trail of wrecked careers, had plunged the country into a fit of moral cowardice. Everyone, in and out of office, trembled in anxiety to prove his anti-Communist credentials. The anxious included Dulles, who, according to an associate, lived in constant apprehension that the McCarthy attack might turn next upon him. Less intensely, it reached up to the President, as shown by Eisenhower's silent acquiescence in McCarthy's attacks on General Marshall. Nothing was so ridiculous, Macaulay once wrote, as the British public in one of its periodical fits of morality—and nothing so craven, it could be added, as the American public in its fit of the 1950s.

During the Eisenhower Administration the New Look had overtaken military strategy. The New Look was nuclear, and the idea behind it, as worked out by a committee of strategists and Cabinet chiefs, was that in the confrontation with Communism, the new weapons offered a means to make prospective American retaliation a more serious threat and war itself sharper, quicker and cheaper than when it relied on vast conventional preparations and "outmoded procedures." Eisenhower was deeply concerned about the prospect of deficit budgets, as was his Secretary of the Treasury George Humphrey, who said flatly that not defense but disaster would result from "a military program that scorned the resources and problems of our economy—erecting majestic defenses and battlements for the protection of a country that was bankrupt." (That was thirty years ago.) The New Look was motivated as much by the domestic economy as by the cold war.

Intending a warning to Moscow, Dulles made the strategy public in his memorable "massive retaliation" speech of January 1954. The idea was to make clear to any "potential aggressor" the certainty and force of American response, but the gun was muffled by the uproar and confusion that greeted the speech. Half the world thought it was bluff and the other half feared it was not. It was in this context that crisis approached in the affairs of Indochina.

In November 1953, General Navarre had sent 12,000 French troops to occupy the fortified area of Dien Bien Phu in the far north, to the west of Hanoi. His purpose was to tempt the enemy into frontal combat, but the position, surrounded by high ground in a region largely controlled by the Viet-Minh, was a rash choice that was to prove disastrous. At about the same time, at the Foreign Ministers' conference in Berlin, Molotov proposed extending the discussions to the problems of Asia at a five-power conference to include the People's Republic of China.

Harried by disturbing reports from Dien Bien Phu, and by extreme pressure at home to end the war, the French clutched at the opportunity to negotiate. The five-power proposal horrified Dulles, who considered any settlement with Communists unacceptable and sitting down with the Chinese, which might be taken to imply recognition of the People's Republic, unthinkable. He believed that Russian overtures ever since Malenkov's coexistence speech were a "phony peace campaign," and a ruse designed to make opponents drop their guard. He set himself to resist the five-power conference by every twist and device of intimidation in his arsenal while at the same time trying to keep France fully committed to the war and yet not so irritated by American pressure as to jeopardize EDC. As the French government, to save its political skin, was bent on putting Indochina on the agenda, Dulles could persist only at the cost of a quarrel he could not risk. He had to give way. The five-power meeting was scheduled for Geneva at the end of April.

The prospect it raised of having to acknowledge a Communist presence in Vietnam and of France giving up the war induced a spasm of horror in the planning centers of American policy. Contingency plans for American armed intervention to replace the French took formal shape, and the strenuous Chairman of the Joint Chiefs produced a policy paper in preparation for the Geneva Conference that carried exaggeration to dizzying heights. A former carrier commander in World War II, Admiral Radford was a forthright apostle of air power and the New Look, and his political perceptions were melodramatic. Presenting the reasons for American intervention, he argued that if Indochina were allowed to fall to the Communists, the conquest of all Southeast Asia would "inevitably follow"; long-term results involving the "gravest threats" to "fundamental" United States security interests in the Far East and "even to the stability and security of Europe" would ensue. "Communization of Japan" would be a probable result. Control of the rice, tin, rubber and oil of Southeast Asia and of the industrial capacity of a Communized Japan would enable Red China "to build a monolithic military structure more formidable than that of Japan prior to World War II." It would then command the western Pacific and much of Asia and exercise a threat extending as far as the Middle East.

The specters that thronged Admiral Radford's imagination—which have so far fallen rather short of being realized—raise an important question for the study of folly. What level of perception, what fiction or fantasy, enters into policy-making? What wild flights soar over reasonable estimates of reality? What degree of conviction or, on the contrary, conscious exaggeration is at work? Is the argument believed or is it inventive rhetoric employed to enforce a desired course of action?

Whether Radford's views were shaped by Dulles or Dulles' by Radford is uncertain but either way they reflected the same over-reaction. Dulles now bent his energies to ensure that the Geneva Conference would allow no inch of compromise with Hanoi, no relaxation by the French, and that the terrible danger inherent in the meeting be understood by his countrymen. He summoned Congressmen, news-papermen, businessmen and other persons of prestige to briefings on the American stake in Indochina. He showed them color charts of Communist influence radiating outward in a red wave from Indochina to Thailand, Burma, Malaya and Indonesia. His spokesmen listed strategic raw materials which would be acquired by Russia and China and denied to the West, and they raised the specter, if America should fail to hold the bulwarks, of Communist gains across Asia from Japan to India. Dulles left the impression, according to one listener, that if the United States could not hold the French in line then we would have to commit our own forces to the conflict. The impression con-veyed itself to Vice-President Nixon, who, in a supposedly off-the-record speech naturally widely quoted, said, in a foreshadowing of Executive war, "If to avoid further Communist expansion in Asia and Indochina, we must take the risk now of putting our boys in, I think the Executive has to take the politically unpopular decision and do it."

The President made the most important contribution to the hypnosis at a press conference on 7 April 1954 when he used the phrase "falling dominoes" to express the consequences if Indochina should be the first to fall. The theory that neighboring countries of Southeast Asia would succumb one after the other by some immutable law of nature had long been voiced. Eisenhower's press conference gave it a name as instantly accepted in the annals of Americana as the Open Door. Whether it was realistic was not questioned, although it encountered some skepticism abroad, as Eisenhower attests in his memoirs. "Our main task was to convince the world that the Southeast Asia war was an aggressive move by the Communists to subjugate that entire area." Americans "as well as the citizens of the three Associated States had to be assured of the true meaning of the war." The hypnosis, in short, had to be extended and war's "true meaning" conveyed by outsiders to a people on whose soil it had been fought for seven years. The need for so much explaining and justifying suggested an inherent flaw which, as time went on, was to widen.

Anticipating Geneva, the Viet-Minh gathered forces for a major show of strength. By raids and artillery they laid siege to Dien Bien Phu, destroyed the French airstrips in March 1954, cut off French supply lines and with the aid of augmented Chinese supplies, which reached a peak of 4000 tons a month during the battle, reduced the fortress to desperate straits.

The crisis echoed in Washington. General Paul Ely, French Chief of Staff, arrived with an explicit request for an American air strike to relieve Dien Bien Phu. The emergency moved Admiral Radford to offer a raid by B-29s from Clark Field in Manila. He had tentatively raised among a few selected officials at State and Defense the possibility of asking for French approval in principle of using tactical atomic weapons to save the situation at Dien Bien Phu. A study group at the Pentagon had concluded that three such weapons properly employed would be sufficient to "smash the Viet-Minh effort there," but the option was not approved and not even broached to the French.* Radford's proposal for conventional Air Force intervention, although

---

* Radford had in mind, it has been said, provoking a Chinese military response in order to precipitate a war with the United States before China was strong enough to

it acquired the historical dignity of a code name, Operation Vulture, was unauthorized by the Joint Chiefs as a whole and, as the Admiral stated later, was "conceptual" only. Ely went home with nothing definite except a promise of 25 additional bombers for French use.

At the same time Dulles was grasping for the conditions that would permit American armed intervention in the event of French collapse. He summoned eight members of Congress, including the Majority and Minority leaders of the Senate, William Knowland and Lyndon Johnson, to a secret conference and asked them for a Joint Resolution by Congress to permit the use of air and naval power in Indochina. Radford, who was present, explained the nature of the emergency and proposed an air strike by 200 planes from the aircraft carriers in the South China Sea. Dulles at high voltage expounded his vision of encirclement if Indochina should be lost. Discovering that Radford's plan did not have the approval of the other Joint Chiefs and that Dulles did not have allies lined up for united action, the Congressmen would go no further than to say that they could probably obtain the resolution if allies were found and the French promised to stay in the field and "accelerate" independence.

In Paris the French Cabinet summoned Ambassador Douglas Dillon to an emergency Sunday meeting to ask for "immediate armed intervention of United States carrier aircraft." They said the fate of Southeast Asia and of the forthcoming Geneva Conference "now rested on Dien Bien Phu." Meeting with Dulles and Radford, Eisenhower remained adamant on his conditions for intervention. His firmness had two foundations: an innate respect for the constitutional processes of government and a recognition that air and naval action would draw in ground forces, whose employment he opposed. He told a press conference in March that "There is going to be no involvement of America in war unless it is the result of the constitutional process that is placed

---

threaten American security. His suggested use of A-weapons in Indochina was submitted orally by the Admiral's assistant to General Douglas MacArthur, then acting as Counselor to the Defense Department, who firmly discouraged the idea. "If we approached the French," he wrote to Dulles, "the story would certainly leak . . . and cause a great hue and cry throughout the parliaments of the free world," particularly among the NATO allies, especially Britain. America would then be pressured to give assurances that she would not use A-weapons in the future without consultation. Furthermore, Soviet propaganda would portray "our desire to use such weapons in Indochina as proof of the fact we were testing out weapons on native peoples." According to an attached note by one of Dulles' staff, "Sec did not want to raise this now with Adm. R—and the latter I gather did not raise it with Sec."

upon Congress to declare it. Now let us have that clear; and that is the answer." Further he agreed with the military conclusion that air and naval action without ground forces could not gain the American objective, and he did not believe ground forces should again be committed, as in Korea, without prospect of decisive result.

In the military discussions, the resolute opponent of ground combat was the Army Chief of Staff, General Matthew B. Ridgway, who had saved the situation in Korea. Sent to take over the command from MacArthur, he had pulled the 8th Army out of disarray and led it to a fight that frustrated North Korea's attempt to take over the country. If not victory, the outcome had at least restored the status quo ante and contained Communism. Ridgway's views were emphatic and subsequently confirmed by a survey team he sent to Indochina in June when the issue of United States intervention became critical. Headed by General James Gavin, Chief of Plans and Development, the team reported that American ground combat would take "heavy casualties" and require five divisions at the outset and ten when fully involved. The area was "practically devoid of those facilities which modern forces such as ours find essential to the waging of war. Its telecommunications, highways, railroads, all the things that make possible the operations of a modern force on land, were almost nonexistent." To create these facilities would require "tremendous engineering and logistical efforts" at tremendous cost, and in the team's opinion "this ought not to be done."

Eisenhower agreed, and not only for military reasons. He believed unilateral United States intervention would be politically disastrous. "The United States should in no event undertake alone to support French colonialism," he said to an associate. "Unilateral action by the United States in cases of this kind would destroy us." The principle of united action should apply too, he emphasized, in case of overt Chinese aggression.

The threat of a settlement with Communism threw Dulles into a fury af activity to round up allies, especially the British, for united action, to keep the French in combat, to scare the Chinese from intervention by hints of atomic warfare, to thwart coalition, partition, ceasefire or any other compromise with Ho Chi Minh and in general to scuttle the Geneva Conference either before or after it convened.

Like fibers of a cloth absorbing a dye, policy-makers in Washington were by now so thoroughly imbued, through repeated assertions, with the vital necessity of saving Indochina from Communism that they believed in it, did not question it and were ready to act on it. From rhetoric it had become doctrine, and, in the excitement of the crisis, evoked from the President's Special Committee on Indochina a policy advice with respect to the Geneva Conference that in simple-minded arrogance might have been Lord Hillsborough come back to life. Comprising Defense, State and CIA, the Committee included among its members Deputy Secretary of Defense Roger Kyes, Admiral Radford, Under-Secretary of State Walter Bedell Smith, Assistant Secretary Walter Robertson and Allen Dulles and Colonel Edward Lansdale of CIA. On April 5 it recommended as a first principle that "It be United States policy to accept nothing short of a military victory in Indochina." Considering that the United States was not a belligerent, an element of fantasy seems to have entered into this demand.

Secondly, if failing to obtain French support for this position, the United States should "initiate immediate steps with the governments of the Associated States aimed toward continuation of the war in Indochina to include active United States participation" with or without French agreement. In plainer language that meant that the United States should take over the war by request of the Associated States. Further, that there should be "no cease-fire in Indochina prior to victory" whether the victory came by "successful military action or clear concession of defeat by the Communists." Since, with Dien Bien Phu falling, military action hardly pointed toward success, and since concession of defeat by the Viet-Minh was a hypothesis made of air, and since the United States was in no position to decide whether or not there should be a cease-fire, this provision was entirely meaningless. Finally, to combat a certain passivity with regard to the American thesis, the Committee urged that "extraordinary" efforts be made "to give vitality in Southeast Asia to the concept that Communist imperialism is a transcending threat to each of the Southeast Asia states."

The fate of this document, whether discussed, rejected or adopted, is not recorded. It does not matter, for the fact that it could be formulated at all reflects the thinking—or what passes for thinking by government—that conditioned developments and laid the path for future American intervention in Vietnam.

Dulles' efforts to assemble united action were unavailing. The British proved recalcitrant and, unpersuaded of the American view that Australia, New Zealand and Malaya were candidates for the domino list, firmly refused to commit themselves to any course of action prior to the outcome of the Geneva discussions. The French, in spite of their crisis and their request for an air strike, refused to invite the United States to take part in their war, feeling that outright partnership would damage their prestige, which no nation takes so seriously as the French. They wanted to keep Indochina their own affair, not part of a united front against Communism. The reluctance Dulles met in both cases was in part of his own making because the alarm raised by his "massive retaliation" speech of the previous January caused the allies to worry about America initiating atomic warfare.

On 7 May, Dien Bien Phu fell, giving the Viet-Minh a stunning triumph to support their claims at Geneva. Braving it out, Dulles assured a press conference that "Southeast Asia could be secured even without perhaps Vietnam, Laos and Cambodia"—in other words, the dominoes would not be falling as expected.

In the gloom of the day after the news from Dien Bien Phu, the parley on Indochina opened in Geneva. It was held at the upper level, with France represented by Premier Joseph Laniel and the other powers by their Foreign Ministers—Anthony Eden and Molotov as co-chairmen, Dulles and Under-Secretary Bedell Smith for the United States, Chou En-lai for China, Pham Van Dong for the Viet-Minh, and representatives of Laos, Cambodia and the Associated States of Vietnam. Tension was high because Premier Laniel had to bring home a cease-fire to save his government, while the Americans were bending their efforts to prevent it. The Europeans pressed, terms acceptable to both sides were hard to find, coalition government was abandoned in favor of partition, the demarcation line and withdrawal zones were fiercely disputed, arguments festered, emotions rose.

As the weeks went by, Laniel's government fell and was replaced by one under Pierre Mendès-France, who believed that continuation of the war in Indochina "does much less to bar the road to Communism in Asia than to open it in France." He announced that he would end the war in thirty days (by 21 July) or resign, and he bluntly told the National Assembly that if no cease-fire were obtained at Geneva, it would be necessary for the Assembly to authorize conscription to supplement the professional army in Indochina. He said his last act before resigning would be to introduce a bill for that purpose and the Assembly would be required to vote on it the same day. To enact conscription for an already unpopular war was not a measure the members cared to contemplate. With that threat in his pocket, Mendès-France went at once to Geneva to make good his self-imposed deadline.

The Conference struggled through a thicket of antagonisms. Partition of Vietnam was pressed as the only means of separating the belligerents; the French claimed the 18th parallel, as opposed to the Viet-Minh's claim of the 13th, later of the 16th, which would have included the ancient capital of Hue in their zone. The Associated States balked at all arrangements. Dulles, refusing to join in any concession to the Communists, departed, then returned. While back in Washington, he renewed his drum-beating about Chinese intervention. "If such overt military aggression occurred," he said in a public speech, "that would be a deliberate threat to the United States itself." He thus firmly placed United States security out on the limb of Indochina.

As Mendès' deadline approached at Geneva, breakdown threatened over the demarcation line and the timing of elections for eventual reunification. Bargainings and bilateral conferences took place behind the scenes. The Soviet Union, moving toward détente after Stalin, exerted pressure on Ho Chi Minh to settle. Chou En-lai, China's delegate, told Ho that it was in his interest to take half a loaf in order to get the French out and keep the Americans out, and that he would gain the whole eventually. He was prevailed upon very unwillingly to settle for the 17th parallel and a two-year lapse before elections. Settlement was reached in time for a final declaration on July 21 that brought the French war to an end. Insofar as France had to acknowledge defeat by conceding half of Vietnam to the rebels, the result was more damaging to her prestige than if she had conceded voluntarily at the start. In this error too the United States would later follow.

The Geneva Accord declared a cease-fire, confirmed under international auspices the independence of Laos and Cambodia and partitioned Vietnam into separate North and South zones, under the specific provision that "the military demarcation is provisional and should not in any way be interpreted as constituting a political or territorial boundary." The Accord further permitted French forces to remain until requested to leave by the Associated States, provided for elections by July 1956, for limits and regulations on foreign military bases, armaments and personnel and for an International Control Commission to supervise implementation of the terms. The government of neither Hanoi nor Saigon signed the agreement, nor did the United States, which would go no further than a sulky declaration to refrain from "the threat or the use of force" to disturb the arrangements.

The settlement at Geneva ended a war and averted wider participation by either China or the United States, but lacking satisfied sponsors anxious to sustain it, and including dissatisfied parties looking to reverse it, it was born defective. Not the least of the dissatisfied was the United States.

Geneva represented defeat for Dulles in all aspects of his Indochina policy. He had failed to prevent establishment of a Communist regime in North Vietnam, failed to gain Britain or anyone else for united action, failed to keep France actively in the field, failed to gain approval for American military intervention from the President, even failed to gain EDC, which the French Assembly unkindly rejected in August. These results left little impression; he was not prepared to infer from them any reason to re-examine policy. As in the case of Philip II, "no experience of the failure of his policy could shake his belief in its essential excellence." He called a press conference in Geneva not to "mourn the past," as he said, but to "seize the future opportunity to prevent the loss of Northern Vietnam from leading to the extension of Communism throughout Southeast Asia and the Southwest Pacific." The refrain was the same as before. He adduced one lesson, however, from the experience: "that resistance to Communism needs popular support . . . and that the people should feel that they are defending their own national institutions." That was indeed the lesson and it could not have been better stated, but as events were to show, it had only been stated, not learned.

3. Creating the Client:
1954-60

At this stage, with eight years of American effort in aid of the French having come to nothing, and with the French effort having failed at a cost in French Union troops of 50,000 killed and 100,000 wounded, the United States might have seen indications for disengagement from Indochina's affairs. The example of futility in China was fresh, where a longer and greater effort to direct that country's destinies had been dissipated by the Communist Revolution like sand before the wind. No inference from the Chinese experience—that Western wishes might not apply to the situation, that foreign politics, too, is the art of the possible —had been derived. The American government reacted not to the Chinese upheaval or to Vietnamese nationalism per se, but to intimidation by the rabid right at home and to the public dread of Communism that this played on and reflected. The social and psychological sources of that dread are not our subject, but in them lie the roots of American policy in Vietnam.

The United States had no thought either of disengaging from Indochina or of acquiescing in the Geneva settlement. Dulles' immediate task as he saw it was two-fold: to create a non-colonial Southeast Asia treaty organization like NATO which should provide authority in advance for collective defense—or its image—against the advance of Communism in the area; and secondly, to ensure the functioning of a valid national state in South Vietnam able to hold the line against the North and eventually recapture the country. The Secretary of State was already engaged in both efforts in advance of the Geneva Declaration.

Dulles had begun drum-beating for a SEA mutual security pact in May as part of his campaign to counteract Geneva. Whether consciously or not, he was moving to bring the United States into position as the controlling power in the situation, replacing the colonial powers. He wanted a legal international basis for intervention as had existed in Korea because of violation of a boundary established by the UN. The implications alarmed observers, among others the *St. Louis Post-Dispatch*, which asked in a series of editorials before the Geneva cease-fire whether Dulles' purpose was "to provide a backdoor method by which the United States can intervene in the Indochina war." Do the people of the United States wish "to organize the use of armed forces against internal revolt of the kind that started the Indochina war"? Answering in the negative, the *Post-Dispatch* reiterated the theme "This is a war to stay out of." It foresaw that intervention would commit the United States to a "limited" war which probably "could only be won by making it unlimited." For further emphasis, the newspaper published a cartoon by Daniel Fitzpatrick showing Uncle Sam gazing into a dark swamp labeled "French Mistakes in Indochina." The caption asked, "How would another mistake help?" The fact that the cartoon won a Pulitzer Prize is evidence that its message, as early as 1954, was not obscure.

Tragedy deeper than a mistake was seen in the same year by an observer deeply concerned with the American relation to Asia. In his book *Wanted: An Asian Policy*, Edwin O. Reischauer, Far East specialist and future Ambassador to Japan, located the tragedy in the West's having allowed Indochinese nationalism to become a Communist cause. This is what had come of American support of the French in "an extremely ineffective and ultimately hopeless defense of the status quo." The result "shows how absurdly wrong we are to battle Asian nationalism instead of aiding it."

Under Dulles' relentlessly organizing hand, a conference to establish the Southeast Asia Treaty Organization (SEATO) met at Manila in September 1954. By involving only three Asian nations, and only two—Thailand and the Philippines—from Southeast Asia (the third was Pakistan), and only one contiguous to Indochina and none from Indochina itself, it lacked a certain authenticity from the start. The other members were Britain, France, Australia, New Zealand and the United States. Combatively as ever, Dulles informed the delegates that their purpose was to agree in advance on a response "so united, so strong and so well-placed" that any aggression against the treaty area would lose more than it could gain. Since the Asian members of the conference had no appreciable military power, and the others were either in no geographical position to deploy it or were already withdrawing from the area, and since the United States itself had reached no settled commitment of forces for the defense of Southeast Asia, the Secretary's demand was an exercise in make-believe. In Article IV, the operative core of the treaty, he obtained a commitment by each member to "meet the common danger in accordance with its constitutional processes." This was not exactly the ready sword Excalibur.

In a separate protocol, Dulles managed to bring the Associated States of Indochina under the protection of Article IV and to define its obligations, to his own satisfaction, as a "clear and definite agreement on the part of the signatories" to come to the aid of any member of the pact subjected to aggression. In real terms, as a delegate from the Defense Department, Vice-Admiral Davis, said, the treaty left Southeast Asia "no better prepared than before to cope with Communist aggression."

In the meantime a new premier of South Vietnam had been installed who from the start to violent finish was an American client. Chosen not from within the country but from the circle of Vietnamese exiles outside, he was elevated by French and American manipulations in which France was a very reluctant partner. For the sake of motivating greater energy and self-reliance in South Vietnam, the United States was determined to remove the French presence apart from the unfortunate necessity of retaining France's armed forces until a reliable Vietnamese army could be officered and trained to take their place. Under the Geneva arrangements, the French were obligated to supervise the armistice and the eventual elections, and for them it was hard not to assume that during the transition period their commercial and administrative and cultural ties could be maintained and developed toward a voluntary inclusion of Indochina in the French Union.

The United States wanted the contrary and found a player in Ngo Dinh Diem, an ardent nationalist of a Catholic mandarin family whose father had been a Lord Chamberlain at the Imperial Court of Annam. Diem had served as a provincial governor in the French Colonial service and as Minister of Interior under Bao Dai, but had resigned in 1933 in protest against French rule and the cancellation of promised reforms. He retired to Japan and after his return had refused a Japanese offer in 1945 to form a government under the ever available Bao Dai. As fervent an anti-Communist as he was a nationalist, he had likewise rejected the alternative of joining Ho Chi Minh, who had offered him a post at Hanoi. This non-cooperation led to his arrest and detainment for six months by the Viet-Minh. Recognized as the leading non-Communist nationalist, he had refused to serve under the Elysée Agreement as incompatible with sovereignty, and in 1949 went again into exile in Japan. In 1950 he came to the United States, where by virtue of a brother who was a Catholic bishop he made contact with Cardinal Spellman of New York.

Introduced by the Cardinal to influential circles, Diem met Justice Douglas in Washington soon after Douglas' discovery of the "five fronts" of Southeast Asia. Impressed by Diem's vision of a future for his country combining independence and social reform, Douglas believed he had found the man who could be a real alternative to both the French puppet Bao Dai and the Communist Ho Chi Minh. He conveyed his discovery to the CIA and introduced his candidate to Senators Mansfield and John F. Kennedy, both Catholics. Thereafter, Diem was on his way.

Here at last was the American candidate, a valid Vietnamese nationalist whose Francophobia absolved him of any taint of colonialism and whose approval by Cardinal Spellman certified his anti-Communism. He was safe from Senator McCarthy. He went to Europe in 1953 to promote his candidacy among the Vietnamese expatriates in France and was actively lobbying in Paris in 1954 during the Geneva parley when discovery of a promising leader was urgent. Diem was certainly not a French choice, but France's need of a cease-fire was more compelling than her dislike of the candidate. With American backing and the wire-pulling of various factions among the expatriates, and with Mendès-France's deadline drawing close, Diem was reluctantly accepted. Bao Dai, still Chief of State in a comfortable retreat on the Riviera, was prevailed upon to appoint him premier just before the Geneva Accord was signed.

Around this figure, over the next nine years, the effort to construct a viable democratic self-sustaining state of South Vietnam centered and collapsed. Diem proved ill-equipped. Living on theory and high principle, he had no experience of national independent government; he shared the general antagonism to the French, yet inherited the colonial legacy through the class that benefited from it and to which he belonged; he was a devout Catholic in a largely Buddhist society; he had to contend with divisive sects and Mafia-type factions with private armies and gangster methods. Rigid in his ideas, unschooled in compromise, unacquainted with democracy in practice, he was unable to deal with dissent or opposition except by fiat or force. In one of the sad betrayals that high office inflicts on good intentions, circumstances turned him into a dictator without giving him a dictator's iron means.

Now, with an American Ambassador and full-scale Embassy in Saigon, and with proliferating advisers and agencies in addition to MAAG, United States policy injected itself more purposefully than ever, taking as its first task the training of an effective and, it was to be hoped, loyal and motivated Vietnamese army. MAAG wanted to do it alone without participation by the French, on the theory that American influence would thereby be differentiated from the French. That we would inherit the distaste felt for any white intrusion was not contemplated. Americans saw themselves as "different" from the French, to be welcomed as well-wishers of Vietnamese independence, while the fact that it was the United States which had brought back the French and financed their war was mentally swept under the rug. By helping an independent South Vietnam to establish itself, it was thought we could prove our good intentions.

Requirements for the training program brought out in discussion the reluctance of military policy-makers in Washington to become further involved. But given a mission, the good soldier carries it out without question. General O'Daniel, the MAAG commander, drew up a schedule of procedures and requirements for the training program and pleaded for an enlarged staff to be despatched before the Geneva cut-off for additional personnel.

With ample reports about the mood and uncertain loyalties of the Vietnamese army, the Joint Chiefs were thoroughly skeptical; they did not want to be held responsible for failure, or worse, in case of a clash, having American troops drawn in to rescue an inadequate force. They concluded in an unambiguous memorandum of August 1954 that it was "absolutely essential" to have "a reasonably strong stable civil government in control," and that it was "hopeless to expect a United States training mission to achieve success" unless the nation concerned could effectively perform all functions necessary to recruitment and maintenance. They foresaw "a complete military vacuum" if French forces were withdrawn and, if the United States took over, an unwanted American "responsibility for any failure of the program," and they judged in conclusion that the United States "should not participate." They hastened to add, with the care of government advisers never to be too definitive, that if "political considerations are overriding" they would "agree to the assignment of a training mission." In official process, advice tends to be flexible because it is afraid of closed options.

Strenuous arguing ensued about the force levels to be trained, the cost of maintaining the French army in place—$100 million for 1955, $193 million for 1956—and the timing of phased French withdrawals, while the Joint Chiefs' doubts of success grew all the while stronger. In November 1954, given the chaotic internal political situation in Vietnam, they found "no assurance . . . of loyal and effective support for the Diem Government" or of "political and military stability within South Vietnam." Unless the Vietnamese themselves showed the will to resist Communism, "no amount of external pressure and assistance can long delay complete Communist victory in South Vietnam." With hindsight, it is impossible to avoid asking why the American government ignored the advice of the persons appointed to give it.

Harassed by internal opponents and rivals, and by incompetence, dissent and corruption, Diem had also to cope with an influx of nearly a million refugees from the North during the 300 days allowed by Geneva for exchange of populations. In response to Catholic propaganda spreading the word that "Christ has moved south" and "the Virgin Mary has moved south," the mass movement was 85 percent Catholic. It represented nevertheless a significant group who did not want to live under Communism, and by providing Diem with a coherent body of support actually helped to consolidate his rule, although his favoring them in official positions aroused antagonism. The United States assumed much of the burden; the Navy transported 300,000 of the refugees and their resettlement was underwritten by an outpouring of funds raised by Catholic Charities and others.

"Highly placed officials from Washington," after visiting Saigon, according to one report, privately indicated their conclusion that "Vietnam probably would have to be written off at a loss." Assailed by contrary advice, struggling with the problem of how to strengthen and stabilize Diem, of how to retain the French forces while eliminating their interests, of what to decide about training the Vietnamese army, of what degree of investment to make in general, American policy found itself in a morass. The French, who never liked Diem, reported him, in the words of Premier Faure, "not only incapable but mad." Senator Mansfield, on the other hand, after a second fact-finding trip, reported him to be a genuine nationalist whose survival was essential to American policy. Mansfield's report to the Senate, however, was more discouraged than in the previous year. He said the situation had "seriously deteriorated" owing to a "consistent underestimating" by everyone of the political and military strength of the Viet-Minh. Because of dissatisfaction with Diem's policies, there appeared to be "scant hope of achieving our objectives in Indochina in the near future." If Diem fell, Mansfield believed, his successors would be even less democratic, and in that event the United States "should consider an immediate suspension of all aid to Vietnam and the French Union forces there." He concluded with a cold dose of common sense: "Unless there is reasonable expectation of fulfilling our objectives, the continued expenditure of the resources of the citizens of the United States is unwarranted and inexcusable."

Eisenhower hesitated. He addressed a letter to Diem in October expressing his grave concern for the future of a country "temporarily divided by an artificial military grouping" (not the "international boundary" that his successors liked to claim) but advising that he was ready to work out with Diem "an intelligent program of American aid given directly to your Government," provided that Diem gave assurance of the "standards of performance" his government would maintain if the aid were supplied. With little confidence in promises, the President sent General J. Lawton Collins, a trusted colleague from World War II, on a special mission to work out relations with the French and the "standards" expected of Diem.

Collins' report was negative. He found Diem "unready to assert the type of leadership that can unify this country and give it a chance of competing with the hard, effective, unified control of Ho Chi Minh." The choices open to American policy, as he saw them, were either to support Diem for a little while longer without commitment or, if he failed to make progress, to bring back Bao Dai, and if that was unacceptable, "I recommend re-evaluation of our plans for assisting Southeast Asia with special attention to earlier proposal," namely, "the gradual withdrawal of support from Vietnam." This was "the least desirable [but] in all honesty, and in view of what I have observed here to date, this may be the only solution."

Asked to stay on to work out a program of support with General Ely, the French commander, Collins reaffirmed his advice five months later. Vietnam would not be saved from Communism, he reported, unless a sound program of political, economic and military reforms were put into effect based on wholehearted coordination among Vietnamese, Americans and French, and if this were not secured, "in my judgment we should withdraw from Vietnam."

Why, in the light of all these doubts and negatives, did the United States not take the opportunity to pull back? It did not because always the argument arose that if American support were withdrawn, South Vietnam would disintegrate and the front against Communism would give way in Indochina just when it faced a new threat elsewhere. The Quemoy-Matsu crisis over the Chinese offshore islands erupted at this time, bringing Dulles to his most paranoid and to the "brink"—in his terms—of war with Red China. The crisis quelled any impulse to look at Vietnam with realism or to consider General Collins' alternative.

Collins himself, though convinced of Diem's incapacity, was working energetically to make the regime qualify as a client worth American support, and in response to his pressure a program of land reform was drawn up and a provisional assembly appointed to draft a constitution. Washington seized on these signs of progress and, motivated also by desire to frustrate French overtures to Diem's rivals, officially con-. firmed American support of his government. At the same time, in February 1955, the decision to undertake the training of a "completely autonomous" Vietnamese army was taken, and with it a deep step into Vietnamese affairs.

The assumption of American responsibility had already brought with it the creeping companion of all interventions, covert operations. A combat team calling itself the Saigon Military Mission had begun operating in North Vietnam under the direction of General O'Daniel and the command of Colonel Lansdale, an officer of the Air Force and later of the CIA who had led activities against the Huk guerrillas in the Philippines. Conceived and organized before the Geneva Agreement, its operations were conducted for a year after the Geneva provisions made them illegitimate. The Mission's original assignment was to "undertake paramilitary operations against the enemy"—although technically speaking the United States as a non-belligerent had no "enemy." Its purpose was modified after Geneva to read "prepare the means" for such operations. To that end the Lansdale Mission engaged in the sabotage of trucks and railroads, undertook the recruiting, training and infiltrating of two covert South Vietnamese "paramilitary" teams, and planted for their use caches of smuggled supplies, arms and ammunition. Since the Geneva Agreement had prohibited the introduction of all war matériel and personnel after 23 July 1954, and the United States had pledged not to "disturb" these provisions, the Mission after that date violated the pledge. While not very heinous per se and normal enough if the nation had been at war, the violation began the series of falsehoods that were to widen until they engulfed the reputation and damaged the self-respect of the United States.

A feasible alternative to the embracing of an infirm client was possible, and attempted, in fact, by the French. Accommodation with Hanoi was now openly the French aim, not only for the sake of French investments and commercial interests in both North and South, but also to test Mendès-France's political philosophy of peaceful coexistence. The French government, reported Ambassador Douglas Dillon from Paris, was more and more "disposed to explore and consider . . . an eventual North-South rapprochement," and in pursuit of this aim sent a major figure, Jean Sainteny, to Hanoi. A former colonial official and a Free

French officer during the war, he had maintained relations with Ho Chi Minh and served during the Indochina war as French Commissioner for the North. Ostensibly his mission in Hanoi was to protect French business interests, but Ambassador Dillon learned that Sainteny had convinced his government that South Vietnam was doomed and that "the only possible means of salvaging anything was to play the Viet-Minh game and woo the Viet-Minh away from Communist ties in the hope of creating a Titoist Vietnam which would cooperate with France and might even adhere to the French Union."

While the Titoist solution now seems illusory, it was no more so than the American belief in building a strong capable democratic alternative to Ho Chi Minh in the Diem regime; one scenario could have been tried as easily as the other. The French program did not work out because Mendès-France lost office in 1955 and because French businessmen, unable to realize profits under Communist restrictions, gradually withdrew from the North while the French hold in general was being reduced by the United States.

Failure, however, does not necessarily mean that the goal was impossible. Ho's primary object at this time was to gain and maintain Vietnam's independence of France just as it was Marshal Tito's to gain Yugoslavia's independence of Russia. If the United States could aid Tito, why should it have to crush Ho? The answer is that the self-hypnosis had worked: mixed with a vague sense of the Yellow Peril advancing with hordes of now-Communist Chinese, there was felt to be something peculiarly sinister about Communism in Asia. As its agent, North Vietnam remained "the enemy."

The client was not doing well. An attempted coup d'état by Diem's antagonists in April 1955, a Cabinet crisis and the active disloyalty of his Chief of Staff revived American anxiety. According to a *New York Times* correspondent, his government "has proven inept, inefficient and unpopular," the "chances of saving it were slim" and "brooding civil war threatens to tear the country apart." Even Dulles had said to General Collins when Collins left to take up his post that "the chances of our saving the situation there are not more than one in ten." In the light of Diem's further troubles, he now concluded that "the only serious problem we have not yet solved is that of indigenous leadership." The implications of this stunning assessment did not occur to him.

Washington was in a quandary, vainly seeking an alternative to Diem, anxiously questioning whether to invest more support in a wavering regime. General Collins was re-called for consultation. At a press conference, President Eisenhower allowed an almost painful glimpse of his hesitation: "In Vietnam there have occurred lots of difficulties. People have left the Cabinet and so on . . . it is a strange and almost inexplicable situation. . . . What the exact terms of our future policy will be I can't say."

Here was another opportunity for disengagement. Diem's government had not lived up to the "standards of performance" on which Eisenhower had conditioned American aid. The implications of the French defeat, the refusal of the British to commit themselves to united action, the pallid partnership of the NATO nations—why did not the Eisenhower Administration put it all together and, given the President's great prestige at home, detach itself from a losing proposition? In the bureaucracy, doubtless no one did put it all together; and besides, the fear of being "soft on Communism" abided.

Diem's success in smashing the coup d'état with troops loyal to the source of American largesse gave him a reprieve. He tightened his government by bringing in his three brothers to replace opponents and took on the appearance of a strong man. The United States, relieved of the pain of re-thinking, publicly reaffirmed its support for him, chiefly because it feared the consequences of letting him fall. Donald Heath, the new Ambassador in Saigon, stated the choice: committing "over $300 million plus our national prestige" on the retention of a Free Vietnam was a gamble, but withholding support would be worse by assisting a Communist takeover. The choice, as all too often, was between two undesirables.

Enforcing the choice was always the fear of domestic outcry. Mansfield, the influential Senator, "believes in Diem," it was said, and the reaction to be expected from Cardinal Spellman if his protégé were dumped was unpleasant to contemplate. "Alas! for the newly betrayed millions of Indochinese," he had declared after Geneva, "who must now learn the awful facts of slavery from their eager Communist masters" in repetition of "the agonies and infamies inflicted upon the hapless victims of Red Russia's bestial tyranny." Communism had been following a "carefully set-up timetable for the achievement of a world plan." Red rulers knew what they wanted with "terrible clarity" and pursued it with "violent consistency." The Cardinal had continued in this vein, rousing a convention of the American Legion to unanimous bristle. In mid-1955, when Eisenhower was preparing to run for a second term, he had no desire to let loose more tirades of this kind.

Adoption of the client made the United States a sponsor in Diem's fateful denial of the nationwide elections to be held in 1956 as agreed on at Geneva. The North, with a population of 15 million to South

Vietnam's 12 million, and a general acknowledgment of the greater popularity of the Viet-Minh, had counted on the elections to gain command of the country as a whole. When in July 1955 it invited the South to consult on preparations for the event, Diem refused on the ground that no election under the Hanoi regime would allow a free vote, that enforced results would overwhelm the votes of the South and that in any event he was not bound by the Geneva Accord. While valid, his objection lost something of its force when three months later, in a referendum held in the South to depose the absent Bao Dai as Chief of State and confer the Presidency on Diem, the desired result was achieved by what a foreign observer called "outrageous" methods that delivered 98.8 percent of the vote. A free expression of the voters' will was obviously not to be expected on either side, nor could it have been otherwise in a country devoid of democratic experience. As a solution for Vietnam's civil conflict, the election—supposed to have been supervised by a powerless International Control Commission—was never more than a charade devised at Geneva as a desperate expedient to allow temporary partition and a cease-fire.

No one questioned that if the elections were held, as one official reported, "the overwhelming majority of Vietnamese would vote Communist." In the course of a speech opposing equal status for a Communist regime, Senator John F. Kennedy acknowledged "the popularity and prevalence" of Ho Chi Minh's party "throughout Indochina"—which seemed to him reason *not* to allow its participation in a national government. Eisenhower, informed by advisers that Ho would certainly win the election, "refused to agree" (according to General Ridgway) to its taking place. While Diem did not need American advice in the matter, his refusal rested on American support. By 1956 more evidence of harsh measures in the North, including widespread killing of landlords on the Chinese pattern, was at hand. Terrorist tactics in an election could be assumed. In June 1956 the State Department officially announced that "We support President Diem fully in his position that when conditions do not exist that could preclude 'intimidation or coercion' . . . there can be no free choice."

The consequence was that, failing reunification by election, North Vietnam resorted to other means—the encouragement of insurgency followed by the so-called War of Liberation. No egregious folly may be charged to the United States in this affair except that, by backing Diem's decision, America seemed to share in what critics of the war were to claim was a brazen suppression of the people's will, leaving the North no alternative but insurgency. Suppression it was not, because the people's will would not have found a free voice in any case. The non-holding of the elections was an excuse for, not a cause of, renewed war. "We shall achieve unity," the North's Deputy Premier Pham Van Dong had warned at Geneva. "No force in the world, internal or external, can make us deviate from our path."

In the next five years, with a flow of American funds that paid 60 to 75 percent of its budget, including the total cost of its army, and supported an unfavorable trade balance, South Vietnam appeared to flourish in unanticipated order and prosperity. The French armed forces, under insistent American pressure, gradually departed in phased withdrawals until the French High Command was dissolved in February 1956. The American Friends of Vietnam, organized by the Catholic Relief Services and the International Rescue Committee (originally formed to save victims of Nazism and having a list of the most respectable liberal names running down its letterhead), spread word with the assistance of a public relations agent in Saigon, on a $3000 monthly retainer, of the "miracle" of South Vietnam. It seemed, during these five years, as if progress had been made and the gamble would work.

Behind the miracle, facts were less favorable. Ill-planned land reforms alienated more than they helped the peasants; "Communist denunciation" programs, in which neighbors were induced to inform on one another, and endless busy and corrupt official interferences in peasant lives turned sentiment against Diem. Critics and dissenters were arrested, sent to "re-education camps," or otherwise silenced. The flood of imports paid for by the United States was used as a political instrument to win middle-class support through a generous supply of consumer goods. A study by American political scientists reported that South Vietnam "is becoming a permanent mendicant" dependent on external support, and concluded that "American aid has built a castle on sand."

Peasant discontent supplied ready ground for insurgents. Operating on the move, Viet-Minh partisans native to the South, who had stayed behind after partition, formed guerrilla groups, which were joined by partisans who had gone North at the partition and, after training and indoctrination, filtered back over the border. By 1959 insurgents controlled large areas of South Vietnam. "If you drew a paint brush across the South," an intelligence agent told Senator Mansfield, "every hair of the brush would touch a Viet-Minh."

In the same years the North too suffered disaffection, owing partly to food scarcity as a result of being cut off from the rice bowl of the South, and partly to Communist oppression. In a public confession to Party colleagues, General Giap acknowledged in 1956 that "We executed too many honest people . . . resorted to terror . . . disciplinary punishments . . . torture." Internal stresses kept Hanoi too preoccupied in its own territory to launch war against the South, but reunification remained the fixed goal. While crushing resistance and establishing control during the period 1955–60, Hanoi enlarged and trained its forces, accumulated arms from China and by degrees built up connections with the insurgents in the South.

By 1960 between 5000 and 10,000 guerrillas, called by the Saigon government Viet-Cong, meaning "Vietnamese Communist," were estimated to be active in the South. While the Vietnamese army, under American advice, was mainly stationed along the partition line to guard against a Korea-style attack, the insurgents were spreading havoc. According to Saigon, they had in the past year assassinated 1400 officials and civilians and kidnapped 700 others. Diem's most stringent measures, including death sentences authorized for terrorists, subversives and "rumor spreaders," and relocation of peasant communities into fortified village clusters, proved ineffective. The population felt no active loyalty either to Diem or, on the other hand, to Communism or the cause of reunification. They wanted safety, land and the harvest of their crops. "The situation may be summed up," reported the American Embassy in January 1960, "in the fact that the government has tended to treat the population with suspicion or to coerce it and has been rewarded with apathy and resentment."

In that year the Manifesto of the Eighteen, issued by a Committee for Progress and Liberty that included ten former Cabinet members, called for Diem's resignation and sweeping reforms. He had all of them arrested. Six months later a military coup attempted his overthrow on the ground that he had "shown himself incapable of saving the country from Communism and of protecting national unity." With the aid of troops summoned from outside the city, Diem suppressed the coup within 24 hours. He received Washington's congratulations and expression of the hope that with strengthened power, he could now proceed to "rapid implementation of radical reforms." This American hope was conveyed with monotonous regularity, always with the hint behind it that continuance of aid depended on "standards of performance." Yet when reforms failed to follow, American aid did not stop, for fear that if it were withdrawn Diem would fall.

American confidence vis-à-vis the Soviet Union suffered another shock in 1957 when the Russians launched *Sputnik* into orbit to a height of 560 miles and a speed around the globe of 18,000 miles per hour. In the year before this dismaying feat, Soviet armed forces had taken over Hungary while the United States, for all Dulles' boasts, remained passive. In the year after *Sputnik*, Communists under Fidel Castro took over Cuba, likewise watched helplessly by the United States, though only 90 miles away. Yet the Communists in faraway Vietnam were perceived as a direct threat to American security.

In consultation between Washington and Saigon, a counter-guerrilla or counter-insurgency plan was developed to coordinate the work of American agencies with the Vietnamese army. MAAG's personnel was doubled to 685 for the program. The new Ambassador, Elbridge Durbrow, had misgivings. He did not think the additional military aid the plan called for should be delivered, or would be effective, without political improvement. But Diem exerted the perverse power of the weak: the greater his troubles, the more support he demanded—and received. In a dependent relationship the protégé can always control the protector by threatening to collapse.

In September 1960 the Communist Party Congress in Hanoi called for the overthrow of the Diem regime and of "American imperialist rule." Formation of the National Liberation Front (NLF) of South Vietnam followed in December. Though nominally native to the South, it echoed the call for the overthrow of Diem and the "camouflaged colonial regime of the American imperialists" and announced a ten-point program of Marxist social reforms dressed in the usual garments of "democracy," "equality," "peace" and "neutrality." Overt civil war was thus declared just as a new American President, John F. Kennedy, took office in the United States.

4. *"Married to Failure":*
1960-63

The new Administration came into office equipped with brain power, more pragmatism than ideology and the thinnest electoral majority of the 20th century, barely half of one percent. Like the President, his associates were activists, stimulated by crises, eager to take active measures. As far as the record shows, they held no session devoted to re-examination of the engagement they had inherited in Vietnam, nor did they ask themselves to what extent the United States was committed or what was the degree of national interest involved. Nor, so far as appears in the mountains of memoranda, discussions and options flowing over the desks, was any long-range look taken at long-range strategy. Rather, policy developed in ad hoc spurts from month to month. A White House official of the time, asked in later years how the American interest in Southeast Asia was defined in 1961, replied that "it was simply a given, assumed and unquestioned." The given was that we had to stop the advance of Communism wherever it appeared and Vietnam was then the place of confrontation. If not stopped there, it would be stronger the next time.

As a young Congressman, Kennedy had visited Indochina for himself in 1951, reaching the conclusion obvious to most American observers, that to check the Communist drive South it was essential to "build strong native non-Communist sentiment." To act "apart from and in defiance of innately nationalistic aims spells foredoomed failure." It is a dismaying fact that throughout the long folly of Vietnam, Americans kept foretelling the outcome and acting without reference to their own foresight.

By 1956 Kennedy had moved closer to cold war orthodoxy, talking less of "strong native sentiment" and more of dominoes in a variety of metaphor: Vietnam was the "cornerstone of the free world in Southeast Asia, the keystone of the arch, the finger in the dike." To the usual list of neighbors who would fall "if the red tide of Communism overflowed into Vietnam" he added India and Japan. The current of rhetoric carried him forward into two traps: Vietnam was "a proving ground of democracy in Asia" and "a test of American responsibility and determination in Asia."

Two weeks before Kennedy entered the White House, the Soviet Premier, Nikita Khrushchev, offered the decisive challenge of the time in the form of his announcement that national "wars of liberation" were to be the vehicle for advancing the Communist cause. These "just wars," he said, wherever they occurred, in Cuba, Vietnam, Algeria, would receive full Soviet support. Kennedy responded in his Inaugural Address with alarming reference to the defense of freedom "at its hour of maximum danger."

The first test was, unhappily, a grotesque and humiliating fiasco. Initiated under Eisenhower, the attempt made in April 1961 to liberate Cuba from Communism at the Bay of Pigs was a joint venture of Cuban exiles and the CIA with frivolously insufficient means and over-confident procedures. Though it was not Kennedy's plan, he was briefed on it before taking office, and given his go-ahead—impelled by the awful momentum that makes carrying through easier than calling off a folly—it was his responsibility. The invasion foreshadowed Vietnam in underestimating the opponent. Castro's regime proved well-organized, on guard, alert and ready for combat. The landings were discovered quickly and opposed vigorously, and the expected sympathetic uprisings were either effectively suppressed or never took place. Castro proved, in fact, more popular with his countrymen than the exiles whom the United States was supporting—another situation to be duplicated in Vietnam. With admirable resolve, Kennedy took the hard decision not to send in Air Force and Marines to the rescue, leaving many to perish. The effect of this spectacular snafu in the first ninety days of the Administration was to make all its members grimly determined to prove their muscle in the contest against Communism.

Neither a liberal nor a conservative, Kennedy was an operator of quick intelligence and strong ambition who stated many elevated principles convincingly, eloquently, even passionately, while his actions did not always match. In the major offices of government and the White House staff, he put men of active mind, proven ability and, as far as possible, a hardheaded attitude to match his own. Mostly men of his age, in their forties, they were not the social philosophers, innovators and idealists of the New Deal. In the Kennedy camp the word usually attached to idealist was "slob" or "bleeding heart." The New Deal was another era; world war and cold war had intervened and the far right still rumbled. The new men in government, whether

Rhodes Scholars, academics from Harvard and Brookings or recruits from Wall Street, politics and the law, were expected to be realistic, sophisticated, pragmatic, tough. Toughness was the tone, and whatever their varying characters and capacities, Kennedy's group adopted it, as the court around a monarch or a working group around a dominant chief to whom the members owe appointment is likely to do.

Robert McNamara, a prodigy of the Harvard Business School, of "systems analysis" for the Air Force during World War II and of rapid rise afterward to presidency of the Ford Motor Company, was a characteristic and outstanding choice as Secretary of Defense. Precise and positive, with slicked-down hair and rimless glasses, McNamara was a specialist of management through "statistical control," as he had demonstrated both in the Air Force and at Ford. Anything that could be quantified was his realm. Though said to be as sincere as an Old Testament prophet, he had the ruthlessness of uninterrupted success, and his genius for statistics left little respect for human variables and no room for unpredictables. His confidence in the instrumentality of matériel was perfect and complete. "We have the power to knock any society out of the 20th century," he once said at a Pentagon briefing. It was this gift of certainty that made two Presidents find McNamara so invaluable and was to make him the touchstone of the war.

No less significant was the man not chosen as Secretary of State, Adlai Stevenson, who because he was thoughtful was seen as a Hamlet, as indecisive, as that unforgivable thing, "soft." Although heavily favored for the State Department by the Eleanor Roosevelt wing of the party, he was avoided and the appointment given instead to Dean Rusk. Sober, judicious, reserved, Rusk did not share the Kennedy style, but he had the advantage of experience at the State Department and status as current President of the Rockefeller Foundation, and he would never be a challenge to the President as Stevenson might have been. As a staff colonel in charge of war planning in the China-Burma-India theater during the war, he had had the opportunity to learn from the American experience in China, but what he chiefly took from that experience was a pronounced and rigid antagonism to Chinese Communism. As Assistant Secretary for Far Eastern Affairs at the time of China's belligerency during the Korean war, Rusk had firmly and wrongly predicted that the Chinese would not enter, and thereafter felt deeply a sense of responsibility for the losses that followed.

In command of the National Security Council (NSC), with an office in the White House, was McGeorge Bundy of Boston, cool, confident, impeccable, and able to utilize his mental equipment so effectively that a schoolmate at Groton said he was ready to become dean of the school at age twelve. In fact, he became Dean of Harvard at 34. Although Bundy was a Republican in politics and family background who had twice voted for Eisenhower over Stevenson, this was no deterrent; if anything, it was a recommendation to Kennedy, who wanted connections to the respectable right. With his paper-thin mandate and a majority of only six in the Senate, he believed the problems of his Administration would come primarily from the right, and felt impelled to make overtures. One of the more extreme was his appointment as head of the CIA of John McCone, a reactionary Republican millionaire from California, a disciple of massive retaliation who, in the opinion of the Neanderthal Senator Strom Thurmond, "epitomizes what has made America great."

Like the President, many of his associates were combat veterans of World War II, having served as Navy officers and fliers, as bombardiers and navigators, and in the case of Roger Hilsman, the new Assistant Secretary of State for Far Eastern Affairs, as leader of an OSS unit behind Japanese lines in Burma. Accustomed to success in the war and in their postwar careers, they expected no less in Washington. None of the leading newcomers had ever held elective office. Power and status exhilarated these men and their fellows; they enjoyed the urgencies, even the exhaustion, of government; they liked to call themselves "crisis managers"; they tried hard, applied their skills and intelligence, were reputed "the best and the brightest"—and were to sadly discover, like others before and after them, that rather than their controlling circumstances, circumstances controlled them: that government, in the words of one of the group, J. K. Galbraith, was rarely more than a choice between "the disastrous and the unpalatable."

Creeping escalation began in Kennedy's first ten days in office, when he approved a counter-insurgency plan previously drawn up by the Pentagon to invigorate South Vietnam's operations against the Viet-Cong. It authorized additional American personnel and expenditures to train and equip a Vietnamese Civil Guard of 32,000 for anti-guerrilla activity and to increase the Vietnamese army by 20,000. The President's approval was given in response to a report by General Lansdale of increased Viet-Cong activity. Although he believed in Diem as the necessary governing figure, Lansdale had found him losing ground, unprepared to fight the kind of contest confronting him, unwilling for fear of yielding authority to institute political reforms. Comprehension was lacking in both his Vietnamese and his American advisers that tactics other than simple military formations were needed to cope with the guerrilla warfare and propaganda of the enemy. Reading the report, Kennedy commented, "This is the worst we have had yet, isn't it?"

Lansdale advocated a thorough renovation of the advisory role, which would put experienced and dedicated Americans "who know and really like Asia and the Asians" in the field to work and live alongside the Vietnamese and "try to influence and guide them toward United States policy objectives." He outlined a program of procedures and personnel. Much impressed, Kennedy attempted to push through the program with Lansdale himself in charge, or alternatively in charge of an interdepartmental Washington task force for Vietnam, but bureaucratic barriers in the State and Defense departments resisted. Lansdale's program was not implemented, but even if it had been, however sincere and sympathetic, it suffered from the missionary compulsion to guide the Vietnamese "toward United States policy objectives," not toward their own. This flaw, too, with its implications, Kennedy recognized when he said, "If it were ever converted into a white man's war, we should lose it as the French had lost a decade earlier." Here was a classic case of seeing the truth and acting without reference to it.

The American failure to find any significance in the defeat of the French professional army, including the Foreign Legion, by small, thin-boned, out-of-uniform Asian guerrillas is one of the great puzzles of the time. How could Dien Bien Phu be so ignored? When David Schoenbrun, correspondent for CBS, who had covered the French war in Vietnam, tried to persuade the President of the realities of that war and of the loss of French officers equivalent each year to a class at St. Cyr, Kennedy answered, "Well, Mr. Schoenbrun, that was the *French*. They were fighting for a colony, for an ignoble cause. We're fighting for freedom, to free them from the Communists, from China, for their independence." Because Americans believed they were "different" they forgot that they too were white.

Failing the Lansdale program, regular personnel were added to MAAG to accelerate the training program, raising its numbers to over 3000, and a 400-man group from the Special Warfare Training Center at Fort Bragg was sent to Vietnam for counter-insurgency operations. This violation of the Geneva rules was justified on the ground that North Vietnam too was infiltrating arms and men across the border.

. . .

Military theory and strategy underwent a major change with the advent of the Kennedy Administration. Appalled by the plans based on "massive retaliation" which the military under Eisenhower had embraced because they promised quick solutions and less expense in preparedness, Kennedy and McNamara turned to the ideas of the new school of defense intellectuals expressed in their doctrine of limited war. Its aim was not conquest but coercion; force would be used on a rationally calculated basis to alter the enemy's will and capabilities to the point where "the advantages of terminating the conflict were greater than the advantages of continuing it." War would be rationally "managed" in such a way as to send messages to the opposing belligerent, who would respond rationally to the pain and damage inflicted on him by desisting from the actions that caused them. "We are flung into a straitjacket of rationality," wrote the formulator of the doctrine, William Kaufman. That was a condition that exactly suited Secretary McNamara, the high priest of rational management. One thing was left out of account—the other side. War is polarity. What if the other side failed to respond rationally to the coercive message? Appreciation of the human factor was not McNamara's strong point, and the possibility that humankind is not rational was too eccentric and disruptive to be programmed into his analysis.

Prompted by Khrushchev's challenge of wars of liberation, a by-product of the limited-war theory emerged: counter-insurgency, which blossomed into the great cult of the Kennedy years with the President himself as its prophet. The no-nonsense men of his Administration embraced the doctrine with muscular enthusiasm. It would show them awake to the new conditions of the contest. It would meet the insurgents on their own ground, deal with social and political causes of insurgency in the developing countries, catch the Communists bathing, as Disraeli once said of the Whigs, and walk away with their clothes.

Stimulated by Lansdale's report, the President read the treatises of Mao and Che Guevara on guerrilla warfare and assigned them for reading in the Army. At his order, a special Counter-Insurgency Program was established to inculcate recognition "throughout the United States government that subversive insurgency ('wars of liberation') is a major form of politico-military conflict equal in importance to conventional warfare." The doctrine was required to be reflected in the organization, training and equipment of United States armed forces and civilian agencies abroad so as to ensure programs for prevention or defeat of insurgency or indirect aggression with special reference to Vietnam, Laos and Thailand. On discovering that enrollment at Fort Bragg was fewer than a thousand, the President ordered its mission expanded and the green beret of the Special Forces restored as a symbol of the new program. His Special Military Representative, General Maxwell Taylor, propagated the gospel, as did other disciples, including even Robert Kennedy out of his expertise as Attorney-General.

Papers on doctrine and methods poured from Walt Rostow, the voluble professor from MIT who held the number-two post at NSC. Speaking on guerrilla warfare at the graduation exercises at Fort Bragg in June 1961, he brought the "revolutionary process" in the Third World under the American wing by calling it "modernization." America, he said, was dedicated to the proposition that "Each nation will be permitted to fashion out of its own culture and ambitions the kind of modern society it wants." America respects "the uniqueness of each society," seeks nations which shall "stand up straight . . . to protect their own independence," undertake to "protect the independence of the revolutionary process now going forward." Thomas Jefferson himself could not have better expressed America's true principles—spoken here by one who consistently advocated their contradiction in practice.

Although the doctrine emphasized political measures, counter-insurgency in practice was military. Since it was not held in great favor by the military establishment, which did not welcome elite commands or intrusions into regular routines and regarded all this emphasis on reforms as getting in the way of its proper task of training men to drill and shoot, counter-insurgency in operation did not live up to the high-minded zeal of the theory. All the talk was of "winning the allegiance" of the people to their government, but a government for which allegiance had to be won by outsiders was not a good gamble.

What, in fact, did the United States and Diem have to offer an apathetic or alienated population? Flood control, rural development, youth groups, slum clearance, improved coastal transport, educational assistance were among the American-sponsored programs, all worthy but not of the essence. To successfully counteract the insurgents, counter-insurgency would have had to redistribute land and property to the peasants, redistribute power from the mandarins and mafias, disband the security forces that were filling Saigon's prisons—in short, remake the old regime and pledge it to a cause, as Lansdale was to say, "which makes a stronger appeal to the people than the Communist cause." Diem and his family, especially his younger brother Ngo

Dinh Nhu and Mme. Nhu, and their fellows of the governing class had no such intentions, nor indeed did their American sponsors.

The United States was still demanding reform as a quid pro quo of American aid, as if meaningful reform that could "win the allegiance" of the population were something that could be accomplished in a few months. It took some 25 centuries in the West, with a much faster rate of change than in the East, before government began to act in the interest of the needy. The reason why Diem never responded to the American call for reform was because his interest was opposed. He resisted reform for the same reason as the Renaissance popes, because it would diminish his absolute power. American insistence on his need of popular support was mere din in his ears, irrelevant to Asian circumstances. Asia presumes an obligation of citizens to obey their government; Western democracy regards government as representing the citizens. There was no meeting ground nor likely to be one. But because South Vietnam was a barrier to Communism, the United States, impervious to the obvious, persisted in trying to make Diem's government live up to American expectations. The utility of "perseverance in absurdity," Edmund Burke once said, "is more than I could ever discern."

With a crisis erupting over the threatened "loss" of Laos, the Joint Chiefs in May 1961 recommended that if Southeast Asia were to be held from the Communists, sufficient United States forces should be deployed to deter action by North Vietnam and China and to assist training of the South Vietnamese for more active counter-insurgency. At the Pentagon discussions began of "the size and composition which would be desirable in the case of a possible commitment of United States forces to Vietnam." This was contingency planning, while attention that summer was focused on Laos rather than on Vietnam.

Laos was the mouse that roared. In this landlocked upland country lying lengthwise between Vietnam and Thailand, with a population believed to number hardly more than two million, another Communist specter was abroad. This was the Pathet Lao, the nationalist-Communist Laotian version of the Viet-Minh. Because Laos touched China at its northern border and opened onto Cambodia in the south, it assumed in foreign eyes extraordinary importance as a corridor through which Ho's and Mao's Communists would pour, on some awful day of Red advance. Without deeply disturbing the easygoing life of the Laotians, sovereignty swayed among multiple rivals, of whom the leading figures were the legitimate ruler, Prince Souvanna Phouma, a neutralist in cold war politics; his half-brother, another Prince who was leader of the

Pathet Lao; and a third claimant, who was the American client and had been in place for a while, installed by CIA manipulations, and had subsequently been ousted.

Because the half-brothers were negotiating a coalition which could have neutralized their country and left the Pathet Lao in control of the mountain passes, Laos suddenly became during the Eisenhower-Dulles period a small oriental Ruritania, "a vital factor in the free world," a "bulwark against Communism," "a bastion of freedom." American money and matériel inundated and bewildered the parties. Briefing Kennedy before his inauguration, Eisenhower promoted the country to primary domino, saying, "If we permitted Laos to fall, then we would have to write off the whole area." He advised that every effort be made to persuade SEATO members to join in common action, but contemplated "our unilateral intervention" if they did not. Since Laos was rough in terrain and unreachable by Pacific-based sea and air power, clearly no place for effective combat, Eisenhower's astonishing remark, in contrast to his resistance to active intervention in much more accessible Vietnam, suggests that Laos had some peculiar faculty of bemusing men's minds.

In one of those minor frenzies that periodically craze international relations, the situation by 1961 had reached a crisis of complex cabals. Coalition in Laos threatened to become a casus belli. The Geneva Accord was invoked by Britain and France and a fourteen-nation conference re-convened at Geneva. In Washington all-day meetings ran late into the night at the White House. Kennedy, still sweating from the Bay of Pigs fiasco only days before, was determined to show that America meant business against Communism and to avert an outcry on the right if coalition should succeed. He authorized movement of the 7th Fleet to the South China Sea, helicopters and combat units to Thailand and alert of forces in Okinawa.

When advised by General Lyman K. Lemnitzer, the new Chairman of the Joint Chiefs, that if China and North Vietnam interfered they could be contained by nuclear arms, Kennedy was shocked into a less inflated view of the issue. He decided to accept neutralization and the return of Souvanna Phouma and sent the veteran diplomat Averell Harriman to Geneva to arrange an agreement to that effect. The solution was feasible because it was acceptable to both the Soviets and the United States and because the Laotians preferred to be let alone rather than to fight. While neutralization blocked intervention, it also had a negative effect: by leaving the Pathet Lao in place, it raised doubts in the local SEATO nations of the firmness of America's commitment against Communism in Asia. Loudly professed, these doubts made a great impression on the next visitor, Vice-President Lyndon Johnson.

Johnson was despatched in May 1961 to Taiwan, South Vietnam and the SEATO neighbors to reassure the region of American support. The Vice-President's interest in and experience of foreign affairs were minimal. When forced to pay attention as Senator and Majority Leader, he adjusted his attitude to fit conventional cold war orthodoxy. Although foreign affairs were not for him a major concern—Johnson's major concern was the advancement of his own career—the cold war dogma organized his impressions and reactions. His public pronouncements were addressed to the lowest common denominator of the public, as when in Saigon he announced that Diem was "the Winston Churchill of Asia." Less fatuous, his report to the President was manfully interventionist. He was ready for the United States to shoulder the burden of responsibility for Asia. "The key to what is done by Asians in defense of Southeast Asia's freedom," he wrote, "is confidence in the United States. There is no alternative to United States leadership in SEA. Leadership in individual countries . . . rests on the knowledge and faith in United States power, will and understanding." While his words may show a profound ignorance of what leadership rests on in Asia, they perfectly express the sense of omnipotent capacity with which the United States emerged from World War II. We had crushed the war machines of Germany and Japan, crossed oceans to do so, restored Europe, ruled Japan; we were a Paul Bunyan straddling two hemispheres.

"I recommend," Johnson continued emphatically, "that we move forward promptly with a major effort to help these countries defend themselves. . . . I cannot stress too strongly the extreme importance of following up this mission with other measures, other actions, other efforts"—presumably military. With realism he was not always to retain, he advised that the decision "must be made in full realization of the very heavy and continuing costs in terms of money, of effort and of United States prestige," and that "At some point we may be faced with the further decision of whether we commit major United States forces to the area or cut our losses and withdraw should our other efforts fail."

He warned, "There is no mistaking the deep and long-lasting impact of recent developments in Laos . . . which have created doubt and concern about the intentions of the United States throughout Southeast Asia." With no experience of Eastern habits of speech that conceal a kernel of substance—or sometimes no substance—under voluminous wrappings of form, Johnson took all he was told at face value, urging that it was of "the first importance" that his mission "bear fruit immediately." He proposed that the "real enemies"—hunger, ignorance, poverty and disease—be combatted by "imaginative use of American scientific and technological capacity" and concluded, "The battle against Communism must be joined in Southeast Asia with the strength and determination to achieve success there—or the United States must inevitably surrender the Pacific"—here he threw away 6000 miles of ocean together with Okinawa, Guam, Midway and Hawaii—"and pull back our defenses to San Francisco."

It was a mixed bag of characteristic American ideas. The simplistic either/or about defeating Communism or surrendering the Pacific probably did not influence the President, who was out of sympathy with his Vice-President and vice versa. But the doubts of America's steadfastness that so affected Johnson raised the issue of credibility that was to swell until in the end it seemed to be all we were fighting for.

Credibility emerged in the Berlin crisis of that summer when, after a harsh and intimidating meeting with Khrushchev in Vienna, Kennedy said to James Reston, "Now we have a problem in making our power credible, and Vietnam looks like the place." But Vietnam was never the place, because the American government itself never totally believed in what it was doing. The contrast with Berlin was only too plain. "We cannot and will not permit the Communists to drive us out of Berlin either gradually or by force," Kennedy said in July, and he was ready in his own mind, according to associates, to risk war, even nuclear war, over the issue. Despite all the protestations of equal firmness, Vietnam never received a comparable status in American policy, while at the same time no American government was ever willing to let it go. It was this split that tortured the whole endeavor, beginning with Kennedy himself.

Berlin provided another lesson in the fact that "the essential point," in the words of Assistant Secretary of Defense Paul Nitze, "was that the value to the West of the defenses of Berlin was far greater than the value to the Soviet Union of taking Berlin." His observation might have suggested that the value to North Vietnam of gaining control of the country for which they had fought so long was far greater to them than the value of frustrating them was to the United States. They were fighting on their own soil, determined to be at last its rulers. Good or bad, unyielding firmness of purpose lay with Hanoi, and because it was unyielding was likely to prevail. Neither Nitze nor anyone else perceived the analogy.

In South Vietnam "The situation gets worse and worse almost week by week," reminding him of Chungking, the correspondent Theodore White wrote to the White House in August 1961. "The guerrillas now control almost all the southern delta, so much so that I could find no American who would drive me outside Saigon in his car even by day without military convoy." This matched the "gloomy evaluation" of General Lionel McGarr, now chief of MAAG, who estimated that Diem controlled only 40 percent of South Vietnam and that the insurgents immobilized 85 percent of his military forces.

White's letter further reported "a political breakdown of formidable proportions," and his own puzzlement that while "Young fellows of 20–25 are dancing and jitterbugging in Saigon nightclubs," twenty miles away "The Commies on their side seem to be able to find people willing to die for their cause." It was a discrepancy that was beginning to bother other observers. In closing, White asked, if we decided to intervene, "Have we the proper personnel, the proper instruments and the proper clarity of objectives to intervene successfully?" "Clarity of objectives" was the crucial question.

Uncertain, Kennedy despatched the first and best known of an endless series of upper-level official missions to assess conditions in Vietnam. Secretary McNamara was later to go no fewer than five times in 24 months, and missions at the secondary level went back and forth to Saigon like bees flying in and out of a hive. With Embassy, MAAG, intelligence and aid agencies already on location and reporting back, Washington's incessant need of new assessments testifies to the uncertainty in the capital.

The mission of General Maxwell Taylor and Walt Rostow in October 1961 was prompted nominally by Diem's request for a bilateral defense treaty and the possible introduction of American combat troops to which so far he had been averse. A surge in Viet-Cong attacks and fear of infiltration across the Laos border had raised his alarm. Though ambivalent, Kennedy, seeking credibility in Vietnam, was for the moment in favor of increased effort and wanted affirmation rather than information, as his choice of envoys indicates. Taylor was obviously chosen to make a military estimate. Handsome and suave, with piercing blue eyes, he was admired as a "soldier-statesman" who spoke several languages, could quote Polybius and Thucydides and had written a book, *The Uncertain Trumpet.* He had commanded the 101st Airborne Division in World War II, served as Superintendent of West Point, as Ridgway's successor in Korea, as Chief of Staff during the last Dulles years. Out of sympathy with the doctrine of massive retaliation, he retired in 1959 to become president of Lincoln Center for the Performing Arts in New York. This cultivated figure was a natural attraction for Kennedy, but for all his repute as an intellectual general, not a brass hat, his ideas and recommendations tended to be conventional.

His fellow-voyager Walt Rostow (named for Walt Whitman) was a fervent believer in the American capacity to guide and develop the underdeveloped world. A hawk in the cause of halting Communism before the word "hawk" came into use, he had already proposed a plan calling for the introduction of 25,000 American combat troops. As a target selector in the European war, he had emerged as an enthusiast of air power, although post-war surveys of strategic bombing had concluded that the results were not decisive. Rostow was a positivist, a Dr. Pangloss who, as described by a fellow-worker, would advise the President on learning of a nuclear attack on Manhattan that the first phase of urban renewal had been accomplished at no cost to the Treasury. When because of left-wing activity during his student days his security clearances were frequently held up, Kennedy complained, "Why are they always picking on Walt as soft-headed? Hell, he's the biggest Cold Warrior I've got." That he would find reasons for going forward in Vietnam was a foregone conclusion.

Accompanied by officials of State, Defense, Joint Chiefs and the CIA, the mission visited South Vietnam for a week, 18–25 October, and retired to the Philippines to compose its report. This document, together with "Eyes Only" cables from Taylor to the President and annexes and supplements by individual members of the mission, has defied coherent summary ever since. It said something of everything, combined yes and no, pessimism and optimism, and on the whole, with many qualifications, argued that the program to "save South Vietnam" would be made to work only by the infusion of American armed forces to convince both sides of our seriousness. It recommended the immediate deployment of 8000 troops "to halt the downward trend" of the regime and "a massive joint effort to deal with Viet-Cong aggression." It quite accurately foresaw the consequences: American prestige, already engaged, would become more so; if the ultimate object was to eliminate insurgency in the South, "There is no limit to our possible commitment (unless we attack the source in Hanoi!)." Here, both in statement and in parenthesis, the future military problem was formulated.

The report contained other formulations equally basic if less well judged. Without having viewed the enemy's terrain or industrial base,

Taylor reported that North Vietnam was "extremely vulnerable to conventional bombing." Rarely has military judgment owed so much to imagination.

In referring to Hanoi's role as aggressor across an "international boundary," the report picked up the inventive rhetoric that marked the Vietnam affair throughout its duration. The Geneva Declaration had specifically stated that the partition line was "provisional" and not to be interpreted "as constituting a political or territorial boundary." Eisenhower had specifically recognized it as that and nothing more. Yet like "vital" national interest, "international boundary" was one of the inventions by policy-makers used to justify the case for intervention, or even to convince themselves that they had a case. Rostow had already used it in his speech at Fort Bragg. Rusk used it three months after Taylor in a public address in which he went further than anyone to speak of "external aggression" across "international boundaries." By repeated usage, the transformation of partition line into international boundary became the norm.

In describing South Vietnam's military performance as "disappointing," and making the routine acknowledgment that "Only the Vietnamese can defeat the Viet-Cong," Taylor stated his belief that Americans "as friends and partners can show them how the job might be done." This was the elemental delusion that underwrote the whole endeavor.

The pattern that military intervention was bound to follow was thus laid out by the chosen adviser. No one advised against it, as Ridgway unequivocally had in the past. State Department members of the mission in their annexes described the situation as "deteriorating" with increasing Viet-Cong successes, and pointed out that the Communist effort started at the lowest social level, in the villages. That was where "The battle must be lost and won"; the fact that foreign troops, though they could assist, could not win that battle should rule out "any full United States commitment to eliminate the Viet-Cong threat." Nevertheless, the author of this report, Sterling Cottrell, chairman of the inter-departmental Vietnam Task Force, fully supported the Taylor-Rostow forward march. Rather than admit the inference that is knocking at the gate, a second-level official will generally prefer to associate himself with superior opinion.

Secretary Rusk too, despite his total commitment to stopping Communism, felt it was inadvisable to commit American prestige too deeply for the sake of what he called "a losing horse." This flaw in the client bothered him, for on another occasion, testifying in camera before the Senate Foreign Relations Committee, he brooded aloud about consistently finding the United States tied to weak allies of the old regime and the need to determine in what circumstances "can you or should you invest in a regime when you know in your heart that that regime is not viable." American foreign policy was never asked a more significant question and it was left, as might be expected, unanswered.

Departmental reactions to Taylor's report, starting with Mc-Namara's, were muddled. Training and mental habits had formed in McNamara a man of the implicit belief that, given the necessary material resources and equipment and the correct statistical analysis of relative factors, the job—any job—could be accomplished. In response, he and the Joint Chiefs made a fundamental point in stating that military intervention required a clear commitment to an objective, in this case, preventing the fall of South Vietnam to Communism. They estimated that the necessary forces, taking into consideration possible Soviet and Chinese reactions, would reach a probable limit of six divisions, or 205,000 men, who should be reinforced by a warning to Hanoi that continued support of Viet-Cong insurgency in the South "will lead to punitive retaliation against North Vietnam."

Kennedy was wary of the military option, and may have orally asked for modified advice. Obligingly, McNamara had second thoughts and, jointly with Rusk, forwarded a second memorandum suggesting that for the time being the deployment of combat forces could be deferred but should be prepared for introduction at any time. Warning both ways, the two Secretaries, who did not think alike, said that without a strong effort by South Vietnam, "United States forces could not accomplish their mission in the midst of an apathetic or hostile population." On the other hand, the fall of South Vietnam would "undermine the credibility of American commitments elsewhere" and "stimulate domestic controversies." Offering a little bit of everything, and avoiding a strong yes or no, this suited Kennedy's uncertainty. Doubting the efficacy of "a white man's war," and warned by Taylor of the inevitable pressure to reinforce, he did not want his Administration to be saddled by this distant and unpromising entanglement. Yet the alternative of disengagement was always seen to be worse—loss of faith in the American shield abroad and accusations at home of weakness and infirmity against Communism.

Kennedy's instinct was caution, subject to ambivalence. At first he accepted deferral of a combat force, carefully avoiding an explicit negative which might open the gates of wrath on the right. He informed

Diem that additional advisory and technical troops would be sent in the hope that they would "galvanize and supplement" Vietnamese effort, for which "no amount of extra aid can substitute." The option of combat troops was being held in abeyance. In the regular reference to political and administrative reforms, the President asked for a "concrete demonstration" of progress, and added a reminder that advisory duties were more suitable for "white foreign troops than . . . missions involving the seeking out of Viet-Cong personnel submerged in the Vietnamese population"—which was true but disingenuous, since this was what the Special Forces in counter-insurgency were supposed to do. In language that was vague but not vague enough, Kennedy boxed himself in by assuring Diem that "We are prepared to help the Republic of Vietnam to protect its people and preserve its independence." In effect, he held to the objective while taking no action.

Diem reacted badly and "seemed to wonder," according to the American Ambassador, "whether the United States was getting ready to back out on Vietnam as, he suggested, we had done in Laos." Credibility had to be maintained and deterioration halted. Without any clear-cut decision or plan of mission, the troops began to go. United States instruction teams required combat support units, air reconnaissance required fighter escorts and helicopter teams, counter-insurgency required 600 Green Berets to train the Vietnamese in operations against the Viet-Cong. Equipment kept pace—assault craft and naval patrol boats, armored personnel carriers, short-take-off and transport planes, trucks, radar installations, Quonset huts, airfields. Employed in support of ARVN (South Vietnamese Army) combat operations, all these required manning by United States personnel, who willy-nilly entered a shooting war. When Special Forces units directed ARVN units against the guerrillas and met fire, they returned it. Helicopter gunships, when fired on, did the same.

Increased activity required more than a training command. In February 1962 a full field command under the acronym MACV (Military Assistance Command Vietnam) superseded MAAG with a three-star general, Paul D. Harkins, former Chief of Staff to Maxwell Taylor in Korea, in command. If a date is needed for the beginning of the American war in Vietnam, the establishment of Mac-Vee, as it became known, will serve.

By mid-1962 American forces in Vietnam numbered 8000, by the end of the year over 11,000, ten months later, 17,000. United States soldiers served alongside ARVN units at every level from battalion to division and general staff. They planned operations and accompanied

Vietnamese units into the field from six to eight weeks at a time. They airlifted troops and supplies, built jungle airstrips, flew helicopter rescue and medical evacuation teams, trained Vietnamese pilots, coordinated artillery fire and air support, introduced defoliation flights north of Saigon. They also took casualties: 14 killed or wounded in 1961, 109 in 1962, 489 in 1963.

This was war by the Executive, without Congressional authorization, and in the face of evasions or denials by the President, war virtually without public knowledge, though not without notice. Accused by the Republican National Committee of being "less than candid with the American people" about the involvement in Vietnam, and asked if it were not time to "drop the pretense" about "advisers," Kennedy, evidently stung, replied at a news conference in February 1962, "We have not sent combat troops there—in the generally understood sense of the word. We have increased our training mission and our logistics support . . ." and this was "as frank as he could be" consistent with that unfailing refuge, "our security needs in the area." It did not satisfy. "The United States is now involved in an undeclared war in South Vietnam," wrote James Reston on the same day. "This is well known to the Russians, the Chinese Communists and everyone else concerned except the American people."

The American infusion succeeded for a while in strengthening the Vietnamese effort. Operations began going well. The "strategic hamlet" program, most acclaimed and favored project of the year, sponsored by Diem's brother Nhu and highly regarded by the Americans, succeeded in actually turning back the Viet-Cong in many places, if it did not endear the Diem government to the rural population. Designed to isolate the guerrillas from the people, depriving them of food and recruits, the program forcibly relocated villagers from their own communities to fortified "agrovilles" of approximately 300 families, often with little but the clothes on their backs, while their former villages were burned behind them to deprive the Viet-Cong of shelter. Besides ignoring the peasant's attachment to his ancestral land and his reluctance to leave it for any reason, the program levied forced labor to construct the "agrovilles." With elaborate effort invested in and hopes attached to them, the "strategic hamlets" cost as much in alienation as they gained in security.

With ARVN under American tutelage, increasing its missions, with the Viet-Cong defection rate rising and many of its bases abandoned, confidence recovered. Nineteen sixty-two was Saigon's year, unsuspected to be its last. American optimism swelled. Army and

Embassy spokesmen issued positive pronouncements. The war was said to be "turning the corner." The body count of VC against ARVN was estimated at five to three. General Harkins was consistently bullish. Secretary McNamara, on an inspection trip in July, declared characteristically, "Every quantitative measurement we have shows we are winning this war." At a military conference at CINCPAC (Commander in Chief, Pacific) headquarters in Honolulu on his way home, he initiated planning for a gradual phase-out of United States military involvement in 1965.

At the ground level, colonels and non-coms and press reporters were more doubtful. The most cogent doubter was J. K. Galbraith, who, on his way to India as Ambassador at the time of the Taylor report in November 1961, was asked by Kennedy to stop off at Saigon for yet another assessment. Galbraith received the impression that Kennedy wanted a negative one, and gave it unsparingly. The situation was "certainly a can of snakes." Diem's battalions were "unmotivated malingerers." Provincial army chiefs combined military command with local government and political graft; intelligence on insurgent operations was "non-existent." The political reality was "total stasis" arising from Diem's greater need to protect himself from a coup than to protect the country from the Viet-Cong. The ineffectuality and unpopularity of his government conditioned the effectiveness of American aid. When Diem drove through Saigon, his movement, reminiscent of the Japanese Emperor's, "requires the taking in of all laundry along the route, the closing of all windows, an order to the populace to keep their heads in, the clearing of all streets, and a vast bevy of motorcycle outriders to protect him on his dash." The effort to bargain for reform with promises of aid was useless because Diem "will not reform either administratively or politically in any effective way. That is because he cannot. It is politically naive to expect it. He senses that he cannot let power go because he would be thrown out."

Galbraith advised resisting any pressure for introducing American troops because "Our soldiers would not deal with the vital weakness." He had as yet no solution to "the box we are now in," except to dispute the argument that there was no alternative to Diem. He thought a change and a new start were essential, and though no one could promise a safe transition, "We are now married to failure."

Again in March 1962 he wrote to urge that the United States should keep the door wide open for any kind of political settlement with Hanoi and "jump at the chance" if any appeared. He believed Jawaharlal Nehru would help and the Russians could be approached by

Harriman to find out if Hanoi would call off the Viet-Cong in return for American withdrawal and an agreement to talk about ultimate unification. Returning home in April, he proposed to Kennedy an internationally negotiated settlement for a non-aligned government on the Laos model. By continuing to support an ineffectual government, he predicted, "We shall replace the French as the colonial force in the area and bleed as the French did." In the meantime all steps to commit American soldiers to combat should be resisted, and it would be well to disassociate ourselves from such unpopular actions as defoliation and the "strategic hamlets."

Galbraith's proposal, put in writing, was squelched by the Joint Chiefs, who saw it as an effort to disengage from "what is now a well-known commitment to take a forthright stand against Communism in Southeast Asia." They cited in evidence the President's ill-advised promise to Diem to preserve the Republic's independence. They advocated no change in American policy, but rather that it be "pursued vigorously to a successful conclusion." This was the general consensus; Kennedy did not contest it; Galbraith's suggestion died.

A successful conclusion was already fading. Discontent was rising around Diem like mist from a marsh. Peasants were further alienated by Saigon's full-time draft for military service in place of the traditional six months' service each year allowing a man to return to his home for labor in his fields. In February 1962 two dissident air force officers bombed and strafed the Presidential Palace in a vain attempt to assassinate Diem. American reporters were probing the chinks and finding the short-falls and falsehoods in the compulsive optimism of official briefings. In increasing frustration, they wrote increasingly scornful reports. As one of them wrote long afterward, "Much of what the newsmen took to be lies was exactly what the Mission genuinely believed and was reporting back to Washington," on the basis of what it was told by Diem's commanders. Since American intelligence agents swarmed through the country, taking Diem's commanders on faith was hardly an excuse, but having committed American policy to Diem, as once to Chiang Kai-shek, officials felt the same reluctance to admit his inadequacy.

The result was a press war: the angrier the newsmen became, the more "undesirable stories" they wrote. The government sent Robert Manning, the Assistant Secretary of State for Public Affairs, himself a former newspaperman, to Saigon to try to subdue the storm, hoping, according to a memorandum by Manning, to "see the American involvement in Vietnam minimized, even represented as something less than in reality it is." Although the public paid little attention, a few became aware that something was going wrong in this far-off endeavor. Dissent began to sprout here and there, small, scattered and of no great significance. The public as a whole knew vaguely that Communism was being combatted somewhere in Asia and in general approved of the effort. Vietnam was a distant unvisualized place, no more than a name in the newspapers.

One individual critic, the strongest in knowledge and status, was Senator Mike Mansfield, now Majority Leader and the Senator most deeply concerned with Asia. He felt that the United States, drawing upon old missionary tradition, was obsessed by a zeal to improve Asia, re-animated by the anti-Communist crusade, and that the effort would be the undoing of both America and Asia. On returning in December 1962 from an inspection tour made at the President's request, his first visit since 1955, he told the Senate that "Seven years and $2 billion of United States aid later . . . South Vietnam appears less not more stable than it was at the outset." He aimed a slap at the optimists and another at the strategic hamlets, in regard to which "The practices of the Central Government to date are not reassuring."

To Kennedy in person he was more outspoken, saying that the infusion of American troops would come to dominate a civil war that was not our affair. Taking it over would "hurt American prestige in Asia and would not help the South Vietnamese to stand on their own feet either." Growing more disturbed and red in the face as Mansfield talked, Kennedy snapped at him, "Do you expect me to take this at face value?" Like all rulers, he wanted to be confirmed in his policy and was angry at Mansfield, as he confessed to an aide later, for disagreeing so completely, "and angry at myself because I found myself agreeing with him."

Nothing changed. The President sent other investigators, Roger Hilsman, head of State Department Intelligence, and Michael Forrestal of Bundy's staff, a team closer to the Mansfield than to the Taylor-Rostow view. They reported that the war would last longer, cost more in money and lives than anticipated, and that "The negative side of the ledger is still awesome," but as office holders without Mansfield's independent base, they did not dispute the prevailing policy.

Buried in Hilsman's intensively detailed report were many specific negatives, but no moves were made to adjust to the information the investigators brought back. Adjustment is painful. For the ruler it is easier, once he has entered a policy box, to stay inside. For the lesser official it is better, for the sake of his position, not to make waves, not to press evidence that the chief will find painful to accept. Psychologists call the process of screening out discordant information "cognitive dissonance," an academic disguise for "Don't confuse me with the facts." Cognitive dissonance is the tendency "to suppress, gloss over, water down or 'waffle' issues which would produce conflict or 'psychological pain' within an organization." It causes alternatives to be "deselected since even thinking about them entails conflicts." In the relations of subordinate to superior within the government, its object is the development of policies that upset no one. It assists the ruler in wishful thinking, defined as "an unconscious alteration in the estimate of probabilities."

Kennedy was no wooden-head; he was aware of the negatives and bothered by them, but he made no adjustment, nor did any of his chief advisers suggest making one. No one in the Executive branch advocated withdrawal, partly in fear of encouragement to Communism and damage to American prestige, partly in fear of domestic reprisals. And for another reason, the most enduring in the history of folly: personal advantage, in this case a second term. Kennedy was smart enough to read signs of failure, to sense in Vietnam an ongoing disaster. He was annoyed by it, angered to be trapped in it, anxious that his second term not be spoiled by it. He would have liked to win, or to find a reasonable facsimile of winning, to cut losses and get out.

The trend of his thinking emerged at a Congressional breakfast in the White House in March 1963 when Mansfield renewed his arguments. Drawing him aside, the President said, perhaps because he knew it was what the influential Senator wanted to hear, that he was beginning to agree about a complete military withdrawal. "But I can't do it until 1965—until after I'm re-elected." To do it before would cause "a wild conservative outcry" against him. To his aide Kenneth O'Donnell, Kennedy repeated, "If I tried to pull out completely now, we could have another Joe McCarthy scare on our hands"; only after re-election, and he added sharply, "So we'd better make damn sure I am re-elected." To other friends he implied his doubts, but argued that he could not give up Vietnam to the Communists and ask American voters to re-elect him.

His position was realistic, if not a profile in courage. Re-election was more than a year and a half away. To continue for that time to invest American resources and inevitably lives in a cause in which he no longer had much faith, rather than risk his own second term, was a decision in his own interest, not the country's. Only an exceedingly rare ruler reverses that order.

· · ·

In the interval, the supreme confrontation of the Cuban missile crisis had been skillfully mastered, and its setback for Khrushchev and successful outcome for the United States had invigorated the Administration's confidence and prestige. One reason the Soviets had backed away offered the same lesson as Berlin—placing the missiles in Cuba was a daring gamble, not a vital interest for the USSR, whereas preventing missile sites so near our shores *was* a vital interest of the United States. On the basis of the law of vital interest, it was predictable that the United States would ultimately back down in Vietnam and the North prevail.

With the blow to Communism in Cuba and enhanced American prestige, it would have been a moment to disengage from Vietnam with every hope of overriding a domestic uproar. But this was the time of official optimism, with no current running for withdrawal. Kennedy did, at about this time, instruct Michael Forrestal to think about preparing a plan for post-election withdrawal, saying it would take a year to prepare acceptance by Congress and by the allies in Asia and Europe. Nothing came of this, but when asked privately how he would manage withdrawal without damage to American prestige, he replied, "Easy; put a government in there that would ask us to leave." Publicly he was saying that for the United States to withdraw "would mean a collapse not only of South Vietnam but Southeast Asia. So we are going to stay." He was thinking both ways and was never to resolve the duality.

A constant factor in the policy process was fear of what China might do. The Sino-Soviet split was by now apparent, and as the Russian threat seemed to shrink in a period of détente, the Chinese, behind the curtain of severed relations, loomed more menacing than before. The impression of Korea had not faded; the bellicose show over Quemoy-Matsu, the annexation of Tibet, the border war with India taken together made a picture of infinite mischief. When asked in a television interview if he had any reason to doubt the validity of the domino theory, Kennedy said, "No, I believe it, I believe it. . . . China looms so high just beyond the frontiers that if South Vietnam went, it would not only give them an improved position for guerrilla assault on Malaysia, but would also give the impression that the wave of the future in Southeast Asia was China and the Communists."

In fact, if Americans could have seen the value of accepting a strongly nationalist North Vietnam, Communist or not, a vigorous, independent, intensely anti-Chinese nation would have been a far better barrier against the feared Chinese expansion than a divided warring country offering every opportunity for interference from across the border. This did not occur to the best and the brightest. China, in any event, was then struggling in the economic ditch into which the Great Leap Forward had landed her, and in no shape for foreign adventure. "Know your enemy" is the most important precept in any adversary relationship, but it is the peculiar habit of Americans, when dealing with the Red menace, to sever relations and deal from ignorance.

The military establishment, fulfilling McNamara's order at Honolulu, was now busy in drawing up a comprehensive plan, absorbing miles of memoranda and months of paper work, for withdrawal of a not very imposing total of 1000 men by the end of 1963 and the build-up and financing of ARVN to the point where in training and numbers it could be expected to take over the war. While MACV and CINCPAC and Defense Department were up to their knees in figures and acronyms and exchange of documents, progress soured in South Vietnam and brought on the crisis that ended in Diem's fall and death, dragging behind it the moral responsibility of the United States.

Diem's mandate to govern, never thoroughly accepted by the mixture of sects, religions and classes, was finally shattered by the Buddhist revolt in the summer of 1963. Long resentment of the favored treatment of Catholics practiced by the French and continued by Diem fired the Buddhist cause and gave it a native appeal. In May, when Saigon prohibited celebrations of Buddha's birthday, riots followed and government troops fired on the demonstrators, killing several. Renewed riots and martial law were given a terrible notoriety by the desperate act of self-immolation by a Buddhist monk who set himself on fire in a public square of Saigon. The protest spread, gathering in all opponents of the regime: anti-Catholics, anti-Westerners, dissidents of the lower and middle classes. Repression and violence rose, known to be guided by Diem's brother Nhu and culminating in a raid on the main Buddhist pagoda and the arrest of hundreds of monks. The Foreign Minister and the Ambassador to the United States resigned in protest; Diem's government began to crack.

American intelligence, which seems not to train its sights on popular feeling, had not foreseen the revolt. Two weeks before the outbreak, Secretary Rusk, deceived by the barrage of optimism from MACV, was led to speak of the "steady movement" in South Vietnam "toward a constitutional system resting on popular consent" and the evidence of rising morale indicating that the people were "on their way to success."

In the army too Diem had enemies. A generals' coup was simmering. War effort had dwindled as the government struggled against plots and conspiracies. Nhu and the sinister Mme. Nhu began to appear in intelligence reports as communicating with the enemy, with the suspected object of reaching a "neutralist" settlement through French intermediaries for the advancement of their own fortunes. All America's investment seemed in jeopardy. Was this the preferred protégé for nation-building, the reliable candidate to bar the way to the implacably motivated North?

Discussions in Washington about what to do were heated, the more so as the government, in fact, did not know what course to take. Was there an alternative to Diem? If he remained, could the insurgency ever be defeated under his government? Argument concentrated on the pros and cons of Diem and how to get rid of the Nhus, not on any reconsideration of what America was doing in this *galère*. Less because of their oppression of the Buddhists than because of their neutralist overtures, the Nhus had to be eliminated. The hope was to force Diem to that point by judicious cut-off of aid, but Diem, confident of the American commitment against the Communists, was impervious to these threats. They were made rather nervously in anxiety at the State Department that Diem might see in them a sign that action against him and the Nhus was imminent and "take some quite fantastic action such as calling on North Vietnam for assistance in expelling the Americans." This interesting notion suggests a certain frailty in Washington's own sense of its role in Vietnam.

Gradually policy-makers reached the conclusion, not that South Vietnam as a barrier to Communism was a losing proposition, but that Diem was and would have to go, with the help of the United States. In short, Washington should support the plotted military coup. It was an assumption of the right—or, if not the right, the pragmatic imperative —to protect investment in a client company under failing management.

A classic covert CIA agent, Colonel Lou Conein, opened liaison with the plotting generals, and the new Ambassador, Henry Cabot Lodge, vigorously took charge, completely convinced of the need to end American partnership with "this repressive regime with its bayonets at every corner." Responding to his advice, Washington instructed him that if Diem did not get rid of the Nhus, "We are prepared to accept the obvious implication that we can no longer support Diem," and empowered him to tell "appropriate military commanders we will give them direct support in any interim period of breakdown central government mechanism." In the yes-no style of government instructions, Lodge was told by the White House that "no initiative" should be taken for "active covert encouragement to a coup," but on the other hand "urgent covert effort" should be made to "build contacts with possible alternative leadership"—which should of course be "totally secure and fully deniable."

As the recent Republican Vice-Presidential candidate, Lodge had been appointed to the Embassy not only for his political ability and fluency in French, but as a means of involving his party in the Vietnamese entanglement. No pushover, he took care to put the Kennedy government on record so that it could not later repudiate him. "We are launched," he wired, "on a course from which there is no respectable turning back: the overthrow of the Diem government." He informed State that Colonel Conein had made the desired contact with the coup leader, General "Big" Minh, who had outlined three possible plans of action of which the first was the "assassination" of the Nhus while keeping Diem in office; "this was the easiest plan to accomplish."

In the ongoing conferences in Washington, a larger issue than the fate of Diem and the Nhus occasionally raised its head, as when Robert Kennedy said the primary question was "whether the Communist takeover could be successfully resisted by any government. If it could not, now was the time to get out of Vietnam entirely, rather than waiting." If it could be resisted under a different government, then we should go ahead with plans for a change, but he felt that basic question "had not been answered."

Some tried to answer. Field officers who had accompanied ARVN units into combat, and learned in bitterness that American training and weapons could not supply the will to fight, did their best to circumvent General Harkins' suppression of negative reports and gave their accounts of sorry performance at debriefings in the Pentagon. One in particular, the battle at Ap Bac in January 1963 involving an ARVN battalion of 2000 equipped with artillery and armored personnel carriers, had been expected to demonstrate triumphantly the newly acquired fire power and aggressiveness. Caught under the sudden fire of 200 Viet-Cong guerrillas, the ARVN troops cowered behind grounded helicopters, refused to stand up to shoot, refused orders to counterattack. The Province Chief commanding a Civil Guard unit refused to permit his troops to engage. In the slaughter three American advisory officers were killed. Ap Bac bared the failings of ARVN, the inutility of the American program and the hollowness of Headquarters optimism, although no one was allowed to say so. Colonel John Vann, the senior American at Ap Bac, was back at the Pentagon in the summer of 1963 trying to inform the General Staff. As Maxwell Taylor was the particular patron of General Harkins and upheld his view, Vann's message could make no headway. A Defense Department spokesman announced that "The corner has definitely been turned toward victory," and CINCPAC foresaw the "inevitable" defeat of the Viet-Cong.

Foreign aid officers, too, voiced discouragement. Rufus Phillips, director of rural programs, reported the strategic hamlet program in "shambles," and made the point that the war was not primarily military but a political conflict for the allegiance of the people, and that the Diem regime was losing it. John Macklin, director of the United States Information Service, who had taken leave of absence in 1962 as *Time* correspondent to try to help turn the Vietnamese people against the Viet-Cong, resigned after 21 months with his assignment ending "in despair." The chief of the interdepartmental Working Group on Vietnam, Paul Kattenburg of State, startled a conference with Rusk, McNamara, Taylor, Bundy, Vice-President Johnson and others present by his recommendation that, given the certainty that Diem would not separate from his brother and would get less and less support from the people and go "steadily down hill," it would be better for the United States to decide to get out now. No one present agreed, and the suggestion was firmly quelled by Rusk, who said that policy should proceed on the assumption that "We will not pull out until the war is won." Subsequently, Kattenburg was eased out of the Working Group and transferred to another post, predicting as he left that the war could draw in 500,000 Americans and extend into a five- to ten-year conflict.

A Delphic voice spoke out at this moment: Charles de Gaulle proposed a neutralist solution. In one of his shrouded statements, delivered at a French Cabinet meeting but given an unusual authorization for publication verbatim, clearly intended for overseas ears, de Gaulle expressed the hope that the Vietnamese people would make a "national effort" to attain unity and "independence from exterior influences." In spectral phrases about French concern for Vietnam, he said every effort made toward this end would find France ready to cooperate. His demarche was taken by diplomats, poring over his language, to mean a "neutralized" solution on the pattern of Laos, independent of both Communist China and the United States. "Authoritative sources" indicated that the North Vietnamese had been showing themselves receptive and that French officials had been passing on feelers from Hanoi in other capitals.

This could have been the opening to "jump at the chance" of a possible negotiated settlement, as Galbraith had once advised. De Gaulle was offering an out if Washington had been wise enough to want one.

"Wide annoyance," however, was reported in the American government, a frequent reaction to de Gaulle's pomposities. Yet, given political disintegration and military inadequacy and lack of any real progress in South Vietnam, and the hints from Hanoi, the American government could have used the opportunity of Diem's coming collapse and de Gaulle's implied good offices to say it had done all it could by way of support; it could not do more; the rest was up to the Vietnamese people to settle for themselves. This would have meant sooner or later a Communist take-over. With the future not foreseen, and with the confidence of 1963 in American power, that outcome was still unacceptable.

Matters proceeded on the chosen course toward coup d'état. That it violated a basic principle of foreign relations did not bother the realists of the Kennedy school. That it made nonsense of the reiterated American insistence that Vietnam's conflict was "their" war does not seem to have been considered. "Their" war was a ceaseless refrain; Dulles said it, Eisenhower said it, Rusk said it, Maxwell Taylor said it, all the Ambassadors said it, Kennedy himself said it many times: "In the final analysis it is their war. They are the ones who have to win it or lose it." If it was their war, it was also their government and their politics. For the defenders of democracy to conspire with plotters of a coup d'état, no matter how cogent the reasons, could not be hailed in the history books as the American way. It was a step in the folly of self-betrayal.

Troubled by his role and the smell of the swamp he was getting into, Kennedy resorted to another fact-finding mission, the now traditional Washington substitute for policy. A rapid but intensive four-day tour was made by General Victor Krulak, special adviser to Maxwell Taylor, who was now Chief of Staff and Chairman of the Joint Chiefs, and Joseph Mendenhall of State, an old Vietnam hand with a large acquaintance among Vietnamese civilians. Their reports to the White House on return, one hearty and promising from military sources, the other caustic and gloomy, were so at variance as to evoke the President's puzzled query "You two did visit the same country, didn't you?" On their heels followed another mission at the highest level, General Taylor himself and Secretary McNamara with the assignment to find out how far the political chaos had affected the military effort. Their report on 2 October, while positive on military prospects, was full of political negatives that belied their hopes. All contradictions were muffled by McNamara's public announcement, with the President's approval, that 1000 men could be withdrawn by the end of the year and that "The major part of the United States military task can be completed by the end of 1965." The confusion and contradiction in fact-finding did nothing to clarify policy.

On 1 November the generals' coup took place successfully. It included, to the appalled discomfort of the Americans, the unexpected assassinations of Diem and Nhu. Less than a month later, President Kennedy too was in his grave.

5. Executive War:
1964-68

From the moment he took over the presidency, according to one who knew him well, Lyndon Johnson made up his mind that he was not going to "lose" South Vietnam. Given his forward-march proposals as Vice-President in 1961, this attitude could have been expected, and while stemming from cold war credos it had even more to do with the demands of his own self-image—as became overt at once. Within 48 hours of Kennedy's death, Ambassador Lodge, who had come home to report on post-Diem developments, met with Johnson to brief him on the discouraging situation. Political prospects under Diem's successor, he reported, held no promise of improvement but more likely of further strife; militarily, the army was shaky and in danger of being over-whelmed. Unless the United States took a much more active role in the fighting the South might be lost. Hard decisions, Lodge told the President squarely, had to be faced. Johnson's reaction was instant and personal: "I am not going to be the first President of the United States to lose a war," alternatively reported as "I am not going to lose Vietnam. I am not going to be the President who saw Southeast Asia go the way that China went."

In the nervous tension of his sudden accession, Johnson felt he had to be "strong," to show himself in command, especially to overshadow the aura of the Kennedys, both the dead and the living. He did not feel a comparable impulse to be wise; to examine options before he spoke. He lacked Kennedy's ambivalence, born of a certain historical sense and at least some capacity for reflective thinking. Forceful and domineering, a man infatuated with himself, Johnson was affected in his conduct of Vietnam policy by three elements in his character: an ego that was insatiable and never secure; a bottomless capacity to use and impose the powers of office without inhibition; a profound aversion, once fixed upon a course of action, to any contra-indications.

Speculations about a neutralist solution were floating in South Vietnam after Diem's assassination, and it is possible that Saigon might have come to terms with the insurgents at this point but for the American presence. A broadcast by the clandestine Viet-Cong radio was heard suggesting negotiations for a cease-fire. A second broadcast suggesting accommodation with the new President in Saigon, General Duong Van Minh, leader of the coup against Diem, if he were to detach himself from the United States was picked up and reported in Washington by the Foreign Broadcasting Intelligence Service. These were not hard offers and probably intended merely to probe Saigon's political chaos. Saigon was listening if Washington was not. The six-foot President, General "Big" Minh, a former Buddhist peasant, who though well-meaning and popular had no control over a nest of rivals, was rumored to be considering contact with the Viet-Cong. After three months in office he in turn became the victim of a coup. The same rumor clung to successors who followed each other through coups and ousters during the next months. American opposition to any such feelers was actively exerted by the Embassy and its agents.

During this time U Thant, the Burmese Secretary General of the UN, was testing receptivity to a neutralist coalition government. Though coalition between fundamental enemies is an illusion, it can be used for temporary settlement. It did not interest Washington. Nor did Senator Mansfield's rather desperate proposal in January to open the way for American withdrawal by dividing South Vietnam itself between Saigon and the Viet-Cong. Although Johnson was demanding "solutions" from his advisers, these compromises with Communism were not what he had in mind.

The hard decisions were already forming. On return from a fact-finding mission in December, McNamara reported that unless current trends were reversed within "the next two or three months," they would "lead to neutralization at best and more likely to a Communist-controlled state." The stakes in preserving a non-Communist South were so high, he told the President, "that in my judgment we must go on bending every effort to win."

Enormity of the stakes was the new self-hypnosis. To let North Vietnam win would give incalculable encouragement to Communism everywhere, erode confidence everywhere in the United States and arouse the right at home to political slaughter. The *New York Times* affirmed it in an editorial of fearful portent: the roll of Southeast Asian nations, Laos, Cambodia, Burma, Thailand, Malaysia, Indonesia, would be endangered if South Vietnam fell; the "entire Allied position in the Western Pacific would be in severe jeopardy"; India would be "outflanked," Red China's drive for hegemony "enormously enhanced"; doubts of United States ability to defend other nations against Communist pressure would spread around the world; the impact on revolutionary movements would be profound; neutralism would spread and with it a sense that Communism might be the wave of the future. As of 1983, Vietnam has, unhappily, been under Communist control for eight years and except for Laos and Cambodia, none of these terrors has been realized.

By 1964, ten years had passed since America undertook to save South Vietnam after Geneva. Circumstances had changed. The Soviet Union had been faced down in the Berlin and Cuban missile crises; Soviet influence over the European Communist parties was much less; NATO was firmly established. Why then were stakes still considered so high in remote unimportant Vietnam? Communism had made European advances without engendering the hysteria that seemed to infect us out of Asia. If Communist advance anywhere was so to be feared, why did we fling a harebrained strike at Cuba and make our stand in Vietnam? Perhaps, perversely, because it *was* Asia, where Americans took it for granted they could impose their will and the might of their resources on what a United States Senator, Thomas Dodd of Connecticut, referred to in his wisdom as "a few thousand primitive guerrillas." To be frustrated in Asia seemed unacceptable. The stake had become America's exercise of power and its manifestation called "credibility." Despite old counsel that a land war in Asia was unwinnable, despite disillusioning experience in China and Korea, despite French experience on the very spot where Americans now stood, this perception of what was at stake was overriding.

Reminiscent of British visions of ruin if they lost the American colonies, prophecies of exaggerated catastrophe if we lost Vietnam served to increase the stakes. Johnson voiced this over-reaction in his initial scenario of pulling back to San Francisco; Rusk voiced it in 1965 in his advice to the President that withdrawal "would lead to our ruin and almost certainly to catastrophic war," and again in 1967 when he drew a picture at a press conference of "a billion Chinese armed with nuclear weapons." The *New York Times*' military correspondent, Hanson Baldwin, voiced it in 1966, writing that withdrawal from Vietnam would result in "political, psychological and military catastrophe" and would mean that the United States "had decided to abdicate as a great power" and be "reconciled to withdrawal from Asia and the Western Pacific." Fear too conjured visions: "I am scared to death," said Senator Joseph Clark in the Senate Foreign Relations Committee, that "we are on our way to nuclear World War Three."

. . .

North Vietnam was now sending units of its regular army across the line to exploit the disintegration of the South. To prevent collapse of America's client, President Johnson and his circle of advisers and the Joint Chiefs came to the conclusion that the moment had come when they must enter upon coercive war. It would be war from the air though it was understood that this would inevitably draw in ground forces. Civilian and military agencies began drawing operational plans, but though Saigon's situation was growing daily more precarious, action could not be initiated yet because Johnson faced the presidential election of 1964. Since his opponent was the bellicose Senator Barry Goldwater, he had to appear as the peace candidate. He took up the chant about "their" war: "We are going . . . to try to get them to save their own freedom with their own men." "We are not going to send American boys nine or ten thousand miles away from home to do what Asian boys ought to be doing for themselves." "We don't want our American boys to do the fighting for Asian boys." When, six months later, American boys were sent into combat with no dramatic change of circumstances, these phrases were easily recalled, beginning the erosion of Johnson's own credibility. Long accustomed to normal political lying, he forgot that his office made a difference, and that when lies came to light, as under the greater spotlight on the White House they were bound to, it was the presidency and public faith that suffered.

Public response to the campaign of Goldwater the hawk denouncing a "no win" policy versus Johnson the peacemaker flowed steadily one way. After World War II and Korea, and in the shadow of the atomic bomb, Americans, however anti-Communist, wanted no war. Women especially were to vote disproportionately for Johnson, testifying to the reservoir of anti-war sentiment. The Administration might have taken heed but did not, because it never stopped believing its troubles would come from the right.

While giving one signal to voters, Johnson had to give another of fiercer intent to Hanoi in the hope of holding back a challenge, at least until after the election. Naval units in the Gulf of Tonkin, including the destroyer *Maddox*, soon so notorious, went beyond intelligence gathering to "destructive" action against the coast, which was supposed to convey a message to Hanoi to "desist from aggressive policies." The real message, which by now virtually everyone believed necessary, was to be American bombing.

Johnson, Rusk, McNamara and General Taylor flew to Honolulu in June for a meeting with Ambassador Lodge and CINCPAC to consider a program of American air action and the probable next step of ground combat. The rationale for the bombing was two-thirds political: to bolster the sinking morale in South Vietnam, strongly urged by Lodge, and to break the will to fight of the North Vietnamese and cause them to cease supporting the Viet-Cong insurgency and ultimately to negotiate. The military aim was to stop infiltration and supply. Recommendations and caveats were tossed and turned and argued, for the planners were not eager for belligerency in a civil conflict in Asia, even while pretending it was "external aggression." The underlying need, given the rapid failing of the South, was to redress the military balance so that the United States should not ne- gotiate from weakness. Until that could be achieved, any move toward negotiations "would have been an admission that the game was up."

As it was bound to, the uncomfortable question of nuclear weapons came up without arousing anyone's advocacy. The only case in which their use was even theoretically contemplated was against the vast peril, as it was seen, of the Communist Chinese if they should be provoked into entering the war. Secretary Rusk, whose adrenaline always rose on that subject, believed that in view of China's enormous population, "we could not allow ourselves to be bled white fighting them with conven- tional weapons." This meant that if escalation brought about a major Chinese attack, "it would also involve use of nuclear arms." He was nevertheless aware that Asian leaders opposed it, seeing in it an element of racial discrimination, "something we would do to Asians but not to Westerners." Possible circumstances of tactical use were briefly dis- cussed. General Earle Wheeler, new Chairman of the Joint Chiefs, was unenthusiastic; Secretary McNamara said he "could not imagine a case where they would be considered," and the matter was dropped.

Operational plans for the bombing were drawn, but the order for action postponed, for while the election still lay ahead, Johnson's peace image had to be protected. The graver question of ground combat was left in abeyance until a dependable government could be installed in the political shambles of Saigon. Further, as General Taylor pointed out, the American public would have to be educated to appreciate the United States interest in Southeast Asia. Secretary McNamara, with his usual precision, thought this "would require at least thirty days," as if it were a matter of selling the public a new model automobile.

Johnson was intensely nervous about expanding American bellig- erency for fear of precipitating intervention by the Chinese. Neverthe- less, if escalation was inevitable, he wanted a Congressional mandate. At Honolulu the text of a draft resolution was read and discussed, and on his return home the supreme manipulator prepared to obtain it.

The Tonkin Gulf Resolution of 7 August 1964 has been so exhaustively examined that it can afford to rest under more cursory treatment here. Its importance was that it gave the President the mandate he was seeking and left Congress suddenly staring helplessly and to some extent resentfully at its empty hands. Not a Fort Sumter or a Pearl Harbor, Tonkin Gulf was no less significant; in a cause of uncertain national interest, it was a blank check for Executive war.

The cause was the claim of the destroyer *Maddox* and other naval units that they had been fired upon at night by North Vietnamese torpedo patrol boats outside the three-mile limit recognized by the United States. Hanoi claimed sovereignty up to a twelve-mile limit. A second clash followed the next day under obscure conditions never fully clarified and subsequently, during re-investigation in 1967, thought to have been imagined or invented.

White House telecommunications to Saigon crackled with crisis. Johnson promptly asked for a Congressional Resolution authorizing "all necessary measures to repel armed attack," and Senator J. William Fulbright, as Chairman of the Senate Foreign Relations Committee, undertook to guide it through the Senate. While aware that he was not altogether upholding the constitutional authority of Congress, Fulbright believed in Johnson's earnest assurances of having no wish to widen the war and thought the Resolution would help the President withstand Goldwater's calls for an air offensive and also help the Democratic Party by showing it to be tough against Communists.

The personal ambition that so often shapes statecraft has also been cited in the suggestion that Fulbright had hopes of replacing Rusk as Secretary of State after the election, which depended on retaining Johnson's goodwill. Whether true or not, Fulbright was correct in supposing that one purpose of the Resolution was to win over the right by a show of force.

Senator Gaylord Nelson of Wisconsin tried to limit the Resolution by an amendment against "any extension of the present conflict," but this was quashed by Fulbright, who said that since the President had no such intentions, the amendment was not needed. Senator Sam Ervin of North Carolina, working the famous eyebrows, hinted at the lurking uneasiness among some Senators about the whole involvement when he asked, "Is there any reasonable or honorable way we can extricate ourselves without losing our face and probably our pants?" The most outspoken opponent was, as always, Senator Wayne Morse, who denounced the Resolution as a "pre-dated declaration of war," and, having been tipped off by a telephone call from a Pentagon officer, questioned

McNamara closely about suspicious naval actions in the Gulf. Mc-Namara firmly denied any "connection with or knowledge of" any hostile actions. Morse was often right but fulminated so regularly against so many iniquities that he was discounted.

The Senate, a third of whom were also up for re-election, did not wish to embarrass the President two months before the national vote or show themselves any less protective of American lives. After a one-day hearing, the Resolution authorizing "all necessary measures" was adopted by the Foreign Relations Committee by a vote of 14 to 1 and subsequently approved by both Houses. It justified the grant of war powers on the rather spongy ground that the United States regards as "vital to its international interests and to world peace, the maintenance of international peace and security." Neither the prose nor the sense carried much conviction. By its ready acquiescence, the Senate, once so jealous of its constitutional prerogative to declare war, had signed it over to the Executive. Meanwhile, with evidence accumulating of confusion by radar and sonar technicians in the second clash, Johnson said privately, "Well, those dumb stupid sailors were just shooting at flying fish." So much for casus belli.

Alternatives for the United States were offered at this time by U Thant's proposal to reconvene the Geneva Conference and by a second summons from de Gaulle for a negotiated peace. De Gaulle proposed settlement by a conference of the United States, France, Soviet Russia and China to be followed by evacuation of the entire Indochina peninsula by all foreign forces and by a big powers guarantee of the neutrality of Laos, Cambodia and the two Vietnams. It was a feasible—and probably at that time achievable—alternative, except that it would not have ensured a non-Communist South Vietnam, and for that reason it was ignored by the United States.

An American emissary, Under-Secretary of State George Ball, had been sent a few weeks previously to explain to de Gaulle that any talk of negotiations could demoralize the South in its current fragile condition, even lead to its collapse, and that the United States "did not believe in negotiating until our position on the battlefield was so strong that our adversaries might make the requisite concessions." De Gaulle rejected this position outright. The same illusions, he told Ball, had drawn France into such trouble; Vietnam was a "hopeless place to fight"; a "rotten country," where the United States could not win for all its great resources. Not force but negotiation was the only way.

Although he might have gloated to see the United States discomfited as France had been, de Gaulle let a larger consideration govern him.

The reason why he and other Europeans in many subsequent efforts tried so earnestly to disengage the United States from Vietnam was fear of American attention and resources being diverted from Europe to an Asian backwater.

U Thant had meanwhile ascertained through Russian channels that Hanoi was interested in talks with the Americans, and he so informed the United States Ambassador to the UN, Adlai Stevenson. U Thant proposed a cease-fire across both Vietnam and Laos and offered to let the United States write the terms as it saw fit and to announce them unchanged. On conveying this message, Stevenson met only stalling in Washington, and after the election a negative response on the ground that the United States had learned through other channels that Hanoi was not really interested. Further, Rusk said, the United States would not send a representative to Rangoon, where U Thant had arranged for the talks to take place, because any hint of such a move would cause panic in Saigon—or, what the United States really feared and did not say, renewed feelers toward neutralism.

Not concealing his displeasure at this rejection, U Thant pointedly told a press conference in February that further bloodshed in Southeast Asia was unnecessary and that only negotiation could "enable the United States to withdraw gracefully from that part of the world." By that time the American bombing campaign called ROLLING THUNDER had begun and under the crashing and killing of American air raids the opportunity for graceful exit would never come again.

Johnson had already let pass a greater opportunity for disengagement—his own election. He defeated Goldwater by the largest popular majority in American history and gained unassailable majorities in Congress of 68–32 in the Senate and 294–130 in the House. The vote was largely owed to the split among Republicans between the Rockefeller moderates and the Goldwater extremists and to the widespread fear of Goldwater's warlike intentions, and the result put Johnson in a position to do anything he wanted. His heart was in the welfare programs and civil rights legislation that were to create the Great Society, free of poverty and oppression. He wanted to go down in history as the great benefactor, greater than FDR, equal to Lincoln. Failure to seize his chance at this moment to extricate his Administration from an unpromising foreign entanglement was the irreparable folly, though not his alone. His chief advisers in government believed with him that they would take greater punishment from the right by withdrawing than from the left by pursuing the fight. Confident in his own power, Johnson believed he could achieve both his aims, domestic and foreign, at once.

Reports from Saigon told of progressive crumbling, riots, corruption, anti-American sentiment, neutralist movement by the Buddhists. "I feel," declared one American official in Saigon, "as though I were on the deck of the *Titanic*." These signals did not suggest to Washington a useless effort and a time to cut losses, but rather a need for greater effort to redress the balance and gain the advantage. Officials, civilian and military, agreed on the necessity of intervention in the form of air war to convince the North to give up its attempted conquest. That the United States could accomplish its aim by superior might no one doubted.

Like Kennedy, Johnson believed that to lose South Vietnam would be to lose the White House. It would mean a destructive debate, he was later to say, that would "shatter my Presidency, kill my Administration, and damage our democracy." The loss of China, which had led to the rise of Joe McCarthy, was "chickenshit compared with what might happen if we lost Vietnam." Robert Kennedy would be out in front telling everyone that "I was a coward, an unmanly man, a man without a spine." Worse, as soon as United States weakness was perceived by Moscow and Peking, they would move to "expand their control over the vacuum of power we would leave behind us ... and so would begin World War III." He was as sure of this "as nearly as anyone can be certain of anything." No one is so sure of his premises as the man who knows too little.

A feasible alternative, on the strength of the electoral mandate, might have been to pursue U Thant's overtures to Hanoi and even use his influence to install a government in Saigon (as Kennedy had suggested) that would invite the United States to depart, leaving Vietnam to work out its own settlement. Since this would inevitably lead to a Communist take-over, it was a course the United States refused to contemplate, although it would have cast off a devouring incubus.

A good look would have revealed that the raison d'être for American intervention had slipped considerably. When the CIA was asked by the President for its estimate of the crucial question whether, if Laos and South Vietnam fell to Communist control, all Southeast Asia would necessarily follow, the answer was in the negative; that except for Cambodia, "It is likely that no other nation in the area would quickly succumb to Communism as a result of the fall of Laos and Vietnam." The spread of Communism in Southeast Asia "would not be inexorable" and America's island bases in the Pacific "would still enable us to employ enough military power in the area to deter Hanoi and Peking." We would not, after all, have to pull back to San Francisco.

Another advice came from the inter-agency Working Group on Vietnam, composed of representatives from State, Defense, Joint Chiefs and CIA, who bravely undertook after the election in November to "consider realistically what our overall objectives and stakes are." This unprecedented endeavor led the group, after long and careful review, to deliver a serious warning: that the United States could not guarantee a non-Communist South Vietnam "short of committing ourselves to whatever degree of military action would be required to defeat North Vietnam and possibly Communist China." Such action could lead to a major conflict and "possibly even the use of nuclear weapons at some point."

At the same time, Under-Secretary of State George Ball, who as a believer in the primacy of Europe and a specialist in economic problems took a sour view of the whole Vietnam affair, exerted a major effort to deter the decision for combat. In a long memorandum he made the point that bombing, rather than persuading the North to abandon its aims, was likely to provoke Hanoi to send in more ground forces, its largest resource, which would in turn require larger United States forces to meet them. Already, Ball said, our allies believed the United States was "engaged in a fruitless struggle in Vietnam, and if expanded to a land war would divert America from concern with Europe. What we had most to fear was a general loss of confidence in American judgment." His recommendation was to warn Saigon of possible disengagement on the basis of its failing war effort. This would probably precipitate a deal with the insurgents, which he privately thought was the best result attainable.

In discussion, Ball found the three chief officers of the Administration, McGeorge Bundy, McNamara and Rusk, "dead set" against his views and interested only in one problem: "how to escalate the war until the North Vietnamese were ready to quit." When his memorandum was submitted to the President, the result was the same. Johnson looked it over, asked Ball to go through it with him point by point and handed it back without comment.

Why did these advisory voices of the CIA, the Working Group, the Under-Secretary of State, have so little impact? Advice on the basis of collected information was the business of the first two, of the Working Group specifically on Vietnam. If Johnson read its report—and one would like to think that government agencies write reports for more than wallpaper—he refused the message. Ball could be tolerated as an "in-house devil's advocate," and was in fact useful in that role as showing the White House open to dissenters. But minds at the top were locked in the vise of 1954—that Ho was an agent of world Communism, that the lesson of appeasement precluded yielding at any point, that the United States' undertaking to frustrate North Vietnam's drive to control the country was right and must be carried out. How could it *not* succeed against what Johnson called "that raggedy-ass little fourth-rate country"? Despite the Working Group's warning, the President, his Secretaries and the Joint Chiefs were sure that American power could force North Vietnam to quit while the United States carefully avoided a clash with China.

Hanoi too could be ill-advised. Two days before the American election, as if to provoke belligerency, the Viet-Cong took the first offensive action against a specifically American facility—a mortar attack on the Bien Hoa airfield. This was an American training base where a squadron of old B-57s had recently been moved in from the Philippines for training purposes, making it a tempting target. Six of the planes were demolished, five Americans killed, and 76 other casualties sustained. Certain that the attack was instigated by Hanoi, General Taylor, then Ambassador in Saigon, telephoned Washington for authority to take immediate reprisals. All chief advisers in the capital concurred. Waiting for the election, Johnson held back, and because of his nagging worries about China and despite reports of accelerating decay in Saigon, he was to hold back for three months more.

Cautious and hesitating, he sent McGeorge Bundy and McNamara's Assistant Secretary, John McNaughton, to find out whether air war was really necessary to save the South. While they were in South Vietnam, the Viet-Cong made another attack, this time on American barracks at Pleiku, in which eight Americans were killed and 108 injured. Inspecting the shattered field, Bundy was said to have been outraged by the deliberate challenge and to have telephoned a highly charged demand for reprisals to the President. Whether he did or not, emotion was not the deciding factor. Bundy's memorandum, drafted on his way home in company with Taylor and General William C. Westmoreland (the commander who had replaced Harkins), was cold and hard: without "new United States action, the defeat of South Vietnam appears inevitable. . . . The stakes in Vietnam are extremely high. . . . The international prestige of the United States is at risk. . . . There is no way of negotiating ourselves out of Vietnam which offers any serious promise at present." Consequently, "The policy of graduated and continuing reprisal," as planned, was the most promising course. Negotiations of any sort should not now be accepted except on the basis of an end to Viet-Cong violence.

Here were the essentials that were to hold United States policy in their grip: that the stakes were high, that protecting United States prestige from failure was primary, that graduated escalation of bombing was to be the strategy, that negotiations were not wanted until the scale of punishment softened the resolve of North Vietnam. Explaining gradualism, Maxwell Taylor wrote later, "We wanted Ho and his advisers to have time to meditate on the prospects of a demolished homeland." A source of trouble was detected here by John McNaughton, a former professor of law given to hard analysis. With uncomfortable foresight, he included in a list of war aims "To emerge from crisis without unacceptable taint from methods used."

In response to Pleiku, an immediate reprisal had been carried out within hours of the attack, with the Majority Leader and the Speaker of the House summoned to the White House to witness the decision. After three more weeks of anxious discussion, on 2 March, the program for a three-month bombing campaign called ROLLING THUNDER was begun.

Johnson's anxiety lest the bombing overstep some unknown line of Russian or Chinese tolerance required ROLLING THUNDER to be supervised directly from the White House. Each week CINCPAC sent the program for the next seven days, with munitions dumps, warehouses, fuel depots, repair shops and other targets described and located and the number of sorties estimated, to the Joint Chiefs, who passed them to McNamara and he to the White House. Here they were carefully examined at the highest level of government by a group consisting initially of the President, the Secretaries of Defense and State and the chief of NSC, who assembled for the task at lunch every Tuesday. Their selections, made 9000 miles from the spot by men immersed in a hundred other problems, were conveyed back to the field by the same route. Afterward, the results of each sortie, reported by each pilot to his base commander, were collated and communicated back to Washington. McNamara was always the best informed because, it was said, in driving over from the Pentagon he had eight more minutes than the others to study his target list.

The presiding presence at the Tuesday lunches was the wallpaper of the second-floor dining room depicting scenes of Revolutionary triumphs at Saratoga and Yorktown. Ever hungering for history's favor, Johnson invited a professor of history, Henry Graff of Columbia University, to attend several sessions of the Tuesday lunches and interview the members. The resulting account did not erect the monument he hoped for. In his own version, possibly embroidered for effect, the President lay awake at night worrying about the trigger that might activate "secret treaties" between North Vietnam and its allies, sometimes to the point of putting on his bathrobe at 3:00 a.m. and going down to the Situation Room, where air raid results were marked on a wall map.

A greater danger than China lay on the American home front. While national sentiment, insofar as it paid attention, on the whole supported the war, the bombing campaign brought explosions of dissent on the campuses. The first "teach-in" of faculty and students, at the University of Michigan in March, attracted an unexpected mass of 3000 participants and the example soon spread to universities on both coasts. A meeting held in Washington was connected to 122 campuses by telephone. The movement was less a sudden embrace of Asia than an extension of the civil rights struggle and the Free Speech and other student radical enthusiasms of the early sixties. The same groups now found a new cause and provided the organizing energy. At Berkeley 26 faculty members joined in a letter stating that "The United States government is committing a major crime in Vietnam" and expressing their shame and anger that "this blood bath is made in our name." Though mauled by the feuds of rival factions, the protest movement lent a fierce energy, much of it mindless, to the opposition.

The need of a "convincing public information campaign" to accompany military action had been foreseen by the policy-makers, but its efforts accomplished little. Speaking teams of government officers sent to debate in the universities only supplied more occasions for protest and victims for the students to heckle. A White Paper entitled "Aggression from the North" issued by the State Department, designed to show the infiltration of men and arms by North Vietnam as "aggressive war," was feeble. In all their public justifications, the President, the Secretary of State and other spokesmen harped on "aggression," "militant aggression," "armed aggression," always in comparison with the failure to stop the aggressions that brought on World War II, always implying that Vietnam too was a case of foreign aggression. They made the point so insistently that they sometimes said it explicitly, as when McNamara in 1966 called it "the most flagrant case of outside aggression." The ideological division in Vietnam may have been real and insuperable, just as was the division between South and North in the American Civil War, but it is not recorded in the American case that the North's war against the South's secession was considered "outside aggression."

By April it was apparent that ROLLING THUNDER was having no visible effect on the enemy's will to fight. Bombing of the supply trails in Laos had not prevented infiltration; Viet-Cong raids showed no signs of faltering. The decision to introduce American infantry seemed ineluctable and the Joint Chiefs so recommended. Fully recognized as portentous, the question was exhaustively discussed, with the confident assurances of some matched by the doubts and ambivalence of others, both military and civilian. The decisions taken in April and May were piecemeal, based on a strategy of continued bombing supplemented by ground combat with the aim of breaking the will of the North and the Viet-Cong "by effectively denying them victory and bringing about negotiations through the enemy's impotence." This impotence it was thought possible to achieve by attrition, that is, by killing off the Viet-Cong rather than trying to defeat them. United States troops were to be raised initially to a combat strength of 82,000.

Wanting it both ways, battle axe and olive branch, Johnson delivered a major speech at Johns Hopkins University on 7 April offering prospects of vast rural rehabilitation and a flood control program for the Mekong Valley, supported by $1 billion of United States funds, in which North Vietnam, after accepting peace, would share. The United States would "never be second in the search . . . for a peaceful settlement," Johnson declared, and was ready now for "unconditional discussions." It sounded open and generous, but what "unconditional" meant in American thinking was negotiations when the North was sufficiently battered to be prepared to concede. Matched by an equal and opposite insistence on certain *pre*conditions by the other side, these were the fixed premises that were to nullify all overtures for the next three years.

The billion-dollar carrot attracted no bites. Rejecting Johnson's overture, Hanoi announced its four preconditions the next day: 1) withdrawal of United States military forces; 2) no foreign alliances or admission of foreign troops by either side; 3) adoption of the NLF (National Liberation Front or Viet-Cong) program by South Vietnam; 4) reunification of the country by the Vietnamese without outside interference. Since point 3 was exactly what the South and the United States were fighting against, it was the obvious nullifier. International interest in sealing off the conflict found itself blocked. A conference of seventeen non-aligned nations convened by Marshal Tito appealed for negotiations without effect; contacts with Hanoi pursued by J. Blair Seaborn, Canadian member of the International Control Commission, went unrequited; the prime ministers of four

British Commonwealth countries on a mission to urge negotiation in the capitals of the parties to the struggle were refused admission by Moscow, Peking and Hanoi. An envoy of the United Kingdom on the same mission, admitted to Hanoi a few months later, found the response still negative.

In May 1965, the United States, making its own effort, initiated a pause in the bombing which it was hoped might evoke from Hanoi a sign of willingness to talk. At the same time a note from Rusk was delivered to the North Vietnamese Embassy in Moscow suggesting reciprocity in reducing "armed action." The note was returned without reply and American bombing resumed a few days later.

On 9 June the fateful decision to authorize "combat support" of South Vietnam by American ground forces was publicly announced by the White House, embedded in verbiage intended to show it as merely an increase in effort, not a basic change. The first "search and destroy" mission took place on 28 June. In July the President announced an increase in draft quotas along with the addition of 50,000 troops to bring strength in Vietnam to 125,000. Further additions brought the total to 200,000 by the end of 1965. The purpose of these escalations, as General Taylor later explained to the Senate, was to inflict "continued increasing loss on the Viet-Cong guerrillas so that they cannot replace their losses" and by this attrition convince the North that it could not win a military victory in the South. "Theoretically, they would virtually run out of trained troops by the end of 1966," and at that point, rather than negotiate, they might simply give up the attempt and fade away. It was in pursuit of this process that the necrophiliac body count became such an unpleasant feature of the war. That the North, with a regular army of over 400,000, could in fact activate any number of men to replace Viet-Cong losses for some reason escaped the sophisticated statistical analyses of the Pentagon.

Belligerency was now a fact. United States soldiers were killing and being killed, United States pilots were diving through anti-aircraft fire and, when crashing, were being captured to become prisoners of war. War is a procedure from which there can be no turning back without acknowledging defeat. This was the self-laid trap into which America had walked. Only with the greatest difficulty and rarest success, as belligerents mired in futility have often discovered, can combat be terminated in favor of compromise. Because it is a final resort to destruction and death, war has traditionally been accompanied by the solemn statement of justification, in medieval times a statement of "just war," in modern times a Declaration of War (except by the Japanese, who launch their wars by surprise attack). However false and specious the justification may be, and usually is, a legalism of this kind serves to state the case and automatically endows the government with enlarged powers.

Johnson decided to do without a Declaration, partly because neither cause nor aims were clear enough in terms of national defense to sustain one, partly because he feared a Declaration might provoke Russia or China to a response in kind, mainly because he feared it would divert attention and resources from the domestic programs which he hoped would make his reputation in history. Fear of touching off a right-wing stampede in favor of invasion and unrestricted bombing of the North if the deteriorating plight of the South were made known was a further reason for concealing and obfuscating the extent of involvement. Johnson thought he could pursue the war without the nation noticing. He did not ask Congress for a Declaration because he was advised or worried that he might not get it, nor did he ask for a renewed vote on the Tonkin Gulf Resolution for fear of being embarrassed by reduced majorities.

It would have been wiser to face the test and require Congress to assume its constitutional responsibility for going to war. The President should likewise have asked for an increase in taxes to balance war costs and inflationary pressures. He avoided this in his hope of not arousing protest. As a result his war in Vietnam was never legitimized. By forgoing a Declaration he opened a wider door to dissent and made the error, fatal to his presidency, of not assuring the ground of public support.

By-passing a Declaration was one result of the limited-war concept developed during the Kennedy Administration. In a remarkable statement of that time* McNamara had said, "The greatest contribution Vietnam is making . . . is developing an ability in the United States to fight a limited war, to go to war without arousing the public ire." He believed this to be "almost a necessity in our history, because this is the kind of war we'll likely be facing for the next fifty years."

Limited war is basically a war decided on by the Executive, and "without arousing the public ire"—meaning the public notice—means parting company with the people, which is to say discarding the principle of representative government. Limited war is not nicer or

* Previously cited in two scholarly works (see Reference Notes), this statement, which Mr. McNamara does not recall, has defied all efforts to trace it to a documented primary source. It is included here because the ring is authentic and the implications serious, then and now.

kinder or more just than all-out war, as its proponents would have it. It kills with the same finality. In addition, when limited on one side but total for the enemy, it is more than likely to be unsuccessful, as rulers more accustomed to the irrational have perceived. Urged by Syria and Jordan to launch a limited war against Israel in 1959, President Nasser of Egypt replied that he was willing to do so if his allies could obtain Ben-Gurion's assurance that he too would limit it. "For a war to be limited depends on the other side."

Johnson's resort to war as soon as the election was over received the appropriate comment in a cartoon by Paul Conrad showing him looking into a mirror and seeing Goldwater's face looking back at him. Dissent from this point on, though as yet confined mainly to students, extremists and pacifists, grew loud and incessant. A National Coordinating Committee to End the War in Vietnam was formed, which organized protest rallies and assembled a crowd of 40,000 to mount a picket line around the White House. Draft-card-burning spread, following the example of a young man, David Miller, who courted arrest by ceremoniously burning his card in the presence of Federal agents and who suffered two years in prison for the act. In horrible emulation of the Buddhist monks, a Quaker of Baltimore burned himself alive on the Pentagon steps on 2 November 1965, followed by a second such suicide in front of the UN a week later. The acts seemed too crazed to influence the American public, except perhaps negatively, as equating anti-war protest in the public mind with emotional misfits.

If dissent was passionate, it was far from general. Hard-hat sentiment, which so distinguishes organized labor in America from its counterpart abroad, was expressed by the AFL-CIO Council. In an unveiled warning to members of Congress in the mid-term election of 1966 the Council resolved, "Those who would deny our military forces unstinting support are in effect aiding the Communist enemy of our country." Labor's rank and file shared the sentiment. When an unorthodox mayor of Dearborn, Michigan, the Ford suburb, put a referendum on the municipal ballot in the 1966 election calling for a cease-fire followed by American withdrawal "so the Vietnamese people can settle their own problems," he was answered by an overwhelming vote in the negative.

Influential voices, however, were taking up the dissent. Even Walter Lippmann sacrificed his carefully cultivated cordiality with Presidents to the demands of truth. Denying the argument of "external aggression," he stated the obvious: that there were never two Vietnams but only "two zones of one nation." He poured scorn on the policy of globalism that committed the United States to "unending wars of liberation" as a universal policeman. The conversion of Lippmann and of the *New York Times*, which now opposed deeper involvement, added respectability to the opposition, while inside the government doubts that the war could be militarily resolved were coming into the open. The President's close and trusted press secretary, Bill Moyers, tried steadily to outflank the hawks at the government's top by reporting the disillusions of lesser officers, agents and observers. The Moyers network, initially created at Johnson's request for contrary views, proved too uncomfortable for the President, who did not like "dissonance" or having to face multiple options. He shared the problem if not the flash of insight of Pope Alexander VI in his one moment of remorse when he acknowledged that a ruler never hears the truth and "ends by not wanting to hear it." Johnson wanted his policies to be ratified, not questioned, and as the issues hardened, he avoided listening to Moyers' reports.

Advisers who worried about the inevitable escalation of combat were proposing alternatives. The Embassy in Saigon under Maxwell Taylor, who despite responsibility for the first combat initiative was not an advocate of expanded belligerency, proposed early in 1965 a plan for "terminating our involvement." It advocated a return to Geneva, using as bargaining chips the progressive reduction of American forces plus "amnesty and civil rights" for the Viet-Cong and an American-sponsored program for the economic development of all Indochina. The plan was drafted by Taylor's deputy, U. Alexis Johnson, a career foreign service officer, and a hint of it entered the Johns Hopkins speech and ended there. George Ball followed with repeated memoranda urging disengagement of our interests from those of Saigon before some major disaster cut off choices. Of communications to a President, Galbraith has written that "the overwhelming odds are that he will never read them."

Two men deeply respected by the President, Senator Richard Russell of Georgia and Clark Clifford, former White House counsel to Truman, tried to divert him from the course he was taking. Russell, as chairman until 1969 of both the all-powerful Approrpiations Committee and the Armed Services Committee and a colleague throughout Johnson's senatorial years, was expected by many to become the first Southern President, if chance had not inserted Johnson ahead of him. Though publicly a hawk, in 1964 he had privately exhorted Johnson to keep out of war in Asia and now proposed, in a rare example of creative thinking, that a public opinion poll be taken in Vietnamese cities on whether American help was wanted and that if the results were negative, the United States should withdraw. The ascertaining of Vietnamese opinion on American appropriation of "their" war was an original idea that had not previously occurred to anyone and was, of course, despite its eminent source, not adopted.

A clue to the answer might have been seen in the eyes of Vietnamese villagers. A journalist who had covered the war in Europe recalled the smiles and hugs and joyous offers of wine when GIs came through liberated areas of Italy. In Vietnam, the rural people, when American units passed them on the streets or in the villages, kept their eyes down or looked the other way and offered no greetings. "They just wanted us to go home." Here was a sign of the vanity of "nation-building." What nation has ever been built from outside?

Clifford, an important Washington lawyer and intimate of the President, warned in a private letter that on the basis of CIA assessments, further build-up of ground forces could become an "open-end commitment . . . without realistic hope of ultimate victory." Rather, he advised, the President should probe every avenue leading to possible settlement. "It won't be what we want but we can learn to live with it." The gist of his and the other counsels was confirmed by a foreign observer, the distinguished Swedish economist Gunnar Myrdal, who wrote in the *New York Times* in July 1965 that "The conviction that this policy will end in failure is commonly held in all countries outside the United States."

None of the American advisers' doubts was stated publicly, and none except Ball's proposed outright withdrawal. Rather they advised holding on without escalating while seeking a negotiated settlement. Negotiation, however, faced a rigid impasse. Quite apart from preconditions, Hanoi would accept no settlement short of coalition or some other form of compromise leading to its absorption of the South; for the United States any such compromise would represent acknowledgment of American failure, and this the Administration, all the more now for having made itself hostage to its own military, could not accept. It was chained to the aim of ensuring a non-Communist South Vietnam in order to make its exit with credibility intact. The goal had subtly changed from blocking Communism to saving face. McNaughton, one official who did not allow himself self-deception, put it caustically when he placed first on his list of United States war aims, "70 percent to avoid a humiliating defeat to our reputation as guarantor."

The Administration at this stage began to study the chances of "winning." Given a military task, the military had to believe they could accomplish it if they were to believe in themselves and quite naturally demanded more and more men for the purpose. Their statements were positive and the requisitions large. Facing escalation, McNamara asked General Wheeler, Chairman of the Joint Chiefs, what assurance the United States could have "of winning in South Vietnam if we do everything we can." If "winning" meant suppressing all insurgency and eliminating Communists from South Vietnam, Wheeler said, it would take 750,000 to a million men and up to seven years. If "winning" meant demonstrating to the Viet-Cong that they could not win, a lesser force would be enough. What national interest warranted the investment of such forces, lesser or larger, did not enter the discussion; the Administration simply went forward because it did not know what else to do. When all options are unpromising, policy-makers fall back on "working the levers" in preference to thinking.

Johnson's idea was to fight and negotiate simultaneously. The difficulty was that the limited war aim of causing North Vietnam to leave South Vietnam alone was unachievable by limited war. The North had no intention of ever conceding a non-Communist South, and since such a concession could have been forced upon them only by military victory, and since such a victory was unattainable by the United States short of total war and invasion, which it was unwilling to undertake, the American war aim was therefore foreclosed. If this was recognized by some, it was not acted upon because no one was prepared to admit American failure. Activists could believe the bombing might succeed; doubters could vaguely hope some solution would turn up.

Unpleasantly for the President, Adlai Stevenson's sudden death in London brought to light the circumstances of the rebuff to U Thant's mediation. Eric Sevareid, reporting what Stevenson had told him just before his death, revealed for the first time that Hanoi had in fact agreed to the meeting proposed by U Thant, whereas Johnson had recently told a press conference that there had not been the "slightest indication" of interest on the other side. The *St. Louis Post-Dispatch* thereupon recalled that in the year prior to America's entering active belligerency, Johnson or his White House spokesman had stated no less than seven times that the United States was seeking no wider war. The President's personal credibility suffered accordingly.

On top of the Stevenson story, another failed peace overture became known. At the request of the United States, the Italian Foreign

Minister, Amintore Fanfani, then a delegate to the UN, arranged for two Italian professors, one a former acquaintance of Ho Chi Minh, to go to Hanoi. While encountering "a strong desire to find a peaceful solution," they also reported, as Fanfani wrote to Johnson, that Ho's conditions included a cease-fire throughout North and South, in addition to the Four Points previously announced. He had, however, agreed to begin talks without requiring withdrawal of American forces. Since a cease-fire in place would have left North Vietnamese units inside the South, it was not acceptable to the United States, but Rusk conveyed the American rejection on the grounds of finding "no real willingness for unconditional negotiations" in Hanoi. The episode leaked to the press as such things do when someone wants them known.

Disconcerted at being exposed as uninterested in peace, the President ordered a bombing halt at Christmas time and launched a spectacular flying peace circus. Officials were despatched like carrier pigeons to capitals east and west, ostensibly to seek paths to negotiation—Harriman on a round-the-world tour to Warsaw, Delhi, Teheran, Cairo, Bangkok, Australia, Laos and Saigon; Arthur Goldberg, Stevenson's successor at the UN, to Rome, Paris and London; McGeorge Bundy to Ottawa; Vice-President Hubert Humphrey to Tokyo and two Assistant Secretaries of State to Mexico City and the African states, respectively. Nothing came of this display except stimulation of heavy public pressure on Johnson to extend the bombing halt. It was extended for 37 days with the announced purpose of testing Hanoi's willingness to talk, in vain. Looking toward its ultimate goal, Hanoi had little to expect from negotiations.

While bombing resumed and the war grew harsher, the search for settlement continued. Talks in Warsaw with Polish intermediaries in mid-1966 seemed to be making progress until, at a delicate point, American air strikes, directed for the first time at targets in and around Hanoi, caused North Vietnam to cancel the contacts. The episode showed that neither side basically wanted negotiations to succeed. In his unsparing way, McNaughton stated the dilemma for the United States: aiming for victory could end in compromise but aiming for compromise could end only in defeat, because to reveal "a lowering of sights from victory to compromise . . . will give the DRV [North Vietnam] the smell of blood."

The war was turning nasty with napalm-burned bodies, defoliated and devastated croplands, tortured prisoners and rising body counts. It was also becoming expensive, now costing $2 billion a month. Progressive escalation bringing troop strength to 245,000 in April 1966 required a request to Congress for $12 billion in supplemental war costs. In the field, the entry of American combat forces had stopped the Viet-Cong in its progress toward gaining control. The insurgents were reportedly losing their sanctuaries, forced to keep moving, finding it harder to re-group, with consequent demoralization and desertions. Their casualties and those of North Vietnamese units, according to American counts, were satisfactorily rising; prisoners' interrogation was said to show loss of morale; success of the American aim seemed within reach.

The price was a confirmation of the French view of a "rotten war." In pursuit of attrition, Westmoreland deployed combat units as lures to provoke attack so that American artillery and air force could close in for a kill and a gratifying body count. "Search and destroy" missions using tanks, artillery strafing and defoliation from the air left ruined villages and ruined crops and destitute refugees living in festering camps along the coast in growing resentment of the Americans. Bombing strategy too was directed toward attrition by famine through the destruction of dikes, irrigation ditches and the means of agriculture. Defoliation missions could destroy 300 acres of rice within three to five days and strip an equal area of jungle within five to six weeks. Napalm amounted to official terrorism, corrupting the users, who needed only to press the firing button to watch "huts go up in a boil of orange flame." Reports of American fighting methods written by correspondents in chronic antagonism to the military were reaching home. Americans who had never before seen war now saw the wounded and homeless and the melted flesh of burned children afflicted thus by their own countrymen. When even the *Ladies Home Journal* published an account with pictures of napalm victims, McNaughton's hope of emerging "without taint" vanished.

Reciprocal violence added to the spiral. Viet-Cong terrorism by means of rockets, shelling of villages, booby traps, kidnappings and massacres was indiscriminate and deliberate, designed to instill insecurity and demonstrate the lack of protection by the Saigon authorities. While American armed intervention had prevented the insurgents' victory, it had not brought closer their defeat. Progress was deceptive. When the balance wavered, Russia and China sent in more supplies to the North, refreshing its strength. The low morale deduced from prisoners was a misinterpretation of the stoicism and fatalism of the East. In the American forces, short-term one-year tours of duty, intended to avoid discontent, prevented adaptation to irregular jungle warfare, thereby increasing casualties since the rate was always highest in the early months of duty. Adaptation never matched circumstances. American fighting tactics were designed in terms of large troop formations making use of mobility, and in terms of industrial targets for the exercise of air power. Once in motion the American military machine could not readjust to a warfare in which these elements did not exist. The American mentality counted on superior might, but a tank cannot disperse wasps.

Needs other than military absorbed equal concern. The "pacification" program was a strenuous American effort to strengthen the social and political fabric of South Vietnam in the interests of democracy. It was supposed to build confidence in Saigon and stabilize its footing. But the successive governments of Generals Khanh, Ky and Thieu, all of whom resented the patronage they depended upon, were not helpful collaborators. Nor were the white men's forces in their massive material presence the agents to "win hearts and minds." That program, known as WHAM to Americans in the field, failed of its object despite all the energy Washington invested in it and in some sectors turned sentiment against Saigon and the United States. Opposition to the generals' regime grew overt, with demands being made for civilian rule and a constitution. The Buddhist anti-government movement revived and again clashed in open struggle with Saigon's troops. At Hue, the ancient capital, demonstrators sacked and burned the American consulate and the cultural center.

Sentiment in the United States was also turning, with a noticeable rise in anti-war feeling when bombing resumed after the Christmas halt. Members of Congress, whom Maxwell Taylor had found, when briefing them on his return as Ambassador, "surprisingly patient and uncritical," were forming pockets of dissent. During the bombing pause, 77 members of the House, mostly Democrats, urged the President to extend the pause and submit the conflict to the UN. When the bombing resumed, fifteen Senators, all Democrats, made public a letter to the President, opposing the renewal. When Senator Morse proposed repeal of the Tonkin Gulf Resolution as an amendment to an appropriations bill for Vietnam, three Senators—Fulbright, Eugene McCarthy of Minnesota and Stephen Young of Ohio—joined the undeviating Morse and Gruening in its favor. It was defeated 92 to 5.

While not very bold, these were signals of opposition to the President from within his own party. They were the beginnings of a peace bloc that would split the Democratic Party over Vietnam, but they had no convinced and determined leadership in either House or Senate that was ready to oppose the majority.

Disaffection was deeper than the meager votes indicated. Congress continued to vote obediently for appropriations because most members could not bring themselves to reject Administration policy when the alternative meant admission of American failure. Further, they were in large part willing captives of the giant identified by Eisenhower as the military-industrial complex. Defense contracts were its currency, manipulated by more than 300 lobbyists maintained by the Pentagon on the Hill. The military provided V.I.P. tours, dinners, films, speakers, planes, sporting weekends and other perquisites, especially to senior committee chairmen in both Houses. A quarter of the membership of Congress held reserve commissions. Criticism of military procurements made a Congressman vulnerable to the charge of undermining national security. At the convening of the 89th Congress in 1965, that bold leader Vice-President Hubert Humphrey advised new members, "If you feel an urge to stand up and make a speech attacking Vietnamese policy, don't make it." After a second or third term, he said, they could afford to be independent, "but if you want to come back in '67 don't do it now."

Fulbright's vote on the Morse amendment signified an open break with Johnson. He felt betrayed by the move into active combat, contrary to Johnson's assurances, and was one day to confess that he regretted his role in the Tonkin Gulf Resolution more than anything else he had ever done. He now organized, in January–February 1966, in six days of televised hearings before the Senate Foreign Relations Committee, the first serious public discussion at an official level of the American intervention in Vietnam. More than was appreciated at the time, basic issues emerged—alleged "commitment," national interest, disproportion of effort to interest and the nascent recognition of American self-betrayal. Secretary Rusk and General Taylor made the case for the Administration; Ambassador George Kennan, General James M. Gavin, Fulbright himself and several colleagues spoke for the dissent.

Secretary Rusk insisted as always that the United States had "a clear and direct commitment" to secure South Vietnam against "external attack" deriving from the SEATO Treaty and Eisenhower's letter to Diem, and that this imposed an "obligation" to intervene. With the inventive rhetoric characteristic of true believers, he asserted that "the integrity of our commitments is absolutely essential to the preservation of peace right around the globe." When the supposed commitment was punctured by Senator Morse, who cited a recent denial by Eisenhower that he had "ever given a unilateral commitment to the government of South Vietnam," Rusk retreated to the position that the United States was "entitled" by the SEATO Treaty to intervene and that the commitment derived from policy statements by successive Presidents and from the appropriations voted by Congress itself. General Taylor acknowledged under questioning that insofar as the use of our combat ground forces was concerned, the commitment "took place of course only in the spring of 1965."

With regard to national interest, Taylor claimed that the United States had a "vital stake" in the war without defining what it was. He said that Communist leaders, in their drive to conquer South Vietnam, expected to undermine the position of the United States in Asia and prove the efficacy of wars of national liberation, which it was incumbent on the United States to show were "doomed to failure." Senator Fulbright was moved to ask if the American Revolution was not a "war of national liberation."

General Gavin questioned whether Vietnam was worth the investment in view of all other American commitments abroad. He believed we were being "mesmerized" by the endeavor, and that the contemplated troop strength of half a million, reducing our capacity everywhere else, suggested that the Administration had lost all sense of proportion. South Vietnam was simply not that important.

The charge that public opposition to the war represented "weakness" and failure of will (today being revived by the revisionists of the 1980s) was briefly touched by General Taylor in describing the French public's repudiation of the war as demonstrating "weakness." Senator Morse replied that it would not be "too long before the American people repudiate our war in Southeast Asia," as the French had theirs, and when they did, would that be "weakness"?

In sober words Ambassador Kennan brought out the question of self-betrayal. Success in the war would be hollow even if achievable, he said, because of the harm being done by the spectacle of America inflicting "grievous damage on the lives of a poor and helpless people, particularly on a people of different race and color. . . . This spectacle produces reactions among millions of people throughout the world profoundly detrimental to the image we would like them to hold of this country." More respect could be won by "a resolute and courageous liquidation of unsound positions" than by their stubborn pursuit. He quoted John Quincy Adams' dictum that wherever the standard of liberty was unfurled in the world, "there will be America's heart . . . but she goes not abroad in search of monsters to destroy." Pursuing monsters meant endless wars in which "the fundamental maxim of [American] policy would insensibly change from liberty to force." No harder truth was spoken at the hearings.

For all their truths, the Fulbright hearings were not a prelude to action in the only way that could count, a vote against appropriations, so much as an intellectual exercise in examination of American policy. The issue of longest consequence, Executive war, was not formulated until after the hearings, in Fulbright's preface to a published version. Acquiescence in Executive war, he wrote, comes from the belief that the government possesses secret information that gives it special insight in determining policy. Not only was this questionable, but major policy decisions turn "not upon available facts but upon judgment," with which policy-makers are no better endowed than the intelligent citizen. Congress and citizens can judge "whether the massive deployment and destruction of their men and wealth seem to serve their overall interests as a nation."

Though he could bring out the major issues, Fulbright was a teacher, not a leader, unready himself to put his vote where it counted. When a month after the hearings the Senate authorized $4.8 billion in emergency funds for the war in Vietnam, the bill passed against only the two faithful negatives of Morse and Gruening. Fulbright voted with the majority.

The belief that government knows best was voiced just at this time by Governor Nelson Rockefeller, who said on resumption of the bombing, "We ought all to support the President. He is the man who has all the information and knowledge of what we are up against." This is a comforting assumption that relieves people from taking a stand. It is usually invalid, especially in foreign affairs. "Foreign policy decisions," concluded Gunnar Myrdal after two decades of study, "are in general much more influenced by irrational motives" than are domestic ones.

After World War II a Strategic Bombing Survey by scientists, economists and other specialists had concluded that strategic bombing in the European theater (as distinct from tactical bombing in conjunction with ground action) had not been decisive. It had not significantly reduced Germany's physical fighting capacity or induced an earlier readiness to come to terms. The survey discovered extraordinary rapidity of repairs and no diminution of morale; in fact, bombing could raise morale. In March 1966, when the three allotted months of ROLLING THUNDER had extended to more than a year without noticeable "will-breaking," a group of prominent scientists at MIT and Harvard, including some who had served on the earlier survey, proposed a similar hard look at bombing results in Vietnam. Commissioned by the Institute of Defense Analysis under the code name JASON, a body of 47 specialists in various disciplines went through ten days of briefings by Defense, State, CIA and White House, followed by two months of technical studies. The group concluded that effects on North Vietnam's will to fight and on Hanoi's appraisal of the cost of continuing to fight "have not shown themselves in any tangible way." Bombing had not created serious difficulties in transportation, the economy or morale. The surveyors found no basis for concluding that "indirect punitive effects of the bombing will prove decisive in these respects."

The main reason, JASON stated, for the relative ineffectiveness of the air offensive was "unrewarding targets." The study concluded that a "direct frontal attack on a society" tended to strengthen the fabric, increase popular determination and stimulate protective devices and capacity for repair. This social effect was not unpredictable; it was the same as had been found in Germany, and indeed in Britain, where heightening of morale and hardening of determination as a result of the German terror bombing of 1940–41 was well known.

As an alternative to bombing, JASON recommended construction of an "anti-infiltration" barrier across Vietnam and Laos for a distance of about 160 miles. Fully presented in the study with detailed technical plans, it was to consist of minefields, walls, ditches and strong points strung with electronic barbed wire and flanked by defoliated strips on either side, at an estimated cost of $800 million. Whether it might have worked cannot be known. Ridiculed by Air Force commanders at CINCPAC who could not allow an alternative to their function, it was never tried.

Like every other "dissonant" advice, JASON bumped against a stone wall. Strategy remained unchanged because the Air Force, in concern for its own future role, could not admit that air power could be ineffective. CINCPAC continued to raise the punitive level of the bombing on a basis of calculated pain according to a calculated "stress theory" of human behavior: Hanoi should respond to "stress" by ceasing the actions that produced it. "We anticipated that they would respond like reasonable people," an official of the Defense Department said afterward. By the end of 1966 the bombs dropped reached an annual rate of 500,000 tons, higher than the rate used against Japan in World War II. Instead of rationally, Hanoi reacted humanly in anger and defiance, as the British had done under the German blitz, as no doubt Americans would have done if bombed. Instead of bringing the enemy chastened to the negotiating table, the air offensive made them more adamant: they now insisted on cessation of bombing as a fixed precondition of negotiation.

Overtures continued through Chester Ronning of Canada and other intermediaries, because by now all parties would have welcomed an end to the war, each on its own terms, which remained irreconcilable. When Washington learned from visitors to Hanoi of finding readiness to talk if the bombing was stopped, the conclusion derived by the United States was that the bombing was hurting and should therefore be augmented to achieve the desired result. The result of course was a hardening of Hanoi's intransigence.

JASON penetrated one significant spot in the stone wall. It confirmed doubts beginning to concern Secretary McNamara. His own Systems Analysis at the Department of Defense concluded that military benefits were not worth the economic cost. Though he gave no public indication, he seemed in private remarks to show a dawning recognition of futility. Believing, as he wrote to the President, that the prognosis for a "satisfactory solution" was not good, he declared in favor of the anti-infiltration barrier as a substitute for bombing and for further increase of ground forces. He failed to carry his point.

Elsewhere in government the sense of futility had spread, causing departures. Few resigned; most were eased out by skillful maneuvers of the President, who whatever his own misgivings did not welcome those of others, outspoken or even unspoken. Hilsman was eased out of the State Department in 1964, Forrestal from the White House staff in 1965, McGeorge Bundy from the NSC early in 1966, followed by the voluntary departures of George Ball and Bill Moyers in September and December 1966. Without exception, all went quietly, silent Laocoons who did not voice, much less shout, their warnings or disagreements at the time.

Silent departure of its members is an important property of government. To speak out even after leaving is to go into the wilderness; by exhibiting disloyalty to bar return within the circle. The same reasons account for reluctance to resign. The official can always convince himself that he can exercise more restraining influence inside, and he then remains acquiescent lest his connection with power be terminated. The effect of the American Presidency with its power of appointment in the Executive branch is overbearing. Advisers find it hard to say no to the President or to dispute policy because they know that their status, their invitation to the next White House meeting, depends on staying in line. If they are Cabinet officers, they have in the American system no parliamentary seat to return to from which they may retain a voice in government.

Rusk remained the rock. If he had doubts, he was able as the classic civil servant to convince himself that American policy was right and to reiterate that regardless of all other considerations the original goal of preserving a non-Communist South Vietnam must be maintained. In tribute to his steadfastness, someone in his own department scrawled inside a telephone booth, "Dean Rusk is a recorded announcement." Replacing Bundy, Walt Rostow, who had been predicting the imminent collapse of Viet-Cong insurgency since 1965, remained an enthusiast. At the top, Johnson was less so. Asked once how long the war might last, he answered, "Who knows how long, how much? The important thing is, are we right or wrong?" To pursue the killing and devastation of war with that question in doubt was unwise in relation to the public, to his own presidency and to history.

Through the draft, required by repeated escalations, the war was now affecting the general public directly. In mid-1966, the Pentagon announced that the troop level in Vietnam would reach 375,000 by the end of the year, with 50,000 more to follow in the next six months. By mid-1967, the level reached 463,000, with Westmoreland asking for 70,000 more for a total over 525,000 as a "minimum essential force" and Johnson announcing that the Commander's needs and requests "will be supplied." To the young answerable to the draft, this war made no appeal, especially not to those who saw it as mean and inglorious. Everyone who could took advantage of the draft extension allowed during the pursuit of higher education, while the less advantaged classes entered uniform. The inequitable draft, first sin of the Vietnam war on the home front, and intended to reduce cause for disaffection in the social sector, dug a cleavage in American society in addition to the cleavage in opinion.

Public protest meetings gathered members, campus demonstrations and anti-war marches swelled in stridency and violence, with waving of Hanoi's flag and slogans shouted in favor of Ho Chi Minh. A huge rally clashed against soldiers in battle dress on the steps of the Pentagon with protesters arrested and women beaten. Because protest was associated in the public mind with drugs and long hair and the counterculture of the decade, it may have slowed rather than stimulated general dissent. By the public on the whole, anti-war demonstrations were seen, according to a poll, as "encouraging the Communists to fight all the harder." Draft evasion and flag-burning outraged the patriots. Nevertheless, a sense of discomfort, animated by a perception of the war as cruel and immoral, was spreading. Bombing of a small rural Asian country, Communist or not, could not be seen as imperative necessity. Eyewitness reports to the *New York Times* by Harrison Salisbury of hits on the civilian areas of Hanoi—first denied, then admitted by the Air Force—raised an uproar. Johnson's rating in the polls for handling of the war slid over into the negative and would never again regain a majority of support. Accounts of prisoners casually tossed from helicopters and other incidents of callous brutality showed Americans that their country too could be guilty of atrocity. Opprobrium abroad, the mistrust of our closest allies, Britain, Canada and France, made themselves felt.

War is supposed to unite a people, but a war that excites disapproval, like that in the Philippines in 1900 or Britain's Boer War, divides a country more deeply than its normal divisions. As the New Left and other radicals became more offensive and unkempt, they deepened the rift with the respectable middle class and excited the hatred and reciprocal violence of the unions and hard hats. How long could we stand the "spiritual confusion," asked Reischauer in 1967 in a book called *Beyond Vietnam*. For some, perception of their country turned negative. The National Council of Churches claimed that America "was seen as a predominantly white nation using our overwhelming strength to kill more Asians." Martin Luther King, Jr., said he could no longer reprove acts of violence by his own people without speaking out against "the greatest purveyor of violence in the world today—my own government."

His was a terrible recognition. To see ourselves newly and suddenly as the "bad guys" in the world's polarity and to know the agent was "my own government" was a development with serious consequences. Distrust for and even disgust with government were the most serious, beginning with alienation from the vote. "You voted in '64 and got Johnson—why bother?" read a banner at an anti-war rally in New York. Vice-President Humphrey was unmercifully heckled at Stanford University. "The deterioration of every government," Montesquieu wrote in the 18th century in his *Spirit of the Laws*, "begins with the decay of the principles on which it was founded."

The Administration's war reports eroded its credibility at home, for which much of the blame rested with the military. Indoctrinated in deception for purposes of misleading the enemy, the military misleads from habit. Each of the services and major commands manipulated the news in the interests of "national security," or to make itself look good, or to win a round in the ongoing interservice contest, or to cover up mistakes or glamorize a commander. With an angry press eager to expose, the public was not left in the usual ignorance of the often shabby deceptions lying beneath the hocus-pocus of communiqués.

Dissent spread to the establishment. Walter Lippmann spent an evening in 1966 persuading Katharine Graham, publisher of the *Washington Post*, hitherto firmly among the hawks, that "decent people could no longer support the war." The alarming cost, reaching into the billions, mortgaging the future to deficit spending, causing inflation and unfavorable balance of payments, worried many in the business world. Some businessmen formed opposition groups, small in relation to the business community as a whole, but encouraged when the imposing figure of Marriner Eccles, former chairman of the Federal Reserve Board, spoke publicly for a group called Negotiation Now, organized by Galbraith and Arthur Schlesinger, Jr. An occasional ex-government voice broke silence. James Thomson, one of the internal dissenters who had left the Far East staff of the State Department in 1966, stated in a letter to the *New York Times* that there had always been "constructive alternatives" and, in an echo of Burke, that the United States as the greatest power on earth had "the power to lose face, the power to admit error, and the power to act with magnanimity."

General Ridgway's dislike of the war was well known. Reaching the independence of retirement, another of his stature, General David M. Shoup, recently retired Commandant of the Marine Corps and a hero of the Pacific war, joined him. The government's contention that Vietnam was "vital" to United States interests was, he said, "poppycock"; the whole of Southeast Asia was not "worth a single American life. . . . Why can't we let people actually determine their own lives?" Senator Robert Kennedy, the President's nemesis, or so perceived, called for a halt to the bombing as futile and in another speech infuriating to the White House proposed that the NLF should have a voice in any negotiations. A milestone was passed when a single Senator, Gaylord Nelson of Wisconsin, joined the lonely pair of Morse and Gruening to vote against a new appropriation bill of $12 billion for the war. In the House, Representative George Brown of California offered a Resolution to be added to this bill stating that it be the "sense of the Congress" that none of the funds authorized should be used for "military operations in or over North Vietnam." Though only a Resolution and not obligatory upon the Executive, it was nevertheless overwhelmingly defeated by 372 to 18.

Despite twenty years of pronouncements ever since Truman about the "vital" interest of Southeast Asia to the United States and the dire necessity of stopping Communism, the purpose of the war to the general public remained unclear. In May 1967, when a Gallup poll asked respondents if they knew why the United States was fighting in Vietnam, 48 percent answered yes and 48 percent answered no. The absent Declaration of War might have made a difference.

The purpose of the war was not gain or national defense. It would have been a simpler matter had it been either, for it is easier to finish a war by conquest of territory or by destruction of the enemy's forces and resources than it is to establish a principle by superior force and call it victory. America's purpose was to demonstrate her intent and her capacity to stop Communism in a framework of preserving an artificially created, inadequately motivated and not very viable state. The nature of the society we were upholding was an inherent flaw in the case, and despite all the efforts at "nation-building," it did not essentially change.

How then to terminate the squandering of American power in this unpromising, unprofitable, potentially dangerous conflict? Confident that North Vietnam must be hurting and could be brought to bend to the American purpose, the Administration attempted repeatedly in 1966–67 to bring Hanoi to the point of talks, always on American terms. The terms were a seemingly open-minded "unconditional," ignoring the fact that Hanoi insisted on a condition: cessation of the bombing. United States overtures carried various pledges to end the bombing, to stop the increase of United States forces "as soon as possible and not later than six months" after North Vietnam pulled back its forces from the South and ceased the use of violence. All the offers depended on reciprocal reduction of combat by Hanoi. Hanoi offered no reciprocity unless the bombing stopped first.

Foreign powers added their efforts. Pope Paul appealed to both sides for an armistice leading to negotiations. U Thant, asked by Washington to exercise his good offices, urged the United States and both Vietnams to meet on British territory for negotiations. To all the overtures from whatever quarter, through public statements by Ho Chi Minh and other officials and interviews with visiting journalists, Hanoi reiterated its insistence as prerequisite to negotiation upon an "unconditional" end to the bombing, cessation of all other acts of war by the United States, withdrawal of United States forces and acceptance of the Four Points. While modification of the other conditions was made from time to time, the demand to cease bombing was basic and never varied.

When the Premier, Pham Van Dong, referred to the Four Points as a "basis for settlement" rather than a prerequisite condition, Americans thought they detected a signal, and again in a statement that Hanoi would "examine and study proposals" for negotiation if the United States stopped the bombing. On this occasion, American and North Vietnamese representatives from their respective embassies in Moscow actually conferred, but since no bombing pause accompanied the meeting to indicate serious American intent, it had no result.

On another occasion, two Americans acquainted with Hanoi personally carried a message drafted by the State Department which proposed secret discussions on the basis of "some reciprocal restraint." The wording was milder, and airplanes, though not grounded, were for a time held away from the Hanoi area. Failing a response, they returned, hitting Haiphong for the first time and railroad yards and other targets in the capital. U Thant suggested the obvious test to cut through all the maneuvers. He urged the United States to "take a calculated risk" in a bombing halt, which, he believed, would lead to peace talks in "a few weeks' time." America did not make the test.

For domestic consumption, President Johnson described his country as ready to do "more than our part in meeting North Vietnam halfway in any possible cease-fire, truce or peace conference negotiations," but "more than our part" did not include grounding the B-52s. A letter from Johnson addressed directly to Ho Chi Minh repeated the formula of reciprocity: bombing and augmentation of United States forces would cease "as soon as I am assured that infiltration into South Vietnam by land and sea has stopped." Ho's reply repeated his formula as before.

Analysis of North Vietnam's responses indicated to Washington "a deep conviction in Hanoi that our resolves will falter because of the cost of the struggle." The analysts were correct. Hanoi's intransigence was indeed tied to a belief that the United States, whether from cost or from rising dissent, would tire first. When Secretary Rusk indignantly added up 28 American proposals of peace, he was half right; they did not want it until they could get it on their own terms. Since the American overtures not only met none of their required conditions but never indicated the extent and nature of the ultimate political settlement, Hanoi was not interested.

At one moment real movement seemed to take place when the Soviet Premier, Aleksei Kosygin, visited Prime Minister Harold Wilson in Britain. Acting as intermediaries in communication with the principals, they came close to arranging an agreed basis for talks. It was shattered when Johnson, at the last moment, as Kosygin was already leaving London, unaccountably altered the wording of the final communiqué, too late for consultation. "Peace was almost in our grasp," Wilson ruefully said. That is doubtful. The impression is hard to avoid that Johnson was indulging in all these maneuvers in order to placate criticism at home and abroad, but that he and the advisers he listened to still aimed at negotiations imposed by superior strength.

A cloud was rising on the domestic horizon. Progressive escalation, growing like the appetite that increases by what it feeds on, with no stated limits, was not accepted without question for a war only vaguely understood. Westmoreland's method of calling for increments of 70,000 to 80,000 at a time postponed the issue of calling up the Reserves but, as McNaughton warned his chief, only postponed it "with all its horrible baggage" to a worse time, the election year of 1968. McNaughton drew attention to mounting public dissent, fed by American casualties (there were to be 9000 killed and 60,000 wounded in 1967), by popular fear that the war might widen and by "distress at the amount of suffering being visited" on the people of both Vietnams. "A feeling is widely and strongly held that 'the Establishment' is out of its mind . . . that we are carrying the thing to absurd lengths. . . . Most Americans do not know how we got where we are. . . . All want the war ended and expect their President to end it. Successfully, or else."

If the "or else" meant "or out he goes," that alternative was not unimaginable. It was slowly becoming clear to Johnson that there was no way the Vietnam entanglement could end to his advantage. Military success could not end the war within the eighteen months left of his present term, and with an election ahead, he could not disengage and "lose" Vietnam. The Reserves, the casualties, the public protest would have to be faced. He was caught and, in Moyers' judgment, "He knew it. He sensed that the war would destroy him politically and wreck his presidency. He was a miserable man."

Johnson was under pressure too from the right and from the growing resentment of the military and their spokesmen at the restraints holding them back. The Armed Services Committee gave the resentment a public forum in August 1967 in subcommittee hearings under the chairmanship of Senator John Stennis. Even before taking testimony, Stennis stated his opinion that it was a "fatal mistake" to suspend or restrict the bombing.

Admiral Ulysses Grant Sharp, Air Force Commander at CINCPAC, carried the point further in a passionate argument for air power. He proclaimed a splendid record for the B-52s of damage inflicted on barracks, ammunition depots, power plants, railroad yards, iron, steel and cement plants, airfields, naval bases, bridges and in general a "widespread disruption of economic activity" and transportation, damaged harvests and increased food shortages. Without the bombing, he said, the North could have doubled its forces in the South, requiring the United States to bring in as many as 800,000 additional troops at a cost of $75 billion just to stay even. He condemned all suggestion of bombing pauses on the ground that they allowed the enemy to repair his supply lines, re-supply his forces in the South and build up his formidable anti-aircraft defenses. Sharp's scorn for civilian selection of targets as slow and too far removed was outspoken. If civilian authorities, he asserted in recognizable reference to the Tuesday lunch system, heeded the advice of the military, lifted restraints on "lucrative" targets in the vital Hanoi and Haiphong areas, eliminated long delays in approving targets, the bombing would be far more effective. Its cessation would be a "disaster," indefinitely prolonging the war.

Secretary McNamara's testimony brought all this into question. In an impressive presentation, he cited evidence to show that the bombing program had not significantly reduced the flow of men and supplies, and he disputed the military advice to lift restraints and allow a greater target range. "We have no reason to believe that it would break the will of the North Vietnamese people or sway the purpose of their leaders . . . or provide any confidence that they can be bombed to the negotiating table." Thus the whole purpose of American strategy was admitted to be futile by the Secretary of Defense. By revealing the open rift between civilian and military, the testimony created a sensation.

Senator Stennis' report on the hearings was an unrestrained assault on civilian interference. He said the overruling of military by civilian judgment has "shackled the true potential of air power." What was needed now was a hard decision "to take the risks that have to be taken, and apply the force that is required to see the job through."

Johnson was determined not to take any such risks, which still so worried him that he had apologized to the Kremlin for an accidental hit on a Soviet merchant vessel in a North Vietnamese harbor. Nor could he cease or halt the bombing as a means to peace because his military advisers assured him that this was the only way to bring the North to its knees. He felt obliged to call a press conference after the Stennis hearings to deny rifts in his government and to declare his support of the bombing program, although without relinquishing authority over selection of targets. In deference to the military, General Wheeler, Chairman of the Joint Chiefs, was thereafter invited to be a regular member of the Tuesday lunch and, with McNamara overruled, the target range gradually crept north, specifically taking in Haiphong.

With McNamara's testimony, the Johnson Administration had cracked. The strongest prop until now, the most hardheaded of the team inherited from Kennedy, the major manager of the war, had lost faith in it and from then on McNamara lost his influence with the President. When at a Cabinet meeting he said that the bombing, besides failing to prevent infiltration, was "destroying the countryside in the South; it's making lasting enemies," his colleagues stared at him in uncomfortable silence. The anti-war public waited, yearning for his disavowal of the war, but it did not come. Loyal to the government game, McNamara, like Bethmann-Hollweg in Germany in 1917, continued in the Pentagon to preside over a strategy he believed futile and wrong. To do otherwise, each would have said, would be to show disbelief, giving comfort to the enemy. The question remains where duty lies: to loyalty or to truth? Taking a position somewhere in between, McNamara did not last long. Three months after the Stennis hearings, Johnson announced, without consulting the person in question, McNamara's nomination as president of the World Bank. The Secretary of Defense at his departure was discreet and well-behaved.

By this time the government's pursuit of the war was domestically on the defensive. To shore up his political position and restore public confidence in him, Johnson brought home General Westmoreland, Ambassador Ellsworth Bunker, Lodge's successor, and other important personages to issue optimistic predictions and declare their firm faith in the mission "to prevail over Communist aggression." Incoming evidence not shared with the public was less encouraging. CIA estimates concluded that Hanoi would accept no level of air or naval action as "so intolerable that the war had to be stopped." A CIA study of bombing, unkindly calculated in terms of dollar value, brought out the fact that each $1 worth of damage inflicted on North Vietnam cost the United States $9.60. Systems Analysis at the Department of Defense found that the enemy could construct alternative supply routes "faster than we could choke them off," and estimated that more American troops would do more harm than good, especially to the economy of South Vietnam. The Institute of Defense Analysis, in a renewal of the JASON study, could find no new evidence to modify its earlier conclusions, and contrary to the claims of the Air Force, frankly stated, "We are unable to devise a bombing campaign in the North to reduce the flow of infiltrating personnel."

When objective evidence disproves strongly held beliefs, what occurs, according to theorists of "cognitive dissonance," is not rejec-

tion of the beliefs but rigidifying, accompanied by attempts to ration-
alize the disproof. The result is "cognitive rigidity"; in lay language,
the knots of folly draw tighter. So it was with the bombing. The more
punitive and closer it came to Hanoi, the more it foreclosed the Administration's own desire to negotiate itself out of the war. At the end of
1967 the Defense Department was to announce that the total tonnage
of bombs dropped on North and South together was over 1.5 million,
surpassing by 75,000 tons the total dropped on Europe by the Army
Air Force in World War II. Slightly more than half had been dropped
on North Vietnam, surpassing the total dropped in the Pacific theater.

One limit had been reached. In July, Johnson had placed a ceiling
on the escalation of ground forces at 525,000, just over the figure
General Leclerc, 21 years before, had declared would be required, "and
even then it could not be done." At the same time a new overture had
been made by the United States with a slight relaxation of insistence
on reciprocity. Two Frenchmen, Raymond Aubrac and Herbert
Marcovich, the former a friend from old times of Ho Chi Minh and
both eager to help end the war, had offered, through conversations
with Henry Kissinger at a Pugwash conference, to act as envoys to
Hanoi. After consultation with the State Department, they carried the
message that the United States would stop the bombing if Hanoi gave
assurance that this would lead to negotiations and on the "assumption"
that the North would reciprocally reduce infiltration. The reply
seemed to imply that talks might go forward on this basis, but further
discussion was angrily cut off by Hanoi when Admiral Sharp launched
a major bombing campaign to isolate Hanoi and Haiphong from each
other and from their supply routes. The Tuesday lunch must have
been napping over target selection on that day—unless the carelessness
was deliberate.

A month later, with the noise of dissent rising and evidence that a
political challenge to Johnson within his party was in the making, the
President made a major effort of his own. In a speech at San Antonio
on 29 September he publicly repeated the formula of the Aubrac-
Marcovich mission, saying that "We and our South Vietnamese allies
are wholly prepared to negotiate tonight. . . . The United States is
willing to stop all . . . bombardment of North Vietnam when this will
lead promptly to productive discussions." The United States would
"of course assume" that while talks were in progress the North
Vietnamese would not take advantage of the bombing halt. Hanoi
flatly rejected the overture as a "faked peace" and "sheer deception."
As their channel, Wilfred Burchett, a pro-Communist Australian journalist in Hanoi, reported "deep skepticism" about public or private

feelers from Washington. "I know of no leader who believes that President Johnson is sincere in stating that he really wants to end the war on terms that would leave the Vietnamese free to settle their own affairs."

The folly of missed opportunity was now Hanoi's. By accepting Johnson's public offer, the North Vietnamese could have held him to it and tested the results. If peace could have been plucked from the tangle, their country would have been spared much agony. But the bombing had made them paranoid, and having perceived a hint of give in their enemy's position, they were determined to outlast him until they could negotiate from strength.

Within days the event took place in the United States that turned the anti-war movement from dissent to political challenge. A presidential candidate came forward to oppose Johnson within his own party. Without a political challenge, anti-war organizers knew the movement could make little headway, and they had been active in the search. Robert Kennedy, though prodded by his circle, would not declare himself. On 7 October Senator Eugene McCarthy of Minnesota, in the long line of political independents bred in that region, filled the void with the announcement of his candidacy. Enthusiasm of the anti-war group enveloped him. Radicals, moderates, anyone regardless of politics who wanted to be rid of the war, rallied to him. Students poured from the colleges to work in his campaign. Until the first primary, Johnson and the old pros, with scorn for McCarthy's followers as a bunch of amateurs, did not take the challenge seriously. In fact, it was the beginning of the end. One month later the *Saturday Evening Post*, organ of middle America, presented the sum of American intervention in a stark editorial that said, "The war in Vietnam is Johnson's mistake, and through the power of his office he has made it a national mistake."

When the Tet offensive by the enemy exploded in Vietnam at the end of January 1968, the turn in American opinion against the war and against the President gathered force swiftly. Unlike the Viet-Cong's previous war against the rural villages, this was a massive coordinated assault against more than 100 towns and cities of South Vietnam at once, where the insurgents had for the most part not been visible before. Now, in the ferocity of attack, which succeeded in penetrating the grounds of the American Embassy in Saigon, American television viewers saw fighting in the streets, gunfire and death in American precincts, and gained a fearful impression. Hue, the ancient capital, was held for several weeks by the Viet-Cong, with thousands of inhabitants massacred before it was relieved. The fighting lasted a month, with many towns dangerously besieged, and it seemed unclear which side the outcome favored. But that such offensive strength could be mobilized at all by a supposedly tottering enemy blasted all confident assessments, punctured Westmoreland's credibility and stunned both the American public and the government.

The intention of the offensive may have been to provoke an uprising or seize a major foothold or demonstrate an impressive degree of strength as a preliminary to negotiations. Although it failed to shatter the South, and cost the Viet-Cong and Northerners heavy casualties, estimated at 30,000 to 45,000, it succeeded in shock value. A sense of disaster pervaded the United States, sharpened by the most widely quoted remark of the war: "It becomes necessary to destroy the town in order to save it." The American major meant that the town had to be razed in order to rout the Viet-Cong, but his phrase seemed to symbolize the use of American power—destroying the object of its protection in order to preserve it from Communism. As the fighting drew to a close, the sober voice of the *Wall Street Journal* declared, "We think the American people should be getting ready to accept, if they have not already, the prospect that the whole Vietnam effort may be doomed."

Westmoreland at once demanded an emergency airlift of 10,500 troops, and followed with a request, in which General Wheeler and the Joint Chiefs concurred, for additional forces numbering 206,000, well over the ceiling Johnson had set in July. Troop strength in Vietnam at this point was just under 500,000. An escalation of such magnitude, which was certain to raise a domestic outcry, faced the Executive with the moment when a choice had to be made between intensified combat and a non-military solution. With an election campaign about to begin, acceptance of Westmoreland's request was daunting, yet mentally locked in the belief that superior force must prevail, Johnson was not ready to negotiate or disengage on any terms that could be construed as "losing."

He appointed a task force under Clark Clifford, the Secretary of Defense–designate, to examine the costs and effects of mobilizing another 200,000 men. When asked if their addition would make the difference between victory and stalemate, the Joint Chiefs could offer no assurance that it would. Although the task force endeavored to keep within their assignment, "fundamental questions" kept recurring: at home, call up of Reserves, extension of the draft, lengthened and perhaps repeated tours of duty, additional billions in cost, increased taxes, wage and price control; on the military front, the inescapable fact that 90,000 Northerners had infiltrated in 1967, that the current rate was three or four times that of the previous year, that the enemy could out-escalate us every time, that the bombing evidently could not stop them, that no level of attrition of their forces had proved "unacceptable." In the fierce, in some places suicidal, assaults of the Tet offensive, the enemy had not hesitated to spend lives prodigally, in some cases at a 50 percent casualty rate. What rate of attrition would they ever find "unacceptable"?

Among the Joint Chiefs and the inner circle of the President's advisers, of whom Rusk, Rostow, Generals Wheeler and Taylor were members of the task force, no inference seemed to be drawn from all this. They were frozen in the posture of the last three years, determined on pursuing combat and giving Westmoreland what he wanted. They were "like men in a dream," in George Kennan's words, incapable of "any realistic assessment of the effects of their own acts." Clifford and others were doubtful, arguing for limiting the war effort while negotiating a settlement. Withdrawal was not an option, for after three years of devastating war and destruction, the revenge of the North was likely to be harsh and the United States could not now walk out and leave the people of South Vietnam to be slaughtered by their enemies. With something less than consensus, the task force recommended on 4 March an increment of 13,500 to meet immediate demands, while the rest of its report, according to a member, "was an effort to get the attention of the President—to get him to focus on the wider questions."

Clifford, chosen by Johnson to restore the support lost with McNamara, ironically absorbed McNamara's disillusion as soon as he took his place. He had already been shaken the previous summer, when on a tour of the SEATO nations to urge a greater contribution of their forces, by the nonchalant attitude toward his mission. The allies, so called, who were the putative "dominoes," were less than seriously engaged. Thailand, next door to the threat, had a contingent of 2500 in Vietnam out of its population of 30 million. Clifford had found esteem and encouragement for America's effort but no disposition to enlarge forces and no serious concern. The view from within Southeast Asia of its own situation raised a serious question about what America was defending.

On entering the Pentagon, Clifford found no plan for military victory but rather a series of limitations—no invasion of the North, no pursuit into Laos and Cambodia, no mining of Haiphong harbor—that precluded it. Among his civilian Assistant and Under-Secretaries, he found disenchantment, ranging from Townsend Hoopes' memorandum on "Infeasibility of Military Victory" to Paul Nitze's offer to resign rather than try to defend the Administration's war policy to the Senate.

He found a report by Systems Analysis stating that "despite a massive influx of 500,000 United States troops, 1.5 million tons of bombs a year, 400,000 attack sorties a year, 200,000 enemy KIA [killed in action] in three years, 20,000 United States KIA, etc., our control of the country-side and urban areas is now essentially at pre–August 1965 levels."

Further, Clifford found dire estimates of the effect on public opinion of each renewed escalation, and prognoses of budget increases of $2.5 billion in 1968 and $10 billion in 1969. He saw the national investment in Vietnam draining our disposable strength from Europe and the Middle East and the likelihood that the more we Americanized the war, the less South Vietnam would do for itself. He became convinced that the "military course we were pursuing was not only endless but hopeless." The war had reached a dead end. Not a man to sink his high-powered talents and polished reputation in a failing cause, Clifford set himself to dislodge the President from his frozen stance. Against the "men in a dream" of the inner group, he was one against eight, but he had realities on his side.

Political forces were aiding. Anti-war sentiment had mounted against the Democrats because they were Johnson's party. The war had become such an albatross, Senator Millard Tydings of Maryland told Johnson's speech writer, that "Any reasonably good Republican could clobber me if the election were held today." Tydings' advisers told him he could save himself only by attacking the President, and though he would not do that, he would have to "speak out against the war. It's dragging the country down and the Democrats along with it." He named several other Senators who reported the same situation in their states. It was confirmed by the California State Democratic Committee, which sent a telegram to the President signed by 300 members saying that in their judgment "The only action which can avert major Democratic party losses in this state in 1968 is an immediate all-out effort to secure a non-military settlement of the Vietnam war." Polls at this time showed the incumbent President trailing any one of six potential Republican opponents in the coming election.

An even stronger signal was Walter Cronkite's broadcast of 27 February, upon his return from the "burned, blasted and weary land" still smoking from the Tet offensive. He described the new refugees, estimated at 470,000, living in "unbelievable squalor" in sheds and shanties and added to the 800,000 already officially listed as refugees. On the political front, he said, "Past performance gives no confidence that the Vietnamese government can cope with its problems." He said the Tet offensive required the realization "that we should have had all along," that negotiations had to be just that, "not the dictation of peace terms. For now it seems more certain than ever that the bloody experience of Vietnam is to end in stalemate." The only "rational way out" was to negotiate our way out, but "not," he warned again, "as victors."

The nation's "uncle" had rendered judgment and "the shock waves," said George Christian, the President's press secretary, "rolled through the Government" up to the top. "If I've lost Walter," the President commented, "I've lost middle America."

A week later Senator Fulbright announced that the Senate's reinvestigation of the Tonkin Gulf Resolution had shown it to have been obtained by "misrepresentation," and it was therefore "null and void." News that the President was considering Westmoreland's request for 200,000 men and had agreed with the Joint Chiefs on a call-up of 50,000 Reserves for strategic back-up leaked to the press, evoking the expected outcry. In dissatisfaction with the war, the public, if accurately reflected by press comment, was readier than the Administration to let go in Southeast Asia, and readier to acknowledge, according to *Time*, "that victory in Vietnam—or even a favorable settlement—may simply be beyond the grasp of the world's greatest power." That thought marked a rite of passage in the era of Vietnam.

Emerging not too energetically from passivity, the Senate Foreign Relations Committee opened hearings at which Fulbright, in his opening speech, declared that the country was witnessing a "spiritual rebellion" among its youth against "what they regard as a betrayal of a traditional American value." With the support of other Senators, Fulbright questioned the authority of the President to "expand the war without the consent of Congress." Members of the Committee informed Clifford and General Wheeler privately that "We just couldn't support a large increase in the number of troops in Vietnam—and if we wouldn't support it, who would?" Called to testify at the hearings, Rusk maintained aims unchanged since Dulles, but admitted that the Administration was re-examining Vietnam policy "from A to Z" and considering alternatives.

The next day, in the New Hampshire primary, Senator McCarthy won an astonishing 42 percent of the vote, and worse followed. Robert Kennedy, recognizing a good thing after someone else had tested the waters, declared himself a candidate. The fiend (in Johnson's eyes) was in the ring and, given the aura of Kennedy popularity, was a more realistic political threat than Senator McCarthy. With both of them stumping the country as peace candidates, Johnson was now Goldwater, without his sharp convictions. He faced an electoral campaign which would tear apart the Democratic Party and in which he, the incumbent, would be permanently on the defensive, trying to justify a war policy that lacked any shine of success. Where nothing else—not JASON, not McNamara's defection, not the non-results of attrition strategy, not Tet—had caused him to re-think, where everything only stiffened "cognitive rigidity," the political prospect penetrated.

It did not shake his resolve about the war, now too rigid to alter, but it raised the humiliating prospect of domestic defeat. At the same time that Kennedy announced, Dean Acheson, whom Johnson after Tet had asked privately for a review of the war effort, brought in his conclusion. After rejecting "canned briefings," and consulting his own choices of sources at State, CIA and Joint Chiefs, he told Johnson that the military were going after an unachievable goal, that we could not win without an unlimited commitment of forces—just as the Working Group had said in 1964—that Johnson's speeches were so out of touch with reality that he was no longer believed by the public and that the country no longer supported the war.

This was the judgment of someone Johnson could neither bully nor ignore, whom indeed he respected; nevertheless, he was not ready to be told he was wrong. In the same week he delivered a bellicose speech to the National Farmers Union in which, pounding the lectern and jabbing his finger at the audience, he demanded a "total national effort" to win the war and the peace. He said he was not going to change his policy in Vietnam because of Communist military successes and denounced critics who would "tuck our tail and violate our commitments." It was a last angry echo of the original vow not to be the first President to lose a war, and it was not admired. James Rowe, the President's longtime friend and adviser, reported to him that calls came in after the speech from people "infuriated" by his impugning their patriotism and unmoved by his "win the war" oratory. "The fact is," was Rowe's hard summary, "hardly anyone today is interested in winning the war. Everyone wants to get out and the only question is how." Three days later, Johnson suddenly announced the recall of Westmoreland and summoned the deputy commander, General Creighton Abrams, home for consultations with the Joint Chiefs. In the course of the consultations, the decision was taken against sending the additional 200,000 troops, but without any definitive change of policy. The Joint Chiefs' price was Johnson's agreement to call up 60,000 for strategic reserve.

To convince the President once and for all of a dead end in Vietnam, Clifford proposed a conference of senior former statesmen to render a verdict. The "Wise Men," as they were later dubbed, included three outstanding military figures, Generals Ridgway, Omar Bradley and Maxwell Taylor; former Secretary of State Acheson; former Secretary of the Treasury Douglas Dillon; former Ambassador Lodge; John McCloy, former High Commissioner for Germany; Arthur Dean, negotiator of the Korean armistice; Robert Murphy, veteran diplomat; George Ball; Cyrus Vance; Arthur Goldberg, and his successor on the Supreme Court, Justice Abe Fortas, Johnson's close friend. These were men of the linked power centers of law, finance and government, not dissenters or peaceniks or long-haired radicals, but persons concerned with maintaining the vested interests of the system who had wider connections in the outside world than were available to the insulated incumbent in the White House.

Their discussions gave serious attention to the increasing economic harm being done to the United States and the bitter public sentiments that were rising. Although some continued to support the bombing, most did not, and the majority agreed that insistence on military victory had trapped the United States in a position that could only get worse and that was not compatible with the national interest. Ridgway argued that if the assumption that Vietnamese leadership could be developed was valid, such development should with American support be accomplished in the space of two years and that Saigon could be given notice of this time limit, after which "We begin a phase-down of our forces." While not a solid consensus, the argument conveyed to the President was that a change of policy was unavoidable; the unspoken advice pointed to negotiation and disengagement.

A nationwide television speech by the President to explain Tet had been scheduled for 31 March. Meeting with several of the "men in a dream"—Rusk, Rostow and William Bundy—and with the President's speech writer Henry Macpherson, who shared his disillusionment, Clifford insisted that the speech must make a sharp departure from past policy. As approved so far, it would be a "disaster." What the advisers still did not understand, he told them, was that among influential people there had been "a tremendous erosion of support, maybe in reaction to Tet, maybe from a feeling that we are in a hopeless bog. The idea of going deeper into the bog strikes them as mad." Major groups in national life, he went on inexorably, "the business community, the press, the churches, professional groups, college presidents, students and most of the intellectual community have turned against the war."

For public consumption, the speech was redirected toward a serious offer of negotiated peace and a unilateral bombing halt. The intention behind it remained unmodified. Johnson had been assured by the military that because the rainy season would enforce reduced operations, a bombing pause would not cost him anything. Moreover, the White House circle and the Joint Chiefs believed that no offer of peace talks would inhibit pursuit of the goal by force of arms because Hanoi was certain to turn it down. Their thinking was made plain in a significant cable to the American ambassadors in the SEATO nations advising them on the day before the scheduled speech of the new overture. The ambassadors were instructed that when informing their host governments they should "Make it clear that Hanoi is most likely to denounce the project and then free our hand after a short period." Clearly, Johnson and his circle were contemplating no change in conduct of the war; the problem was domestic public opinion in the context of the coming election. In the same spirit as the ambassadors were alerted, so were the commanders at CINCPAC and in Saigon. Among the factors "pertinent to the President's decision," General Wheeler informed them, was the fact that the support of the public and Congress since Tet "has decreased at an accelerating rate," and if the trend continued "public support of our objectives in Southeast Asia will be too frail to sustain the effort." But he concluded with the hope that the President's decision to offer the bombing halt "will reverse the growing dissent."

As delivered, Johnson's public address was noble and open-handed. "We are prepared to move immediately toward peace through negotiations. So tonight, in the hope that this action will lead to early talks, I am taking the first step to de-escalate the conflict . . . and doing so unilaterally and at once." Aircraft and naval vessels had been ordered to make no attack on North Vietnam north of the 20th parallel, but only in the critical battlefield area at the DMZ, "where the continued enemy build-up directly threatens allied forward positions." The area to be free of bombing contained 90 percent of the Northern population and the principal populated and food-producing areas. The bombing might be completely stopped "if our restraint is matched by restraint in Hanoi." Johnson called upon Britain and the Soviet Union, as co-chairmen of the Geneva Conference, to help move the unilateral de-escalation toward "genuine peace in Asia," and upon President Ho Chi Minh to "respond positively and favorably." Making no mention of an assumed rejection by Hanoi or of a return to combat by the United States thereafter, he looked forward to a peace "based on the Geneva Accords of 1954," permitting South Vietnam to be "free of any outside domination or interference from us or anybody else." No reference was made to the requested addition of 200,000 men; the possibility of future escalation was left open.

After a moving peroration about divisiveness and unity, Johnson came to the unexpected announcement that electrified the nation and a good part of the world: that he would not "permit the Presidency to become involved in the partisan divisions that are developing in this political year," and accordingly, "I shall not seek and I will not accept the nomination of my Party for another term as your President."

It was abdication, not in recognition of a dead end in the war or abandoning combat but in recognition of a political reality. Johnson was a political animal to the marrow of his bones. His unpopularity was now patent, dragging down with it the Democratic Party. As the incumbent President, Johnson was not prepared to have to struggle for and quite possibly lose re-nomination; he could not suffer such humiliation. The Wisconsin primary, in a state loud with student protest, was scheduled for 2 April, two days ahead, and field agents had telephoned blunt predictions that he would run behind Eugene McCarthy and Robert Kennedy. And so with righteous words about "divisiveness among us all tonight," and his duty to bind up wounds, heal our history, keep the American commitment and other commendable restorative tasks, he took himself grandly and in good timing out of the contest.

Three days later, on 3 April 1968, Hanoi astonished its opponents by announcing its readiness to make contacts with representatives of the United States with a view to determining "unconditional cessation" of the bombing and all other acts of war "so that talks might start."

The 22-year folly since American troopships brought the French back to Indochina was now complete—though not finished. Five more years of American effort to disengage without losing prestige were to compound it. In paucity of cause, vain perseverance and ultimate self-damage, the belligerency that Johnson's Administration initiated and pursued was folly of an unusual kind in that absolutely no good can be said to have come of it; all results were malign—except one, the awakening of the "public ire." Too many Americans had come to feel that the war was wrong, out of all proportion to the national interest and unsuccessful besides. Populists like to speak of the "wisdom of the people"; the American people were not so much wise as fed up, which in certain cases is a kind of wisdom. Withdrawal of public support proved the undoing of an Executive that believed it could conduct limited war without engaging the national will of a democracy.

6. Exit: 1969-73

Use of mustard gas in World War I had to be abandoned because it had an erratic tendency to blow back on the user. The war in Vietnam in its final period turned back upon the United States, deepening disesteem and distrust of government and, in reverse, breeding a hostility in government toward the people that was to have serious consequences. Although the lesson of Lyndon Johnson was plain, the legacy of folly gripped his successor. No better able to make the enemy come to terms acceptable to the United States, the new Administration, like the old, could find no other way than to resort to military coercion, with the result that a war already rejected by a large portion of the American people was prolonged, with all its potential for domestic damage, throughout another presidential term.

Johnson's last year in office, despite the bombing halt and Hanoi's agreement to talk, had brought the war no nearer to an end. Meetings were talks about where to hold the talks, about protocol, about participation by South Vietnam and the NLF, about seating and even the shape of the table. Keeping to their original demand for "unconditional cessation" of bombing as a pre-condition for negotiations, the North Vietnamese would not move from procedure to substance. The United States, while maintaining the bombing halt north of the 20th parallel, tripled its air strikes against infiltration routes below the line and kept search-and-destroy missions at maximum pressure in the effort to improve Saigon's position for a settlement. Two hundred Americans a week were killed in these combats, and the total number of Americans killed in action in 1968 reached 14,000.

The year flared into violence and hatred at home, marked by the assassinations of Robert Kennedy and Martin Luther King, Jr., the riots following King's death, the anarchy and vandalism of student radicals, the vicious reaction and police savagery of the Democratic Convention in Chicago. Domestic intelligence agencies expanded activity against possible subversives, opening private mail, employing agents provocateurs, compiling dossiers on citizens who through some suspect association might be considered dangers to the state.

For the sake of progress in the Vietnam talks, the American delegates, Ambassador Harriman and Cyrus Vance, urged the President to declare a total bombing halt. Johnson refused without reciprocity by Hanoi in reducing military activity, which Hanoi in turn refused unless the bombing ceased first. At the desperate pleas of his party as election approached, Johnson declared a total bombing halt on 1 November, but progress was then frustrated by President Thieu of South Vietnam, who, expecting greater support from a Republican victory in the United States, balked, refusing to participate in the talks. When at last substantive negotiations began in January 1969, a new team under President Richard Nixon and his foreign policy adviser, Henry Kissinger, was in command.

In words reminiscent of Eisenhower's electoral pledge to "go to Korea" to end an unpopular war, Nixon in his campaign for the presidency assured voters, "We will end this one and win the peace." He did not say how, justifying reticence on the ground that he was not going to say anything that could upset Johnson's negotiations in Paris and not "take any position that I will be bound by at a later point." But by stressing the theme "End the war and win the peace," he managed to give the impression that he had a plan. He appeared to take a realistic view. "If the war goes on six months after I become President," he privately told a journalist, "it will be *my* war," and he said he was determined not to "end up like LBJ, holed up in the White House, afraid to show my face in the street. I'm going to stop that war—fast." If this determination was genuine, it indicated common sense, a faculty that has a hard time surviving in high office. Once Nixon was installed in the presidency, the promised process of stopping the war was stood on its head to become one of prolonging it. The new President was discovered to be as unwilling as his predecessor to accept non-success of the war aim and as fixed in the belief that additional force could bring the enemy to terms.

Inheriting a bad situation that could bring them nothing but trouble, Nixon and Kissinger, whom the President had chosen to head the National Security Council, would have done well to consider their problem as if there were a sign pinned to the wall, "Do Not Repeat What Has Already Failed." That might have suggested a glance back to Dien Bien Phu; a clear appraisal of the enemy's stake and his will and capacity to fight for it; and a close look at the reasons for the consistent failure of all Johnson's efforts to negotiate. Reflection thereafter might have led to the conclusion that to continue a war for the sake of consolidating a free-standing regime in South Vietnam was both vain and non-essential to American security, and that to try to gain by negotiation a result which the enemy was determined not to cede was a waste of time—short of willingness to apply *un*limited force. Even if negotiation under military pressure could bring the desired result, it would contain no guarantee, as already pointed out by Reischauer in 1967, that ten or twenty years later "political rule over South Vietnam would not be more or less what it would have been if we had never got involved there."

The logical course was to cut losses, forgo assurance of a viable non-Communist South Vietnam and leave *without* negotiating with the enemy except for a one-condition agreement buying back American prisoners of war in exchange for a pledged time limit on American withdrawal. Just such an option was in fact presented as the least militant in a range of several options proposed, at the request of the Administration, by specialists of the Rand Corporation; it was eliminated from the list by Kissinger and his military advisers before the proposals were presented to the President, but it would not have appealed to him if he had seen it. From being a fiction about the security of the United States, the point of the war had now been transformed into a test of the prestige and reputation of the United States—and, as he was bound to see it, of the President personally. Nixon too had no wish to preside over defeat.

He did have a plan and it did involve a radical reversal of Johnson's course—up to a point. The intention was to dissolve domestic protest by ending the draft and bringing home American ground combat forces. This did not mean relinquishing the war aim. The American air war in Vietnam would be intensified and if necessary extended further against the North's supply lines and bases in Cambodia. To compensate for American troop withdrawal, a program of vastly increased aid, arming, training and indoctrinating would enable South Vietnam's forces to take over the war, with continued American air support. Known as "Vietnamization," this effort was perhaps belated in what had always been supposed to be "their" war. The theory was that floods of matériel would somehow accomplish what had not been accomplished over the past 25 years—the creation of a motivated fighting force able to preserve a viable non-Communist state, at least for an "acceptable interval."

Besides appeasing Americans, unilateral withdrawal of American troops was designed to demonstrate to Hanoi "that we were serious in seeking a diplomatic settlement" and thus encourage the enemy to negotiate acceptable terms. If, however, the North Vietnamese proved intractable, the punitive level of the bombing would be raised until, convinced of the impossibility of victory, they would be forced to give up or let the war simply fade away. To assist in persuading Hanoi, hints were conveyed through the Soviet Union that blockade and mining and more forceful action against supply lines and sanctuaries in Cambodia and Laos were in prospect. As a gesture of intent, the first secret bombing of Cambodia took place in March 1969, when Nixon had been only two months in office; a second followed in April, and the raids became regular and frequent in May.

"Vietnamization" in effect amounted to enlarging and arming ARVN. Considering that arming, training and indoctrinating under American auspices had been pursued for fifteen years without spectacular results, the expectation that these would now enable ARVN successfully to take over the war could qualify as wooden-headedness. Recalling the conditions of 1970, an American sergeant who had been attached to a South Vietnamese unit said, "We had 50 percent AWOLs all the time and most of the [ARVN] company and platoon leaders were gone all the time." The soldiers had no urge to fight under officers "who spent their time stealing and trafficking in drugs."

The grander folly was to reverse the conduct of the war only halfway—that is, by taking out the Americans while maintaining the strategy of increasing punitive pressure from the air (or "negative reinforcement," as it was called). Apart from its domestic purpose, disengagement on the ground would have made sense only if the objective it had been intended to achieve had been given up at the same time.

Withdrawal of combat troops is an unusual way to win a war, or even to force the way to a favorable settlement. Once started, it could not easily be halted and would, like escalation, build its own momentum and, as forces dwindled, become irreversible. Understandably bitter, the American military saw it as precluding success and, since they had small confidence in Vietnamization, making even a tenable settlement unlikely. It had become necessary because the idea that the war could be fought without arousing the public ire had proved an illusion. Nixon and Kissinger, for all their hard-headed calculations, were apparently victims of another illusion. They appear to have thought that American withdrawal from ground combat could be accomplished without weakening South Vietnam's already infirm morale and without re-affirming the determination of the North. Of course it did both.

Reduction of effort does not signal to the enemy stern and determined intentions, but rather the reverse, as in the case of General Howe's evacuation of Philadelphia. American colonists saw in that departure a trend that was drawing the British away, and knew they need make no terms with the Carlisle Peace Commission. Hanoi received the same message. When Nixon announced the withdrawal program in June 1969 and the first American contingent of 25,000 sailed for home in August, the North Vietnamese knew the contest would end in their favor. Whatever the cost, they had only to hold out. As if in recognition, Ho Chi Minh, after half a century's struggle, died in September.

At home, Nixon's plan failed to recognize that something more than distress at casualties was active in the dissent; that many people felt a sense of wrong in the war, a violation of the way they felt about their country; that although protest would subside for a while with the return of troops, the deeper feeling was a corollary of the war itself and would grow stronger with continued belligerence.

In its assured belief that the Americans, like the French, would lose the war at home, Hanoi remained intransigent. In anger and frustration, the United States turned to "negative reinforcement." Plans for a "savage blow" or a "decisive blow" or the "November option," as it was variously called, were drawn. Blockade would be established, harbors, rivers and coastal waters mined, dikes broken, Hanoi carpet-bombed. "I refuse to believe that a little fourth-rate power like North Vietnam doesn't have a breaking point," Kissinger said in the course of the planning. He was correct in that everything has a breaking point; the test is the degree of force required. Faced by the objections of civilian analysts who argued that the proposed measures would not significantly reduce the North's capacity to fight in the South, and by fear of awakening what Kissinger called the "dormant beast of public protest," the November option was called off.

Frenzied Vietnamization was pursued with ARVN doubled in numbers and gorged with arms, ships, planes, helicopters, more than a million M-16 rifles, 40,000 grenade launchers, 2000 heavy mortars and howitzers. Even with 10,000 ARVN officers, pilots, mechanics and intelligence analysts sent abroad for training in advanced skills, it was late in the day. Through the process, a stronger hold was gained for a while in South Vietnam, mainly because the Viet-Cong had never recovered from their losses in the Tet offensive, but with 150,000 American troops scheduled to leave in 1970 and more to follow, it looked like a race between Vietnamization and the withdrawals.

Protest, far from dormant, did not fade. An organized Vietnam Moratorium Day to demand "peace now" was marked in October

1969 by demonstrations across the country, with 100,000 rallying on Boston Common to hear Senator Edward Kennedy call for withdrawal of all ground forces within a year and all air and support units within three years, by the end of 1972. A sign carried by a demonstrator in San Francisco read, "Lose the war in Vietnam—Bring the boys home." In a planned reply to the Moratorium, the President appealed in a national address to the "silent majority" that he said supported him, promising to complete the withdrawals according to a scheduled though unspecified timetable, and to "end the war in a way we could win the peace."

If there was a majority of the silent, it was mainly from indifference, whereas protest was active and vocal and unfortunately a focus for people Nixon, in an unguarded if justified response to campus bombings, called "bums." A second Vietnam Moratorium Day, in November, mobilized 250,000 demonstrators in Washington. Watching from a balcony, Attorney-General John Mitchell, Nixon's former law partner, thought "It looked like the Russian Revolution." In that comment, the anti-war movement took its place in the eyes of the government, not as citizens' rightful dissent against a policy that large numbers wanted their country to renounce, but as the malice and threat of subversion. It was this view that produced the "enemies list."

Because the dissent was voiced by the press and shared by prominent figures of the establishment, Nixon perceived it as a conspiracy against his political existence by the "liberals" who he believed had "sought to destroy him since the Alger Hiss case." Kissinger, disturbed and often angered, as his memoirs attest, regarded the protest as interference with the conduct of foreign affairs, a necessary nuisance of democracy that had to be endured but should not be allowed to influence a serious statesman. It did not tell him anything, even when voiced by a delegation of colleagues from the Harvard faculty. It did not tell the President anything he thought worth listening to about the constituency in whose name he acted. Neither man heard anything valid in the dissent. Like the clamor for reform that assailed the ears of the Renaissance Popes, it conveyed no notice of an urgent need, in the rulers' own interest, for a positive response.

Negotiations, whether in secret meetings between Kissinger and Hanoi's emissary Le Duc Tho or in the four-party talks in Paris, could make no progress because each side still insisted on conditions unacceptable to the other. North Vietnam demanded the ouster of the Thieu-Ky government and its replacement by a nominal "coalition" to include the NLF. As this would amount to abandonment of its client, it was obviously rejected by the United States, which in turn demanded the withdrawal of all Northern forces from the Southern zone. As violating their right to be in any part of what they never ceased to consider one country, this was adamantly rejected by the North Vietnamese. Although their concept was the same as Abraham Lincoln's insistence on the immutability of union, the Americans gave it no credit or else believed that Hanoi must be brought by force to give up.

"To end the war in a way we could win the peace," that is, by preserving a non-Communist South Vietnam, was the ball and chain of American negotiations. It was equated with credibility, now called "peace with honor," as endlessly asserted by Nixon and Kissinger. "Peace with honor" had become the "terrible encumbrance" of America in Vietnam. "Show the thing you contend for to be reason," Burke had said, "show it to be common sense, show it to be the means of attaining some useful end, and then I am content to allow it what dignity you please." Instead, what the United States was contending for was a "hopeless enterprise," as Jean Sainteny, from his long French experience in Vietnam, told Henry Kissinger. If Kissinger had read more Burke than Talleyrand, the course of his policy might have been different.

The alternatives were either to batter North Vietnam into defeat by a degree of force the United States was unwilling to use, or else to relinquish American conditions, leaving South Vietnam, when sufficiently strengthened by Vietnamization, to defend itself and, as envisaged by Kissinger himself, "end our involvement *without* agreement with Hanoi." The major obstacle was the American prisoners of war, whom Hanoi refused to surrender unless its conditions were met, but a promised deadline for withdrawal of all combat air and ground forces could have bought their release. This alternative, for the sake of a quick end and the health of the American nation, was feasible, and there were those who called for it. It was disallowed because of assumed damage to America's reputation. That cutting losses and getting back to the proper business of the nation might have aided rather than harmed America's reputation was not weighed in the balance of policy-making. As between battering and relinquishing, Nixon and Kissinger chose the so-far-sterile middle way of trying by graduated force to make "continuation of the war seem less attractive to Hanoi than a settlement." That program had been around for years.

It now took the form of intensified bombing directed not at North Vietnam's own territory but at its supply lines, bases and sanctuaries in Cambodia. The sorties were systematically falsified in military records for convoluted reasons having to do with Cambodia's neutrality, but since an excuse was at hand in the fact of the enemy's having long violated that neutrality, the secrecy probably had more to do with concealing extension of the war from the American public. Given the anti-war sentiments of the press and of many government officials, the supposition that the raids could be kept secret was one of the curious delusions of high office. A Pentagon correspondent of the *New York Times* picked up evidence and reported the strikes. Although the story excited no public attention, it started the process that was to make Cambodia Nixon's nemesis. Enraged at what he believed were "leaks" on the secret bombing, he called in the FBI, which under Kissinger's direction established the first of the wire-taps on a member of his own staff, Morton Halperin, who had access to classified reports. A long sequence that was to end in the first resignation of a President in the history of the Republic was begun.

Nixon's secret operations were still in the dark, but in April 1970, furor erupted when American ground forces together with ARVN invaded Cambodia. To widen the war to another, nominally neutral, country when the cry in America was to reduce rather than extend belligerence was—like Rehoboam's summoning the overseer of forced labor to quell the Israelites—the most provocative choice possible in the circumstances. An act perfectly designed to bring down trouble upon the perpetrator, it was the kind of folly to which governments seem irresistibly drawn as if pulled by a mischievous fate to make the gods laugh.

Military reasons for the invasion were seemingly cogent: to pre-empt an expected offensive by North Vietnam supposedly intended to gain control of Cambodia and place the enemy in a position of serious threat to South Vietnam during the period of American withdrawals; to buy time for Vietnamization; to cut off a major supply line from the Cambodian port of Sihanoukville; and to support a new and friendlier regime in Phnom Penh that had ousted the left-leaning Prince Sihanouk. Yet if it were in Nixon's and America's interest to end the war, wisdom in government could have counseled equally cogent reasons against the operation.

Nixon supposed that his previously announced schedule of withdrawing 150,000 troops in 1970 would cancel protest or, if "those liberal bastards" were going to make trouble anyway, that he might as well be hanged for a wolf as a sheep. He announced the campaign in a combative speech as a response to North Vietnamese "aggression," with familiar references to not being a President who would preside over American defeat. An objective of the invasion was said to be destruction of an alleged enemy headquarters, or "nerve center," labeled COSVN (Central Office of South Vietnam). Tactically the invasion succeeded in capturing significant quantities of North Vietnamese arms, destroying bunkers and sanctuaries, adding 200 to the body count and causing the enemy enough damage to set back the purported offensive by a year, even if the mysterious "nerve center" was never discovered, despite its majestic acronym. The overall result was negative: a weakened government in Phnom Penh left in need of protection, land and villages wrecked, a third of the population made homeless refugees, and the pro-Communist Khmer Rouge greatly augmented by recruits. The North Vietnamese soon returned to overrun large areas, arm and train the insurgents and lay the ground for the ultimate tragic suffering of another nation of Indochina.

Reaction in America to the invasion was explosive, antagonizing both political extremes, impassioning debate, kindling the hate of dissenters for the government and vice versa. While polls often showed spurts of support for Nixon's more aggressive actions, anti-war sentiment was louder and the press outspokenly hostile. The *New York Times* called Nixon's reasons for the invasion "Military Hallucination—Again" and affirmed that "Time and bitter experience have exhausted the credulity of the American people." Revelation a few months previously of the Mylai massacre, in which American soldiers in a burst of crazy brutality had killed over 200 unarmed villagers, including old men, women and helpless crying children, had already horrified the public. The shock was greater when, following Cambodia, Americans killed Americans. On 4 May, at Kent State University in Ohio, the National Guard, called out by the Governor to contain what appeared to him dangerous campus violence, opened fire on the demonstrators, killing four students. The picture of the girl student kneeling in agonized unbelief over the body of a dead companion became a memorial more familiar than any picture since the raising of the flag on Iwo Jima. The war had indeed blown back upon America.

Protest blazed after Kent State. Student strikes, marches, bonfires caught up the campuses. An angry crowd of close to 100,000 massed in the park across from White House grounds, where a ring of sixty buses with police was drawn up like a wagon circle against Indians. At the Capitol, Vietnam veterans staged a rally marked by each man tossing away his medals. At the State Department, 250 staff members signed a statement of objection to the extended war. All this was denounced as aiding the enemy by encouraging them to hold out, which was true, and as unpatriotic, which was also true, for the saddest consequence was loss of a valuable feeling by the young, who laughed at patriotism.

Protest had its lunatic fringe in idiocy of rhetoric and in lawless destruction, and this outraged the righteous, not necessarily because they were hawks, but because they considered such actions an offense against respectability and law and order. The antagonism was epitomized in physical clash when construction workers in hard hats attacked a march of student protesters in Wall Street, beating them with whatever they had at hand for use as weapons. It reached a peak in October at San Jose, where Nixon came to speak in the mid-term election campaign of 1970. He was greeted by a mob screaming oaths and obscenities and, when he left the hall, throwing eggs and rocks, one just grazing him. It was the first mob assault on a President in American history. "We could see the hate in their faces . . . hear the hate in their voices," he said afterward in a statement denouncing the rioters as "violent thugs" representative of "the worst in America."

The clouds of criticism of his Cambodian action infuriated the President even before the San Jose incident and sharpened his always active sense of persecution. "A siege mentality" pervaded the White House, according to Charles Colson of the staff. "It was now 'us' against 'them.'" The palace guard, according to another observer, "genuinely believed that a left-wing revolution was a distinct possibility." The resort to secret surveillance of "enemies," undercover methods of harassment and espionage, breaking and entering, wiretapping without warrants became a full-fledged operation. A White House staff member assigned to watch radical terrorist groups drew up a plan for unleashed police power and unauthorized entry as a tool of law enforcement. Signed by the President, the program existed as policy for five days until the FBI, perhaps jealous of its own prerogatives, advised its abandonment. The search for the source of leaks on the secret bombing expanded until it reached seventeen wire-taps on members of the National Security Council and on several newspapermen. As with the elusive COSVN, no leaks were discovered; the stories proved to be the ordinary enterprise of the press.

Right of dissent is an absolute of the American political system. The readiness to attempt its suppression by and on behalf of the Chief of State and to undertake and tolerate illegal procedures laid the lines

to Watergate. With continued frustration in negotiations, and prolonging of the war into another year, these procedures increased and grew
to excess on publication of the Pentagon Papers in June 1971. A collected record of mostly classified government documents originally
authorized by McNamara in an effort to uncover the roots of American involvement, the Papers were purloined by Daniel Ellsberg, a
former Pentagon official now an ideologue of anti-war convictions,
and made available to the press and certain members of the House and
Senate. Although the record did not go beyond 1968, the sensitivity
to leaks of the Nixon-Kissinger team was extreme, especially so because they were working in secret to bring off the re-opening of relations with China and a summit meeting with Moscow and did not
wish Washington to be regarded as incapable of confidential relations.
A "plumbers" group to locate leaks was established in a basement
office next door to the White House, and orders came "right out of
the Oval Office" (according to later testimony) to get something on
Ellsberg. The result was the burglary of Ellsberg's psychiatrist's office
with the object of framing him as a Soviet agent, an enterprise of
doubtful utility for, if successful, it could well have spiked Nixon's
intensely desired summit with the Russians. Fortunately for their
employer, the plumbers came away empty-handed, but no matter
what they might have discovered about Ellsberg it could not in any
case have discredited fourteen volumes of photocopied government
documents. Folly at the top was clearly seeping down. Here too, in
the absence of scruple against lawbreaking, the morality of the Renaissance Popes re-appears.

Signals of trouble were rising from Congress, which had been content so far to be hardly more than a spectator of the affair tormenting
the nation. Congress, said a member, "is a body of followers not
leaders." Since it may be presumed to follow what it senses to be the
trend of public opinion, its torpor is evidence that until Cambodia the
silent majority probably *was* a majority. When Nixon's first six months
in office brought no cease-fire as his campaign had promised, the anti-
war Senators, Mansfield, Kennedy, Gaylord Nelson, Charles Goodell
and others, began to call publicly for measures to end the war. Invasion of Cambodia without Congressional authority galvanized efforts
in the Senate to reassert the prerogatives vis-à-vis the Executive it had
allowed to lapse in self-enfeeblement. One thing the Pentagon Papers
had revealed was the conspicuous absence in any of the discussions or
documents of concern about the share of Congress in determining
defense and foreign policy. After the invasion of Cambodia was a fact,

Nixon offered assurances to a selected group from both Houses that American troops would not penetrate deeper than 30 to 35 miles without Congressional approval being sought—he did not say obtained—and that all troops would be withdrawn within three to seven weeks.

Senators were not reassured. Amendments to appropriation bills, to cut off funds, to curb or put time limits on military involvement in one way or another, were introduced, approved in committee, debated by an aroused chamber and adopted by ample majorities. In each case, under the autocratic management of super-hawk committee chairmen of the lower House, they were emasculated or thrown out in conference or stifled by parliamentary tactics to cut off debate. The Tonkin Gulf Resolution was finally repealed, but only when the Administration, outfoxing opponents, itself sponsored repeal on the ground that authority for war lay in the constitutional powers of the President as Commander-in-Chief. That ground was muddy—for was he in fact Commander-in-Chief without a declared state of war?—but the Supreme Court, confronted by several tests, walked carefully around it.

Nevertheless, anti-war votes in the lower House were rising. When 153 Representatives, the largest number so far, voted against tabling, that is killing, the Cooper-Church Amendment to cut off funds for operations in Cambodia after July, it was a rumble of revolt. In the following year the number rose to 177 in favor of the Mansfield Amendment, originally fixing a deadline of nine months (modified by the House to "as soon as possible") for withdrawal, pending release of the POWs. Though small, the rise implied growing opposition, even the possible approach of that unimaginable moment when the Legislature might say "Stop" to the Executive.

In 1971, ARVN forces with American air support, although without American ground forces, invaded Laos in a repeat of the Cambodian operation. The cost of "Vietnamization" for ARVN proved to be a 50 percent casualty rate, with the added impression that they were now fighting and dying to permit Americans to depart. This was reinforced by Washington's tendency to herald all operations as designed to "save American lives." Anti-Americanism in Vietnam spread, and with it undercover cooperation with the NLF and open demands for a political compromise. Protest movements revived—this time against Thieu in place of Diem. Morale among the remaining American forces sank, with units avoiding or refusing combat, wide use of drugs, and—something new to the American Army—cases of "fragging," or murder by hand grenade, of officers and NCOs.

At home, polls showed a majority beginning to emerge in favor of removal of all troops by the end of the year, even if the result were Communist control of South Vietnam. For the first time a majority agreed to the proposition that "It was morally wrong for the U.S. to be fighting in Vietnam," and that getting involved in the first place was a "mistake." The public is volatile, polls are ephemeral, and answers may respond to the language of the question. Immorality was discovered because, as Lord North said of his war, "Ill success rendering it at length unpopular, the people began to cry out for peace."

By 1972, the war had lasted longer than any foreign conflict in American history, and the six months Nixon had given himself had stretched out to three years, with 15,000 additional American casualties and the end not yet in sight.

All the Paris talks and Kissinger's secret missions failed of result, essentially because the United States was trying to negotiate itself out of a war it could not win and look good at the same time. North Vietnam was equally to blame for the prolongation, but the stakes were not equal. It was their land and their future that for them were at stake. In March 1972, when most American combat forces had gone, North Vietnam mounted an offensive that was at last to propel the war to an end.

Launched across the DMZ, 120,000 North Vietnamese troops with Soviet tanks and field guns pierced ARVN defenses and advanced against the populated centers around Saigon. Unable to respond on the ground, the United States re-activated the first stage of the "savage blow" planned in 1969, sending the B-52s over the North for heavy attacks on fuel depots and transportation targets in Hanoi and Haiphong. Nixon announced the campaign as the "decisive military action to end the war." A month later Kissinger offered a plan for a standstill cease-fire which for the first time omitted the requirement of Northern withdrawal from the South and which declared American readiness to withdraw all forces within four months after return of the prisoners. Political settlement was left open. The four-month deadline might have summoned in Hanoi the wisdom to accept, but having always refused to negotiate under bombing, they did so again.

With re-election on his mind, Nixon was enraged by the enemy's recalcitrance and swore among associates that "The bastards have never been bombed like they're going to be bombed this time." Against advice of a fearful domestic reaction and the risk that the Russians might cancel the Moscow summit scheduled in two weeks along with the signing of the painfully negotiated SALT agreement, he announced the second half of the "savage blow"—naval blockade and mining of Haiphong harbor and round-the-clock raids by the B-52s. Because of nervousness about damage to Soviet and other foreign shipping, resort to blockade and mining had long been avoided and were expected to arouse howls of censure at home. The White House staff, in its hopped-up state of nerves, believed the decision "could make or break the President" and spent over $8000 from election funds to elicit a flood of phony telegrams of approval and concocted advertisements in newspapers so that the White House could announce opinion running in support of the President. They might have spared themselves the exertion; while the press and articulate dissenters condemned the blockade, public opinion was not outraged but seemed rather to appreciate tough American action in the face of North Vietnamese intransigence.

Another incident of sharp practice came to light shortly afterward when five agents of CREEP (Committee to Re-elect the President), connected to the two chief plumbers (Howard Hunt and Gordon Liddy) who had staged the Ellsberg raid, were caught in the act of rifling the files and bugging the phones of the headquarters of the Democratic National Committee in the Watergate office building. Ultimate revelations of what the presidency was engaged in at this time were not to become public knowledge until the trials of the five agents and the hearings of Senator Ervin's special investigating committee in the following year. They were to uncover an accumulated tale of cover-up, blackmail, suborned testimony, hush money, espionage, sabotage, use of Federal powers for the harassment of "enemies," and a program by some fifty hired operators to pervert and subvert the campaigns of Democratic candidates by "dirty tricks," or what in the choice language of the White House crew was referred to as "ratfucking." The final list of indictable crimes would include burglary, bribery, forgery, perjury, theft, conspiracy and obstructing justice, most of it over-reacting and, like the tape that was to bring down the edifice in ruins, self-inflicted.

Character again was fate. When worked on by the passions of Vietnam, Nixon's character, and that of the associates he recruited, plunged his Administration into the stew that further soured respect for government. Disgrace of a ruler is no great matter in world history, but disgrace of government is traumatic, for government cannot function without respect. Washington suffered no physical sack like that which disrespect for the Papacy visited upon Rome, but the penalty has not been negligible.

While only the tip of the Watergate scandal so far showed, the explosion of combat in Vietnam brought results. Blockade combined with destruction of fuel and ammunition stores drastically reduced North

Vietnam's supplies. The Russians proved to be more concerned about détente with the United States than about Hanoi's need. They welcomed Nixon in Moscow and advised their friends to come to terms. China too wanted to dampen the conflict. In the flush of re-opened relations recently brought off by Nixon and Kissinger, they were now interested in playing off the United States against Russia, which led Mao Tse-tung, during a visit by NLF leaders, to advise them to give up their insistence on the overthrow of Thieu, until now their sine qua non. "Do as I did," he said. "I once made an accord with Chiang Kai-shek when it was necessary." Persuaded that their day too would come, the NLF agreed.

The North too, suffering under the B-52s, was ready to yield the political condition. From the evidence of polls in the United States, where the Democratic candidate was floundering in the gaffes of an inept campaign, Hanoi realized that Nixon would be in command for the next four years and concluded that it could get better terms from him before the election. Negotiations were renewed, complicated compromises and intricate arrangements were hammered out to permit United States disengagement behind a facade of Thieu's survival, and Kissinger was able to announce on 31 October, prematurely as it proved, that "Peace is at hand."

Thieu refused absolutely to accept the draft treaty, which allowed 145,000 North Vietnamese troops to remain in the South and recognized the NLF as a participant in the future political solution under its newly assumed title of Provisional Revolutionary Government (PRG). Considering that to do otherwise would have been to acquiesce in his own demise, his position was not unnatural. At this juncture, Nixon was stunningly re-elected by the largest popular and electoral majority ever recorded, an extraordinary triumph for a President who not long afterward was driven to assure the American people that "I am not a crook." The landslide was the result of many causes: the weakness and vacillations of his opponent, Senator McGovern, whose ill-chosen declaration that he would go "on his knees" to Hanoi and his proposal of a $1000 welfare give-away to every family repelled the voters; the success of the "dirty tricks," which had destroyed a stronger candidate in the primaries; public relief in the expectation of peace at last; and perhaps in the background a reaction of middle America against the counterculture of long hair, hippies, drugs and radicals with all their implied threat to accepted values.

Invigorated by his mandate, Nixon exerted the strongest pressure on both sides in Vietnam for a settlement. He assured Thieu in a letter that while his concern about the remaining presence of North Vietnamese forces in the South was understandable, "You have my absolute assurance that if Hanoi fails to abide by the terms of this agreement, it is my intention to take swift and severe retaliatory action." The intention was undoubtedly just that, for the Paris agreement had not undertaken to withdraw air power from carriers in nearby waters or from bases in Thailand and Taiwan. The Joint Chiefs were in fact directed to draw plans for possible retaliatory action, using air power from Thailand, and $1 billion worth of arms were ordered for delivery to Saigon. Thieu was also told that if he continued obdurate, the United States could make peace without him, which failed to move him. In re-opened secret negotiations with the North, Kissinger backed away from the agreed terms; he now asked for a token withdrawal of Northern troops from the South, lowered status for the NLF and other changes, accompanied by threats of renewed military coercion.

Re-confirmed in its belief in the perfidy of the United States, Hanoi refused to make the required adjustments. Freed of concern about public protest, Nixon responded with a ferocious blow, the notorious Christmas bombing, heaviest American action of the war. In twelve days of December the Air Force pounded North Vietnam with a greater tonnage of bombs than the total of the past three years, reducing areas of Hanoi and Haiphong to rubble, destroying Hanoi's airport, factories and power plants. One effect blew back. Plane losses owed to North Vietnam's strong concentration of SAM missile defenses cost America 95 to 100 new prisoners of war and the worrisome price of 15 heavy bombers (or 34, according to Hanoi). The purpose of the Christmas bombing was twofold: to bring about a sufficient weakening of North Vietnam to permit the survival of Saigon for long enough to allow the United States to be gone and, by this proof of America's determination, to overcome Thieu's resistance or else to provide the excuse to proceed without him. "We had walked the last mile with him," according to a later explanation, "and as a consequence we could settle."

The fierce attack so near the end darkened America's reputation at home and abroad, enhancing its image of brutality. New members elected to Congress by the revised rules in Democratic primaries promised an approaching challenge, which took visible shape when the Democratic caucus of both Houses voted on 2 and 4 January for an "immediate" cease-fire and cut-off of all funds for military operations in any of the countries of Indochina, contingent only upon release of the POWs and safe withdrawal of American forces. Faced by the long-discounted possibility of revolt by Congress, and with Watergate disclosures rising in Judge John J. Sirica's courtroom, the Administration proposed to call off the bombing if Hanoi would resume peace talks. Hanoi agreed; negotiations of desperation were resumed; a treaty was drawn and Thieu given an explicit ultimatum that unless he complied, the United States would terminate economic and military support and conclude the treaty without him.

In the final treaty, the two conditions for which North Vietnam and the United States had prolonged the war for four years—overthrow of Thieu's regime on the one hand and removal of North Vietnam's forces from the South on the other—were both abandoned; political status of the old Viet-Cong, now metamorphosed into the PRG, was acknowledged, though to spare Thieu's feelings not explicitly; the DMZ or partition line, whose elimination Hanoi had demanded, was retained but—going back to Geneva—as a "provisional not a political or territorial boundary." The unity of Vietnam was implicitly recognized in an article providing that "The reunification of Vietnam shall be carried out" by peaceful discussion among the parties, thereby relegating "external aggression" across an "international boundary"—America's casus belli for so many years—to the dustbin of history.

Thieu gripped refusal with the rigor of death until the last hour of Nixon's ultimatum, then gave way. Signed in Paris on 27 January 1973, the treaty left the situation on paper no different from the insecure settlement of Geneva nineteen years before. To the physical reality had since been added more than half a million deaths in North and South, hundreds of thousands of wounded and destitute, burned and crippled children, landless peasants, a ravaged land deforested and pitted with bomb craters and a people torn by mutual hatred. The procedures for eventual agreement by the two zones were generally recognized as unworkable and an early resort to force widely assumed. The viability of a non-Communist South Vietnam, for which America had wrecked Indochina and betrayed herself, inspired confidence in no one—unless in Nixon and Kissinger, who convinced themselves that the United States could still retrieve the situation if necessary. What was left standing by the treaty was a temporary screen behind which America, clutching a tattered "peace with honor," could escape.

In the aftermath, as everyone knows, Hanoi overcame Saigon within two years. When Nixon had been destroyed by Watergate and Congress had finally gathered the votes to preclude, by cutting off funds,

American re-intervention, North Vietnam launched a final offensive and the disheartened South failed to withstand the onslaught. For all that some units fought hard, ARVN as a national army, in the words of an American soldier, "was like a house without any foundation—the collapse came naturally." The Communists established their rule over the whole of Vietnam, and similar results were accomplished in Cambodia. The new political order in Vietnam was approximately what it would have been if America had never intervened, except in being far more vengeful and cruel. Perhaps the greatest folly was Hanoi's—to fight so steadfastly for thirty years for a cause that became a brutal tyranny when it was won.

Congressional refusal to allow the United States to re-intervene represented the functioning, not, as Kissinger lamented, "the breakdown of our democratic political process." Rather than weakness of American will to see the task through, it was belated recognition of a process clearly contrary and damaging to self-interest, and the summoning of political responsibility to terminate it. It came too late, however, for the country to escape punishment. Human casualties are bearable when they are believed to have served a purpose; they are bitter when, as in this case, 45,000 killed and 300,000 wounded were sacrificed for nothing. Expenditures of about $20 billion annually for nearly a decade, amounting to a total of about $150 billion over and above what would have been the normal military budget, contorted the economy to a condition that has not since been righted.

More important than the physical effects was the lowered trust in and authority of government. Legislation by Congress in the post-Vietnam years was repeatedly directed to restricting the Executive in various kinds of conduct on the assumption that without such restrictions, it would act irregularly or illegitimately. The public too learned suspicion, and many would have felt their attitude expressed in two words by one of the White House staff, Gordon Strachan, who on being asked by the Ervin committee what advice he would give to other young people wishing to serve in government, answered, "Stay away." For many, confidence in the righteousness of their country gave way to cynicism. Who since Vietnam would venture to say of America in simple belief that she was the "last best hope of earth"? What America lost in Vietnam was, to put it in one word, virtue.

The follies that produced this result begin with continuous over-reacting: in the invention of endangered "national security," the invention of "vital interest," the invention of a "commitment" which rapidly assumed a life of its own, casting a spell over the inventor. In this process the major mover was Dulles, who, by setting out to wreck the compromise of Geneva and install America as the keeper of one zone and relentless opponent of the other, was the begetter of all that followed. His zeal as a Savonarola of foreign policy mesmerized associates and successors into parroting "national security" and "vital interest," not so much in belief as in lip service to the cold war, or as scare tactics to extract appropriations from Congress. As late as 1975, President Ford told Congress that unwillingness to vote aid for South Vietnam would undermine "credibility" as an ally, which is "essential to our national security." Kissinger repeated the theme two months later, telling a press conference that if South Vietnam were allowed to go under it would represent "a fundamental threat over a period of time to the security of the United States."

Over-reacting was present in the conjuring of specters, of falling dominoes, of visions of "ruin," of yielding the Pacific and pulling back to San Francisco, of minor dragons like the invisible COSVN, and finally the paranoia of the Watergate White House. More serious, over-reacting led to the squandering of American power and resources in a grand folly of disproportion to the national interest involved. The absence of intelligent thought on this issue was astonishing for, as General Ridgway wrote in 1971, "it should not have taken great vision to perceive . . . that no truly vital United States interest was present . . . and that the commitment to a major effort was a monumental blunder."

A second folly was illusion of omnipotence, cousin to the Popes' illusion of invulnerability; a third was wooden-headedness and "cognitive dissonance"; a fourth was "working the levers" as a substitute for thinking.

In the illusion of omnipotence, American policy-makers took it for granted that on a given aim, especially in Asia, American will could be made to prevail. This assumption came from the can-do character of a self-created nation and from the sense of competence and superpower derived from World War II. If this was "arrogance of power," in Senator Fulbright's phrase, it was not so much the fatal hubris and over-extension that defeated Athens and Napoleon, and in the 20th century Germany and Japan, as it was failure to understand that problems and conflicts exist among other peoples that are not soluble by the application of American force or American techniques or even American goodwill. "Nation-building" was the most presumptuous of the illusions. Settlers of the North American continent had built a nation from Plymouth Rock to Valley Forge to the fulfilled frontier, yet failed to learn from their success that elsewhere, too, only the inhabitants can make the process work.

Wooden-headedness, the "Don't-confuse-me-with-the-facts" habit, is a universal folly never more conspicuous than at upper levels of Washington with respect to Vietnam. Its grossest fault was under-estimation of North Vietnam's commitment to its goal. Enemy motiva-tion was a missing element in American calculations, and Washington could therefore ignore all the evidence of nationalist fervor and of the passion for independence which as early as 1945 Hanoi had declared "no human force can any longer restrain." Washington could ignore General Leclerc's prediction that conquest would take half a million men and "Even then it could not be done." It could ignore the demonstration of élan and capacity that won victory over a French army with modern weapons at Dien Bien Phu, and all the continuing evidence thereafter.

American refusal to take the enemy's grim will and capacity into account has been explained by those responsible on the ground of ignorance of Vietnam's history, traditions and national character: there were "no experts available," in the words of one high-ranking official. But the longevity of Vietnamese resistance to foreign rule could have been learned from any history book on Indochina. Attentive consulta-tion with French administrators whose official lives had been spent in Vietnam would have made up for the lack of American expertise. Even superficial American acquaintance with the area, when it began to supply reports, provided creditable information. Not ignorance, but refusal to credit the evidence and, more fundamentally, refusal to grant stature and fixed purpose to a "fourth-rate" Asiatic country were the determining factors, much as in the case of the British attitude toward the American colonies. The irony of history is inexorable.

Underestimation was matched by overestimation of South Vietnam because it was the beneficiary of American assistance, and because Washington verbiage equated any non-Communist group with the "free" nations, fostering the delusion that its people were prepared to fight for their "freedom" with the will and energy that freedom is sup-posed to inspire. Such was the stated anchor of our policy; dissonant evidence had to be rejected or it would have made it obvious that this policy was built on sand. When dissonance disturbed attitudes toward either enemy or client, the attitudes, following the rules of wooden-headedness, rigidified.

A last folly was the absence of reflective thought about the nature of what we were doing, about effectiveness in relation to the object sought, about balance of possible gain as against loss and against harm both to the ally and to the United States. Absence of intelligent think-ing in rulership is another of the universals, and raises the question

whether in modern states there is something about political and bureau-
cractic life that subdues the functioning of intellect in favor of "working the levers" without regard to rational expectations. This would
seem to be an ongoing prospect.

The longest war had come to an end. Faintly from a distance of
200 years might have been heard Chatham's summary of a nation's
self-betrayal: "by the arts of imposition, by its own credulity, through
the means of false hope, false pride and promised advantages of the
most romantic and improbable nature." A contemporary summing up
was voiced by a Congressman from Michigan, Donald Riegle. In
talking to a couple from his constituency who had lost a son in
Vietnam, he faced the stark recognition that he could find no words
to justify the boy's death. "There was no way I could say that what
had happened was in their interest or in the national interest or in
anyone's interest."

Epilogue

"A LANTERN ON THE STERN"

If pursuing disadvantage after the disadvantage has become obvious is irrational, then rejection of reason is the prime characteristic of folly. According to the Stoics, reason was the "thinking fire" that directs the affairs of the world, and the emperor or ruler of the state was considered to be "the servant of divine reason [appointed] to maintain order on earth." The theory was comforting, but then as now "divine reason" was more often than not overpowered by non-rational human frailties—ambition, anxiety, status-seeking, face-saving, illusions, self-delusions, fixed prejudices. Although the structure of human thought is based on logical procedure from premise to conclusion, it is not proof against the frailties and the passions.

Rational thought clearly counseled the Trojans to suspect a trick when they woke to find the entire Greek army had vanished, leaving only a strange and monstrous prodigy beneath their walls. Rational procedure would have been, at the least, to test the Horse for concealed enemies as they were urgently advised to do by Capys the Elder, Laocoon and Cassandra. That alternative was present and available yet discarded in favor of self-destruction.

In the case of the Popes, reason was perhaps less accessible. They were so imbued by the rampant greed and grab and uninhibited self-gratification of their time that a rational response to the needs of their constituency was almost beyond their scope. It would have required a culture of different values. One might suppose that an ordinary instinct of self-preservation would have taken notice of the rising dissatisfaction lapping like flood water at their feet, but their view of the Papacy was temporal and secular, and they were too immersed in princely wars and in private consumption and display to take alarm at the intangible of discontent. The Papacy's folly lay not so much in being irrational as in being totally estranged from its appointed task.

The successive measures taken with regard both to the American colonies and to Vietnam were so plainly grounded in preconceived

fixed attitudes and so regularly contrary to common sense, rational inference and cogent advice that, as folly, they speak for themselves.

In the operations of government, the impotence of reason is serious
because it affects everything within reach—citizens, society, civilization.
It was a problem of deep concern to the Greek founders of Western
thought. Euripides, in his last plays, conceded that the mystery of moral
evil and of folly could no longer be explained by external cause, by the
bite of Atē, as if by a spider, or by other intervention of the gods. Men
and women had to confront it as part of their being. His Medea knows
herself to be controlled by passion "stronger than my purposes." Plato,
some fifty years later, desperately wanted man to grasp and never let go
of the "sacred golden cord of reason," but ultimately he too had to
acknowledge that his fellow-beings were anchored in the life of feelings,
jerked like puppets by the strings of desires and fears that made them
dance. When desire disagrees with the judgment of reason, he said,
there is a disease of the soul, "And when the soul is opposed to knowledge, or opinion or reason which are her natural laws, that I call folly."

When it came to government, Plato assumed that a wise ruler would
take most care of what he loved most, that is, what fitted best with his
own interests, which would be equivalent to the best interests of the
state. Since he was not confident that the rule always operated the way it
should, Plato advised as a cautionary procedure that the future guard-
ians of the state should be watched and tested during their period of
maturing to ensure that they conducted themselves according to the
rule.

With the advent of Christianity, personal responsibility was given
back to the external and supernatural, at the command of God and the
Devil. Reason returned for a brief brilliant reign in the 18th century,
since when Freud has brought us back to Euripides and the controlling
power of the dark, buried forces of the soul, which not being subject
to the mind are incorrigible by good intentions or rational will.

Chief among the forces affecting political folly is lust for power,
named by Tacitus as "the most flagrant of all the passions." Because it
can only be satisfied by power over others, government is its favorite
field of exercise. Business offers a kind of power, but only to the very
successful at the very top, and without the dominion and titles and red
carpets and motorcycle escorts of public office. Other occupations—
sports, sciences, the professions and the creative and performing arts—
offer various satisfactions but not the opportunity for power. They may
appeal to status-seekers and, in the form of celebrity, offer crowd worship and limousines and prizes, but these are the trappings of power, not

the essence. Government remains the paramount area of folly because it is there that men seek power over others—only to lose it over themselves.

Thomas Jefferson, who held more and higher offices than most men, took the sourest view of it. "Whenever a man has cast a longing eye on [office]," he wrote to a friend, "a rottenness begins in his conduct." His contemporary across the Atlantic, Adam Smith, was if anything more censorious. "And thus *Place* . . . is the end of half the labors of human life; and is the cause of all the tumult and bustle, all the rapine and injustice which avarice and ambition have introduced into this world." Both were speaking of moral failure, not of competence. When that comes into question, it gains no higher rating from other statesmen. In the 1930s, when a chairman was being sought for the Senate investigation of the munitions industry, a leader of the peace movement asked the advice of Senator George Norris. Ruling himself out as too old, Norris went down the list of his colleagues, crossing off one after the other as too lazy, too stupid, too close to the Army, as moral cowards or overworked or in poor health or having conflict of interest or facing re-election. When he had finished he had eliminated all but Senator Gerald Nye, the only one out of the 96 whom he deemed to have the competence, independence and stature for the task. Much the same opinion in different circumstances was pronounced by General Eisenhower in discussing the need for inspired leaders to create a United States of Europe as the only way to preserve Europe's security. He did not think it would happen, because "Everyone is too cautious, too fearful, too lazy, and too ambitious (personally)." Odd and notable is the appearance of lazy in both catalogues.

A greater inducement to folly is excess of power. After he had conceived his wonderful vision of philosopher-kings in the Republic, Plato began to have doubts and reached the conclusion that laws were the only safeguard. Too much power given to anything, like too large a sail on a vessel, he believed, is dangerous; moderation is overthrown. Excess leads on the one hand to disorder and on the other to injustice. No soul of man is able to resist the temptation of arbitrary power, and there is "No one who will not under such circumstances become filled with folly, the worst of diseases." His kingdom will be undermined and "all his power will vanish from him." Such indeed was the fate that overtook the Renaissance Papacy to the point of half, if not all, of its power; and Louis XIV, although not until after his death; and—if we consider the American Presidency to confer excess of power—Lyndon Johnson, who was given to speaking of "*my* air force" and thought his position entitled him to lie and deceive; and, most obviously, Richard Nixon.

Mental standstill or stagnation—the maintenance intact by rulers and policy-makers of the ideas they started with—is fertile ground for folly. Montezuma is a fatal and tragic example. Leaders in government, on the authority of Henry Kissinger, do not learn beyond the convictions they bring with them; these are "the intellectual capital they will consume as long as they are in office." Learning from experience is a faculty almost never practiced. Why did American experience of supporting the unpopular party in China supply no analogy to Vietnam? And the experience of Vietnam none for Iran? And why has none of the above conveyed any inference to preserve the present government of the United States from imbecility in El Salvador? "If men could learn from history, what lessons it might teach us!" lamented Samuel Coleridge. "But passion and party blind our eyes, and the light which experience gives us is a lantern on the stern which shines only on the waves behind us." The image is beautiful but the message misleading, for the light on the waves we have passed through should enable us to infer the nature of the waves ahead.

In its first stage, mental standstill fixes the principles and boundaries governing a political problem. In the second stage, when dissonances and failing function begin to appear, the initial principles rigidify. This is the period when, if wisdom were operative, re-examination and re-thinking and a change of course are possible, but they are rare as rubies in a backyard. Rigidifying leads to increase of investment and the need to protect egos; policy founded upon error multiplies, never retreats. The greater the investment and the more involved in it the sponsor's ego, the more unacceptable is disengagement. In the third stage, pursuit of failure enlarges the damages until it causes the fall of Troy, the defection from the Papacy, the loss of a trans-Atlantic empire, the classic humiliation in Vietnam.

Persistence in error is the problem. Practitioners of government continue down the wrong road as if in thrall to some Merlin with magic power to direct their steps. There are Merlins in early literature to explain human aberration, but freedom of choice does exist—unless we accept the Freudian unconscious as the new Merlin. Rulers will justify a bad or wrong decision on the ground, as a historian and partisan wrote of John F. Kennedy, that "He had no choice," but no matter how equal two alternatives may appear, there is always freedom of choice to change or desist from a counter-productive course if the policy-maker has the moral courage to exercise it. He is not a fated creature blown by the whims of Homeric gods. Yet to recognize error, to cut losses, to alter course, is the most repugnant option in government.

For a chief of state, admitting error is almost out of the question. The American misfortune during the Vietnam period was to have had Presidents who lacked the self-confidence for the grand withdrawal. We come back again to Burke: "Magnanimity in politics is not seldom the truest wisdom, and a great Empire and little minds go ill together." The test comes in recognizing when persistence in error has become self-damaging. A prince, says Machiavelli, ought always to be a great asker and a patient hearer of truth about those things of which he has inquired, and he should be angry if he finds that anyone has scruples about telling him the truth. What government needs is great askers.

Refusal to draw inference from negative signs, which under the rubric "wooden-headedness" has played so large a part in these pages, was recognized in the most pessimistic work of modern times, George Orwell's *1984*, as what the author called "Crimestop." "Crimestop means the faculty of stopping short, as though by instinct, at the threshold of any dangerous thought. It includes the power of not grasping analogies, of failing to perceive logical errors, of misunderstanding the simplest arguments . . . and of being bored and repelled by any train of thought which is capable of leading in a heretical direction. Crimestop, in short, means protective stupidity."

The question is whether or how a country can protect itself from protective stupidity in policy-making, which in turn raises the question whether it is possible to educate for government. Plato's scheme, which included breeding as well as educating, was never tried. A conspicuous attempt by another culture, the training of the mandarins of China for administrative function, produced no very superior result. The mandarins had to pass through years of study and apprenticeship and weeding out by a series of stiff examinations, but the successful ones did not prove immune to corruption and incompetence. In the end they petered out in decadence and ineffectiveness.

Another such scheme used aliens. The Turkish Janissaries were the better-known military arm of a larger body—the Kapi Kullari, or Slave Institution—which filled every civil post from palace cook to Grand Vizier. Made up of Christian children taken from their parents and brought up and exhaustively trained by the Ottoman Turks for official functions in what may have been the most complete educational system ever devised, they were legally slaves of the Sultan, converted to Islam, forbidden to have families or own property. Free of these distractions, it was supposed they would be able to devote themselves singlemindedly to the state and its sovereign, on whom they were entirely dependent for pay and the necessities of life. The Sultan thus acquired a body not only of first-class administrators, but of strong supporters of his absolutism. Although the system worked to excellent effect, it did not save the Ottoman Empire from slow degeneration; nor, in the end, could the system save itself. In the course of time, the military branch gained growing power, defied the marriage ban and assumed hereditary rights, perpetuated themselves as a permanent and dominant clan, and eventually, in inevitable challenge to the ruler, attempted to seize power in overt revolt. They were slaughtered and destroyed, bringing down the rest of the Slave Institution with them, while the Grand Turk dwindled into dotage.

In 17th-century Europe, after the devastation of the Thirty Years' War, Prussia, when it was still Brandenburg, determined to create a strong state by means of a disciplined army and a trained civil service. Applicants for the civil positions, drawn from commoners in order to offset the nobles' control of the military, had to complete a course of study covering political theory, law and legal philosophy, economics, history, penology and statutes. Only after passing through various stages of examination and probationary terms of office did they receive definitive appointments and tenure and opportunity for advancement. The higher civil service was a separate branch, not open to promotion from the middle and lower levels.

The Prussian system proved so effective that the state was able to survive both military defeat by Napoleon in 1807 and the revolutionary surge of 1848. But by then it had begun to congeal, like the mandarins, losing many of its most progressive citizens in emigration to America. Prussian energies, however, succeeded in 1871 in uniting the German states in an empire under Prussian hegemony. Its very success contained the seed of ruin, for it nourished the arrogance and power-hunger that from 1914 through 1918 was to bring it down.

Political shock moved the English to give attention to the problem. Neither the loss of America nor the storm waves of the French Revolution shook their system of government, but in the mid-19th century, when the rumble from below was growing louder, the revolutions of 1848 on the Continent had effect. Instead of taking refuge in reactionary panic, as might have been expected, the authorities, with commendable enterprise, ordered an investigation of their own government practices, which were then virtually the private preserve of the propertied class. The result was a report on the need for a permanent civil service to be based on training and specialized skills and designed to provide continuity and maintenance of the long view as against transient issues and political passions. Though strongly resisted, the system was adopted in 1870. It has produced distinguished civil servants, but also Burgess, MacLean, Philby and Blunt. The history of British government in the last hundred years suggests that factors other than the quality of its civil service determine a country's fate.

In the United States, the civil service was established chiefly as a barrier to patronage and the pork-barrel, rather than in search of excellence. By 1937, a presidential commission, finding the system inadequate, was urging the development of a "real career service . . . requiring personnel of the highest order, competent, highly trained, loyal, skilled in their duties by reason of long experience, and assured of continuity." After much effort and some progress, that goal is still not reached, but even if it had been, it would not affect elected officials and high appointments—that is, government at the top.

In America, where the electoral process is drowning in commercial techniques of fund-raising and image-making, we may have completed a circle back to a selection process as unconcerned with qualifications as that which made Darius King of Persia. When he and six fellow conspirators, as recorded by Herodotus, overthrew the reigning despot, they discussed what kind of government—whether a monarchy of one or an oligarchy of the wisest men—they should establish. Darius argued that they should keep to the rule of one and obtain the best government by choosing "the very best man in the whole state." Being persuaded, the group agreed to ride out together next morning and he whose horse was the first to neigh at sunrise should be King. By ruse of a clever groom who tethered a favorite mare at the critical spot, Darius' horse performed on time and his fortunate master, thus singled out as the best man for the job, ascended the throne.

Factors other than random selection subdue the influence of the "thinking fire" on public affairs. For the chief of state under modern conditions, a limiting factor is too many subjects and problems in too many areas of government to allow solid understanding of any of them, and too little time to think between fifteen-minute appointments and thirty-page briefs. This leaves the field open to protective stupidity. Meanwhile bureaucracy, safely repeating today what it did yesterday, rolls on as ineluctably as some vast computer, which, once penetrated by error, duplicates it forever.

Above all, lure of office, known in our country as Potomac fever, stultifies a better performance of government. The bureaucrat dreams of promotion, higher officials want to extend their reach, legislators and the chief of state want re-election; and the guiding principle in these pursuits is to please as many and offend as few as possible. Intelligent government would require that the persons entrusted with high office should formulate and execute policy according to their best judgment, the best knowledge available and a judicious estimate of the lesser evil. But re-election is on their minds, and that becomes the criterion.

Aware of the controlling power of ambition, corruption and emotion, it may be that in the search for wiser government we should look for the test of character first. And the test should be moral courage. Montaigne adds, "Resolution and valor, not that which is sharpened by ambition but that which wisdom and reason may implant in a well-ordered soul." The Lilliputians in choosing persons for public employment had similar criteria. "They have more regard for good morals than for great abilities," reported Gulliver, "for, since government is necessary to mankind, they believe . . . that Providence never intended to make management of publick affairs a mystery, to be comprehended only by a few persons of sublime genius, of which there are seldom three born in an age. They suppose truth, justice, temperance and the like to be in every man's power: the practice of which virtues, assisted by experience and a good intention, would qualify any man for service of his country, except where a course of study is required."

While such virtues may in truth be in every man's power, they have less chance in our system than money and ruthless ambition to prevail at the ballot box. The problem may be not so much a matter of educating officials for government as educating the electorate to recognize and reward integrity of character and to reject the ersatz. Perhaps better men flourish in better times, and wiser government requires the nourishment of a dynamic rather than a troubled and bewildered society. If John Adams was right, and government is "little better practiced now than three or four thousand years ago," we cannot reasonably expect much improvement. We can only muddle on as we have done in those same three or four thousand years, through patches of brilliance and decline, great endeavor and shadow.

REFERENCE NOTES
AND WORKS CONSULTED

INDEX

Chapter One

PURSUIT OF POLICY
CONTRARY TO SELF-INTEREST

REFERENCE NOTES

p. 5 JOHN ADAMS: Letter to Thomas Jefferson, 9 July 1813, in *The Adams-Jefferson Letters*, ed. L. J. Cappon, Chapel Hill, 1959, II, 351.

5 ENGLISH HISTORIAN, "NOTHING IS MORE UNFAIR . . .": Denys A. Winstanley, *Lord Chatham and the Whig Opposition*, Cambridge, 1912, 129.

7 PLATO ON PHILOSOPHER-KINGS: *Republic*, V, 473.

7 HISTORIAN ON PHILIP II: *Encyclopaedia Britannica*, 14th ed., anon.

8 OXENSTIERNA: *Bartlett's Familar Quotations*.

8 REHOBOAM: I Kings 11:43, 12:1 and 4; II Chronicles 9:31, 10:1 and 4.

10 "AMPLE IN FOLLY": *Ecclesiasticus (Book of Sirach)* 48:6.

11 MONTEZUMA: William H. Prescott, *The Conquest of Mexico*, New York, 1843; C. A. Burland, *Montezuma*, New York, 1973.

13 THIRTEEN MUSKETS: *New Cambridge Modern History*, I, 442.

14 VISIGOTHS: Dr. Rafael Altamira, "Spain Under the Visigoths," in *Cambridge Medieval History*, II, chap. 6.

17 SOLON, "LEARNED SOMETHING NEW": Plutarch's *Lives*.

18 SCHLESINGER, SR., QUOTED: *The Birth of a Nation*, New York, 1968, 245–6.

20 VOLTAIRE QUOTED: M. A. François, *The Age of Louis XIV*, Everyman ed., New York, 1966, 408.

20 LOUIS XIV AS GOD'S INSTRUMENT: G.R.R. Treasure, *Seventeenth Century France*, New York, 1966, 368.

21 DAUPHIN'S CAUTIONS: G. A. Rothrock, *The Huguenots: Biography of a Minority*, Chicago, 1973, 173.

21 SAINT-SIMON'S COMMENT: *Memoires* in Sanche de Gramont, *The Age of Magnificence*, New York, 1963, 274.

22 HUGUENOT OFFICERS JOIN WILLIAM III: Estimate submitted to the King by Marshal Vauban in 1689; Rothrock, op. cit., 179.

23 FRENCH HISTORIAN ON "GREAT DESIGNS": C. Picavet in *La diplomatie au temps de Louis XIV*, 1930; q. Treasure, op. cit., 353.

23 EMERSON: *Journals, 1820–72*, Boston, 1909–14, IV, 160.

p. 24   CHARLES X WOULD RATHER BE A WOODCUTTER: Alfred Cobban, *A History of Modern France*, 2 vols., Penguin ed., 1961, II, 72.

24   300 FRANCS FOR QUALIFICATION: ibid., II, 77.

25   CHIEF OF STAFF TO CHANCELLOR, "IT WAS MORE LIKELY . . .": Fritz Fischer, *Germany's Aims in the First World War*, New York, 1967, 184–5.

26   BETHMANN, "INEVITABLY CAUSE AMERICA . . .": Speech in Reichstag, 10 Jan 1916, q. Hans Peter Hanssen, *Diary of a Dying Empire*, Bloomington, Indiana Univ. Press, 1955.

26   "GASPING IN THE REEDS . . .": in Reichstag, 31 Jan 1917, q. Hanssen, op. cit., 165.

26   HELFFERICH, "LEAD TO RUIN": *Official German Documents Relating to the World War*, 2 vols., Carnegie Endowment for International Peace, New York, I, 150.

26   TWO LEADING BANKERS: Max Warburg and Bernhard Dernburg, see Fischer, op. cit., 307.

27   ZIMMERMANN, "TO RISK BEING CHEATED . . .": Fischer, op. cit., 299.

27   CONFERENCE OF 9 JAN 1917, ALL QUOTATIONS: A verbatim report of the conference is in *German Documents*, I, 340, 525; II, 1219–77, 1317–21.

28   BETHMANN, "FINIS GERMANIAE": q. G. P. Gooch, *Recent Revelations of European Diplomacy*, London, 1927, 17.

28   RIEZLER, "GERMANY IS LIKE A PERSON . . .": q. Fritz Stern, *The Responsibility of Power*, ed. L. Krieger, and Stern, New York, 1967, 278.

30   ADMIRAL YAMAMOTO QUOTED: Gordon W. Prange, *At Dawn We Slept*, New York, 1981, 10, 15, 16.

31   ADMIRAL NAGANO DOUBTFUL IF JAPAN WOULD WIN: from the diary of Marquis Kido, Lord Privy Seal, 31 July 1941, q. Herbert Feis, *The Road to Pearl Harbor*, Princeton, 1950, 252.

Chapter Two

PROTOTYPE: THE TROJANS TAKE
THE WOODEN HORSE WITHIN THEIR WALLS

WORKS CONSULTED

APOLLODORUS. *The Library [and Epitome]*. 2 vols. Trans. Sir James George Frazer. London and New York, 1921.

ARNOLD, MATTHEW. "On Translating Homer" in *The Viking Portable Arnold*. New York, 1949.

BOWRA, C. M. *The Greek Experience*. Mentor ed. New York, n.d. (orig. pub. 1957).

DICTYS OF CRETE AND DARES THE PHRYGIAN. *The Trojan War*. Trans. R. M. Frazer, Jr. Bloomington, Indiana Univ. Press, 1966.

DODDS, E. R. *The Greeks and the Irrational*. Berkeley, Univ. of California Press, 1951.

EURIPIDES. *The Trojan Women*. Trans. with notes, Gilbert Murray. Oxford Univ. Press, 1915.

FINLEY, M. I. *The World of Odysseus*, rev. ed. New York, 1978.

GRANT, MICHAEL, AND HAZEL, JOHN. *Gods and Mortals in Classical Mythology.* Springfield, Mass., 1973.

GRAVES, ROBERT. *The Greek Myths.* 2 vols. Penguin ed. Baltimore, 1955.

GROTE, GEORGE. *History of Greece.* 10 vols. London, 1872.

HERODOTUS. *The Histories.* 2 vols. Trans. George Rawlinson. Everyman ed. New York.

HOMER. *The Iliad.* Trans. Richmond Lattimore. Chicago, Univ. of Chicago Press, 1951.

——. *The Iliad.* Trans. Robert Fitzgerald. New York, 1974.

——. *The Odyssey.* Trans. Robert Fitzgerald. New York, 1963.

KIRK, G. S. *The Nature of Greek Myths.* Penguin ed. Baltimore, 1974.

KNIGHT, W.F.J. "The Wooden Horse at the Gates of Troy." *Classical Quarterly.* Vol. 28, 1933, 254.

MACLEISH, ARCHIBALD. "The Trojan Horse," in *Collected Poems.* Boston, 1952.

MACURDY, GRACE A. "The Horse-Training Trojans." *Classical Quarterly* (O.S. 1923). Vol. XVII, 51.

QUINTUS OF SMYRNA. *The War of Troy.* Trans., with intro. and notes, Frederick M. Combellach. Norman, Oklahoma Univ. Press, 1968.

SNELL, BRUNO. *The Discovery of the Mind: Greek Origins of European Thought.* Cambridge, Mass., 1953.

SCHERER, MARGARET S. *The Legend of Troy in Art and Literature.* New York and London, 1963.

STEINER, GEORGE, AND FAGLES, ROBERT. *Homer: A Collection of Critical Essays.* Englewood Cliffs, N.J., 1962.

VIRGIL. *The Aeneid.* Trans. Rolfe Humphries. New York, 1951.

REFERENCE NOTES

Note: Numerals in reference notes to the *Iliad*, *Odyssey* and *Aeneid* refer to lines (which vary somewhat according to translation), not to pages.

p. 36 STORYTELLER, "WHAT HAS HAPPENED . . .": Powys, preface to "Homer and the Aelther" in Steiner and Fagles, 140.

37 DEMODOCUS' TALE OF THE WOODEN HORSE: *Odyssey*, Bk VIII, 499–520.

37 HOMER'S SUCCESSORS: The verse narratives between Homer and Virgil, which exist mainly in fragments or epitomes, are: the *Cypria*, c. 7th century B.C.; the *Little Iliad* by Lesches of Lesbos; *The Sack of Ilium* by Arctinus of Miletus. Post-*Aeneid* treatments of the Trojan War are: Apollodorus; Hyginus' *Fabulae*; Quintus Smyrnaeus' *Posthomerica*; Servius on the *Aeneid*; Dictys the Cretan; and Dares the Phrygian.

38 POSEIDON AND APOLLO AS BUILDERS OF TROY: from Servius, discussed in Frazer's Notes to Apollodorus, II, 229–35; Murray's Notes to Euripides, 81.

38 WOODEN HORSE BUILT ON ATHENA'S ADVICE: *Aeneid*, Bk II, 13–56; Lesches' *Little Iliad*, q. Scherer, 110; Graves, II, 331.

39 HORSE SACRED TO TROY, AND SACRED VEIL: *Odyssey*, Bk VIII, 511 ff.; *Little Iliad*, q. Knight; *Aeneid*, Bk II, 234.

39 EPEIUS: Quintus, 221–2, 227.

39 "HALF WAY BETWEEN VICTORY AND DEATH": Quintus, 227.

p. 39   THYMOETES AND CAPYS: *Aeneid*, Bk II, 46–55.

39   PRIAM AND COUNCIL DEBATE: Arctinus, *Sack of Ilium*, q. Scherer, 111.

39   CROWD CRIES "BURN IT! . . .": *Odyssey*, Bk VIII, 499; Graves, II, 333.

39   LAOCOON'S WARNING: *Aeneid*, Bk II, 56–80, 199–231; Hyginus, *Fabulae.*

40   SINON: *Aeneid*, II, 80–275; Quintus, 228.

40   SERPENTS: *Aeneid*, Bk II, 283–315.

41   PLINY ON STATUE: q. Scherer, 113.

41   OTHER PORTENTS: Quintus, 231–2.

41   CASSANDRA: *Aeneid*, Bk II; Quintus, 232–3; Hyginus and Apollodorus, q. Graves, II, 263–4, 273; Frazer's Notes to Apollodorus, II, 229–35.

42   "TREMBLING IN THEIR LEGS": Odysseus reports this to Achilles in Hades, *Odyssey*, Bk XI, 527.

42   FATE OF TROJANS AFTER THE FALL: *Aeneid*, Bk II, 506–58.

44   PAUSANIAS AND SIEGE ENGINE: Grote, I, 285; Graves, II, 335.

45   A MILITARY HISTORIAN: Yigael Yadin in *World History of the Jewish People*, Rutgers Univ. Press, 1970, II, 159; also *Art of Warfare in Biblical Lands*, London, 1965, 18.

45   HERODOTUS ON HELEN: Bk II, chap. 113–19; "INFATUATED": ibid., chap. 120.

46   PRIAM, "TO THE GODS I OWE . . .": *Iliad*, Bk III, c. 170.

46   ZEUS, "WHEN IT IS THROUGH BLINDNESS . . .": *Odyssey*, Bk I, 30; ON AEGISTHUS: ibid., 32 ff.

46   ATĒ: appears first in Hesiod, predating Homer; sometimes called Eris or Erinys; sometimes figures as daughter of Eris, Goddess of Discord; in *Iliad*, Bk IX, 502–12; Bk XIX, 95–135; in various classical dictionaries.

47   FLOOD LEGEND: Kirk, 135–6, 261–4; Graves, II, 269.

48   LITAI: *Iliad*, Bk IX, 474–80, Fitzgerald translation.

48   AGAMEMNON BLAMES ATĒ: *Iliad*, Bk XIX, 87–94.

48   BRUTUS' VISION: Shakespeare, *Julius Caesar*, Act. 3, Sc. 1.

Chapter Three

THE RENAISSANCE POPES PROVOKE
THE PROTESTANT SECESSION: 1470–1530

WORKS CONSULTED

The most inclusive source for the history of the Papacy in this period, to which all later studies must be indebted, is Ludwig von Pastor's *History of the Popes from the Close of the Middle Ages* in 14 volumes, first published in German in the 1880s and '90s. Jacob Burckhardt's classic *The Civilization of the Renaissance in Italy*, first published in German in his native Switzerland in 1860, is equally indispensable.

    Primary sources, on which the following works are based, are the Vatican archives; letters, diplomatic correspondence and reports and other miscellaneous sources collected in Muratori's *Annals*; individual chronicles, especially the diary of John Burchard, Vatican Master of Ceremonies under Alexander VI and Julius

II; and the major contemporary histories, Guicciardini's *Storia d'Italia*, Francesco Vettori's *Storia d'Italia*, Machiavelli's *The Prince* and *The Discourses*, Vasari's *Lives of the Painters*.

AUBENAS, ROGER, AND RICARD, ROBERT. *L'Eglise et la Renaissance.* Vol. 15 of *Histoire de l'Eglise.* Ed. A. Fliche and V. Martin. Paris, 1951.

BRION, MARCEL. *The Medici.* Trans. New York, 1969.

BURCHARD, JOHN. "Pope Alexander VI and His Court" (Extracts from the Latin diary of the Papal Master of Ceremonies, 1484–1506). Ed. F. L. Glaser. New York, 1921.

BURCKHARDT, JACOB. *The Civilization of the Renaissance in Italy.* Vol. I. Colophon ed., New York, 1958.

CALVESI, MAURIZIO. *Treasures of the Vatican.* Trans. J. Emmons, Geneva, 1962.

CATHOLIC ENCYCLOPEDIA, 1907–12, and NEW CATHOLIC ENCYCLOPEDIA, 1967.

CHADWICK, OWEN. *The Reformation.* London, 1964.

CHAMBERLIN, E. R. *The Bad Popes.* New York, 1969.

CHAMBERS, DAVID SANDERSON. "The Economic Predicament of Renaissance Cardinals," *Studies in Medieval and Renaissance History.* Vol III. Lincoln, Neb., 1966.

COUGHLAN, ROBERT. *The World of Michelangelo: 1475–1564.* New York, 1966.

DICKENS, A. G. *Reformation and Society in 16th Century Europe.* New York, 1966.

ERASMUS, DESIDERIUS. *The Praise of Folly.* Trans. H. H. Hudson. Princeton, 1941.

FUNCK-BRENTANO, FRANTZ. *The Renaissance.* Trans. New York, 1936.

GILBERT, FELIX. *Machiavelli and Guicciardini.* Princeton, 1965.

GILMORE, MYRON P. *The World of Humanism, 1453–1517.* New York, 1958.

GREGOROVIUS, FERDINAND. *History of Rome.* 13 vols. Trans. A. Hamilton. London, 1894–1902.

GUICCIARDINI, FRANCESCO. *The History of Italy.* Trans. S. Alexander. New York, 1969.

HALE, J. R. *Renaissance Europe: 1480–1520.* Berkeley, 1971.

HIBBERT, CHRISTOPHER. *The House of Medici: Its Rise and Fall.* New York, 1975.

HILLERBRAND, HANS J. *The World of the Reformation.* New York, 1973.

HOWELL, A. G. FERRERS. *S. Bernardino of Siena.* London, 1913.

HUGHES, PHILIP. *A History of the Church.* Vol III. New York, 1947.

HUIZINGA, JOHAN. *Erasmus and the Age of the Reformation.* Trans. New York, 1957.

JEDIN, HUBERT. *A History of the Council of Trent.* Vol I. Trans. London, 1957.

LEES-MILNE, JAMES. *St. Peter's.* Boston, 1967.

LOPEZ, ROBERT S. *The Three Ages of the Italian Renaissance.* Boston, 1970.

LORTZ, JOSEPH. *How the Reformation Came.* Trans. New York, 1964.

MACHIAVELLI, NICCOLO. *The Prince and The Discourses.* Modern Library ed. New York, 1940.

MALLETT, MICHAEL. *The Borgias: The Rise and Fall of a Renaissance Dynasty.* New York, 1969.

MATTINGLY, GARRETT. *Renaissance Diplomacy.* Boston, 1955.

MCNALLY, ROBERT E., S.J. *Reform of the Church.* New York, 1963.

MITCHELL, BONNER. *Rome in the High Renaissance: The Age of Leo X.* Norman, Univ. of Oklahoma Press, 1973.

The New Cambridge Modern History. Vol I. *The Renaissance: 1493–1520.* Cambridge, 1957.

OECHSLI, WILHELM. *History of Switzerland, 1499–1914.* Trans. Cambridge, 1922.

OLIN, JOHN C. *The Catholic Reformation: Savonarola to Ignatius Loyola, 1495–1540.* New York, 1969.

O'MALLEY, JOHN. "The Discovery of America and Reform Thought at the Papal Court in the Early Cinquecento," in Fredi Chiapelli, ed., *First Images of America.* Vol I. Berkeley, 1976.

——. *Praise and Blame in Rome: Renaissance Rhetoric, Doctrine and Reform in the Sacred Orators of the Papal Court, 1450–1521.* Durham, N.C. Duke Univ. Press, 1972.

OWST, G. R. *Preaching in Medieval England, 1350–1450.* Cambridge, 1926.

PARTNER, PETER. "The Budget of the Roman Church in the Renaissance Period," in *Italian Renaissance Studies.* Ed. E. F. Jacob. London, 1960.

——. *Renaissance Rome, 1500–1559.* Berkeley, 1972.

PASTOR, LUDWIG VON. *The History of the Popes from the Close of the Middle Ages.* Vols. V–IX. Trans. Ed. F. I. Antrobus and R. F. Kerr, London and St. Louis, 1902–10.

PORTIGLIATTI, GIUSEPPE. *The Borgias.* New York, 1928.

PREZZOLINI, GIUSEPPE. *Machiavelli.* New York, 1967.

RANKE, LEOPOLD VON. *History of the Popes . . . in the 16th and 17th Centuries.* 3 vols. Trans. London, 1847.

RIDOLFI, ROBERTO. *The Life of Niccolò Machiavelli.* Trans. Chicago, 1954.

RODOCANACHI, E. *Histoire de Rome: Le pontificat de Jules II.* Paris, 1928. *Les pontificats d'Adrien VI et de Clément VII.* Paris, 1933.

ROUTH, C.R.N., ED. *They Saw It Happen in Europe, 1450–1600* (anthology of eye-witnesses' accounts). Oxford, 1965.

SCHAFF, DAVID S. *History of the Christian Church.* Vol 6. Grand Rapids, Mich., 1910.

SCHEVILL, FERDINAND. *The Medici.* New York, 1949.

——. *History of Florence.* New York, 1961.

TODD, JOHN M. *The Reformation.* New York, 1971.

DE TOLNAY, CHARLES. *The Medici Chapel.* Princeton, 1948.

ULLMANN, WALTER. *A Short History of the Papacy in the Middle Ages.* London, 1972.

VASARI, GIORGIO. *Lives of the Artists.* Ed. Betty Burroughs. New York, 1946.

YOUNG, G. F. *The Medici.* Modern Library ed. New York, 1930.

REFERENCE NOTES

The wars, politics and international relations of the Papacy and the Italian states, and the circumstances of Luther's break and its aftermath, are not annotated below because they are amply recorded in standard secondary histories and studies of the Renaissance and Reformation.

p. 55 "STAKE IN A GAME OF TENNIS": G. G. Coulton, *Social Life in Britain from the Conquest to the Reformation,* Cambridge, 1918, 204.

55 "STARVED FOR THE WORD OF GOD": q. Owst, 31–2.

55 "IF THE PREACHER": q. Howell, 251–2.

p. 56   "TO TRANSFORM ALL CHRISTIANS": Todd, 97; Olin, xxi.
56   DOMENICHI's *Tractatus*: O'Malley, 211–14. "BABYLON, THE MOTHER OF . . .":
q. ibid., 211. "DIGNITY OF THE CHURCH": q. ibid., 86, n. 33.
57   MACHIAVELLI, "SUPREME FELICITY": *The Prince*, Bk II, chap. II.
58   JACOB THE RICH: Gilmore, 60. AGOSTINO CHIGI: Funck-Brentano, 37.
59   ASSASSINATION OF GIULIANO DE MEDICI: Burckhardt, 78.
59   "CRUELEST, WORST . . .": q. ibid., 52.
59   "FULL OF CONTEMPT": q. ibid., 42.
60   HE "LEFT THE HOSPITAL": Burchard, 130.
60   PANDOLFO PETRUCCI: Burckhardt, 50. FEDERIGO OF URBINO: ibid., 65.
61   NICHOLAS V, "TO CREATE SOLID . . .": q. Lees-Milne, 124, and Mallett, 47.

1. Sixtus IV

p. 62   "THREE EVIL GENIUSES": *New Cambridge*, 77.
62   SIXTUS' CAREER AND CHARACTER: Burckhardt, 123; Hughes, 389–90; Mallett,
53–6; Aubenas, 87–90.
63   SIXTUS MADE 34 CARDINALS: Chambers, 290; Jedin, 88.
63   ARCHEPISCOPAL SEES TO BOYS OF EIGHT AND ELEVEN: Hughes, 442.
63   CARDINAL RIARIO'S BANQUET: Pastor, IV, 243–5.
63   PIUS II'S LETTER TO BORGIA: q. Routh, 83.
64   MANIFESTO EQUATING SIXTUS WITH SATAN: Aubenas, 88, and Pastor, IV, 136,
n. 2.
64   PAZZI PLOT: Aubenas, 76–7; Hughes, 393–4.
64   "PLEASE GOD THAT YOUR HOLINESS . . .": q. Aubenas, 77.
64   ARCHBISHOP ZAMOMETIC, FORTUNES OF: Jedin, 105.

2. Innocent VIII

p. 66   INNOCENT'S CHARACTER AND HABITS: Pastor, V, 246–70; Burckhardt, 126.
66   BORGIA BRIBES OF 25,000 DUCATS: Mallett, 100. "SO FALSE AND PROUD": q.
Pastor, V, 237.
67   "SEND A GOOD LETTER . . .": ibid., 242.
67   MORTGAGED THE PAPAL TIARA: Ullmann, 319.
67   "THE LORD DESIRETH NOT . . .": q. *New Cambridge*, 77.
67   FORGING FIFTY PAPAL BULLS: Hughes, 402.
68   CARDINAL ANTOINE DUPRAT: ibid., 447, n. 1.
68   LIVES OF THE CARDINALS: Pastor, V, 354, 370; Chambers, 291, 304, 307.
69   GIOVANNI DE' MEDICI'S ECCLESIASTICAL ADVANCEMENT: Chamberlin, 211.
69   LORENZO'S LETTER TO HIS SON: q. Pastor, V, 358–9; Olin, xv; Mallett, 52.
First published in Fabroni's *Life of Lorenzo*, 1784.
70   GENOA "WOULD NOT HESITATE . . .": q. Pastor, V, 246.
71   "PUSILLANIMITY . . . OF THE POPE": q. Pastor, V, 269.
71   "GENOESE SAILOR": q. ibid., 269.
72   "THE BEAST OF THE APOCALYPSE": q. O'Malley, 234.
72   "WHAT MORTAL POWER": q. Hughes, 345.
73   PRINCE DJEM, RIVALRY FOR AND SUBSIDIES: Guicciardini, 70; Aubenas, 140.
73   DJEM'S ARRIVAL IN ROME: Pastor, V, 299.
74   INNOCENT'S DYING WISH: Pastor, V, 320.

3. Alexander VI

p. 75 "FLEE, WE ARE IN THE HANDS . . .": q. Mallett, 120. BULLFIGHT: Schaff, 442; Mallett, 108.

75 FOUR MULE-LOADS OF BULLION: Mallett, 115, from Stefano Infessura's *Diario della città di Roma*. Borgia's buying of votes, with sums and promises given to each of the cardinals, is detailed in Pastor, V, 418.

75 CALIXTUS' SENILITY: *Cambridge Medieval History*, VIII, 175.

75 BORGIA'S CHARACTER, RICHES AND CONDUCT: Guicciardini, chaps. II and XIII; Routh, 92–3; Mallett, 84–6; Ullmann, 319; Chamberlin, 166–71.

76 "DO UNPLEASANT THINGS": q. Burckhardt, xix. "TOOK PAINS TO SHINE": Sigismondo de Conti, q. Burchard, xvii. "BRILLIANTLY SKILLED": Jacopo Gherardi da Volterra, q. Mallett, 84. "IRON TO A MAGNET": q. Routh, 93. "UNDERSTOOD MONEY MATTERS": q. Burchard, xvii.

76 BORGIA'S FAMILY: Guicciardini, 124; Ullmann, 319. VANOZZA REPLACED HER MOTHER: Burchard, xv.

77 PATERNITY OF THE EIGHTH CHILD: Mallett, 181.

77 ALEXANDER'S PROCESSION TO THE LATERAN: Burchard, q. Mallett, 120.

78 ELEVEN NEW CARDINALS: Chamberlin, 199.

78 DELLA ROVERE, A "LOUD EXCLAMATION": Pastor, V, 418.

78 TOTAL OF 43 CARDINALS: Jedin, 88.

79 REFORM THE MOST FREQUENT TOPIC: Chadwick, 20.

79 CHARLES VIII'S PLANS FOR INVASION OF ITALY: Guicciardini, 46–8. INTENTION TO DEPOSE POPE: *New Cambridge*, 302. CARDINAL DELLA ROVERE'S ROLE: ibid., 348–50.

79 "SO FULL OF VICES": Guicciardini, 69.

79 "TERRIBLE BEYOND ANYTHING": ibid., 68.

80 GEORGE MEREDITH: *The Egoist*.

80 LUDOVICO IL MORO INVITES CHARLES VIII: *New Cambridge*, 296.

80 "INNUMERABLE CALAMITIES": Guicciardini, 48.

81 ARMED PARADE OF THE FRENCH IN ROME: Pastor, V, 451–2.

81 "REQUISITIONS ARE FEARFUL": ibid., 454.

82 SAVONAROLA: Aubenas, 130–36; Schevill, *Florence*, 433–55.

83 "CAUSED SUCH TERROR": q. Coughlan, 69. HIS PROPHECY: ibid.

83 "POPES AND PRELATES": Pastor, VI, 14–15.

83 HAILED CHARLES VIII: Schevill, *Florence*, 444.

84 POPE "NO LONGER A CHRISTIAN": q. Jedin, 40.

84 15,000 HEAR ROBERTO DA LECCE: Pastor, V, 177.

84 TWENTY IN FLORENCE ELECT OWN "POPE": Pastor, V, 215.

85 DEATH OF JUAN, DUKE OF GANDIA: Mallett, 154–5; Chamberlin, 187–90.

85 "THE MOST GRIEVOUS DANGER": q. Jedin, 126.

85 PROPOSED PROGRAM OF REFORM: Hale, 228; Hughes, 450.

86 LOUIS XII: Guicciardini, 139; Aubenas, 143–4.

86 "*Tutto va al contrario*": Marino Sanuto, *Diarii*, Tom. I, Venezia, 1879, p. 1054, para. 127.

87 PORTUGUESE AND SPANISH ENVOYS: Pastor, VI, 62–4.

87 CESARE'S CAREER: Pastor, VI, 61–8. MURDERS: ibid., 75; Burckhardt, 132. WEARING A MASK: Burchard, xxii.

88 ALFONSO HACKED TO DEATH: Mallett, 177–8.

p. 88   BALLET OF THE CHESTNUTS: Burchard, 155. MARES AND STALLIONS: ibid.

89   100,000 DUCATS FOR DOWRY: Burchard, 157. EIGHTY NEW OFFICES: Hughes, 413–14.

89   CARDINAL SANGIORGIO: Jedin, 97.

89   GHASTLY TALES: Burchard, 186–7; Jedin, 97; LETTER OF FRANCESCO GONZAGA, 22 DEC 1503: q. Routh, 95.

90   "NO LAW, NO DIVINITY": q. O'Malley, 187, n. 2.

4. Julius II

p. 91   CONCLAVE IN CASTEL SANT' ANGELO: Pastor, VI, 186.

91   ELECTION OF PICCOLOMINI: ibid., 199–201.

92   PIUS III, "STOREHOUSE OF ALL VIRTUES": q. ibid. "HIGHEST HOPES": ibid., 200.

92   "IMMODERATE . . . PROMISES": Guicciardini, q. Routh, 99.

93   JULIUS, CHARACTER AND CONDUCT: Pastor, VI, 213; Gilbert, 125–7. LITTLE BELL ON TABLE: Gilbert, 124.

94   IN HELMET AND MAIL: Guicciardini, q. Routh, 100–1. "CERTAINLY A SIGHT VERY UNCOMMON": ibid.

95   "DETERMINED TO VINDICATE": Pastor, VI, 329–31. "TO HANG A COUNCIL": ibid. "TO LEAD AN ARMY TO ROME": ibid.

95   "THE FRENCH IN ROME . . .": q. ibid. "*Fuori i barbari!*": Aubenas, 156.

95   MATTHÄUS SCHINNER: Pastor, VI, 325; Oechsli, 33, 54.

95   ERASMUS ON JULIUS: *Querela Pacis* of 1517, q. *New Cambridge*, I, 82; Aubenas, 243.

96   "A MONK DANCING IN SPURS": q. Pastor, VI, 360.

96   "OUTSIDE OF ALL REASON": q. Gilbert, 123.

96   CRITIC QUOTED, "BECAUSE THEY GRIEVED": q. Young, 276.

96   BUILDING ST. PETER'S: Vasari; Ullmann, 317; Mitchell, 52.

97   *Il ruinante*: Lees-Milne, 142.

97   JULIUS AND MICHELANGELO: Vasari, chap. on Michelangelo, passim.

97   "PUT A SWORD THERE": Vasari, 266.

98   REDISCOVERY OF LAOCOON: Pastor, VI, 488; Calvesi, 125; Hibbert, Notes, 325; Coughlan, 103; Lees-Milne, 141; Rodocanachi, *Jules II*, 58–60.

99   CARDINAL WROTE AN ODE TO IT: Rodocanachi, *Jules II*, 60, n. 2. FRANCIS I TRIED TO CLAIM IT: Hibbert, 222.

100   JOHN COLET'S SERMON: Olin, 31–9.

100   BOLOGNESE JURIST WARNED: Giovanni Gozzadini, q. Jedin, 40.

100   EGIDIO OF VITERBO'S ORATION: Olin, 44–53; Pastor, VI, 407.

101   PRESERVE HIS ASCETIC PALLOR: Burckhardt, 169.

101   DECREES OF THE FIFTH LATERAN: Hughes, 480; *New Cambridge*, 92.

102   FRENCH "VANISHED LIKE MIST": q. Pastor, VI, 416.

102   THANKSGIVING PROCESSION: Aubenas, 165.

103   ERASMUS, *Julius Exclusus*: q. Hale, 226.

103   "VIRTUE WITHOUT POWER": q. Pastor, VI, 452.

5. Leo X

p. 104   "LET US ENJOY IT": Pastor, VIII, 76.

104   LEO'S CHARACTER AND CONDUCT: ibid., 71 ff.; Guicciardini and Vettori, q. Routh, 104–05; Chamberlin, 209–48.

p. 104 LEO'S LATERAN PROCESSION: Gregorovius, VIII, 180–8; Lortz, 92.

105 LEO'S EXPENDITURES: Pastor, VII, 341; VIII, 99–100; Hughes, 434.

105 MARBLE FROM PIETRASANTA: Vasari, 271. "IMPOSSIBLE TO DEAL WITH": de Tolnay, 4.

106 WOULD HAVE MADE RAPHAEL A CARDINAL: Vasari, 231.

106 CHIGI'S BANQUET: Gregorovius, VIII, 244; Pastor, VIII, 117.

106 LEO'S HABITS AND APPEARANCE: Pastor, VII, VIII, passim; Calvesi, 149. PAOLO GIOVIO QUOTED: Chamberlin, 218.

107 MICHELANGELO, "A THOUSAND YEARS FROM NOW": de Tolnay, 68.

107 CARDINAL BIBBIENA: Pastor, VIII, 111–12. "GOD BE PRAISED": Ranke, I, 54; Mitchell, 14.

107 PROCESSION OF THE WHITE ELEPHANT: Pastor, VII, 75.

108 GREEK "IMMORTALS" INVOKED: Mitchell, 88.

108 "HAVING MADE A TREATY . . .": q. Chamberlin, 228.

108 CONCORDAT OF BOLOGNA: Hughes, 448–9.

109 PLANNING TO PALM OFF A COPY: Gregorovius, VIII, 210.

109 LEO'S NEPOTISM: Young, 297, and others.

109 ENVOY SEIZED DESPITE A SAFE-CONDUCT: Chamberlin, 231; WAR ON URBINO: Aubenas, 182; Pastor, VIII, 92.

110 PETRUCCI CONSPIRACY: Hughes, 431; Mitchell, 109–14; Schaff, 486.

110 CREATED 31 CARDINALS IN A DAY: Young, 299.

111 BAGLIONI BEHEADED: ibid., 300.

111 LEO'S BULLFIGHT: Pastor, VIII, 173.

111 RISING DISSENT: ibid., VIII, 177; Hughes, 491.

111 CORTESE AND PICO DELLA MIRANDOLA: Pastor, VIII, 407.

112 ERASMUS, "AS TO THESE SUPREME PONTIFFS": *Colloquies*, 33, 98–9. "PESTILENCE TO CHRISTENDOM": q. Huizinga, 141.

112 MACHIAVELLI CASTIGATES CHURCH: *Discourses*, Bk I, chap. XII.

113 "THIS BARBAROUS DOMINATION": *The Prince*, chap. XXVI. "REVERENCE FOR THE PAPACY": Guicciardini, 149.

113 COLET, CHURCH A MACHINE FOR MAKING MONEY: Hale, 232.

114 INDULGENCES FOR FUTURE SINS: Schaff, 766.

114 TETZEL'S SALES: Dickens, 61. "I HAVE HERE . . .": q. Chamberlin, 241–2.

115 LEO MORE CONCERNED BY RAPHAEL'S DEATH: Lees-Milne, 147.

116 "HELL-HOUND IN ROME": q. Dickens, 23.

116 LEO'S DEATH AND DEBTS: Hughes, 431, 434; Rodocanachi, *Adrian VI*, 7; Vettori, from his *Storia d'Italia*, q. Routh, 104–05. LAMPOON: Mitchell, 122.

117 CARDINALS HISSED: Mitchell, 125.

6. Clement VII

p. 118 CARDINAL SCHINNER MISSED ELECTION BY TWO VOTES: Oechsli, 25.

118 ELECTION OF ADRIAN: Pastor, IX, 25–31, 45; "JUST TO WASTE THE MORNING": ibid., 329. ATTRIBUTED TO THE HOLY GHOST: Guicciardini, 330. HIS CHARACTER: Mitchell, 126; Burckhardt, 169.

118 "UNDER PAIN OF ETERNAL DAMNATION": q. Pastor, IX, 91.

118 "THOSE STEEPED IN SIN": q. ibid., 92.

119 "EVERYONE TREMBLES . . .": q. ibid., 94–5.

p. 119 ADRIAN'S MEASURES: Ranke, I, 73–4; Pastor, IX, 52, 70–4 ff. "SACRED THINGS . . . MISUSED": q. Lortz, 95. "HOW MUCH . . . DEPENDS": Ranke, I, 74; Pastor, IX, 125.

120 CLEMENT'S CHARACTER: Guicciardini, q. Chamberlin, 258; Routh, 104. "GIVES AWAY NOTHING": Marco Foscari, q. Chamberlin, 260. VETTORI, "FROM A GREAT . . .": from his *Sommario*, q. Gilbert, 252.

120 CHARLES V ON POPE'S DOUBLE DEALING: q. Chamberlin, 265.

121 TWO ENGLISH ENVOYS: q. Lopez, 39.

121 COLONNA UPRISING: Guicciardini, 372.

122 "WE ARE ON THE BRINK OF RUIN": Giberti, q. Chamberlin, 273.

122 SACK OF ROME: Pastor, IX, 370–429; Partner, *Renaissance Rome*, 31. "A STONE TO COMPASSION": Pastor, IX, 399, and n. 4.

123 "HELL HAS NOTHING TO COMPARE": ibid., 400.

123 COMMENTS OF IMPERIAL ARMY COMMISSARY: Mercurino de Gattinara, q. Routh, 106–09. CAJETAN: q. Hughes, 474, n. 4.

124 CLEMENT'S SIEGE OF FLORENCE: Brion, 167, and others.

124 CLEMENT'S DEATH: Guicciardini, q. Chamberlin, 285. CORPSE HACKED: Brion, 167.

125 "UNABLE TO RECOVER ANYTHING OF MY OWN": q. Chamberlin, 285.

Chapter Four

THE BRITISH LOSE AMERICA

WORKS CONSULTED

Primary Sources

ALMON, JOHN. *Anecdotes of the Life of William Pitt, Earl of Chatham.* 3 vols. London, 1793.

BARRINGTON, SHUTE, BISHOP OF DURHAM. *The Political Life of William Wildman, Viscount Barrington,* by his brother. London, 1814.

BURKE, EDMUND. *Correspondence.* Ed. C. W. Fitzwilliam and R. Bourke. 4 vols. London, 1844.

——. *Speeches and Letters on American Affairs.* Ed. Canon Peter McKevitt. London, 1961 (orig. 1908).

——. *Writings and Speeches.* 12 vols. Boston, 1901.

CHESTERFIELD, PHILIP STANHOPE, 4TH EARL. *Letters.* Ed. Bonamy Dobrée. 6 vols. London, 1932.

DELANY, MARY GRANVILLE. *Autobiography and Correspondence.* Ed. Lady Llanover. 6 vols. London, 1861–62.

FITZMAURICE, LORD EDMOND. *Life of William, Earl of Shelburne.* 3 vols. London, 1876. (Includes letters and diaries.)

FRANKLIN, BENJAMIN. *Autobiography.* Ed. John Bigelow. Philadelphia, 1881.

——. *Letters and Papers of Benjamin Franklin and Richard Jackson, 1753–85.* Ed. Carl Van Doren. Philadelphia, 1947.

GEORGE III. *Correspondence, 1760–1783.* Ed. Sir John Fortescue. 6 vols. London, 1927–28. (All citations refer to this edition unless otherwise noted.)

——. *Correspondence of, with Lord North.* Ed. W. Bodham Donne. 2 vols. London, 1867.

GRAFTON, AUGUSTUS HENRY, 3RD DUKE. *Autobiography and Political Correspondence.* Ed. Sir William Anson. London, 1898.

HANSARD. *Parliamentary History of England.* 36 vols. London, 1806–20.

PITT, WILLIAM, EARL OF CHATHAM. *Correspondence.* Ed. William S. Taylor and John H. Pringle. 4 vols. London, 1838–40.

ROCKINGHAM, CHARLES, 2ND MARQUESS. *Memoirs.* Ed. Earl of Albemarle. 2 vols. London, 1852.

STEVENS, B. F. *Facsimiles of Mss in European Archives Relating to America.* 25 vols. London, 1889–95.

WALPOLE, HORACE. *Memoirs of the Reign of George III.* Ed. Denis Le Marchant. 4 vols. London, 1845.

——. *Last Journals, 1771–83.* 2 vols. London, 1859.

——. *Correspondence.* Ed. Wilmarth Lewis. 48 vols. New Haven, Yale Univ. Press, 1937–83.

Secondary Sources

ALLEN, H. C. *Great Britain and the United States: A History of Anglo-American Relations, 1783–1952.* New York, 1955.

AYLING, STANLEY. *The Elder Pitt.* New York, 1976.

——. *The Georgian Century, 1714–1837.* London, 1966.

BAILYN, BERNARD. *The Ideological Origins of the American Revolution.* Cambridge, Mass., Harvard Univ. Press, 1967.

——. *The Ordeal of Thomas Hutchinson.* Harvard Univ. Press, 1974.

BARGAR, B. D. *Lord Dartmouth and the American Revolution.* Columbia, Univ. of South Carolina Press, 1965.

BEER, GEORGE L. *British Colonial Policy, 1754–65.* Gloucester, Mass., 1958.

BELOFF, MAX. *The Age of Absolutism, 1660–1815.* London, 1966 (orig. 1954).

——. *The Debate on the American Revolution, 1761–1783.* London, 1949.

BONWICK, COLIN. *English Radicals and the American Revolution.* Chapel Hill, Univ. of North Carolina Press, 1977.

BOULTON, JAMES T. *The Language of Politics in the Age of Wilkes and Burke.* London, 1963.

BREWER, JOHN. *Party Ideology and Popular Politics at the Accession of George III.* Cambridge, Cambridge Univ. Press, 1976.

BROOKE, JOHN. *King George III.* New York, 1972.

BROUGHAM, HENRY, LORD. *Historical Sketches of Statesmen in the Time of George III.* 2 vols. Philadelphia, 1839.

BROWN, WELDON A. *Empire or Independence; a Study in the Failure of Reconciliation, 1774–1783.* Baton Rouge, Louisiana State Univ. Press, 1941.

BUTTERFIELD, SIR HERBERT. *George III and the Historians.* New York, 1959 (orig. 1936).

CLARK, DORA MAE. *British Opinion and the American Revolution.* New Haven, Yale Univ. Press, 1930.

COPEMAN, DR. W.S.C. *A Short History of the Gout.* Berkeley, Univ. of California Press, 1964.

DERRY, JOHN W. *Charles James Fox.* New York, 1972.

Dictionary of National Biography. 22 vols. London, 1908–

FEILING, KEITH GRAHAME. *The Second Tory Party, 1714–1832.* London, 1938.

FOSTER, CORNELIUS. *Charles Townshend and His American Policy.* Providence, R.I., 1978.

GIPSON, LAWRENCE H. *The British Empire Before the American Revolution.* 15 vols. New York, 1958–70.

GRIFFITH, SAMUEL B., II. *In Defense of the Public Liberty: Britain, America and the Struggle for Independence, 1760–81.* New York, 1976.

GUTTRIDGE, G. H. *English Whiggism and the American Revolution.* Berkeley, Univ. of California Press, 1942.

HARLOW, VINCENT T. *The Founding of the Second British Empire, 1763–1793.* Vol. 1. London, 1952.

HINKHOUSE, FRED J. *The Preliminaries of the American Revolution as Seen in the English Press, 1763–75.* New York, Columbia Univ. Press, 1926.

HOFFMAN, ROSS J. S. *The Marquis; a Study of Lord Rockingham, 1730–1782.* New York, 1973.

HYAMS, EDWARD. *Capability Brown.* New York, 1971.

JARRETT, DEREK. *England in the Age of Hogarth.* New York, 1974.

JESSE, JOHN HENEAGE. *Memoirs of the Life and Reign of George III.* 3 vols. London, 1867.

KNOLLENBERG, BERNHARD. *Origin of the American Revolution: 1759–1766.* New York, 1960.

——. *Growth of the American Revolution: 1766–1775.* New York, 1975.

LABAREE, BENJAMIN W. *The Boston Tea Party.* New York, 1964.

LAVER, JAMES. *The Age of Illusion: Manners and Morals, 1750–1848.* New York, 1972.

LECKY, WILLIAM E. H. *History of England in the 18th Century.* Vols. III & IV. London, 1921 & 1923.

MACAULAY, THOMAS BABINGTON, LORD. "William Pitt, Earl of Chatham," in two parts, *Critical and Historical Essays.* Vols. II & III. Boston, 1901.

MACKESY, PIERS. *The War for America, 1775–1783.* Cambridge, Mass., 1964.

MEAD, WILLIAM E. *The Grand Tour in the 18th Century.* Boston and New York, 1914.

MILLER, JOHN C. *Origins of the American Revolution.* Stanford Univ. Press, and London, 1959 (orig. 1943). (All citations from Miller refer to this book unless otherwise noted.)

——. *The Triumph of Freedom.* Boston, 1948.

MINGARY, G. E. *English Landed Society in the 18th Century.* London, 1963.

MORGAN, EDMUND S. *Birth of the Republic, 1763–89.* Chicago, Univ. of Chicago Press, 1956.

——. *The Gentle Puritan: A Life of Ezra Stiles, 1727–95.* New Haven, Yale Univ. Press, 1962.

——, AND MORGAN, HELEN. *The Stamp Act Crisis.* Chapel Hill, Univ. of North Carolina Press, 1953.

MUMBY, FRANK A. *George III and the American Revolution.* London, 1923.

NAMIER, SIR LEWIS. *The Structure of Politics at the Accession of George III.* 2nd ed. London, 1957.

——. *England in the Age of the American Revolution.* London, 1961 (orig. 1930).

——. *Crossroads of Power; Essays on 18th Century England.* New York, 1962.

——, AND BROOKE, JOHN. *Charles Townshend.* London, 1964.

NICOLSON, HAROLD. *The Age of Reason, 1700–1789.* London, 1960.

OLSON, ALISON G. *The Radical Duke: Charles Lennox, Third Duke of Richmond.* Oxford, 1961.

PARES, RICHARD. *King George III and the Politicians.* Oxford Univ. Press, 1953.

PLUMB, J. H. *England in the 18th Century, 1714–1815.* London, 1950.

——. *Chatham.* Hamden, Conn., 1965.

——. *In the Light of History.* Boston, 1973.

RITCHESON, CHARLES R. *British Politics and the American Revolution.* Norman, Univ. of Oklahoma Press, 1954.

ROBERTSON, SIR CHARLES GRANT. *Chatham and the British Empire.* London, 1946.

SACHSE, WILLIAM L. *The Colonial American in Britain.* Madison, Univ. of Wisconsin Press, 1956.

SAINSBURY, JOHN. "The Pro-Americans of London, 1769 to 1782." *William and Mary Quarterly.* July 1978, 423–54.

SCHLESINGER, ARTHUR, SR. *The Colonial Merchants and the American Revolution, 1773–76.* New York, 1939.

SHERSON, ERROL H. S. *The Lively Lady Townshend.* New York, 1927.

THOMAS, PETER D. G. *British Politics and the Stamp Act Crisis.* Oxford Univ. Press, 1975.

TREVELYAN, SIR GEORGE OTTO. *The American Revolution.* 3 vols. London, 1921–22.

VALENTINE, ALAN. *The British Establishment, 1760–1784; An Eighteenth Century Biographical Dictionary.* 2 vols. Norman, Univ. of Oklahoma Press, 1970.

——. *Lord George Germain.* Oxford, 1962.

——. *Lord North.* 2 vols. Norman, Univ. of Oklahoma Press, 1967.

VAN DOREN, CARL. *Benjamin Franklin.* New York, 1952 (orig. 1938).

WATSON, J. STEVEN. *The Reign of George III.* Oxford Univ. Press, 1960.

WICKWIRE, FRANKLIN B. *British Subministers and Colonial America, 1763–1783.* Princeton Univ. Press, 1966.

WILLIAMS, BASIL. *The Life of William Pitt, Earl of Chatham.* 2 vols. London, 1966 (orig. 1913).

——. *The Whig Supremacy.* Oxford Univ. Press, 1962 (orig. 1938).

WINSTANLEY, DENYS A. *Lord Chatham and the Whig Opposition.* Cambridge Univ. Press, 1912.

REFERENCE NOTES

The well-known events and developments of British politics, of colonial affairs leading to the Revolution and of the War of the Revolution itself are not annotated as they can easily be found in the relevant sources listed above. References are reserved for quotations and for the comparatively less well-known facts and incidents. The source for biographical facts and matters of personality, if not otherwise stated, may be understood to be the *DNB* or Valentine's *Estab-*

lishment. Statements in Parliament may be found under the given date in the relevant volumes of Hansard's *Parliamentary History:* XVI (Jan 1765–Nov 1770), XVII (Feb 1771–Jan 1774), XVIII (Nov 1774–Oct 1776), XIX (Jan 1777–Dec 1778).

1. Who's In, Who's Out

p. 128 BURKE, "THE RETENTION OF AMERICA": q. Allen, 239.

129 "TO FIX UPON US . . .": q. Knollenberg, *Origin,* 91. "IN PROPER SUBJECTION": ibid., 92, 318, n. 17.

130 "PARLIAMENTARY CABALS": q. Brooke, 226.

131 "TORRENT OF IMPETUOUS ELOQUENCE": John Adams, q. Bailyn, *Ordeal,* 56.

131 1732, "PARLIAMENT WOULD FIND IT . . .": q. Morgan, *Stamp Act,* 4.

131 WALPOLE, "NO! IT IS TOO HAZARDOUS . . .": q. Jesse, I, 251.

132 PITT, "THE POOREST MAN": Hansard, XV, 1307.

132 DASHWOOD, KNOWLEDGE OF FIGURES: Rockingham, *Memoirs,* I, 117. "PEOPLE WILL POINT AT ME . . .": q. Walpole, *Memoirs,* I, 152.

133 GEORGE III, "LORD NORTH CANNOT SERIOUSLY THINK": q. Pares, 57.

133 GRENVILLE, "THE ABLEST MAN OF BUSINESS": Walpole, *Memoirs,* IV, 188.

134 MRS. ARMSTEAD: Valentine, *Germain,* 471, n. 3.

135 23 ELDEST SONS OF PEERS: Namier, *Structure,* 2.

135 GEORGE SELWYN NEVER WENT TO BARBADOS: Laver, 73.

135 SHELBURNE, "THE ONLY PLEASURE": q. Fitzmaurice, I, 88.

135 WALPOLE, "PASSION FOR THE FRONT RANK": *Memoirs,* II, 164.

136 SHELBURNE, "COME DOWN WITH THEIR LOUNGING OPINIONS": q. in Grafton, Introduction by Anson, xxxiv.

136 LADIES ADVERTISED THEIR CARD PARTIES: Sherson, 44.

136 VILLAGE OF STOWE RELOCATED: Hyams, 15. PLANTINGS AT KNOLE: Valentine, *Germain,* 5.

136 ROME'S GOVERNMENT "THE WORST POSSIBLE": q. Mead, 317.

137 DARTMOUTH SAT FOR EIGHTEEN PORTRAITS: Bargar, 6.

137 DR. JOHNSON, "BUT TWO MEN": q. Lecky, III, 385–6.

137 PITT, "COWED FOR LIFE": q. Fitzmaurice, I, 72.

137 MANSFIELD, "YOU COULD NOT ENTERTAIN ME": q. Hoffman, 11.

138 WALDEGRAVE ON GEORGE III: q. Brooke, 222; Namier, *Crossroads,* 131.

138 GEORGE III ON KING ALFRED: q. Namier, *England,* 93.

138 "BLACKEST OF HEARTS" AND "SNAKE IN THE GRASS": q. Watson, 4.

140 ADMIRAL ANSON, "I MUST NOW BEG": q. Namier, *Structure,* 34.

141 LORD NORTH'S INSTRUCTIONS IN ELECTION OF 1774: q. Trevelyan, I, 201.

141 YORKSHIRE M.P. "SAT TWELVE HOURS": q. Namier, *Crossroads,* 32.

142 RICHARD JACKSON, "I HAVE ACCESS TO": *Letters and Papers of Franklin and Jackson,* 138.

142 BOARD OF TRADE ASKED TO ADVISE ON "LEAST BURTHENSOME": Beer, 275.

143 GRENVILLE, "ALL MEN WISH NOT TO BE TAXED": q. ibid., 285.

143 WALPOLE ON GRANBY: *Memoirs,* IV, 179.

143 FOX, "TEN BOTTLES OF WINE": q. Trevelyan, I, 205.

143 WALPOLE ON EGREMONT: q. Valentine, *Establishment,* II, 950.

144 "TO THE INFINITE PREJUDICE": q. Knollenberg, *Origin,* 105.

145 6500 TONS OF FLOUR: T. H. White, *Age of Scandal* (London, 1950), 32.

p. 145   WOLFE ON AMERICAN SOLDIERS: q. Knollenberg, *Origin*, I, 120, 330, n. 17.
AMHERST ON SAME: ibid., 120. GENERAL MURRAY ON SAME: *Letters from
America, 1775–80, of a Scots Officer, Sir James Murray, During the War
of American Independence*, ed. Eric Robson. Manchester University
Press, 1951. GENERAL CLARKE, "WITH A THOUSAND GRENADIERS": q. Benjamin
Franklin, *Writings*, IX, 261.

145   DIFFERENT NATURE OF MILITARY SERVICE: This point, drawn from im-
pressive original research, has been made very persuasively by F. W.
Anderson in "Why Did Colonial New Englanders Make Bad Soldiers?,"
William and Mary Quarterly, XXXVIII, No. 3, July 1981, 395–414.

147   FOOTNOTE ON FRANKLIN'S MOTIVATION: suggested by Knollenberg, *Origin*,
155.

147   "IN GOD'S NAME": Morgan, *Stamp Act*, 54, n. 3.

148   RESISTANCE TO POLICE FORCE AND CENSUS: Jarrett, 34, 36.

148   THE SPEAKER ON THE CENSUS WAS SIR WILLIAM THORNTON IN PARLIAMENT:
Hansard, XIV, 1318–22.

2. "*Asserting a Right You Know You Cannot Exert*"

p. 150   MACAULAY, "AS LONG AS THE GLOBE LASTS": III, 647.

150   HUTCHINSON'S TREATISE: Bailyn, *Ordeal*, 62–3.

150   FRANKLIN, "A DISGUST OF THESE": q. Van Doren, 333.

151   GRENVILLE'S DISCUSSIONS WITH THE AGENTS AND THEIR OFFERS: Morgan,
Stamp Act, 53–70. MASSACHUSETTS ASSEMBLY: ibid., 60. GARTH'S STATE-
MENT: ibid., 58, n. 15. INGERSOLL ON "DREADFUL APPREHENSIONS": ibid., 62.
WHATELY, "SOME TAXES": q. Wickwire, 103. GOVERNOR HOPKINS'S PAMPHLET:
Morgan, op. cit., 36.

152   NEW YORK ASSEMBLY: ibid., 37.

152   HEARINGS IN PARLIAMENT, JACKSON, GARTH, TOWNSHEND, BARRE, 6–7 FEB 65:
Hansard, XVI. INGERSOLL'S COMMENT: q. Knollenberg, *Origin*, 224.

153   TRINITY COLLEGE, "HALF BEAR GARDEN": q. Valentine, *Germain*, 10.

153   SECOND READING, CONWAY: 15 Feb 65, Hansard, XVI.

154   STAMP TAX ENACTED, COMMENTS ON: WALPOLE, "LITTLE UNDERSTOOD":
Memoirs, II, 49; WHATELY: q. Knollenberg, *Origin*, 225; SEDGEWICK, ibid.;
HUTCHINSON, "WE ARE ALL SLAVES": q. Bailyn, *Ordeal*, 71.

155   "AFRAID OF WHAT?": ibid.; EZRA STILES' REPORT: q. Morgan, *Stiles*, 233.

155   HOMESPUN FLAX "FINE ENOUGH": Mason, George C., *Reminiscences of
Newport*, Newport, 1884, 358.

155   "SEAS ROLL AND MONTHS PASS": Burke, in Parliament, 22 Mar 75.

156   ADAMS, "A VENAL CITY": q. Bailyn, *Ideological*, 136.

156   "SPAWN OF OUR TRANSPORTS": q. Miller, *Origins*, 229. "MONGREL BREED":
q. ibid., 203.

156   "VIRTUAL REPRESENTATION": Miller, 279.

157   BERNARD'S PLAN: Beloff, *Debate*, 86–8; Morgan, *Stamp Act*, 14.

157   HALIFAX' COMMENT: Morgan, *Stamp Act*, 19.

157   FRANKLIN, "AWE THE WORLD!": to Lord Kames, 3 Jan 60, *Writings*, IV, 4.
"I AM STILL OF THE OPINION": *Autobiography*, Part III, 165.

158   SOAME JENYN'S PAMPHLET: q. Beloff, *Debate*, 27, 77.

p. 158 CHESTERFIELD, "ASSERTING A RIGHT": letter of 25 Feb 66, *Letters*, VI, no. 2410. GENERAL GAGE: q. Burke, in Parliament, 19 Apr 74, Hansard, XVIII.

159 PITT, MADNESS IN FAMILY: Fitzmaurice, I, 71. GOUT: cf. Copeman, 95.

160 "I KNOW I CAN SAVE": q. Macaulay, II, 272. WALPOLE, "WE ARE FORCED TO ASK": q. *DNB* on Pitt. "CLUNG TO THE WHEELS": Macaulay, III, 617. "BEING RESPONSIBLE": q. Williams, *Pitt*, II, 113. "UNATTACHED TO ANY PARTY": q. Robertson, 69. "I CANNOT BEAR": ibid., 2.

161 "SAGE AND AWFUL": ibid., 16. "TRIED IT ON PAPER": Fitzmaurice, I, 76, n.

162 NORTHINGTON, "IF I HAD KNOWN": q. Feiling, 93. BARRINGTON, "SOME FORTUNE": q. ibid., 71.

164 GERMAIN, "IF YOU UNDERSTAND": q. Morgan, *Stamp Act*, 274.

164 BEDFORD, DEBATE IN THE LORDS: q. Thomas, 365.

164 ORGANIZED PRESSURE FOR REPEAL: Clark, 41, 44–5; Miller, 155. FRANKLIN, "UNLESS COMPELLED . . . THEY WILL NOT FIND A REBELLION": in Parliament, Hansard, XVI, 137. "AN OVERWHELMING MAJORITY": Winstanley, 109.

165 WALPOLE, "RISK LIGHTING UP": written in 1768, *Memoirs*, II, 218.

165 CAMDEN, "SOME THINGS YOU CANNOT DO": q. Allen, 242.

165 "FACE OF AN ANGEL": *DNB*, Conway. REACTIONS TO REPEAL: Hinkhouse, 74–5; Miller, 159–60; Griffith, 45. ADAMS, "QUIET AND SUBMISSIVE": q. Trevelyan, I, 2.

3. Folly Under Full Sail

p. 167 "WICKED AND DESIGNING MEN": q. Bailyn, *Ideological*, 151.

167 TOWNSHEND, "IF WE ONCE LOSE": q. Miller, 240.

168 "TO DISMISS MY MINISTRY": q. Knollenberg, *Growth*, 35.

168 FRANKLIN ON HILLSBOROUGH: q. Van Doren, 383. BURKE, A "DIVERSIFIED MOSAIC": in Parliament, 19 Apr 74.

169 CONWAY, "SUCH LANGUAGE": q. Macaulay, III, 672. CHATHAM ON NEW YORK: q. Ayling, *Pitt*, 364.

169 "CONTINUOUS CABALS": Franklin, *Autobiography*, Part I, 532. GRAFTON "COMES ONCE A WEEK": Walpole, *Memoirs*, III, 391. GRAFTON KNEW HIMSELF UNFIT: Brooke, 226.

169 TOWNSHEND, BURKE ON: in Parliament, 19 Apr 74. WALPOLE ON, "GREATEST MAN": q. *DNB*; "STUDIED NOTHING": *Memoirs*, II, 275. NEWCASTLE ON: q. Namier, *Crossroads*, 195. DAVID HUME ON: ibid.

170 WALPOLE, "NOT THE LEAST MAD": q. Sherson, 16. "DROPS DOWN IN A FIT": q. Namier, *Crossroads*, 195. TOWNSHEND, "TO HAVE NO PARTY": q. ibid., 201.

170 TOWNSHEND INTRODUCES BUDGET: ibid., 210; Miller, 242, 250.

171 PROPOSES CUSTOMS DUTIES: Winstanley, 111. CABINET SUBMITS: Grafton, 126–7, 175–9; Walpole, *Memoirs*, III, 51, n.; Winstanley, 141, 144; Namier and Brooke, passim.

172 GARTH, "THE FRIENDS OF AMERICA": Knollenberg, *Growth*, 301, n. 33.

172 "POOR CHARLES TOWNSHEND": Sir William Meredith, q. Foster, viii.

173 LADY CHATHAM AND GRAFTON ON CHATHAM'S ILLNESS: Ayling, *Pitt*, 369; Williams, *Pitt*, II, 242.

173 AT PYNSENT AND HAYES: Walpole, *Memoirs*, III, 41–2. THE IRASCIBLE OWNER: Bargar, 16. CAMDEN, "THEN HE IS MAD": ibid.

174 GOUT AND DR. ADDINGTON: Williams, *Pitt*, II, 242–3.

p. 174 MADNESS, OTIS: Bailyn, *Ordeal*, 72; ORFORD: Nicolson, 253. SACKVILLE BROTHERS: Fitzmaurice, I, 343; Valentine, *Germain*, 466–70; Mackesy, 51. DUCHESS OF QUEENSBERRY: Jack Lindsay, *1764*, London, 1959. LORD GEORGE GORDON: Feiling, 136.

174 FEAR OF THE PATRIOTS AS "LEVELLERS": Knollenberg, *Growth*, 48.

176 GEORGE III ON HILLSBOROUGH: q. Miller, 261.

176 "TO HAVE A STANDING ARMY!": Andrew Eliot, q. Bailyn, *Ideological*, 114.

177 NEWCASTLE PROTESTS USE OF FORCE: q. Knollenberg, *Growth*, 14.

177 WEYMOUTH, "TO THE TOTAL NEGLECT": Walpole, *Memoirs*, III, 135–6; See also Macaulay, III, 600.

178 GEORGE III, "IT WAS THE INDISPENSABLE": q. by Shelburne to Sir Henry Moore, Governor of New York, 9 Aug 66, q. Mumby, 161.

178 "NOT A HOBNAIL OR A HORSESHOE": q. Ayling, *Pitt*, 340.

179 GRADUATING CLASS OF HARVARD AND RHODE ISLAND COLLEGE: Alice M. Earle, *Colonial Dames and Goodwives*, Boston, 1895, 241.

179 FRANKLIN ON "LAWLESS RIOTS": *Autobiography*, II, 10.

179 "THE PERSONS WHO WISH": q. Sainsbury, 433. COUNCILMEN AND ALDERMEN: ibid.

180 WILLIAM BECKFORD, WALPOLE ON: q. Valentine, *Establishment*, I, 68.

180 *London Magazine* AND PUBLIC OPINION: Hinkhouse, 20, 147; Bonwick, 64. RALPH IZARD: q. Miller, 449.

180 GRAFTON'S MISTRESS: Jesse, I, 460; Laver, 72–3.

181 "SO ANTI-COMMERCIAL": q. Miller, 277. "SO PREPOSTEROUS": ibid.

181 HILLSBOROUGH RESURRECTS STATUTE OF HENRY VIII: Winstanley, 252.

182 BECKFORD, "A STRANGE PIECE OF POLICY": 14 Mar 69, Hansard, XVI, 605. POWNALL'S SPEECH: 15 Mar 69, ibid., 612–20.

183 HILLSBOROUGH OMITS "SOOTHING . . . EXPRESSION": Valentine, *North*, I, 176.

183 "IF YOU WOULD BE BUT STEADY": q. Bailyn, *Ordeal*, 83–4.

183 BOSTON PRESS REPORTS: Earle, op. cit., 243.

184 CHATHAM, "DISCONTENT OF TWO MILLIONS": in the Lords, 9 Jan 70, Hansard, XVI, 650. CAMDEN HUNG HIS HEAD IN CABINET: ibid., q. Williams, *Pitt*, II, 264.

184 YORKE'S SUICIDE: Walpole, *Memoirs*, IV, 51–2; Feiling, 111.

184 NORTH, DESCRIBES A CHIEF MINISTER: q. Brooks, 187.

185 HIS RESEMBLANCE TO GEORGE III: Feiling, 102. ONLY ONE MAN MADE HIM ANGRY: Jesse, II, 208; Robertson, 137. GIBBON ON: q. *DNB*. "A HUNDRED YEARS TOO SOON": q. Watson, 149. FOX, "HE WAS SO FAR FROM LEADING": q. Valentine, *North*.

186 WISH TO REPEAL TOWNSHEND DUTIES: q. Knollenberg, *Origin*, 244. KING GIVES HIM £20,000: Valentine, *North*, I, 460.

186 DEBATES, MARCH–MAY 1770: Hansard, XVI; BARRÉ, 709–12; POWNALL, 856–69; SIR WILLIAM MEREDITH, 872–3.

187 MOTION DEFEATED, 204–142: 873; POWNALL RETURNS TO OFFENSIVE: 8 May 70, 980–5.

187 BURKE, GOLDSMITH ON: q. Lecky, III, 385; DR. JOHNSON ON: q. ibid., WALPOLE ON: q. ibid., 394. IN COMMONS: 9 Jan 70, Hansard, XVI, 672–3, 720–25.

188 8 MAY 70 RESOLUTIONS: 1001–09. "MALIGNITY OF YOUR WILL": 1005.

p. 188 RICHMOND: PERIODS OF DEPRESSION: letter of 10 Mar 69, q. Olson, 11.
189 "NO, LET ME ENJOY MYSELF": q. Trevelyan, I, 130. ON MINISTERIAL CONDUCT: Hansard, XVI, 1009–13.
189 HILLSBOROUGH'S REPLY: ibid., 1016–19.
189 "DOWDESWELL WAS DEVILISH SULKY": letter of 12 Feb 71, q. Olson, 43.
190 "WITH HOUND AND HORN": q. Trevelyan, I, 131.
190 COLONIES DISAVOW INDEPENDENCE: Schlesinger, 228.

4. "Remember Rehoboam!"

p. 191 *Gaspée* INCIDENT: Wickwire, 142; Miller, 326–9; Morgan, *Birth*, 54–5.
191 "TEN THOUSAND DEATHS": q. Morgan, *Stiles*, 261.
192 THURLOW: Feiling, 81; FOX ON: q. Brougham, I, 116; WEDDERBURN, "EVEN TREACHERY": attributed to Junius, q. Williams, *Pitt*, II, 277.
193 DARTMOUTH: Bargar, passim.
193 "WOMEN ARE SUCH SLAVES TO IT": q. Miller, 343.
194 BARRE, AMERICANS WERE NEGROES: Jesse, II, 400.
194 QUINCY, "IN *all* COMPANIES": q. Bonwick, 78.
194 HILLSBOROUGH, "INHERENT PRE-EMINENCE": q. Miller, 206.
194 ROCKINGHAM, "CHILDREN [WHO] OUGHT TO BE DUTIFUL": q. Valentine, *North*, I, 170.
195 CHATHAM, "IF THIS HAPPENS": q. Williams, *Pitt*, II, 297.
195 CHATHAM, "IF LIBERTY BE NOT COUNTENANCED": speech of 27 Jan 66, q. Williams, *Pitt*, II, 198. "A POOR DESERTED DEPLORABLE KINGDOM": q. Miller, 207. LETTERS TO THE PRESS: Hinkhouse, 106–10.
195 AMERICAN COMMENTS ON TEA DUTY: q. Miller, 342–3.
197 FRANKLIN IN THE COCKPIT: Trevelyan, I, 162. WEARS SAME VELVET SUIT: from *Memoirs* of William Temple Franklin, q. in *Papers of Benjamin Franklin*, ed. William Willcox, New Haven, Yale Univ. Press, 1978. Vol. 21, 41, n. 9.
197 BOSTON PORT BILL DEBATE: Hansard, XVII, 1199–1201, 1210, 1281, 1282–6. JOHNSTONE'S WARNING: q. Gipson, XII, 114.
198 ROARS OF "POPERY": q. Miller, 375–6; Hinkhouse, 172.
199 JOHNSTONE, "A GREAT DISPOSITION": debate of 22 Apr 74, Hansard, XVII, 1281.
199 DUNNING, "WAR, SEVERE REVENGE": q. Labarée, 199. HOWE'S OPINION: q. Trevelyan, I, 262. BURGOYNE, "TO SEE AMERICA CONVINCED": debate on repeal of the Tea Act, 19 Apr 74, Hansard, XVII, 1271.
199 HENRY LAURENS PROPHESIED: q. Sachse, 180.
199 BURKE'S SPEECH OF 19 APR 74: Hansard, XVII.
200 FRANKLIN, "BY PERSISTING IN A WRONG": q. Van Doren, 335.
200 "TO SPRINKLE AMERICAN ALTARS": q. Page Smith, *A New Age Now Begins*, 1976, I, 391. PUTNAM DROVE 130 SHEEP: W. F. Livingston, *Israel Putnam*, New York, 1901, 78.
200 JEFFERSON, "DELIBERATE AND SYSTEMATICAL PLAN": q. Bailyn, *Ideological*, 120; WASHINGTON ON SAME: ibid.; TOM PAINE ON SAME: *Letter to Abbé Raynal on the Affairs of North America*.
201 BURKE, "WHAT ENFORCING AND WHAT REPEALING": Speech of 19 Apr 74, Hansard, XVII.

p. 201   ADAMS, "A HOBGOBLIN": q. Alfred O. Aldridge, *Man of Reason: The Life of Thomas Paine*, Philadelphia, 1959, 34.

     201   JEFFERSON, "UNION ON A GENEROUS PLAN": q. Beloff, *Debate*, 176. GALLOWAY'S PLAN: ibid., 203. FRANKLIN, "EXTREME CORRUPTION": q. Bailyn, *Ideological*, 136.

     202   GEORGE III, "BLOWS MUST DECIDE": to North, 18 Nov 75, *Correspondence*, no. 1556.

     202   BARRINGTON'S DISSENT: Trevelyan, I, 113; Barrington, 141, 144–5.

     203   TWO AMERICANS AS SHERIFFS OF LONDON: Plumb, *Light*, 83.

     203   DR. JOHNSON, "A RACE OF CONVICTS": Boswell's *Life*, Everyman ed., I, 526.

     204   CHATHAM'S MOTION OF 20 JAN 75: Ayling, *Pitt*, 414. "SLEEPING AND CONFOUNDED MINISTRY": q. Williams, *Pitt*, II, 304. "OPPOSITION STARED AND SHRUGGED: Walpole to Conway, 22 Jan 75, *Correspondence*, IV, 91.

     204   CHATHAM'S BILL FOR REPEAL: 1 Feb 75. GOWER'S RESPONSE: Hansard, XVIII, 208.

     205   THE "DELUDED PEOPLE": the phrase was the King's to Lord North, 18 Aug 75, III, 247. AMHERST DECLINES THE COMMAND: Trevelyan, I, 260.

     205   NORTH'S PLAN ELICITS "UNCERTAINTY, SURPRISE": q. Miller, 406.

     205   BURKE, "ABSOLUTE NECESSITY": 22 Mar 75, known as the Conciliation Speech, Hansard, XVIII.

     206   WALPOLE TO MANN, "VICTORY WILL RUIN US": 7 May 75, *Correspondence*, XXIV, 98.

     206   COLONEL GRANT, AMERICANS "WOULD NOT FIGHT": Hansard, XVIII, 226; SANDWICH ON SAME: q. Griffith, 154. GOWER, "LANGUAGE OF THE RABBLE": Hansard, XVIII, 166.

     207   BURGOYNE, "WE TOOK A STEP": q. Trevelyan, George M., *History of England*, New York, 1953, III, 73.

     207   "THE HORRID TRAGEDY": Sayre to Chatham, 20 May 75, q. Ritcheson, 191.

     207   WESLEY'S LETTER TO DARTMOUTH: full text, Luke Tyerman, *Wesley*, 1872, III, 197–200. There is dispute as to whether the letter was addressed to Dartmouth or North; Tyerman does not specify. Caleb T. Winchester, in *Life of John Wesley* (New York, 1906) says that the addressee was North. *DNB* on Dartmouth claims it was Dartmouth, as does Valentine, *North*, I, 349.

5. "... *A Disease, a Delirium*"

p. 208   HARVEY, "AS WILD AN IDEA": George III, *Correspondence*, III, xiii.

     208   NORTH, "THE ARDOR OF THE NATION": q. Brooke, 180.

     209   TO PROSECUTE "WITH VIGOR": George III to Lord North, 18 Aug 75, *Correspondence*, III, 247–8.

     209   GERMAIN, "BRINGING THE REBELS TO THEIR KNEES": q. Valentine, *North*, I, 390.

     210   "I ALWAYS TOLD YOU": Fitzmaurice, I, 345. ANCESTOR "LIVED IN THE GREATEST SPLENDOUR": *DNB*.

     210   COLONIES MUST ACKNOWLEDGE "SUPREME AUTHORITY": q. Valentine, *North*, I, 409.

     211   DR. PRIESTLEY, "ANYTHING LIKE REASON": q. ibid., 406.

     212   REFUSALS TO SERVE, KEPPEL, EFFINGHAM, AND CHATHAM'S SON: Trevelyan,

III, 202, 206–7; CONWAY "COULD NEVER DRAW HIS SWORD": Hansard, XVIII, 998.

p. 212 CAVENDISH, "BURIED IN ONE GRAVE": q. Miller, 452. RICHMOND, "PERFECTLY JUSTIFIABLE": q. *DNB*. PUBLIC SUBSCRIPTION FOR AMERICANS "MURDERED": Hinkhouse, 193; Feiling, 134.

212 WALPOLE, "COUNTRY WILL BE DESERTED": to Countess of Ossory, 15 Oct 76, *Correspondence*, IX, 428. "OH THE FOLLY": to Conway, 31 Oct 76, ibid., 429.

213 BOSWELL, "ILL-DIGESTED AND VIOLENT": letters of 18 Mar 75 and 12 Aug 75, *Letters*, ed. Chauncey Tinker, 2 vols., Oxford, 1924, I, 213, 239. DR. JOHNSON, "EXCEPT AN AMERICAN": Boswell, *Life*, II, 209. CARMARTHEN, "FOR WHAT PURPOSE": debate of 15 Apr 74, Hansard, XVII, 1208.

213 CHATHAM PREDICTED FRENCH ENTRY: q. Donne, editor's preface to *Correspondence of George III with Lord North*, II, 9.

214 RICHMOND, "I FEEL VERY LANGUID": 11 Dec 75, q. Olson, 169. TO BURKE ON A FRENCH PEERAGE: Burke, *Correspondence*, II, 118, 120.

214 FOX, "ON THE ROCKINGHAM WHIGS": q. ibid., II, 182. BURKE, "PLENTIFUL FORTUNES": ibid.

215 WASHINGTON, "NOW THE WHOLE FORCE OF NEW ENGLAND": to General Putnam, *Writings of George Washington*, ed. John C. Fitzpatrick, USGPO, 1931–1944, IX, 115.

215 CHATHAM SPEECH OF 20 NOV 77: Hansard, XIX, 360–75.

216 FOX, "ABSOLUTELY IMPOSSIBLE": ibid., 431–2.

217 CHATHAM SPEECH OF 11 DEC 77: q. Donne in *Correspondence of George III with Lord North*, II, 114.

217 "YOU HAVE NO IDEA," LETTER TO SELWYN: q. Valentine, *Germain*, 265. "UNIVERSAL DEJECTION": ibid. GIBBON, "IF IT HAD NOT BEEN FOR SHAME": Walpole, *Last Journals*, II, 76.

217 GERMAIN, "WILFUL BLINDNESS": q. Valentine, *Germain*, 275.

217 GEORGE III, "I KNOW THAT I AM DOING MY DUTY": 26 July 75, *Correspondence*, III, no. 1683.

218 PRAYED HEAVEN "TO GUIDE ME": ibid., no. 3923.

218 GERMAIN'S CARRIAGE HORSES: Fitzmaurice, I, 358; Valentine, *Germain*, 284.

219 PEACE COMMISSION PROPOSALS: Hansard, XVIII, 443. "FULL MELANCHOLY SILENCE," and "IGNOMINIOUS": Walpole, *Last Journals*, II, 200. DR. JOHNSON, "SUCH A BUNDLE OF IMBECILITY": q. Robertson, 174. IGNOMINIOUS DAY: Walpole to Mann, 18 Feb 78.

220 ROCKINGHAM AND RICHMOND, "INSTANTLY AND PUBLICLY": Olson, 172–3.

221 CHATHAM'S LAST SPEECH: Hansard, XIX, 7 Apr 78. HIS DEATH: Plumb, *Chatham*, 156; Robin Reilly, *William Pitt the Younger*, New York, 1979, 52; DR. ADDINGTON: Williams, *Pitt*, II, 242–3.

221 PREDICTIONS OF RUIN: SHELBURNE: q. Miller, 453; RICHMOND TO ROCKINGHAM: 15 Mar 78, q. Olson, 172–3. WALPOLE, "MISERABLE LITTLE ISLAND": q. Miller, 396.

222 BURKE, TO ROCKINGHAM: 25 Aug 75, q. ibid., 453.

222 FOX, "IN A MANNER CONSISTENT": q. Derry, 87. WALPOLE, "TOO INERT"; *Correspondence*, to Mann, 30 June 79. FOX, "DESPISED EVERYWHERE": q. Derry, 75.

222 CARLISLE PEACE COMMISSION: q. Brown, 266.

p.223 HIS LITTLE DAUGHTER CAROLINE: q. Brown, 266; "OUR OFFERS OF PEACE": ibid., 263; PUBLIC PROCLAMATION OF 3 OCT 78: Stevens, *Facsimiles*, XI, no. 1171–2;

224   CARLISLE'S FIRST DRAFT: 29 Sept 78, ibid., V, no. 529; CONGRESS RECOMMENDS PROCLAMATION PUBLISHED: ibid., XII, 1200–01.

224   EDEN, "THIS NOBLE COUNTRY": Miller, *Triumph*, 5. TO WEDDERBURN, "IT IS IMPOSSIBLE": ibid.

226   YORKSHIRE PETITION: Feiling, 135–6. DUNNING RESOLUTION: Trevelyan, I, 216.

227   CONWAY'S MOTION: Jesse, III, 357; Feiling, 141; all sources.

227   GEORGE III, PROPOSED ABDICATION: Namier, *Crossroads*, 125.

228   ONLY NEGOTIATOR RICHARD OSWALD: Allen, 254 (here erroneously named James).

228   GEORGE III, "DISMEMBERMENT OF AMERICA": to Shelburne, 10 Nov 82, *Correspondence*, VI, no. 3978.

229   ADAMS, "PRIDE AND VANITY": letter written from Holland in 1782, q. Allen, 255; see also Miller, *Triumph*, 632.

230   ROCKINGHAM, "TACIT COMPACT": q. Guttridge, 73–4.

231   IF HAMLET AND OTHELLO HAD BEEN REVERSED: J. G. Adams, q. by William Willcox, *Portrait of a General* (Sir Henry Clinton), New York, 1964, xi.

Chapter Five

AMERICA BETRAYS HERSELF IN VIETNAM

WORKS CONSULTED

ACHESON, DEAN. *Present at the Creation*. New York, 1969.

AMERICAN ENTERPRISE INSTITUTE. *Vietnam Settlement: Why 1973, Not 1969?* Rational Debate Series. Washington, D.C., 1973.

ANDERSON, PATRICK. *The President's Men*. New York, 1968.

AUSTIN, ANTHONY. *The President's War: Tonkin Gulf Resolution*. New York, 1971.

BALL, GEORGE W. *The Past Has Another Pattern*. New York, 1982.

BUNDY, MC GEORGE. "Vietnam, Watergate and Presidential Powers." *Foreign Affairs*. Winter 1979/80.

BUTTINGER, JOSEPH. *The Smaller Dragon: A Political History of Vietnam*. New York, 1958.

——. *Vietnam: A Dragon Embattled*. 2 vols. New York, 1967.

CHICAGO, UNIVERSITY OF, CENTER FOR POLICY STUDIES. *Vietnam: Which Way to Peace?* Chicago, 1970.

CLIFFORD, CLARK. "A Vietnam Reappraisal." *Foreign Affairs*. July 1969.

COHEN, WARREN I. *Dean Rusk (American Secretaries of State and Their Diplomacy*, Vol. 19). Totowa, N.J., 1980.

COLLINS, J. LAWTON, GENERAL. *Lightning Joe: An Autobiography*. Baton Rouge, 1979.

CONGRESSIONAL QUARTERLY SERVICE. *Congress and the Nation.* Vol. III, 1969–72. Washington, D.C., 1973.

COOPER, CHESTER. *The Lost Crusade: America in Vietnam.* New York, 1970.

COUNCIL ON FOREIGN RELATIONS. *American Dilemma in Viet-Nam: A Report on the Views of Leading Citizens in Thirty-three Cities.* Ed. Rolland H. Buskner. New York, 1965.

DE GAULLE, CHARLES. *Memoirs.* (English ed.). 3 vols. New York, 1960.

DONOVAN, ROBERT J. *Conflict and Crisis: The Presidency of Harry S. Truman, 1945–48.* New York, 1977.

DOUGLAS, WILLIAM O. *North from Malaya.* New York, 1953.

DRACHMAN, EDWARD R. *United States Policy Toward Vietnam, 1940–45.* Rutherford, N.J., 1970.

DUNN, PETER. *An Interpretation of Source Materials for the Period September 1945 Until May 1946 in the Region of Cochinchina and South Annam.* Unpublished dissertation. School of Oriental Studies. Univ. of London.

EISENHOWER, DWIGHT D. *Diaries.* Ed. Robert H. Ferrell. New York, 1981.

——. *Mandate for Change, 1953–56.* New York, 1963.

——. *Waging Peace, 1956–61.* New York, 1965.

ELLSBERG, DANIEL. *Papers on the War.* New York, 1972.

EVANS, ROWLAND, AND NOVAK, ROBERT. *Lyndon B. Johnson: The Exercise of Power.* New York, 1966.

EWALD, WILLIAM BRAGG. *Eisenhower, the President.* Englewood, N.J., 1981.

FALL, BERNARD. *The Two Vietnams: A Political and Military Analysis.* New York, 1967.

FIFIELD, RUSSELL H. *Americans in Southeast Asia: The Roots of Commitment.* New York, 1973.

FITZGERALD, FRANCES. *Fire in the Lake.* Boston, 1972.

FRANCK, THOMAS, AND WEISBAND, EDWARD, EDS. *Secrecy and Foreign Policy.* New York, 1974.

FULBRIGHT, SENATOR J. WILLIAM. *The Vietnam Hearings.* See U.S. Congress, Senate.

GALBRAITH, JOHN KENNETH. *A Life in Our Times.* Boston, 1981.

GELB, LESLIE, AND BETTS, RICHARD K. *The Irony of Vietnam: The System Worked.* Washington, D.C., 1980.

GRAFF, HENRY F. *The Tuesday Cabinet.* Englewood Cliffs, N.J., 1970.

GURTOV, MELVIN. *The First Vietnam Crisis: Chinese Communist Strategy and United States Involvement, 1953–54.* New York, 1967.

HALBERSTAM, DAVID. *The Best and the Brightest.* New York, 1972.

HALLE, LOUIS J. *The Cold War as History.* New York, 1967.

HAMMER, ELLEN J. *The Struggle for Indo-China, 1940–1955.* Stanford, 1966.

HARDIN, CHARLES M. *Presidential Power and Accountability.* Chicago, 1974.

HARRIS, LOUIS. *The Anguish of Change.* New York, 1973.

HERRING, GEORGE C. *America's Longest War: The United States and Vietnam, 1950–75.* New York, 1979.

HILSMAN, ROGER. *To Move a Nation.* New York, 1967.

HOOPES, TOWNSEND. *The Limits of Intervention.* New York, 1969.

——. *The Devil and John Foster Dulles.* Boston, 1973. (All references are to this book unless otherwise noted.)

HULL, CORDELL. *Memoirs.* 2 vols. New York, 1948.

ISAACS, HAROLD R. *No Peace for Asia.* New York, 1947.

KAPLAN, FRED. *Wizards of Armageddon.* New York, 1983.

KEARNS, DORIS. *Lyndon Johnson and the American Dream.* New York, 1976.

KENDRICK, ALEXANDER. *The Wound Within: America in the Vietnam Years, 1945–74.* Boston, 1974.

KISSINGER, HENRY. *The White House Years.* Boston, 1979.

KRAFT, JOSEPH. "A Way Out in Vietnam." *Harper's.* Dec 1964.

——. "Washington Insight." *Harper's.* Sept 1965.

KRASLOW, DAVID, AND LOORY, STUART H. *The Secret Search for Peace in Vietnam.* New York, 1968.

LA FEBER, WALTER. "Roosevelt, Churchill and Indochina: 1942–45." *American Historical Review.* Dec 1975.

LAKE, ANTHONY, ED., ET AL. *The Vietnam Legacy.* New York, 1976.

LANCASTER, DONALD. *The Emancipation of French Indo-China.* London, 1961.

LEAHY, ADMIRAL WILLIAM D. *I Was There.* New York, 1950.

LEWY, GUENTER. *America in Vietnam.* New York, 1978.

LOGUE, CAL M., AND PATTON, JOHN H. "From Ambiguity to Dogma: The Rhetorical Symbols of Lyndon B. Johnson on Vietnam," *Southern Speech Communication Journal.* Spring 1982, 310–29.

MACPHERSON, HARRY. *A Political Education.* Boston, 1972.

MANNING, ROBERT, GEN. ED. *The Vietnam Experience:* Vol. I, *Setting the Stage* by Edward Doyle and Samuel Lipsman; Vol. III, *Raising the Stakes* by Terence Maitland and Theodore Weiss. Boston, 1981–82.

MANSFIELD, SENATOR MIKE. See U.S. Congress, Senate.

MARSHALL, D. BRUCE. *The French Colonial Myth.* New Haven, 1973.

MECKLIN, JOHN. *Mission in Torment: An Intimate Account of the United States Role in Vietnam.* New York, 1965.

MILSTEIN, JEFFREY S. *Dynamics of the Vietnam War.* Columbus, Ohio, 1974.

MORGENTHAU, HANS J. *Vietnam and the United States.* Washington, D.C., 1965.

MYRDAL, GUNNAR. "With What Little Wisdom." *New York Times Magazine.* 18 July 1965.

O'DONNELL, KENNETH. "LBJ and the Kennedys." *Life.* 7 Aug 1970.

PATTI, ARCHIMEDES F. A. *Why Viet-Nam?* Berkeley, Univ. of California Press, 1981.

Pentagon Papers. See U.S. Department of Defense.

POWERS, THOMAS. *The War at Home: Vietnam and the American People, 1964–68.* New York, 1973.

RACE, JEFFREY. "Vietnam Intervention: Systematic Distortion in Policy Making." *Armed Forces and Society.* May 1976, 377–96.

——. "The Unlearned Lessons of Vietnam." *Yale Review.* Winter 1977, 162–77.

RASKIN, MARCUS, AND FALL, BERNARD. *The Vietnam Reader.* rev. ed. New York, 1967.

REISCHAUER, EDWIN O. *Wanted: An Asian Policy.* New York, 1955.

——. *Beyond Vietnam: The United States and Asia.* New York, 1967.

RIDGWAY, GENERAL MATTHEW B. "Indochina: Disengaging." *Foreign Affairs.* July 1971.

——. *Soldier.* New York, 1956.

RIEGLE, DONALD. *O Congress.* New York, 1972.

ROBERTS, CHALMERS M. "The Day We Didn't Go to War," in Raskin and Fall, q.v., originally from *The Reporter.* 14 Sept 1954.

RUSSETT, BRUCE M., AND STEPAN, ALFRED. *Military Force and American Society.* New York, 1973.

SAFIRE, WILLIAM. *Before the Fall: An Inside View of the Pre-Watergate White House.* New York, 1975.

St. Louis Post-Dispatch. Richard Dudman et al. Special Supplement on Vietnam, 30 Apr 1975.

SALINGER, PIERRE. *With Kennedy.* New York, 1966.

SCHANDLER, HERBERT Y. *The Unmaking of a President: Lyndon Johnson and Vietnam.* Princeton, 1977.

SCHEER, ROBERT. *How the United States Got Involved in Vietnam.* Santa Barbara, 1965.

SCHLESINGER, ARTHUR, JR. *A Thousand Days.* Boston, 1965.

SEVAREID, ERIC. "The Final Troubled Hours of Adlai Stevenson." *Look.* 30 Nov 1965.

SHAPLEN, ROBERT. *The Lost Revolution.* New York, 1966. (All references are to this book unless otherwise noted.)

——. *The Road from War.* New York, 1970.

SHARP, U. S. GRANT, ADMIRAL. *Strategy for Defeat.* San Rafael, Calif., 1978.

SHAWCROSS, WILLIAM. *Sideshow: Kissinger, Nixon and the Destruction of Cambodia.* New York, 1979.

SMITH, R. HARRIS. *OSS: The Secret History of America's First Central Intelligence Agency.* Berkeley, Univ. of California Press, 1972.

SORENSEN, THEODORE C. *Kennedy.* New York, 1965.

STEEL, RONALD. *Walter Lippmann and the American Century.* Boston, 1980.

SUMMERS, COLONEL HARRY G. *On Strategy: A Critical Analysis of the Vietnam War.* Presidio, Calif., 1982.

SZULC, TAD. *The Illusion of Peace: Foreign Policy in the Nixon Years.* New York, 1978.

TAYLOR, GENERAL MAXWELL D. *Swords and Plowshares.* New York, 1972.

THOMPSON, W. SCOTT, AND FRIZZELL, DONALDSON D., EDS. *The Lessons of Vietnam: A Colloquium in 1973-74 at Fletcher School of Law and Diplomacy on the Military Lessons of the Vietnamese War.* New York, 1977.

THOMSON, JAMES C., JR. "How Could Vietnam Happen?" *The Atlantic.* April 1968.

——. "Resigning from Government," in Franck and Weisband, q. v.

THORNE, CHRISTOPHER. *Allies of a Kind.* London, 1978.

U.S. CONGRESS, SENATE, Committee on Foreign Relations, Mansfield, Senator Mike, Report of, *On a Study Mission to the Associated States of Indo-China, Vietnam, Cambodia, Loas,* 83rd Congress, 1st Session, 27 Oct 1953.

——. Report of . . . , *to Vietnam, Cambodia and Laos,* 83rd Congress, 2nd Session, 15 Oct 1954.

——. Report of . . . , *to Vietnam, Cambodia and Laos,* 84th Congress, 1st Session, 6 Oct 1955.

U.S. CONGRESS, SENATE, 89TH CONGRESS, 2ND SESSION. *Hearings Before the Committee on Foreign Relations; Supplemental Foreign Assistance Fiscal Year 1966 —Vietnam,* S. 2793 (Fulbright Hearings), Part I, pp. 1-743. (The Hearings were also published as a trade book by Random House with an introduction by Sen. Fulbright: *The Vietnam Hearings,* New York, 1966.)

U.S. CONGRESS, 92ND, 2ND SESSION: SENATE COMMITTEE ON FOREIGN RELATIONS. *The United States and Vietnam: 1944–47. A Staff Study based on* "The Pentagon Papers" *by Robert M. Blum* (cited as PP, Senate). USGPO, Washington, D.C., 1972.

U.S. DEPARTMENT OF DEFENSE. *The Pentagon Papers: United States–Vietnam Relations, 1945–1967.* Study prepared in twelve books by the Department of Defense and declassified for the House Armed Services Committee (cited as PP). USGPO, Washington, D.C., 1971.

——. *The Pentagon Papers: History of United States Decision Making on Vietnam,* Senator Gravel edition. 4 vols. and Index volume. Boston, 1971–72. (Citations are from this edition unless otherwise noted.)

——. *The Pentagon Papers:* as published by the *New York Times.* New York, 1971.

U.S. OFFICE OF THE CHIEF OF MILITARY HISTORY: MARCEL VIGNERAS. *Special Studies: Rearming the French.* Washington, D.C., 1957.

U.S. STATE DEPARTMENT. *Foreign Relations of the United States* (annual). USGPO. Washington, D.C.

VIGNERAS, MARCEL. *See* U.S. Office of the Chief of Military History.

WHITE, RALPH K. *Nobody Wanted War: Misperception in Vietnam and Other Wars.* New York, 1968.

WHITE, THEODORE. *The Making of the President, 1968.* New York, 1969.

WICKER, TOM. *JFK and LBJ.* New York, 1968.

WILCOX, FRANCIS O. *Congress, the Executive, and Foreign Policy.* New York, 1971.

PERSONS CONSULTED

GEORGE W. BALL	LESLIE GELB	HARRISON SALISBURY
MC GEORGE BUNDY	DAVID HALBERSTAM	BILL MOYERS
WILLIAM P. BUNDY	MORTON HALPERIN	DAVID SCHOENBRUN
MICHAEL FORRESTAL	CARL KAYSEN	JAMES THOMSON
J. K. GALBRAITH	ROBERT S. MC NAMARA	

REFERENCE NOTES

Abbreviations

ARVN	Army of the Republic of Vietnam (South)
CCS	Combined Chiefs of Staff (Allied in World War II)
CINCPAC	Commander in Chief, Pacific
DRV	Democratic Republic of Vietnam (North)
FRC	(Senate) Foreign Relations Committee
FRUS	*Foreign Relations of the United States* (annual series)
JCS	Joint Chiefs of Staff
MAAG	Military Assistance Advisory Group
MACV	Military Assistance Command Vietnam
NSC	National Security Council
PP	*Pentagon Papers* (all references are to the Gravel edition, except where otherwise noted)
SEA	Southeast Asia

1. In Embryo

p. 235 ROOSEVELT, "SHOULD NOT GO BACK TO FRANCE": Hull, II, 1597.

235 THE PRESIDENT "HAS BEEN MORE OUTSPOKEN": q. Thorne, 468.

235 AT CAIRO, "NOT TO GO BACK!": Stilwell Papers, q. B. W. Tuchman, *Stilwell and the American Experience in China*, New York, 1971, 405. TRUSTEESHIP "FOR 25 YEARS" and "I ASKED CHIANG KAI-SHEK": ibid., 410.

236 GEORGES BIDAULT, "WHOLE-HEARTED COOPERATION": q. La Feber, 1292.

236 FAR EAST DESK URGED INDEPENDENCE: J. C. Vincent Mem. 2 Nov 43, FRUS, 1943, China, 866. See also Fifield, 69 n.

236 "VOLUNTARY" CONSENT OF FORMER COLONIAL POWER: Drachman, 51.

236 ROOSEVELT DID NOT WANT TO GET "MIXED UP": Mem. for Secretary of State, 1 Jan 45, FRUS, 1945, VI, 293. REVERSED HIMSELF: FRUS, 1944, *British Commonwealth and Europe*, FDR to Hull, 16 Oct 44. See also Drachman, 80.

237 ROOSEVELT ON "INDEPENDENCE": to Charles Taussig, Halberstam, 81; Thorne, 630.

237 STETTINIUS ON FRENCH SOVEREIGNTY: State Dept. Bulletin, 8 Apr 45. DE GAULLE, "IF YOU ARE AGAINST US": Caffery to Sec. of State, FRUS, 1945, VI, 300.

237 GREW, "ENTIRELY INNOCENT": Grew to Caffery, FRUS, 1945, VI, 307. See also Grew to Hurley, 2 June 1945, ibid., 312.

237 FRENCH SURVEY OF 1910: Buttinger, I, 450, n. 53.

238 "MORE ILLITERATE THAN THEIR FATHERS": Jules Harmard, *Domination et colonisation*, Paris, 1910, 264, q. Buttinger, *Smaller Dragon*, 425.

238 "REPRESENTATIVES OF THE CONQUERED RACE": q. Manning, *Stage*, 109, from Milton Osborne, *French Presence in Cochin China and Cambodia, 1859–1905*, Ithaca, 1969, 119.

239 OSS AND HO CHI MINH: Smith, 332–4. AMERICA "OPPOSED COLONIALISM": ibid. OSS DISTRICT CHIEF: Col. Paul Halliwell, q. Shaplen, 33.

239 DECISIONS AT POTSDAM: Leahy, 286, 338, 413; also, CCS to St. Didier, 19 July 45, Vigneras, 398.

240 ACCORDING TO ADMIRAL KING: Thorne, 631.

240 TRUMAN, "NO OPPOSITION" TO RETURN OF THE FRENCH: De Gaulle, III, 910. DE GAULLE TO PRESS CONFERENCE: q. Drachman, 90.

240 BRAZZAVILLE DECLARATION: q. Marshall, 107; see also Smith, 324.

240 "WE WILL KEEP ON FIGHTING": q. Shaplen, 30.

240 MESSAGE IN NAME OF BAO DAI: q. Hammer, 102.

241 "FACILITATE RECOVERY . . . BY THE FRENCH": q. Cooper, 39.

241 FRENCH RETURN ON AMERICAN SHIPS: Dunn; also Hammer, 113; Isaacs, 151–7; "TO EMPLOY AMERICAN FLAG VESSELS": PP(HR), Bk I, Part I, A, p. A-24, q. Patti, 380.

241 BRITISH USED JAPANESE UNITS: Isaacs, 151; FOOTNOTE QUOTING MOUNT-BATTEN: q. Dunn from one of the following: *Lord Mountbatten's Report to Combined Chiefs of Staff, 1943–45* (London, HMSO, 1951), *Post Surrender Tasks, Section E of the above* (London, HMSO, 1969); GREAT BRITAIN: *Documents Relating to British Involvement in the Indo-China Conflict, 1945–65*, Command 2834 (London, HMSO, 1965).

241 GENERAL GRACY'S REMARKS: q. Buttinger, I, 327.

p. 242 WEARING AMERICAN UNIFORMS: Cooper, 41; Isaacs, 161; Smith, 344.

242 "STABLE, STRONG AND FRIENDLY": PP (Senate), 13. OSS TO OBSERVE "PUNITIVE MISSIONS": q. Smith, 347.

242 EIGHT APPEALS BY HO TO U.S. UNANSWERED: FRUS, 1946, VIII, 27; also PP, I, 17.

242 ARTHUR HALE REPORT: Gallagher Papers, PP (Senate), Appendix I, 31–6.

243 *Christian Science Monitor*: by Gordon Walker, 2 Mar 46. STATE DEPT., "SERIOUSLY DETERIORATING": 28 Nov 45, FRUS, 1945, VI, 1388, n. 37.

243 CHARLES YOST REPORT: 13 Dec 45, ibid.; see also Fifield, 69–70.

243 MARSHALL, "DANGEROUSLY OUTMODED": drafted by the French Desk for Embassy in Paris, PP, I, 31–2. ACHESON TO MOFFAT: ibid., 20.

244 MOFFAT, "FIFTY YEARS FROM NOW": PP (Senate), 13.

244 AMERICAN CONSUL IN SAIGON, "NO SETTLEMENT": Charles S. Reed to Sec. of State, 22 Dec 46, FRUS, 1946, VIII, 78–9. LECLERC, "IT WOULD TAKE 500,000": q. Halberstam, 84, from Paul Mus orally.

245 TRUMAN AND ACHESON ASSURED THE PUBLIC: FRUS, 1945, VI, 313; Thorne, 632.

245 FRENCH DESK DIRECTIVE ON INDOCHINA: Feb 1947, PP, I, 31.

2. Self-Hypnosis

p. 247 NSC SEA IS "TARGET": June, 49, PP, I, 82. "KEY AREA": ibid., 83.

248 BAO DAI TO PHAN QUANG DAN: PP, I, 71–2. DAN, "WITHOUT IDEOLOGY": ibid.

248 ROBERT BLUM, "GIVES LITTLE PROMISE": Shaplen, 87; PP, I, 73.

249 "VITAL TO THE . . . FREE WORLD": 24 May 51, q. Gelb, 44.

249 TRUMAN, "MONSTROUS CONSPIRACY": radio report to the American people, 11 Apr 51, PP, I, 588.

249 NSC "ANTICIPATED" SEIZURE: 27 Feb 50, PP, I, 83. STATE DEPT., NO TRACES OF KREMLIN: ibid., 34.

250 TRUMAN, SPECIAL MESSAGE TO CONGRESS: 24 May 51, PP, I, 589. ACHESON, "REMOVE ANY ILLUSIONS": q. Gelb, 42.

251 RUSK, "NEW COLONIALISM": q. Cohen, 75. "TOOL OF THE POLITBURO": testimony to Senate FRC, 8 June 1950, q. Cohen, 50.

251 *NYT* EDITORIAL, "IT SHOULD NOW BE CLEAR": 11 June 52. NSC SEES JAPAN SUCCUMBING: PP, I, 84.

251 OHLY MEMORANDUM: Acheson, 674.

251 U.S. NAVAL AND AIR ACTION IN EVENT OF CHINESE ENTRY: NSC 124, PP, I, 88.

252 WALTER ROBERTSON, "NO REGIME AS MALEVOLENT": q. Hoopes, 147.

252 KNOWLAND, "SOVIET CONQUEST": ibid., 203.

252 JOHNSON, "GREAT BEAST": q. Ball, 404. DULLES, "PASSION TO CONTROL EVENTS": Hoopes, 140.

252 DULLES, "PACIFIC FRONT . . . WIDE OPEN": in Senate, 21 Sept 49, q. Hoopes, 78.

253 "PART OF A SINGLE PATTERN": ibid., 115.

253 DULLES, "THESE TWO GENTLEMEN": ibid., 78.

253 AUTHOR OF REPUBLICAN PARTY PLATFORM: Halle, 270. Text in *National Party Platforms*, compiled D. B. Johnson, I, 496–505, Univ. of Illinois Press, Urbana, 1978.

p. 254 DULLES TRIES TO GET KREMLIN PROMISE: Hoopes, 172.

254 GENERAL STAFF, "RE-EVALUATION" IN RELATION TO COST: PP, I, 89.

254 BARRINGTON: q. Barrington, 142–3.

254 ADMIRAL DAVIS, "SHOULD BE AVOIDED": PP, I, 89.

254 PENTAGON CHIEFS' ADVICE, CHINA THE ENEMY: q. Cohen, 174.

255 EISENHOWER'S THREE CONDITIONS: PP, I, 94; *Mandate*, 345.

255 "WILL PROBABLY DETERIORATE": 4 June 53, PP, I, 391–2.

256 "THE FRENCH BLACKMAILED US": Acheson interview with Professor Gaddis Smith, *NYT Book Review*, 12 Oct 69.

256 "THE FREEDOM WE CHERISH": q. Halle, 286–7.

256 TRAPNELL REPORT: PP, I, 487–9.

256 "A LACK OF ENTHUSIASM": 3 Feb 54, q. Gelb, 52.

257 "POPULATION SUPPORTED THE ENEMY": Eisenhower, *Mandate*, 372–3.

257 U.S. PAYING 80 PERCENT: Hammer, 313, n. 20a.

259 JUSTICE DOUGLAS: *North from Malaya*, 10, 208.

259 MANSFIELD REPORT: U.S. Congress, Senate FRC, 83rd Congress, 1st Session: see under U.S. Congress, Senate.

259 DULLES' FEAR OF MCCARTHY: Hoopes, 160.

259 NEW LOOK STRATEGY OF CABINET: Eisenhower, *Mandate*, 451; Hoopes, chap. 13. HUMPHREY COMMENT: q. ibid., 196.

260 DULLES, "PHONY PEACE CAMPAIGN": Hoopes, 173.

261 RADFORD POLICY PAPER FOR GENEVA: PP, I, 448–51.

261 DULLES LEFT THE IMPRESSION: Hoopes, 212. NIXON, "IF TO AVOID": 16 Apr 54, q. Eisenhower, *Mandate*, 353, n. 4.

262 EISENHOWER, "OUR MAIN TASK": *Mandate*, 168.

262 CHINESE SUPPLY 4000 TONS A MONTH: Cooper, 59.

262 ELY MISSION AND OPERATION VULTURE: Roberts, in Raskin and Fall, 57–66; PP, I, 97–106. PROPOSED USE OF ATOMIC BOMBS: FRUS, 1952–54, XIII, 1271. FOOTNOTE, PROVOKING CHINESE RESPONSE: Chalmers Roberts in *Washington Post*, 24 Oct 71, q. Gelb, 57. MACARTHUR COMMENT: FRUS, op. cit., to Sec. of State 7 Apr 54, 1270–2.

263 DULLES MEETING WITH CONGRESSIONAL LEADERS: Roberts, op. cit.; Hoopes, 210–11.

263 FRENCH CABINET ASKS INTERVENTION: PP, I, 100–04; Roberts; Hoopes, 207–08. EISENHOWER, "NO INVOLVEMENT": 10 Mar 54, q. Gurtov, 78.

264 GAVIN REPORT: Ridgway, *Soldier*, 276; also Gavin in Senate FRC Hearings in 1966.

264 EISENHOWER REJECTS UNILATERAL INTERVENTION: *Mandate*, 373; PP, I, 129.

265 SPECIAL COMMITTEE'S REPORT: 5 Apr 54, PP, I, 472–6.

266 DULLES ON FALL OF DIEN BIEN PHU: 11 May 54, PP, I, 106; also *NYT*, 24 June 54.

266 MENDES-FRANCE, "DOES MUCH LESS": q. Hoopes from *Le Monde*, 12 Feb 54. CEASE-FIRE IN THIRTY DAYS: Ambassador Dillon to Sec. of State, 6 July 54, PP (HR), Bk IX, 612. CONSCRIPTION: ibid.

267 DULLES, "DELIBERATE THREAT": 11 June 54, q. Hoopes, 230.

267 CHOU EN-LAI'S ADVICE: as told by Chou to Harrison Salisbury, Salisbury to author, 17 Feb 83.

3. *Creating the Client*

p. 269   FRENCH CASUALTIES: Eisenhower, *Mandate*, 337.

270   *St. Louis Post-Dispatch*, "A WAR TO STAY OUT OF": 5 May 54 and other editorials, May 7, 9, 10, 12, 14, 19, 22, 1954. FITZPATRICK CARTOON: ibid., *wanted*, 8 June 54.

270   REISCHAUER, "AN EXTREMELY INEFFECTIVE": 178–9; 251–7.

270   DULLES, "SO UNITED, SO STRONG": q. Hoopes, 242.

271   ADMIRAL DAVIS, "NO BETTER PREPARED": PP, I, 212.

271   DIEM'S CAREER: Mansfield report to Senate FRC, 15 Oct 54, 83rd Congress, 2nd Session; see also Scheer.

272   JUSTICE DOUGLAS INTRODUCES DIEM: Scheer and Hinckle, "The Viet-Nam Lobby," in Raskin and Fall, 69.

273   AMERICANS "DIFFERENT" FROM THE FRENCH: William Bundy to author, 18 Feb 81.

273   JOINT CHIEFS, "ABSOLUTELY ESSENTIAL": PP, I, 215.

273   JOINT CHIEFS, "NO ASSURANCE": PP, I, 218.

274   "CHRIST HAS MOVED SOUTH": q. Cooper, 130.

274   "VIETNAM PROBABLY WOULD HAVE TO BE WRITTEN OFF": report of the Lansdale Mission, PP, I, 577.

274   FAURE, "NOT ONLY INCAPABLE BUT MAD": PP, I, 241.

274   MANSFIELD REPORT: U.S. Congress, Senate FRC, 83rd Congress, 2nd Session.

275   EISENHOWER LETTER TO DIEM: PP, I, 253.

275   COLLINS' REPORT: PP, I, 226. RE-AFFIRMED: Collins, 408.

276   LANSDALE MISSION: PP, I, 573–83.

276   FRENCH "DISPOSED TO EXPLORE": PP, I, 221. SAINTENY, "ONLY POSSIBLE MEANS": ibid., 222.

277   *NYT*, "PROVEN INEPT": C. L. Sulzberger, 18 Apr 55.

277   DULLES, CHANCES "ONE IN TEN": Collins, 379.

278   EISENHOWER, "LOTS OF DIFFICULTIES": q. Cooper, 142.

278   HEATH, "OVER $300 MILLION": PP, I, 227.

278   SPELLMAN, "ALAS!": *NYT*, 31 Aug 54.

278   DIEM DENIAL OF ELECTIONS: PP, I, 245.

279   "OUTRAGEOUS" METHODS: Buttinger, II, 890.

279   "OVERWHELMING MAJORITY": Leo Cherne in *Look*, 25 Jan 56; see also Cooper, 132.

279   KENNEDY ON HO'S "POPULARITY": in Senate, 6 Apr 54, q. Scheer, 15.

279   EISENHOWER "REFUSED TO AGREE": Ridgway, *Foreign Affairs*, 585; see also Eisenhower, *Mandate*, 372. STATE DEPT., "WE SUPPORT": PP, I, 246.

280   PHAM VAN DONG, "WE SHALL ACHIEVE UNITY": PP, I, 250.

280   A STUDY BY AMERICAN POLITICAL SCIENTISTS: one of a series conducted in Vietnam from 1955 to 1962 by Michigan State University under the direction of Professor Wesley Fishel, q. Scheer, 53.

281   GIAP, "WE EXECUTED": PP, I, 246.

281   AMERICAN EMBASSY, "SITUATION MAY BE SUMMED UP": PP, I, 258.

281   MANIFESTO OF THE EIGHTEEN AND ARRESTS: Cooper, 159; text of Manifesto in Raskin and Fall, 116–21. "INCAPABLE OF SAVING THE COUNTRY": ibid., 483; WASHINGTON'S CONGRATULATIONS: ibid.

282   NLF TEN-POINT PROGRAM: text in Raskin and Fall, 216–21.

4. "Married to Failure"

p. 283 "IT WAS SIMPLY A GIVEN": James Thomson, *NYT* Books, 4 Oct 70.

283 KENNEDY, "CORNERSTONE . . . KEYSTONE": speech on "America's Stake in Vietnam" to American Friends of Vietnam, June 1956, q. Lewy, 12.

285 MC NAMARA, "WE HAVE THE POWER TO KNOCK": reportedly said at a Pentagon briefing, Robert D. Heinl, *Dictionary of Military and Naval Quotations*, Annapolis, 1966, 215.

285 BUNDY, READY TO BE DEAN AT AGE TWELVE: q. Halberstam, 52.

286 THURMOND ON MC CONE: Halberstam, 153.

286 GALBRAITH, "THE DISASTROUS AND THE UNPALATABLE": Galbraith, 477.

287 "THIS IS THE WORST WE HAVE HAD YET": Schlesinger, 320; PP, II, 6, 27.

287 LANSDALE PROGRAM: PP, II, 440–1.

287 KENNEDY, "WHITE MAN'S WAR": Schlesinger, 505, 547.

287 "WELL, MR. SCHOENBRUN": Schoenbrun to author.

288 LIMITED WAR, "ADVANTAGES OF TERMINATING": q. Kaplan, 330. KAUFMAN QUOTED: ibid., 199.

288 KENNEDY READ MAO AND CHE GUEVARA: Schlesinger, 341.

289 ROSTOW'S SPEECH AT FORT BRAGG: Raskin and Fall, 108–16.

289 LANSDALE, "A STRONGER APPEAL": q. Schlesinger, 986.

290 BURKE, "PERSEVERANCE IN ABSURDITY": speech in Commons of 19 April 1774, Hansard XVIII.

290 PENTAGON DISCUSSIONS ON "SIZE AND COMPOSITION": Action Memorandum, 11 May 61, PP, II, 642.

291 EISENHOWER BRIEFING: Gelb and Betts, 29.

291 7TH FLEET TO SOUTH CHINA SEA, AND OTHER MOVEMENTS: Ball, 363.

291 LEMNITZER SUGGESTS NUCLEAR ARMS: Galbraith, 467. KENNEDY SHOCKED: ibid.

292 JOHNSON, "THE WINSTON CHURCHILL": q. Schlesinger, 541. HIS REPORT: text in PP, II, 55–9; see also Ball, 385.

293 KENNEDY TO RESTON: q. Gelb and Betts, 70. "WE CANNOT AND WILL NOT": 25 July 61, q. Sorensen, 583 ff. READY TO RISK NUCLEAR WAR: ibid.

293 NITZE, "VALUE TO THE WEST": Thompson and Frizzell, 6.

294 THEODORE WHITE, "SITUATION GETS WORSE": q. Schlesinger, 544.

294 MC GARR'S ESTIMATE: Taylor, 220–1.

295 ROSTOW AS DR. PANGLOSS: Macpherson, 258. "BIGGEST COLD WARRIOR": q. Halberstam, 161.

295 TAYLOR-ROSTOW REPORT: PP, II, 14–15, 90–98; Taylor, 227–44.

296 "EXTERNAL AGGRESSION": q. Cohen, 184.

296 STATE DEPT. ANNEXES: PP, II, 95–7.

296 RUSK, "A LOSING HORSE": PP, II, 105.

297 "REGIME NOT VIABLE": in camera testimony to Senate FRC, 28 Feb 61, q. Cohen, 111.

297 MC NAMARA-JCS RESPONSE: PP, II, 108–09. MC NAMARA-RUSK SECOND MEMORANDUM: PP, II, 110–16.

297 KENNEDY TO DIEM: ibid., 805–06.

298 DIEM "SEEMED TO WONDER": Acting Defense Minister Thuan Nguyen Dinh to Ambassador Nolting, ibid., 121.

299 CASUALTY FIGURES: PP (*NYT*), 110.

p. 299 REPUBLICAN NATIONAL COMMITTEE: *NYT*, 14 Feb 62. KENNEDY, "WE HAVE
        NOT SENT COMBAT TROOPS": PP, II, 808.

   300 MC NAMARA, "EVERY QUANTITATIVE MEASUREMENT": q. Schlesinger, 549.

   300 GALBRAITH'S REPORT: Galbraith, 471–3; PP, II, 122–4. LETTERS OF NOVEMBER,
        1961 AND MARCH 1962: Galbraith, 477–9; also PP, II, 670–1. "MARRIED TO
        FAILURE": q. Schlesinger, 548.

   301 JCS, "WELL-KNOWN COMMITMENT": Lemnitzer for JCS to Sec. of De-
        fense, 13 Apr 62, ibid., 671–2.

   301 "WHAT THE NEWSMEN TOOK TO BE LIES": Mecklin, 100. MANNING MEMO-
        RANDUM: Salinger, 328; for the press war, see also Manning, ed. *Stakes*,
        58–61.

   302 MANSFIELD, ZEAL WOULD BE THE UNDOING: Macpherson, 45. TOLD THE
        SENATE: 88th Congress, 1st Session, GPO, Washington, D.C., 1963.

   302 MANSFIELD-KENNEDY CONVERSATION: O'Donnell.

   302 HILSMAN REPORT: PP, II, 690–726.

   303 COGNITIVE DISSONANCE, "SUPPRESS, GLOSS OVER": I am indebted to Jeffrey
        Race for bringing this concept to my attention. The quoted passages
        are from his article in *Armed Forces and Society*. See also Leon
        Festinger, *A Theory of Cognitive Dissonance*, Evanston, Ill., 1957.

   303 KENNEDY HINTS WITHDRAWAL TO MANSFIELD: O'Donnell.

   304 INSTRUCTS MICHAEL FORRESTAL: Forrestal to author. "EASY; PUT A GOVERN-
        MENT": O'Donnell. "WOULD MEAN COLLAPSE": q. Schlesinger, 989. "WE
        ARE GOING TO STAY": 17 July 63, PP, II, 824.

   304 "NO, I BELIEVE IT": NBC interview with Chet Huntley, PP, II, 828.

   305 RUSK, "STEADY MOVEMENT": q. Schlesinger, 986.

   305 NHUS SUSPECTED OF DEALING WITH ENEMY: Ball, 370.

   306 "SOME QUITE FANTASTIC ACTION": State to Lodge, 29 Aug 63, unsigned,
        PP, II, 738.

   306 CONEIN LIAISON: Ball, 371; FOR U.S. INVOLVEMENT IN COUP, see PP, II, 256–
        63, Documents, 734–51. LODGE, "THIS REPRESSIVE REGIME": PP, II, 742, para.
        8. WASHINGTON'S INSTRUCTIONS: State to Lodge, 24 Aug 63, PP, II, 734;
        NSC to Lodge, 5 Oct 63, ibid., 257, 766.

   307 LODGE, "WE ARE LAUNCHED": ibid., 738. "ASSASSINATION" OF NHUS: to State
        from Lodge, 5 Oct 63, ibid., 767.

   307 ROBERT KENNEDY, "COMMUNIST TAKE-OVER": Sept 63, PP, II, 243. Hilsman,
        106.

   307 BATTLE OF AP BAC: Manning, ed. *Stakes*, 50–51. COLONEL VANN: Halberstam,
        203–05. DOD AND CINCPAC OPTIMISM: Cooper, 480.

   308 RUFUS PHILLIPS REPORT: PP, II, 245. JOHN MECKLIN "IN DESPAIR": Mecklin,
        x. KATTENBURG CONFERENCE: PP, II, 241; Cohen, 190. KATTENBURG PREDIC-
        TION: Halberstam, 370.

   308 DE GAULLE SPEAKS: *NYT*, 30 Aug 63. "AUTHORITATIVE SOURCES": ibid., from
        Washington. "WIDE ANNOYANCE": ibid.

   309 "THEIR" WAR; KENNEDY, "IN THE FINAL ANALYSIS": interview with Walter
        Cronkite, Sept 1963, q. Wicker, 186.

   309 "YOU TWO DID VISIT": q. PP, III, 23, from Hilsman.

   309 PUBLIC ANNOUNCEMENT, "BY THE END OF 1965": text in Raskin and Fall,
        128–9.

5. Executive War

p. 311 MADE UP HIS MIND NOT TO "LOSE": Bill Moyers to author.

311 "I AM NOT GOING TO BE THE FIRST PRESIDENT": James Reston in *NYT*, 1 Oct 67. ALTERNATIVE VERSION: Wicker, 205.

312 VIET-CONG BROADCAST SUGGESTING CEASE-FIRE: q. Wicker, 189, from Jean Lacouture, *Vietnam: Between Two Truces*, 1966, 170. SECOND BROADCAST PICKED UP IN WASHINGTON: Wicker, ibid.

312 GENERAL "BIG" MINH AND SUCCESSORS' FEELERS OPPOSED BY U.S.: Joseph Kraft, "Washington Insight," *Harper's*, Sept 1965.

312 MC NAMARA, "NEXT TWO OR THREE MONTHS": PP, II, 193.

312 *NYT* EDITORIAL: 3 Nov 63.

313 RUSK, "WOULD LEAD TO OUR RUIN": q. Cohen, 258. "A BILLION CHINESE": at a press conference, *NYT*, 13 Oct 67. HANSON BALDWIN: *NYT Magazine*, 27 Feb 66. SEN. JOSEPH CLARK: at Senate FRC (Fulbright) hearings in 1966.

314 JOHNSON ON "THEIR" WAR: q. Wicker, 231-2.

314 *Maddox*, "DESTRUCTIVE" ACTION: PP, III, 150-1. NAVAL UNITS: Ball, 379. "DESIST FROM AGGRESSIVE POLICIES": JCS Mem. 19 May 64, PP, III. 511.

314 HONOLULU CONFERENCE: PP, III, 171-7; Ball, 375-9.

315 "ADMISSION THAT THE GAME WAS UP": q. Gelb, 115.

315 NUCLEAR OPTION: PP, III, 175; RUSK, PP, II, 322; MC NAMARA, PP, III, 238.

315 MC NAMARA, "AT LEAST THIRTY DAYS": ibid., 176.

316 FULBRIGHT'S MOTIVES FOR TONKIN RESOLUTION: Hoopes, *Limits*, 25-6. TONKIN DEBATE IN FRC: SEN. NELSON: Wicker, 223; SEN. ERVIN: Austin, 78; SEN. MORSE TIPPED OFF BY PHONE CALL: Austin, 68.

317 MC NAMARA'S DENIAL: ibid.

317 "WELL, THOSE DUMB STUPID SAILORS": q. Ball, 379.

317 DE GAULLE PROPOSES SETTLEMENT: PP, II, 193; INTERVIEW WITH BALL: Ball, 377-8.

318 U THANT'S PROPOSAL: Kraslow and Loory, 102; Sevareid in *Look*, 30 Nov 65.

319 "AS THOUGH I WERE ON THE *Titanic*": q. Kraft, *Harper's*, Dec 1967, in Raskin and Fall, 315-22.

319 "SHATTER MY PRESIDENCY" and all other remarks quoted in this paragraph: Kearns, 253, 257.

319 CIA, "LIKELY THAT NO OTHER NATION": PP, III, 178.

320 WORKING GROUP'S WARNING: PP, III, 217.

320 BALL'S MEMORANDUM: Ball, 380-6, 390-2.

321 "RAGGEDY-ASS LITTLE FOURTH-RATE COUNTRY": q. Manning, ed., *Stakes*, 183.

321 BUNDY'S MEMORANDUM: 7 Feb 65, PP, III, 309, 687-9.

322 TAYLOR, "DEMOLISHED HOMELAND": Taylor, 403.

322 MC NAUGHTON, "WITHOUT UNACCEPTABLE TAINT": plan of action addressed to McNamara 24 Mar 65, PP, III, 695.

322 TUESDAY LUNCH: Graff, passim; Evans and Novak, 553-5.

323 PRESIDENT WOULD GET UP AT 3 A.M.: Kearns, 270.

323 MICHIGAN "TEACH-IN" AND 122 CAMPUSES CONNECTED BY TELEPHONE: Powers, 55, 61. BERKELEY FACULTY STATEMENT: ibid., 80.

323 THE WHITE PAPER: 28 Feb 65, PP, III, 728.

p. 323   MC NAMARA, "THE MOST FLAGRANT CASE": q. *St. Louis Post-Dispatch*, Spec. Supp., D7.

324   COMBAT DISCUSSIONS: PP, III, chap. 3, "Air War in North Vietnam"; chap. 4, "American Troops Enter Ground War."

325   RUSK NOTE TO NORTH VIETNAM EMBASSY IN MOSCOW: Kraslow, 122.

325   TAYLOR EXPLAINS ATTRITION: Senate FRC hearings, 1966.

325   ON DECLARATION OF WAR: Summers, 21–9; Nitze, in Thompson and Frizzell, 7.

326   MC NAMARA, "WITHOUT AROUSING THE PUBLIC IRE": q. by Douglas Rosenberg as epigraph for "Arms and the American Way" in Russett, 170. Subsequently quoted in Summers, 18. Mr. Rosenberg lacks record of the original source.

327   NASSER'S REPLY ON LIMITED WAR: q. Roche, Am. Enterprise, Debate, 137, from Mohamed Heikal, *Cairo Documents*, New York, 1973.

327   PAUL CONRAD CARTOON: *Los Angeles Times*, 4 Apr 65.

327   SUICIDE SEEMED TOO CRAZED: *NYT* editorial, 11 Nov 65.

327   AFL-CIO COUNCIL: Hardin, 94.

327   DEARBORN REFERENDUM: *NYT*, 1 Nov and 10 Nov 66.

327   LIPPMANN DENIES "EXTERNAL AGGRESSION": Steel, 565.

328   MOYERS NETWORK: Moyers to author; Anderson, 341.

328   EMBASSY PROPOSES "TERMINATING OUR INVOLVEMENT": Taylor, q. Lake, 297.

328   GALBRAITH, "OVERWHELMING ODDS": Galbraith, 469, n. 7.

328   SEN. RUSSELL PRIVATELY EXHORTED: William P. Bundy to author; PROPOSES POLL OF VIETNAMESE OPINION: PP, IV, 98.

329   A JOURNALIST RECALLS: Herbert Mitgang to author.

329   CLIFFORD IN PRIVATE LETTER: 17 May 65, q. Gelb, 371, from LBJ papers.

329   MC NAUGHTON, "70 PERCENT TO AVOID": PP, III, 695.

330   MC NAMARA-WHEELER ON "WINNING": PP, IV, 290–2.

330   "WORKING THE LEVERS": Ball, 376.

330   SEVAREID, HANOI HAD AGREED: Sevareid, in *Look*, 30 Nov 65.

330   *St. Louis Post-Dispatch* ON JOHNSON DENIALS: Spec. Supp., D4.

330   ITALIAN MISSION: Kraslow, 130–1. All the foreign missions seeking negotiation are detailed in this book.

331   WARSAW TALKS: Gelb, 152 ff. from 4 vols. of PP dealing with foreign negotiations, unpublished at the time of writing.

331   MC NAUGHTON STATES DILEMMA: PP, IV, 48.

331   $2 BILLION A MONTH: Wicker, 271.

332   300 ACRES OF RICE: Powers, 224; on extent of defoliation, see Lewy, 258.

332   "HUTS GO UP IN . . . FLAME": ibid., 223, quoting Frank Harvey, *Air War—Vietnam*, New York, 1968.

332   *Ladies Home Journal*: Jan 1967.

333   CONGRESS "SURPRISINGLY PATIENT": Taylor, 321.

334   300 PENTAGON LOBBYISTS: Hardin, 83.

334   HUMPHREY, "IF YOU FEEL AN URGE": q. Powers, 48.

334   FULBRIGHT REGRETTED TONKIN ROLE: Wilcox, 29.

334   SENATE FRC HEARINGS: see under U.S. Congress. RUSK: on 28 Jan and 18 Feb. EISENHOWER DENIAL OF COMMITMENT: *NYT*, 18 Aug 65, "Military Pledge to Saigon Is Denied by Eisenhower," p. 1.

p. 335   TAYLOR AT HEARINGS: 17 Feb, 450. FULBRIGHT ON AMERICAN REVOLUTION: 17 Feb, 441. GAVIN: 8 Feb. MORSE-TAYLOR ON "WEAKNESS": 17 Feb, 454-5. KENNAN: 10 Feb.

336   ROCKEFELLER, "SUPPORT THE PRESIDENT": *NYT*, 1 Feb 66.

336   GUNNAR MYRDAL: *NYT Magazine*, 18 July 65.

337   JASON BOMBING SURVEY: PP, IV, 115-20, 166, 702-66.

337   "WE ANTICIPATED . . . LIKE REASONABLE PEOPLE": Warnke, q. Gelb, 139, from oral interview in LBJ papers. ANNUAL RATE OF 500,000 TONS: Hanson Baldwin in *NYT*, 30 Dec 66.

338   MC NAMARA'S DOUBTS: Halberstam, 630. PP (*NYT*), 510-16. SYSTEMS ANALYSIS, NOT WORTH THE COST: PP, IV, 136.

338   SILENT DEPARTURES: Thomson, "Resigning from Government"; see also Graff, 24, and Studs Terkel, "Servant of the State: A Conversation with Daniel Ellsberg," *Harper's*, Feb 1972.

339   "DEAN RUSK IS A RECORDED ANNOUNCEMENT": Halberstam, 634.

339   LBJ, "WHO KNOWS HOW LONG": q. Graff, 104.

339   "MINIMUM ESSENTIAL FORCE": PP, II, 511.

339   PROTEST SEEN AS "ENCOURAGING THE COMMUNISTS": Harris, 67.

340   JOHNSON'S RATING TURNS NEGATIVE: ibid., 60.

340   "SPIRITUAL CONFUSION": *Beyond Vietnam*, 6. NATIONAL COUNCIL OF CHURCHES: Logue and Patton, 324. KING, "GREATEST PURVEYOR": *NYT*, 5 Apr 67.

340   "YOU VOTED IN '64 . . .": *NYT*, 6 Nov 66.

341   LIPPMANN, "DECENT PEOPLE NO LONGER SUPPORT": Steel, 571.

341   JAMES THOMSON LETTER: *NYT*, 4 June 67.

341   GENERAL SHOUP, "POPPYCOCK": *NYT* obit., 16 Jan 83.

342   POLL, 48 YES, 48 NO: Logue and Patton, 326.

342   PHAM VAN DONG, "BASIS FOR SETTLEMENT": 3 Jan 67, Cooper, 501.

343   AMERICANS AND NORTH VIETNAMESE CONFERRED: Kraslow, 167-74, Cooper, 346-7.

343   TWO AMERICANS TO HANOI: Ashmore and Baggs, Kraslow, 200. U THANT, "CALCULATED RISK": ibid., 208.

343   LBJ, "MORE THAN OUR PART": 31 Dec 66. LETTER TO HO CHI MINH: Kraslow, 206.

343   "DEEP CONVICTION IN HANOI": q. Gelb, 164, from unpublished PP vols.

343   HAROLD WILSON–KOSYGIN NEGOTIATION: Kraslow, 186-98, Herring, 168-9.

344   MC NAUGHTON, "SUCCESSFULLY, OR ELSE": May 67 Memorandum for President, PP, IV, 477-9.

344   "HE WAS A MISERABLE MAN": Moyers to author.

344   STENNIS HEARINGS: PP, IV, 199-204; Sharp, ibid., 191-7.

346   MC NAMARA, "DESTROYING THE COUNTRYSIDE": q. Macpherson, 430-1. COLLEAGUES STARED: ibid.

346   CIA, "SO INTOLERABLE": q. Cohen, 277. STUDY IN DOLLAR VALUES: PP, IV, 136. SYSTEMS ANALYSIS, SUPPLY ROUTES: ibid., 223. "WE ARE UNABLE TO DEVISE": ibid., 224-5.

347   BOMB TOTAL 1.5 MILLION TONS: PP, IV, 216.

347   AUBRAC-MARCOVICH MISSION: July 67, Kraslow.

347   BURCHETT, "DEEP SKEPTICISM": Kraslow, 227-8.

p. 348 *Saturday Evening Post*: 18 Nov 67.

349 "DESTROY THE TOWN IN ORDER TO SAVE IT": heard by public over TV. The town was Ben Tre. *Wall Street Journal*: 23 Feb 68.

349 CLIFFORD TASK FORCE: Schandler, 121–76; Clifford, *Foreign Affairs*.

350 KENNAN, "MEN IN A DREAM": q. Hoopes, *Limits*, 178.

350 CLIFFORD'S TOUR OF SEATO NATIONS: ibid., 169–71.

350 DISENCHANTMENT: Clifford, *Foreign Affairs;* Hoopes, *Limits*, 186–95. NITZE: ibid., 199.

351 SYSTEMS ANALYSIS: PP, IV, 558.

351 CLIFFORD, "NOT ONLY ENDLESS BUT HOPELESS": Clifford, *Foreign Affairs*.

351 SENATOR TYDINGS: Macpherson, 420. DEMOCRATIC COMMITTEE TELEGRAM: q. Powers, 300.

351 CRONKITE BROADCAST: transcript supplied by Mr. Cronkite.

352 "THE SHOCK WAVES": q. Schandler, 198.

352 *Time*, "VICTORY IN VIETNAM": 15 Mar 68.

352 SENATE FRC HEARINGS: *NYT*, 8 Mar 68. QUESTIONED AUTHORITY OF THE PRESIDENT: Schandler, 211. "WE JUST COULDN'T": Senator Jackson, q. ibid.

353 ACHESON REVIEW: Hoopes, *Limits*, 205; Kendrick, 259.

353 SPEECH TO NATIONAL FARMERS UNION: *NYT*, 19 Mar 68. ROWE REPORTS CALLS: Rowe Mem. to President, 19 Mar 68, q. Schandler, 249.

354 "WISE MEN" CONFERENCE: Ridgway, *Foreign Affairs*; PP, IV, 266–8; Ball, 407–09.

354 CLIFFORD, "TREMENDOUS EROSION": Macpherson, 435; Hoopes, *Limits*, 219.

355 CABLE TO AMBASSADORS: PP, IV, 595.

355 WHEELER TO CINCPAC ON DECREASE OF SUPPORT: q. Schandler, 279.

356 FIELD AGENTS TELEPHONED: Theodore White, 118.

6. Exit

p. 358 "IF THE WAR GOES ON SIX MONTHS": to Harrison Salisbury; Salisbury to author. "END UP LIKE LBJ": q. Herring, 219.

359 REISCHAUER, NO GUARANTEE: *Beyond Vietnam*, 19.

359 RAND RANGE OF OPTIONS: Konrad Kellen, one of the RAND specialists, to author.

359 "ACCEPTABLE INTERVAL": q. *St. Louis Post-Dispatch*, Spec. Supp., D2.

360 AN AMERICAN SERGEANT, AWOLS: q. Richard Dudman, *St. Louis Post-Dispatch*, Spec. Supp., D10.

361 "NOVEMBER OPTION": Szulc, 152.

361 "A LITTLE FOURTH-RATE POWER": q. ibid., 150.

361 "DORMANT BEAST": Kissinger, 244.

361 ARMS FOR VIETNAMIZATION: G. Warren Nutter, Asst. Sec. of Defense under Nixon, in Am. Enterprise *Vietnam Settlement*, 71.

362 "LOSE THE WAR IN VIETNAM—BRING THE BOYS HOME": q. Kissinger, 307. "BUMS": q. Herring, 232. MITCHELL, "LIKE THE RUSSIAN REVOLUTION": q. Kendrick, 296.

362 "SOUGHT TO DESTROY HIM": Kissinger, 299.

362 "TO END THE WAR IN A WAY": q. Theodore White, 130.

Reference Notes

427

p. 363   BURKE, "SHOW THE THING YOU CONTEND FOR": Speech of 19 Apr 1774, Hansard, XVIII.

363   SAINTENY, "HOPELESS ENTERPRISE": q. Ball, 411.

363   *Without* AGREEMENT WITH HANOI": Kissinger, 271.

363   "CONTINUATION . . . LESS ATTRACTIVE": ibid., 262.

364   SORTIES SYSTEMATICALLY FALSIFIED: Shawcross, 19–35; Kissinger, 253.

364   FBI WIRE-TAPS: Kissinger, 252.

364   "THOSE LIBERAL BASTARDS": q. Szulc, 158.

364   NIXON'S SPEECH ANNOUNCING CAMBODIA CAMPAIGN: 30 Apr 70. COSVN: Kissinger, 490, 506.

365   "MILITARY HALLUCINATION": q. ibid., 511, n.d.

365   250 STATE DEPT. STAFF MEMBERS: ibid., 513.

366   SAN JOSE INCIDENT: Safire, 325. "WE COULD SEE THE HATE": q. ibid., 329; *St. Louis Post-Dispatch*, Spec. Supp., D3.

366   COLSON, "SIEGE MENTALITY": q. Herring, 233. "GENUINELY BELIEVED": q. John Roche in Lake, 132. WHITE HOUSE STAFF MEMBER: Thomas Charles Huston, Safire, 297. SEVENTEEN WIRE-TAPS, Kissinger, 252.

367   "RIGHT OUT OF THE OVAL OFFICE": John Dean's testimony, q. Congressional Quarterly Service, 991.

367   CONGRESS "A BODY OF FOLLOWERS": Riegle, diary entry for 9 June 71. On role of Congress on Vietnam in Nixon's term, see Frye and Sullivan in Lake, 199–209, also Congressional Quarterly Service and of course Kissinger, passim.

368   ARVN, FIGHTING TO ALLOW AMERICANS TO DEPART: Fitzgerald, 416.

369   POLL, "MORALLY WRONG": Harris, 73.

369   LORD NORTH, "ILL SUCCESS": in May 1783, q. Valentine, *North*, II, 313.

369   "THE BASTARDS HAVE NEVER BEEN BOMBED": q. Herring, 241.

370   "COULD MAKE OR BREAK": q. Carl Bernstein and Robert Woodward, *All the President's Men*, New York, 1974, 265.

370   "RATFUCKING": ibid., 127–8.

371   MAO, "DO AS I DID": q. Szulc, 610.

372   NIXON, "MY ABSOLUTE ASSURANCE": Kissinger, 1412.

372   AIR POWER FROM BASES IN THAILAND: Gelb, 349.

372   KISSINGER BACKED AWAY FROM AGREED TERMS: Herring, 246.

372   "WE HAD WALKED THE LAST MILE": Paul Warnke, Asst. Sec. of Defense 1967–69, succeeding McNaughton, American Enterprise *Debate*, 125.

372   DEMOCRATIC CAUCUS: *Congress and Nation*, III.

373   ULTIMATUM TO THIEU: Kissinger, 1459.

374   "A HOUSE WITHOUT ANY FOUNDATION": q. Dudman, *St. Louis Post-Dispatch*, Spec. Supp., D10.

374   KISSINGER, "THE BREAKDOWN": Kissinger, 520.

375   FORD, "CREDIBILITY . . . ESSENTIAL": message to Congress, Jan. 75. KISSINGER, "FUNDAMENTAL THREAT": press conference of 26 Mar 75.

375   RIDGWAY, "IT SHOULD NOT HAVE TAKEN": in *Foreign Affairs*.

376   "NO EXPERTS AVAILABLE": McNamara to author.

377   CONGRESSMAN FROM MICHIGAN: Riegle, entry in diary for 20 Apr 71.

Epilogue

"A LANTERN ON THE STERN"

REFERENCE NOTES

p. 380 "SERVANT OF DIVINE REASON": Morton Smith in *Columbia History of the World*, ed. John Garraty and Peter Gay, New York, 1972, 210.

381 PLATO, "GOLDEN CORD," PUPPETS, DISEASE OF THE SOUL: *Laws*, I, 644–5, III, 689B.

381 TACITUS, "MOST FLAGRANT": *Annals*, Bk XV, chap. 53.

382 JEFFERSON, "WHENEVER A MAN": to Tench Coxe, 1799, q. *Oxford Dictionary of Quotations*, 3rd ed., 1980, 272, no. 11. ADAM SMITH, "AND THUS PLACE": *Theory of Moral Sentiments* I, iii, 2, q. *Oxford Dictionary of Quotations*, 509, no. 8.

382 SENATOR NORRIS: Wayne S. Cole, *Senator Gerald P. Nye and American Foreign Relations*, Minneapolis, 1962, 67. EISENHOWER, "EVERYONE IS TOO CAUTIOUS": *Diaries*, for 11 June 51.

382 PLATO, "THE WORST OF DISEASES": *Laws*, III, 691D.

383 "INTELLECTUAL CAPITAL": Kissinger, 54.

383 COLERIDGE, "IF MEN COULD LEARN": *Oxford Dictionary of Quotations*, 157, no. 20.

383 "HE HAD NO CHOICE": Schlesinger, 538.

384 "MAGNANIMITY IN POLITICS": Speech on Conciliation, 22 Mar 1775, Hansard, XVIII.

384 "CRIMESTOP": I owe the citation of this passage to Jeffrey Race, "The Unlearned Lessons of Vietnam," *Yale Review*, Winter 1977, 166.

386 STORY OF DARIUS: Herodotus, Bk III, chaps. 82–6.

387 MONTAIGNE, "RESOLUTION AND VALOR": *Complete Essays*, trans. Donald M. Frame, Stanford, 1965, II, 36.

387 LILLIPUTIANS "HAVE MORE REGARD": Jonathan Swift, *Gulliver's Travels*, Part One, chap. 6.

Index